BUSINESS COMMUNICATION NOW

Third Canadian Edition

Isobel M. Findlay
University of Saskatchewan

Kitty O. Locker

Business Communication NOW
Third Canadian Edition

ISBN-13: 978-1-25-902471-9
ISBN-10: 1-25-902471-7

1 2 3 4 5 6 7 8 9 0 WEB 1 9 8 7 6 5

Printed and bound in Canada

Director of Product Management: *Rhondda McNabb*
Senior Product Manager: *Karen Fozard*
Senior Marketing Manager: *Margaret Greenfield*
Senior Product Developer: *Sara Braithwaite*
Senior Product Team Associate: *Marina Seguin*
Supervising Editor: *Cathy Biribauer*
Photo/Permission Editor: *Marnie Lamb*
Copy Editor: *Kelli Howey*
Plant Production Coordinator: *Scott Morrison*
Manufacturing Production Coordinator: *Emily Hickey*
Cover and Inside Design: *Jennifer Stimson*
Composition: *Laserwords Private Limited*
Cover Photo: *Kakin/Shutterstock Royalty Free*
Printer: *Webcom, Ltd.*

Library and Archives Canada Cataloguing in Publication Data

Locker, Kitty O.
[Business communication now (2014)]
Business communication now / Isobel M. Findlay, Kitty O. Locker. -- Third Canadian edition.

Revision of: Business communication now. 2nd Canadian ed.
McGraw-Hill Ryerson, ©2012.
Includes bibliographical references and indexes.
ISBN 978-1-25-902471-9 (pbk.)

1. Business communication--Textbooks. I. Findlay, Isobel, author II. Title.

HF5718.L6335 2015 658.4'5 C2014-904598-0

BRIEF CONTENTS

CONTENTS

PART 3 LETTERS, MEMOS, AND E-MAIL MESSAGES

7 / ROUTINE MESSAGES 144

8 / NEGATIVE MESSAGES 171

9 / PERSUASIVE AND SALES MESSAGES 194

PART 4 REPORTS

10 / PLANNING, RESEARCHING, AND DOCUMENTING REPORTS 224

PART 5 JOB SEARCH PROCESS

PREFACE

I am delighted to share with you the third Canadian edition of *Business Communication NOW*—an edition carefully revised to meet the needs of my favourite audience: my fellow Canadian teachers and learners, colleagues and students.

Based on extensive faculty and student feedback and my own research and experience in business communications, this edition teaches students to think critically, to manage technological, cultural, and other change, and to improve written and oral business communication skills. These skills will prepare students to grasp opportunities and meet challenges in their academic and professional careers.

This edition explains why communications have moved to the heart of business practice and why communications are the number-one skill expected of job candidates. Students will see the communication tasks they will be likely to encounter in a wide array of occupations, and the strategies most likely to succeed.

Business Communication NOW demonstrates the importance—and ethics—of tailoring business communications to audiences representing different personality types and ethnicities, as well as organizational, political, and economic cultures in a global business environment.

Particular attention has also been paid to new and changing technologies—including blogging, texting, instant messaging, and social media—and the impact these technologies have on the business communication landscape. If students can benefit from speedy access to information, they also face heightened expectations of the accuracy and currency of their own communications. This focus on technology better equips students for the opportunities and challenges of digital media and makes the text more readily accessible and relevant to a student audience.

Balancing theory and practice, expanding understanding of diversity within and beyond Canadian borders, and condensing and clarifying, this third Canadian edition aims to help your students build confidence, invest in their own credibility and authority, and achieve success in your classroom and beyond.

FEATURES

COMMUNICATING IN A DIGITAL WORKPLACE Findlay has a strong focus on contemporary technologies and their impact on business communications—from writing for the Web and Web site design to viral marketing and social media—and heightened expectations of transparency and accountability.

COMMUNICATING IN A DIVERSE WORKPLACE *Business Communication NOW* emphasizes skills and strategies for success in a diverse workplace, including information on working in teams, effective listening, conflict resolution, and collaborative writing.

COMMUNICATING IN A GLOBAL WORKPLACE Findlay focuses on both intercultural and international communications with a discussion of avoiding stereotyping and ethnocentrism, adapting writing for various audiences, and respecting cultural differences.

MAGAZINE LAYOUT AND DESIGN The unique and popular magazine-style design returns in this edition and continues to engage students with its visual appeal and approachable writing style.

FOCUS ON ETHICS Ethics in business and business communications is stressed throughout the text with newsworthy and relevant Canadian examples.

RELEVANT TO ALL STUDENTS The text motivates students in a variety of programs by referring to a wide array of occupations through examples and model documents and showcases a range of businesses from large to small, corporate and co-operative, for-profit and not-for-profit, and Crown corporations.

CHAPTER CHANGES

- Updated coverage and increased focus throughout the textbook on electronic technology and social media.
- Pedagogical boxes have been updated for currency and relevancy to chapter content.

Chapter 1 focuses on motivating students to invest in business communication by linking the communication process to an evolving business environment that increasingly values communication skills. Chapter 1 also underlines a renewed interest in etiquette, demonstrating the costs and benefits of strong communications and reinforcing the power of rhetorical and generic competencies.

Chapter 2 is comprehensive and current and takes the mystery out of audience analysis, channel choice, and goodwill.

Chapter 3 has current and concise advice on the writing process and how to improve writing for online and offline situations.

Chapter 4 offers a broad range of Canadian and other examples showing the importance of visual and verbal rhetoric to the credibility and usability of print and online resources. It includes updated content on online media, and a clearer sense of the continuities between and differences among print and online media.

Chapter 5 makes clear a complex set of challenges and opportunities at the heart of intercultural business communication. It encourages students to learn from their diverse classrooms to navigate diversity in and beyond the workplace and to avoid the huge social and economic costs of cultural incompetence.

Chapter 6 links together active listening, group dynamics, team formation, conflict resolution, meeting management, and collaborative writing with technological and interpersonal considerations—promoting trust and loyalty, diversity and respect, as the keys to team innovation and success.

Chapter 7 is called Routine Messages to emphasize the coverage of general correspondence such as electronic media, letters, and memos. There is a range of Canadian examples, including a new Inside Perspective, and clear step-by-step advice to maximize opportunities and manage risks.

Chapter 8 includes updated Canadian examples, provides advice on how to flexibly and tactfully handle bad news, and includes new exercises and problems to develop skills in handling negative messages in a crisis or on controversial topics.

Chapter 9 combines persuasive messages and sales, fundraising, and promotional messages in a more succinct discussion. There is also an increased focus on the ethics of persuasion.

Chapter 10 covers planning, researching, and documenting proposals and reports and encourages students to see the importance of consistent and credible research, evaluation, and documentation.

Chapter 11 provides clear and careful guidance through the principles of proposal and report writing supported by a range of professional and student examples.

Chapter 12 contains a balance between updated technological advice and reminders about the social aspects of presenting/building relationships with audiences.

Chapter 13 balances coverage of employee and employer perspectives in a changing job market and offers practical advice on how to think about and prepare for each stage of the job search process.

WALKTHROUGH

Opening Vignette An Inside Perspective introduces readers to business professionals who share on-the-job insight that is relevant to the chapter's content and goals.

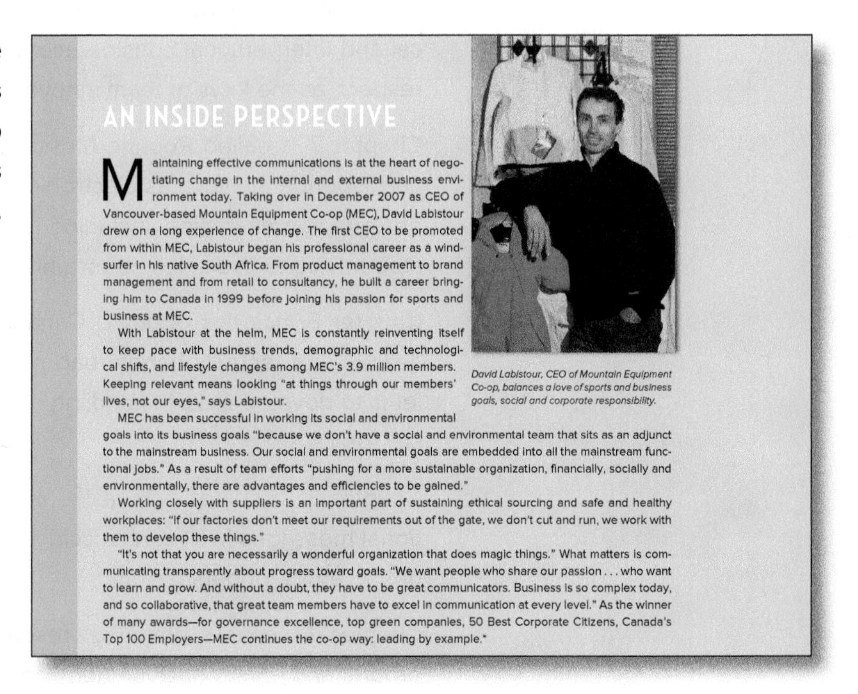

AN INSIDE PERSPECTIVE

Maintaining effective communications is at the heart of negotiating change in the internal and external business environment today. Taking over in December 2007 as CEO of Vancouver-based Mountain Equipment Co-op (MEC), David Labistour drew on a long experience of change. The first CEO to be promoted from within MEC, Labistour began his professional career as a windsurfer in his native South Africa. From product management to brand management and from retail to consultancy, he built a career bringing him to Canada in 1999 before joining his passion for sports and business at MEC.

With Labistour at the helm, MEC is constantly reinventing itself to keep pace with business trends, demographic and technological shifts, and lifestyle changes among MEC's 3.9 million members. Keeping relevant means looking "at things through our members' lives, not our eyes," says Labistour.

David Labistour, CEO of Mountain Equipment Co-op, balances a love of sports and business goals, social and corporate responsibility.

MEC has been successful in working its social and environmental goals into its business goals "because we don't have a social and environmental team that sits as an adjunct to the mainstream business. Our social and environmental goals are embedded into all the mainstream functional jobs." As a result of team efforts "pushing for a more sustainable organization, financially, socially and environmentally, there are advantages and efficiencies to be gained."

Working closely with suppliers is an important part of sustaining ethical sourcing and safe and healthy workplaces: "If our factories don't meet our requirements out of the gate, we don't cut and run, we work with them to develop these things."

"It's not that you are necessarily a wonderful organization that does magic things." What matters is communicating transparently about progress toward goals. "We want people who share our passion . . . who want to learn and grow. And without a doubt, they have to be great communicators. Business is so complex today, and so collaborative, that great team members have to excel in communication at every level." As the winner of many awards—for governance excellence, top green companies, 50 Best Corporate Citizens, Canada's Top 100 Employers—MEC continues the co-op way: leading by example.*

Document Examples Annotated visual examples such as letters, memos, reports, and e-mails explain communication miscues and offer suggestions for improvement.

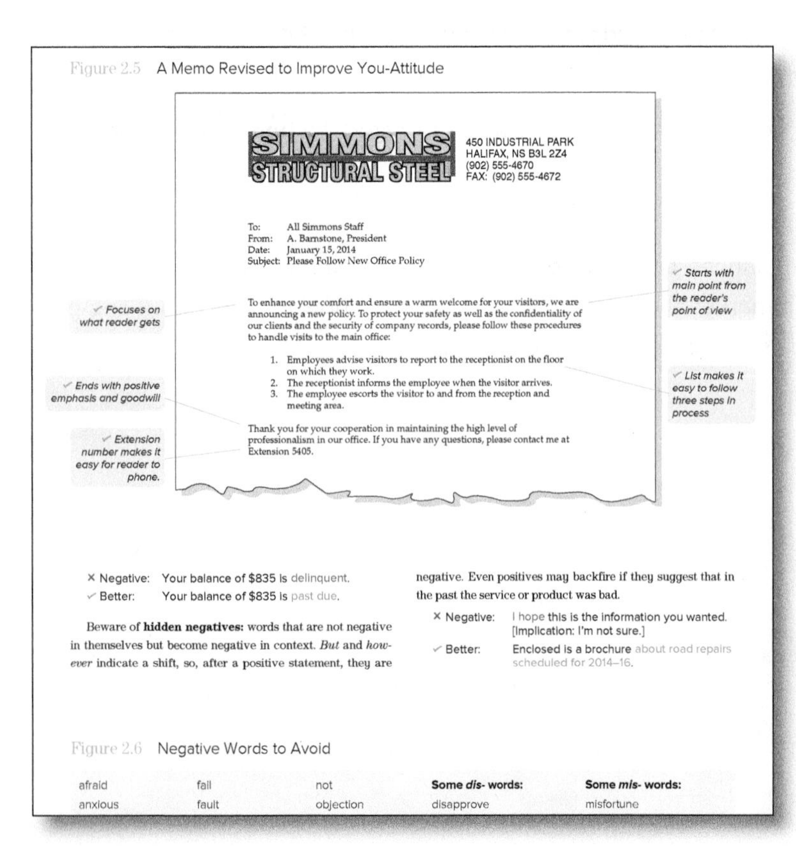

Figure 2.5 A Memo Revised to Improve You-Attitude

SIMMONS STRUCTURAL STEEL
450 INDUSTRIAL PARK
HALIFAX, NS B3L 2Z4
(902) 555-4670
FAX: (902) 555-4672

To: All Simmons Staff
From: A. Barnstone, President
Date: January 15, 2014
Subject: Please Follow New Office Policy

To enhance your comfort and ensure a warm welcome for your visitors, we are announcing a new policy. To protect your safety as well as the confidentiality of our clients and the security of company records, please follow these procedures to handle visits to the main office:

1. Employees advise visitors to report to the receptionist on the floor on which they work.
2. The receptionist informs the employee when the visitor arrives.
3. The employee escorts the visitor to and from the reception and meeting area.

Thank you for your cooperation in maintaining the high level of professionalism in our office. If you have any questions, please contact me at Extension 5405.

× Negative: Your balance of $835 is delinquent.
✓ Better: Your balance of $835 is past due.

Beware of **hidden negatives:** words that are not negative in themselves but become negative in context. *But* and *however* indicate a shift, so, after a positive statement, they are negative. Even positives may backfire if they suggest that in the past the service or product was bad.

× Negative: I hope this is the information you wanted. [Implication: I'm not sure.]
✓ Better: Enclosed is a brochure about road repairs scheduled for 2014–16.

Figure 2.6 Negative Words to Avoid

afraid	fail	not	**Some *dis*- words:**	**Some *mis*- words:**
anxious	fault	objection	disapprove	misfortune

Positive and Negative Examples Effective and ineffective communication examples appear side by side so that students can pinpoint problematic constructions and improve their skills. Annotations indicate weaker and stronger messages for easy comparison.

× Lacks you-attitude: I have negotiated an agreement with Apex Rent-a-Car that gives you a discount on rental cars.

✓ You-attitude: As a Sunstrand employee, you can now get a 20% discount when you rent a car from Apex.

The first sentence focuses on what the writer does, not on what the reader receives. Any sentence that focuses on the writer's work or generosity lacks you-attitude, even if the sentence contains the word *you*. Instead of focusing on what we are giving the reader, focus on what the reader can now do.

× Lacks you-attitude: We are shipping your order of September 21 this afternoon.

✓ You-attitude: The two dozen CorningWare starter sets you ordered will be shipped this afternoon and should reach you by September 28.

The reader is less interested in when we shipped the order than in when it will arrive. Note that the phrase "should reach you by" leaves room for variations in delivery schedules. Give the reader the name of the carrier, so the reader knows whom to contact if the order doesn't arrive promptly.

2. Refer to the Reader's Request or Order Specifically

When you write about the reader's request, order, or policy, refer to it specifically, not as a generic *your order* or *your policy*. If your reader is an individual or a small business, it's friendly to specify the content of the order; if you are writing to a company with which you do a great deal of business, give the invoice or purchase order number.

× Lacks you-attitude: Your order . . .

✓ You-attitude (to individual): The desk chair you ordered . . .

✓ You-attitude (to a large store): Your invoice #783329 . . .

The form letter printed in Figure 2.3 is stuffy and selfish. The comments in blue identify where the letter lacks you-attitude, loses credibility, and generates ill will.

1. **The language is stiff and legalistic.** Note the obsolete (and sexist) "Gentlemen:" "Please be advised," "herein," and "expedite."
2. **The tone is selfish.** The letter is written from the writer's point of view; there are no benefits for the reader. (The writer says there are, but without evidence the claim isn't convincing.)
3. **The main point is buried** in the middle of the long first paragraph. The middle is the least emphatic part of a paragraph.
4. **The request is vague.** How many references does the supplier want? Would credit references, like banks, rather than vendor references work too? Is the name of the reference enough, or is it necessary also to specify the line of credit and/or the years credit has been established? What "additional financial information" does the supplier want? Bank balance? The request sounds like an invasion of privacy, not a reasonable business practice.
5. **Words are misused** (*herein* for *therein*), suggesting either an ignorant writer or one who doesn't care enough about the subject and the reader to use the right word.

3. Don't Talk about Feelings Except to Congratulate or Offer Sympathy

In most business situations, your feelings are irrelevant and should be omitted.

× Lacks you-attitude: We are happy to extend you a credit line of $5,000.

✓ You-attitude: You can now charge up to $5,000 on your Visa card.

Figure 3.12 Questions to Ask Readers Checklist

OUTLINE OR PLANNING DRAFT

- Does the plan seem on the right track?
- What topics should be added? Should any be cut?
- Do you have any other general suggestions?

REVISING DRAFT

- Does the message satisfy all its purposes?
- Is the message adapted to the audience(s)?
- Is the organization effective?
- What parts aren't clear?
- What ideas need further development?
- Do you have any other suggestions?

POLISHING DRAFT

- Are there any problems with word choice or sentence structure?
- Did you find any inconsistencies?
- Did you find any typos?
- Is the document's design effective?

Checklists serve as a handy reference guide when composing and editing messages.

Summary of Key Points provides an overview of the important points students have learned in the chapter.

SUMMARY OF KEY POINTS

- Writing processes can include eight activities: planning, gathering, writing, evaluating, getting feedback, revising, editing, and proofreading. *Revising* means changing the document to make it better satisfy the writer's purposes and the audience. *Editing* means making local changes that make the document grammatically correct. *Proofreading* means checking to be sure the document is free from typographical errors. The activities do not have to come in any set order.
- Good style in business writing is less formal, more friendly, and more personal than the style usually used for term papers.
- To improve your style,
  1. Start a clean page or screen so that you aren't locked into old sentence structures.
  2. Try WIRMI: *What I Really Mean Is*. Then write the words.
  3. Try reading your draft out loud to someone sitting about one metre away. If the words sound stiff, they'll seem stiff to a reader, too.
  4. Ask someone else to read your draft out loud. The places where that person stumbles are places where your writing can be better.
  5. Read widely and write *a lot*.
- To make your writing easier to read,

  As you write and revise paragraphs,
  1. Begin paragraphs with topic sentences.
  2. Use transitions to link ideas.

  As you write and revise sentences,
  3. Use active verbs most of the time.
  4. Use verbs—not nouns—to carry the weight of your sentence.
  5. Tighten your writing.
  6. Vary sentence length and sentence structure.
  7. Use parallel structure.
  8. Put your readers in your sentences.

  As you choose words,
  9. Use words that are accurate, appropriate, ethical, and familiar.
  10. Use technical jargon only when it is essential and known to the reader. Replace business jargon.
- Writing and editing for the Web requires short paragraphs and sentences, 50% less text than in a paper document, good use of transitions, headings, and subheadings, highlighted key words, lists, and links.
- You can improve the quality of the feedback you give and get by focusing on aspects of a draft needing comment. If a reader criticizes something, fix the problem. If you think the reader misunderstood you, revise the draft so that the reader can see what you meant.

Exercises and Problems End of chapter exercises include a range of individual, pair, and group work activities for use in class or as assignments. These exercises encourage students to assume a role or perform a task in a variety of realistic business scenarios and to see the connections between the cultures and activities of the classroom and the workplace.

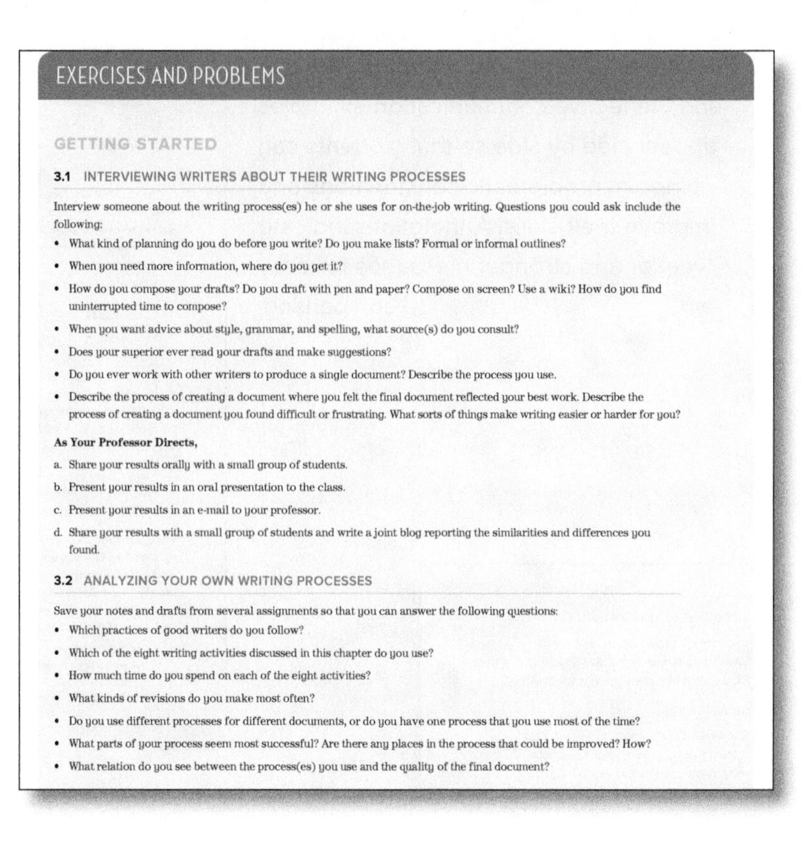

EXERCISES AND PROBLEMS

GETTING STARTED

3.1 INTERVIEWING WRITERS ABOUT THEIR WRITING PROCESSES

Interview someone about the writing process(es) he or she uses for on-the-job writing. Questions you could ask include the following:

- What kind of planning do you do before you write? Do you make lists? Formal or informal outlines?
- When you need more information, where do you get it?
- How do you compose your drafts? Do you draft with pen and paper? Compose on screen? Use a wiki? How do you find uninterrupted time to compose?
- When you want advice about style, grammar, and spelling, what source(s) do you consult?
- Does your superior ever read your drafts and make suggestions?
- Do you ever work with other writers to produce a single document? Describe the process you use.
- Describe the process of creating a document where you felt the final document reflected your best work. Describe the process of creating a document you found difficult or frustrating. What sorts of things make writing easier or harder for you?

As Your Professor Directs,

a. Share your results orally with a small group of students.

b. Present your results in an oral presentation to the class.

c. Present your results in an e-mail to your professor.

d. Share your results with a small group of students and write a joint blog reporting the similarities and differences you found.

3.2 ANALYZING YOUR OWN WRITING PROCESSES

Save your notes and drafts from several assignments so that you can answer the following questions:

- Which practices of good writers do you follow?
- Which of the eight writing activities discussed in this chapter do you use?
- How much time do you spend on each of the eight activities?
- What kinds of revisions do you make most often?
- Do you use different processes for different documents, or do you have one process that you use most of the time?
- What parts of your process seem most successful? Are there any places in the process that could be improved? How?
- What relation do you see between the process(es) you use and the quality of the final document?

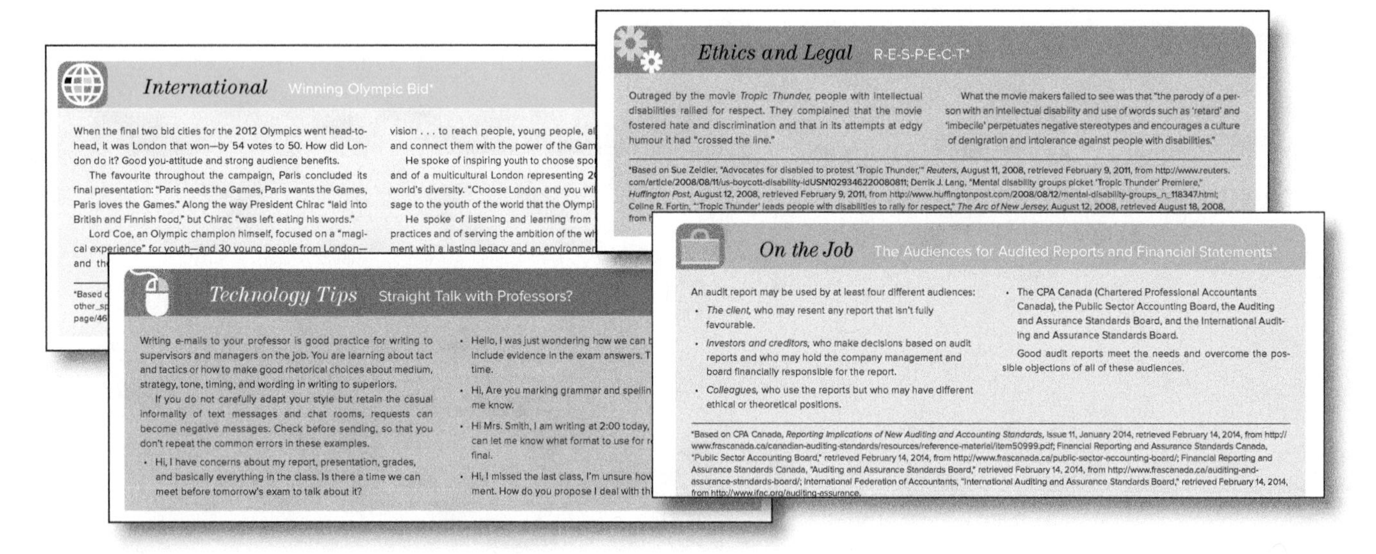

International Winning Olympic Bid*

When the final two bid cities for the 2012 Olympics went head-to-head, it was London that won—by 54 votes to 50. How did London do it? Good you-attitude and strong audience benefits.

The favourite throughout the campaign, Paris concluded its final presentation: "Paris needs the Games, Paris wants the Games, Paris loves the Games." Along the way President Chirac "laid into British and Finnish food," but Chirac "was left eating his words."

Lord Coe, an Olympic champion himself, focused on a "magical experience" for youth—and 30 young people from London—

vision . . . to reach people, young people, a[ll] and connect them with the power of the Ga[mes]

He spoke of inspiring youth to choose spo[rt] and of a multicultural London representing 2[00] world's diversity. "Choose London and you wi[ll] sage to the youth of the world that the Olymp[ic]

He spoke of listening and learning from practices and of serving the ambition of the w[orld] ment with a lasting legacy and an environme[nt]

Ethics and Legal R-E-S-P-E-C-T*

Outraged by the movie *Tropic Thunder*, people with intellectual disabilities rallied for respect. They complained that the movie fostered hate and discrimination and that in its attempts at edgy humour it had "crossed the line."

What the movie makers failed to see was that "the parody of a person with an intellectual disability and use of words such as 'retard' and 'imbecile' perpetuates negative stereotypes and encourages a culture of denigration and intolerance against people with disabilities."

*Based on Sue Zeidler, "Advocates for disabled to protest 'Tropic Thunder,'" *Reuters*, August 11, 2008, retrieved February 9, 2011, from http://www.reuters.com/article/2008/08/11/us-boycott-disability-idUSN1029346220080811; Derrik J. Lang, "Mental disability groups picket 'Tropic Thunder' Premiere," *Huffington Post*, August 12, 2008, retrieved February 9, 2011, from http://www.huffingtonpost.com/2008/08/12/mental-disability-groups_n_118347.html; Celine R. Fortin, "'Tropic Thunder' leads people with disabilities to rally for respect," *The Arc of New Jersey*, August 12, 2008, retrieved August 18, 2008,

Technology Tips Straight Talk with Professors?

Writing e-mails to your professor is good practice for writing to supervisors and managers on the job. You are learning about tact and tactics or how to make good rhetorical choices about medium, strategy, tone, timing, and wording in writing to superiors.

If you do not carefully adapt your style but retain the casual informality of text messages and chat rooms, requests can become negative messages. Check before sending, so that you don't repeat the common errors in these examples.

- Hi, I have concerns about my report, presentation, grades, and basically everything in the class. Is there a time we can meet before tomorrow's exam to talk about it?
- Hello, I was just wondering how we can [...] include evidence in the exam answers. T[...] time.
- Hi, Are you marking grammar and spellin[g...] me know.
- Hi Mrs. Smith, I am writing at 2:00 today, [...] can let me know what format to use for r[...] final.
- Hi, I missed the last class, I'm unsure ho[w...] ment. How do you propose I deal with th[...]

On the Job The Audiences for Audited Reports and Financial Statements*

An audit report may be used by at least four different audiences:

- *The client*, who may resent any report that isn't fully favourable.
- *Investors and creditors*, who make decisions based on audit reports and who may hold the company management and board financially responsible for the report.
- *Colleagues*, who use the reports but who may have different ethical or theoretical positions.
- The CPA Canada (Chartered Professional Accountants Canada), the Public Sector Accounting Board, the Auditing and Assurance Standards Board, and the International Auditing and Assurance Standards Board.

Good audit reports meet the needs and overcome the possible objections of all of these audiences.

*Based on CPA Canada, *Reporting Implications of New Auditing and Accounting Standards*, Issue 11, January 2014, retrieved February 14, 2014, from http://www.frascanada.ca/canadian-auditing-standards/resources/reference-material/item50999.pdf; Financial Reporting and Assurance Standards Canada, "Public Sector Accounting Board," retrieved February 14, 2014, from http://www.frascanada.ca/public-sector-accounting-board/; Financial Reporting and Assurance Standards Canada, "Auditing and Assurance Standards Board," retrieved February 14, 2014, from http://www.frascanada.ca/auditing-and-assurance-standards-board/; International Federation of Accountants, "International Auditing and Assurance Standards Board," retrieved February 14, 2014, from http://www.ifac.org/auditing-assurance.

International, Ethics and Legal, On the Job, and Technology Tips boxes enhance the chapter content and provide current and relevant facts and articles.

SUPPLEMENTS

INSTRUCTOR RESOURCES

McGraw-Hill Connect™ is a Web-based assignment and assessment platform that gives students the means to better connect with their coursework, with their instructors, and with the important concepts that they will need to know for success now and in the future.

With Connect, instructors can deliver assignments, quizzes, and tests online. Instructors can edit existing questions and author entirely new problems. Track individual student performance—by question, assignment, or in relation to the class overall—with detailed grade reports. Integrate grade reports easily with Learning Management Systems (LMS).

By choosing Connect, instructors are providing their students with a powerful tool for improving academic performance and truly mastering course material. Connect allows students to practise important skills at their own pace and on their own schedule. Importantly, students' assessment results and instructors' feedback are all saved online—so students can continually review their progress and plot their course to success.

Connect also provides 24/7 online access to an eBook—an online edition of the text—to aid students in successfully completing their work, wherever and whenever they choose.

Additional resources for the Instructor available within Connect include the following:

- An **Instructor's Manual** with teaching strategies and tips, sample syllabi, and creative classroom activities.
- **PowerPoint slides** for each chapter that offer instructional support and provide a visual complement to lectures. The slides are comprehensive and can be adapted to meet the needs of any course.
- A **Test Bank** for each chapter that offers a variety of multiple choice, true and false, and short-answer questions.

CONNECT INSIGHT NEW to the third edition of Findlay! Visualized data tailored to your needs as an instructor makes it possible to quickly confirm early signals of success, or identify early warning signs regarding student performance or concept mastery—even while on the go.

STUDENT RESOURCES

Connect provides students with a powerful tool for improving academic performance and truly mastering course material, plus 24/7 online access to an interactive and searchable eBook. Connect allows students to practise important skills at their own pace and on their own schedule. Importantly, students' assessment results and instructors' feedback are all saved online—so students can continually review their progress and plot their course to success. Additional resources available within Connect include Model Documents, Grammar Review, Videos, Writing Tutors, and more!

SUPERIOR LEARNING SOLUTIONS AND SUPPORT

The McGraw-Hill Ryerson team is ready to help you assess and integrate any of our products, technology, and services into your course for optimal teaching and learning performance. Whether it's helping your students improve their grades, or putting your entire course online, the McGraw-Hill Ryerson team is here to help you do it. Contact your Learning Solutions Consultant today to learn how to maximize all of McGraw-Hill Ryerson's resources!

For more information on the latest technology and Learning Solutions offered by McGraw-Hill Ryerson and its partners, please visit us online: **www.mheducation.ca/highereducation/educators/digital-solutions/**

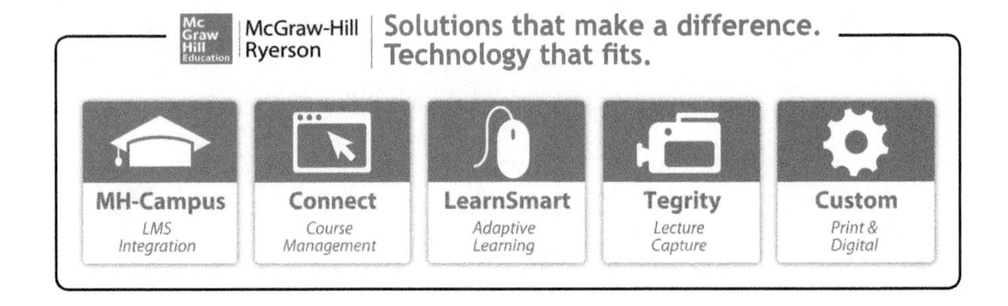

ABOUT THE AUTHOR

DR. ISOBEL M. FINDLAY

Dr. Isobel M. Findlay is a professor in the Department of Management and Marketing; University Co-director, Community-University Institute for Social Research; and Scholar, Centre for the Study of Co-operatives, University of Saskatchewan, where she teaches business communications, business and community, co-operative studies, and law and culture.

She has special research interests in communications, cultures, and communities; diversity in the workplace; Aboriginal and associative organizations; and corporate social responsibility, performance indicators, and reporting standards. After six years on a Social Sciences and Humanities Research Council of Canada (SSHRC) research project on Social Enterprises, Knowledgeable Economies, and Sustainable Communities, she is currently completing work on another SSHRC-funded project on Animating Mi'kmaw Humanities in Atlantic Canada and beginning a three-year Canadian Institutes of Health Research project on Workplace Harassment among Caregivers: Fostering Communicative Action and Ethical Practice through Participatory Theatre.

She is also pursuing her research interests in the context of the Sectoral Commission on Culture, Communication and Information of the Canadian Commission for UNESCO, where she is completing her second three-year term.

In addition to essays on Aboriginal justice, economic development, and co-operatives, she is editor, co-author, or co-editor of the following:

- Co-editor (with Bonnie Jeffery, Diane Martz, and Louise Clarke), *Journeys in Community-based Research* (2014)
- Co-editor (with Ana Maria Peredo and Fiona Duguid) of a special issue of the *Journal of Co-operative Studies 47.1* (2014)
- Co-editor (with Warren Weir and Louise Clarke) of a special issue of the *Journal of Aboriginal Economic Development 4.1* (2004) on Value(s) Added: Sharing Voices on Aboriginal CED
- Editor, *Introduction to Literature,* 4th and 5th editions (2000, 2004)
- Co-author with James (Sakej) Youngblood Henderson and Marjorie L. Benson, *Aboriginal Tenure in the Constitution of Canada* (2000)
- Co-editor (with L. M. Findlay), *Realizing Community: Multidisciplinary Perspectives* (1995)

A member of the Canadian Communication Association and the International Association of Business Communicators, she has operated her own writing and editing business; facilitated workshops and consulted with the public and private sectors, profit and non-profit organizations; and written many successful grant applications and proposals. A proud recipient of a University of Saskatchewan Students' Union Teaching Excellence Award, she is also co-winner of the Saskatchewan Book Awards Scholarly Writing Award, 2000.

TO LEN, ANDREW, AND NICK—ISOBEL M. FINDLAY

ACKNOWLEDGMENTS

I continue to owe an enormous debt to Kitty Locker whose work has inspired my own contributions to the field of business communication. I am also grateful to colleagues and students at the Edwards School of Business, University of Saskatchewan. Thanks especially to my friends and former colleagues Neil Balan and Susan McDonald for sharing my enthusiasms and their own good examples. Thanks also to the many organizations in the public and private sectors with whom I have consulted and worked. All have added immeasurably to my own learning, to my sense of research opportunities, to my understanding of barriers to effective communication—and of models of professional communication.

The efforts of many people are needed to develop and improve a text. Among these people are the reviewers who point out areas of concern, cite areas of strength, and make recommendations for change. In this regard the instructors named here provided feedback that was enormously helpful in preparing this third edition.

Jay Dolmage, *University of Waterloo*

Paul Finlayson, *George Brown College*

Karen Grandy, *Saint Mary's University*

Gail Rees, *Canadore College*

Erika Whelan, *Fleming College*

To my editors at McGraw-Hill Ryerson I am especially grateful for their support, wise counsel, good humour, and creativity. The book has been greatly enriched by them: senior product manager Karen Fozard, senior product developer Sara Braithwaite, supervising editor Cathy Biribauer, permissions editor Marnie Lamb, and copy editor Kelli Howey. To the formatters and designers my sincere thanks for their work in transforming the manuscript into an eminently readable and visually engaging text.

And to my dear friends and research partners (Linda and Sue, Sakej and Marie, Lynne, and Len), thanks for the support, the critical input—and for the very necessary social diversions.

Finally, I want to thank my sons Andrew and Nick for their love, support, and resilience. My greatest debt I owe to my husband, Len Findlay, whose own scholarly engagement and intellectual rigor continue to inspire and sustain.

COMMUNICATING IN A CHANGING BUSINESS WORLD

1

Learning Outcomes

LO1 Explain the importance of effective communications to personal and organizational success

LO2 List five questions you need to ask in analyzing business communication situations

LO3 Identify five criteria of good writing

LO4 Describe the communication process

LO5 Discuss eight principles that help you improve communications

LO6 Explain the managerial functions of communication

LO7 Describe ten trends impacting business communication

AN INSIDE PERSPECTIVE

David Labistour, CEO of Mountain Equipment Co-op, balances a love of sports and business goals, social and corporate responsibility.

Maintaining effective communications is at the heart of negotiating change in the internal and external business environment today. Taking over in December 2007 as CEO of Vancouver-based Mountain Equipment Co-op (MEC), David Labistour drew on a long experience of change. The first CEO to be promoted from within MEC, Labistour began his professional career as a windsurfer in his native South Africa. From product management to brand management and from retail to consultancy, he built a career bringing him to Canada in 1999 before joining his passion for sports and business at MEC.

With Labistour at the helm, MEC is constantly reinventing itself to keep pace with business trends, demographic and technological shifts, and lifestyle changes among MEC's 3.9 million members. Keeping relevant means looking "at things through our members' lives, not our eyes," says Labistour.

MEC has been successful in working its social and environmental goals into its business goals "because we don't have a social and environmental team that sits as an adjunct to the mainstream business. Our social and environmental goals are embedded into all the mainstream functional jobs." As a result of team efforts "pushing for a more sustainable organization, financially, socially and environmentally, there are advantages and efficiencies to be gained."

Working closely with suppliers is an important part of sustaining ethical sourcing and safe and healthy workplaces: "If our factories don't meet our requirements out of the gate, we don't cut and run, we work with them to develop these things."

"It's not that you are necessarily a wonderful organization that does magic things." What matters is communicating transparently about progress toward goals. "We want people who share our passion . . . who want to learn and grow. And without a doubt, they have to be great communicators. Business is so complex today, and so collaborative, that great team members have to excel in communication at every level." As the winner of many awards—for governance excellence, top green companies, 50 Best Corporate Citizens, Canada's Top 100 Employers—MEC continues the co-op way: leading by example.*

*Based on Beedie Newsroom, "BBA student facilitates debate among Vancouver's top CIOs," December 12, 2013, retrieved from http://beedie.sfu.ca/blog/2013/10/mec-ceo-talks-about-the-importance-of-corporate-social-responsibility-ceo-series/#more-7341; David Ebner, "Shaking it up for the ever-evolving outdoors market," *The Globe and Mail,* February 1, 2011, B3; Lauren McKeon, "Q&A with David Labistour," *Canadian Business,* March 18, 2008, 10; Fiona Anderson, "MEC gets award for sustainable business," *Vancouver Sun,* February 14, 2008.

In diverse situations within the family, in the classroom, at work, or at play, you have been communicating for results throughout your life. Consciously or unconsciously, you have been thinking about your purposes (what action, reaction, result, or reward you want) and your audiences (parents, siblings, teachers, teammates, or colleagues) in choosing what, when, and how to communicate. You have been learning about what works (or not) and have been adapting to change.

You have been learning about the power of argument, your own character and credibility, and audience interests and beliefs—about the art of persuasion or rhetoric (⏩ Chapter 9)—to get the results you want. You have been learning the codes of behaviour or social norms, what is acceptable and what is not, and developing the judgment and cultural competency to make things happen in your community.[1]

Business similarly depends on communication to plan products; hire, train, and motivate workers; coordinate manufacturing and delivery; persuade customers to buy; bill them for the sale; and prepare for and manage change. In fact, for many businesses and non-profit and government organizations, the "product" is information or services created and delivered by communication. In every organization, communication is the way people build working relationships, get their points across, and get work done.

Communication takes many forms: face-to-face, phone, or cell conversations, informal or even virtual meetings, **Skype,**

On the Job Lessons from the Best*

When Watson Wyatt & Co. examined communications of 267 companies and their return to shareholders in a 2003–04 study, co-author Kathryn Yates found, "The bottom line is that employee communications is no longer a 'soft' function, but rather a business function that drives performance and contributes to a company's financial success."

Studies from 2003 to 2007 confirmed that effective employee communications was a leading predictor of financial performance. Disengaged employees cost the United States alone between $250 billion and $350 billion annually, according to Mark Attridge.

Even in financially challenging times, the 2009–10 Watson Wyatt study of 5 million employees confirms that effective communication is key to engaging employees, promoting safety and productivity, and enhancing financial performance. By 2013–2014, companies with effective communications were "three and a half times more likely to significantly outperform their industry peers than firms that are not effective in these areas."

*Based on Towers Watson, *How the Fundamentals Have Evolved and the Best Adapt: 2013–2014 Change and Communication ROI Study Report*, retrieved from http://www.towerswatson.com/en-CA/Insights/IC-Types/Survey-Research-Results/2013/12/2013-2014-change-and-communication-roi-study; Watson Wyatt, *Capitalizing on Effective Communication: How Courage, Innovation and Discipline Drive Business Results in Challenging Times: 2009–2010 Communication ROI Study Report*, retrieved from http://www.watsonwyatt.com/research/pdfs/NA-2009-14356.pdf; Mark Attridge, "Measuring and managing employee work engagement: A review of the research and business literature," *Journal of Workplace Behavioral Health*, 24 (2009): 383–98; "Better communication pays off for companies," *The Globe and Mail*, November 7, 2003, C1.

e-mail, **blogs, wikis, Twitter, Facebook,** text, instant messages, letters, memos, and reports. All of these methods are forms of **verbal communication,** or communication that uses words. **Nonverbal communication** does not use words. Pictures, computer graphics, and company logos are nonverbal. **Pinterest, Instagram,** and **Flickr** are sites that host photo and video sharing among online communities. **Vine** is a mobile app that allows users to create and share six-second video clips or embed them in **social media.** Interpersonal nonverbal signals include smiles, who sits where at a meeting, the size of an office, and how long someone keeps a visitor waiting.

This chapter explains why changes in the business environment—see ►► "Trends in Business Communication" in this chapter—require the superior communication skills MEC CEO David Labistour emphasizes (◄◄ An Inside Perspective) and move communication from a secondary to a central role. It also explains how technological change has given voice to diverse stakeholders in conversations in which businesses participate, though never fully control, and raised expectations of the correctness, clarity, currency, and content of communications. This chapter and those that follow guide you through the principles and practice of effective business communication, offering incentives and examples while sharing tools that will help you improve communication skills and meet current standards of professionalism.

LO1

COMMUNICATION ABILITY = PROMOTABILITY

Even "entry-level" jobs require high-level skills in reasoning, mathematics, and communicating. You'll read information; you'll listen to instructions; you'll ask questions; you may solve problems in teams. As a result, communication ability ranks first among the qualities that employers look for in job and promotion candidates.

For the full text of the Conference Board of Canada's "Employability Skills 2000+," see Figure 1.7 later in this chapter. These valuable soft skills have become even more important in an online world—where, author Charles Rubin argues, "you are what you write."[2]

According to Darlene Bailey, vice-president human resources and field operations, WCG International Consultants in Victoria: "If you have those [soft] skills, you have a better chance of getting a job and keeping the job . . . Perhaps everyone knows a teacher has to be a good communicator, but it's a skill that many others have to call on, whether it's to deal with co-workers, customers, suppliers, or others they encounter even in the most solitary of positions."[3]

In a work world where the ability to "analyze, write, persuade, and manage" can "facilitate career change,"[4] good writers—not surprisingly—earn more. Linguist Stephen Reder has found that among people with two- or four-year degrees, workers in the top 20% of writing ability earn, on average, more than three times as much as workers whose writing falls into the worst 20%.[5] For Canadian men, the lifetime reward for higher literacy skills is $585,000; for women, the reward is $683,000.[6]

"I'LL NEVER HAVE TO WRITE BECAUSE . . ."

Some students think that a secretary will do their writing, that they can use form letters, that only technical skills matter, that they'll call rather than write, or that rules and etiquette are things of the past in the world of texting and Twitter. Each of these claims is fundamentally flawed.

Claim 1: Secretaries will do all my writing.

Reality: Downsizing and technology have cut support staffs nationwide. Of the secretaries who remain, 71% are administrative assistants whose duties are managerial.[7]

Claim 2: I'll use form letters or templates when I need to write.

Reality: A **form letter** is a prewritten, fill-in-the-blanks letter designed to fit standard situations. The higher you rise, the more frequently you'll face situations that aren't routine, that demand creative solutions.

Claim 3: I'm being hired as an accountant, not a writer.

Reality: *The Chartered Professional Accountant Competency Map* (2012) identifies five enabling competencies for accountants: professional and ethical behaviour, problem solving and decision making, communication, self-management, teamwork, and leadership. In particular, "CPAs must communicate effectively through listening, understanding, speaking, and writing with clarity, and through the art of persuasion and negotiation. CPAs must be able to clearly communicate complex matters to all levels of an entity."[8] To be competitive in a global economy, accountants, like engineers, need these so-called soft skills: "communications, team building, report writing and preparing presentations."[9]

Claim 4: I'll just pick up the phone or use my cell.

Reality: Important calls require follow-up letters, memos, or e-mail messages. People in organizations put things in writing to make themselves and their accomplishments visible, create a record, convey complex data, make things convenient for the reader, save money, and convey their own messages more effectively. "If it isn't in writing," says one manager, "it didn't happen."

Claim 5: Nobody cares about the old rules any more. Anything goes in texts or tweets.

Reality: The shorter the message, the more opportunities for ambiguity and miscommunication. That's why ever more concerns exist in classrooms and workplaces about how and when we text and tweet, what we disclose, and who or what might be impacted. Coming across as spontaneous and sincere takes preparation and planning. Industry Canada, for instance, follows the Treasury Board Standard on Social Media Account Management. A 12-step protocol means that tweets can be planned for weeks, go through dozens of edits and approvals (for policy compliance), and have retweets by other agencies pre-arranged.[10]

LO2

UNDERSTANDING AND ANALYZING BUSINESS COMMUNICATION SITUATIONS

In the face of massive technological, cultural, and demographic change impacting business communications, the best communicators remain conscious of the context in which they make their choices; they're aware of options.

Ask yourself the following questions:

- **What's at stake—to whom?** Think not only about your own purpose and needs but also about the concerns your boss and your readers may have. Your message will be most effective if you think of the organizational context—and

Technology Tips No Substitute for Proofreading*

Computer software can make writing easier, but there's still no substitute for careful writing. Before you let your spell checker and grammar checker do your editing, consider these results of a study of graduate students proofreading a business letter. When the students with the highest verbal SAT scores proofread on their own, they made, on average, five errors. Students with lower verbal SATs made an average of 12.3 errors. When students turned on the spell checker, they made more mistakes! The students with the highest verbal SAT scores averaged 16 errors, and those with lower scores averaged 17 errors.

A Prime Minister's Office news release about Prime Minister Harper's itinerary also failed the proofreading test when it listed Iqualuit rather than Iqaluit as Nunavut's capital. The extra "u" changed the meaning from "many fish" to people with an intimate part of their anatomy unwiped!

If that error cost embarrassment, a single proofreading error cost Penguin Group Australia the equivalent of Cdn$20,000 when 7,000 copies of *The Pasta Bible* cookbook had to be destroyed because a recipe called for "freshly ground black people" instead of pepper.

When typos are a major turnoff to prospective employers and customers, it makes sense to practise your proofreading skills.

*Based on Terry Pedwell, "PMO's spelling mistake gives Iqaluit a bum rap," *Winnipeg Free Press*, August 19, 2009, retrieved February 4, 2011, from http://www.winnipegfreepress.com/canada/pmos-spelling-mistake-gives-iqaluit-a-bum-rap-53673857.html; Adam Arnold, "Book axed over 'ground black people' typo," *SkyNews*, April 19, 2010; Jay Greene, "Spell-cheque nation," *BusinessWeek*, May 5, 2003.

the larger context of stakeholders including shareholders, customers, and regulators. When the stakes are high, you'll need to take into account people's emotional feelings as well as objective facts.

- **Should you send a message?** Sometimes, especially when you're new on the job, silence can be the tactful response. But be alert to opportunities to learn, to influence, to make your case. Your communications can build your career.
- **What channel should you use?** Paper documents and presentations are formal and give you considerable control over the message. E-mail, blogs, text messages, phone and cell calls, and stopping by someone's office are less formal. Oral channels promote group decision making, allow misunderstandings to be cleared up more quickly, and seem more personal. Sometimes you may need more than one message, in more than one channel.
- **What should you say?** Content for a message may not be obvious. How detailed should you be? Should you repeat information that the audience already knows? The answers will depend on the kind of document, your purposes, audiences, and the corporate culture. And you'll have to figure these things out for yourself, without detailed instructions. Your judgment is at stake.
- **How should you say it?** The form of your ideas—what comes first, second, and last—and the words you use shape the audience's response. A well-designed, visually attractive document enhances readability whether you are speaking for your organization or selling your skills to a potential employer.

THE COST OF WRITING

Despite—or because of—proliferating technologies, writing costs time and money. A study of Canadian workers reported that 58% spend two to four hours per day reading text (print or online), 28% miss important information often, and 63% miss key content "once in a while." Complaints about poor written communications were reported by 71%, with 85% citing "wasted time," 70% "lost productivity," and 63% "errors."[11] In reduced productivity alone, low literacy costs Canadian organizations $2.5 million annually.[12] Improved literacy means increased productivity and bottom-line business performance and improved learning, greater participation, and higher earning power for employees.[13]

In many organizations, all external documents must be approved before they go out. A document may **cycle** from writer to superior to writer to another superior to writer again 3 or 4 or even 11 times before it is finally approved. The cycling process increases the cost of writing while adding to its accuracy and credibility.

Long documents can involve large teams of people and take months to write. Whether in the public or private sector, strong writing skills are therefore at a premium.

Good communication is worth every minute it takes and every penny it costs. In fact, in a survey conducted by the International Association of Business Communicators, CEOs said that communication yielded a 235% return on investment.[14]

THE COST OF POOR WRITING

When writing isn't as good as it could be, you and your organization pay a price in wasted time, wasted efforts, and lost goodwill.

Bad writing has these costs:

- **Takes longer to read** (up to 97% of reading time involves trying to understand what we're reading)
- **Needs revision** (involving disproportionate managerial time on explaining how to revise)
- **Obscures ideas** and needlessly protracts discussions and decisions
- **Requires requests for further information** (and further delays)
- **Does not get results**—or gets the wrong results
- **Undermines the image of the organization**
- **Loses goodwill**

Messages can also create a poor image because of poor audience analysis and inappropriate style (see ⏩ Chapter 2).

BENEFITS OF IMPROVING WRITING

Better writing has these benefits:

- **Saves time.** Reduces reading and revision time and the time taken asking writers "What did you mean?"
- **Makes your efforts more effective.** Increases the number of requests that are answered positively and promptly—on the first request. Presents your points more forcefully.
- **Communicates your points more clearly.** Reduces the misunderstandings that occur when the reader has to supply missing or unclear information.
- **Builds goodwill.** Builds a positive image of your organization. Builds an image of yourself as a knowledgeable, intelligent, capable person.

LO3

CRITERIA FOR EFFECTIVE MESSAGES

Good business writing meets five basic criteria:

1. **It's clear.** The meaning the reader gets is the meaning the writer intended. The reader doesn't have to guess.
2. **It's complete.** All of the reader's questions are answered. The reader has enough information to evaluate the message and act on it.

3. **It's correct.** All of the information in the message is accurate. The message is free from errors in punctuation, spelling, grammar, word order, and sentence structure.
4. **It's concise.** It saves the reader's time. The style, organization, and visual impact of the message help the reader to read, understand, and act on the information promptly.
5. **It's courteous.** It builds goodwill. The message presents a positive image of the writer and his or her organization. It treats the reader as a person, not a number. It cements a good relationship between the writer and the reader.

Whether a message meets these five criteria depends on the interactions among the writer, the audience, the purposes of the message, and the situation. No single set of words will work in all possible situations.

LO4

PRINCIPLES THAT CAN HELP IMPROVE YOUR COMMUNICATIONS

Many miscommunications arise not because people genuinely disagree but because they make different assumptions and use symbols to mean different things. **Communication theory** and **semantics** can help us understand how, why, and where communication, perhaps the most complex human activity, can break down, and what we can do to communicate more effectively. Communication theory attempts to explain what happens when we communicate. Semantics is the study of the way our behaviour is influenced by the words and other symbols we use to communicate.

Never merely a matter of transmitting information, communication is a socio-cultural process negotiating differences of power and cultural competency in building the credibility, goodwill, and trust that sustain business relationships. The process is so complex because it is negotiated within contexts from the immediate situation to the broader culture and legal, ethical, ecological, political, and economic environment.

Speakers negotiate meanings in particular contexts that are themselves always changing (see ▸▸ "Trends in Business Communication" in this chapter). The eight principles of semantics help us understand and take account of the ways that those contexts shape and are shaped by communications.

Communication theory is likewise useful in helping us understand where and why miscommunication occurs at each stage from stimulus and **perception** to **encoding** the message to **transmission** through channels to **decoding,** interpreting, choosing and selecting, and **feedback.**

Feedback may be direct and immediate or indirect and delayed; it may be verbal or nonverbal. Each person in the process is responsible for feedback that clarifies and confirms understanding.

Noise can interfere with every aspect of the communication process. Noise may be physical, psychological, or socio-cultural. Physical noise could be a phone line with static, or handwriting that is hard to read. Psychological noise could include not liking a speaker, being preoccupied, or having one's mind already made up on an issue. Socio-cultural noise may include failures to follow etiquette or to adopt appropriate levels of formality (see Figure 1.1).

Channels—formal and informal—vary in speed, accuracy of transmission, cost, number of messages carried, number

Figure 1.1 A Model of the Communication Process

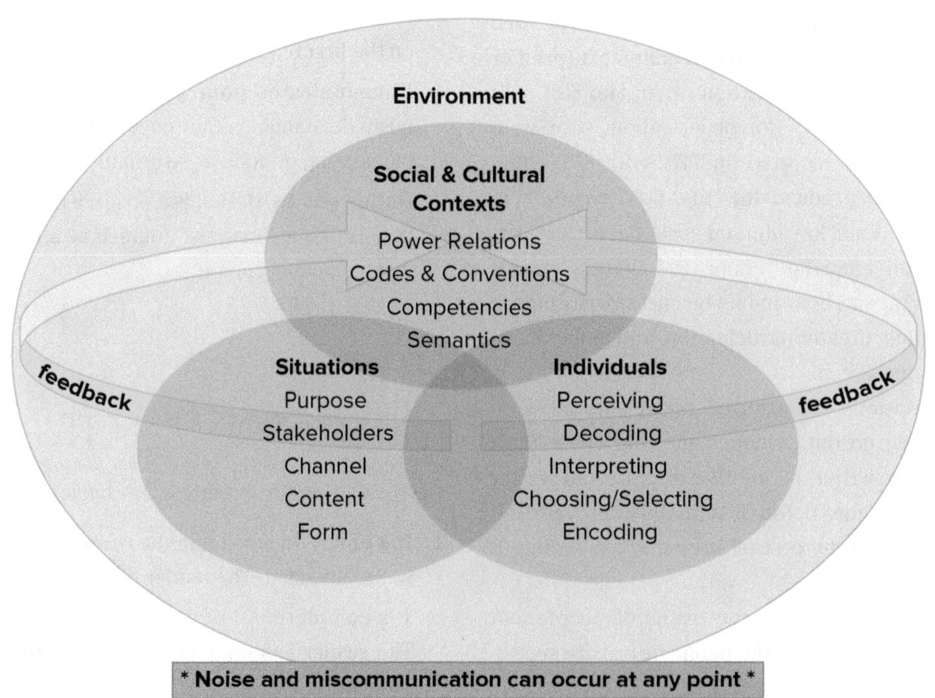

Technology Tips Choosing the Right Channel*

In creating the right impression, channel choice plays an important role. E-mail may not be the most tactful choice when ending a professional or personal relationship. An e-mail sent in haste can return to haunt the sender.

When artist Sophie Calle received a breakup e-mail from her partner concluding with the wish that she take care of herself, she did just that by asking 107 female experts for their opinion of the e-mail. Their responses became the basis of her exhibition *Take Care of Yourself* shown at the Venice Biennale in summer 2007 and on a world tour in 2008.

Before going public, Calle showed the sender the work. Although she has never revealed his identity, he "wasn't very happy." Still, in the end "he had respect for the project" and did not resist.

When Prime Minister Stephen Harper and Industry Minister Tony Clement chose Twitter to disclose government intentions on the CRTC's 2011 Internet user-based billing decision, their channel choice was widely criticized.

By contrast, Mayor Naheed Nenshi of Calgary has been widely praised for his use of Facebook, Twitter, and YouTube to engage voters. Nenshi won 40% of the ballots in a vote that increased participation from 32.9% in 2007 to 53.24% in October 2010. His win, he argues, "proves voters care deeply about big ideas": "We called it politics in full sentences."

*Based on Iain Marlow and Susan Krashinsky, "Telecoms faced with new uncertainty," *Report on Business*, February 4, 2011, B1; Craig Wong, "Harper tweets promise of Internet billing review," *TheStar.com*, February 1, 2011, retrieved February 4, 2011, from http://www.thestar.com/business/article/931674–harper-tweets-promise-of-internet-billing-review; "CRTC must reverse Internet usage ruling: Clement," retrieved June 19, 2011, from http://www.cbc.ca/news/canada/story/2011/02/03/crtc-internet-clement.html; "Calgary chooses Nenshi as new mayor," retrieved June 24, 2011, from http://www.cbc.ca/news/canada/calgary/story/2010/10/19/calgary-election-mayor.html; Chrystia Freeland, "Calgary mayor gives his own Twitter revolution lesson," *Report on Business*, April 1, 2011, B2; Sarah Milroy, "Romantic revenge, served in multimedia," *The Globe and Mail*, August 2, 2008, R4.

of people reached, efficiency, and ability to promote goodwill. Depending on your purpose, audience, and situation, one channel may be better than another (▸▸ Chapter 2).

Oral channels are better for group decision making, allow misunderstandings to be cleared up more quickly, and seem more personal. Shorter communication channels are more accurate than longer chains of communications that increase the potential for error. For important messages when the cost of miscommunication is high, managers usually use two different channels—for example, talking to someone about a written memo.

Channel choice may also be influenced by organizational culture. Waterloo-based BlackBerry gives its employees a device, inviting them to join a business without borders or boundaries and renew inventiveness and opportunity.

Channel overload occurs when the channel cannot handle all the messages. Websites can crash when subjected to unusually high traffic. **Information overload** occurs when more messages are transmitted than the human receiver can handle. Some receivers process information "first come, first served." Some may try to select the most important messages and ignore others. A third way is to depend on abstracts or summaries. None of these ways is completely satisfactory.

At every stage, people may misperceive, misinterpret, choose badly, encode poorly, and choose inappropriate channels. Miscommunication can also occur because different people have different frames of reference. We always interpret messages in light of our personal experiences, our cultures (▸▸ Chapter 5) and subcultures, and even the point in history at which we live.

Semantic principles offer eight practical tools for negotiating barriers and improving communication. They help us recognize bias, monitor assumptions, and moderate claims so that messages can be more effectively relayed, received, and understood. They help us analyze and recognize logical flaws in our own and others' arguments.

LO5

1. Perception Involves the Perceiver as Well as the Perceived

What we perceive is conditioned by what we are able to see, what we have seen, what we are prepared to see, and what we want to see—all of which are affected by our cultural and other experience. For example, some Canadians see an exploitable commodity when they look at the land, while many Aboriginal people see Mother Earth. Such differences can cause serious miscommunications in discussions about resource exploitation.

Most people have a tendency to attribute their own feelings or perceptions to other people as well. We may tune out messages we think will challenge our own positions; we seek messages that support our positions.

Use these correctives to check the accuracy of your perceptions:

1. Recognize that everyone's perception will in some measure be biased.
2. Recognize that different positions cause us to view reality differently and to draw different conclusions from what we observe.
3. If a new idea does not fit neatly into your worldview, recognize that your worldview, not the idea, may need rethinking.

2. Observations, Inferences, and Judgments Are Not the Same

Ten minutes before lunchtime, Jan is talking on the phone. Her manager thinks, "She's talking again. Doesn't she ever work?" Jan is talking to a potential customer; she sees the call as essential, since it may eventually lead to a sale. She can't understand why her manager doesn't think she's serious about her career.

Jan's manager has jumped to the wrong conclusion. He is confusing observations and inferences.

An **observation** is a statement that you yourself have verified. An **inference** is a statement that you have not personally verified, but whose truth or falsity could be established. A **judgment** or an **opinion** is a statement that can never be verified, since it includes terms that cannot be measured objectively.

Usually, we call statements facts if nearly everyone in our culture accepts them as true. But remember that before Columbus's arrival in North America, nearly everyone believed that the world was flat. Almost everything we know we take on someone else's authority.

In everyday life and in business, you have to make decisions based on inferences ("The sales figures I've been given are accurate") and even on judgments ("We have too much money tied up in long-term investments"). What should you as a reader or writer do?

1. Check to see whether a statement is an observation, an inference, or a judgment.
2. Estimate the accuracy of the inference by comparing it to your experiences with the source and with this kind of situation. If the cost of making a mistake is high, try to get more information.
3. Distinguish between what you know to be the case and what you think, assume, or judge to be true. In the following example, the italicized words remind readers that the statements are inferences.

He predicts that the stock market *could* move up an additional 10% to 20% during the next 12 to 18 months.

3. No Two Things Are Exactly Alike

We make sense of the world by grouping things into categories. Once we have categories, we often simply assign each new experience to a category and then make the response we think appropriate to that category.

Unfortunately, this convenient lumping can lead to **stereotyping** (⏩ Chapter 5): putting similar people or events into a single category, even though significant differences exist.

To guard against stereotyping, do the following:

1. Recognize differences as well as similarities. The members of any one group are not identical.
2. Be sure that any analogy you use to make your point clear is accurate at the point of comparison.

4. Things Change Significantly with Time

If you keep up with the stock market, with commodity prices, or with interest rates, you know that things (as well as people) change significantly with time.

Someone who does not recognize that prices, situations, and people change is guilty of making a **frozen evaluation.** The following corrections help us remember not to freeze evaluations:

1. Date statements. The price of Research In Motion (RIM) stock on October 20, 2001 is not the price of BlackBerry stock on June 24, 2014.
2. Provide a frame of reference so that your reader can compare profits or percentages.
3. Periodically retest assumptions about people, businesses, products, and services to ensure that your evaluations still apply.

International The Word Is Not Connected to the Object

- In Germany, Oktoberfest is held in September.
- The Big Ten athletic conference has 12 teams.
- The principal ingredient in sweetbread is neither sugar nor bread but the cooked pancreas or thymus of a young animal, usually a calf.
- Wild rice isn't necessarily wild. Nearly all the wild rice on grocery-store shelves is commercially cultivated in rice paddies and turned and watered by machines. For centuries before Europeans came to North America, the Algonquin and Siouan peoples harvested wild rice, a seed from an aquatic grass rather than a member of the rice family. Canadian "Lake Wild Rice" is harvested from natural bodies of water rather than cultivated or paddy-grown as in the United States.*

*Adapted from Agriculture and Agri-Food Canada, "Canada's wild rice industry," retrieved March 3, 2005, from http://www.agr.gc.ca.

5. Most *Either–Or* Classifications Are Not Legitimate

A common logical fallacy (or error in reasoning) is **polarization:** trying to force the reader into a position by arguing that there are only two possible positions, one of which is clearly unacceptable:

> Either the supervisor runs this department with a firm hand, or anarchy will take over and work will never get done.

Running a department "with a firm hand" is only one leadership style; sharing authority with or even transferring it entirely to subordinates need not result in anarchy.

Even people who admit that there are more than two possible positions may still limit the options unnecessarily. Such **blindering,** after the blinders that horses wear, can lead to polarization.

Sometimes blindering is responsible for bad questions in surveys:

> Do you own ____, rent ____, or live with your parents ____?

What about someone who lives with a friend or with relatives other than parents?

Polarization unnecessarily sharpens divisions between people and obscures the common ground; blindering prevents our seeing creative solutions to the problems we face. Here are some correctives:

1. Recognize the complexities of a situation. Resist the temptation to oversimplify.
2. Whenever you see only two alternatives, consciously search for a third or more before making your decision.
3. Redefine the question or problem to get at the real issue.

× Don't ask:	How can I as a team leader show that I'm in control?
✓ Ask:	How can we improve the effectiveness of our report?

6. A Statement Is Never the Whole Story

It is impossible to know everything; it is impossible to tell someone everything. When we assume that a statement contains all the important information, or when the context is omitted (deliberately or inadvertently), meanings are inevitably twisted.

For example, media widely reported that Canada "fizzled" in the swimming pool at the 2008 Olympics. When a CBC reporter asked Canadian 4x200 relay swimmers how they might get to the "world stage," swimmers responded that they were on the world stage, having just finished fifth and broken the Canadian record in an Olympic final![15]

What can we do to avoid misstatements by implication?

1. Recognize that reports are filtered; you are not getting all the facts, and you are almost certainly getting inferences as well as observations.
2. Check the messages you send out to make sure you have provided the background information the reader needs to interpret your message accurately.

7. Words Are Not Identical to the Objects They Represent

People, who name things and use words, provide the only connection between the thing and the word.

We often respond to the word or label rather than to reality. Our degree of distress during a bleak economic period is affected by the label: a *slowdown* doesn't sound as bad as a *recession,* and even that is better than a *depression.* Advertisers understand that labelling a book a *best-seller* is sure to increase sales.

Try these correctives:

1. Support **claims** with specific **evidence** or **data.**
2. Check your own responses to make sure your decisions are based not on labels but on valid, logical arguments.
3. If your claims cause a **counterclaim, limit** your claim or provide a **rebuttal** to be convincing.

8. Communication Symbols Must Stand for Essentially the Same Thing in the Minds of the Sender and the Receiver

Communication depends on symbols. **Bypassing** occurs when two people use the same symbol to mean different things.

Bypassing creates misunderstandings. When employees hear communication skills described as "soft skills," they may assume that they are as easy, simple, and natural as the label implies. They may understand communication only as a means of transmitting information and may therefore ignore complex issues of audience, purpose, and context. They may fail to invest the sort of time, planning, and effort that effective communication takes. They may also blame themselves or become frustrated when they discover that communicating is among the most challenging things we do in business.

Here are some measures that will help us avoid bypassing:

1. Be sensitive to contexts.
2. Consider the other person's background and situation. What is he or she likely to mean?
3. Mirror what the other person has said in your own words and check for accuracy. Be sure to use different words for the key ideas.
4. Ask questions.

LO6

THE MANAGERIAL FUNCTIONS OF COMMUNICATION

According to McGill professor Henry Mintzberg, managers have three basic jobs: to collect and convey information, to make decisions, and to promote interpersonal unity.[16] All of those jobs are carried out through communication. Managers collect relevant information from conversations, the grapevine, phone and mobile calls, memos, reports, databases, social media, and the Internet. They convey information and decisions to other people inside or outside the organization through meetings, speeches, press releases, videos, **podcasts,** blogs, wikis, Skype, Facebook, Twitter, memos, letters, e-mail and text messages, and reports. Managers motivate organizational members in speeches, memos, conversations at lunch and over coffee, bulletin boards, and through "management by walking around."

Effective managers are able to use a wide variety of media and strategies to communicate. They know how to interpret comments from informal channels such as the company grapevine; they can speak effectively in small groups and in formal presentations; they write well.

Communication—oral, nonverbal, and written (print or digital)—goes to both internal and external audiences. **Internal audiences** (Figure 1.2) are other people in the same organization: subordinates, superiors, peers. **External audiences** (Figure 1.3) are people outside the organization: customers, suppliers, unions, shareholders, potential employees, government agencies, the press, and the general public.

Listening, Speaking, and Interpersonal Communication

Informal listening, speaking, and working in groups are just as important as writing formal documents and giving formal oral presentations. As a newcomer in an organization, you'll need to listen to others both to find out what you're supposed to do and to learn about the organization's values and culture, and what behaviours and communication styles it favours.

Informal chat, both about yesterday's game and about what's happening at work, connects you to the **grapevine,** an informal source of company information. Savvy employers and employees know when and "what kind of chatter is harmful or helpful"; "whom to talk to and what to talk about"; and when they have crossed the ethical line to spread hurtful gossip or rumours.[17] Networking with others in and beyond your office and working with others in workgroups will be crucial to your success.

These skills remain important as you climb the corporate ladder. In fact, a study of 15 executives judged good performers by their companies showed that these executives spent most of their time in informal contact with other people. These informal discussions, taking 76% of these executives' work time, enabled them to promote their agendas.[18]

Knowing Your Purpose

People in organizations produce a large variety of documents. Your own and your organization's success depends on your ability to understand the functions, formats, and conventions of different genres or kinds of documents, what standards

Figure 1.2 The Internal Audiences of the Sales Manager—West

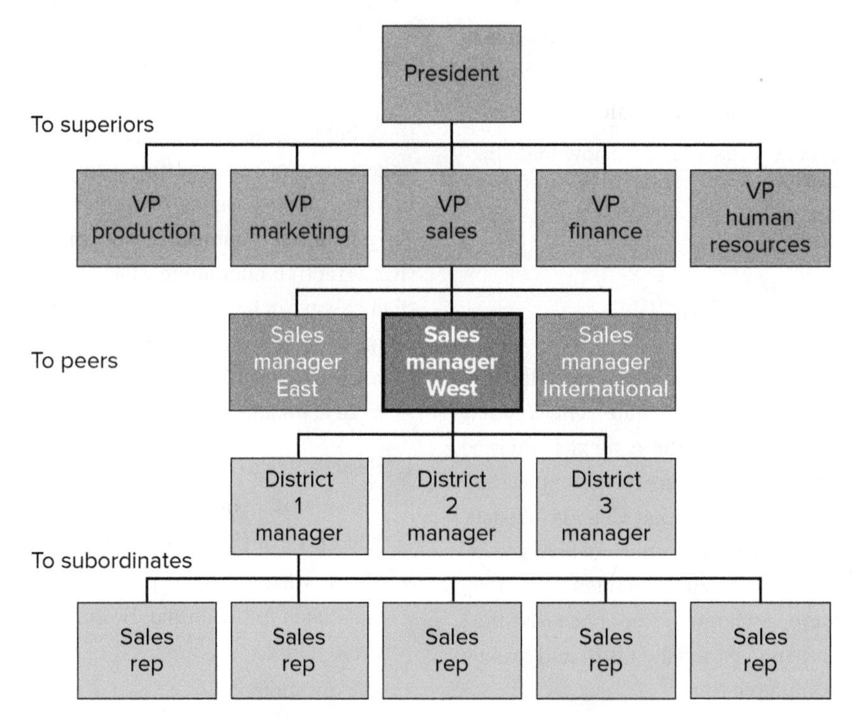

On the Job The Payoff from Listening*

In business settings, listening skills are more than courteous; they also provide value to the organization. Managers who listen carefully enable others to share ideas and knowledge. Smart managers invite feedback and then listen actively.

Inattentive listening can be costly in time, effort, mistakes, misaligned priorities, and uncoordinated activities.

Weak listeners

- Tune out spoken messages
- Focus on their own response rather than on the speaker
- Become distracted easily
- Fail to see relevance
- Do not seek clarification
- Judge delivery rather than content
- Avoid eye contact
- Take extensive notes without evaluating or prioritizing

Effective listeners

- Stop talking
- Maintain an open mind and concentrate on the speaker
- Resist and manage distractions
- Recognize what's in it for them
- Think, evaluate, and summarize
- Attend to tone of voice, nonverbals, and subtexts
- Maintain eye contact and respond to the speaker
- Tailor note taking to the occasion

*Based on Carter McNamara, "Habits to differentiate good from poor listening," retrieved February 4, 2011, from http://www.managementhelp.org/commskls/listen/gd_vs_pr.htm; PAR Group, "The secrets to listening well," retrieved February 4, 2011, from http://www.thepargroup.com/article_SecretsListenWell.html; "Listen up, leaders: Let workers do the talking," *HRMagazine,* October 2003, downloaded from http://findarticles.com/p/articles/mi_m3495; Sherman K. Okum, "How to be a better listener," *Nation's Business,* August 1975; Philip Morgan and Kent Barker, "Building a professional image: Improving listening behavior," *Supervisory Management,* November 1995.

are current, where flexibility is possible, how and where you might creatively improvise and innovate, and how documents fit with organization goals. Understanding how conventional formats enable common codes allows you to achieve your communication purpose.

All of the documents in Figures 1.4 and 1.5 have one or more of the *three basic purposes of business writing:* to inform, to request or persuade, and to build goodwill. When you **inform,** you explain something or tell readers something. When you **request** or **persuade,** you want the reader to act.

Figure 1.3 The Corporation's External Audiences

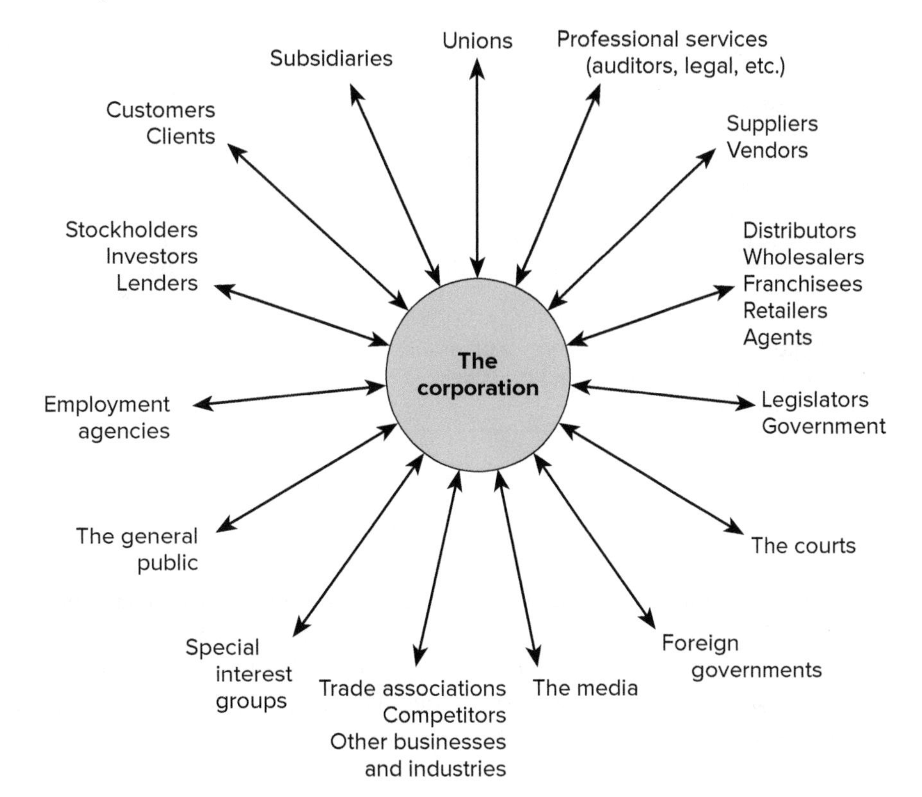

Source: Daphne A. Jameson

Figure 1.4 Internal Documents Produced in One Organization

DOCUMENT	DESCRIPTION OF DOCUMENT	PURPOSE(S) OF DOCUMENT
Transmittal	Memo accompanying document, telling why it's being forwarded to the receiver	Inform; persuade reader to read document; build image and goodwill
Monthly or quarterly report	Report summarizing profitability, productivity, and problems during period. Used to plan activity for next month or quarter	Inform; build image and goodwill (report is accurate, complete; writer understands company)
Policy and procedures bulletin	Statement of company policies and instructions (e.g., how to run fire drills, how to use social media professionally)	Inform; build image and goodwill (procedures are reasonable)
Request to deviate from policy and procedures bulletin	Persuasive memo arguing that another approach is better for a specific situation than the standard approach	Persuade; build image and goodwill (request is reasonable; writer seeks good of company)
Performance appraisal	Evaluation of an employee's performance, with recommended areas for improvement or recommendation for promotion	Inform; persuade employee to improve
Memo of congratulations	Congratulations to employees who have won awards, been promoted, or earned community recognition	Build goodwill

Figure 1.5 External Documents Produced in One Organization

DOCUMENT	DESCRIPTION OF DOCUMENT	PURPOSE(S) OF DOCUMENT
Quotation	Letter giving price for a specific product, fabrication, or service	Inform; build goodwill (price is reasonable)
Claims adjustment	Letter granting or denying customer request to be given credit for defective goods	Inform; build goodwill
Job description	Description of qualifications and duties of each job. Used for performance appraisals, setting salaries, and hiring	Inform; persuade good candidates to apply; build goodwill (job duties match level, pay)
10-K report	Report filed with the Securities and Exchange Commission detailing financial information	Inform
Annual report	Report to shareholders summarizing financial information for year	Inform; persuade shareholders to retain stock and others to buy; build goodwill (company is a good corporate citizen)
Thank-you letter	Letter to suppliers, customers, or other people who have helped individuals or the company	Build goodwill

The word *request* suggests that the action will be easy or routine; *persuade* suggests that you will have to motivate and convince the reader to act. When you **build goodwill,** you create a good image of yourself and of your organization—the kind of image that makes people want to do business with you.

Most messages have multiple purposes. When you answer a question, you're informing, but you can also build goodwill by showing that you are competent and perceptive and that your answer is correct and complete. In a claims adjustment, whether you answer *yes* or *no,* you want to suggest that the reader's claim received careful consideration and that the decision is fair, businesslike, and justified.

Two of the documents listed in Figure 1.5 package the same information in different ways for different audiences. The 10-K report is informative, designed merely to show that a Canadian company trading in the United States is complying with SEC regulations. The annual report, in contrast, has multiple purposes and audiences. Its primary purpose is to convince shareholders that the company is a good investment and a good corporate citizen. Annual reports will also be read by employees, stockbrokers, potential shareholders, job applicants, and other stakeholders, so the firm creates a report that is persuasive and builds goodwill as well as presenting information.

LO7

TRENDS IN BUSINESS COMMUNICATION

In an ever-changing business environment, business communication is changing—and moving to the heart of business. If business communication personnel used to work behind the scenes translating business goals, they are now front and centre in the decision-making process. Kellie Garrett, for instance, became senior vice-president of strategy, knowledge, and reputation at Farm Credit Canada in Regina and a 2010 Master Communicator honoured by IABC Canada.[19]

Rapid change means that no college or university course or executive MBA program can teach you everything you need to know for your working life. You'll need to remain open to new ideas. You'll need to view situations critically, so that you can evaluate new conditions and recognize opportunities. The skills you learn can stand you in good stead: critical thinking, computer savvy, problem solving, and the ability to write, to speak, and to work well with other people.

Understanding trends can help you in targeting job applications and can enable businesses to position themselves for new opportunities. Ten trends affect business communication: a focus on quality and customers' needs, entrepreneurship and outsourcing, teams, diversity, globalization, legal and ethical concerns, balancing work and family, corporate social responsibility, reputation management, and technology.

WestJet maintains a corporate culture that nourishes customer satisfaction and employee loyalty.

Focus on Quality and Customers' Needs

In general, expectations of quality and customer service are rising in a social media world where customer knowledge and power are increasing.[20] That's a problem for companies, notes direct marketing expert James Rosenfield:

> Unhappy customers in industrialized countries historically tell 15 people about their experiences. [On the Internet] with one keystroke, you can now tell 150 or 1,500 or 15,000![21]

Superior customer service pays. Bank customers who described themselves as most satisfied were much more profitable for the company than were customers who were merely "satisfied."[22] Research suggests that the most effective workers don't see work as assigned tasks. Instead, they define their own goals based on the needs of customers and clients.[23]

Offering superior customer service doesn't always mean spending extra money. Learning from the example of Southwest Airlines in the United States, Clive Beddoe, first president and CEO of WestJet, was determined to get people where they wanted to go on time and at the right price. And the passengers—or "guests"—bought his plan. WestJet was showing a profit within its first six months in 1996. The corporate culture is informal, friendly, good humoured: the executive area at the Calgary headquarters is for the "Big Shots," and human resources is handled in the "People Department." Like Beddoe, current president and CEO Gregg Saretsky is serious about his business—and caring for the community on whose trust the business depends. That means he is ready to adapt to a changing environment to pursue partnerships and new possibilities.[24]

Communication is at the centre of the focus on quality and customers' needs, as the MEC team understands (◀◀ An Inside Perspective). Brainstorming and group problem solving are essential to develop more efficient ways to do things. Then the good ideas have to be communicated throughout the company. Innovators need to be recognized. And only by listening to what customers say can an organization know what its customers really want.

Entrepreneurship and Outsourcing

Entrepreneurship is a fast-growing and increasingly diverse sector of the Canadian economy, with women, youth, ethnic groups, and social entrepreneurs adding to the traditional players. Contributing over $12 billion annually to the Canadian economy, women entrepreneurs start four of five Canadian businesses. One in ten women in Canada is self-employed, many of them combining motherhood and entrepreneurship in what has been termed "mompreneurship."[25]

The Canadian Youth Business Foundation (CYBF), a non-profit, volunteer-based organization founded in 1996, provides mentoring and financing to support young Canadian entrepreneurs (18–34 years) achieve social and economic success. Supporting more than 5,600 young or emerging entrepreneurs to 2014, it has created more than 23,000 new jobs and generated hundreds of millions in gross sales and export revenue as well as $163.6 million in tax revenue.[26]

Although the participation of immigrant communities in entrepreneurship is well known, Aboriginal participation is perhaps less familiar. The 2001 Census identified more than 27,000 Aboriginal people who have their own businesses in primary and traditional industries as well as the knowledge economy. By the 2006 Census numbers had reached 37,000, with marked growth among Aboriginal youth and women.[27]

In the public, private, and non-profit sectors, social entrepreneurship responds to demands for corporate social responsibility and for answers to some complex social problems. Stressing hybrid models of activity, social entrepreneurship draws on the innovation, resourcefulness, and vision of traditional entrepreneurship "to combine the heart of business with the heart of the community through the creativity of the individual."[28] Entrepreneurship is so popular that many business schools now offer courses, internships, or whole programs in starting and running a business.

Some companies are trying to match the success and growth rate of start-ups by nurturing an entrepreneurial spirit in **intrapreneurs** within their organizations. Google Inc.'s "20% work" is a celebrated example of such workplace initiatives to motivate innovation, while Xerox Research Centre in Mississauga credits brainstorming among diverse team members for its record of 220 patentable ideas each year. Fairmont Hotels & Resorts in Toronto similarly credits the "green team" of "ground-level" employees in each hotel with cost-saving measures to reduce the carbon footprint.[29]

Some businesses have had to become entrepreneurial because of outsourcing. **Outsourcing** means going outside the company for products and services that once were provided by the company's employees. Companies can outsource manufacturing, customer service, and accounting. Canada's technology expertise makes it a leading player in outsourced service provision.[30]

Outsourcing makes communication more difficult—and more important—than it was when jobs were done in-house. It's harder to ask questions, since people are no longer down the hall. And it's easier for problems—from intellectual property and currency issues to labour, health and safety, delivery delays, and quality problems—to turn into major ones. Some companies now are creating a "chief resource officer" to monitor contracts with vendors so that lines of communication and responsibility will be clear. Like Mountain Equipment Co-op (◀◀ An Inside Perspective), many are working with suppliers to ensure quality and other standards.

Teams

More and more companies are getting work done through teams. Teamwork brings together people's varying strengths

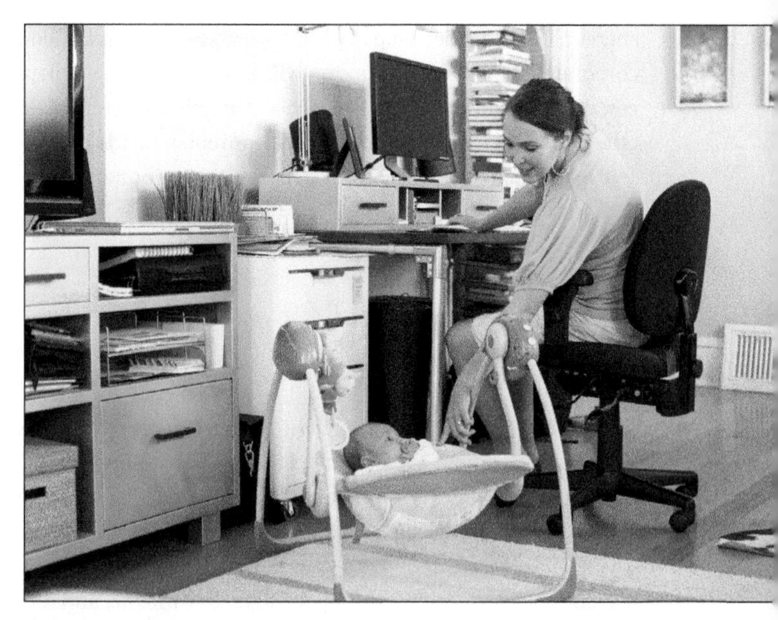

Balancing childcare and running a business is the goal of many women entrepreneurs.

and talents to solve problems and make decisions. Often, teams are cross-functional (drawing from different jobs or functions) and/or cross-cultural (including people from different nations or ethnic or cultural groups served by the company).

Teams helped BC Biomedical Laboratories Ltd. meet client needs, enhance employee satisfaction—and become one of Canada's 50 Best Employers 12 years running to 2012. There's a "family feel" among the more than 650 employees of this Vancouver diagnostic testing service. The management structure is unusually flat (less hierarchical) in an organization where management and employees share goals and leadership. With about half the staff in 45 patient service centres and half at head office, Biomedical Laboratories relies on its strengths: its flexibility, culture of trust, strong communications, and network of team leaders.[31]

Teams—often supported by technology—put a premium on learning to identify and solve problems, to share leadership, to work *with* other people rather than merely delegating work *to* other people, to resolve conflicts constructively, and to motivate people to do their best (▶▶ Chapter 6).

Diversity

Teams put a premium on being able to work with people from different backgrounds.

Although women, Aboriginal people, persons with disabilities, and members of visible minorities have always been part of the workforce, they have not enjoyed equitable participation in the Canadian mainstream. Even when education became more accessible after World War II and women and other marginalized groups began to enter the professions in the 1960s and 1970s, few made it into management.

Now Canadian business is realizing that barriers to recruitment and promotion are hurting the bottom line as well as individuals. Toronto alone is estimated to lose to the underemployment of diverse, qualified people $2.25 billion annually.[32] Helping each worker reach his or her potential requires more flexibility from managers as well as more knowledge about intercultural communication. And it's crucial to help workers from different backgrounds understand each other—especially when layoffs make many workers fear that increased opportunities for someone else will come only at a cost to themselves.

Treating readers with respect has always been a principle of good business communication. The emphasis on diversity simply makes it an economic mandate as well. To learn more about diversity and the workforce, read ⏩ Chapter 5.

Diversity allows businesses to draw on many traditions. When problem solving, organizations from Concentra Financial to Xerox turn to Aboriginal talking circles where co-workers pass an object (rock, feather, or stick). Only the person holding the object may speak, encouraging everyone to listen and learn from one another.

Globalization

In the global economy, importing and exporting are just the start. More and more companies have offices and factories around the world. To sell $200 million worth of appliances in India, Whirlpool adapts appliances to local markets and uses local contractors who speak India's 18 languages to deliver appliances by truck, bicycle, and even oxcart.[33]

From his vantage 250 kilometres above Earth, Canadian astronaut Chris Hadfield acquired a unique perspective on collaborative leadership in a global context: "if you can give [people] enough autonomy, time at the wheel, patience and feedback, you may in fact change the direction everybody is going because you see it's better than the one you originally chose." With over one million followers on Twitter, Chris Hadfield is in demand for his unique insights and power to engage diverse people worldwide.[34]

All the challenges of communicating in one culture and country increase exponentially when people communicate across cultures and countries. Succeeding in a global market requires **intercultural competence,** the ability to communicate sensitively with people from other cultures and countries based on an understanding of cultural differences. Nezar Freeny, founder of international hosting provider Amanah Tech Inc., headquartered in Toronto, has the intercultural competence to command trust—Amanah is Arabic for "trust"—so necessary to successful operations in the global economy.[35] To learn more about international communication, see ⏩ Chapter 5.

Canadian astronaut Chris Hadfield is pictured with the new $5 bank note on the International Space Station, April 30, 2013, in a public relations coup that was more than a year in planning.

Legal and Ethical Concerns

Legal fees cost businesses hundreds of thousands of dollars. The price of many simple items, such as ladders, is inflated greatly by the built-in reserve to protect the manufacturer against lawsuits. Companies are finding that clear, open communication can reduce lawsuits by giving all the parties a chance to shape policies and by clarifying exactly what is and isn't being proposed.

Ethical concerns don't carry the same clear dollar cost as legal fees. But when the Internet stock bubble burst, news stories featured unethical and illegal corporate practices. As investors and consumers heard the accusations of accounting fraud at WorldCom, Enron, and Adelphia Communications, many felt distrustful of businesses in general. The public outcry motivated the U.S. Congress to pass the Sarbanes-Oxley Act in 2002, requiring corporations to engage in much more careful control and reporting of their financial activities.[36] The 2008 economic and financial meltdown did little to renew trust. In fact, the 2013 Edelman Trust Barometer survey of informed publics in 20 countries worldwide found banks and financial services were still the least trusted.[37]

Such public distrust and government regulation have also renewed attention to corporate ethics in Canada, where both Nortel Networks and Hollinger International Inc. became associated with unethical corporate practices—*Canadian Business*'s Matthew McClearn asks whether "anybody even read" the code of ethics at Hollinger.[38] As a result, Canadian companies now face new regulations and reporting standards. Efforts to right wrongs have not always gone as planned. When Nortel CEO Bill Owens announced efforts to regain trust, he named his "first" chief ethics officer as "testimony to our commitment to the highest standards of ethics and integrity in all of our company's operations." Unfortunately, Susan Shepard was not the first ethics officer at Nortel! Megan Barry had held that position from 1994 to 1999, though the department "grew increasingly invisible within the organization" under John Roth's leadership, according to *Maclean's* reporter Steve Maich.[39]

Business schools are increasingly responding to the interest in corporate governance and business ethics. Pointing to gaps in educational offerings, the Association to Advance Collegiate Schools of Business (AACSB International) wants to see more done to teach about stewardship obligations, the concerns of stakeholders, and "the responsible use of power." To that end, Professor Tima Bansal at the Ivey School is teaching University of British Columbia professor Joel Bakan's *The Corporation*, showing the corporation as psychopath.[40]

As Figure 1.6 suggests, language, graphics, and document design—basic parts of any business document—can be ethical or manipulative. Persuasion and gaining compliance—activities at the heart of business and organizational life—can be done with respect or contempt for customers, co-workers, and subordinates.

Organizations must be concerned about broader ethical issues as well: being good environmental citizens, offering a good workplace for their employees, and contributing to the needs of the communities in which they operate.

Balancing Work and Family

One out of every three Canadians aged 19–64 self-identifies as a workaholic, according to a May 2007 study. These individuals—much more likely to be dissatisfied with their work and with the balance between work and family time than other workers—report fair or poor health.[41] By 2012, a study of 25,000 Canadian full-time employees found 60% worked more than 45 hours per week and 54% of knowledge workers took work home to complete outside office hours. Half also managed child care and 23% had elder care duties. Highly dependent on e-mail, 28% reported that e-mail increased their stress. Only 3% reported low stress levels; 76% reported moderate to high levels of depressed mood.[42]

Many companies now recognize that workplace quality and employee engagement can have "an almost magical effect on the bottom line"—especially when generations succeeding the boomers place a high premium on work–life balance. Christine Kirkland of IKEA Canada, for instance, finds that flextime "takes a lot of the stress off." Xerox is among companies finding that flexible, family-friendly policies produce clear gains in productivity and customer service.[43] To make itself more family friendly, Ernst & Young tells people not to check their e-mail on weekends or vacations, limits consultants' travel, and tries to redesign workloads so people won't burn out.[44]

Figure 1.6 Ethical Issues in Business Communication

MANNER OF CONVEYING THE MESSAGE

Language, Graphics, and Document Design

- Is the message audience friendly? Does it respect the audience?
- Do the words balance the organization's right to present its best case with its responsibility to present its message honestly?
- Do graphics help the audience understand? Or do graphics distract or confuse?
- Does document design make reading easy? Does document design attempt to make readers skip key points?

Tactics Used to Shape Response

- Are the arguments logical?
- Are the emotional appeals used fairly? Do they supplement logic rather than substituting for it?
- Does the organizational pattern lead the audience without undue manipulation?
- Are the tactics honest? Do they avoid deceiving the audience?

QUALITIES OF THE MESSAGE

- Is the message an ethical one that treats all parties fairly and is sensitive to all stakeholders?
- Have interested parties been able to provide input into the decision or message?
- Does the audience get all the information it needs to make a good decision?
- Is information communicated in a timely way, or is information withheld to reduce the audience's power?
- Is information communicated in a schema the audience can grasp, or are data "dumped" without any context?

LARGER ORGANIZATIONAL CONTEXT OF THE MESSAGE

- How does the organization treat its employees? How do employees treat each other?
- How sensitive is the organization to stakeholders such as the people who live near its factories, stores, or offices, and to the general public?
- Does the organization support employees' efforts to be honest, fair, and ethical?
- Do the organization's actions in making products, buying supplies, and marketing goods and services stand up to ethical scrutiny?
- Is the organization a good corporate citizen, helpful rather than harmful to the community in which it exists?
- Are the organization's products or services a good use of scarce resources?

The downside of this trend is that sometimes work and family life are not so much balanced as blurred. Many employees study training videos and DVDs, write e-mail, check their mobile, and participate in conference calls on what used to be "personal time." Flexibility is necessary in an age of downsizing and doing business in many time zones, but it means that many managers are essentially on call all the time. Instead of resorting to "guerrilla telework" (working from home rather than booking time off to deal with family emergencies) or "buying balance" (paying for services that free up more time for work), Professors Chris Higgins and Linda Duxbury recommend just saying no.[45]

Corporate Social Responsibility

In the light of legal and ethical concerns, business schools, like businesses, are more and more preoccupied with issues of corporate social responsibility—the relationship between a corporation and all its stakeholders both inside and outside the corporation. As recently as a generation ago, "few people would have had a very clear idea of what you were talking about had you mentioned corporate social responsibility (CSR)," says *The Globe and Mail*'s J. McFarland. They might even have thought of it as oxymoronic when businesses understood their responsibilities only to shareholders and to the financial bottom line.[46]

One commentator has warned about communications pitfalls for reporting CSR activities to financial communities: "Don't tell them about saving the Earth; they want to know about the value creation realized through sustainable development."[47]

Despite the challenges of measuring and reporting performance, more and more organizations like MEC, winner of the Conference Board of Canada's 2008 award for governance innovation (◀◀ An Inside Perspective), are making the effort and discovering it is good business. Some also recognize that clean water and air are "not strictly 'environmental' issues. They are *business* issues." In this context, taking care of the triple bottom line—economic, environmental, and social performance—"is key to success, even survival, in today's competitive business climate."[48] Indeed, a PricewaterhouseCoopers global CEO survey found that 70% of CEOs believe CSR programs enhance profitability.[49]

Reputation Management

Despite the diversity of size, shape, and structure of organizations, many have an interest in **social accounting,** reporting, and auditing to assess performance because they confront the same challenges of "reputation and legitimacy," especially in the face of media "judgement by anecdote."[50] If businesses used to think in terms of ethics or profits, and some currently offer little more than window dressing—"a public relations device designed to throw sand in our eyes"[51]—many are increasingly recognizing that their own interests cannot be separated from those of all other stakeholders. In 2010 *Canadian Business* published its first annual ranking of Canadian company reputations.[52]

Peri Lynn Turnbull, co-author of a Conference Board of Canada report on CSR and reputation, finds that consumers are demanding more responsible behaviour from companies and value such behaviour over brand reputation and price. Still, linking reputation and CSR can be risky, especially for companies that do not live up to their claims. Bob Stamnes advises linking mission-based marketing to branding, and a strategic stakeholder approach fully integrating social issues into corporate identity.[53]

In the context of shareholder activism and class-action lawsuits, in the view of reporters Janet McFarland and Elizabeth Church, reputation and crisis management are now high on "the boardroom agenda": "The costs of mishandling bad news have never been so high." David Beatty, managing director of the Canadian Coalition for Good Governance, agrees: planning is now more proactive because the consequences are "more serious in terms of the financial consequences to the corporation, and potentially to the directors in terms of loss of reputation."[54]

Technology

Technology is so pervasive that students and office employees must be able to navigate the Web and social media and to

Ethics and Legal Should Companies Care?*

If 40 years ago economist Milton Friedman famously advised companies to care about nothing but the economic bottom line, many companies are listening to what consumers and investors have to say about what matters to them.

Environics International's Corporate Social Responsibility Millennium Poll of 25,000 in 23 countries shows that "Canadians have the second highest expectations for corporate behavior" in the world. Only Australians have higher expectations.

The poll reports that "people around the world focus on corporate citizenship ahead of either brand reputation or financial factors."

The Edelman Trust Barometer's study of informed publics in 20 countries confirmed the trend, reporting that financial performance of a company went from the third most important measure of corporate reputation in 2006 to the bottom of a list of ten in 2010 and to 14th in a list of 16 measures in 2013.

*Based on Milton Friedman, "The social responsibility of business is to increase profits," *The New York Times Magazine*, September 13, 1970; Environics International Ltd., *The Millennium Poll on Corporate Social Responsibility*, retrieved August 14, 2008, from http://www.globescan.com/news_archives/MPExecBrief.pdf; *Edelman Trust Barometer*, 2010, retrieved February 4, 2011, from http://www.edelman.com/trust/2010/; *Edelman Trust Barometer*, 2013, retrieved February 8, 2014, http://www.edelman.com/insights/intellectual-property/trust-2013/.

Technology Tips Big Brother Watching?*

Although the Internet has democratized communications, it has a dark side related to the surveillance, transparency, and universal morality that Jeremy Bentham's Panopticon promised in the 18th century. If it allows protestors to mobilize, it can also be used to trace and punish them. In January 2011, two activists were hanged for posting on the Internet footage from the 2009 Iranian "Twitter Revolution."

Before Egypt's then President Mubarak cut off Internet and mobile access, protestors were urging use of photocopies and e-mail rather than the social media monitored by the security police.

Closer to home, University of Toronto professor David Zweig warns employees to assume that their e-mail, instant messaging, blog, and Internet activity is being monitored.

Montreal journalist Craig Silverman warns that employees are increasingly under watch via:

- Cameras in the hallway
- Snoopware on the computer
- Worker drug testing
- Access key cards that record every move

Although workers are more accepting of monitoring when they are consulted, a British survey found that "a watched worker is also an unproductive worker."

*Based on Doug Sanders, "Just watch us," *The Globe and Mail*, December 18, 2010, F4; Evgeny Morozov, "So, you think the Internet will set you free? Think again," *The Globe and Mail*, January 29, 2011, F7; Virginia Galt, "Keyword for workplace messaging? Caution," *Report On Business*, October 7, 2006, B14; Craig Silverman, "Smile, Big Brother's watching," *The Globe and Mail*, March 24, 2008, L3.

use word processing, e-mail, spreadsheet, database, and presentation software. Most colleges and universities have short courses to help students master program technicalities, and longer courses on technology's changing impacts on how—and how often—we communicate.

If new communications technologies allow for speedy, efficient management and transmission of information, they have simultaneously raised expectations of the correctness, currency, quality, and speed of written communications as well as concerns about high levels of distraction and rudeness, even bullying, associated with mobile phones, posting, texting, and tweeting at work and school. According to Simon Fraser University communications professor Peter Chow-White, online anonymity simply reveals what is hidden in everyday life.[55]

Technology provides new opportunities and can save companies money. While online ticket sales have brought in new patrons for many a cultural organization, online donations through CanadaHelps.org have contributed over $300 million to Canada's charities since 2000.[56]

Intranets—Web pages just for employees—give everyone in an organization access to information. Ace Hardware started its message board to cut the cost of mailing out weekly newsletters to franchise owners and answering their phone questions. But an added benefit is that dealers share ideas with each other. Royal Dutch/Shell Group earned $5 million in new revenue when an engineering team in Africa was able to get the solution to a problem from teams in Europe and Asia that had already faced similar situations.[57]

Building on these interactive initiatives, social media are now at the heart of **social intranets** that integrate knowledge management, community building, training, and workplace collaboration. If social intranets meet expectations of open communications, they also present risk to privacy, disclosure, and intellectual property, according to Canadian lawyer Karl Gustafson.[58]

Extranets—Web pages for customers or suppliers—save time and money and improve quality. Two hours after dropping off a load of cranberries, growers can log on to Ocean Spray's extranet to find out how much they earned and how their berries compare to those of other growers. The information helps growers make decisions about harvesting the rest of the crop. Growers benefit by earning more money; Ocean Spray gets higher quality and cuts waste by 25%.[59]

Internet connections, BlackBerrys, cell phones, **VoIP (Voice over Internet Protocol),** Skype, and other devices allow employees to work at home rather than commute to a central office, enhance access for people with disabilities, and make it easy to communicate across oceans and time zones.

Technological change also carries costs in upgrades and training. Technology makes it easier for companies to monitor employees, send and process messages—and produce more public and permanent records (e-mail, blog, video, etc.) of business activities that may come back to damage reputations and haunt in legal or ethical terms.

Technology can also distract and reduce productivity, or reduce readers to skimmers with limited attention spans.[60] Laptop use in the classroom, for example, has been linked to 11% lower test results and reduced understanding of and performance on course content.[61]

The addition of social media, including Facebook, Twitter, **YouTube,** and **LinkedIn,** responds to heightened expectations of interactive communications beyond the traditional media that push information on employees and consumers. With less reported trust in traditional media and corporate-controlled messaging, people are having a say on social media. They are also renewing interest in the social cues of face-to-face communications.[62]

In the information age, effective time and knowledge management depends on identifying which messages are

Ethics and Legal Can Business Change the World?*

Young Canadians value opportunities to volunteer during working hours—and more employers are designing volunteer programs to attract and retain employees.

Yet a study of 990 Canadian companies reports that support remains more passive (adjusting work schedules and permitting time without pay) than strategic. Even passive support yields higher employee morale and enhanced public image, but strategic approaches can strengthen competitive advantage through better integration with company priorities, policies, and social goals.

According to Statistics Canada, 92% of Canadians volunteer to make a difference in their community; only 22% volunteer to advance their careers. Still, employers see benefits in broader employee skill sets.

Even in difficult times, workplace giving continues to rise. Whereas overall giving dropped by 0.1 percent in 2009, United Way of Canada enjoyed a 0.5% increase in employee-driven support.

*Based on Debra Z. Basil, Mary S. Runte, M. Easwaramoorthy, and Cathy Barr, "Company support for employee volunteering: A national survey of companies in Canada," *Journal of Business Ethics* (2009): 387–98; Jennifer Myers, "Giving spirit untarnished by recession," *The Globe and Mail,* November 28, 2009, B17; Virginia Galt, "A new generation discovers the benefits of 'giving back,'" *Report on Business,* June 17, 2006, B10.

Technology Tips The Cost of E-Mail*

"The irony of e-mail is that it is a productivity tool that, through misuse, has become unproductive in our workplace," says Richard Ivey School of Business Professor Christina Cavanagh. She calculates that only 65% of e-mail merits responses. The other 35% comprises spam and other unnecessary messages sent largely on business intranets because they can be.

Information overload is estimated to cost workers eight hours weekly in productivity; e-interruptions reduce the typical day of a knowledge worker by 28%.

Instead of succumbing to the supposed efficiencies of multitasking, Maggie Jackson recommends working on your active listening and attention span. John Freeman warns of the dangerous blurring of public and private lives and urges a disciplined management of e-mail to preserve media-free time for reflection.

One British company with 2,500 employees (Phones4U) has banned internal e-mail. The saving? Three hours per day per employee and Cdn$1.6 million a month. Yet many companies neither monitor e-mail use (despite daily tabulation by their systems) nor recognize high volumes, poor e-mail messages, and management as "a corporate expense."

*Adapted from Christina Cavanagh, "Time is money—and so is e-mail," *The Globe and Mail,* October 24, 2003, C1, C4; Roberto Rocha, "Information overload hurts productivity, *The StarPhoenix,* August 29, 2009, F14; Maggie Jackson, *Distracted: The Erosion of Attention and the Coming Dark Age* (New York: Barnes & Noble, 2009); John Freeman, *The Tyranny of E-mail* (New York: Scribner, 2009).

important so as not to be buried in trivia and on understanding what company and personal information to disclose or not. Asking yourself the five questions described previously in this chapter (◂◂ "Understanding and Analyzing Business Communication Situations") can help avoid damaging disclosures that could lose you your job or harm job opportunities (▸▸ "Ten Deadly Job Search Sins," Chapter 13). Effective knowledge management also requires individuals and organizations to know that new technologies have not simply replaced but supplemented old technologies and to choose well the channels that are best for particular audiences, purposes, and situations. The "personal touch" remains an asset in business communication.[63]

Communications technology affects the way people interpret messages. Readers expect all documents to be well designed and error-free—even though not everyone has access to a laser printer or even to a computer. E-mail, text, and instant messaging lead people to expect instant responses, even though thinking and writing still take time.

Technology plays a large role in the changing face of business communications. High-end videoconferencing makes virtual meetings much more appealing at a time when air travel is becoming less convenient.

Figure 1.7 Employability Skills 2000+

THE SKILLS YOU NEED TO ENTER, STAY IN, AND PROGRESS IN THE WORLD OF WORK—WHETHER YOU WORK ON YOUR OWN OR AS A PART OF A TEAM.

These skills can also be applied and used beyond the workplace in a range of daily activities.

Fundamental Skills

The skills needed as a base for further development.

You will be better prepared to progress in the world of work when you can:

Communicate
- read and understand information presented in a variety of forms (e.g., words, graphs, charts, diagrams)
- write and speak so others pay attention and understand
- listen and ask questions to understand and appreciate the points of view of others
- share information using a range of information and communications technologies (e.g., voice, e-mail, computers)
- use relevant scientific, technological and mathematical knowledge and skills to explain or clarify ideas

Manage Information
- locate, gather and organize information using appropriate technology and information systems
- access, analyze and apply knowledge and skills from various disciplines (e.g., the arts, languages, science, technology, mathematics, social sciences, and the humanities)

Use Numbers
- decide what needs to be measured or calculated
- observe and record data using appropriate methods, tools and technology
- make estimates and verify calculations

Think & Solve Problems
- assess situations and identify problems
- seek different points of view and evaluate them based on facts
- recognize the human, interpersonal, technical, scientific and mathematical dimensions of a problem
- identify the root cause of a problem
- be creative and innovative in exploring possible solutions
- readily use science, technology and mathematics as ways to think, gain and share knowledge, solve problems and make decisions
- evaluate solutions to make recommendations or decisions
- implement solutions
- check to see if a solution works, and act on opportunities for improvement

Personal Management Skills

The personal skill, attitudes, and behaviours that drive one's potential for growth

You will be able to offer yourself greater possibilities for achievement when you can:

Demonstrate Positive Attitudes & Behaviours
- feel good about yourself and be confident
- deal with people, problems and situations with honesty, integrity and personal ethics
- recognize your own and other people's efforts
- take care of your personal health
- show interest, initiative and effort

Be Responsible
- set goals and priorities balancing work and personal life
- plan and manage time, money and other resources to achieve goals
- assess, weigh and manage risk
- be accountable for your actions and the actions of your group
- be socially responsible and contribute to your community

Be Adaptable
- work independently or as a part of a team
- carry out multiple tasks or projects
- be innovative and resourceful; identify and suggest alternative ways to achieve goals and get the job done
- be open and respond constructively to change
- learn from your mistakes and accept feedback
- cope with uncertainty

Learn Continuously
- be willing to continuously learn and grow
- assess personal strengths and areas for development
- set your own learning goals
- identify and access learning sources and opportunities
- plan for and achieve your learning goals

Work Safely
- be aware of personal and group health and safety practices and procedures and act in accordance with these

Teamwork Skills

The skills and attributes needed to contribute productively

You will be better prepared to add value to the outcomes of a task, project or team when you can:

Work with Others
- understand and work within the dynamics of a group
- ensure that a team's purpose and objectives are clear
- be flexible: respect, be open to and supportive of the thoughts, opinions and contributions of others in a group
- recognize and respect people's diversity, individual differences and perspectives
- accept and provide feedback in a constructive and considerate manner
- contribute to a team by sharing information and expertise
- lead or support when appropriate, motivating a group for high performance
- understand the role of conflict in a group to reach solutions
- manage and resolve conflict when appropriate

Participate in Projects & Tasks
- plan, design or carry out a project or task from start to finish with well-defined objectives and outcomes
- develop a plan, seek feedback, test, revise and implement
- work to agreed quality standards and specifications
- select and use appropriate tools and technology for a task or project
- adapt to changing requirements and information
- continuously monitor the success of a project or task and identify ways to improve

The Conference Board of Canada

255 Smyth Road, Ottawa
ON K1H 8M7 Canada
Tel. (613) 526-3280
Fax (613) 526-4857
Internet: http://www.conferenceboard.ca/education

Source: *Employability Skills 2000+* Brochure, 2000, EF (Ottawa: The Conference Board of Canada, 2000).

SUMMARY OF KEY POINTS

- Communication helps organizations and the people in them achieve their goals. The ability to write and speak well becomes increasingly important as you rise in an organization.
- Conscious of the contexts within which they make choices, the best communicators ask the following five questions in analyzing business communication situations:
  - What's at stake—to whom?
  - Should you send a message?
  - What channel should you use?
  - What should you say?
  - How should you say it?
- Good business writing meets five basic criteria: it's clear, complete, correct, concise, and courteous.
- Communication theory attempts to explain what happens when we communicate. Semantics is the study of the way our behaviour is influenced by words and symbols. Communication theory and semantics both show why and where communication can break down and what we can do to communicate more effectively.
- Communication is a socio-cultural process negotiating differences of power and cultural competency within the broader environment (legal, ethical, ecological, political, and economic) in building the credibility, goodwill, and trust that sustain business relationships. Communication theory helps us understand where and why miscommunication may occur at each stage from perceiving to decoding and interpreting to choosing/selecting, encoding and feedback. Each person in the process is responsible for feedback that clarifies and confirms understanding.
- Noise—physical, psychological, or socio-cultural—can interfere with every aspect of the communication process.
- Eight principles of semantics help us avoid errors in perception, interpretation, and argument.
- Managers collect and convey information, make decisions, and promote interpersonal unity—all carried out through formal and informal communication. Listening, speaking, and interpersonal communication skills remain important for executives.
- Ten trends affecting business communication are a focus on quality and customers' needs, entrepreneurship and outsourcing, teams, diversity, globalization, legal and ethical concerns, balancing work and family, corporate social responsibility, reputation management, and technology.

EXERCISES AND PROBLEMS

GETTING STARTED

1.1 CHOOSING A CHANNEL TO CONVEY A SPECIFIC MESSAGE

Your group is designing the campaign for a campus, municipal, or provincial election. What would be the advantages and disadvantages of each of the following channels as media to carry ads for your side?

a. Ad in the campus newspaper.

b. Ad in the local newspaper.

c. Ad on a local radio station after midnight.

d. Ad on the local TV station during the local news show.

e. Ads on billboards.

f. Ad posted on Web site.

g. Flyers distributed door to door.

h. Blog posting on campus Web site.

i. Facebook page.

1.2 EXPLAINING BYPASSING

1. Show how the following statements could produce bypassing.
   a. The house needs painting badly.
   b. I made reservations for seven.
   c. If you think our servers are rude, you should see the manager.
2. Bypassing is the basis of many jokes. Find a joke that depends on bypassing and share it with the class.

1.3 IDENTIFYING LOGOS

Find four corporate logos. Do all your classmates recognize all the logos? Which logos seem to be especially effective symbols for their organizations? What makes them so effective?

1.4 ANALYZING ARGUMENTS

In pairs or in groups, analyze the arguments in one or more of the following kinds of documents. For each, identify the claim and (if present) the evidence or data, and attempts to anticipate and counter opposing arguments. What additional parts (if any) are needed to make the argument convincing?

1. An article in a business periodical or Web site recommending that it is or is not a good idea to buy a particular company's stock.
2. A recruiting brochure or Web or Facebook page explaining why a company is a good place to work.
3. The CEO's letter in an annual report arguing that the company is well positioned for the coming year.
4. A fundraising letter arguing that the organization is doing good work and is a deserving candidate for financial gifts.
5. An article on social networking sites and the dangers of content that can damage the organization's reputation.
6. Material from your city's chamber of commerce presenting your city as a good place to live and work.

COMMUNICATING AT WORK

1.5 UNDERSTANDING THE ROLE OF COMMUNICATION IN YOUR ORGANIZATION

Interview your supervisor to learn about the kinds and purposes of communication in your organization. Your questions could include the following:

- What channels of communication (e.g., memos, e-mail, Twitter, Facebook, YouTube, presentations) are most important in this organization?
- What documents or presentations do you create? Are they designed to inform, to persuade, to build goodwill—or to do all three?
- What documents or presentations do you receive? Are they designed to inform, to persuade, to build goodwill—or to do all three?
- Who are your most important audiences within the organization?
- Who are your most important external audiences?
- What are the challenges of communicating in this organization?
- What kinds of documents and presentations does the organization prefer?

As Your Professor Directs,

a. Share your results with a small group of students.

b. Present your results in an e-mail to your professor.

c. Join with a group of students to make a group presentation to the class.

d. Post your results online to the class.

e. Draft a series of tweets.

COMMUNICATING IN COLLEGE OR UNIVERSITY

1.6 INTRODUCING YOURSELF TO YOUR PROFESSOR

Write a memo (at least one page) introducing yourself to your professor. Use complete memo format with appropriate headings. (See ⏩ Chapter 7 for examples of memo format.) Use a conversational writing style; check your draft to polish the style and edit for mechanical and grammatical correctness. A good memo will enable your instructor to see you as an individual. Use specific details to make your memo vivid and interesting. Remember that one of your purposes is to interest your reader!

Include the following topics:

Background: Where did you grow up? What have you done in terms of school, extracurricular activities, jobs, and family life?

Interests: What are you interested in? What do you like to do? What do you like to think about and talk about? What kind of writing have you done? Have you found different classes/instructors have different standards? What are your writing strengths and weaknesses? What percentage of your day do you devote to using technology?

Achievements: What achievements have given you the greatest personal satisfaction? List at least five. Include things that gave you a real sense of accomplishment and pride, whether or not they're the sort of thing you'd list on a résumé.

Goals: What do you hope to accomplish this term? Where would you like to be professionally and personally five years from now?

1.7 INTRODUCING YOURSELF TO YOUR COLLABORATIVE WRITING GROUP

Write an e-mail or online post (at least one page) introducing yourself to the other students in your collaborative writing group. Include the following topics:

Background: What is your major? What special areas of knowledge do you have? What have you done in terms of school, extracurricular activities, jobs, and family life?

Previous experience in groups: What groups have you worked in before? Are you usually a leader, a follower, or a bit of both? Are you interested in a quality product? In maintaining harmony in the group? In working efficiently? What do you like most about working in groups? What do you like least?

Work and composing style: Do you like to talk out ideas while they're in a rough stage or work them out on paper before you discuss them? Or do you prefer interacting and sharing ideas electronically? Would you rather have a complete outline before you start writing or just a general idea? Do you want to have a detailed schedule of everything that has to be done and who will do it, or would you rather "go with the flow"? Do you work best under pressure, or do you want to have assignments ready well before the due date?

Areas of expertise: What can you contribute to the group in terms of knowledge and skills? Are you good at brainstorming ideas? Researching? Designing charts? Writing? Editing? Word processing? Managing the flow of work? Maintaining group cohesion?

Goals for collaborative assignments: What do you hope to accomplish this term? Where does this course fit into your priorities?

ADAPTING TO AUDIENCES

2

Learning Outcomes

LO1 Explain the multiple audiences of organizational messages

LO2 Illustrate ways to analyze individuals, organizations, and groups

LO3 List six questions that help you adapt messages to audiences

LO4 Explain four criteria for reader benefits

LO5 Illustrate the importance of you-attitude, positive emphasis, and bias-free language

AN INSIDE PERSPECTIVE

Once you know your project purpose, the next priority is to analyze your audience. Only when you have a clear profile—nationality, culture, gender, age, abilities, socio-economic status, education, language, for example—and understand how their characteristics relate to particular messages can you effectively address audience needs, motivations, and benefits.

The more you research and attend to the complexities of cultural identities and the more you understand your audience's psychographics (attitudes and beliefs), the better prepared and more effective you will be in engaging them in relevant and meaningful communications. That understanding was the basis of journalist Michelle Hugli Brass's success as editor of *Shout* magazine, which struck a chord with its Aboriginal youth audience. Her own Saulteaux, Swiss, and British ancestry helped her target audience needs.

When you know who your audience is, you can identify what your audience knows and needs to know to respond to your message. What is your message purpose? Do you want readers to act, think, or feel? You may have multiple purposes: to inform your audience about a program, to persuade them that your program will benefit them, and to consolidate the credibility of your organization as well as you as a writer.

Print and media journalist and social media director Michelle Hugli Brass relishes interviewing people, debating, and challenging people's thinking. Letters from youth and friends on Facebook tell her how well she reaches her audiences.

What is the best channel for your purposes and budget? Internet, television, radio, print, or another medium? Whether she is writing, interacting on Facebook, hosting a radio show, interviewing when she hosted the CBC Afternoon Edition in Regina, or designing social media strategies, Michelle knows how to make the most of her channel to reach her audience.

What information must your message include? Where and how should it be included for appropriate emphasis? What is the logic of your claims? How can you rephrase to meet audience objections? How can you make clear what is in it for them? In whatever field—journalism, business, health care, tourism, trades, or the service sector—putting yourself in your audience's shoes is key, according to journalist Michelle Hugli Brass.

LO1

IDENTIFYING YOUR AUDIENCES

To begin to match your purpose and audience needs (◂◂ An Inside Perspective), it is important to understand the multiple audiences of organizational messages:[1]

1. The **initial audience** is the first audience to get your message. Sometimes the initial audience tells you to write the message.
2. A **gatekeeper** has the power to stop your message instead of sending it on to other audiences, including the primary audience. Sometimes the supervisor who assigns the message is also the gatekeeper; sometimes the gatekeeper is higher in the organization. In some cases, gatekeepers may exist outside the organization.
3. The **primary audience** will decide whether to accept your recommendations or act on the basis of your message. You must reach the primary audience to fulfill your purposes in any message.
4. The **secondary audience** may be asked to comment on your message or to implement your ideas after they've been approved. Secondary audiences also include lawyers who may use your message—perhaps years later—as evidence of your organization's culture and practices.
5. A **watchdog audience,** though it does not have the power to stop the message and will not act directly on it, has political, social, or economic power. The watchdog—members of boards of directors, regulatory bodies, or the media—pays close attention to the transaction between you and the primary audience and may base future actions on its evaluation of your message.

As the following example shows, one person can be part of two audiences. Frequently, a supervisor is both the initial audience and the gatekeeper. Sometimes the initial audience is also the primary audience who will act on the message.

Dawn is an assistant account executive in an ad agency. Her boss asks her to write a proposal for a marketing plan for a client's new product. Her *primary audience* is the executive committee of the client company, who will decide whether to adopt the plan. The *secondary audience* includes the client's marketing staff, who will be asked for comments on the plan, as well as the artists, writers, and media buyers who will carry out details of the plan if it is adopted. Her boss, who must approve the plan before it is submitted to the client, is both the *initial audience* and the *gatekeeper*.

LO2

WAYS TO ANALYZE YOUR AUDIENCE

The most important tool in audience analysis is empathy. **Empathy** is the ability to put yourself in someone else's shoes, to feel with that person. In all probability, the audience is *not* just like you. Nor do people fit neatly into distinct personality types. Analyze yourself so that you see what you and your audience share and how you differ., Know that your audiences may represent multiple personality and other types, and take care not to oversimplify on the basis of generalizations. Use what you know about people and about organizations to predict likely responses, and design your approach.

Analyzing Individuals

When you write or speak to people in your own organization and in other organizations you work closely with, you may be able to analyze your audience as individuals. It will usually be easy to get information by talking to and observing members of your audience, as well as talking to people who know your audience.

Although the **Myers-Briggs Type Indicator** of four personality dimensions—introvert-extrovert, sensing-intuitive, thinking-feeling, and perceiving-judging—is still used in some organizations,[2] many more organizations find it unhelpful when few people have access to reliable sources of information and can risk stereotyping. Instead, consider the broader socio-cultural influences on audience attitudes and behaviours and the evidence of audience practices you see daily in your college, university, or workplace.

Analyzing the Organizational Culture and the Discourse Community

Be sensitive to the culture in which your audiences work and the discourse community or community of practice of which they are a part. **Organizational culture** is a set of values, attitudes, and philosophies. An organization's culture is revealed verbally in its myths, stories, and heroes, and nonverbally in the allocation of space, money, and power—as well as in the clothes people wear and the styles they prefer.

When corporate culture is "a strategic competitive advantage" and "cultural fit" is trumping skills in hiring and promotion decisions, you want to be watching for conventional cues that help you fit in.[3] What are the dress codes? What flexibility is there? What signals are being sent about normative values in the organization? How do you dress for credibility and success? (See ⏩ Chapter 5.)

A **discourse community** is a group of people who share assumptions about what channels, formats, and styles to use for communication, what topics to discuss and how to discuss them, and what constitutes evidence.

A **community of practice** is a group of people who work together, share a sense of purpose, engage in learning together, produce meaning, develop identities, and add value to an organization. People may belong to more than one community of practice within an organization.

In an organization that values equality and individualism, you can write directly to the CEO. In other companies, you'd be expected to follow a chain of command. Some organizations prize short messages; some expect long, thorough documents. Messages, styles, and channels that are consistent with the organization's culture have a greater chance of succeeding—and of reshaping that culture.

Every organization—businesses, government agencies, non-profit organizations, colleges and universities—has a culture. An organization's culture is constructed by the people who founded the organization, who participate in it, and who change it. Vancity staff, board, and members put their words together to tell their story of passion and commitment: "Sometimes audacious. Occasionally irreverent." As a member-owned financial co-operative, Vancity aims to "redefine wealth in a way that furthers the financial, social and environmental well-being of our members and their communities." Its values are clear in its daily activities, its governance, lending practices, grants, and investments in community, ethical principles, environmental choices, and consistent record of award and achievement.[4]

You can begin to analyze an organization's culture by asking the following questions:

- Is the organization tall or flat? How many levels between the CEO and the lowest worker?
- How do people get ahead? Are the organization's rewards based on seniority, education, being well liked, making technical discoveries, or serving customers? Are rewards restricted to a few top people, or is everyone expected to succeed?
- Does the organization value diversity or homogeneity? Does it value independence and creativity or being a team player and following orders? What stories do people tell? Who are the organization's heroes and villains?
- How important are friendship and sociability? To what extent do workers agree on goals, and how intently do they pursue them?

Vancity is close to having 100% of its locations Safe Harbour–certified as a mark of its dedication to an inclusive workplace.

- How formal are behaviour, language, and dress?
- What are the organization's goals? Making money? Serving customers and clients? Advancing knowledge? Contributing to the community?

The Toronto Blue Jays baseball club knows the business benefits—from enhanced morale to increased efficiencies and the bottom line—of a corporate culture that makes employees feel part of a family. That culture sustained people even when the team didn't meet expectations in the 2013 season. In a 2006 study, 99.9% of 185 executives believed that corporate culture impacted financial results, although only 60% reward results, 7% reward innovation and creativity, and 12% reward teamwork. Clearly, a gap remains between words and deeds. Although discomfort with the "softness" of cultural issues offers some explanation, the financial results associated with effective corporate cultures are anything but soft: 38.9% annual revenue growth rate, or three times larger than results for companies on the S&P/TSX 60 over the same period.[5]

Organizations, like nations, can have subcultures (see ⏩ Chapter 5). For example, members of information technology and marketing subcultures in the same organization may dress differently and have different values.

To analyze an organization's discourse community, ask the following questions:

- What channels, formats, and styles are preferred for communication?
- What do people talk about? What topics are not discussed?
- What kind of and how much evidence is needed to be convincing?

A discourse community, like a community of practice, may be limited to a few people in an organization. However, some discourse communities span an entire organization or even everyone in the same field. You will be a member of several overlapping discourse communities (academic, professional, sports, political, for example). In many organizational situations, then, you'll analyze your audience as members of a group: "taxpayers who must be notified that they owe more income tax," or "employees with small children." Focus on what group members have in common. In some cases, no research is necessary: in other cases, Statistics Canada and other databases may yield useful information. In still other cases, you may want to do original research using surveys or interviews (⏩ Chapter 10).

On the Job Costly Cultural Mismatches*

Culture is more than a values statement on a Web site. A company's true culture is evident in the way people behave. Cultural mismatches across or within organizations can be costly.

Walmart faced a $1 billion loss when it pulled out of Germany after overestimating the transferability of its culture and misreading its audience's cultural cues. German consumers did not appreciate greeters, big-box stores, or plastic bags; employees were accustomed to workers' councils and having a say in decisions.

Cultural mismatches or gaps between what companies say and do can reduce employee morale, increase turnover, and hit stock value. If an employee appreciation day comes with a ticket price, or if you are team leader and the team is posting Dilbert cartoons, then you know you have a problem.

*Based on Harvey Schachter, "Adapting for success on foreign shores," *Globe Careers*, November 11, 2009, B15; "Wal-Mart: Struggling in Germany," *BusinessWeek*, April 11, 2005; Parmy Olson, "Wal-Mart bids Germany auf wiedersehen," retrieved February 8, 2011, from http://www.forbes.com/2006/07/28/walmart-germany-metro-cx_po_0728walmart.html; Pamela Babcock, "Is your company two-faced?" *HRMagazine*, January 2004, retrieved February 8, 2011, from http://www.shrm.org/Publications/hrmagazine/EditorialContent/Pages/0104covstory.aspx.

Even within student subcultures on their campus, Enactus Ryerson team members stand out beside the trophy for winning the 2013 Tim Hortons Cup—and a place at the Enactus World Cup in Mexico.

Marketing and communications professionals research their audience's geographic, demographic, psychographic, and behavioural characteristics. Fredericton-based Los Cabos Drumsticks used the Internet to locate music stores before visiting each one personally to pitch its drumsticks. The reward? A tripling of sales.[6] If you know where your audience lives, databases enable you to map demographic and psychographic profiles of customers or employees. **Demographic characteristics** are measurable features that can be counted objectively: age, gender, race, religion, education level, income, and so on (▸▸Chapter 5). Statistics Canada, Citizenship and Immigration Canada, Health Canada, and Canada Post Corporation are among the most useful sources of demographic data in Canada.

Sometimes demographic information is irrelevant; sometimes it's important. Does age matter? Sometimes. "Generational marketing" is helping manufacturers design and market products. Ford develops vehicles to meet the profile of each group of six generations, while Toyota Canada is targeting Scion models to Generation Y, who expect mobile and Internet access to get to know new products and maintain control and choice.[7] But other marketers are finding that considering age alone is inadequate to sell to the "mature market."[8]

In efforts to maintain television advertising market share, Cogeco Cable Inc. is testing a Canadian invention that divides 30-second television spots into different advertisements targeting different geographic or demographic segments. One audience can see alcohol while another sees home improvement options.[9]

Psychographic characteristics are qualitative rather than quantitative: values, beliefs, goals, and lifestyles. Knowing what your audience finds important allows you to organize information in a way that seems natural to your audience and to choose appeals that the audience will find persuasive.

For example, a long-distance phone company used psychographics to understand the characteristics of people who are heavy users of long-distance service. This knowledge helped the company select a spokesperson the heavy users could relate to.[10] Tim Hortons diversified its menu to add to its client base by appealing to important weight-conscious customers—and is continuing to expand in Canada, where it ranked first among the top 50 companies in a 2010 study of corporate reputation, first in a 2013 *Canadian Business* ranking of top Canadian brands, and among the top 100 "most loved companies in the world" in a 2013 APCO Insight study.[11]

CHOOSING CHANNELS TO REACH YOUR AUDIENCE

Communication channels vary in reach, speed, cost, efficiency, accuracy of transmission, number of messages carried, and ability to promote goodwill. Depending on the audience, your purposes, and the situation, one channel may be better than another.

On the Job Reading Levels*

Increasingly complex workplaces—whether in mines equipped with complicated technology (and intimidating instruction manuals) or in factories, offices, or retail stores—require higher communication skills than ever.

- 48% of Canadian adults (over 16) do not have minimum literacy for everyday life and work.
- Canadian Council on Learning predicts that 15 million adult Canadians will have low literacy by 2031.
- Low literacy costs Canadian business $2.5 billion annually.
- Workers with higher literacy skills earn more.
- Literacy is arguably "the single best predictor of good health and longevity."

Research shows that investing in literacy is good for the bottom line, for enhanced health and safety, for employee satisfaction, and for a strong culture.

*Adapted from ABC Life Literacy Canada Web site, retrieved February 9, 2014, from http://abclifeliteracy.ca/literacy-facts-statistics-and-myths; Canadian Council on Learning, "The future of literacy in Canada's largest cities," retrieved February 9, 2011, from http://www.ccl-cca.ca/CCL/Reports/ReadingFuture/index.html; "Benefits of workplace literacy," retrieved February 9, 2011, from http://dev.creativate.ca/westshore/news/benefits-workplace-literacy; André Picard, "Read a book—your health depends on it," *The Globe and Mail*, March 13, 2008, L6.

E-mail, text, or instant messages are appropriate for routine interchanges with people you already know. Twitter is a useful tool for updates and even for timely responses to a crisis (⏩Chapter 8). Twitter and Facebook support engagement with employees and with external stakeholders, while podcasts can be the right choice for recruitment, training, or product launches. E-mail (online for large businesses) is the channel of choice for submitting job applications and circulating formal proposals and reports. Scheduled meetings and oral presentations are more formal than phone calls or stopping someone in the hall. Important messages should use more formal channels, whether they're oral or written.

Figure 2.1 explains the advantages of written and oral messages, while underlining what they have in common.

Your channel choice is typically determined by the audience. Some organizations still post announcements and job openings on bulletin boards because some staff don't have computers. Other organizations overwhelmed by online applications have turned to LinkedIn, Facebook, and Twitter for recruitment purposes (⏩Chapter 13).

Increasingly, organizations are integrating social and traditional media to remain relevant, consolidate reach, build trust, and address concerns around privacy and security. They are making efforts to connect with audiences where and how they want to participate and have their voices heard.

For both internal and external audiences, Lululemon finds social networking "helps to keep everyone connected at every level and empowered," according to online community manager Carolyn Coles.[12] While social networking puts a human face to the company, feedback about products and sizes on Twitter and Facebook can also prove a practical resource for managing inventory.[13]

To reach younger audiences, Sears Canada has invested in Skype and 58-inch screens in ten of its "modern shops" so that customers can get instant feedback from friends and family on outfits they try on. In 2010, sales grew 32 percent.[14] Similarly, with its "Le Club Perrier" party video, Perrier turned to YouTube to connect with young audiences. It reached a million views on day three![15]

Small businesses are similarly learning to make social media work for them. In British Columbia, Salt Spring Coffee Co.'s Twitter, Facebook, and blogging have built a loyal customer base for its fair trade products. That loyalty translates into retweets and even "buycotts" at one of its coffee shops. Organizers described the buycott as a "carrot mob" rewarding the company for its good corporate record. Video of source farms in Nicaragua is adding to the emotional appeal of the Salt Spring story.[16]

The non-profit sector is finding that Twitter is a powerful way to build community and galvanize people when it is guided by clear organizational goals.[17] Blogging is also proving a cost-effective means for sharing non-profit stories and engaging supporters.[18]

Even people who have access to the same channels may prefer different ones. When a university updated its employee benefits manual, the computer scientists and librarians wanted the information online. Faculty wanted to be able to read the information on paper. Maintenance workers and carpenters wanted to get answers on voice mail.[19]

Figure 2.1 Choosing Oral and Written Channels

WRITTEN MESSAGES	• Present extensive or complex financial data. • Present many specific details of a law, policy, or procedure.	• Minimize undesirable emotions (see ⏩ "You-Attitude" and "Positive Emphasis" later in this chapter). • Provide record.
ORAL MESSAGES	• Use emotion to help persuade the audience. • Focus the audience's attention on specific points. • Answer questions, resolve conflicts, and build consensus.	• Modify a proposal that may not be acceptable in its original form. • Get immediate action or response.
ORAL AND WRITTEN MESSAGES	• Adapt the message to the specific audience. • Show the audience how they would benefit from the idea, policy, service, or product. • Overcome any objections the audience may have (⏩ Chapter 9)	• Use you-attitude and positive emphasis. • Use visuals to clarify or emphasize material (⏩ Chapters 4, 11, and 12). • Specify exactly what the audience should do.

Companies that learn and laugh together succeed together. Lululemon pays particular attention to its relationships with its employees; its interactions with its audience; its relationships with business partners, suppliers, and community neighbours; and the environmental impact of its activities.

The bigger your audience, the more complicated channel choice becomes, since few channels reach everyone in your target audience. When United Airlines experienced a computer system crash for five hours in June 2011, passengers and media were frustrated by the lack of information. A few apologetic tweets were unclear about the causes, effects, and implications of the crash for passengers and left those trying to connect by e-mail, telephone, or Web site out in the cold.[20]

When possible, use multiple channels. For example, print ads and customer service materials should contain not only toll-free numbers but also street, e-mail, and Web site addresses, and Facebook, Twitter, or other profiles, to increase access to those who don't like to make phone calls or who have hearing impairments.

Motivated by her 18-month-old sister's illness, seven-year-old Sydney Whyte began to learn how to adapt messages to specific audiences—from friends to school principals, church groups, company presidents, and reporters. To 2011 she raised over $22,000 for cancer research and the James Fund at Toronto's SickKids Foundation.

LO3

USING AUDIENCE ANALYSIS TO ADAPT YOUR MESSAGE

If you know your audience well and if you use words well, much of your audience analysis and adaptation will be unconscious. If you don't know your audience, or if the message is very important, take the time to analyze your audience formally using the following six questions and to revise your draft with your analysis in mind.

As you answer these six questions for a specific audience, think about the organizational culture in which the person works, the political environment, the economy, and current events:

1. How Will the Audience React to the Message?

Audiences will read and act on messages they see as important. The audience's experience with you, your organization, and your subject, as well as your channel choice and tone of voice, shapes response to this new message. Someone who thinks well of you and your organization will be prepared to receive your message favourably.

When the audience may see your message as unimportant, you might do the following:

- In a subject line (▶▶ Chapter 7) or first paragraph, show that this message is important and relevant.
- Make the action as easy as possible.
- Suggest a realistic deadline for action.
- Keep the message as short as possible.

When you must write to someone who has negative feelings about your organization, your position, or you personally, these tactics will help:

- Avoid phrases that could seem condescending, arrogant, rude, hostile, or uncaring.
- Use positive emphasis (see ▶▶ "Positive Emphasis" later in this chapter) to counteract the natural tendency to sound defensive.
- Develop logic and reader benefits fully.

2. How Much Information Does the Audience Need?

It's easy to overestimate the knowledge an audience has. Even people who once worked in your unit may have forgotten

On the Job The Audiences for Audited Reports and Financial Statements*

An audit report may be used by at least four different audiences:

- *The client,* who may resent any report that isn't fully favourable.
- *Investors and creditors,* who make decisions based on audit reports and who may hold the company management and board financially responsible for the report.
- *Colleagues,* who use the reports but who may have different ethical or theoretical positions.
- The CPA Canada (Chartered Professional Accountants Canada), the Public Sector Accounting Board, the Auditing and Assurance Standards Board, and the International Auditing and Assurance Standards Board.

Good audit reports meet the needs and overcome the possible objections of all of these audiences.

*Based on CPA Canada, *Reporting Implications of New Auditing and Accounting Standards,* Issue 11, January 2014, retrieved February 14, 2014, from http://www.frascanada.ca/canadian-auditing-standards/resources/reference-material/item50999.pdf; Financial Reporting and Assurance Standards Canada, "Public Sector Accounting Board," retrieved February 14, 2014, from http://www.frascanada.ca/public-sector-accounting-board/; Financial Reporting and Assurance Standards Canada, "Auditing and Assurance Standards Board," retrieved February 14, 2014, from http://www.frascanada.ca/auditing-and-assurance-standards-board/; International Federation of Accountants, "International Auditing and Assurance Standards Board," retrieved February 14, 2014, from http://www.ifac.org/auditing-assurance.

specific details now that their daily work is in management. A prefatory "as you know" will tactfully suggest that the reader does know what you're saying. People outside your organization won't know how *your* organization does things.

When some of your information is new to the audience, take these actions:

- Make a special effort to be clear. Define terms, explain concepts, use examples.
- Link new information to information that the reader already knows.
- Use paragraphs and headings (⏩ Chapter 4) to break up new information into related chunks that are easier to digest.
- Test your draft document with a subset of your intended audience to see whether the audience can understand and use it.

3. What Obstacles Must You Overcome?

People who have already made up their minds are highly resistant to change. When the audience will oppose what you have to say (⏩ Chapter 9), you need to do the following:

- Start your message with any agreement or common ground that you share with your reader.
- Make a special effort to be clear, courteous, and unambiguous.
- Limit your statement or request. If parts of your message could be delivered later, postpone them.
- Show that your solution is the best solution currently available, even though it isn't perfect.

When your request is time consuming, complicated, or physically or psychologically difficult, try the following:

- Make the action as easy as possible. Provide a form (online or print) that can be filled out quickly.
- Break down actions into a list, so the audience can check off each step as it is completed.
- Show how the audience (not just you or your organization) will benefit when the action is completed.

4. What Positive Aspects Can You Emphasize?

Benefits help persuade the audience that your ideas are good ones. A sense of solidarity with someone can be an even more powerful reason to agree than the content of the message itself. Use all the ethical strategies available to win support for your ideas.

- Put good news in the first paragraph.
- Use reader benefits that go beyond the basic good news of the first paragraph.
- Consider using a vivid anecdote to remind the audience of what you share. If it is not vivid, you may seem to be lecturing the audience.
- Make a special effort to make your writing style friendly and informal.
- Use a salutation and close that remind the audience of their membership in this formal or informal group.

5. What Are the Audience's Expectations about Style and Format?

Good writers adapt their style to suit the reader's preferences. A reader who sees the contractions and shorthand of text messages as too informal needs a different style and format from one who sees traditional business writing as too stuffy.

- Use what you know about your reader to choose a more or less friendly style.
- Use the reader's first name in the salutation only if you use that name when you talk to him or her.

On the Job Write Your Way into the Discourse Community

You can learn about your organization's discourse community by listening to people and reading the documents that they write. But the best way to learn is to write.

The feedback you get from your supervisor will show you how to adapt your writing for the particular organization. To make the feedback most useful, categorize the comments and generalize.

Are you being asked to provide specific supporting details? To write so that people can understand what you say without having to reread? To use a more or less formal style? To include lots of charts or none at all?

Learning to adapt your content, structure, and style to the organization will make you a more effective writer and a more effective worker.

- Avoid terms that carry emotional charges for many readers: for example, criminal, radical.
- Revise your document carefully to ensure that a short document covers the essential points and that a long one is free from wordiness and repetition.
- Pretest the message on a subset of your audience to see if the format enhances or interferes with comprehension and action.

6. How Will the Audience Use the Document?

Reading a document in a quiet office calls for no special care. But suppose the reader will be reading your message on the train commuting home or on a mobile device. Then the physical preparation of the document can make it easier or harder to use.

When the reader will use your document outside an office,

- Use lots of white space (▸▸ Chapter 4).
- Make the document small enough to hold in one hand or to read on a mobile screen.
- Number items so the reader can find his or her place after an interruption.

Understanding how your audience will use the document will enable you to choose the best pattern of organization and the best level of detail. A memo within a company urging the adoption of pollution control equipment needs less information than one to a regulatory body. Different information is needed for instructions explaining how to install and maintain the equipment.

If the document will serve as a general reference,

- Use a specific subject line to aid in storing and retrieval. If online, consider using keywords to make it easy to find in a database search program.
- Use headings within the document so that readers can skim it.
- Give the office as well as a contact person so that the reader can get in touch some time from now.
- Spell out details that may be obvious now but might be forgotten in six months; check for accuracy, completeness, and friendliness.

If the document will be a detailed guide or contain instructions,

- Check to be sure that steps are in chronological order.
- Number steps or provide boxes to check the steps completed.
- Group steps into five to seven subprocesses if there are many individual steps.
- Put any warnings at the beginning; then repeat them just before the specific step to which they apply.

If the document will be used as the basis for a lawsuit,

- Give specific observations with dates and exact measurements as well as any inferences you've drawn from those observations.
- Give a full report with all the information you have. The lawyer can then decide which parts of the information to use in preparing the case.

LO4

READER BENEFITS

Use your analysis of your audience to create effective reader benefits. **Reader benefits** are benefits or advantages that the reader gets by using your services, buying your products, following your policies, or adopting your ideas.

Physiological needs are often considered more basic than needs for safety and security, for love and a sense of belonging, for esteem and recognition, and for self-actualization or self-fulfillment. All of us go back and forth between so-called higher- and lower-level needs. But University of British Columbia economist John Helliwell encourages rethinking of common-sense views of what people value and what motivates them, urging greater investment in trust, well-being, and social capital.[21]

Sometimes just listing the reader's needs makes it obvious which feature meets a given need. Sometimes several features together meet the need.

Suppose that you want to persuade people to come to the restaurant you manage. Depending on what features your

SUBGROUP	FEATURES TO MEET THE SUBGROUP'S NEEDS
People who work outside the home	A quick lunch; a relaxing place to take clients or colleagues
Parents with small children	High chairs, child-size portions, and things to keep the kids entertained
People who eat out a lot	Variety both in food and in décor
People on tight budgets	Economical food; a place where they don't need to tip (cafeteria or fast food)
People on special diets	Low-sodium and low-calorie dishes; vegetarian, kosher, or gluten-free food; locally grown and produced food
People to whom eating out is part of an evening's entertainment	Music or a floor show; elegant surroundings; reservations so they can get to a show or event after dinner; late hours so they can come to dinner after a show or game

restaurant offered, you could appeal to one or more of the following subgroups:

If your benefit or selling point is your relaxing atmosphere, think about the specific details that make the restaurant relaxing. If your strong point is elegant dining, think about all the details that contribute to that elegance.

In routine messages, reader benefits give reasons to comply with the policies you announce and suggest that the policies are good ones. In persuasive messages, reader benefits give reasons to act and help overcome reader resistance. Negative messages do not use reader benefits.

Good reader benefits meet four criteria. Each of these criteria suggests a technique for writing good reader benefits:

1. Adapt Reader Benefits to the Audience
2. Stress Intrinsic as Well as Extrinsic Motivators
3. Prove Reader Benefits and Provide Enough Detail
4. Phrase Reader Benefits in You-Attitude

1. Adapt Reader Benefits to the Audience

When you write to different audiences, you may need to stress different reader benefits. Suppose that you manufacture a product and want to persuade dealers to carry it. The features you may cite in ads directed toward customers—stylish colours, sleek lines, convenience, durability, good price—won't convince dealers. Shelf space is at a premium, and most dealers don't carry all the models of all the brands available for any given product. To be persuasive, talk about benefits from the dealer's point of view: turnover, profit margin, the national advertising campaign that will build customer awareness and interest, and the special store displays.

Features alone rarely motivate readers. Instead, link the feature to the reader's needs—and provide details to make the benefit vivid.

× Weak: We have placemats with riddles.

✓ Better: Answering all the riddles on Monical's special placemats will keep the kids happy till your pizza comes. If they don't have time to finish (and they may not, since your pizza will be ready so quickly), just take the riddles home—or answer them on your next visit.

Reader benefits improve both the attitudes and the behaviour of the people you work with and write to. They make it easier for you to accomplish your goals. Reader benefits tell readers that they can do the job and that success will be rewarded.[22] Thus, they help overcome two problems that reduce motivation: people may not think of all the possible benefits, and they may not understand the relationships among efforts, performance, and rewards.[23]

2. Stress Intrinsic as Well as Extrinsic Motivators

Intrinsic motivators come automatically from using a product or doing something. **Extrinsic motivators** are "added on." Someone in power decides to give them; they do not necessarily come from using the product or doing the action. Figure 2.2 gives examples of extrinsic and intrinsic motivators for three activities.

Figure 2.2 Extrinsic and Intrinsic Motivators

ACTIVITY	EXTRINSIC MOTIVATOR	INTRINSIC MOTIVATOR
Making a sale	Getting a commission	Pleasure in convincing someone; pride in using your talents to develop and execute a strategy
Turning in a suggestion to a company suggestion system	Getting a monetary reward when the suggestion is implemented	Solving a problem at work; making the work environment a little more pleasant
Writing a report that solves an organizational problem	Getting praise, a good performance appraisal, and maybe a raise	Pleasure in having an effect on an organization; pride in using your skills to solve problems; solving the problem itself

Intrinsic motivators or benefits are better than extrinsic motivators for two reasons:

1. You can't give a prize to customers every time they place an order, or to employees who do what they are supposed to do.
2. Research shows that extrinsic motivators may actually make people *less* satisfied with the products they buy or the procedures they follow.

John Helliwell studies the links between job satisfaction, general happiness, and business bottom lines. His work shows that trust, the respect and recognition of superiors, and the opportunity to have ideas adopted are more important than salary and bonuses. Happy employees are engaged ones who attend and perform better, yielding higher returns to the business.[24]

Since money is not the only motivator, choose reader benefits that identify intrinsic as well as extrinsic motivators for following policies and adopting ideas.

3. Prove Reader Benefits and Provide Enough Detail

A reader benefit is a claim or assertion that the reader will benefit if he or she does something. Convincing the reader, therefore, involves two steps: making sure that the benefit will occur, and explaining it to the reader.

If the logic behind a claimed reader benefit is faulty or inaccurate, there's no way to make that particular reader benefit convincing. Revise the benefit to make it logical.

✕ Faulty logic:

Using a computer will enable you to write letters, memos, and reports much more quickly.

Analysis:

If you've never used a computer, in the short run it will take you longer to create a document using a computer. The real time savings come when a document incorporates parts of previous documents or goes through several revisions. Creating a first draft from scratch will still take planning and careful composing; the time savings may or may not be significant.

✓ Revised reader benefit:

Using a computer allows you to revise and edit a document more easily. It eliminates rekeying as a separate step and reduces the time to proofread revisions. It allows you to move the text around on the page to create the best layout.

Always provide enough detail to be vivid and concrete. You'll need more detail in these situations:

a. The reader may not have thought of the benefit before.
b. The benefit depends on the difference between the long run and the short run.
c. The reader will be hard to persuade, and you need detail to make the benefit vivid and emotionally convincing.

4. Phrase Reader Benefits in You-Attitude

Reader benefits in you-attitude (see ⏩ "You-Attitude" later in this chapter) sound less selfish and will be as effective as they could be. A sales letter with strong you-attitude as well as reader benefits got a far bigger response than did an alternate version with reader benefits but no you-attitude.[25] In your final draft, check to be sure that you've used you-attitude.

Psychological description (⏩ Chapter 9) can help you make reader benefits vivid.

WRITING OR SPEAKING TO MULTIPLE AUDIENCES WITH DIFFERENT NEEDS

Many business messages go not to a single person but to a larger audience. When the members of your audience share the same interests and the same level of knowledge, you can use the principles outlined above for individual readers or for members of homogeneous groups. But often different members of the audience have different needs.

Professor Rachel Spilka has shown that talking to readers both inside and outside the organization helped corporate engineers adapt their documents successfully. Talking to readers and reviewers helped writers involve readers in the planning process, understand the social and political relationships among readers, and negotiate conflicts orally rather than depending solely on the document. These writers were then able to think about content as well as about organization and style, appeal to common grounds (such as reducing waste or increasing productivity) that several readers shared, and reduce the number of revisions needed before documents were approved.[26]

When it is not possible to meet everyone's needs, meet the needs of gatekeepers and decision makers first.

Content and Choice of Details

- Provide an overview or executive summary for readers who want just the main points.
- In the body of the document, provide enough detail for decision makers and for anyone else who could veto your proposal.
- If the decision makers don't need details that other audiences will want, provide those details—statistical tabulations, survey findings, or earlier reports—in appendices.

Document Organization

- Use headings and a table of contents so readers can turn to the portions that interest them.
- Organize your message based on the decision makers' attitudes toward it.

International Winning Olympic Bid*

When the final two bid cities for the 2012 Olympics went head-to-head, it was London that won—by 54 votes to 50. How did London do it? Good you-attitude and strong audience benefits.

The favourite throughout the campaign, Paris concluded its final presentation: "Paris needs the Games, Paris wants the Games, Paris loves the Games." Along the way President Chirac "laid into British and Finnish food," but Chirac "was left eating his words."

Lord Coe, an Olympic champion himself, focused on a "magical experience" for youth—and 30 young people from London—and the Olympic ideal and legacy. Coe spoke of "London's vision . . . to reach people, young people, all around the world and connect them with the power of the Games."

He spoke of inspiring youth to choose sport, of a global voice, and of a multicultural London representing 200 nations and the world's diversity. "Choose London and you will send a clear message to the youth of the world that the Olympics is for you."

He spoke of listening and learning from the Olympics' best practices and of serving the ambition of the whole Olympic movement with a lasting legacy and an environmentally friendly Olympics where nothing would be wasted.

*Based on Francis Keogh and Andrew Frase, "Why London won the Olympics," *BBC Sport*, July 6, 2005, retrieved from http://news.bbc.co.uk/sport2/hi/other_sports/olympics_2012/4618507.stm; "Cities make final Olympic pleas," *BBC Sport*, July 6, 2005, retrieved from http://news.bbc.co.uk/sport2/hi/front_page/4654037.stm; "London beats Paris to 2012 Games," *BBC Sport*, July 6, 2005, retrieved from http://news.bbc/co.uk/sport1/hi/front_page/4655555.stm.

Level of Formality

- Avoid personal pronouns. *You* ceases to have a specific meaning when different audiences use a document.
- If both internal and external audiences will use a document, use a slightly more formal style than you would in an internal document.
- Use a more formal style when you write to international audiences (⏩ Chapter 5).

Use of Technical Terms and Theory

- In the body of the document, assume the degree of knowledge that decision makers will have.
- Put background information and theory under separate headings. Then readers can use the headings and the table of contents to read or skip these sections, as their knowledge dictates.
- If decision makers will have more knowledge than other audiences, provide a glossary of terms (refer readers to the glossary early in the document).

GOODWILL

In accounting terms, goodwill is an intangible asset that goes beyond the fair book value of a business. It is a valuation based on reputation and potential that explains why companies competed for Twitter as an acquisition prospect worth an estimated $8 billion or more despite annual revenues that had not yet reached $100 million.[27]

That business principle has translated into an important rhetorical concept of goodwill that smooths the challenges of business. Companies have long been aware that treating customers well pays off in more sales and higher profits. More and more organizations are realizing that treating employees well is financially wise as well as ethically sound. MCI Communications and Electronic Data Systems have also found that internal goodwill has a measurable effect on the bottom line.[28] Researcher Jim Collins found that the most financially successful companies put "people first, strategy second." Another study found that companies that "manage people right" outperformed other companies by 30% to 40%.[29]

You-attitude, positive emphasis, and bias-free language are three ways to help build goodwill. All three help you achieve your purposes and make your messages friendlier, more persuasive, and more professional. They suggest that you care not just about money but also about your readers and their needs and interests.

LO5

YOU-ATTITUDE

You-attitude is a style of writing that looks at things from the reader's point of view, emphasizing what the reader wants to know, respecting the reader's intelligence, and protecting the reader's ego. To apply you-attitude, use the five techniques discussed below.

Note that many you-attitude revisions are *longer* and have *more* information. They are not wordy, however. **Wordiness** means having more words than the meaning requires. We can add information and still keep the writing tight.

1. Talk about the Reader, Not about Yourself

Readers want to know how they benefit or are affected. When you provide this information, you make your message more complete and more interesting.

× Lacks you-attitude: I have negotiated an agreement with Apex Rent-a-Car that gives you a discount on rental cars.

✓ You-attitude: As a Sunstrand employee, you can now get a 20% discount when you rent a car from Apex.

The first sentence focuses on what the writer does, not on what the reader receives. Any sentence that focuses on the writer's work or generosity lacks you-attitude, even if the sentence contains the word *you.* Instead of focusing on what we are giving the reader, focus on what the reader can now do.

× Lacks you-attitude: We are shipping your order of September 21 this afternoon.

✓ You-attitude: The two dozen CorningWare starter sets you ordered will be shipped this afternoon and should reach you by September 28.

The reader is less interested in when we shipped the order than in when it will arrive. Note that the phrase "should reach you by" leaves room for variations in delivery schedules. Give the reader the name of the carrier, so the reader knows whom to contact if the order doesn't arrive promptly.

2. Refer to the Reader's Request or Order Specifically

When you write about the reader's request, order, or policy, refer to it specifically, not as a generic *your order* or *your policy.* If your reader is an individual or a small business, it's friendly to specify the content of the order; if you are writing to a company with which you do a great deal of business, give the invoice or purchase order number.

× Lacks you-attitude: Your order . . .

✓ You-attitude (to individual): The desk chair you ordered . . .

✓ You-attitude (to a large store): Your invoice #783329 . . .

The form letter printed in Figure 2.3 is stuffy and selfish. The comments in blue identify where the letter lacks you-attitude, loses credibility, and generates ill will.

1. **The language is stiff and legalistic.** Note the obsolete (and sexist) "Gentlemen:" "Please be advised," "herein," and "expedite."
2. **The tone is selfish.** The letter is written from the writer's point of view; there are no benefits for the reader. (The writer says there are, but without evidence the claim isn't convincing.)
3. **The main point is buried** in the middle of the long first paragraph. The middle is the least emphatic part of a paragraph.
4. **The request is vague.** How many references does the supplier want? Would credit references, like banks, rather than vendor references work too? Is the name of the reference enough, or is it necessary also to specify the line of credit and/or the years credit has been established? What "additional financial information" does the supplier want? Bank balance? The request sounds like an invasion of privacy, not a reasonable business practice.
5. **Words are misused** (*herein* for *therein*), suggesting either an ignorant writer or one who doesn't care enough about the subject and the reader to use the right word.

3. Don't Talk about Feelings Except to Congratulate or Offer Sympathy

In most business situations, your feelings are irrelevant and should be omitted.

× Lacks you-attitude: We are happy to extend you a credit line of $5,000.

✓ You-attitude: You can now charge up to $5,000 on your Visa card.

Figure 2.3 A Form Letter That Generated Ill Will

Nelson Manufacturing

600 Main Street 204-281-3000
Winnipeg, MB R3T 5V5 fax 204-281-3001

Gentlemen:

Please be advised that upon reviewing your credit file with us, we find the information herein outdated. In an effort to expedite the handling of your future orders with us, and to allow us to open an appropriate line of credit for your company, we ask that you send an updated list of vendor references. Any other additional financial information that you can supply would be to both of our benefits.

May we hear from you soon?

Sincerely,

International You-Attitude with International Audiences

When businesses communicate with international audiences, they need to adjust their point of view. Communicators need to know and prepare for Canada's top trading partners: the United States, United Kingdom, China, Japan, Mexico, South Korea, Netherlands, Germany, France, and Hong Kong, according to Foreign Affairs, Trade and Development Canada, Update 2012.

Some companies consider the cost of translating for international audiences an unnecessary one, but misunderstandings can be costlier.

How formal should protocols be? What channels will work for what audiences? Will face-to-face meetings be needed to build relationships in Asia, Africa, or Latin America? What dress is appropriate?

Even pronouns and direction words need attention. *We* may not feel inclusive to readers with different assumptions and backgrounds. *Here* won't mean the same thing to a reader in Bonn as it does to one in Baie Comeau. Likewise, words such as *soon, many,* and *expensive* have meaning in relation to particular socioeconomic and cultural contexts. Be specific about times, figures, money.

The reader cares about the situation from his or her point of view.

It is appropriate to talk about your own emotions in a message of congratulations or condolence.

✓ You-attitude: Congratulations on your promotion to district manager! I was really pleased to read about it.

In internal memos, it may be appropriate to comment that a project has been gratifying or frustrating. In the letter of transmittal that accompanies a report, it is permissible to talk about your feelings about doing the work. But even other readers in your own organization are primarily interested in their own concerns, not in your feelings.

Don't talk about the reader's feelings, either. It's distancing to have someone else tell us how we feel—especially if the writer is wrong.

× Lacks you-attitude: You'll be happy to hear that the new Agrigrip procedures meet OHS requirements.

✓ You-attitude: The new Agrigrip procedures meet OHS requirements.

When you have good news for the reader, simply give the good news.

× Lacks you-attitude: You'll be happy to hear that your scholarship has been renewed.

✓ You-attitude: Congratulations! Your scholarship has been renewed.

4. In Positive Situations, Use *You* More Often Than *I*. Use *We* When It Includes the Reader

Whenever possible, focus on the reader, not on you or your company.

× Lacks you-attitude: We provide health insurance to all employees.

✓ You-attitude: You receive health insurance as a full-time Procter & Gamble employee.

Most readers are tolerant of the word *I* in e-mail messages, which seem like conversation. Edit paper documents to use *I* rarely if at all. *I* suggests you're concerned about personal issues, not about the organization's problems, needs, and opportunities. Overused *I*'s in job letters send clear messages to prospective employers about whose needs and opportunities are on the writer's mind. *We* works well when it includes the reader. Avoid *we* if it excludes the reader (as it would in a letter to a customer or supplier, or as it might in a memo about what *we* in management want *you* to do).

5. In Negative Situations, Avoid the Word *You*. Use Passive Verbs and Impersonal Expressions to Avoid Assigning Blame

When you report bad news, use a noun for a group of which the reader is a part instead of *you* so readers don't feel they're singled out for bad news.

× Lacks you-attitude: You must get approval from the director before you publish any articles or memoirs based on your work in the agency.

✓ You-attitude: Agency personnel must get approval from the director to publish any articles or memoirs based on their work at the agency.

Use passive verbs and impersonal expressions to avoid blaming the reader. **Passive verbs** describe the action performed on something, without necessarily saying who did it. (See ▸▸ Chapter 3 for a full discussion of passive verbs.) **Impersonal expressions** omit people and talk only about things.

In most business writing, active verbs are better. But when your reader is at fault, passive verbs may be useful to avoid assigning blame.

× Lacks you-attitude: You made no allowance for inflation in your estimate.

✓ You-attitude (passive): No allowance for inflation has been made in this estimate.

✓ You-attitude (impersonal): This estimate makes no allowance for inflation.

Though some might argue that an estimate, for example, is inanimate and can't "make" anything, in the pragmatic world of business writing, impersonal expressions often help you convey criticism tactfully.

Good messages apply you-attitude beyond the sentence level by using content and organization as well as style to build goodwill. Be guided by this chapter's advice on adapting your message to your audience (see ◂◂ "Using Audience Analysis to Adapt Your Message" previously in this chapter).

Consider the memo in Figure 2.4. As the marginal notes indicate, many individual sentences in this memo lack you-attitude. Fixing individual sentences could improve the letter. However, it really needs to be totally rewritten.

Figure 2.5 shows a possible revision of this memo. The revision is clearer, easier to read, and friendlier.

POSITIVE EMPHASIS

Some negatives are necessary. As Merrill Lynch Vice President Stephen Hlibok points out, when you have bad news to give the reader—announcements of layoffs, product defects and recalls, price increases—straightforward negatives build credibility. (See ▸▸ Chapter 8 on how to present bad news.) Sometimes negatives are needed to make people take a problem seriously. And sometimes negatives create a "reverse psychology" that makes people look favourably at your product. Rent-a-Wreck is thriving. (The cars really don't look so bad.)[30]

But in most situations, it's better to be positive. Researchers Annette N. Shelby and N. Lamar Reinsch, Jr., found that business people responded more positively to positive than to negative language and were more likely to say they would act on a positively worded request.[31] Create positive emphasis by using the following five techniques.

1. Avoid Negative Words and Words with Negative Connotations

If you find one of the common negative words listed in Figure 2.6 in a draft, try to substitute a more positive word. When you must use a negative, use the *least negative* term that will convey your meaning.

The following examples show how to replace negative words with positive words.

× Negative: We have failed to finish taking inventory.
✓ Better: We haven't finished taking inventory.
✓ Still better: We will be finished taking inventory Friday.

× Negative: If you can't understand this explanation, feel free to call me.
✓ Better: If you have further questions, just call me.
✓ Still better: Omit the sentence.

If a sentence has two negatives, substitute one positive term.

× Negative: Never fail to back up your files.
✓ Better: Always back up your files.

When you must use a negative term, use the least negative word that is accurate.

Figure 2.4 A Memo Lacking You-Attitude

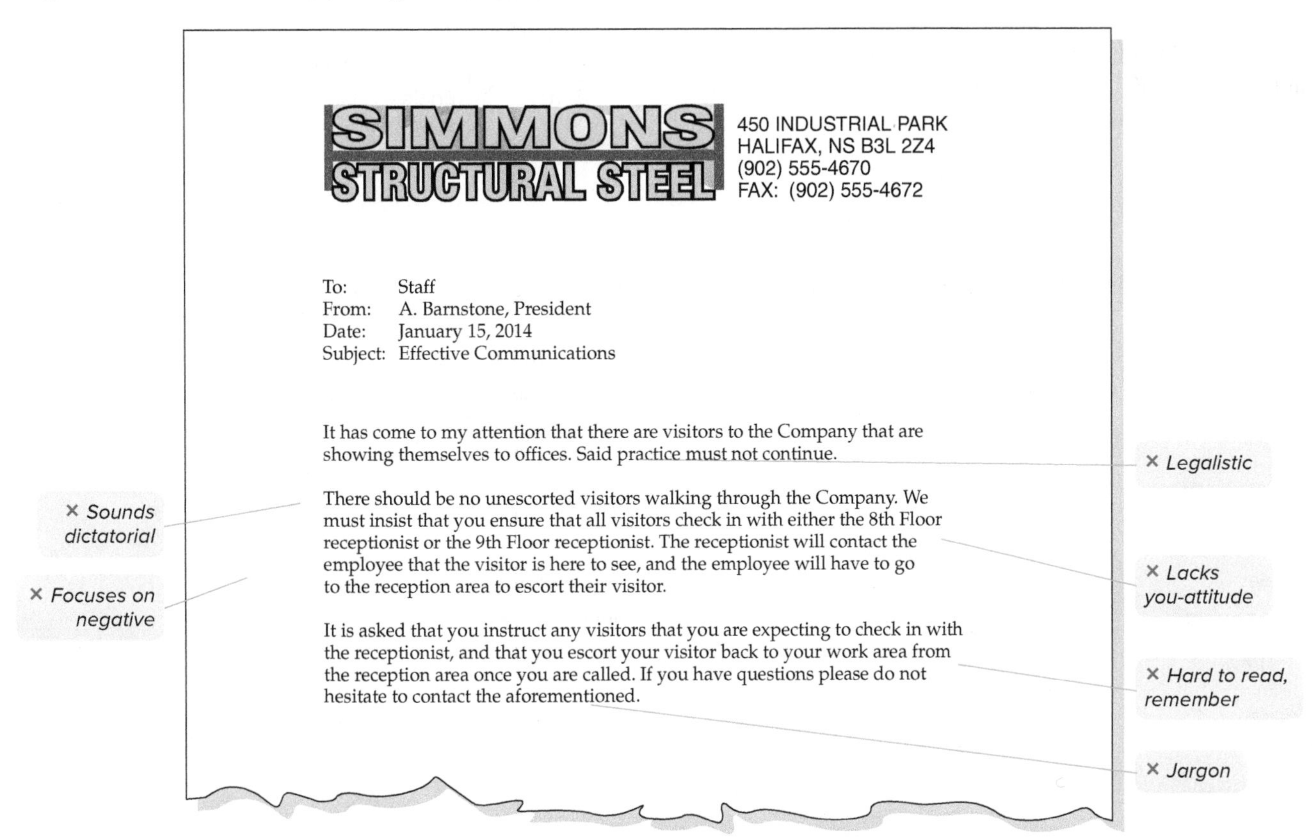
SIMMONS STRUCTURAL STEEL
450 INDUSTRIAL PARK
HALIFAX, NS B3L 2Z4
(902) 555-4670
FAX: (902) 555-4672

To: Staff
From: A. Barnstone, President
Date: January 15, 2014
Subject: Effective Communications

It has come to my attention that there are visitors to the Company that are showing themselves to offices. Said practice must not continue.

There should be no unescorted visitors walking through the Company. We must insist that you ensure that all visitors check in with either the 8th Floor receptionist or the 9th Floor receptionist. The receptionist will contact the employee that the visitor is here to see, and the employee will have to go to the reception area to escort their visitor.

It is asked that you instruct any visitors that you are expecting to check in with the receptionist, and that you escort your visitor back to your work area from the reception area once you are called. If you have questions please do not hesitate to contact the aforementioned.

Figure 2.5 A Memo Revised to Improve You-Attitude

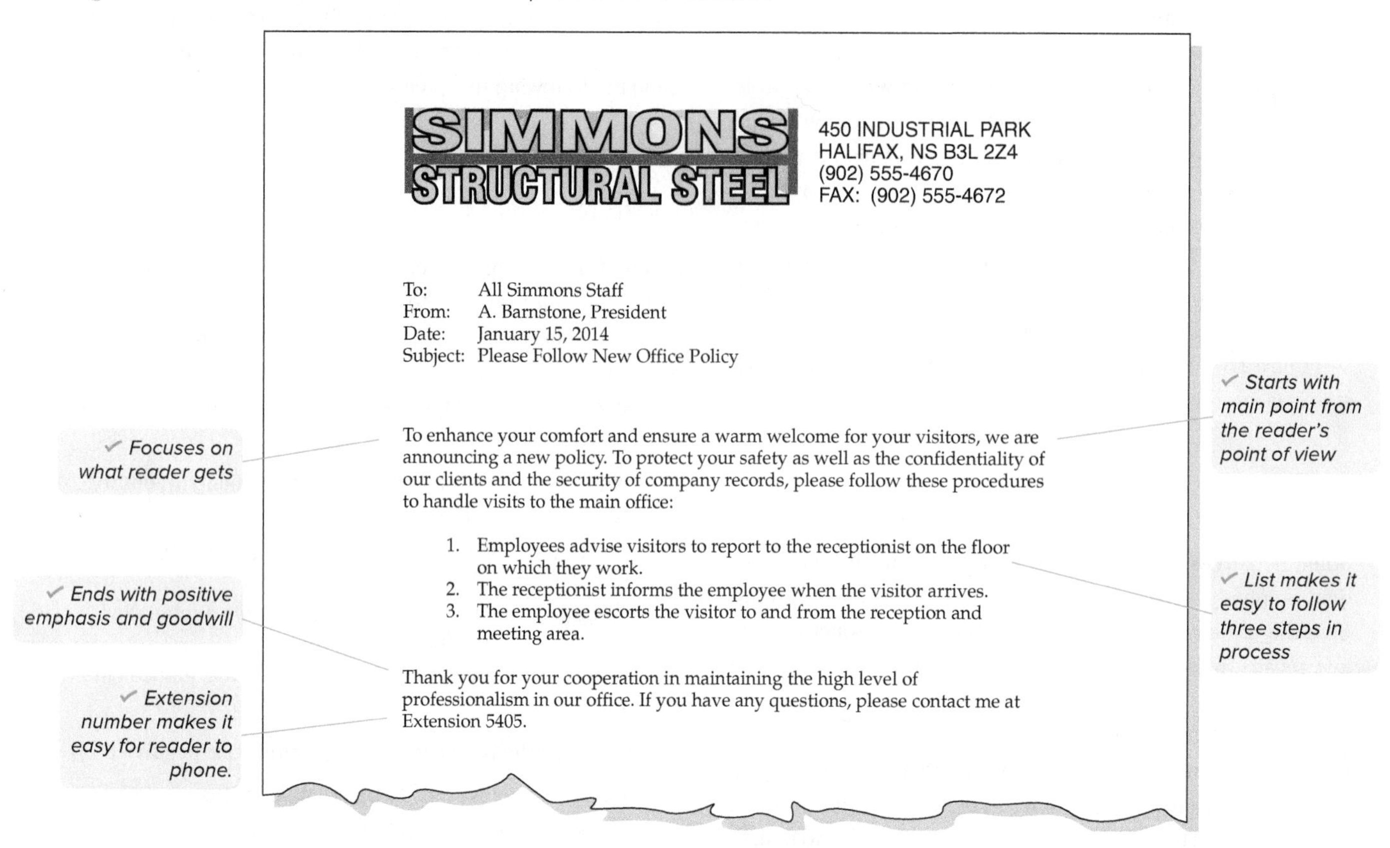
SIMMONS STRUCTURAL STEEL
450 INDUSTRIAL PARK
HALIFAX, NS B3L 2Z4
(902) 555-4670
FAX: (902) 555-4672

To: All Simmons Staff
From: A. Barnstone, President
Date: January 15, 2014
Subject: Please Follow New Office Policy

To enhance your comfort and ensure a warm welcome for your visitors, we are announcing a new policy. To protect your safety as well as the confidentiality of our clients and the security of company records, please follow these procedures to handle visits to the main office:

1. Employees advise visitors to report to the receptionist on the floor on which they work.
2. The receptionist informs the employee when the visitor arrives.
3. The employee escorts the visitor to and from the reception and meeting area.

Thank you for your cooperation in maintaining the high level of professionalism in our office. If you have any questions, please contact me at Extension 5405.

× Negative: Your balance of $835 is delinquent.

✓ Better: Your balance of $835 is past due.

Beware of **hidden negatives:** words that are not negative in themselves but become negative in context. *But* and *however* indicate a shift, so, after a positive statement, they are negative. Even positives may backfire if they suggest that in the past the service or product was bad.

× Negative: I hope this is the information you wanted. [Implication: I'm not sure.]

✓ Better: Enclosed is a brochure about road repairs scheduled for 2014–16.

Figure 2.6 Negative Words to Avoid

afraid	fail	not	**Some *dis-* words:**	**Some *mis-* words:**
anxious	fault	objection	disapprove	misfortune
avoid	fear	problem	dishonest	mistake
bad	hesitate	reject	dissatisfied	missing
careless	ignorant	sorry	**Many *in-* words:**	**Many *un-* words:**
damage	ignore	terrible	inadequate	unclear
delay	impossible	trivial	incomplete	unfair
delinquent	injury	trouble	inconvenient	unfortunate
deny	lacking	wait	insincere	unfortunately
difficulty	loss	weakness		unpleasant
eliminate	neglect	worry		unreasonable
error	never	wrong		unreliable
except	no			unsure

✓ Still better: The brochure contains a list of all roads and bridges scheduled for repair during 2014–16. Call Gwen Wong at 555-3245 for specific dates when work will start and stop, and for alternate routes.

× Negative: Now Krispy Krunch tastes better. [Implication: it used to taste terrible.]

✓ Better: Now Krispy Krunch tastes even better.

When you eliminate negative words, be sure to maintain accuracy. Words that are exact opposites will usually not be accurate. Instead, use specifics to be both positive and accurate.

× Negative: Customers under 60 are not eligible for the Prime Time discount.

× Not true: You must be over 60 to be eligible for the Prime Time discount.

✓ True: If you're 60 or older, you can save 10% on all your purchases with RightWay's Prime Time discount.

Legal phrases also have negative connotations for most readers and should be avoided whenever possible. The idea will sound more positive if you use normal English.

× Negative:

If your account is still delinquent, a second legal notice will be sent to you informing you that cancellation of your policy will occur 30 days after the date of the legal notice if we do not receive your cheque.

✓ Better:

Even if your cheque is lost in the mail and never reaches us, you still have a 30-day grace period. If you do get a second notice, you will know that your payment hasn't reached us. To keep your account in good standing, stop payment on the first cheque and send a second one.

2. Focus on What the Reader Can Do

When there are limits, or some options are closed, focus on the alternatives that remain.

× Negative: We will not allow you to charge more than $1,500 on your Visa account.

✓ Better: You can charge $1,500 on your new Visa card.

✓ or: Your new Visa card gives you $1,500 in credit that you can use at thousands of stores nationwide.

When you have a benefit and a requirement the reader must meet to get the benefit, the sentence is usually more positive if you put the benefit first.

× Negative: You will not qualify for the student membership rate of $25 a year unless you are a full-time student.

✓ Better: You get all the benefits of membership for only $25 a year if you are a full-time student.

Some stores might say, "Put books you don't want here." But bookseller Joseph Best in Lexington, KY, uses positive emphasis.

3. Justify Negative Information by Giving a Reason or Linking It to a Reader Benefit

A reason can help your reader see that the information is necessary; a benefit can suggest that the negative aspect is outweighed by positive factors.

× Negative: We cannot sell compact discs in lots of less than 10.

× Loophole: To keep down packaging costs and to help you save on shipping and handling costs, we sell compact discs in lots of 10 or more.

Suppose the customer says, "I'll pay the extra shipping and handling. Send me seven." If you can't or won't sell in lots of less than 10, you need to write:

✓ Better: To keep down packaging costs and to help customers save on shipping and handling costs, we sell compact discs only in lots of 10 or more.

If you link the negative element to a benefit, be sure it is a benefit the reader will acknowledge. You may think you're doing customers a favour by limiting their credit so they don't get in over their heads. They may prefer more credit so they could expand in hopes of making more sales and more profits.

Ethics and Legal Health Promotion?*

The *Food and Drug Act* of 1952 prohibits direct-to-consumer advertising of prescription pharmaceuticals in Canada, though 1975 amendments opened the door to practices that may not respect the spirit and letter of the law. Public and policy makers are debating the ethical and legal implications of relaxing Canadian regulations.

Studies show that advertising may be more influential than scientific evidence in driving prescription decisions. In the case of a cholesterol-lowering drug, Vytorin, a $200-million direct-to-consumer advertising budget in 2007 produced $5 billion in sales. In 2006 the drug (of which Vytorin is one brand name) was prescribed 33 million times in the U.S. compared with 824,000 in Canada.

Lead researcher Jack Tu underlines the larger message: "It shows the potential downsides to . . . too much advertising, without the evidence behind it."

The results in a study of Vytorin published in the *New England Journal of Medicine* (March 2008) show "no result—zilch. In no subgroup, in no segment, was there any added benefit," said Dutch lead scientist John Kastelein.

Celebrex advertisements highlight the energy of aging and active swimmers and gardeners before urging viewers to talk to their doctors. What they don't mention are side effects at high doses: cardiovascular problems and strokes.

Whether the rules change or not, it isn't ethical to omit negatives customers need to know to make informed decisions.

*Based on Barbara Mintzes et al., "Influence of direct to consumer pharmaceutical advertising and patients' requests on prescribing decisions: Two site cross sectional survey," *BMJ* 324, February 2, 2002, 277–79; John Lorinc, "The side effects of a 30-second spot," *The Globe and Mail*, August 11, 2007, F1–6; Carly Weeks, "Advertising may have more influence on prescriptions than science," *The Globe and Mail*, March, 31, 2008, L3; Marilynn Marchione, "New heart disease drug shows no result—zilch," *The Globe and Mail*, April 1, 2008, L4.

4. If the Negative Is Truly Unimportant, Omit It

Omit negatives only in these situations:

- The reader does not need the information to make a decision.
- You have already given the reader the information, and he or she has access to the previous communication.
- The information is trivial.

The following examples suggest the kind of negatives you can omit:

× Negative:	A one-year subscription to *PC Magazine* is $49.97. That rate is not as low as the rates charged for some magazines.
✓ Better:	A one-year subscription to *PC Magazine* is $49.97.
✓ Still better:	A one-year subscription to *PC Magazine* is $49.97. You save 43% off the newsstand price of $87.78.

5. Put the Negative Information in the Middle

The beginning and end are always positions of emphasis. Put negatives in the middle of a paragraph rather than in the first or last sentence and in the middle of the message rather than in the first or last paragraphs.

Giving a topic lots of space emphasizes it. Therefore, you can de-emphasize negative information by giving it as little space as possible. Give negative information only once in your message. Don't list negatives vertically on the page since lists take space and emphasize material.

TONE, POWER, AND POLITENESS

Tone is the implied attitude of the writer toward the reader. If the words of a document seem condescending or rude, tone is a problem. Tone is tricky because it interacts with power: the words that might seem friendly from a superior to a subordinate may seem snobbish or impertinent if used by the subordinate to the superior. Norms for politeness are cultural and generational. Language that is acceptable within one group may be unacceptable if used by someone outside the group.

The desirable tone for business writing is businesslike but not stiff, friendly but not phony, confident but not arrogant, polite but not grovelling. The following guidelines will help you achieve the tone you want.

- **Use courtesy titles for people outside your organization whom you don't know well.** Many Canadian organizations use first names for everyone, whatever their age or rank. But some people don't like being called by their first names by people they don't know or by someone much younger. When you talk or write to people outside your organization, use first names only if you've established a personal relationship. Otherwise, use a courtesy title:

  Dear Mr. Reynolds:

  Dear Ms. Lee:
- **Be aware of the power implications of the words you use.** "Thank you for your co-operation" is generous coming from a superior to a subordinate; it's not appropriate in a message to your superior.

Different ways of asking for action carry different levels of politeness.[32]

Technology Tips Straight Talk with Professors?

Writing e-mails to your professor is good practice for writing to supervisors and managers on the job. You are learning about tact and tactics or how to make good rhetorical choices about medium, strategy, tone, timing, and wording in writing to superiors.

If you do not carefully adapt your style but retain the casual informality of text messages and chat rooms, requests can become negative messages. Check before sending, so that you don't repeat the common errors in these examples.

- Hi, I have concerns about my report, presentation, grades, and basically everything in the class. Is there a time we can meet before tomorrow's exam to talk about it?
- Hello, I was just wondering how we can be expected to include evidence in the exam answers. Thank you for your time.
- Hi, Are you marking grammar and spelling in the exam? Let me know.
- Hi Mrs. Smith, I am writing at 2:00 today, so hopefully you can let me know what format to use for report answers in the final.
- Hi, I missed the last class, I'm unsure how to do the assignment. How do you propose I deal with this?

× Order:	Turn in your time card by Monday. (lowest politeness)
✓ Polite order:	Please turn in your time card by Monday. (mid-level politeness)
✓ Indirect request:	Time cards should be turned in by Monday. (higher politeness)
✓ Question:	Would you be able to turn in your time card by Monday? (highest politeness)

You need more politeness if you're asking for something that will inconvenience the reader and help you more than the person who does the action (see "Straight Talk with Professors?"). Generally, you need less politeness when you're asking for something small, routine, or to the reader's benefit. Some discourse communities, however, prefer that even small requests be made politely.

× Lower politeness:	To start the scheduling process, please describe your availability for meetings during the second week of the month.
✓ Higher politeness:	Could you let me know what times you'd be free for a meeting the second week of the month?

Generally, requests sound friendliest when they use conversational language.

× Poor tone:	Return the draft with any changes by next Tuesday.
✓ Better tone:	Let me know by Tuesday whether you'd like any changes in the draft.

- **When you must give bad news, consider hedging your statement.** Auditors' opinion letters rarely say directly that firms are using unacceptable accounting practices. Instead, they use three strategies to be more diplomatic: specifying the time ("currently, the records are quite informal"), limiting statements ("it appears," "it seems," "except for the items noted below, these financial statements present fairly"), and using impersonal statements that do not specify who caused a problem or who will perform an action; for example, "the financial statements do not conform to GAAP."[33]

REDUCING BIAS IN BUSINESS COMMUNICATION

Bias-free language and bias-free visuals help sustain the goodwill we work so hard to create in business.

Bias-free language is language that does not discriminate against people on the basis of gender, abilities, race,

Ethics and Legal R-E-S-P-E-C-T*

Outraged by the movie *Tropic Thunder,* people with intellectual disabilities rallied for respect. They complained that the movie fostered hate and discrimination and that in its attempts at edgy humour it had "crossed the line."

What the movie makers failed to see was that "the parody of a person with an intellectual disability and use of words such as 'retard' and 'imbecile' perpetuates negative stereotypes and encourages a culture of denigration and intolerance against people with disabilities."

*Based on Sue Zeidler, "Advocates for disabled to protest 'Tropic Thunder,'" *Reuters,* August 11, 2008, retrieved February 9, 2011, from http://www.reuters.com/article/2008/08/11/us-boycott-disability-idUSN1029346220080811; Derrik J. Lang, "Mental disability groups picket 'Tropic Thunder' Premiere," *Huffington Post,* August 12, 2008, retrieved February 9, 2011, from http://www.huffingtonpost.com/2008/08/12/mental-disability-groups_n_118347.html; Celine R. Fortin, "'Tropic Thunder' leads people with disabilities to rally for respect," *The Arc of New Jersey,* August 12, 2008, retrieved August 18, 2008, from http://www.nj.com/helpinghands/arc/index.ssf/2008/08/people_with_disabilities_rally_1.html.

age, or any other category. It includes all readers, helps to sustain goodwill, is fair and friendly, and complies with the law. Since the 1980s in Canada, bias-free language has been at the heart of policies promoting multiculturalism (Canadian Multiculturalism Act, 1988), advancing human rights, reducing barriers to the participation in the workforce of equity groups, advancing their participation in the public service, and extending access to information and access to programs and services for all Canadians. With similar goals in mind, provinces, universities and colleges, non-governmental organizations, and businesses have developed bias-free language policies and guidelines.

Check to be sure your language is non-sexist, non-racist, and non-ageist. When you talk about people with disabilities or diseases, talk about the people, not the condition. When you produce Facebook pages, videos, newsletters, or other documents with photos and illustrations, choose a sampling of the whole population, not just part of it.

Making Language Non-Sexist

Non-sexist language treats both sexes neutrally. Be sure that your writing is free from sexism in four areas: words and phrases, job titles, courtesy titles, and pronouns. If you find any of the terms in the first column in Figure 2.7 in your writing, replace them with terms from the second column.

Not every word containing *man* is sexist. For example, manager is not sexist. The word comes from the Latin *manus* meaning hand; it has nothing to do with maleness.

Avoid terms that assume everyone is married or is heterosexual.

× Biased: You and your husband or wife are cordially invited to the dinner.

✓ Better: You and your guest are cordially invited to the dinner.

Use neutral titles that do not imply a job is held only by men or only by women. Many job titles are already neutral: accountant, banker, doctor, engineer, inspector, manager, nurse, pilot, secretary, technician, to name a few. Other titles reflect gender stereotypes and need to be changed.

INSTEAD OF	USE
Businessman	A specific title: executive, accountant, department head, business person
Chairman	Chair, chairperson, moderator
Foreman	Supervisor
Salesman	Salesperson, sales representative
Waitress	Server
Woman lawyer	Lawyer
Workman	Worker, employee. Or use a specific title: crane operator

Memos normally use first and last names without courtesy titles. Letters, however, require courtesy titles in the salutation unless you're on a first-name basis with your reader. (See ▸▸ Chapter 7 for examples of memo and letter formats.)

- When you know your reader's name and gender, use courtesy titles that do not indicate marital status: *Mr.* for men and *Ms.* for women. There are, however, two exceptions:
  1. If the woman has a professional title, use that title if you would use it for a man.
     Dr. Kristen Sorenson is our new company physician.
     The Rev. Elizabeth Townsley gave the invocation.
  2. If the woman prefers to be addressed as *Mrs.* or *Miss,* use the title she prefers rather than *Ms.* (You-attitude takes precedence over non-sexist language: address the reader as she or he prefers to be addressed.) To find out if a woman prefers a traditional title, attend to these cues:
     a. Check the signature block in previous correspondence. Use the title she designates.

Figure 2.7 Getting Rid of Sexist Terms and Phrases

INSTEAD OF	USE	BECAUSE
The girl at the front desk	The woman's name or job title: "Ms. Browning," "Rosa," "the receptionist"	Call female employees *women* just as you call male employees *men.* When you talk about a specific woman, use her name, just as you use a man's name to talk about a specific man.
The ladies on our staff	The women on our staff	Use parallel terms for males and females. Few businesses refer to their staff as *gentlemen,* since social distinctions are rarely at issue.
Manpower; manhours; manning	Personnel hours or worker hours Staffing	The power in business today comes from both women and men. If you have to write to Manpower, you are stuck with the term. When you talk about other organizations, however, use non-sexist alternatives.
Managers and their wives	Managers and their guests	Managers may be female; not everyone is married.

b. Notice the title a woman uses in introducing herself on the phone. If she says, "This is Robin Stine," use *Ms.* when you write to her. If she says, "I'm Mrs. Stine," use the title she specifies.

c. Check your company directory. In some organizations, women who prefer traditional titles can list them with their names.

d. When you're writing job letters or crucial correspondence, call the company and ask the receptionist which title your reader prefers.

Ms. is particularly useful when you do not know a woman's marital status.

In addition to using parallel courtesy titles, use parallel forms for names.

NOT PARALLEL	PARALLEL
Members of the committee will be Mr. Jones, Mr. Yacone, and Lisa.	Members of the committee will be Mr. Jones, Mr. Yacone, and Ms. Melton. or Members of the committee will be Irving, Ted, and Lisa.

- When you know your reader's name but not the gender, you have these options:
  1. Call the company and ask the receptionist, or
  2. Use the reader's full name in the salutation:
     Dear Chris Crowell:
     Dear J. C. Meath:
- When you know neither the reader's name nor gender, you have three options:
  1. Omit the salutation and use a subject line.
     SUBJECT: RECOMMENDATION FOR BEN WANDELL
  2. Use the reader's position or job title:
     Dear Loan Officer:
     Dear Registrar:
  3. Use a general group to which your reader belongs:
     Dear Investor:
     Dear Admissions Committee:

Terms that are meant to be positive (Dear Careful Shopper: or Dear Concerned Citizen:) may backfire if readers see them as manipulative flattery.

Although many people claim to dislike Dear Friend: as a salutation in a form letter, research shows that letters using it bring in a higher response than letters with no salutation.

Pronouns

When you write about a specific person, use the appropriate gender pronouns:

In his speech, John Jones said that . . .

In her speech, Judy Jones said that . . .

When you are writing not about a specific person but about anyone who may be in a given job or position, traditional gender pronouns are sexist.

✕ Sexist:

a. Each supervisor must certify that the time sheet for his department is correct.

✕ Sexist:

b. When the nurse fills out the accident report form, she should send one copy to the Central Division Office.

There are four ways to eliminate sexist generic pronouns: use plurals, use second-person you, revise the sentence to omit the pronoun, or use pronoun pairs.

1. Use plural nouns and pronouns.

✓ Non-sexist:

a. Supervisors must certify that the time sheets for their departments are correct.

International Ms. in Any Language*

Other countries have developed non-sexist courtesy titles for women.

Canada	France	Spain	Denmark	Japan
Mrs.	Madame (Mme.)	Señora (Sra.)	Frøken	San
Miss	Mademoiselle (Mlle.)	Señorita (Srta.)	Fru	San
Ms.	Mad.	Sa.	Fr.	San

* Based on Mary Ritchie Key, *Male/Female Language* (Metuchen, NJ: Scarecrow Press, 1975), 50; John C. Condon and Fathi Yousef, *An Introduction to Intercultural Communication* (Indianapolis: Bobbs-Merrill, 1975), 50; and Silvia Fuduric, Letter to the Author, January 19, 1998.

Note: When you use plural nouns and pronouns, other words in the sentence may need to be made plural too (here, *time sheets* and *departments*).

Avoid mixing singular nouns and plural pronouns.

✕ Non-sexist but lacks agreement:

a. Each supervisor must certify that the time sheet for their department is correct.

The lack of agreement between singular *supervisor* and plural *their* is acceptable orally but is not yet acceptable to many readers in writing.

2. Use *you*.

✓ Non-sexist:

a. You must certify that the time sheet for your department is correct.

✓ Non-sexist:

b. When you fill out an accident report form, send one copy to the Central Division Office.

You is particularly good for instructions and statements of the responsibilities of someone in a given position. Using *you* may shorten sentences and make your writing more direct.

3. Substitute an article (*a, an,* or *the*) for the pronoun, or revise the sentence so that the pronoun is unnecessary.

✓ Non-sexist:

a. The supervisor must certify that the time sheet for the department is correct.

✓ Non-sexist:

b. The nurse will
   1. Fill out the accident report form.
   2. Send one copy of the form to the Central Division Office.

4. When you must focus on the action of an individual, use pronoun pairs.

✓ Non-sexist: a. The supervisor must certify that the time sheet for his or her department is correct.

✓ Non-sexist: b. When the nurse fills out the accident report form, she or he should send one copy to the Central Division Office.

Making Language Non-Racist and Non-Ageist

Language is **non-racist** and **non-ageist** when it treats all races and ages fairly, avoiding negative stereotypes of any group. Use these guidelines to check for bias in documents you write or edit:

- **Give someone's race or age only if it is relevant to your story.** When you do mention these characteristics, give them for everyone in your story—not just the non-Caucasian, non-young-to-middle-aged adults you mention.
- **Refer to a group by the term it prefers. As preferences change, change your usage.** The naming of Aboriginal peoples in Canada has undergone significant change since the 1970s and 1980s as many First Nations discard the names assigned to them by Europeans and assert their right to determine their own identities—and to use their own languages and spelling systems. Thus, Anishnabe is preferred to *Ojibwa(y), Mi'kmaq* to *Micmac,* for instance. Because of her mixed heritage, Michelle Hugli Barr (◀◀ An Inside Perspective) often finds herself mistakenly taken for Métis. A Métis is, however, "a person who self-identifies as Métis, is of historic Métis Nation Ancestry, is distinct from other Aboriginal Peoples and is accepted by the Métis Nation."[34]

  The Government of Canada Terminology and Language Standardization Board (Public Works) recommended that Aboriginal and Native (and Indigenous for international groups) be capitalized in line with other ethnic, geographic, and linguistic designations: Asian, Hispanic, Nordic. Aboriginal was to be used as an adjective (as in *Aboriginal peoples*) and not Aboriginals.

  Similarly, it is important not to talk about *Canada's Aboriginal peoples* or *Aboriginal Canadians,* but to respect Aboriginal peoples in Canada. First Nations is preferred to *Status Indians; First Peoples* includes Indians of all statuses.[35]

  Sixty years ago, *Negro* was preferred as a more dignified term than *colored* for African Americans. As times changed, *Black* and *African American* replaced it. Surveys in the mid-1990s showed that almost half of blacks aged 40 and older preferred *Black,* but those 18 to 39 preferred *African American.*[36] Black, Caribbean, or African Canadian are preferred terms.

  Oriental has now been replaced by *Asian.*

  Older people and *mature customers* are more generally accepted terms than *senior citizens* or *golden agers.*
- **Avoid terms that suggest competent people are unusual.** The statement "She is an intelligent black woman" suggests that the writer expects most black women to be stupid. "He is an asset to his race" suggests that excellence in the race is rare. "He is a spry 70-year-old" suggests that the writer is amazed that anyone that old can still move.

Talking about People with Disabilities and Diseases

A disability is a physical, mental, sensory, or emotional impairment that interferes with the major tasks of daily living. According to a 2006 Canadian survey of the ten provinces (but excluding those living in institutions, in the territories, or on First Nations reserves), 4.4 million Canadians (an increase of 21.2% since 2001) currently have a disability; the number of people with disabilities will rise as the population ages. Almost one-third of Aboriginal peoples report a disability.[37]

Chris Danielsen, a National Federation of the Blind spokesman, demonstrates how a cell phone can photograph a document and convert the text into speech.

- **People-first language focuses on the person, not the condition. People-first language** names the person first, then adds the condition.

INSTEAD OF	USE	BECAUSE
The mentally retarded	People with intellectual disabilities	The condition does not define the person or his or her potential.
Cancer patients	People being treated for cancer	

- **Avoid negative terms, unless the audience prefers them.** You-attitude takes precedence over positive emphasis: use the term a group prefers. People who lost their hearing as infants, children, or young adults often prefer to be called deaf, or Deaf, in recognition of Deafness as a culture. But people who lose their hearing as older adults often prefer to be called hard of hearing.

Just as people in a single ethnic group may prefer different labels based on generational or cultural divides, so do differences exist within the disability community.

Some negative terms, however, are never appropriate. Negative terms such as *afflicted, suffering from,* and *struck down* also suggest an outdated view of any illness as a sign of divine punishment.

INSTEAD OF	USE	BECAUSE
Confined to a wheelchair	Uses a wheelchair	People use wheelchairs to go to school, play sports, or participate in the workplace.
AIDS victim	Person with AIDS	Someone can have a disease without being victimized by it.
Abnormal	Atypical	People with disabilities are atypical but not necessarily abnormal.

Choosing Bias-Free Photos and Illustrations

When you produce a document, check the visuals for possible bias. Do they show people of both sexes and various ages and races? People using wheelchairs? It's OK to have individual pictures that have just one gender or one race. But the general impression should suggest that diversity is desirable and normal.

Check relationships and authority figures as well as numbers. If all the men appear in business suits and the women in servers' uniforms, the pictures are sexist. If the only First Nations or Métis people pictured are in similarly subordinate roles, the photos support racism even when an equal number of people from each race are shown.

As Marilyn Dyrud has shown, only 22% of the images of humans in clip art files were women, and most of those showed women in traditional roles. An even smaller percentage pictured members of minority groups.[38] Don't use biased clip art or stock photos: create your own bias-free illustrations.

SUMMARY OF KEY POINTS

- The *primary audience* will make a decision or act on the basis of your message. The *secondary audience* may comment on your message or implement your ideas after they've been approved. The *initial audience* routes the message to other audiences and may assign the message. A *gatekeeper* controls whether the message gets to the primary audience. A *watchdog audience* has political, social, or economic power and may base future actions on its evaluation of your message.
- Empathy is crucial to good audience analysis.
- Communicators can analyze an audience's geographic, demographic, psychographic, and behavioural characteristics, as well as organizational culture, discourse community, and community of practice.
- Six questions help you adapt messages to audiences:
  1. How will the audience react to the message?
  2. How much information does the audience need?
  3. What obstacles must you overcome?
  4. What positive aspects can you emphasize?
  5. What are the audience's expectations about style and format?
  6. How will the audience use the document?
- *Reader benefits* are benefits or advantages that the reader gets by using the writer's services, buying the writer's products, following the writer's policies, or adopting the writer's ideas.
- Good reader benefits meet four criteria:
  1. Adapt reader benefits to the audience
  2. Stress intrinsic as well as extrinsic motivators
  3. Prove reader benefits and provide enough detail
  4. Phrase reader benefits in you-attitude
- You-attitude, positive emphasis, and bias-free language are three ways to help build goodwill.
- *You-attitude* is a style of writing that looks at things from the reader's point of view.
- *Positive emphasis* means focusing on the positive rather than the negative aspects of a situation.
- Bias-free language is fair and friendly, complies with the law, includes all readers, and sustains goodwill.

EXERCISES AND PROBLEMS

GETTING STARTED

2.1 IDENTIFYING AUDIENCES

Discuss in your groups each of the following situations. Label the audiences as initial, gatekeeper, primary, secondary, or watchdog—a valuable stage in understanding and adapting to your audience:

1. Maria is seeking venture capital so that she can expand her business of offering soccer camps to youngsters. She's met an investment banker whose clients regularly hear presentations from business people seeking capital. The investment banker decides who will get a slot on the program, based on a comprehensive audit of each company's records and business plan.
2. Russell has created a Web page for his travel agency. He hopes to sell tickets for both leisure and business travel.
3. Paul works for the mayor's office in a big city. As part of a citywide cost-cutting measure, a blue-ribbon panel has recommended requiring employees who work more than 40 hours in a week to take compensatory time off rather than being paid overtime. The only exceptions will be the police and fire departments. The mayor asks Paul to prepare a proposal for the city council, which will vote on whether to implement the change. Before they vote, council members will hear from (1) citizens, who will have an opportunity to read the proposal and communicate their opinions to the city council; (2) mayors' offices in other cities, who may be asked about their experiences; (3) union representatives, who may be concerned about the reduction in income that will occur if the proposal is implemented; (4) department heads, whose ability to schedule work might be limited if the proposal passes; and (5) the blue-ribbon panel and good-government lobbying groups. Council members come up for re-election in six months.

2.2 IDENTIFYING AND DEVELOPING READER BENEFITS

Listed here are several things an organization might like its employees to do:

1. Use less paper.
2. Attend a brown-bag lunch to discuss ways to improve products or services.
3. Become more physically fit.
4. Volunteer for community organizations.
5. Ease a new hire's transition into the unit.

As Your Professor Directs,

a. Identify the motives or needs that might be met by each of the activities.
b. Take each need or motive and develop it as a reader benefit in a full paragraph. Use additional paragraphs for the other needs met by the activity. Remember to use you-attitude!

2.3 SENDING A QUESTION TO A WEB SITE

Using what you have learned about using audience analysis to adapt your message, send a question or other message that calls for a response to a Web site. You could

- Ask a question about a product.
- Apply for an internship or a job (assuming you'd really like to work there).
- Ask for information about an internship or a job.
- Ask a question about an organization or a candidate before you donate money or volunteer.
- Offer to volunteer for an organization or a candidate. You can offer to do something small and one-time (e.g., spend an afternoon stuffing envelopes, put up yard signs), or you can, if you want to, offer to do something more time consuming or even ongoing.

Pick a specific organization you might use and answer the following questions about it:

1. Does the organization ask for questions or offers? Or will yours come out of the blue?
2. How difficult will it be for the organization to supply the information you're asking for or to do what you're asking it to do? If you're applying for an internship or offering to volunteer, what skills can you offer? How much competition do you have?
3. What can you do to build your own credibility so that the organization takes your question or request seriously?

2.4 IMPROVING YOU-ATTITUDE AND POSITIVE EMPHASIS

(a) Rewrite the examples from the Technology Tips box "Straight Talk with Professors?" to improve you-attitude and positive emphasis. OR (b) Revise these sentences to improve you-attitude and positive emphasis. Eliminate any awkward phrasing. In some cases, you may need to add information to revise the sentence effectively. As your professor directs, peer grade answers.

1. We cannot provide vegetarian meals unless you let us know at least three days in advance.
2. We are pleased to provide free e-mail accounts to students.
3. You'll be happy to know that we have installed an ATM for your convenience.
4. We're swamped. We won't be able to get your order out to you until Friday morning.
5. If the above information is unclear, or if further information on this or any other topic is necessary, please do not hesitate to contact me.
6. I have been using e-mail both in my internship and in classes. I realize that almost everyone now does have experience with e-mail, but at least I won't be behind.
7. I am anxious to discuss this problem with you.
8. Medical certification can delay shutoff of electrical service for non-payment of bills. If someone in your home needs electricity to assure health and well-being, signing up for our medical certification will delay disconnection for 30 days.
9. I had a difficult time evaluating the Web site. The sheer size of the site made it difficult to browse. After considerable time, I decided that, although it is huge, the site is thorough and well designed.
10. We cannot process your request for a reservation because some information is missing.

2.5 ELIMINATING BIASED LANGUAGE

Explain the source of bias in each of the following, and revise to remove the bias. Peer grade answers.

1. We recommend hiring Jim Ryan and Elizabeth Shuman. Both were very successful summer interns. Jim drafted the report on using rap music in ads, and Elizabeth really improved the looks of the office.
2. All sales associates and their wives are invited to the picnic.
3. Although he is blind, Mr. Morin is an excellent group leader.
4. Unlike many blacks, Yvonne has extensive experience designing Web pages.
5. Chris Renker

   Pacific Perspectives

   Centennial Square

   Victoria, BC

   Gentlemen:
6. Serge Dagenais has very good people skills for a man.
7. *Parenting 2014* shows you how to persuade your husband to do his share of child care chores.
8. Mr. Paez, Mr. O'Connor, and Tonya will represent our office at the convention.
9. Sue Corcoran celebrates her 50th birthday today. Stop by her cubicle at noon to get a piece of cake and to help us sing "The Old Grey Mare Just Ain't What She Used to Be."
10. Because older customers tend to be really picky, we will need to give a lot of details in our ads.

E-MAIL MESSAGES

2.6 RESPONDING TO A COMPLAINT

You're the Director of Corporate Communications; the employee newsletter is produced by your office. Today you get this e-mail message from Caroline Huber:

> Subject: Complaint about Sexist Language
>
> The article about the "Help Desk" says that Martina Luna and I "are the key customer service representatives 'manning' the desk." I don't MAN anything! I WORK.

Respond to Caroline. And send a message to your staff, reminding them to edit newsletter stories as well as external documents to replace biased language.

COMMUNICATING AT WORK

2.7 EVALUATING BIAS IN VISUALS

In pairs or groups, evaluate the portrayals of people in one of the following:

- Ads in one issue of a business magazine
- A company's annual report
- A company's Web page.

Do the visuals show people of both genders and all races? Is there a sprinkling of people of various ages and physical conditions? What do the visuals suggest about who has power?

2.8 REVISING A FORM LETTER

You've taken a part-time job at a store that sells fine jewellery. In orientation, the manager tells you that the store photographs jewellery it sells or appraises and mails the photo as a goodwill gesture after the transaction. However, when you see the form letter, you know that it doesn't build much goodwill—and you say so. The manager says, "Well, you're taking a business communication course. Suppose you rewrite it."

Rewrite the letter. Use square brackets for material (like the customer's name) that would have to be inserted in the form letter to vary it for a specific customer. Add information that would help build goodwill.

> Dear Customer:
>
> We are most happy to enclose a photo of the jewellery that we recently sold you or appraised for you. We feel that this added service, which we are happy to extend to our fine customers, will be useful should you wish to insure your jewellery or need to identify it should you have the misfortune of suffering a loss.
>
> We trust you will enjoy this additional service. We thank you for the confidence you have shown by coming to our store.
>
> Sincerely,
>
> Your Sales Associate

PLANNING, COMPOSING, AND REVISING

3

Learning Outcomes

LO1 Describe eight activities in the writing process

LO2 Explain how to build a strong business writing style

LO3 List ten ways to make your writing easier to read

LO4 Discuss successful Web writing and editing

LO5 Explain the importance of getting and using feedback

AN INSIDE PERSPECTIVE

Chartered accountants Uzma Rayani of Alberta Health Services External Financial Reporting, and her twin cousins Sameer Bhojani of BMO Financial, Toronto, and Saira Bhojani of Torys LLP, Toronto, have more than a profession in common: they share a record of achievement and awards and a passion for volunteering.

Chartered accountants Uzma Rayani, Saira Bhojani, and Sameer Bhojani defy stereotypes of number-crunching accountants. They are as concerned with the accuracy of their writing as with the currency of their image and their commitment to community.

Auditing financial statements is one part of an auditor's responsibility. Numbers are not the end of the process. The task of communicating findings—timely, relevant, clear, concise, and factual—requires planning that can take about one-third of the writing time. Analyzing the purpose—informative, persuasive, and so on—and audience before beginning to write is the basis of writing success.

These professionals think about what information is needed, when, and where, so that the audience can easily follow and make good use of the document. When you have multiple audiences (including the media and general public), you face added challenges in finding the language and organization that will satisfy needs.

As a tax lawyer, Saira can influence multi-million-dollar acquisitions or public offerings. She demands as much clarity from Canadian tax legislation as she does from her own writing: "Without clarity, taxpayers face considerable difficulty in determining and paying their tax obligations, and administrators face challenges in effectively enforcing such obligations."

Creating an outline or overview helps identify the messages, the parts, and the headings that will orient and guide readers. Developing an overview is as helpful to writers as to readers, simplifying the choices writers have to make and saving valuable time.

Even the best of planning does not eliminate revising, editing, and proofreading. Skilled performances look easy and effortless. In reality, as every dancer, musician, and athlete knows, they're the products of hard work, hours of practice, attention to detail, and intense concentration. Like skilled performances in other arts, writing rests on a base of work.*

*Based on Saira Bhojani, "Lack of legislative clarity increases burden of Canadian tax compliance," *Ontario Bar Association*, 20, no. 2, retrieved February 14, 2011, from http://www.oba.org/En/tax_en/newsletter_en/v21N1.aspx#Article_3; Torys LLP, "Saira Bhojani," retrieved February 14, 2011, from http://www.torys.com/OurTeam/Pages/BhojaniSaira.aspx; "Profile: Uzma Rayani, Sameer Bhojani, Saira Bhojani," *Spotlight U* (Fall 2007), p. 8.

HOW GOOD WRITERS WRITE

If you have found it difficult to know where to begin a piece of creative writing or an academic paper, know that your choices in writing business documents can be easier. Different genres in business writing (reports, proposals, request letters, résumés, financial statements, and so on) follow conventional order. Résumés, for example, begin with your name and contact information. To be persuasive in getting your audience to read and respond as you wish still takes creativity—and a sure sense of audience, purpose, and context. Above all, business writing is audience-centred, purposeful or action-oriented, and attuned to its situation.

No single writing process works for all writers all the time. However, good writers and poor writers seem to use different processes.[1] Good writers are more likely to do the following:

- Realize that the first draft will not be perfect.
- Write regularly.
- Break big jobs into small chunks.
- Have clear goals focusing on purpose and audience.
- Have several different strategies to choose from.
- Use rules flexibly.
- Wait to edit until after the draft is complete.

Research shows that experts differ from novices in identifying and analyzing the initial problem more effectively, understanding the task more broadly and deeply, drawing from a wider repertoire of strategies, and seeing patterns more clearly. Experts actually compose more slowly than novices, perhaps because they rarely settle for work that is just "OK." Finally, experts are better at evaluating their own work.[2]

Figure 3.1 The Writing Process

Planning	Gathering	Writing	Evaluating
Analyze the situation Define your purpose Analyze your audience(s) Choose the channel Brainstorm Outline Choose organization and design	Gather data Complete formal and informal research	Organize Design Draft	Reread your writing Does it support purpose? Does it meet audience needs?
Getting Feedback	**Revising**	**Editing**	**Proofreading**
Ask someone to evaluate your writing Is purpose clear? Is organization appropriate? Tone? Phrasing?	Check for Readability Usability Reorganize Add Delete Substitute	Check for Clarity Completeness Correctness Conciseness Courtesy Consistency with standards and conventions	Check for Spelling Punctuation Names Facts and figures Format Typos

Thinking about the writing process and consciously adopting "expert" processes will help you become a more expert writer able to impress professors and potential employers or influence people's behaviours or attitudes (see Figure 3.1).

LO1

ACTIVITIES IN THE WRITING PROCESS

Most researchers agree that writing processes can include eight activities: planning, gathering, writing, evaluating, getting feedback, revising, editing, and proofreading. The activities do not have to come in this order. Nor does every writing task demand all eight.

If you are e-mailing, texting, instant messaging, tweeting, or blogging and your audience is within your organization or close friends, the process may be simplified. Otherwise, these electronic media need as much planning and careful revision as any message on which your own and your organization's credibility depend. To support good business outcomes and avoid risks, even legal liabilities, e-communications need to be as clear as they are concise (see ▸▸ "Writing and Editing for the Web" later in this chapter).

Planning includes all the thinking you do. It includes such activities as analyzing the situation or problem, defining your purpose(s), and analyzing the audience(s) (◂◂ Chapters 1 and 2); thinking of ideas; choosing a channel and pattern of organization; considering design issues (▸▸ Chapter 4); or making an outline. Planning includes not only devising strategies for the document as a whole but also generating "mini-plans" for sections of the document. Planning focuses efforts and narrows the scope of your project, simplifying writing decisions and helping match audience and writer needs.

Gathering includes physically getting the data you need. It can mean informal as well as formal research—everything from consulting with colleagues to reviewing examples of similar documents to researching databases or library or Web resources to administering a questionnaire or conducting a focus group (▸▸ Chapter 10). Good research is at the heart of good writing.

Writing is the act of putting words on paper or on a screen. Writing can take the form of lists, fragmentary notes, formal drafts, or stream-of-consciousness writing where you allow your thoughts and associations to go where they will without concern for editing. Stream-of-consciousness can be a useful way of overcoming writer's block and clarifying your thinking. However you approach the writing task, you will also be reconsidering and refining your outline, organization, and design as you draft with your purpose and audience needs in mind.

Evaluating means rereading your work and measuring it against your goals and the requirements of the situation and audience. The best evaluation results from *re-seeing* your draft as if someone else had written it. For long documents, this means setting them aside for a time. Will your audience understand it? Is it complete? Consistent? Convincing? Courteous?

You can evaluate *every* activity in the process, not just your draft. Is your view of purposes adequate? Do you have enough information to write? Are your sources believable? Do your revisions go far enough? Is the design user-friendly?

Getting feedback means asking someone else to evaluate your work. Again, you could get feedback on every activity, not just your draft. Is your pattern of organization appropriate? Does a revision solve an earlier problem? Are there any typos in the final copy?

Revising means making changes in the draft suggested by your own evaluation or by feedback from someone else: adding, deleting, substituting, or rearranging. Revision can be changes in single words, but more often it means major additions, deletions, or substitutions as the writer measures (evaluates) the draft against purpose and audience, and reshapes the document to make it more effective—more readable, user-friendly, and action-oriented.

Editing means checking the draft to see that it satisfies the requirements of standard English and the principles of business writing. Here you'd correct grammatical errors, check word choice and format, and address vagueness and wordiness, ensuring fluency and accuracy. Unlike revision, which can produce major changes in meaning, editing focuses on the local aspects of writing.

Proofreading means checking the final copy to see that it's accurate and free from typographical errors. Spellings and names, facts and figures, format consistency, and punctuation should get one last check.

Source: Used with the permission of ezinearticles.com.

Note the following points about these eight activities:

- **The activities do not have to come in this order.** Some people may gather data *after* writing a draft when they see that they need more specifics to achieve their purposes.
- **You do not have to finish one activity to start another.** Some writers plan a short section and write it, plan the next short section and write it, and so on through the document. Evaluating what is already written may cause a writer to do more planning or to change the original plan.
- **Most writers do not use all eight activities for all the documents they write.** You'll use more activities when you write a kind of document, about a subject, or to an audience that's new to you.

Research about what writers really do has destroyed some of the stereotypes we used to have about the writing process. Consider planning. Traditional advice stressed the importance of planning and sometimes advised writers to make formal

Ethics and Legal Lie-detection On- and Offline*

Although telephone and face-to-face communications involve more deception, Jeffrey Hancock, a Canadian professor at Cornell University, finds that 14% of e-mails involve deception, which is marked by five linguistic indicators:

- Uses 28% more words than truth-telling in efforts to persuade
- Uses third-person pronouns to increase distance from deception
- Includes negative emotion words ("sorry")
- Increases number of sense terms ("feel")
- Is vague and uses fewer "causal phrases" to explain

Those writing in e-mail rather than with pen and paper are more likely to lie and to rationalize their lies. They are also more likely to be negative. The distancing effect of e-mail, texting, or social media permits people to downplay the consequences of their actions.

Although deception is identified only 54% of the time, lying on instant messaging can be detected by these indicators:

- Uses fewer words than honest messages
- Is carefully worded
- Takes 10% longer to write

Executive lies about earnings are signalled by these linguistic cues that similarly aim to distance from communicators' actions:

- "Inflated language" ("outstanding quarter")
- Third-person phrases ("the organization")
- "Generalities rather than specifics"
- Passive constructions ("This has been certified")

*Based on Zosia Bielski, "Digital liars take longer to reply to a message," *The Globe and Mail,* September 13, 2013, L2; Abul Taher and Dipesh Gadher, "Lie detector software catches e-mail fibbers," *The Sunday Times,* February 25, 2007, retrieved March 3, 2011, from http://www.timesonline.co.uk/tol/news/uk/article1434927.ece; Charles E. Naquin, Terri R. Kurtzberg, and Liuba Y. Belkin, "The finer points of lying online: E-mail versus pen and paper," *Journal of Applied Psychology* 95, no. 2: 387–394; Wallace Immen, "Leadership and the language of lying," *Globe Careers,* August 18, 2010, B14.

outlines for everything they wrote. But we know now that not all good documents are based on outlines.[3] A study on writer's block found that some ineffective writers spent so much time planning that they left too little time to write the assignment.[4]

"Plan!" is too simplistic to be helpful. Instead, we need to talk about how much and what kind of planning for what kind of document—and displayed on what medium. Research tells us that reading on the screen affects the ways that we read, limiting attention, encouraging skimming, and reducing reading speed by 25 percent.[5] When that screen is on a mobile device, for instance, the text needs to be redesigned for the specific format to avoid negative effects on readability.[6]

PLANNING, BRAINSTORMING, AND ORGANIZING BUSINESS DOCUMENTS

When you get an assignment, think about all the steps you'll need to go through so that you can plan your time for that project. To get the best results, spend about one-third of your time analyzing the situation and your audience, gathering information, and organizing what you have to say. You may spend even more of your time on a report requiring primary and secondary research. Spend about one-third of your time actually "writing." Spend the final one-third evaluating what you've said, revising the draft(s) to meet your purposes and the needs of the audience and the organization, editing to remove any errors in grammar and mechanics, and proofreading the final copy.

The better your ideas are when you start, the fewer drafts you'll need to produce a good document. Start by asking questions from ◀◀ Chapter 1 to identify what's at stake and what message and channel are appropriate. Use the strategies described in ◀◀ Chapter 2 to analyze audience and identify reader benefits. Gather information you can use for your document.

Sometimes your content will be determined by the situation. Sometimes, even when it's up to you to think of reader benefits or topics to include in a report, you'll find it easy. If ideas won't come, try the following techniques:

- **Brainstorming.** Think of all the ideas you can, without judging them. Consciously try to get at least a dozen different ideas before you stop. The first idea you have may not be the best. Remember that more and better ideas are often generated by teams (▶▶ Chapter 6).

Figure 3.2 Clustering Helps Generate Ideas

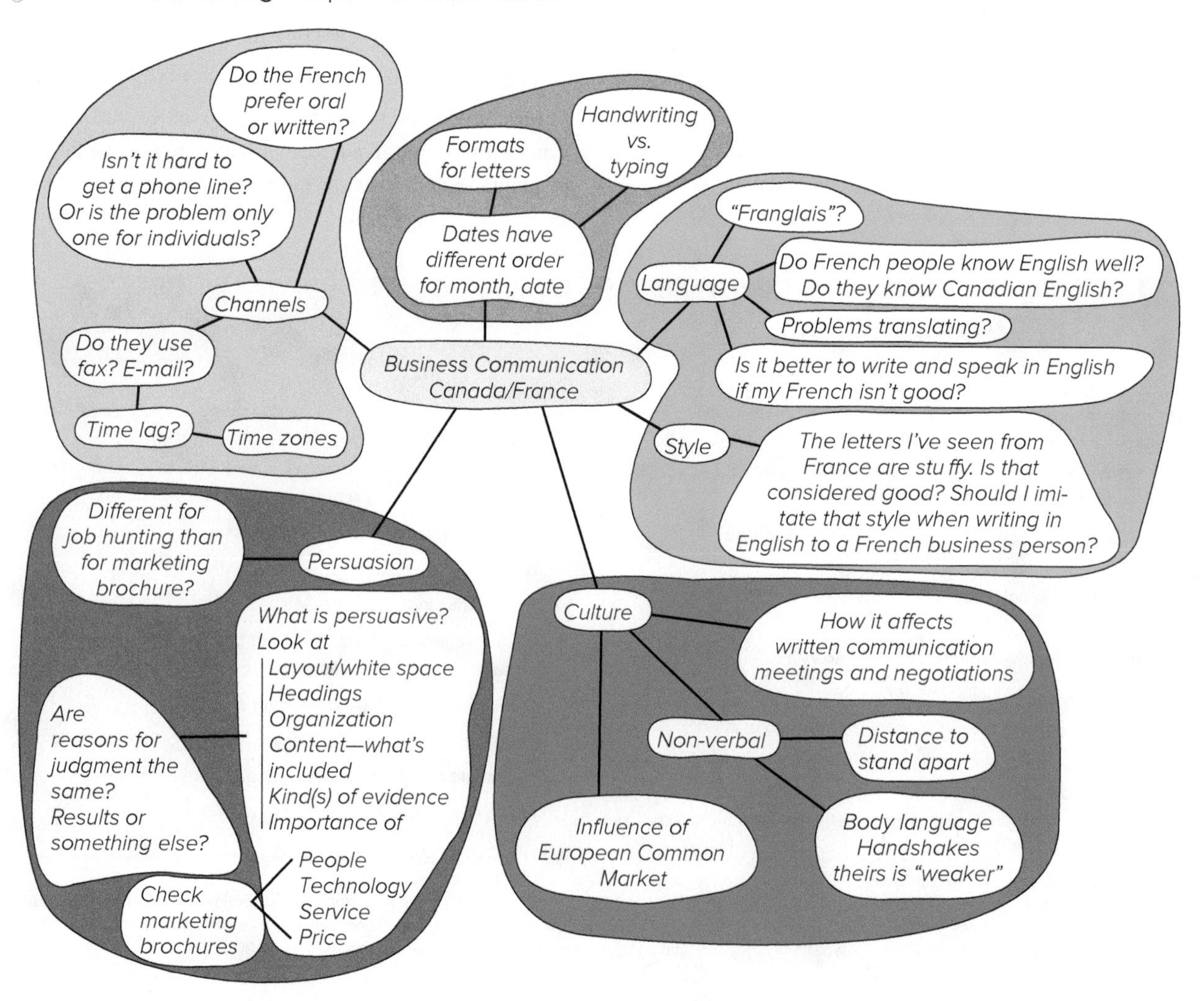

- **Freewriting.**[7] Make yourself write, without stopping, for 10 minutes or so, even if you must write "I will think of something soon." At the end of 10 minutes, read what you've written, identify the best point in the draft, then set it aside, and write for another 10 uninterrupted minutes. Read this draft, marking anything that's good and should be kept, and then write again for another 10 minutes. By the third session, you will probably produce several sections that are worth keeping—maybe even a complete draft that's ready to be revised.
- **Clustering.**[8] Write your topic in the middle of the page and circle it. Write down the ideas the topic suggests, circling them, too. (The circles are designed to tap into the non-linear half of your brain.) When you've filled the page, look for patterns or repeated ideas. Use different coloured pens to group related ideas. Then use these ideas to develop reader benefits in a memo, questions for a survey, content for a blog, or for the body of a report. Figure 3.2 presents the clusters that one writer created about business communication.
- **Talk to your audiences.** As researcher Rachel Spilka shows, talking to internal and external audiences helped writers involve readers in the planning process, understand the social and political relationships among readers, and negotiate conflicts orally rather than depending solely on the document. These writers were then able to think about content as well as about organization and style, appeal to common grounds (such as reducing waste or increasing productivity) that several readers shared, and reduce the number of revisions needed before documents were approved.[9]

Some find inspiration in the applications on their mobile devices—including dictionaries, style guides, and quotations. Others find thinking about the content, layout, or structure of your document can also give you ideas.

For long documents, write out the headings you'll use.

You may use an alphabetized or numbered list of ideas. Or you may use a **sentence outline,** a **key word outline** that focuses the mind and clarifies messages for online writing or short presentations, or **storyboard** for visual communications (see ▸▸ Chapter 12). For anything that's under five pages, less formal notes will probably work. You may want to jot down ideas to use as the basis for a draft.

If you are writing a long report that you may also present, consider using PowerPoint or another presentation program to organize or outline your thinking before writing the report. It may help keep you focused on your purpose, background or context, key messages, and audience.

There is no one right way to generate and organize ideas. Your learning style will often dictate what strategy helps you organize. When you are organizing, you are giving meaning and shape to the ideas you have generated. You are determining the order and importance of ideas, what is included, highlighted, or de-emphasized. You are creating relationships with readers, ideas, and outcomes, helping shape whether they will read and how they will use documents.

Effective design (▸▸ Chapter 4) is as important as organizational choices (see ▸▸ Chapters 7, 8, and 9 on organizing routine, negative, and persuasive messages; see ▸▸ Chapter 11 on organizing reports). Remember that technology has raised readers' expectations about reader-friendly, attractive, and engaging documents and different media require rethinking how much to write and how best to present it. If you are writing for online readers, you typically need 50 percent less text than for paper documents and need to orient readers with clear headings, subheadings, highlighted key words, links, and lists.[10]

Letters and memos will go faster if you choose a basic organizational pattern before you start. You may want to customize common patterns of organization with a planning guide[11] to help you keep the "big picture" in mind as you write. Figure 3.3 shows planning guides developed for specific kinds of documents.

As you plan your document, pay attention to signals from your boss and the organization's culture (see ◂◂ "Ways to Analyze Your Audience" in Chapter 2). For example, if the organization has a style manual that specifies data are plural, follow its guidelines.

If the organization has an ethics counsellor, think about consulting him or her as you decide what to write in a situation with ethical implications. Talk to people in the organization who will

Figure 3.3 Customized Planning Guides for Specific Documents

Planning guide for a trip report	**Planning guide for a proposal**
• The Big Picture from the Company's Point of View: We Can Go Forward on the Project. • Criteria/Goals • What We Did • Why We Know Enough to Go Forward • Next Steps	• Customer's Concern #1 Our Proposal/Answer • Customer's Concern #2 Our Proposal/Answer • Customer's Concern #3 Our Proposal/Answer • Customer's Concern #4 Our Proposal/Answer • Ask for Action
Planning guide for an e-mail message • My Purpose • Points I Want to Make • Document(s) to Attach • Next Steps	**Planning guide for a credit rejection** • Reason • Refusal • Alternative (Layaway/ Co-signer/Provide more information) • Goodwill Ending

Source: E-mail and proposal guides based on Fred Reynolds, "What adult work-world writers have taught me about adult work-world writing," *Professional Writing in Context: Lessons from Teaching and Consulting in Worlds of Work* (Hillsdale, NJ: Lawrence Erlbaum Associates, 1995), 18, 20.

be affected by what you are announcing or proposing, to better understand their concerns. In some organizations, your boss may want to see an early planning draft (see ▸▸ Figure 3.12 later in this chapter) to check that you're on the right track. In other organizations, you may be expected to do a great deal of revising on your own before anyone else sees the document.

REVISING, EDITING, AND PROOFREADING

Good writers make their drafts better by careful revising, editing, and proofreading. Good writers also know when they should invest time and energy in revising, editing, and proofreading. They know that too much concern with correctness in early drafts can block writing.

What to Look for When You Revise

Every chapter in this book suggests questions you should ask as you revise. When you write to an audience you know well, you may be able to check everything at once. When you're writing to a new audience or have to solve a particularly difficult problem, plan to revise the draft at least three times.

The first time, look for content and clarity. Go back to the analysis questions in ◂◂ Chapters 1 and 2 to make sure you've fulfilled all the necessary purposes and have reader benefits for each audience. The second time, check the organization and layout. Finally, check style and tone.

Use the information in ◂◂ Chapter 2 to check for you-attitude, positive emphasis, and bias-free language. Use the techniques in ▸▸ "Ten Ways to Make Your Writing Easier to Read" later in this chapter to make sure sentences and paragraphs are tight, smooth, and friendly. Figure 3.4 summarizes the questions you should ask. Check whether your design supports a visually inviting, readable document (▸▸ Chapter 4).

Often you'll get the best revision by setting aside your draft and redrafting. This strategy takes advantage of the thinking you did on your first draft without locking you into the sentences in it. Use WIRMI (What I Really Mean Is; see ▸▸ "Ten Ways to Make Your Writing Easier to Read") to replace awkward phrasing with what you really mean to say.

Figure 3.4 Thorough Revision Checklist

CONTENT AND CLARITY

- Is your view of purposes complete? Does your document meet the needs of the organization and of the reader—and make you look good?
- Have you given readers all the information they need to understand and act on your message?
- Is all the information accurate?
- Is each sentence clear? Is the message free from apparently contradictory statements?
- Is the logic clear and convincing? Are generalizations and benefits backed up with adequate detail?

ORGANIZATION AND LAYOUT

- Is the pattern of organization appropriate for your purposes, audience, and situation?
- Are transitions between ideas and paragraphs smooth? Do ideas within paragraphs flow smoothly?
- Does document design make it easy for readers to find the information they need?
- Is the document visually inviting?
- Are the right points emphasized by layout?
- Are the first and last paragraphs effective?

STYLE AND TONE

- Is the message easy to read?
- Is the message free from bias?
- Does the message build goodwill?

As you revise, read the document through from start to finish. This is particularly important if you've composed in several sittings or if you've used text from other documents. Researchers have found that such documents tend not to flow well.[12] You may need to add transitions, cut repetitive parts, or change words to create a uniform level of formality throughout the document.

What to Look for When You Edit

Even good writers need to edit, since no one can pay attention to surface correctness while thinking of ideas. Editing should

Technology Tips Using Spell- and Grammar-Checkers

If you use a computer to prepare your documents, use a spell-checker to catch typos.

But you still need to proofread by eye.

Spell-checkers work by matching words: they will signal any group of letters not listed in their dictionaries. However, they cannot tell that a word is missing or that the meaning demands *of* rather than *or*, *not* rather than *now*, or *manager* rather than *manger*.

The right-click thesaurus of synonyms is another useful aid when you are looking for the right word.

Grammar-checkers can help a writer whose command of grammar and mechanics is weak. However, since grammar-checkers do not catch all errors, it's worth taking the time to master grammar and mechanics so you can edit and proofread yourself.

always *follow* revision. There's no point in taking time to fix formatting or correct a grammatical error in a sentence or section that may be cut when you clarify your meaning or tighten your style.

Most writers edit more accurately when they print out a copy of a document and edit the hard copy. But beware: laser printing makes a page look good but does nothing to correct errors. Watch for consistency of content and style across parts of a document (tables of contents, headings, appendices, for example).

Check to be sure that the following are accurate:

- Sentence structure
- Subject–verb and noun–pronoun agreement
- Punctuation
- Word usage
- Spelling—including spelling of names
- Numbers

You need to know the rules of grammar and punctuation to edit (⏩ Appendix A). Most writers make a small number of errors over and over. If you know that you have trouble with dangling modifiers or subject–verb agreement, for example, specifically look for them in your draft. Also look for any errors that especially bother your boss and correct them.

A command of standard grammar will help you build the credible, professional image you want to create with everything you write.

How to Catch Typos

Proofread every document both with a spell-checker and by eye (and ear) to catch the errors a spell-checker can't find (see ⏪ Technology Tips: "Using Spell- and Grammar Checkers").

Proofreading is hard because writers tend to see what they know should be there rather than what really is there. Since it's always easier to proof something you didn't write, you may want to swap papers with a colleague. (Be sure the person looks for typos, not content.) Also read aloud. You will often noticeably stumble over typos or omitted or unnecessary words!

To proofread,

- Read once quickly for meaning, to see that nothing has been left out.
- Read a second time, slowly. When you find an error, correct it and then *reread that line.* Readers tend to become less attentive after they find one error and may miss other errors close to the one they've spotted.
- To proofread a document you know well, read the lines backward or the pages out of order.

Always triple-check title pages, tables of contents, headings, the first and last paragraphs, numbers, and names.

Use the proofreading symbols (⏩ Appendix A) to make corrections when you are working on a hard copy.

LO2

GOOD STYLE IN BUSINESS WRITING

Good business writing is closer to conversation and less formal than the style of writing that has traditionally earned high marks in college and university essays and term papers. Many business professors also like term papers that are easy to read and use good visual impact.

Using an easy-to-read style makes the reader respond more positively to your ideas. You can make your writing easier to read in two ways. First, you can make individual sentences and paragraphs easy to read, so that skimming the first paragraph or reading the whole document takes as little work as possible. Second, you can make the document look visually inviting with signposts to guide readers through it. Now that we have discussed the writing process from planning to proofreading, in this section we focus on ways to make paragraphs, sentences, and words easier to read. See ⏩ Chapter 4 for ways to make the document as a whole easier to read.

Most people have several styles of talking, which they vary instinctively depending on the audience. Good writers have several styles, too. An e-mail to your boss complaining about the delays from a supplier will be informal; a letter to the supplier demanding better service will be more formal.

Reports tend to be more formal than letters and memos, since they may be read many years in the future by audiences the writer can barely imagine. In reports, avoid contractions, spell out acronyms and abbreviations the first time you use them, and avoid personal pronouns. Since so many people read reports, *you* doesn't have much meaning. See ⏩ Chapter 11 for more about report style.

Keep the following points in mind as you choose a level of formality for a specific document:

- Use a friendly, informal style to someone you've talked with.
- Avoid contractions, clichés, slang, and even minor grammatical lapses in documents to people you don't know. Abbreviations are OK in e-mail messages if they're part of the group's culture.
- Pay particular attention to your style when you write to senior management or when you must give bad news. When people are under stress or feel insecure, they rely on nouns rather than on verbs, which deadens their style.[13] Confident people are more direct. Edit your writing so that you sound confident, whether you feel that way or not.

Good business style allows for individual variation. The personal style of the opening paragraphs of PotashCorp CEO William J. Doyle's annual report letter (Figure 3.5) suggests energy and drive, engagement and empathy. The 2014 letter positions the outlook in relation to world economic trends and dietary change in developing countries as well as specific competitor initiatives. Feeding changing appetites in sustainable ways in the context of climate change is both a challenge

Figure 3.5 PotashCorp CEO William J. Doyle's Letter Uses Good Business Style

Short sentences, personal pronouns, parallel constructions, and action verbs mark a good business style. For visual impact, the green colour ties the headings, featured quotation, and bar charts to key messages about productivity and sustainability in an uncertain global environment, and about the values of the corporation—a Canadian and world leader in fertilizers.

Source: http://www.potashcorp.com/irc/overview/our-company-and-operations/executive-letters/ceo-letter.

FOOD AND FERTILIZER MATTER

Dear Shareholders,

At PotashCorp, we manage with a long-term perspective. With every decision we make, we strive to better position your company to deliver on the potential—and the responsibility—that come from being able to help farmers grow more food for an ever-hungry world.

I'm sure those of you who have followed the company for a long time have often heard me speak about the challenge of producing enough food in the years and decades ahead. To understand the complexity of this undertaking, just ask any of the hundreds of millions of farmers around the world about the amount of time, resources and sweat equity they put into growing a crop—and the uncertainty around growing conditions that every season brings with it.

Today the world faces the challenge of producing enough food to feed more than seven billion people, with hundreds of millions added every decade. At the same time, the improving economic position for a large portion of that population means diets will continue to shift to more nutrient-intensive foods.

With limited additional arable land, it is clear that ensuring adequate global food production will continue to be a huge feat—one that we at PotashCorp think about every day.

What motivates us is that meeting future food production needs is not an insurmountable challenge. We can help overcome it by improving the productivity of every acre of farmland. While better practices and new technology are important parts of that equation, such advancements cannot replace the scientific need for essential nutrients in the soil.

This creates a growing need for our products. As the world's largest fertilizer company by capacity, we are uniquely positioned to deliver.

Strategy Matters: Protecting and Building Value

The fundamental drivers that fuel our potential are compelling. Yet the inherent variability in agriculture—driven by often unpredictable growing conditions, changing farmer economics and evolving government policy—has caused fluctuations in an upward-sloping demand growth trend line for fertilizer.

This has been especially true in potash and there could be no better example than the last 10 years. After robust consumption growth in nearly every major market through 2007, global potash shipments have grown little.

With a future that is highly leveraged to global growth and the continued advancement of agronomic practices in the world's developing regions, we expect bumps along the way. We have seen agronomic and economic conditions provide opportunities and challenges that highlight the variable nature of the potash business. In certain regions, such as Brazil, farmers have taken the steps necessary to improve crop production, and fertilizer consumption—including potash—is surpassing record levels. Yet in India, fiscal and political barriers continue to weigh on farmers' ability to improve fertility practices and crop yields.

We began 2013 optimistic that potash markets would experience renewed growth. We saw it happen through the first six months as global shipments moved at a record pace. However, a change in strategy announced by a competitor in late July created significant market uncertainty, causing a sharp decline in shipments and prices in the second half of the year.

While we remain confident in our long-term outlook, we know that forecasting growth in a sometimes unpredictable environment can be difficult. Therefore, we remain focused on the things we can control and on ensuring that every action we take solidifies the competitive position of our company today and in the years ahead.

In late 2013, we took difficult but necessary steps to make operational changes and reduce our workforce by approximately 18 percent, with the biggest impact in our potash and phosphate segments. This was not an easy decision, and resulted in the loss of some great people. By taking these actions, however, we are helping to protect long-term value for all those who depend on our continued success.

For nearly 25 years as a publicly traded company, PotashCorp's Board of Directors and management team have focused on building a company that is ready to respond to a rising need for fertilizer, while remaining competitive and flexible enough to manage through challenging times.

We believe we are positioned to achieve both of these goals. We have developed the production capacity to drive our future growth, particularly in potash. This, coupled with a world-class distribution system, gives us the ability to respond efficiently to our customers' needs. At the same time, we have plans that provide operational flexibility while improving the cost position of each of our three nutrients to protect the company's long-term profitability. As demand grows, PotashCorp and our people are ready to deliver.

We work in a remarkable and critically important industry with a proud history and a bright future. After all, food matters—and matters a lot—and we are proud to play an instrumental role in the global solution while building long-term value for our stakeholders.

William J. Doyle

President and Chief Executive Officer

February 20, 2014

Courtesy of PotashCorp

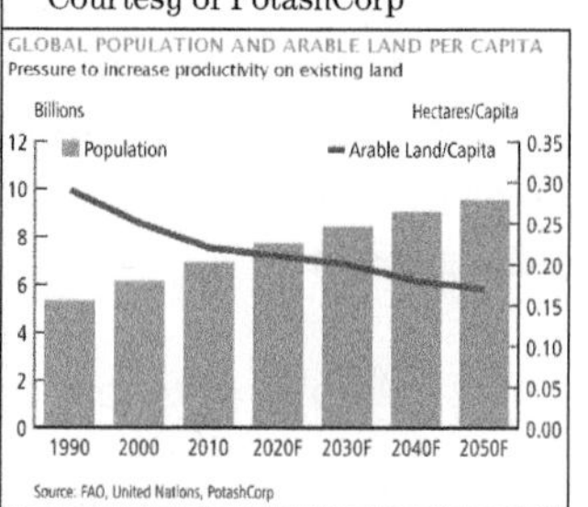

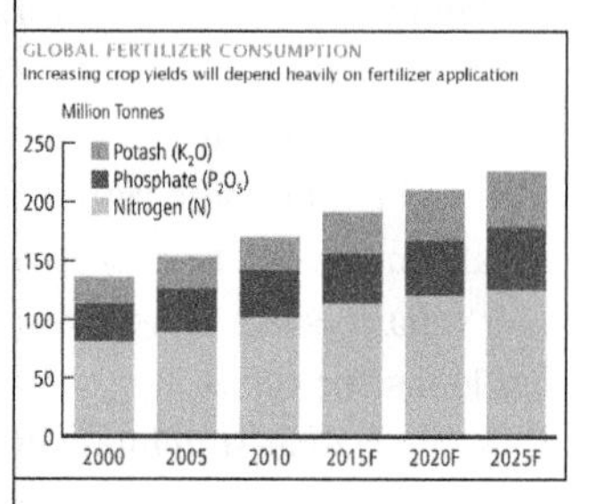

and an opportunity. PotashCorp's 2013 online annual report finds dynamic opportunity unavailable in print (see http://www.potashcorp.com/irc/what-we-report-and-why/about-this-report), while maintaining the theme of "Food Matters."

Evaluating "Rules" About Writing

Some "rules" are grammatical conventions. For example, standard edited English requires that each sentence has a subject and verb, and that the subject and verb agree. Business writing normally demands standard grammar, but exceptions exist. Promotional materials such as brochures, advertisements, and sales and fundraising letters may use sentence fragments to mimic the effect of speech.

Other "rules" may be conventions adopted by an organization so that its documents will be consistent. For example, a company might decide to capitalize job titles (e.g., *Production Manager*) even though grammar doesn't require the capitals.

Still other "rules" are attempts to codify "what sounds good." To evaluate these "rules," you must consider your audience, the community of practice, discourse community, and organizational culture (see ◂◂ "Ways to Analyze Your Audience" in Chapter 2), your purposes, and the situation. If you want the effect produced by an impersonal style and polysyllabic words, use them. But use them only when you want the distancing effect they produce.

Building a Better Style

To improve your style and make it vivid and vigorous,

- Start a clean page or screen, so that you aren't locked into old sentence structures.
- Try WIRMI: *What I Really Mean Is.*[14] Then write the words.
- Try reading your draft out loud to someone sitting about one metre away—about as far away as you'd sit in casual conversation. If the words sound stiff, they'll seem stiff to a reader, too.
- Ask someone else to read your draft out loud. Readers stumble because the words on the page aren't what they expect to see. The places where that person stumbles are places where your writing can be better.
- Read widely and write *a lot.*
- Get and act on feedback.
- Study revised sentences, like the examples in ▸▸ "As You Write and Revise Paragraphs" in the next section.
- Use the ten techniques in Figure 3.6 to polish your style.

The home page of the Canadian federal government's Plain Language Online Training (www.plainlanguagenetwork.org/plaintrain/) practises what it preaches in welcoming people to Plain Train and inviting them to "Click on the Conductor for the guided tour. Click on the Train for the digest."

Plain language is about access and equity, respect and responsibility, transparency and accountability. It is less about following rules and using simple rather than complex language than it is about adopting a new attitude or approach to writing. Plain language helps make our writing clear because it begins with the needs of the reader and matches those with the needs of the writer. The result is both effective and efficient because the reader can understand the message.

Like other provincial commissions, the BC Securities Commission publishes online (www.bcsc.bc.ca) its invaluable *Plain Language Style Guide* and *Continuous Disclosures* documents.

LO3

TEN WAYS TO MAKE YOUR WRITING EASIER TO READ

Direct, simple writing is easier to read. James Suchan and Robert Colucci tested two versions of a memo report. The "high-impact" version had

Technology Tips Tracking Changes*

To make revision easier, you can give or get feedback with the track changes feature in Microsoft Word.

- Open the document you are revising
- Click on the Review menu on your toolbar
- Select Track Changes
- Select Show Markup and enable these features:
  - Comments
  - Ink
  - Insertions and Deletions
  - Formatting
  - Balloons
  - All Reviewers

Once you have accepted (or not) suggested changes, you will want to remove permanently changes and comments:

- Select All Changes in Document (in Reviewing Toolbar)
- Turn Tracked Changes off
- Save and rename your document

*Check out Stephen H. Wildstrom's "Don't Let Word Give Away Your Secrets" (*BusinessWeek*, April 19, 2004, p. 26) to read about costly corporate failures to delete tracking permanently.

Figure 3.6 Ten Ways to Make Your Writing Easier to Read

As you write and revise paragraphs,

1. Begin paragraphs with topic sentences so that readers know what to expect in the paragraph.
2. Use transitions to link ideas.

As you write and revise sentences,

3. Use active verbs most of the time.
4. Use verbs—not nouns—to carry the weight of your sentence.
5. Tighten your writing.
6. Vary sentence length and sentence structure.
7. Use parallel structure. Use the same grammatical form for ideas that have the same logical function.
8. Put your readers in your sentences.

As you choose words,

9. Use words that are accurate, appropriate, ethical, and familiar.
10. Use technical jargon only when it is essential and known to the reader. Replace business jargon.

- The "bottom line" (the purpose of the report) in the first paragraph
- Simple sentences in normal word order (subject, verb, object)
- Active verbs and concrete language
- Short paragraphs, headings, and lists
- First- and second-person pronouns.

The high-impact version took 22% less time to read. Readers said they understood the report better, and tests showed that they really did understand it better.[15] Another study showed that high-impact instructions were more likely to be followed.[16] We'll talk about layout, headings, and lists in ▸▸Chapter 4.

As You Write and Revise Paragraphs

1. Begin with topic sentences.

Paragraphs are visual and logical units. Use them to organize your sentences into blocks. Remember that online writing requires short paragraphs and sentences and good use of transitions.

A good paragraph has **unity;** that is, it discusses only one idea, or topic. The **topic sentence** states the main idea and provides a scaffold to structure your document. Your writing will be easier to read if you make the topic sentence explicit and put it at the beginning of the paragraph.[17]

✕ HARD TO READ (NO TOPIC SENTENCE):

In fiscal 2014, the company filed claims for refund of federal income taxes of $3,199,000 and interest of $969,000 paid as a result of an examination of the company's federal income tax returns by the Canada Revenue Agency (CRA) for the years 2011 through 2013. It is uncertain what amount, if any, may ultimately be recovered.

✓ BETTER (PARAGRAPH STARTS WITH TOPIC SENTENCE):

The company and the Canada Revenue Agency (CRA) disagree about whether the company is owed back taxes. In fiscal 2014, the company filed claims for a refund of federal income taxes of $3,199,000 and interest of $969,000 paid as a result of an examination of the company's federal income tax returns by the CRA for the years 2011 through 2013. It is uncertain what amount, if any, may ultimately be recovered.

A good topic sentence forecasts the structure and content of the paragraph.

Plan B also has economic advantages.

(Prepares the reader for a discussion of B's economic advantages.)

We had several personnel changes in June.

(Prepares the reader for a list of the month's terminations and hires.)

When the first sentence of a paragraph is not the topic sentence, readers who skim may miss the main point. Move the topic sentence to the beginning of the paragraph. If the paragraph does not have a topic sentence, you will need to write one. If you can't think of a single sentence that serves as an "umbrella" to cover every sentence, the paragraph lacks unity. To solve the problem, either split the paragraph into two or eliminate the sentence that digresses from the main point.

2. Use transitions to link ideas.

Transition words and sentences signal the connections between ideas to the reader. **Transitions** tell whether the next sentence continues the previous thought or starts a new idea; transitions can tell whether the idea that comes next is more or less important than the previous thought. Figure 3.7 lists some of the most common transition words and phrases.

As You Write and Revise Sentences

3. Use active verbs most of the time.

At the sentence level, you can do many things to make your writing easy to read.

"Who does what" sentences with active verbs make your writing more forceful.

Passives are usually made up of a form of the verb *to be* plus a past participle. *Passive* has nothing to do with *past.* Passives can be past, present, or future:

were received	(in the past)
is recommended	(in the present)
will be implemented	(in the future)

To spot a passive, find the verb. If the verb describes something that the grammatical subject is doing, the verb is active. If the verb describes something that is being done to the grammatical subject, the verb is passive.

Figure 3.7 Transition Words and Phrases

To show addition or continuation of the same idea	To introduce an example	To show that the contrast is more important than the previous idea	To show time
And	for example (e.g.)	but	after
Also	for instance (i.e.)	however	as
first, second, third	indeed	nevertheless	before
in addition	to illustrate	on the contrary	in the future
Likewise	namely	**To show cause and effect**	next
Similarly	specifically	as a result	then
To introduce the last or most important item	**To contrast**	because	until
Finally	in contrast	consequently	when
Furthermore	on the other hand	for this reason	while
Moreover	or	therefore	**To summarize or end**
			in conclusion
			finally

ACTIVE	PASSIVE
The customer received 500 widgets.	Five hundred widgets were received by the customer.
I recommend this method.	This method is recommended by me.
The federal agencies will implement the program.	The program will be implemented by the federal agencies.
The committee will decide next month.	A decision will be made next month. [No agent in sentence.]
[You] Send the customer a letter informing her about the change.	A letter will be sent informing the customer of the change. [No agent in sentence.]

Passive verbs have at least three disadvantages:

a. Passive verbs make the sentence longer. Passives take more time to understand.[18]

b. If the agent is omitted, it's not clear who is responsible for doing the action.

c. Using many passive verbs, especially in material that has a lot of long words, can make the writing boring, pompous, and vague.

Passive verbs are desirable in these situations:

a. Use passives to emphasize the object receiving the action, not the agent.

Your order was shipped November 15.

The customer's order, not the shipping clerk, is important.

b. Use passives to provide coherence within a paragraph. A sentence is easier to read if "old" or familiar information comes at the beginning of a sentence. When you have been discussing a topic, use the word again as your subject even if that requires a passive verb.

The bank made several risky loans in 2013. These loans were written off as "uncollectable" in 2014.

Using *loans* as the subject of the second sentence provides a link between the two sentences, making the paragraph as a whole easier to read.

c. Use passives to avoid assigning blame.

The order was damaged during shipment.

An active verb would require the writer to specify *who* damaged the order. The passive here is more tactful.

4. Use verbs—not nouns—to carry the weight of your sentence.

Put the weight of your sentence in the verb to make your sentences more forceful and up to 25% easier to read.[19] When the verb is a form of the verb *to be,* revise the sentence to use a more forceful verb.

✕ Weak: The financial advantage of owning this equipment instead of leasing it is 10% after taxes.

✓ Better: Owning this equipment rather than leasing it will save us 10% after taxes.

Nouns ending in *-ment, -ion,* and *-al* often hide verbs.

~~make an adjustment~~	adjust
~~make a payment~~	pay
~~make a decision~~	decide
~~reach a conclusion~~	conclude
~~take into consideration~~	consider
~~make a referral~~	refer
~~provide assistance~~	assist

Use verbs to present the information more forcefully.

✕ Weak: We will perform an investigation of the problem.

✓ Better: We will investigate the problem.

✕ Weak: Selection of a program should be based on the client's needs.

✓ Better: Select the program that best fits the client's needs.

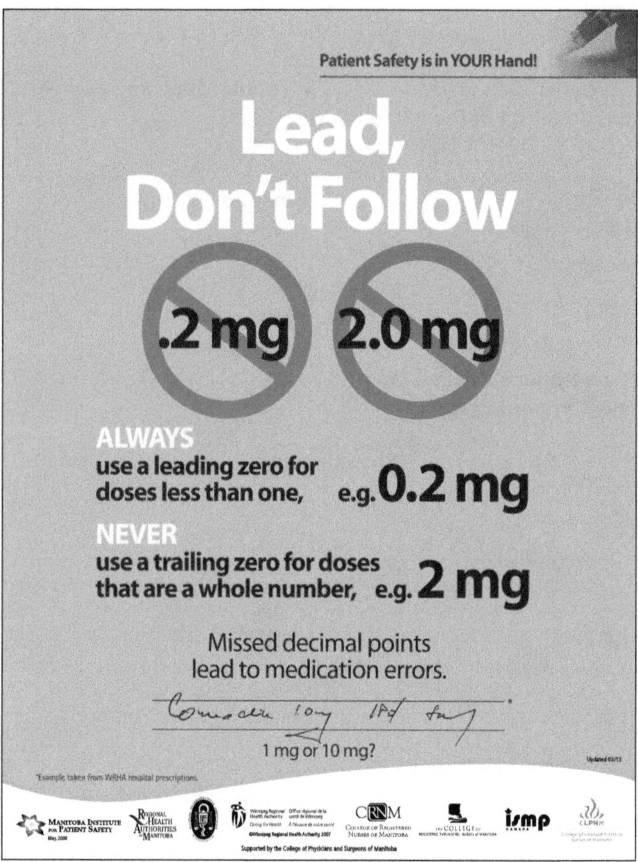

Winnipeg Regional Health Authority posters take aim at hastily scrawled prescriptions and overused abbreviations that can be misinterpreted after an audit showed one-third compromised patient safety. Studies show that Canadian patients have been harmed or killed by medication errors.

Source: Used with the permission of the Winnipeg Regional Health Authority.

5. Tighten your writing.

Writing is wordy if the same idea can be expressed in fewer words. Unnecessary words increase keying and reading time, bore your reader, and make your meaning more difficult to decipher.

Good writing is tight; however, tight writing may be long because it is packed with ideas. In ◀◀ Chapter 2, we saw that revisions to create you-attitude and positive emphasis and to develop reader benefits were frequently *longer* than the originals because the revision added information to the original.

Sometimes you may be able to look at a draft and see immediately how to tighten it. When the solution isn't obvious, try the following strategies for tightening your writing.

a. **Eliminate words that say nothing.** Cut words if the idea is already clear from other words in the sentence. Substitute single words for wordy phrases.

× Wordy: Keep this information on file for future reference.

✓ Tighter: Keep this information for reference.

✓ or: File this information.

Phrases beginning with *of, which,* and *that* can often be shortened.

× Wordy: the question of most importance

✓ Tighter: the most important question

× Wordy: the estimate that is enclosed

✓ Tighter: the enclosed estimate

Sentences beginning with *There are* or *It is* can often be tighter.

× Wordy: There are three reasons for the success of the project.

✓ Tighter: Three reasons explain the project's success.

× Wordy: It is the case that college or university graduates advance more quickly in the company.

✓ Tighter: College or university graduates advance more quickly in the company.

If you find these phrases in your draft, or any of the unnecessary words shown in Figure 3.8, eliminate them.

b. **Use gerunds and infinitives to make sentences shorter and smoother.** A gerund (the -ing form of a verb) is a verb used as a noun. In the sentence, "Running is my favourite activity," running is the subject of the sentence. An **infinitive** is the form of the verb that is preceded by to: *to run* is the infinitive.

In the revision below, a gerund (purchasing) and an infinitive (to transmit) tighten the revision.

× Wordy: A plant suggestion has been made where they would purchase a QWIP machine for the purpose of transmitting test reports between plants.

Figure 3.8 Words to Cut

CUT THE FOLLOWING WORDS	CUT REDUNDANT WORDS	SUBSTITUTE A SINGLE WORD FOR A WORDY PHRASE	
Quite	~~a period of~~ three months	~~at the present time~~	now
Really	during ~~the course of~~ the negotiations	~~due to the fact that~~	because
Very	during ~~the year of~~ 2004	~~in the event that~~	if
	maximum ~~possible~~	~~in the near future~~	soon (or give the date)
	~~past~~ experience	~~prior to the start of~~	before
	plan ~~in advance~~	~~on a regular basis~~	regularly
	refer ~~back~~		
	~~the colour~~ blue		
	~~true~~ facts		

✓ Tighter: The plant suggests purchasing a QWIP machine to transmit test reports between plants.

Even when gerunds and infinitives do not reduce length, they often make sentences smoother and more conversational.

c. **Combine sentences to eliminate unnecessary words.** In addition to saving words, combining sentences focuses the reader's attention on key points, adds energy, and sharpens the relationship between ideas.

× Wordy: I conducted this survey by telephone on Sunday, April 21. I questioned two groups of seniors—male and female—who, according to the Student Directory, were still living in the dorms. The purpose of this survey was to find out why some seniors continue to live in the dorms even though they are no longer required by the University to do so. I also wanted to find out if there were any differences between male and female seniors in their reasons for choosing to remain in the dorms.

✓ Tighter: On Sunday, April 21, I phoned seniors living in the dorms to find out (1) why they continue to live in the dorms even though they are no longer required to do so, and (2) whether men and women had the same reasons for staying in the dorms.

d. **Put the meaning of your sentence into the subject and verb to cut the number of words.** Put the core of your meaning into the subject and verb of your main clause.

× Wordy: The reason we are recommending the computerization of this process is that it will reduce the time required to obtain data and will give us more accurate data.

✓ Better: We are recommending the computerization of this process because it will save time and give us more accurate data.

✓ Tight: Computerizing the process will give us more accurate data more quickly.

6. Vary sentence length and sentence structure.

Readable prose mixes sentence lengths and varies sentence structure. A really short sentence (under 10 words) can add punch to your prose. Really long sentences (over 30 or 40 words) are danger signs. When your subject matter is complicated or full of numbers, make a special effort to keep sentences short.

You can vary sentence patterns in several ways. First, you can mix simple, compound, complex, and **compound-complex sentences** (see ⏩ Appendix A).

You can also vary sentences by changing the order of elements. Normally the subject comes first.

We will survey customers later in the year to see whether demand warrants a third store on campus.

To create variety, occasionally begin the sentence with some other part of the sentence.

Later in the year, we will survey customers to see whether demand warrants a third store on campus.

To see whether demand warrants a third store on campus, we will survey customers later in the year.

Use the following guidelines for sentence length and structure:

a. **Use long sentences to show how ideas are linked to each other; to avoid a series of short, choppy sentences; and to reduce repetition.** The following sentence is hard to read because it is long. Just cutting it into a series of short, choppy sentences doesn't help. The best revision uses medium-length sentences to show the relationship between ideas.

× TOO LONG:

It should also be noted in the historical patterns presented in the summary, that though there were delays in January and February which we realized were occurring, we are now back where we were about a year ago, and that we are not off line in our collect receivables as compared to last year at this time, but we do show a considerable over-budget figure because of an ultraconservative goal on the receivable investment.

× CHOPPY:

There were delays in January and February. We knew about them at the time. We are now back where we were about a year ago. The summary shows this. Our present collect receivables are in line with last year's. However, they exceed the budget. The reason they exceed the budget is that our goal for receivable investment was very conservative.

✓ BETTER:

As the summary shows, although there were delays in January and February (of which we were aware), we have now regained our position of a year ago. Our present collect receivables are in line with last year's, but they exceed the budget because our goal for receivable investment was very conservative.

b. **Group the words in long and medium-length sentences into chunks.**[20] The "better" revision above has seven chunks. Any sentence pattern will get boring if repeated. Use different sentence patterns to keep your prose interesting.

c. **Keep the subject and verb close together.** Often you can move the subject and verb closer together if you put the modifying material in a list at the end of the sentence. For maximum readability, present the list vertically.

× HARD TO READ:

Movements resulting from termination, layoffs and leaves, recalls and reinstates, transfers in, transfers out, promotions in, promotions out, and promotions within are presently documented through the Payroll Authorization Form.

✓ SMOOTHER:

The following movements are documented on the Payroll Authorization Form: termination, layoffs and leaves, recalls and reinstates, transfers in and out, and promotions in, out, and within.

✓ STILL BETTER:

The Payroll Authorization Form documents the following movements:

- Termination
- Layoffs and leaves
- Recalls and reinstates
- Transfers in and out
- Promotions in, out, and within

7. Use parallel structure.

Parallel structure puts words, phrases, or clauses in the same grammatical and logical form (as in the "better" example with a bulleted list). In the following faulty example, *by reviewing* is a gerund, while *note* is an imperative verb. Make the sentence parallel by using both gerunds or both imperatives.

× FAULTY:

Errors can be checked by reviewing the daily exception report or note the number of errors you uncover when you match the lading copy with the file copy of the invoice.

✓ PARALLEL:

Errors can be checked by reviewing the daily exception report or by noting the number of errors you uncover when you match the lading copy with the file copy of the invoice.

✓ ALSO PARALLEL:

To check errors, note

1. The number of items on the daily exception report.
2. The number of errors discovered when the lading copy and the file copy are matched.

Note that a list in parallel structure must fit grammatically into the umbrella sentence that introduces the list.

Words must also be logically parallel. In the following faulty example, *juniors, seniors,* and *athletes* are not three separate groups. The revision groups words into non-overlapping categories.

× Faulty: I interviewed juniors and seniors and athletes.

✓ Parallel: I interviewed juniors and seniors. In each rank, I interviewed athletes and non-athletes.

Parallel structure is a powerful device for making your writing tighter, smoother, and more forceful (see Figures 3.9 and 3.10).

Figure 3.9 Use Parallelism to Tighten Your Writing

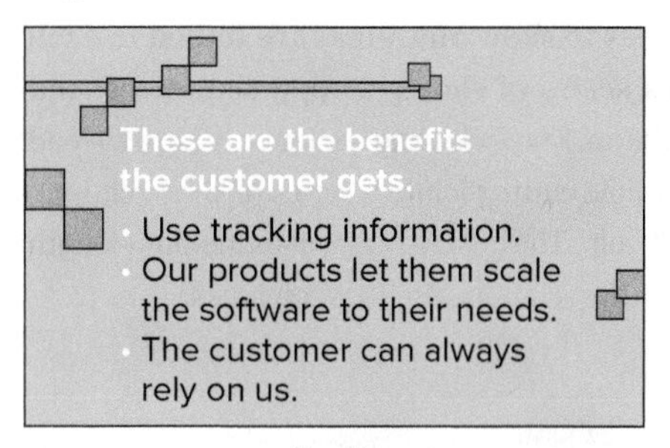

Faulty | Parallel

Figure 3.10 Eliminate Repeated Words in Parallel Lists

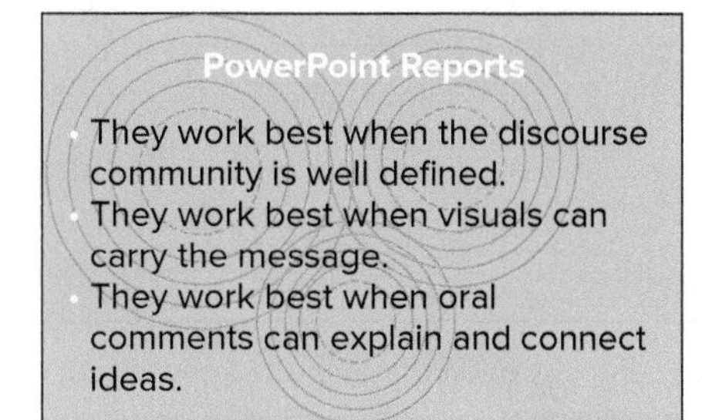

Wordy | Tight

8. Put your readers in your sentences.

Use second-person pronouns (*you*) rather than third-person (*he, she, one*) to give your writing more impact. *You* is both singular and plural; it can refer to a single person or to every member of your organization.

× THIRD-PERSON:

Funds in a participating employee's account at the end of each six months will automatically be used to buy more stock unless a "Notice of Election Not to Exercise Purchase Rights" form is received from the employee.

✓ SECOND-PERSON:

Once you begin to participate, funds in your account at the end of each six months will automatically be used to buy more stock unless you turn in a "Notice of Election Not to Exercise Purchase Rights" form.

Be careful to use *you* only when it refers to your reader.

× Incorrect: My visit with the outside sales rep showed me that your schedule can change quickly.

✓ Correct: My visit with the outside sales rep showed me that schedules can change quickly.

As You Choose Words

9. Use words that are accurate, appropriate, ethical, and familiar.

The best word depends on context: the situation, your purposes, your audience, and the words you have already used. Accurate words mean what you want to say. Appropriate words convey the attitudes you want and fit well with the other words in your document. Familiar words are easy to read and understand.

We learn some meanings by formal and informal study: the importance of "generally accepted accounting principles," the best strategies for increasing the size of donations in a fundraising letter, or what the garbage can on a computer screen symbolizes. Some meanings are negotiated as we interact one-on-one with another person, attempting to communicate. Some words persist, even though the reality behind them has changed: Statistics Canada predicts that by 2017 visible minorities will become the majority in Toronto and Vancouver.[21]

Accurate denotations. To be accurate, a word's denotation must match the meaning the writer wishes to convey. **Denotation** is a word's literal or dictionary meaning. Most common words in English have more than one denotation. The word *pound*, for example, means, or denotes, a unit of weight, a place where stray animals are kept, a unit of money in the British system, and the verb "to hit." Coca-Cola spends an estimated $20 million a year to protect its brand names so that Coke will denote only that brand and not just any cola drink.

When two people use the same word to mean, or denote, different things, bypassing occurs (see ◀◀ Chapter 1). For example, risk may be an economic term dealing with efficiency; for an environmentalist the word may denote health concerns. Progress is possible only when the writer and readers agree on a meaning.

Problems also arise when writers misuse words. The former U.S. President George W. Bush is a major source: "The law I sign today directs new funds and new focus to the task of collecting vital intelligence on terrorist threats and on weapons of mass production [*production* for *destruction*]."[22]

Examples of misused words include these:

Tow the line.

(To *toe* the line is to conform to a general policy or principle.)

Earn a free lunch.[23]

(A lunch one earns isn't free.)

Accurate denotations can make it easier to solve problems. In one production line with a high failure rate, the largest category of defects was *missed operations*. At first, the supervisor wondered if the people on the line were lazy or irresponsible. But some checking showed that several different problems were

On the Job Away with Words?*

Drawing on thousands of nominations for most overused and abused words, Lake Superior State University announces its banished words list for 2014.

- *Selfie:* Received the most nominations.
- *Twerk/Twerking:* Made the Oxford Dictionaries online 2014.
- *Hashtag:* Used to be called the pound symbol.

Entrepreneur James Adonis argues that clichés are symptoms of lazy, unimaginative thinking. To those who say "there is no 'I' in team," he answers that he has often been the only one working on the team.

Similarly, Matt Wilson complains about common phrases that are so embedded in everyday speech—Start at the beginning, Let me begin by saying, At the end of the day—that they are repeated mindlessly and endlessly, and to very little point!

*Based on Lake Superior State University banished words list, retrieved March 6, 2014, from www.lssu.edu/banished/current.php; James Adonis, *Corporate Punishment: Smashing the Management Clichés for Leaders in a New World* (Jossey-Bass, 2010); Harvey Schachter, "Tried and true maxims? More like tired and false," *Report on Business*, December 15, 2010, B18; Matt Wilson, "Meaningless phrases people use every day," posted December 30, 2010, retrieved January 3, 2011, from http://www.ragan.com?Main/Articles/42315.aspx?format=2.

labelled *missed operations:* parts installed backward, parts that had missing screws or fasteners, parts whose wires weren't connected. Each of these problems had a different solution. Using accurate words redefined the problem and enabled the production line both to improve quality and to cut repair costs.[24]

Using words correctly remains a challenge for many. If you can master the distinctions between commonly confused pairs of words, you will communicate more accurately and effectively (▸▸ Appendix A).

Appropriate connotations. Words are appropriate when their **connotations**—that is, their emotional associations or colourings—convey the attitude you want. Many words carry connotations of approval or disapproval, disgust or delight.

POSITIVE WORD	NEGATIVE WORD
Assume	Guess
Curious	Nosy
Cautious	Fearful
Firm	Obstinate
Flexible	Wishy-washy

A supervisor can "tell the truth" about a subordinate's performance and yet write either a positive or a negative performance appraisal, based on the words in the appraisal. Consider an employee who pays close attention to details. A positive appraisal might read, "Terry is a meticulous team member who takes care of details that others sometimes ignore." But the same behaviour might be described negatively: "Terry is hung up on trivial details."

Advertisers carefully choose words with positive connotations. Expensive cars are never *used;* instead, they're *preowned, experienced,* or even *previously adored.*[25]

Words may also connote status. Both *salesperson* and *sales representative* are non-sexist job titles, but the second suggests someone selling important items to corporate customers.

Connotations change over time. The word *charity* had acquired such negative connotations by the 19th century that people began to use the term *welfare* instead. Now, *welfare* carries some negative associations.

Ethical implications of word choice. How positively can we present something and still be ethical? "Pressure-treated" lumber sounds acceptable. But naming the material injected under pressure—"arsenic-treated" lumber—may lead the customer to make a different decision. We have the right to package our ideas attractively, but we have the responsibility to give the public or our superiors all the information they need to make decisions.

Word choices have ethical implications in other contexts as well. For example, as the racial and ethnic makeup of the workforce has changed, more companies have adopted the language of "managing diversity." People tend to view this language as positive, because it presumes employees' differences can be an asset to their employer, not a source of difficulty. However, communication professors Erika Kirby and Lynn Harter point out that referring to employees as resources to be managed places corporate financial interests above employees' human interests. The risk is that managers may lose sight of ethical obligations in "managing" their diverse employees.[26]

Familiar words. Use familiar words that are in almost everyone's vocabulary. Use the word that most exactly conveys your meaning, and try to use specific, concrete words, which are easier to understand and remember.[27]

The following list gives examples of short, simple alternatives:

FORMAL AND STUFFY	SHORT AND SIMPLE
Ameliorate	Improve
Commence	Begin
Enumerate	List
Finalize	Finish, complete
Prioritize	Rank
Utilize	Use
Viable option	Choice

There are four exceptions to the general rule that "shorter is better":

1. Use a long word if it is the only word that expresses your meaning exactly.
2. Use a long word if it is more familiar than a short word. *Send out* is better than *emit* and *a word in another language for a geographic place or area* is better than *exonym* because more people know the first item in each pair.
3. Use a long word if its connotations are more appropriate. *Exfoliate* is better than *scrape off dead skin cells.*
4. Use a long word if the discourse community (see ◂◂ Chapter 2) prefers it.

10. Use technical jargon only when it is essential and known to the reader. Replace business jargon.

There are two kinds of **jargon.** The first is the specialized terminology of a technical field. *LIFO* and *FIFO* are technical terms in accounting; *byte* and *baud* are computer jargon. A job application letter is the one occasion when it's desirable to use technical jargon: using the technical terminology of the reader's field suggests your competence in that field. Vancouver Community College's online multilingual legal glossary (www.legalglossary.ca) available in eight languages can be a useful resource for those in search of the appropriate legal jargon. In other kinds of messages, use technical jargon only when the term is essential and known to the reader. *Wired* magazine's Jargon Watch (www.wired.com) lists fresh and not so fresh examples of jargon.

When a genetic variation on rapeseed was developed by Canadian plant breeders to enhance nutritional value, a change of name to canola allowed trademark registration and clear marketing advantages in differentiating canola and promoting the health advantages of its low saturated fat content (the lowest among oils commonly available in the supermarket). With increasing global demand for oils for cooking and biofuels, canola promises to be a solution. Exports more than doubled in the ten years to 2014.

If a technical term has a "plain English" equivalent, use the simpler term:

× Jargon: Foot the average monthly budget column down to total variable costs, total management fixed costs, total sunk costs, and grand total.

✓ Better: Add the figures in the average monthly budget column for each category to determine the total variable costs, the total management fixed costs, and the total sunk costs. Then add the totals for each category to arrive at the grand total.

The revision here is longer but better because it uses simple words. The original will be meaningless to a reader who does not know what "foot" means.

The second kind of jargon is the **businessese** that some writers still use (Figure 3.11). Some writers call these terms *deadwood,* since they are no longer living words. If any of the terms in the first column of Figure 3.11 show up in your writing, replace them with updated language.

LO4

WRITING AND EDITING FOR THE WEB

Writers preparing content for a Web site, blog, or social media should keep in mind the physical demands of reading a computer screen and the special challenges of mobile devices. Internet users tend to scan to find whatever they are looking for. They want to get things done. Because reading screens is 25% slower than reading from paper and most do not scroll beyond the first screen, Web content should have 50% of a paper document word count.

Figure 3.11 Getting Rid of Business Jargon

INSTEAD OF	USE	BECAUSE
At your earliest convenience	The date you need a response	If you need it by a deadline, say so. It may never be convenient to respond.
As per your request; 65 kilometres per hour	As you requested; 65 kilometres an hour	*Per* is a Latin word for by or for each. Use per only when the meaning is correct; avoid mixing English and Latin.
Enclosed please find	Enclosed is; Here is	An enclosure isn't a treasure hunt. If you put something in the envelope, the reader will find it.
Forward same to this office.	Return it to this office.	Omit legal jargon.
Hereto, herewith	Omit	Omit legal jargon.
Please be advised; Please be informed	Omit—simply start your response	You don't need a preface. Go ahead and start.
Please do not hesitate	Omit	Omit negative words.
Pursuant to	According to; or omit	*Pursuant* does not mean *after.* Omit legal jargon in any case.
Said order	Your order	Omit legal jargon.
This will acknowledge receipt of your letter.	Omit—start your response	If you answer a letter, the reader knows you got it.
Trusting this is satisfactory, we remain	Omit	Eliminate *-ing* endings. When you are through, stop.

If reading on the Web can be physically challenging, writing for the Web must also entice and retain readers faced with incredible choice. That is why except for the most informal of e-communications for friends or family, careful planning, revision, and editing remain critical. Twitter and mobile devices have added to incentives to reduce wordiness and get to the point.

Writer Nicole Henderson offers five tips designed to get you noticed online:

1. Develop content to answer your reader's questions and needs.
2. Craft a concise story to grab readers.
3. Organize with headings, lists, bolding, and value-added sidebars.
4. Use headlines and bold words your readers will be looking for.
5. Be plain and get to the point.[28]

According to corporate writer Barb Sawyers, writing for the Web needs to have a conversational style that draws readers into a "friendly chat." Her advice is to imagine yourself talking face-to-face, using "I" and "you," raise and answer their questions, and discuss the stories that interest them. That will make the writing both easier and more engaging.[29]

In summary, writing for the Web is most effective when it follows these guidelines:

- Write concisely; use fragments.
- Maintain objectivity to enhance credibility.
- Put the main point first; then provide details.
- Break up the text with headings that describe the content.
- Make each page independent (users enter at any page).
- Choose easy-to-read type fonts; highlight key words.
- Use informal and direct language; don't try to be cute and clever.
- Keep hyperlinks to a minimum.
- Link to credible pages.
- Make words and phrases linkable rather than saying "click here."
- Consider key words for search engine optimization.
- Have a call to action on each page (Buy now).
- Update regularly.[30]

READABILITY FORMULAS AND GOOD STYLE

Readability formulas attempt to measure objectively how easy something is to read. However, since they don't take many factors into account, the formulas are at best a limited guide to good style.

Computer packages that analyze style may give you a readability score. Some companies require that guarantees and other consumer documents meet certain scores.

The two best-known readability formulas—the Gunning Fog Index and the Flesch Reading Ease Scale—depend heavily on word length and sentence length. But as Janice C. Redish and Jack Selzer have shown,[31] using shorter words and sentences will not necessarily make a passage easy to read. Short words are not always easy to understand, especially if they have technical meanings (e.g., waive, bear market, liquid). Short, choppy sentences and sentence fragments are actually harder to understand than well-written medium-length sentences.

No reading formula yet devised takes into account three factors that influence how easy a text is to read: the complexity of the ideas, the organization of the ideas, and the layout and design of the document.

Instead of using readability formulas, test your draft with the people for whom it is designed. How long does it take them to find the information they need? Do they make mistakes when they try to use the document? Do they find the document easy to use? Answers to these questions can give much more accurate information than any readability score.

LO5

GIVING, GETTING, AND USING FEEDBACK

Giving, getting, and using feedback almost always improves a document. In many organizations, it's required. All external documents must be read and approved before they go out. The process of drafting, giving and getting feedback, revising, and getting more feedback is called cycling (see ◂◂ Chapter 1). Susan Kleimann studied a 10-page document whose 20 drafts made a total of 31 stops on the desks of nine reviewers on four different levels.[32] Being asked to revise a document is a fact of life in businesses, government agencies, and non-profit organizations.

You can improve the quality of the feedback you get by telling people which aspects you'd especially like comments about. For example, when you give a reader the outline or planning draft,[33] you might want to know whether the general approach is appropriate. After your second draft, you might want to know whether reader benefits are well developed. When you reach the polishing draft, you'll be ready for feedback on style and grammar. Figure 3.12 lists questions to ask when giving or getting feedback. See also the ◂◂ Technology Tip "Tracking Changes" earlier in this chapter, which discusses Microsoft Word's tools for giving and getting feedback.

It's easy to feel defensive when someone criticizes your work—something to remember when giving feedback. If the feedback stings, put it aside until you can read it without feeling defensive. Even if you think the reader hasn't understood what you were trying to say, the fact the reader complained usually means the section could be improved. Rephrasing the statement, giving more information or examples, or documenting the source may clarify.

Reading feedback carefully is a good way to understand the culture of your organization. Are you told to give more details or to shorten messages? Does your boss add headings and bullet points? Look for patterns in the comments, and apply what you learn in your next document. You are also learning how to give useful feedback for your organization.

Technology Tips Blogging Bosses*

Debate rages about the risks and rewards of corporate blogging. Corporate blogging remains the smallest cohort in Technorati's 2010 report; mobile blogging now represents 25% of all blogging.

Technorati tracks 100 million blogs—a number reportedly increasing by 175,000 every day—though Socialtext.net lists only 54 Fortune 500 companies with corporate blogs. Fewer than ten CEOs in Canada write their own blogs. Commentators attribute the numbers to conservative corporate cultures and fear of losing control of the message.

Issues of credibility, authenticity, and confidentiality are also relevant. A Peppercomm survey of 200 marketing executives found more than 70% consider fake, promotional corporate blogs the "biggest blunder" committed by companies. More than 50% criticize "obvious ghostwriting" or blogs started without a clear purpose. Corporate lawyers are concerned about confidentiality.

So why blog? It can be a powerful way to build relationships with staff and other stakeholders; a forum to tell the corporate story—but only if you invest the time, have a gift for writing, and can cope with flaming or negative feedback.

Jim Estell of Synnex Canada Ltd. has a formula: 20% personal and 80% business. He finds, "the more people know me, the more apt they are to do business with me. It gives me a lot of influence."

Sass Peress of ICP Solar Technologies Inc., Montreal, argues, "Keep your family out of it." He finds his blog brings in business and "gives the company credibility as a leader."

*Based on Jon Sobel, "Technorati state of the blogosphere 2010," retrieved March 6, 2011, from http://technorati.com/blogging/article/state-of-the-blogosphere-2010-introduction/; Steve Cody, "The digital debate: Should CEOs blog?" IABC *CW Bulletin*, June 2007; Tony Martin, "They blog, therefore they are . . . better CEOs," *Report on Business Weekend*, March 15, 2008, B18.

Instead of thinking of giving feedback as a chore, consider it an "investment in your people" and be as "prepared to listen as you are to speak."[34]

Remember too that the widespread use of word processors is raising readers' expectations. Readers are now more likely to ask for a revision; they care about the physical appearance of documents. Because word processing makes it easy to correct typos, change spacing and margins, and insert graphics, readers are less tolerant of badly designed documents and of documents with obvious corrections. And wikis are useful resources for giving and getting feedback (see ⏩ Chapter 6).

European researchers Anne Mangen and Jean-Luc Velay argue that the sensory feedback from using pen and paper—the relation between brain and body, between perception and manual skill—helps imprint knowledge.[35]

Figure 3.12 Questions to Ask Readers Checklist

OUTLINE OR PLANNING DRAFT

- Does the plan seem on the right track?
- What topics should be added? Should any be cut?
- Do you have any other general suggestions?

REVISING DRAFT

- Does the message satisfy all its purposes?
- Is the message adapted to the audience(s)?
- Is the organization effective?
- What parts aren't clear?
- What ideas need further development?
- Do you have any other suggestions?

POLISHING DRAFT

- Are there any problems with word choice or sentence structure?
- Did you find any inconsistencies?
- Did you find any typos?
- Is the document's design effective?

ORGANIZATIONAL PREFERENCES FOR STYLE

Different organizations and bosses may legitimately have different ideas about what constitutes good writing. If the style the company prefers seems reasonable, use it. If the style doesn't seem reasonable—if you work for someone who likes flowery language or wordy paragraphs, for example—you have several choices.

- Go ahead and use the techniques in this chapter. Sometimes seeing good writing changes people's minds about the style they prefer.
- Help your boss learn about writing. Show him or her this book or the research cited in the notes to demonstrate how a clear, crisp style makes documents easier to read.
- Recognize that a style may serve purposes other than communication. An abstract, hard-to-read style may help a group forge its own identity. James Suchan and Ronald Dulek have shown that Navy officers preferred a passive, impersonal style because they saw themselves as followers.[36] When big words, jargon, and wordiness are central to a group's self-image, change will be difficult, since changing style will mean changing the corporate culture.
- Ask. Often the documents that end up in files aren't especially good; later, other workers may find these and copy them, thinking they represent a corporate standard. Bosses may in fact prefer better writing.

Building a good style takes energy and effort, but it's well worth the work. Good style can make every document more effective; good style can help make you the good writer so valuable to every organization.

SUMMARY OF KEY POINTS

- Writing processes can include eight activities: planning, gathering, writing, evaluating, getting feedback, revising, editing, and proofreading. *Revising* means changing the document to make it better satisfy the writer's purposes and the audience. *Editing* means making local changes that make the document grammatically correct. *Proofreading* means checking to be sure the document is free from typographical errors. The activities do not have to come in any set order.
- Good style in business writing is less formal, more friendly, and more personal than the style usually used for term papers.
- To improve your style,
  1. Start a clean page or screen so that you aren't locked into old sentence structures.
  2. Try WIRMI: *What I Really Mean Is.* Then write the words.
  3. Try reading your draft out loud to someone sitting about one metre away. If the words sound stiff, they'll seem stiff to a reader, too.
  4. Ask someone else to read your draft out loud. The places where that person stumbles are places where your writing can be better.
  5. Read widely and write *a lot.*
- To make your writing easier to read,

  As you write and revise paragraphs,

  1. Begin paragraphs with topic sentences.
  2. Use transitions to link ideas.

  As you write and revise sentences,

  3. Use active verbs most of the time.
  4. Use verbs—not nouns—to carry the weight of your sentence.
  5. Tighten your writing.
  6. Vary sentence length and sentence structure.
  7. Use parallel structure.
  8. Put your readers in your sentences.

  As you choose words,

  9. Use words that are accurate, appropriate, ethical, and familiar.
  10. Use technical jargon only when it is essential and known to the reader. Replace business jargon.
- Writing and editing for the Web requires short paragraphs and sentences, 50% less text than in a paper document, good use of transitions, headings, and subheadings, highlighted key words, lists, and links.
- You can improve the quality of the feedback you give and get by focusing on aspects of a draft needing comment. If a reader criticizes something, fix the problem. If you think the reader misunderstood you, revise the draft so that the reader can see what you meant.

EXERCISES AND PROBLEMS

GETTING STARTED

3.1 INTERVIEWING WRITERS ABOUT THEIR WRITING PROCESSES

Interview someone about the writing process(es) he or she uses for on-the-job writing. Questions you could ask include the following:

- What kind of planning do you do before you write? Do you make lists? Formal or informal outlines?
- When you need more information, where do you get it?
- How do you compose your drafts? Do you draft with pen and paper? Compose on screen? Use a wiki? How do you find uninterrupted time to compose?
- When you want advice about style, grammar, and spelling, what source(s) do you consult?
- Does your superior ever read your drafts and make suggestions?
- Do you ever work with other writers to produce a single document? Describe the process you use.
- Describe the process of creating a document where you felt the final document reflected your best work. Describe the process of creating a document you found difficult or frustrating. What sorts of things make writing easier or harder for you?

As Your Professor Directs,

a. Share your results orally with a small group of students.

b. Present your results in an oral presentation to the class.

c. Present your results in an e-mail to your professor.

d. Share your results with a small group of students and write a joint blog reporting the similarities and differences you found.

3.2 ANALYZING YOUR OWN WRITING PROCESSES

Save your notes and drafts from several assignments so that you can answer the following questions:

- Which practices of good writers do you follow?
- Which of the eight writing activities discussed in this chapter do you use?
- How much time do you spend on each of the eight activities?
- What kinds of revisions do you make most often?
- Do you use different processes for different documents, or do you have one process that you use most of the time?
- What parts of your process seem most successful? Are there any places in the process that could be improved? How?
- What relation do you see between the process(es) you use and the quality of the final document?

As Your Professor Directs,

a. Discuss your process with a small group of other students. Write a group memo (see ▸▸ Chapter 7 for memo format) to your professor on what the group shared and what not.

b. Write an e-mail to your professor analyzing in detail your process for composing one of the assignments for this class.

c. Write an e-mail to your professor analyzing your process during the term. What parts of your process(es) have stayed the same throughout the term? What parts have changed?

GETTING IT RIGHT

3.3 CHECKING SPELL- AND GRAMMAR-CHECKERS

Each of the following paragraphs contains errors in grammar, spelling, and punctuation. Which errors does your spell- or grammar-checker catch? Which errors does it miss? Does it flag as errors any words that are correct? As your professor instructs, peer grade the answers.

a. Answer to an Inquiry—Enclosed are the tow copies you requested of our pamphlet, "Using the Internet to market Your products. The pamphelt walks you through the steps of planning the Home Page (The first page of the web cite, shows examples of other Web pages we have designed, and provide a questionaire that you can use to analyze audience the audience and purposes.

b. Performance Appraisal—Most staff accountants complete three audits a month. Ellen has completed 21 audits in this past six months she is our most productive staff accountant. Her technical skills our very good however some clients feel that she could be more tactful in suggesting ways that the clients accounting practices courld be improved.

c. Brochure—Are you finding that being your own boss crates it's own problems? Take the hassle out of working at home with a VoiceMail Answering System. Its almost as good as having your own secratery.

d. Presentation Slides

How to Create a Web résumé

- Omit home adress and phone number
- Use other links only if they help an employer evalaute you.
- Be professional.
- Carefully craft and proof read the phrase on the index page.

How to Create a Scannable Résumé

- Create a "plain vanilla" document.
- Use include a "Keywords" section. Include personality trait sas well as accomplishments.
- Be specific and quantifyable.

3.4 IDENTIFYING WORDS WITH MULTIPLE DENOTATIONS

a. Each of the following words has several denotations. How many can you list without going to a dictionary? How many additional meanings does a good dictionary list?

   browser   log   court   table

b. List five words that have multiple denotations.

3.5 EVALUATING THE ETHICAL IMPLICATIONS OF CONNOTATIONS

In each of the following pairs, identify the more favourable term. Is its use justified? Why or why not? As your professor instructs, peer grade answers.

1. wastepaper   recovered fibre
2. feedback   criticism
3. deadline   due date
4. scalper   ticket reseller
5. budget   spending plan

3.6 CHOOSING LEVELS OF FORMALITY

Identify the more formal word in each pair. Which term is better for most business documents? Why? As your professor instructs, peer grade answers.

1. adapted to   geared to
2. befuddled   confused
3. assistant   helper
4. pilot project   testing the waters
5. cogitate   think

CHOOSING YOUR WORDS

3.7 ELIMINATING JARGON AND SIMPLIFYING LANGUAGE

Revise these sentences to eliminate jargon and to use short, familiar words. In some sentences, you'll need to reword, reorganize, or add information to produce the best revision. As your professor instructs, peer grade answers.

1. Computers can enumerate pages when the appropriate keystroke is implemented.
2. Any alterations must be approved during the 30-day period commencing 60 days prior to the expiration date of the agreement.
3. As per your request, the undersigned has obtained estimates of upgrading our computer system. A copy of the estimated cost is attached hereto.
4. Please be advised that this writer is in considerable need of a new computer.
5. Enclosed please find the proposed schedule for the training session. In the event that you have alterations that you would like to suggest, forward same to my office at your earliest convenience.

3.8 CHANGING VERBS FROM PASSIVE TO ACTIVE

In pairs or groups, identify the passive verbs in the following sentences and convert them to active verbs. In some cases, you may need to add information to do so. You may use different words as long as you retain the basic meaning of the sentence. Remember that imperative verbs are active, too.

1. The business plan was written by Tyrone King.
2. The cost of delivering financial services is being slashed by computers, the Internet, and toll-free phone lines.
3. When the vacation schedule is finalized it is recommended that it be routed to all supervisors for final approval.
4. As stated in my résumé, I have designed Web pages for three student organizations.
5. Material must not be left on trucks outside the warehouse. Either the trucks must be parked inside the warehouse or the material must be unloaded at the time of receiving the truck.

3.9 REDUCING WORDINESS

1. Eliminate words that say nothing (the ideas are already clear from other words in the sentence). You may use different words.
   a. There are many businesses that are active in community and service work.
   b. The purchase of a new computer will allow us to produce form letters quickly. In addition, return on investment could be calculated for proposed repairs. Another use is that the computer could check databases to make sure that claims are paid only once.
   c. Our decision to enter the South American market has precedence in the past activities of the company.

2. Use gerunds and infinitives to make these sentences shorter and smoother.
   a. The completion of the project requires the collection and analysis of additional data.
   b. The purchase of laser printers will make possible the in-house production of the newsletter.
   c. The treasurer has the authority for the investment of assets for the gain of higher returns.
3. Combine sentences to show how ideas are related and to eliminate unnecessary words.
   a. Some customers are profitable for companies. Other customers actually cost the company money.
   b. If you are unable to come to the session on dental coverage, please call the human resources office. You will be able to schedule another time to ask questions you may have about the various options.
   c. Major Japanese firms often have employees who know English well. Canadian companies negotiating with Japanese companies should bring their own interpreters.

3.10 USING TOPIC SENTENCES

In pairs or groups, make each of the following paragraphs more readable by opening each paragraph with a topic sentence. You may be able to find a topic sentence in the paragraph and move it to the beginning. In other cases, you'll need to write a new sentence.

1. At Disney World, a lunch put on an expense account is "on the mouse." McDonald's employees "have ketchup in their veins." Business slang flourishes at companies with rich corporate cultures. Memos at Procter & Gamble are called "reco's" because the model P&G memo begins with a recommendation.
2. The first item on the agenda is the hiring for the coming year. George has also asked that we review the agency goals for the next fiscal year. We should cover this early in the meeting since it may affect our hiring preferences. Finally, we need to announce the deadlines for grant proposals, decide which grants to apply for, and set up a committee to draft each proposal.
3. Separate materials that can be recycled from your regular trash. Pass along old clothing, toys, or appliances to someone else who can use them. When you purchase products, choose those with minimal packaging. If you have a yard, put your yard waste and kitchen scraps (excluding meat and fat) in a compost pile. You can reduce the amount of solid waste your household produces in four ways.

3.11 REVISING PARAGRAPHS

Revise each paragraph to make it easier to read. Change, rearrange, add, or delete words and sentences.

a. Once a new employee is hired, each one has to be trained for a week by one of our supervisors at a cost of $1,000 each which includes the supervisor's time. This amount also includes half of the new employee's salary, since new hires produce only half the normal production per worker for the week. This summer $24,000 was spent in training 24 new employees. Absenteeism increased in the department on the hottest summer days. For every day each worker is absent we lose $200 in lost production. This past summer there was a total of 56 absentee days taken for a total loss of $11,200 in lost production. Turnover and absenteeism were the causes of an unnecessary expenditure of over $35,000 this summer.

b. One service is investments. General financial news and alerts about companies in the customer's portfolio are available. Quicken also provides assistance in finding the best mortgage rate and in providing assistance in making the decision whether to refinance a mortgage. Another service from Quicken is advice for the start and management of a small business. Banking services, such as paying bills and applying for loans, have long been available to Quicken subscribers. The taxpayer can be walked through the tax preparation process by Quicken. Someone considering retirement can use Quicken to ascertain whether the amount being set aside for this purpose is sufficient. Quicken's Web site provides seven services.

3.12 WRITING PARAGRAPHS

Write a paragraph on each of the following topics.

a. Discuss your ideal job.

b. Summarize a recent article from a business magazine or newspaper.

c. Explain how technology is affecting the field you plan to enter.

d. Explain why you have or have not decided to work while you attend university.

e. Write a profile of someone who is successful in the field you hope to enter.

As Your Professor Directs,

a. Label topic sentences, active verbs, and parallel structure.

b. Edit a classmate's paragraphs to make the writing even tighter and smoother.

3.13 TRACKING YOUR OWN MECHANICAL ERRORS

Analyze the mechanical errors (grammar, punctuation, word use, and typos) in each of your papers.

- How many different errors are marked on each paper?
- Which three errors do you make most often?
- Is the number of errors constant in each paper, or does the number increase or decrease during the term?

As Your Professor Directs,

a. Correct each of the mechanical errors in one or more papers.

b. Deliberately write two new sentences in which you make each of your three most common errors. Then write the correct version of each sentence.

c. Write an e-mail to your professor discussing your increasing mastery of mechanical correctness during the semester.

d. Briefly explain to the class how to avoid one kind of error in grammar, punctuation, or word use.

DESIGNING DOCUMENTS, SLIDES, AND SCREENS

4

Learning Outcomes

LO1 Explain the importance of effective design

LO2 List eight guidelines for effective page design

LO3 Describe six steps to create good visuals

LO4 Describe special features of Web site design

LO5 Discuss presentation slide design

LO6 Explain how to test design usability

AN INSIDE PERSPECTIVE

President, ISL, an ISO 9001 certified Web marketing and development company in Halifax and Vancouver, Malcolm Fraser is a past chair, Canadian Information Communications and Technology Federation. Named one of Atlantic Canada's top 50 CEOs for five years and inducted into the Top 50 CEO Hall of Fame 2013, he is proud of his design team—including finance and project management, without whom "the project just wouldn't be as smooth."

Good document design focuses on the reader. Imagine a particular reader trying to do something with your document. Document design is not about decoration but rather about guiding the reader through a task. For example, designers at ISL are "problem solvers, not decorators so the design serves the structure and functionality of the Web site while providing a rich interactive experience for the user," says Halifax-based president Malcolm Fraser. ISL designers are extending their award-winning ways with mobile, mapping, and social media technologies.

To test a document, ask people to do something with it, such as fill out a form. Ask them how well it worked; they'll tell you what they understand and what they don't. Observe them; they'll show you when the instructions are unclear or when they can't find the right information.

Good document design is good business. The process begins and ends with people: from those in account management and consulting who ask the right questions and develop the strategies, to those who bring them to life, to those who monitor quality and the end-users themselves.

Good design saves money by preventing errors and reducing phone calls from customers who don't understand what they're supposed to do. Employees can be freed up to provide even better customer service. Good design shows customers that you care about their time and want to make tasks easier for them. Isn't that the best marketing a company can have?

Good document design is as important for your college or university papers, reports, or presentations as it is for your job application package (see also ▸▸ Chapters 11, 12, and 13). Document design is where you can show both your creative flair and your attention to detail.

Research shows that easy-to-read documents enhance your credibility and build an image of you as a professional, competent person.[1] Visual like verbal rhetoric depends on conventions and codes being internalized, adapted, and interpreted by users who consolidate group and other identities in the process. "Conventions," according to Charles Kostelnick and Michael Hassett, "prompt rather than stifle invention" and are shaped and reshaped by social and cultural norms and technological innovations.[2] Good design is as important for short as for long documents: one-page letters and memos, résumés, reports and proposals, Web pages, social media, and newsletters.

LO1

THE IMPORTANCE OF EFFECTIVE DESIGN

Good document design saves time and money, reduces legal liabilities, and builds goodwill. A well-designed document looks inviting, friendly, and easy to read. Effective design also groups ideas visually, making the structure of the document more obvious so the document is easier to read. A visual sign of an organization's identity, design creates brand promise. Picking up on a cruise ship theme of a fundraising event held by the Mental Health Foundation of Nova Scotia, ISL Digital Marketing created a visually pleasing application designed to keep participants engaged through interactivity. The application displayed a race between cruise ships, each tied to one of five performers. Each donation on behalf of performers propelled their cruise ship further in the race. The design kept participants engaged with the event and helped the foundation double its on-site fundraising.[3]

When document design is poor, organizations, individuals, and even society can suffer. The *Challenger* space shuttle blew up because its O-rings failed in the excessive cold. Poor communication—including charts that hid, rather than emphasized, the data—contributed to the decision to launch. Engineer and whistleblower Roger Boisjoly continues to teach what we can learn about communications and ethical design and decision making from events leading to the *Challenger* disaster.[4] In 2008, Canada faced a crisis of medical nuclear isotope supply after the Atomic Energy of Canada Limited (AECL) nuclear research reactor at Chalk River shut down for three weeks. This case had its roots in issues of design, communications, and regulatory oversight. According to a July 2008 report by three independent consultants, a "culture of informality" was "a significant and fundamental flaw" in the "methods of operation" of AECL and

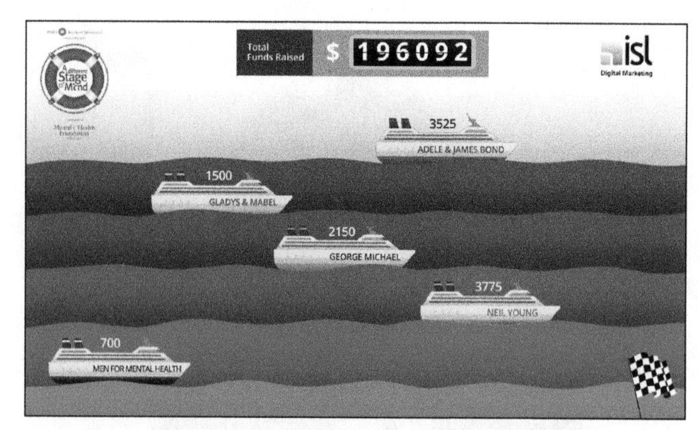

The design of ISL's "Fund-Racer" application added to fun and funds at a February 2014 fundraiser for the Mental Health Foundation of Nova Scotia.

the Canadian Nuclear Safety Commission that "contributed to a series of misunderstandings." Vagueness added to the lack of clarity in the design and communication of operating licences.[5]

DESIGN AS PART OF YOUR WRITING PROCESS(ES)

Design isn't something to "tack on" when you've finished writing. Indeed, the best documents, slides, and screens are created when you think about design at each stage of your writing process(es).

- As you plan, think about your audience. Are they skilled readers? Are they busy? Will they read the document straight through or skip around in it?
- As you write, incorporate lists and headings. Use visuals to convey numerical data clearly and forcefully (see ▸▸ "Designing Visuals" later in this chapter).
- Get feedback from people who will be using your document. What parts of the document do they find hard to understand? Do they need more information?
- As you revise, check your draft against the guidelines in this chapter.

LO2

GUIDELINES FOR PAGE DESIGN

Use the eight guidelines in Figure 4.1 to create visually attractive, user-friendly documents.

1. Use White Space to Separate and Emphasize Points

White space—the empty space on the page—makes material easier to read by emphasizing the material that it separates from the rest of the text. To create white space,

- Use headings.
- Use a mix of paragraph lengths (most no longer than seven keyed lines). It's OK for a paragraph to be just one sentence. First and last paragraphs, in particular, should be short.
- Use lists.
- Use tabs or indents—not spacing—to align items vertically.
- Use numbered lists when the number or sequence of items is exact.
- Use **bullets** (large dots or squares) when the number and sequence don't matter.

Figure 4.1 Guidelines for Page Design

1. Use white space to separate and emphasize points.
2. Use headings to group points and lead the reader through the document.
3. Limit the use of words set in all capital letters.
4. Use no more than two fonts in a single document.
5. Use ragged right margins for business communications.
6. Put important elements in the top left and lower right quadrants of the page.
7. Use a grid of imaginary columns to unify visuals and other elements in a document.
8. Use highlighting, decorative devices, and colour in moderation.

Ethics and Legal A False Sense of Security*

Online bank customers rely on a false sense of security promoted by marketing and the refund guarantees of Canada's five major banks, according to study authors Paul Van Oorschot, Canada Research Chair in Network and Software Security, Carleton University, and PhD student Mohammad Mannan.

If they troubled to check the fine print, customers would find that "100% online security guarantees" are "conditional on fulfilling complicated security requirements."

A survey of 123 technically advanced users showed they failed to fulfill those requirements. To expect average people to do so is "extremely naïve," the study argues. Claims that users could comply "in minutes" are unrealistic. The average user could take hours if not days.

The study concludes that most will be ineligible for the 100% reimbursement guarantees and that reassuring claims about completing online banking with "confidence" and "peace of mind" are "no more than a marketing slogan which misleads users."

A *Vancouver Sun* editorial concludes that the banks need to redesign to make the processes less "complicated and risky." Or, they should "shoulder more of the risk—without hiding behind all the fine print."

*Based on Mohammad Mannan and Paul C. Van Oorschot, "Security and usability: The gap in real-world online banking," *New Security Paradigms Workshop (NSPW) 2007,* retrieved March 7, 2011, from http://www.csl.toronto.edu/~mmannan/publications/online-banking-nspw07.pdf; "The onus for safe online banking falls more on banks than on clients," *Vancouver Sun,* April 15, 2008, retrieved March 7, 2011, from http://www.canada.com/vancouversun/news/editorial/story.html?id=9ba9bb07-4ef6-475b-b70b-79aa99a39802; Sarah Schmidt, "A false sense of security," *Ottawa Citizen,* April 10, 2008.

On the Job Costs and Benefits of Document Design*

- Rewriting its policy and procedures manuals saved FedEx $400,000 in the first year in increased productivity. More searches for information were successful, and more of them could be completed in less than three minutes.
- A Sabre computer reservation manual was cut from 100 pages to 20, saving $19,000 just in producing the document.
- A 2008 study shows that diners will spend on average $5.55 more on a meal if restaurants drop the dollar symbol from their menus. According to lead author Sybil Yang, "Changing the menu typography is like picking the low-hanging fruit when it comes to squeezing every last cent from an existing business."
- Digital photos from photo-sharing Web site Flickr of the 65 parks of the East Bay Regional Park District, California, proved a cost-effective way to update print and Web materials. By January 2010, 540 Flickr members had posted 5,816 photos, while visitors to the park district's Web site had doubled to a million visitors.

*Based on Jay Mead, "Measuring the value added for technical documentation: A review of research and practice," *Technical Communication 45*, no. 3 (August 1998): 353–379; Sarah Schmidt, "Diners will pay more for food without the $," *Vancouver Sun*, August 14, 2008, retrieved August 15, 2008, from http://www.canada.com/vancouversun/news/story.html?id=331b1ee0-447e-4ff0-a81a-2c15cdc073ca; Isa Polt-Jones, "Photo finish," *Communication World*, September–October 2010: 40–42.

When you use a list, make sure all of the items in it are parallel (see ◄◄ Chapter 3) and fit into the structure of the sentence that introduces the list.

× FAULTY:

The following suggestions can help employers avoid bias in job interviews:

1. Base questions on the job description.
2. Questioning techniques.
3. Selection and training of interviewers.

✓ PARALLEL:

The following suggestions can help employers avoid bias in job interviews:

1. Base questions on the job description.
2. Ask the same questions of all applicants.
3. Select and train interviewers carefully.

✓ ALSO PARALLEL:

Employers can avoid bias in job interviews by

1. Basing questions on the job description.
2. Asking the same questions of all applicants.
3. Selecting and training interviewers carefully.

Figure 4.2 shows an original keyed document. In Figure 4.3, the same document has been improved by using shorter paragraphs, lists, and headings. These devices take space. When saving space is essential, it's better to cut the text and keep white space and headings.

Figure 4.2 A Document with Poor Visual Impact

× Full capital letters make the title hard to read

MONEY DEDUCTED FROM YOUR WAGES TO PAY CREDITORS

When you buy goods on credit, the store will sometimes ask you to sign a Wage Assignment form allowing it to deduct money from your wages if you do not pay your bill. When you buy on credit, you sign a contract agreeing to pay a certain amount each week or month until you have paid all you owe. The Wage Assignment Form is separate. It must contain the name of your present employer, your social insurance number, the amount of money loaned, the rate of interest, the date when payments are due, and your signature. The words "Wage Assignment" must be printed at the top of the form and also near the line for your signature. Even if you have signed a Wage Assignment agreement, Roysner will not withhold part of your wages unless all of the following conditions are met: 1. You have to be more than forty days late in payment of what you owe; 2. Roysner has to receive a correct statement of the amount you are in default and a copy of the Wage Assignment form; and 3. You and Roysner must receive a notice from the creditor at least twenty days in advance stating that the creditor plans to make a demand on your wages. This twenty-day notice gives you a chance to correct the problems yourself. If these conditions are all met, Roysner must withhold 15% of each paycheque until your bill is paid and give this money to your creditor.

× Long paragraph is visually uninviting

If you think you are not late or that you do not owe the amount stated, you can argue against it by filing a legal document called a "defence." Once you file a defence, Roysner will not withhold any money from you. However, be sure you are right before you file a defence. If you are wrong, you have to pay not only what you owe but also all legal costs for both yourself and the creditor. If you are right, the creditor has to pay all these costs.

× Important information is hard to find

As George Miller has shown, our short-term memories can hold only seven plus or minus two bits of information.[6] Only after those bits are processed and put into long-term memory can we assimilate new information. Large amounts of information will be easier to process if they are grouped into three to seven chunks rather than presented as individual items.

2. Use Headings to Group Points and Lead the Reader through the Document

Headings (see ▸▸ Chapter 11) are words, short phrases, or short sentences that group points and divide your document into sections. Headings and subheadings enable your reader to see at a glance how the document is organized, to turn quickly to sections of special interest, and to compare and contrast points more easily. Headings also break up the page, making it look less formidable and more interesting.

- Make headings specific.
- Make each heading cover all the material until the next heading.
- Keep headings at any one level parallel: all nouns, all complete sentences, or all questions.

Headings may be **topic** or **functional** (or generic) or **talking** or **informative heads.** Functional headings

Figure 4.3 A Document Revised to Improve Visual Impact

✓ First letter of each main word capitalized—Title split onto two lines

Money Deducted from Your Wages to Pay Creditors

When you buy goods on credit, the store will sometimes ask you to sign a Wage Assignment form allowing it to deduct money from your wages if you do not pay your bill.

✓ Headings divide document into chunks

Have You Signed a Wage Assignment Form?

When you buy on credit, you sign a contract agreeing to pay a certain amount each week or month until you have paid all you owe. The Wage Assignment Form is separate. It must contain the following:

✓ List with bullets where order of items doesn't matter

✓ Single-space list when items are short

- The name of your present employer
- Your social insurance number
- The amount of money loaned
- The rate of interest
- The date when payments are due
- Your signature

The words "Wage Assignment" must be printed at the top of the form and also near the line for your signature.

✓ Headings must be parallel; here all are questions

When Would Money Be Deducted from Your Wages to Pay a Creditor?

Even if you have signed a Wage Assignment agreement, Roysner will not withhold part of your wages unless all of the following conditions are met:

✓ Numbered list where number, order of items matter

✓ White space between items emphasizes them

✓ Double space between items in list when most items are two lines or longer

1. You have to be more than 40 days late in payment of what you owe.

2. Roysner has to receive a correct statement of the amount you are in default and a copy of the Wage Assignment form.

3. You and Roysner must receive a notice from the creditor at least 20 days in advance stating that the creditor plans to make a demand on your wages. This 20-day notice gives you a chance to correct the problem yourself.

If these conditions are all met, Roysner must withhold fifteen percent (15%) of each paycheque until your bill is paid and give this money to your creditor.

What Should You Do If You Think the Wage Assignment Is Incorrect?

If you think you are not late or that you do not owe the amount stated, you can argue against it by filing a legal document called a "defence." Once you file a defence, Roysner will not withhold any money from you. However, be sure you are right before you file a defence. If you are wrong, you have to pay not only what you owe but also all legal costs for both yourself and the creditor. If you are right, the creditor has to pay all these costs.

(*Background, Budget, Recommendations*) describe general topics or functions; informative headings (*Employee Survey Supports New E-Mail Policy*) add information and interest. Functional headings make good sense in regular or routine reports (trip or progress, for instance) and in defusing emotions in response to documents addressing sensitive issues. Informative headings can help readers think about issues when they are clear and concrete. Vagueness (*Moving Forward in a New Era*) will do little to conjure images and clarify areas of emphasis.

In a letter or memo, key main headings even with the left-hand margin in bold. Capitalize the first letters of the first word and of other major words; use lowercase for all other letters. (See Figure 4.4 for an example.) Use subheadings only when you have at least two subdivisions under a given main heading. In a report, you may need more than two levels of headings (see ⏩ Figure 11.7).

3. Limit the Use of Words Set in All Capital Letters

We recognize words by their shapes.[7] (See Figure 4.4.) In capitals, all words are rectangular; letters lose the descenders and ascenders that make reading go 19% more quickly.[8] Use full capitals sparingly.

4. Use No More Than Two Fonts in a Single Document

Fonts are unified styles of type. Each font comes in several sizes and usually in several styles (bold, italic, etc.). Typewriter fonts are **fixed;** that is, every letter takes the same space. An *i* takes the same space as a *w*. Courier and Prestige Elite are fixed fonts. Computers usually offer **proportional** fonts as well, where wider letters take more space than narrower letters. Times Roman, Palatino, Helvetica, and Arial are proportional fonts.

Serif fonts have little extensions, called serifs, from the main strokes. (In Figure 4.5, look at the feet on the *r*'s in New Courier and the flick on the top of the *d* in Lucinda.) New Courier, Elite, Times Roman, Palatino, and Lucinda Calligraphy are serif fonts. Serif fonts are easier to read because the serifs help the eyes move from letter to letter. Helvetica, Arial, Geneva, and Technical are **sans serif** fonts since they lack serifs (*sans* is French for *without*). Sans serif fonts are good for titles and tables.

Most business documents use just one font—usually Times Roman, Palatino, Helvetica, or Arial. Helvetica's popularity was promoted by American typographer Mike Parker, confirmed by its use in early Apple desktops, and achieved "rock star" status in the independent movie *Helvetica* about typography and visual culture.[9]

You can create emphasis and levels of headings by using bold, italics, and different sizes. Bold is easier to read than italics, so use bolding if you need only one method to emphasize text. In a complex document, use bigger type for main headings and slightly smaller type for subheadings and text. If you combine two fonts in one document, choose one serif and one sans serif typeface.

Eleven-point Times Roman is ideal for letters, memos, and reports. Twelve-point type is acceptable, especially for mature readers. Use 9- or 10-point type to get the effect of a printed book or brochure.

Figure 4.4 Full Capitals Hide the Shape of a Word

Full capitals hide the shape of a word and slow reading 19%.

FULL CAPITALS HIDE THE SHAPE OF A WORD AND SLOW READING 19%.

Figure 4.5 Examples of Different Fonts

This sentence is set in 12-point Times Roman.

This sentence is set in 12-point Arial.

This sentence is set in 12-point New Courier.

This sentence is set in 12-point Lucinda Calligraphy.

This sentence is set in 12-point Broadway.

This sentence is set in 12-point Technical.

If your material will not fit in the available pages, cut one more time. Putting some sections in tiny type will save space but creates a negative response—that may extend to the organization that produced the document.

5. Use Ragged Right Margins for Business Communications

Computers often allow you to use **full justification** so that type on both sides of the page is evenly lined up. Books, newspapers, and magazines typically justify margins. Although justification can look formal and professional, it can be challenging to adjust space between words without reducing readability. This paragraph justifies margins.

Margins justified only on the left are sometimes called **ragged right margins.** Lines end in different places because words are of different lengths. Ragged right—with its less formal and more personalized appearance—is now standard in business communications.

In its 2007 redesign, *The Globe and Mail* adopted "a universal ragged-right format" to enable the use of "large-text type in narrow columns, which reduces the need to hyphenate words. This makes for smoother reading." To trace how newspaper design and readability has changed since the first issue on March 5, 1844, with a readership of 300, to today's issue with a readership of 2 million, check out *The Globe and Mail* video *First drafts of history: The Globe and Mail celebrates 170 years.* Recognizing that design matters even more in the competition for print and online readers, the *Globe* launched another redesign in 2010—one that has proven to be an award winner (see Figure 4.6).[10]

6. Put Important Elements in the Top Left and Lower Right Quadrants of the Page

Readers of English start in the upper left-hand corner of the page and read to the right and down. The eye moves in a Z pattern.[11] (See Figure 4.7.) Therefore, as Philip M. Rubens notes, the four quadrants of the page carry different visual weights. The top left quadrant, where the eye starts, is the most important; the bottom right quadrant, where the eye ends, is next most important.[12] Titles should always start in the top left; reply coupons or other important elements should be in the bottom right.

7. Use a Grid of Imaginary Columns to Unify Visuals and Other Elements in a Document

For years, graphic designers have used a **grid system** to design pages. In its simplest form, a grid imposes two or three imaginary columns on the page. In more complex grids, these columns can be further subdivided. Then all the graphic elements—text indentations, headings, visuals, and so on—are lined up within the columns. The resulting symmetry creates a more pleasing page[13] and unifies long documents.

Figure 4.8 uses grids to organize a page with visuals, a newsletter page, and a résumé.

8. Use Highlighting, Decorative Devices, and Colour in Moderation

Many word processing programs have arrows, pointing fingers, and a host of other **dingbats** that you can insert. Clip art packages and presentation software allow you to insert more and larger images into your text. Used in moderation, highlighting and decorative devices make pages more interesting. However, a page or screen that uses every possible highlighting device just looks busy and hard to read.

Colour works well to highlight points. Use colour for overviews and main headings, not for small points. Blue, green, or violet type is most legible for younger readers, but perception

International Cultural Differences in Document Design*

Cultural differences in document design are based on reading practices and experiences with other documents. For example, one laundry detergent company printed ads in the Middle East showing soiled clothes on the left, its box of soap in the middle, and clean clothes on the right. But, because people in that part of the world read not from left to right but from right to left, many people thought the ads meant that the soap actually soiled the clothes.

People in Canada focus first on the left side of a Web site. However, Middle Eastern people focus first on the right side. Web sites in Arabic and Hebrew orient text, links, and graphics from right to left.

If companies' success depends on their communications' consistency with cultural values, Hans Hoeken and Hubert Korzilius caution against treating nationality as cultural difference. Their findings show how difficult it is to compare cultural responses to documents when, for instance, a translated document does not carry the same meaning for different cultures, and some cultures avoid the extremes of rating scales or have less experience with advertisements. In one study they cite, North American participants believed a male figure to be upper class, while Chinese participants read his jeans as evidence of a manual labourer.

*Based on Hans Hoeken and Hubert Korzilius, "Conducting experiments on cultural aspects of document design: Why and how?" *Communications* 28, no. 3 (2003): 285–304; David A. Ricks, *Blunders in International Business* (Cambridge, MA: Blackwell, 1993), 53; and Albert N. Badre, "The effects of cross cultural interface design orientation on World Wide Web user performance," *GVU Technical Report* GIT-GVU-01-03, August 31, 2000, 8, retrieved September 1, 2001, from http://www.cc.gatech.edu/gvu/reports/2001.

Figure 4.6 The Globe and Mail Page Redesign

THE GLOBE AND MAIL • WEDNESDAY, FEBRUARY 23, 2011 NEWS • A3

BEST IN NEWSPAPER DESIGN GLOBE WINNERS » A SELECTION

1. Front pages from the weekday and weekend editions of The Globe submitted in the Overall Newspaper Redesign category.
2. Report on Business pages that were recognized in the Section News Design category.
3. Folios that exhibit not only the depth of The Globe's content but the range of its news design, acknowledged in the Single Page News Design category: Award winners included a piece on outgoing Newfoundland premier Danny Williams, the architecture of ice fishing huts, and the stories behind the medals of three Canadian veterans.

PROUDLY PRINT

New-look Globe wins top redesign award

Vancouver Olympics coverage, Report on Business and Folio also singled out for honours

The Globe's new look has earned international distinction from the Society for News Design just months after the newspaper launched a massive redesign.

The Globe received the award of excellence for its 2010 redesign as part of the 32nd Edition Best of News Design Creative Competition, and was the only paper to win for a revamp of the entire publication, as opposed to individual pages or sections.

"We called the redesign 'Proudly Print.' We are a digital leader, but we're not shy about putting out one of the world's great newspapers," said Globe editor-in-chief John Stackhouse. "Design matters more than ever. We all have countless things fighting for our attention and the ability to use design effectively – to make readers stop and take notice – is essential to journalism in an increasingly crowded space"

The awards also honoured one of the new Globe's products: the Folio pages, which are meant to be a showcase for design and photography that enhance the stories printed there. Three features won awards in the competition.

The Report on Business won an award of excellence in news section design, a feat for a visually challenging part of the newspaper. "Business sections are not about flash or visual spice – although you'll find those in the ROB," Mr. Stackhouse said. "What's really satisfying is that the judges recognized the importance of compact design and efficiency, because there is so much information. It needs to capture the right tone."

Finally, the paper's coverage of the Vancouver Olympics won an award of excellence for special coverage in multiple sections.

"Although these awards were earned by all of our staff, they are really owned by our readers – they drive and inspire us for excellence everyday. This is just the start," said Adrian Norris, The Globe's managing editor of design and presentation.

Permission granted by *The Globe and Mail*

of blue diminishes for readers over 50.[14] Since the connotations of colours vary among cultures, check ⏩ Chapter 5 before you use colour with international or multicultural audiences.

When you use colour,

- Use glossy paper to make colours more vivid.
- Be aware that colours on a computer screen always look brighter than the same colours on paper because the screen sends out light.

DECIDING WHEN TO USE VISUALS

If the Information Age has proliferated sources of information, it has also produced added incentives—and aids—for readers eager to see what information means for them. We will focus here on how visuals can make numbers meaningful and messages memorable by replacing the proverbial 1,000 words (see ⏩ Chapter 12 for visuals in oral presentations).

The 2005 Make Poverty History campaign, for instance, used powerful visual effects to get across its message. From

Figure 4.7 Put Important Elements in the Top Left and Bottom Right Quadrants

Eye movement on the page

Start

Stop

Orange quadrants are most important

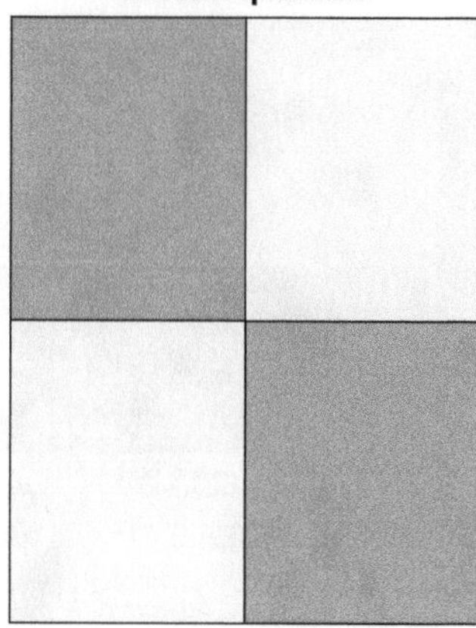

Source: Based on Russel N. Baird, Arthur T. Turnbull, and Duncan McDonald, *The Graphics of Communication: Typography, Layout, Design, Production,* 5th ed. (New York: Holt, Rinehart, and Winston, 1987), 37.

the white wristbands and shoelaces to the white bands wrapped around world landmarks on July 1, 2005, or the Live 8 concert attracting 1 million spectators and 2 billion viewers around the world, the campaign used visual displays to reinforce messages about the 30,000 children who die every day as a result of extreme poverty.

A series of short videos make powerful statements: Bono snapping his fingers in *Make History 2005,* or celebrities in *Click* snapping their fingers to register someone dying from extreme poverty every three seconds. All urged us to make poverty history one by one. In 2008 the campaign continued with member organizations around the world and was adopted in Canada by First Nations intent on making poverty history for their peoples.[15]

The ease of creating visuals by computer may make people use them uncritically. Even though research tells us that 65% of us are visual learners, use a visual only to achieve a specific purpose. Never put in numbers or visuals just because you have them; instead, use them to convey information the audience needs or wants, minimizing "meaningless elements, both in text and pictures."[16]

In your rough draft, use visuals

- **To see that ideas are presented completely.** A table, for example, can show you whether you've included all the items in a comparison.
- **To find relationships.** For example, charting sales on a map may show that the sales representatives who made quota all have territories on the East or the West Coast. Is the product one that appeals to coastal lifestyles? Is advertising reaching the coasts but not the Prairies, Ontario, or Quebec? Even if you don't use the visual in your final document, creating the map may lead you to questions you wouldn't otherwise ask.

In the final presentation or document, use visuals

- **To make points vivid.** Readers skim memos, reports, and Web pages; a visual catches the eye. The brain processes

Figure 4.8 Examples of Grids to Design Pages

A page with visuals

NEWS

Three-column grid.

A newsletter page

Six-column grid.

A résumé page

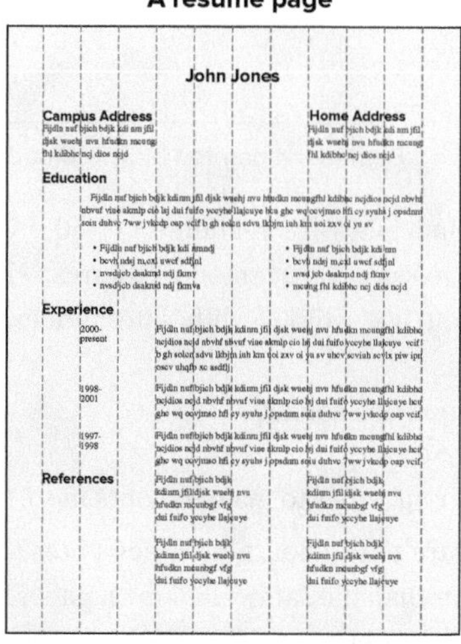

Twelve-column grid.

visuals immediately. Understanding words—written or oral—takes more time.

- **To emphasize material that might be skipped if it were buried in a paragraph.** The beginning and end are places of emphasis. Visuals allow you to emphasize important material, wherever it logically falls.
- **To present material more compactly and with less repetition than words alone would require.** Words can call attention to the main points of the visual, without repeating all of the visual's information.

The number of visuals you will need depends on your purposes, the kind of information, and the audience. You'll use more visuals when you want to show relationships and to persuade, when the information is complex or contains extensive numerical data, and when the audience values visuals.

LO3

DESIGNING VISUALS

Use the following six steps to create good visuals.

1. Check the Source of the Data

Your chart is only as good as the underlying data. Check to be sure that your data come from a reliable source.

2. Determine the Story You Want to Tell

Every visual should tell a story. Stories can be expressed in complete sentences that describe something that happens or changes. The sentence also serves as the title of the visual:

× NOT A STORY

Canadian Sales, 2009–2014

✓ POSSIBLE STORIES

Forty Percent of Our Sales Were to New Customers

Growth Was Highest in Quebec

Sales Increased from 2009 to 2014

Sales Were Highest in the Areas with More Sales Representatives

Stories that tell us what we already know are rarely interesting. Instead, good stories may

- Support a hunch you have
- Surprise you or challenge so-called common knowledge
- Show trends or changes you didn't know existed
- Have commercial or social significance
- Provide information needed for action
- Contain personal relevance for you and the audience

To find stories,

1. **Focus on a topic** (purchases of cars, who likes jazz, etc.)
2. **Simplify the data** on that topic and convert the numbers to simple, easy-to-understand units
3. **Look for relationships and changes.** For example, compare two or more groups: do men and women have the same attitudes? Look for changes over time. Look for items that can be seen as part of the same group. For example, to find stories about entertainers' incomes, you might compare the number of writers, actors, and musicians in three rankings.
4. **Process the data** to find more stories. Calculate the percentage change from one year to the next.

When you think you have a story, test it against all the data to be sure it's accurate.

Some stories are simple straight lines: "Sales Increased." But other stories are more complex, with exceptions or outlying cases. Such stories will need more nuanced titles to do justice to the story. Figure 4.9 tells a predictable story about

Figure 4.9 Alberta GPI Environmental Sustainability Index Compared with GDP Growth, 1961–1999

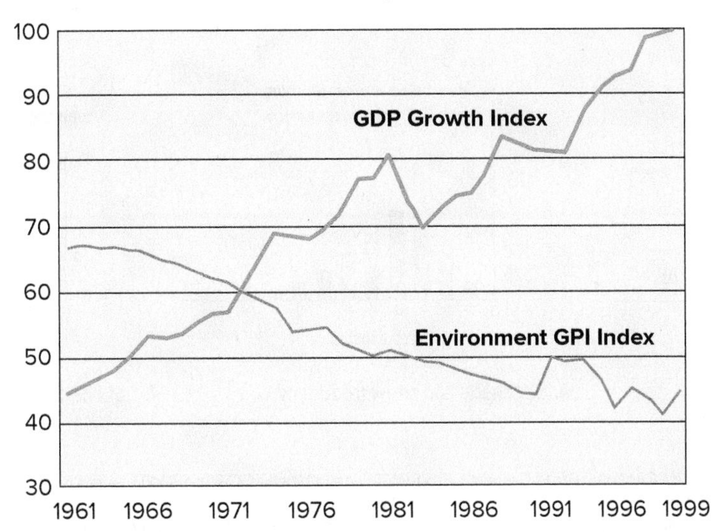

Source: The Alberta GPI Accounts 1961–1999; rptd. from Mark Anielski & Mark Winfield, "A Conceptual Framework for Monitoring Municipal and Community Sustainability in Canada." Report prepared by the Pembina Institute for Environment Canada, June 17, 2002.

growth in Alberta together with a powerful message about its unsustainability—a prediction leading to some tough decisions in Alberta's 2014 budget.[17]

Almost every data set allows you to tell several stories. You must choose the story you want to tell. Dumps of uninterpreted data confuse and frustrate your audience; they undercut the credibility and goodwill you want to create.

3. Choose the Right Visual for the Story

Visuals are not interchangeable. Good writers choose the visual that best matches the purpose of presenting the data:

- Use a table when the reader needs to be able to identify exact values. (See Figure 4.10a.)
- Use a chart or graph when you want the reader to focus on relationships.[18]
- To compare a part to the whole, use a **pie chart.** (See Figure 4.10b.)
- To compare one item to another item, use a map or a **bar chart.** (See Figure 4.10c.)
- To compare items over time, use a bar chart or a **line graph.** (See Figure 4.10d.)
- To show frequency or distribution, use a line graph or bar chart. (See Figure 4.10e.)
- To show correlations, use a bar chart, a line graph, or a **dot chart.** (See Figure 4.10f.)
- Use **infographics** to show complex data in visual form. (See Figure 4.11.)
- Use photographs to create a sense of authenticity or show the item in use. If the item is especially big or small, include something in the photograph that can serve as a reference point: a dime, a person.
- Use drawings to show dimensions or emphasize detail.
- Use maps to emphasize location.

4. Follow the Conventions for Designing Typical Visuals

Every visual should contain six components:

1. A title that tells the story that the visual shows
2. A clear indication of what the data are. For example, what people *say* they did is not necessarily what they really did. An estimate of what a number will be in the future differs from numbers that have already been measured.
3. Clearly labelled units
4. Labels or legends identifying axes, colours, and symbols

Figure 4.10 Choose the Visual to Fit the Story

Canadian sales reach $44.5 million.

	Millions of dollars		
	2000	2005	2010
Atlantic	10.2	10.8	11.3
Southern Ontario	7.6	8.5	10.4
Quebec	8.3	6.8	9.3
Prairies	11.3	12.1	13.5
Totals	37.4	38.2	44.5

a. Tables show exact values.

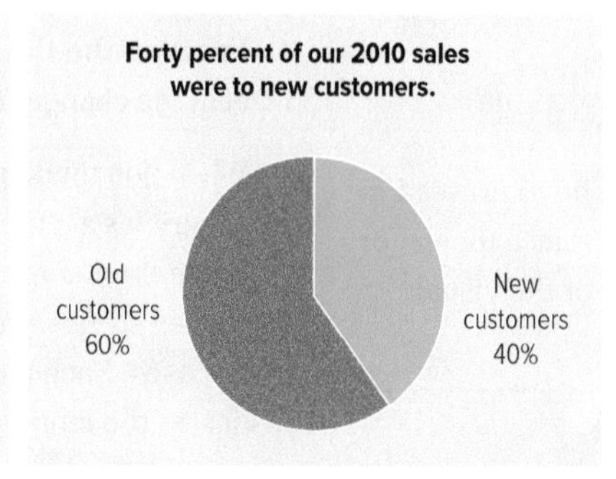

b. Pie charts compare a component to the whole.

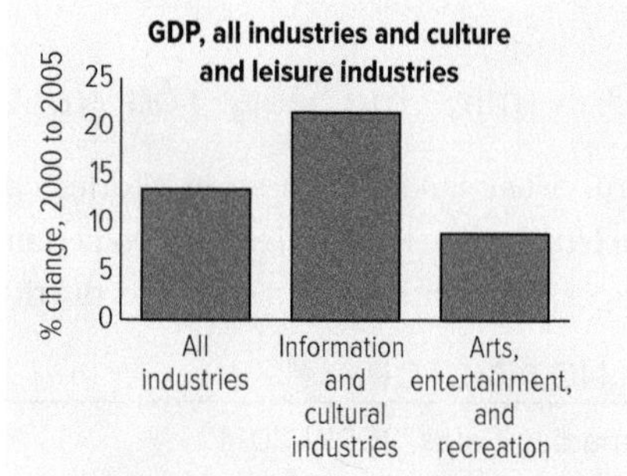

c. Bar charts compare items or show distribution or correlation.

d. Line charts compare items over time or show distribution or correlation.

e. Bar charts can show frequency.

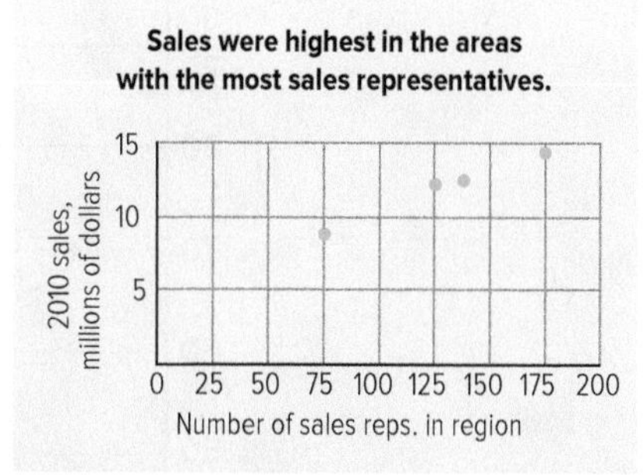

f. Dot charts show correlation.

Source: Figure 4.10c: Adapted from Statistics Canada, "Gross Domestic Product, All Industries and Culture and Leisure Industries," CANSIM table 379-0017, http://www41.statcan.ca/2007/3955/ceb3955_000-eng.htm, retrieved Apr. 15, 2014. This does not constitute an endorsement by Statistics Canada of this product. Figure 4.10d: Adapted from Statistics Canada, "Trade in Culture Goods with the United States," Catalogue no. 87-007-XIE, http://www41.statcan.ca/2007/3955/ceb3955_002-eng.htm, retrieved Apr. 15, 2014. This does not constitute an endorsement by Statistics Canada of this product.

Figure 4.11 Canadian Internet Use Survey Infographic

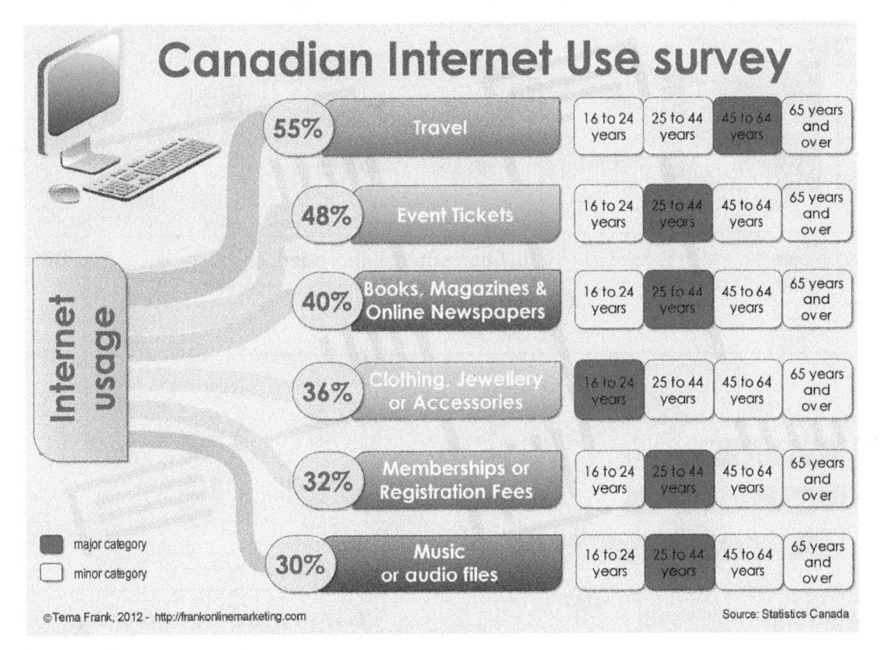

Source: Tema Frank, Web Mystery Shoppers Inc. & Frank Online Marketing, http://temafrank.com.

5. The source of the data, if you created the visual from data someone else gathered and compiled
6. The source of the visual, if you reproduce a visual someone else created

Formal visuals are divided into tables and figures (see ▸▸ "List of Illustrations" in Chapter 11).

Tables

Use tables only when you want the audience to focus on specific numbers. Graphs convey less specific information but are always more memorable.

- Round off to simplify the data (e.g., 35% rather than 35.27%; 44.5 million rather than 44,503,276).
- Provide column and row totals or averages when they're relevant.
- Put the items you want readers to compare in columns rather than in rows to facilitate mental subtraction and division.

Suppose you want to give investors information about various stocks' performance. Organizing the daily numbers into tables would be much more useful than paragraph after paragraph of statements. Tables of stock prices have been the norm until recently. Now, on the Internet, SmartMoney.com offers subscribers Market Map 1000, a graphics tool that helps them see the top performers. Each company is shown as a rectangle, and companies are clustered into industry groups. Users can click on industry groups for a more detailed view.[19]

Pie Charts

Pie charts help the audience to measure area. Research shows that people can judge position or length (which a bar chart uses) much more accurately than they judge area. The data in any pie chart can be put in a bar chart.[20] Therefore, use a pie chart only when you are comparing one segment to the whole. When you are comparing one segment to another segment, use a bar chart, a line graph, or a map—even though the data may be expressed in percentages.

- Make the chart a perfect circle. Perspective circles distort the data.
- Limit the number of segments to no more than seven. If your data have more divisions, combine the smallest or the least important into a single "miscellaneous" or "other" category.
- Label the segments outside the circle. Internal labels are hard to read.

Bar Charts

Bar charts (Figure 4.12) are easy to interpret because they ask people to compare distance along a common scale, which most people judge accurately. Bar charts are useful in a variety of situations: to compare one item to another, to compare items over time, and to show correlations. Use horizontal bars when your labels are long; when the labels are short, either horizontal or vertical bars will work.

- Order the bars in a logical or chronological order.
- Put the bars close enough together to make comparison easy.
- Label both horizontal and vertical axes.
- Put all labels inside the bars or outside them. When some labels are inside and some are outside, the labels carry the visual weight of longer bars, distorting the data.
- Make all the bars the same width.

Figure 4.12 Varieties of Bar Charts

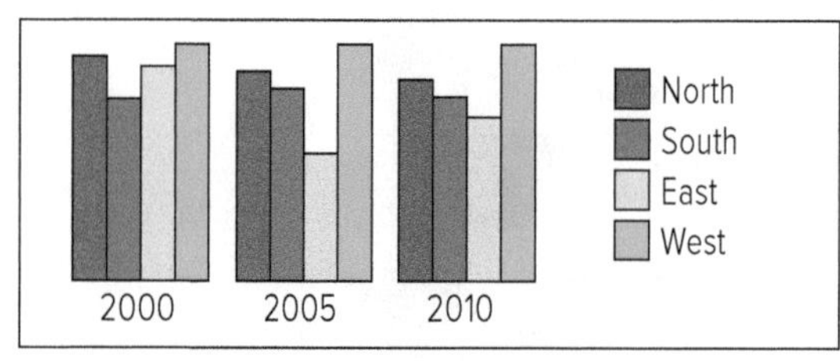

a. Grouped bar charts compare several aspects of each item, or several items over time.

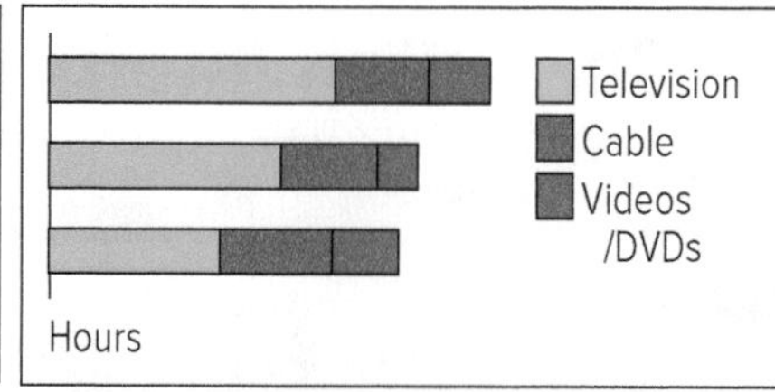

b. Segmented, subdivided, or **stacked bars** sum the components of an item.

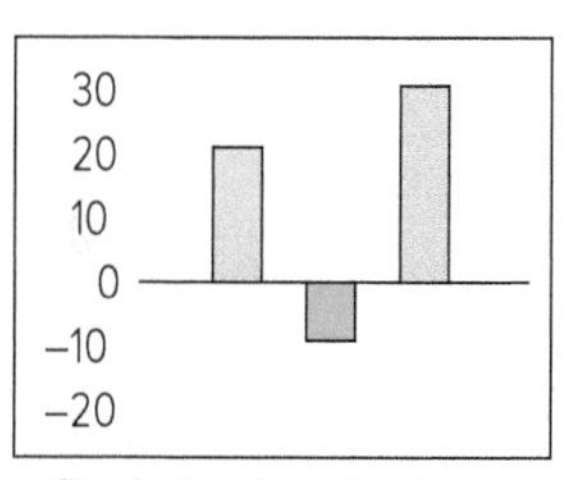

c. Deviation bar charts identify positive and negative values.

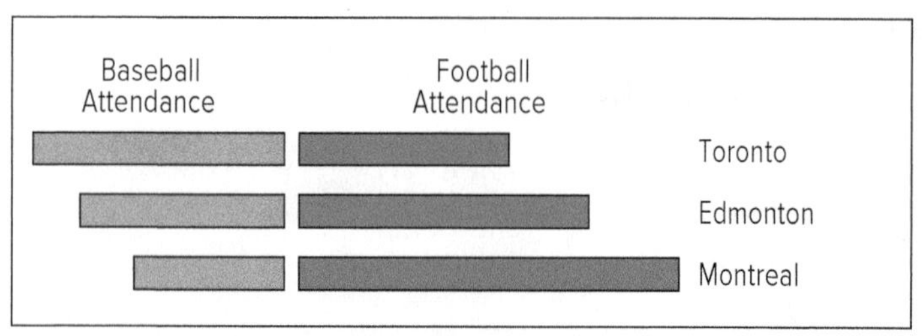

d. Paired bar charts show the correlation between two items.

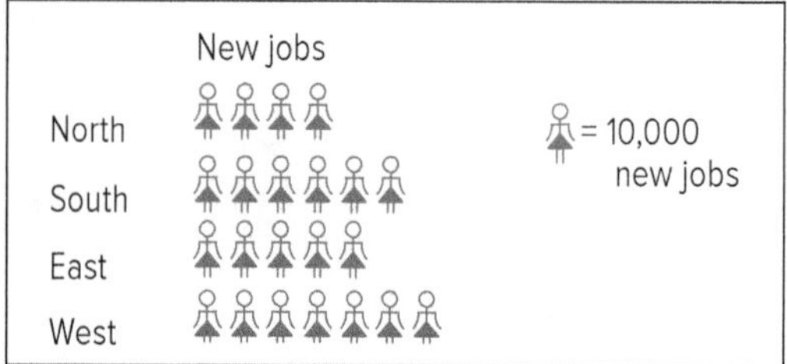

e. Histograms or **pictograms** use images to create the bars.

- Use different colours for different bars only when their meanings are different: estimates as opposed to known numbers, negative as opposed to positive numbers.
- Avoid using perspective. Perspective makes the values harder to read and can make comparison difficult.
- **Grouped bar charts** allow you to compare either several aspects of each item or several items over time. Group together the items you want to compare.
- **Segmented, subdivided,** or **stacked bars** sum the components of an item. It's hard to identify the values in specific segments; grouped bar charts are almost always easier to use.
- **Deviation bar charts** identify positive and negative values, or winners and losers.
- **Paired bar charts** show the correlation between two items.
- **Histograms** or **pictograms** use images to create the bars.

Line Graphs

Line graphs are also easy to interpret. Use line graphs to compare items over time, to show frequency or distribution, and to show correlations.

- Label both horizontal and vertical axes.
- When time is a variable, put it on the horizontal axis.
- Avoid using more than three different lines on one graph. Even three lines may be too many if they cross each other.
- Avoid using perspective. Perspective makes the values harder to read and can make comparison difficult.

Dot Charts

Dot charts show correlations or other large data sets.

- Label both horizontal and vertical axes.
- Keep the dots fairly small. If they get too big, they no longer mark data "points"; some of the detail is lost.

Photographs

Photographs convey a sense of authenticity. The photo of a prototype helps convince investors that a product can be manufactured; the photo of a devastated area can suggest the need for government grants or private donations.

You may need to **crop**, or trim, a photo for best results.

A growing problem with photos is that they may be edited or staged, purporting to show something as reality even though it never occurred. Still, it is important to remember that photos have never been as objective as many took them to be; all photos involve human decisions about what to include and exclude.[21]

Drawings

With a drawing, the artist can provide as much or as little detail as is needed to make the point; different parts of the drawing can show different layers or levels of detail. Drawings are also useful for showing structures underground, undersea, or in the atmosphere.

Maps

Use maps to emphasize location or to compare items in different locations. Several computer software packages now allow users to generate municipal, provincial, national, or global maps, adding colour or shadings, and labels. Google Earth has added to our navigational toolkit.

- Label cities, provinces, or countries if it's important that people be able to identify levels in areas other than their own.

- Avoid using perspective. Perspective makes the values harder to read and can make comparison difficult.

5. Use Colour and Decoration with Restraint

Colour makes visuals more dramatic, but it creates at least two problems. First, readers try to interpret colour, an interpretation that may not be appropriate. (Perhaps the best use of colour occurs in the weather maps printed daily in many newspapers. Blue seems to fit cold; red seems to fit hot temperatures.) Second, meanings assigned to colours differ depending on the audience's national background and profession (see ▸▸Chapter 5).

These general cultural associations may be superseded by corporate, national, or professional associations. Some people associate blue with IBM or Hewlett-Packard and red with Coca-Cola, communism, or Japan. People in specific professions learn other meanings for colours. Blue suggests *reliability* to financial managers, *water* or *coldness* to engineers, and *death* to health care professionals. Red means *losing money* to financial managers, *danger* to engineers, but *healthy* to health care professionals. Green usually means *safe* to engineers, but *infected* to health care professionals.[22]

Resist the temptation to make your visual "artistic" or "relevant" by turning it into a picture or adding clip art. **Clip art** consists of predrawn images that you can import into your newsletter, sign, or graph. A small drawing of a car in the corner of a line graph showing the number of kilometres driven is acceptable in an oral presentation but out of place in a written report. Edward Tufte uses the term **chartjunk** for decorations that at best are irrelevant to the visual and at worst mislead the reader.[23] If you use clip art, be sure that the images of people show a good mix of both sexes, various races and ages, and various physical conditions.

6. Be Sure the Visual Is Accurate and Ethical

Always double-check your visuals to be sure the information is accurate; many visuals have accurate labels but misleading visual shapes. Visuals communicate quickly; audiences remember the shape, not the labels. Resource-sharing sites such as Creative Commons Canada and Flickr are important open sources that allow ethical uses of images based on a community-centred framework and commitment to collaboration as innovation. If the reader has to study the labels to get the right picture, the visual is unethical even if the labels are accurate.

For ethical use of photographs, award-winning photographer Suzanne Salvo recommends checking the following:

- Source of the photo
- Context of the photo
- Whether and how it has been manipulated
- Copyright constraints on alterations
- Possible audience interpretation of altered images[24]

Two-dimensional figures distort data by multiplying the apparent value by the width as well as by the height—four times for every doubling in value. Perspective graphs are especially hard for readers to interpret and should be avoided.[25]

Even simple bar and line graphs may be misleading if part of the scale is missing or truncated. **Truncated graphs** are most acceptable when the audience knows the basic data set well. For example, graphs of the stock market almost never start at zero; they are routinely truncated. This omission is acceptable for audiences who follow the market closely.

To make your visuals more accurate,

- Differentiate between actual and estimated or projected values
- When you must truncate a scale, do so clearly with a break in the bars or in the background
- Avoid perspective and three-dimensional graphs
- Avoid combining graphs with different scales
- Use images of people carefully in histographs to avoid sexist, racist, or other exclusionary visual statements

INTEGRATING VISUALS

Refer to every visual in your text. Normally one gives the table or figure number in the text but not the title. Put the visual as soon after your reference as space and page design permit. If the visual will not be immediately obvious to the reader, provide a page reference:

As Figure 3 shows (page 10), . . .

(See Table 2 on page 14.)

Summarize the main point of a visual *before* you present the visual itself. Then when readers get to it, they'll see it as confirmation of your point.

✗ Weak: Listed below are the results

✓ Better: As Figure 4 shows, sales doubled in the last decade

Visuals for presentations need to be simpler than visuals the audience reads on paper. You may want to cut out one of the columns, round off the data even more, or present the material in a chart rather than a table.

Visuals for presentations should have titles but don't need figure numbers. Do know where each visual is so that you can return to one if someone asks about it during the question period.

Rather than reading the visual to the audience, summarize the story and then elaborate on what it means for the audience. If you have copies of all the visuals for your audience, hand them out at the beginning of the talk.

LO4

DESIGNING WEB SITES

The Nielsen Norman advice on home page design—the source of first and lasting impressions—is to "treat it like the front page of a major newspaper." The content depends on user needs and tasks as well as business or organizational goals. At a glance, it needs to communicate memorably and distinctly:

- Where users are (company name and logo; link to About Us and Contact Us)
- What the company does (tag line)
- What users can do on the site (1–4 tasks)[26]

Donald Norman insists that design is "a social activity," not just a technical one, so the social impact should be front and centre.[27] ISL Web designers (see ◀◀ An Inside Perspective) similarly focus on people, conversations, creativity, and "sound business strategy." They build Web sites for clients' customers, because "in a crowded web environment if their experience is bad, they won't return." User-centric Web sites like the Maritime Inns and Resorts site (see ▶▶ Figure 4.16 later in this chapter) have these benefits, according to ISL:

- Drive more qualified traffic to your Web site and increase awareness
- Increase purchases, leads, referrals, and word of mouth
- Reduce support costs[28]

The story you want to tell remains as important on the Web as in any other medium. If the Web has made us "content snackers," there is another important fact of the Web: it is a "link economy." Every story requires "a beginning, a middle and a hyperlink." Communications consultant Angelo Fernando argues that we need to be less "content machines" than "link machines." Hyperlinks connect your story to those of others, to broader networks and to fuller contexts. Newspapers such as *The New York Times* and *The Washington Post* and magazines such as *Esquire* are experimenting with Web delivery of news, organizing dynamic pages with the latest developments on stories and incorporating voice and cuts from albums in music reviews, for example.[29]

Standards continue to evolve for online documents. Open Source Web Design (www.oswd.org) offers Web design templates that you can build on and share. To see what *not* to do, check out some of the worst Web sites around at www.webpagesthatsuck.com.

LO5

DESIGNING PRESENTATION SLIDES

As you design slides for PowerPoint and other presentation programs such as Prezi, keep the following guidelines in mind (see also ▶▶ Chapter 12). For large rooms you may need to increase the font sizes recommended here:

- Use a big font size: 44 or 50 point for titles, 32 point for subheads, and 28 point for examples.
- Use bullet-point phrases rather than complete sentences (see Figure 4.13).

Figure 4.13 Presentation Slide Putting Principles into Practice

Why Design Matters

- Looks inviting and easy to read
- Saves time and money
- Reduces legal liabilities
- Builds goodwill

- Use clear, concise language.
- Make only three to five points on each slide. If you have more, consider using two slides.
- Customize your slides with the company logo, charts, downloaded Web pages, podcasts, and scanned-in photos and drawings.
- Use animation to make words and images appear and move during your presentation—but only in ways that help you control information flow and build interest. Avoid using animation just to be clever; it will distract your audience.

Use clip art only if the art is really appropriate to your points and only if you use non-sexist and non-racist images. Marilyn Dyrud has found the major clip art packages to be biased. Today, however, Internet sources have made such a wide variety of drawings and photos available that designers really have no excuse for failing to pick an inclusive and visually appealing image. Even organizations on tight budgets can find free public domain (not copyrighted) and low-cost resources.[30]

Choose a consistent template, or background design, for the entire presentation. Make sure that the template is appropriate for your subject matter. For example, use a globe only if your topic is international business and palm trees only if you're talking about tropical vacations. One problem with PowerPoint is that the basic templates may seem repetitive to people who see lots of presentations made with the program. For a very important presentation, you may want to consider customizing the basic template.

Choose a light background if the lights will be off during the presentation and a dark background if the lights will be on. Slides will be easier to read if you use high contrast between the words and backgrounds. See Figure 4.14 for examples of effective and ineffective colour combinations.

DESIGNING BROCHURES

Walk into any bank, municipal office, hospital, or political campaign office and you will find brochures. Brochures remain efficient and cost-effective channels for many in the

Figure 4.14 Effective and Ineffective Colours for Presentation Slides

Effective

Use high contrast between words and background.

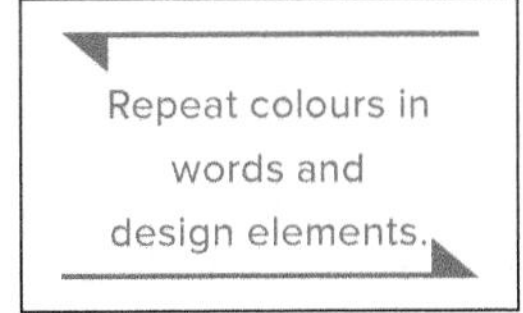

Ineffective

Limit the number of bright colours.

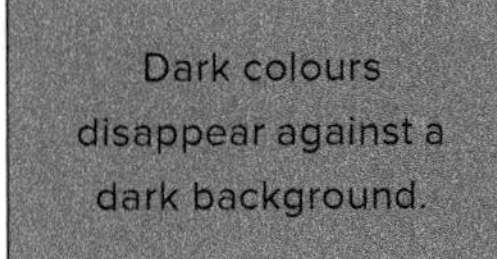

Light colours disappear against a light background.

business, non-profit, and government sectors. They remain as useful for those in tourism and hospitality as for banking, health, and education—all of which need to accommodate the needs of diverse audiences. To design brochures and newsletters, first think about purpose and audience. An "image" brochure designed to promote awareness of your company will have a different look than an "information" brochure telling people how to do something and persuading them to do it.

Use this process to create effective brochures.

1. Determine your objective(s).
2. Identify your target audience(s).
3. Identify a *central selling point:* one overarching reader benefit the audience will get (▸▸ Chapter 9).
4. Choose the image you want to project. (Clean and clear? Trendy? Or what?)
5. Identify objections and brainstorm ways to deal with them (▸▸ Chapter 9).
6. When text is important, draft text to see how much room you need. Do tighten your writing (◂◂ Chapter 3). But when you really need more room, use a bigger brochure layout or a series of brochures.
7. Experiment with different sizes of paper and layout. Consider how readers will get the brochure—must it fit in a standard rack? Use thumbnail sketches to test layouts.
8. Make every choice—colour, font, layout, paper—a conscious one. The three-fold brochure shown in Figure 4.15

On the Job Say It with Colour*

Research tells us that colour can be a powerful ally when you are trying to engage, inform, or persuade your audience. Saying it with colour has these results:

- Increases brand recognition by up to 80%
- Improves readership by 40%
- Speeds up learning from 55 to 78%
- Enhances comprehension by 73%
- Increases engagement by 42% (colour rather than black and white ads)

Consultant G. Michael Campbell finds colour is a useful tool for coding information and affecting the reader's reaction. Here are some of his ideas for using colour:

- Identify ideas according to common associations with colour—red for stop or danger, green for go or money.
- Match colours to the moods they tend to evoke. Red demands attention (but is easy to overuse); yellow is cheery. Blue and green tend to have a calming effect.
- Avoid colour combinations that would confuse people who are colourblind. About 10 percent of men and 0.5 percent of women cannot distinguish between red and green.

Toronto's Strategic Objectives created buzz with a redesigned fashion show sponsored by Cashmere bath tissue in support of the Canadian Breast Cancer Foundation (CBCF). When it became clear that Cashmere's support of CBCF was not registering, a limited edition of Pink Cashmere (25 cents per sale going to CBCF) became the focus of the "A Touch of Pink" fashion show with pink tissue accessories. Professional photos and social media tactics added to the success: 97.3 million impressions in Eastern Canada, 61 media reports, 22,400 visits to the Cashmere Web site, and $35,000 to CBCF.

*Based on "Color printing center—Tips for color use," Hewlett-Packard Public Sector Web, retrieved March 9, 2011, from http://www.hp.com/sbso/productivity/color/use/tips.html; G. Michael Campbell, *Bulletproof Presentations* (Franklin Lakes, NJ: Career Press, 2002), 190–193; Linda Mastaglio, Robert Brown, and Steve Freeman, "Above the fold," *Communication World*, January-February 2010, 18–19.

Figure 4.15 Three-Fold Brochure on 8½-by-11-inch (22 × 28 cm) Paper

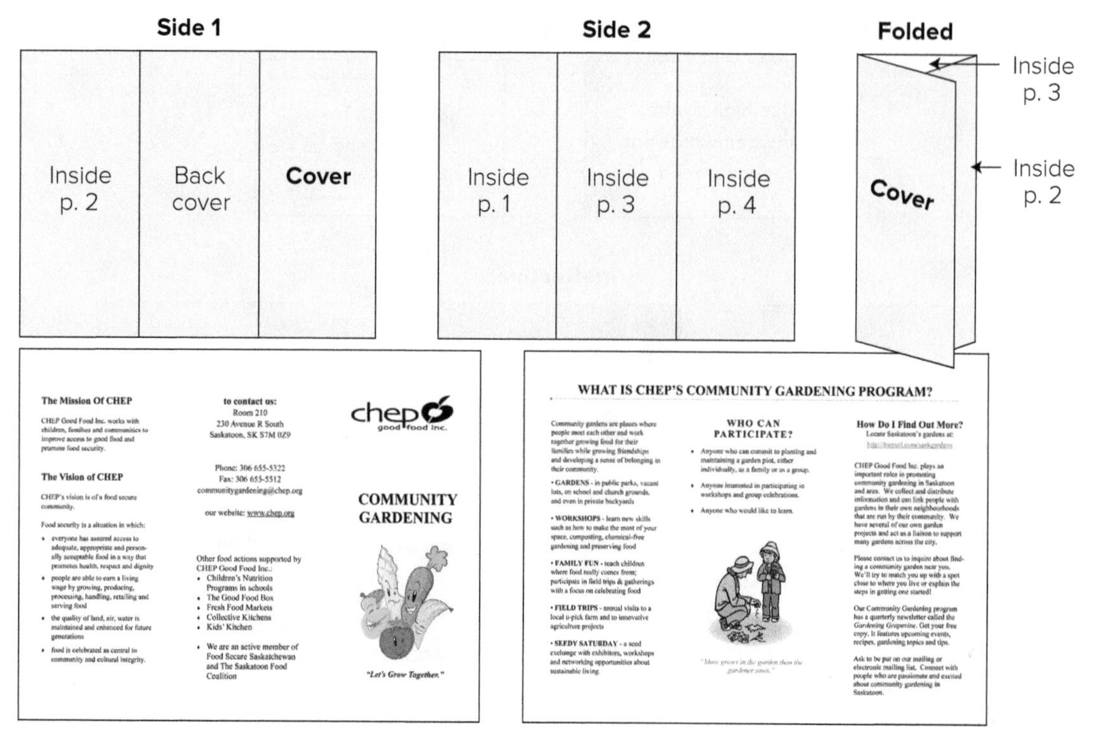

Source: Used with the permission of CHEP Good Food Inc.

is the most common, but many other arrangements are possible.

9. Polish the prose and graphics. Use you-attitude and positive emphasis.

Follow these design principles:

- Use the cover effectively.
  - Put your central selling point on the cover.
  - Use a photo that tells a story—and works for the audience. A photo of a campus landmark may not mean much to an audience thinking about attending a summer program on campus. Know that what people want to see in photos are people (dogs are a close second).[31]
- Use a grid to align the elements within the panels. Make sure that the Z pattern emphasizes important points for each spread the reader sees. In a three-fold brochure, the Z pattern needs to work for the cover alone, for inside pages 1 and 2, and for inside pages 1, 3, and 4 (when the brochure is fully opened).
- Effective brochures not only repeat graphic elements (headings, small photos) across panels to create a unified look but also contain contrast (between text and images, and between a larger font for headings and a smaller one for text).

Technology Tips Making Your Web Page Accessible

Users with hearing impairments need captions for audio material on the Web.

Blind users need words, not images. Words can be voiced by a screen reader or translated into Braille text. Canadian screen reader programs go from left to right, then down line by line. Keystrokes can let users skip to a specific letter in a list. To make your Web page accessible for people with vision impairments,

- Put a link to a text-only version of the site in the upper-left-hand corner.
- Put navigation links, a site map, and search box at the top of the screen, preferably in the upper-left-hand corner.
- Arrange navigation links alphabetically so that blind users can jump to the links they want.
- Provide alternative text (an "Alt tag") for all images, applets, and submit buttons.
- Provide a static alternative to flash or animation.

Technology Tips Well-Designed Web Sites Keep Customers*

Imagine going to a supermarket where 75% of the customers abandon their carts half full in the aisles because they are so frustrated they decide to shop somewhere else. It would be a lot like shopping online.

In a recent poll, almost half the online retailers said they don't know what percentage of their customers abandon shopping carts. Among the rest, 87% reported abandonment rates above 20%. Because the Internet makes it easy for shoppers to go to other sites, Jakob Nielsen says, "People don't have to use bad sites."

What keeps online shoppers happy? Other polls ask customers what they look for when they shop on the Internet. Recent answers indicate they want pages that load quickly and make it easy to find what they want. They like basics such as search tools and clear labels. Few online shoppers care about bells and whistles like personalized recommendations.

*Based on Robyn Greenspan, "E-commerce mainstream, measurements lacking," *ClickZ Internet Marketing Statistics*, April 9, 2004, downloaded at http://www.clickz.com; ClickZ Stats staff and Sharon Gaudin, "Personalization not the secret to e-commerce," *ClickZ Internet Marketing Statistics*, November 14, 2003, downloaded at http://www.clickz.com; David Neal, "Interview: Good design pays off," *IT Week*, May 19, 2003, downloaded at http://www.itweek.co.uk/articles/print/2086589; Reid Goldsborough, "Substance, not style, draws hits," *Philadelphia Inquirer*, May 20, 2004, downloaded at http://www.philly.com.

- Use colour effectively.
  - Restraint usually works best for informative brochures. To get the effect of colour with the least expense, use black print on coloured paper.
  - If you use four-colour printing, use glossy paper.
  - Readers over 50 may have trouble reading text in some shades of blue.
- Make the text visually appealing.
  - Use no more than two fonts—just one may be better.
  - Use proportional fonts.
  - Avoid italic type and underlining, which make text hard to read. To emphasize text, use bold (sparingly).
  - Most brochures use 8-, 9-, or 10-point type. Use 10-point rather than 8-point for readers over 40.
  - Use small tab indents.
  - Make sure that you have enough white space in your copy. Use lists and headings. Use short paragraphs with extra space between paragraphs.
- Ragged right margins generally work better with short line lengths.
- If you use a reply coupon, make sure its reverse side doesn't have crucial information the reader needs to keep.

To make the brochure worth keeping, provide useful information. Make the text candid, believable, and human.

LO6

TESTING THE DESIGN FOR USABILITY

A design that looks pretty may or may not work for the audience. To know whether your design is functional, test it with your audience.

Testing a draft with five users will reveal 85% of the problems with the document.[32] If time and money permit additional testing, revise the document and test the new version with another five users. Test the document with the people who are most likely to have trouble with it: very old or young readers, people with little education, people who read English as a second language.

Three tests yield useful information:

- Watch someone as he or she uses the document to do a task. Where does the reader pause, reread, or seem confused? How long does it take? Does the document enable the reader to complete the task accurately?
- Ask the reader to "think aloud" while completing the task, interrupt the reader at key points to ask what he or she is thinking, or ask the reader to describe the thought process after completing the document and the task. Learning the reader's thought processes is important, since a reader may get the right answer for the wrong reasons. In such a case, the design still needs work.
- Ask readers to put a plus sign (+) in the margins by any part of the document they like or agree with, and a minus sign (−) by any part of the document that seems confusing or wrong. Then use interviews or focus groups to find out the reasons for the plus and minus judgments.

Faced with heightened customer expectations, Maritime Inns and Resorts commissioned a new website (Figure 4.16) to enhance usability and to communicate the comfort that is the hallmark of the Maritime resort experience. ISL (see ◀◀ An Inside Perspective) optimized the search engine for "find-ability," linked the online reservation system, developed an Internet marketing strategy, and integrated design and photography in building atmosphere.[33]

Figure 4.16 Maritime Inns and Resorts

Source: Used with the permission of the Maritime Inns and Resorts.

SUMMARY OF KEY POINTS

- An attractive document looks inviting, friendly, and easy to read. The visual grouping of ideas also makes the structure of the document more obvious so it is easier to read.
- Good document design can save time and money, prevent legal liabilities, and build goodwill.
- Eight guidelines help writers create visually attractive documents:
  1. Use white space.
  2. Use headings.
  3. Limit the use of words set in all capital letters.
  4. Use no more than two fonts in a single document.
  5. Use ragged right margins for business communications.
  6. Put important elements in the top left and lower right quadrants.
  7. Use a grid to unify visuals and other graphic elements.
  8. Use highlighting, decorative devices, and colour in moderation.
- Follow these six steps to create good visuals:
  1. Check the source of the data.
  2. Determine the story you want to tell.
  3. Choose the right visual for the story.
  4. Follow the conventions for designing typical visuals.
  5. Use colour and decoration with restraint.
  6. Be sure the visual is accurate and ethical.
- Good Web site design is user-centred.
  - Content depends on user needs and tasks as well as business goals.
  - The story you want to tell is as important on the Web as in any other media.
  - Hyperlinks connect your story to others and give fuller contexts.
- As you design slides for PowerPoint and other presentation programs,
  - Use a big font.
  - Use bullet-point phrases.
  - Make only three to five points on each slide.
  - Customize your slides.
- To test a document, observe readers, ask them to “think aloud” while completing the task, interrupt them at key points to ask what they are thinking, or ask them to describe the thought process after completing the document and the task.

EXERCISES AND PROBLEMS

GETTING STARTED

4.1 EVALUATING PAGE DESIGNS

In pairs or groups, use the guidelines in this chapter to evaluate each of the following page designs. Do they use white space, headings, and fonts appropriately? How well do they use the quadrants and grid of columns? How well are visuals integrated? What are their strong points? What could be improved?

As Your Professor Directs,

a. Present your findings to the class.

b. Write an e-mail to your professor on your findings.

c. Design a prototype implementing your findings.

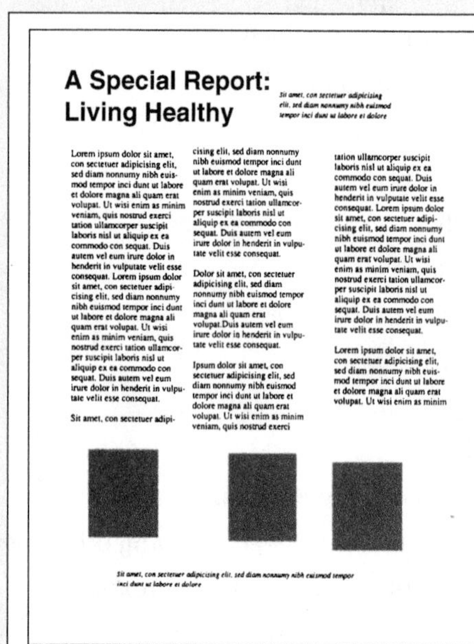

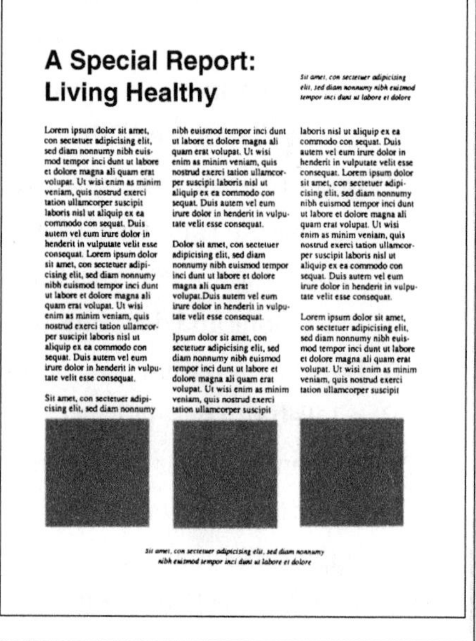

4.2 EVALUATING POWERPOINT SLIDES

Evaluate the following drafts of PowerPoint slides.

- Are the slides' backgrounds appropriate for the topic?
- Do the slides use words or phrases rather than complete sentences?
- Is the font big enough to read from a distance?
- Is the art relevant and appropriate?
- Is each slide free from errors?

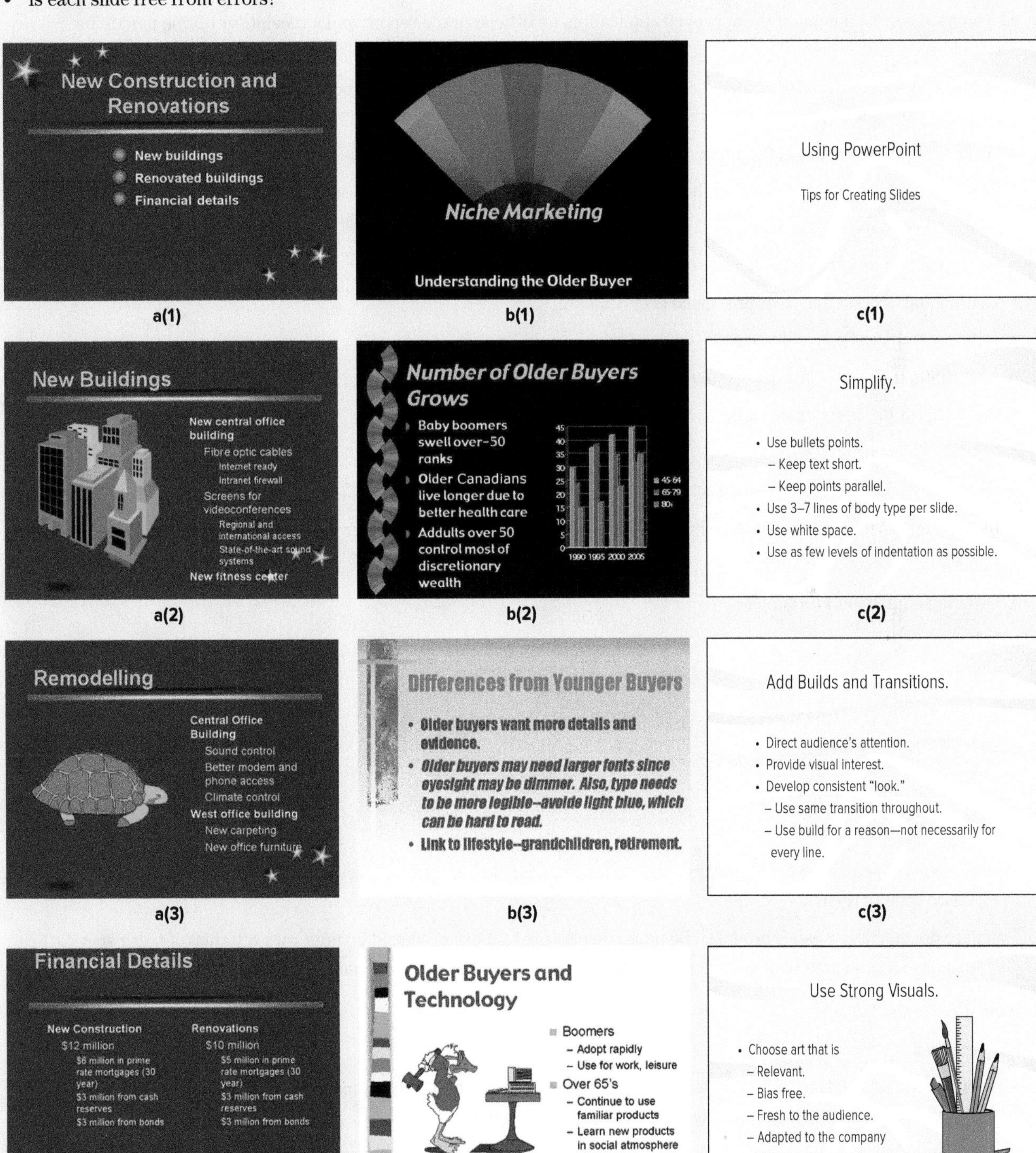

4.3 USING HEADINGS

Reorganize the items in each of the following lists, using appropriate headings. Use bulleted or numbered lists as appropriate. As your professor directs, peer grade answers.

a. Rules and Procedures for a Tuition Reimbursement Plan

1. You are eligible to be reimbursed if you have been a full-time employee for at least three months.
2. You must apply before the first class meeting.
3. You must earn a "C" or better in the course.
4. You must submit a copy of the approved application, an official grade report, and a receipt for tuition paid to be reimbursed.
5. You can be reimbursed for courses related to your current position or another position in the company, or for courses that are part of a degree related to a current or possible job.
6. Your supervisor must sign the application form.
7. Courses may be at any appropriate level (high school, college, or graduate school).

b. Activities in Starting a New Business

- Getting a loan or venture capital
- Getting any necessary city or provincial licences
- Determining what you will make, do, or sell
- Identifying the market for your products or services
- Pricing your products or services
- Choosing a location
- Checking zoning laws that may affect the location
- Identifying government and university programs for small business development
- Figuring cash flow
- Ordering equipment and supplies
- Selling
- Advertising and marketing

COMMUNICATING AT WORK

4.4 ANALYZING DOCUMENTS AT WORK

1. Collect several documents: letters and memos, newsletters, ads and flyers, and reports. Use the guidelines in this chapter to evaluate each of them.
2. Compare documents or pages produced by your competitors to those produced by your own organization in a specific category (for example, brochures, blogs, instructions, Web pages, Facebook). Which documents are more effective? Why?

As Your Professor Directs,

a. Discuss the documents with a small group of classmates.

b. Write a memo (see ▸▸ Chapter 7 for format) to your professor evaluating three or more of the documents. Include originals or photocopies of the documents you discuss as an appendix to your memo.

c. Write an e-mail to your supervisor recommending ways the organization can improve its documents.

d. In an oral presentation to the class, explain what makes one document good and another one weak. If possible, use high-quality images (use your snipping tool, for example) so that classmates can see the documents as you evaluate them.

DOCUMENT ASSIGNMENTS

4.5 EVALUATING PAGE DESIGNS

Collect several documents that you receive as a consumer or a student: forms, letters, newsletters, announcements, ads, and flyers. Use the guidelines in this chapter to evaluate each of them.

As Your Professor Directs,

a. Discuss the documents with a small group of classmates.

b. Write an e-mail to your professor evaluating three or more of the documents. Include scanned copies of the documents you discuss as an attachment to your e-mail.

c. Write a letter (see ➧ Chapter 7 for format) to an organization recommending ways it can improve the design of the documents.

d. In an oral presentation to the class, explain what makes one document good and another one weak. Use high-quality images so that classmates can see the documents as you evaluate them.

4.6 EVALUATING WEB PAGES

Compare three Web pages in the same category (for example, official provincial or territorial tourism sites, helping the homeless organizations, trade associations, car companies, university departments, sports information). Which page(s) are most effective? Why? What weaknesses do the pages have? What changes would you recommend?

As Your Professor Directs,

a. Discuss the pages with a small group of classmates.

b. Write a memo (see ➧ Chapter 7 for format) to your professor evaluating the pages. Include URLs of the pages in your memo.

c. In an oral presentation to the class, explain what makes one page good and another one weak. If possible, put the pages on screen so that classmates can see the pages as you evaluate them.

d. Post your evaluation to the class blog. Include the URLs so classmates can click to the pages you discuss.

4.7 CREATING A BROCHURE OR NEWSLETTER

In groups or pairs, create a brochure or newsletter for a campus, non-profit, government, or business organization. Write an e-mail to your professor explaining your choices for content and design.

4.8 CREATING A WEB OR FACEBOOK PAGE

Create a Web or Facebook page for an organization that does not yet have one. Write an e-mail to your professor explaining your choices for content and design.

4.9 TESTING A DOCUMENT

Ask someone to follow a set of instructions or to fill out a form. (Consider consumer instructions, forms for financial aid, and so forth.)

- Time the person. How long does it take? Is the person able to complete the task?
- Observe the person. Where does he or she pause, reread, seem confused?
- Interview the person. What parts of the document were confusing?

As Your Professor Directs,

a. Discuss the changes needed with a small group of classmates.

b. Write a memo (see ➧ Chapter 7 for format) to your professor evaluating the document and explaining the changes that are needed. Include the document as an appendix to your memo.

c. Write to the organization that produced the document recommending necessary improvements.

d. In an oral presentation to the class, evaluate the document and explain what changes are needed. If possible, use a transparency of the document so that classmates can see it.

COMMUNICATING ACROSS CULTURES

5

Learning Outcomes

LO1 Explain the importance of cultural competence

LO2 Define culture and explain how culture affects communications

LO3 Discuss the classification of high-context and low-context cultures

LO4 Explain monochronic and polychronic cultures

LO5 Discuss conversational style

LO6 Explain how to adapt writing for international audiences

AN INSIDE PERSPECTIVE

Tacita Lewars, Global HR Management Practitioner.
Source: Courtesy of Tacita Lewars.

My interest in Global Human Resources Management began with a lesson on a public transit bus.

I was in university at the time and on my way to an early morning class. I boarded the bus and sat next to a friendly looking gentleman. As we greeted our "hellos," his accent indicated that he was an immigrant to Canada.

"Are you a girl?" he asked after we had travelled a few minutes. I was taken aback by the question. I thought I was obviously female.

"Yes." I responded stiffly.

We travelled for a few more minutes in silence while I absorbed the impact of my neighbour's question. What did he mean by asking me that? Couldn't he tell I was a girl? Were other people also questioning themselves when they saw me, wondering whether I was a girl or a boy?

My thoughts were interrupted when my neighbour turned to me again and repeated the question, "Are you a girl?"

I could barely keep my composure. Wasn't he convinced?

"Yes, I'm a girl!" I tensed. "Would you like to see evidence?"

The man looked embarrassed. "Oh . . . I just wanted to know whether you were a girl or a wife," he explained. Flatteringly, my neighbour was assessing my status, whether I was married or single, and not my gender, whether I was male or female. Two perspectives were at play and two interpretations of common English language were in conflict. Our exchange allowed me to see firsthand how unintentional miscommunication across cultures can easily occur.

The lesson is this: we each filter communication through our own cultural frame of reference. The result is that individuals of differing cultural orientations may use the same terminology, but mean completely different things. This can lead to distorted messages, misjudgments, and conflict.

How can we alleviate cross-cultural communication challenges? Firstly, as one's own cultural context is often dominant, seeking to fully understand others' points of reference (as opposed to jumping to conclusions, as I did) is paramount. This includes asking clarifying questions to ensure both parties are aligned in their understanding. Secondly, in exchanging information, using plain language and minimizing the use of acronyms or cultural idioms helps to keep the message clear. In addition, being open to and respectful of viewpoints that differ from one's own encourages dialogue.

In business, communication is essential to leveraging the innovation that results from diverse perspectives and experiences. In order for strategies to be developed and executed, and a diverse workforce to be aligned and engaged, effective communication across cultures is key.

*Tacita Lewars, CHRP, GMS, GPHR, is a Global Human Resources Management practitioner and university course instructor.

Our values, priorities, and practices are shaped by the **culture** in which we grow up. We learn our culture and patterns of acceptable behaviour and beliefs at home and at school, at work and at play, and may internalize it to the point that we do not even recognize its power to shape our thoughts, feelings, and behaviours. It may feel so logical as to seem natural. We may not be aware of the most basic features of our own culture until we come into contact with people who do things differently. If we come from a culture where dogs are pets, that interpretation may seem "natural" until we learn that in other cultures dogs, like chickens, are raised for food.

Our culture is not simply decorative (dress, dance, or diet, powwows or tea ceremonies) but dynamic, changing in response to travel and trauma and to economic, political, and environmental change. In fact, Western uses of the word *culture* trace the historical shift from rural to urban living, from tilling the soil ("coulter" means the blade of a ploughshare) to cultivating the mind.[1]

If our cultures are logical and learned, they are also complex, contested, and contradictory. What does it mean to be a Canadian, for example? To a Quebecker? To a Newfoundlander? To someone on the Prairies or in the Northwest Territories? To a new Canadian who has just taken the oath of loyalty?

Understanding our own as well as other cultures is crucial if you want to volunteer overseas, go on a student exchange, work for a multinational company headquartered in another

On the Job Beyond Stereotypes*

Learning about different cultures is important for understanding the different kinds of people we work with. However, leadership coaches Keith Caver and Ancella Livers caution that people are individuals, not just representatives of a cultural group. Caver and Livers have found that co-workers sometimes treat black individuals first as representatives of black culture, and only second as talented and experienced managers.

African American clients of Caver and Livers have complained that they are often called upon to answer diversity questions or to interpret the behaviour of famous black Americans such as Clarence Thomas or Jesse Jackson, and they wonder whether their white colleagues would feel their race qualifies them to interpret the deeds of famous white Americans.

A 2007 Ryerson RBC Foundation Institute for Disability Studies report found:

- Practising concealment is a "second job" for people with disabilities.
- People with disabilities have to educate their colleagues while "keeping it light" with humour.

In a 2010 study of 22,338 non-unionized employees in the information and communications technology sector, Canadian researchers Margaret Yap and Alison Konrad found that women and visible minorities still face "unconscious bias" in the workplace. They face a sticky floor, middle management bottleneck, and glass ceiling: "On average, men were 4.5 per cent more likely to receive promotions than white females, 7.9 per cent more likely than minority males and 16.1 per cent more likely than minority females."

*Based on Keith A. Caver and Ancella B. Livers, "Dear white boss," *Harvard Business Review*, November 2002, 76–8; Kathryn Frazee et al., *Doing Disability at the Bank: Discovering the Work of Learning/Teaching Done by Disabled Bank Employees* (October 2007), retrieved March 11, 2011, from http://www.rbc.com/diversity/pdf/Ryerson_Report_Oct-07.pdf; Margaret Yap and Alison Konrad, "Gender and racial differences in promotions: Is there a sticky floor, a mid-level bottleneck, or a glass ceiling?" *Relations industrielles/Industrial relations* 64, no. 4 (2009): 593–619.

country, sell your products or services in other countries, or manage an international plant or office.

The first step in understanding another culture is to realize that it may do things very differently, and that the difference is not bad or inferior. People inhabit several cultures (national, ethnic, religious, professional, and so on) simultaneously. Even within a single culture people differ. The kinds of differences summarized in this chapter can turn into stereotypes, which can be just as damaging as ignorance. Don't try to memorize the material here as a rigid set of rules. Instead, use the examples to get a sense for the kinds of things that differ from one culture to another. Test these generalizations against your experience. When in doubt, ask.

LO1

UNDERSTANDING DIVERSITY IN CANADA

Cultural competence, the capacity to communicate effectively across cultural differences, is as valuable at home as abroad. The successful intercultural communicator is

- Aware that his or her preferred values and behaviours are influenced by culture and are not necessarily "right"
- Flexible and open to change
- Sensitive to verbal and nonverbal behaviour
- Aware of the values, beliefs, and practices in other cultures
- Sensitive to differences among individuals within a culture[2]

Even if you stay in Canada, you'll work with people whose backgrounds differ from yours. Residents of small towns and rural areas have different notions of friendliness than do people from big cities. British Columbians may talk differently than people in the Maritimes.

Bilingual Canada has long compared the diversity of its people to a mosaic. Now immigrants from Philippines, China, India, United States, United Kingdom, Pakistan, France, Iran, Haiti, and United Arab Emirates—the top ten source countries for permanent residents in 2012 (see Figure 5.1)—add their voices to the medley of French, English, and Aboriginal languages. Radio station CHIN in Toronto broadcasts in 32 languages.[3]

Widely recognized for its multilateralism, peacekeeping, social programs, official bilingualism, and multiculturalism, Canada is arguably the most culturally diverse country and Toronto one of the world's most diverse cities. In 1931, 81% of Toronto's population of 631,207 was British in origin; by 1996 only 16% of 4.2 million self-identified as exclusively British. In 1998, Toronto adopted its motto "Diversity, Our Strength." By 2031, Toronto's visible minorities will represent 63% of the population (54% in Vancouver and 31% in Montreal). Meantime, the increasing trend of intermarriage is rendering the concept of race less and less important.[4]

In this context, cultural and subcultural groups define themselves by virtual affiliations (Facebook, LinkedIn, YouTube), by their allegiance to one or another platform (BlackBerry versus Apple, Microsoft versus Google, PC versus Mac), by appeals to musical preferences (heavy metal, rap, hip hop), or by commitment to a movement (women's, environmental, labour, anti-globalization). See too ◀◀ Chapter 2 on organizational cultures and subcultures.

Figure 5.1 Canada—Permanent Residents by Top Source Countries, 2010–2012

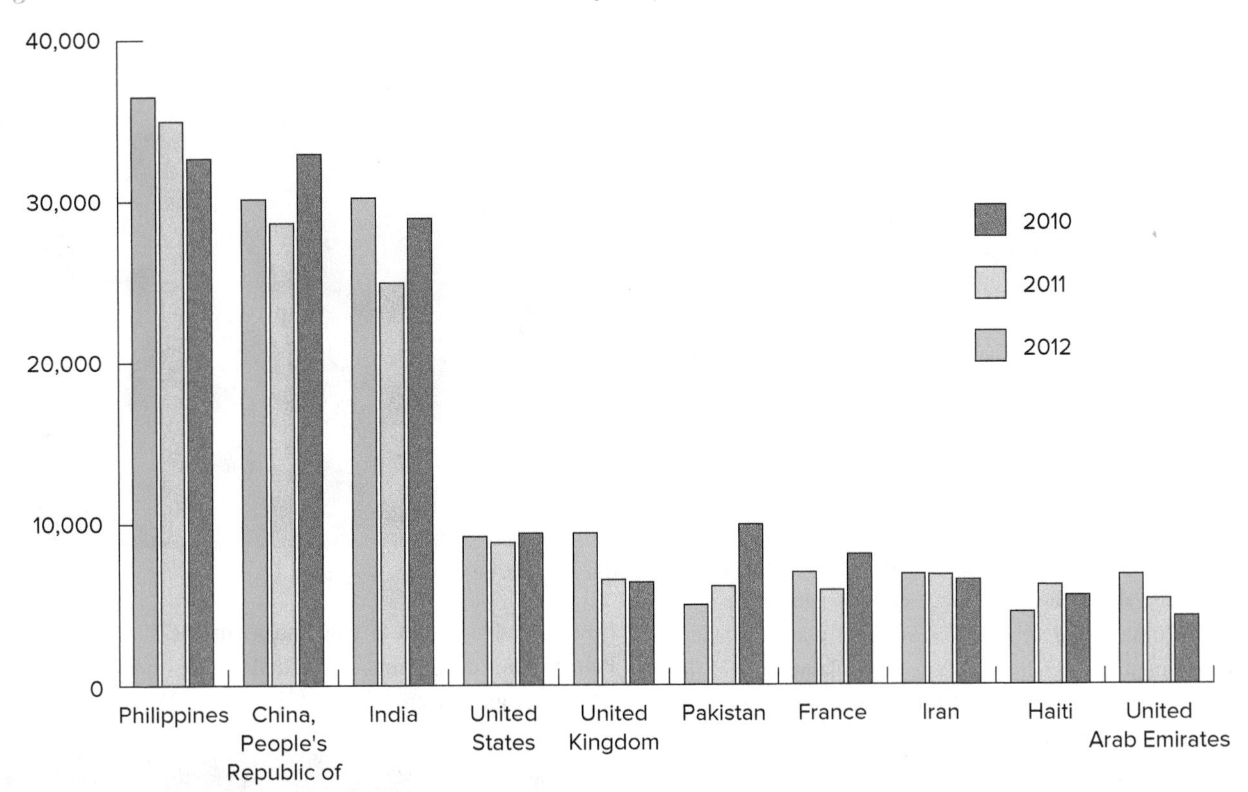

Source: Citizenship and Immigration Canada, "Facts and figures 2012—Immigration overview: Permanent and temporary residents." August 7, 2013. Retrieved March 25, 2014, from http://www.cic.gc.ca/english/resources/statistics/facts2012/permanent/10.asp. Reproduced with the permission of Citizenship and Immigration Canada.

By at least one account, Canada's global success is due in large measure to its multiculturalism, which teaches empathy, and to the fact that it is not a dominant power that thinks only of its own stakeholders.[5]

When Canada came of age with the signing of the *Constitution Act, 1982,* it recognized the Aboriginal and treaty rights of Aboriginal peoples. In recognizing and naming Aboriginal peoples, however, Canada simultaneously obscured the great diversity of those peoples: Mi'kmaq, Cree, Dene, Anishnabe, Algonquin, Nisga'a, Inuit, and Métis, to name but a few (see ◀◀ Chapter 2 on naming and spelling preferences).

Organized by SUCCESS Foundation, Walk with the Dragon is an annual community fundraising event in Vancouver's Stanley Park that attracts more than 13,000 people.

Diversity in the Workplace

The last 30 years have seen a growing emphasis on diversity in the workplace. But ordinary people have always worked. In the past, such people (including non-elite white males) may have been relegated to low-status and low-paying jobs, to agricultural or domestic work, or to staff rather than line work and management.

"Diversity" in the workplace comes from many sources: gender, race and ethnicity, regional and national origin, social class, religion, age, sexual orientation, abilities (see ◀◀ Chapter 2 on reducing bias in business communication). In the classroom you are already likely experiencing, negotiating, and celebrating the multicultural realities of Canada today. Listening to and learning from students with very different backgrounds is a rich resource that will prepare you to appreciate different styles and avoid some of the miscommunications discussed in this chapter and ▶▶ Chapter 6.

The workplace is not always as welcoming of diversity as Canadian multiculturalism would have us believe (see the ◀◀ On the Job feature "Beyond Stereotypes"). The experience of those who are perceived as different explains something of the human and financial costs of mainstream cultural values and practices that appear so natural as to be invisible (see the ▸▸ On the Job feature "Valuing Diversity?"). Even multigenerational diversity has been presented as a workplace problem, especially with the ending of mandatory retirement in many jurisdictions.

Generation X (born between 1965 and 1980), popularized by Canadian author Douglas Coupland and pilloried by the media as "alienated, overeducated, underachieving slackers," and Generation Y, born to boomers since the 1980s, have been represented as "the generation that won't grow up."[6] But what does it mean to label people as if their ages told you all you need to know, or to think that age has more explanatory power than geography, gender, abilities, ethnicity, and so on? Does labelling produce the identities it presumes to discover, encouraging the very alienation it deplores? Do we understand how communication produces and reproduces identities?[7]

Generational differences at a glance.

Does talk about the novelty of current generation gaps forget while recycling ancient stories about younger generations? We might remember Socrates' complaints about children as "tyrants": "They contradict their parents, gobble their food, and terrorize their teachers."

If the cultural icons that resonate for baby boomers may mean little to members of Generation X or Y (or millennials), and far less to those born in 2000 or later (Generation Z, or the so-called media generation), family enjoyment of multigenerational exchanges suggests that generations can and do work, play, and learn well together.

A 2010 Canadian study of professionals found more similarities than differences among different age groups in their loyalty, concern to do a good job, interest in work–life balance, and preference for small to medium business.[8] In a blog posting, millennial Becky Johns challenges supervisors to stop perpetuating the myths and stereotypes, to stop "whining about why we suck, and start teaching us" to become better writers, think more critically, be better listeners, defend arguments, and "package research in a way that's helpful to others."[9]

OPERATING IN A GLOBAL BUSINESS WORLD

As we saw in ◂◂ Chapter 1, exports are essential both to the success of individual businesses and to a country's economy as a whole. Sixty percent of 833 surveyed Canadian companies are engaged in global business, though no country represents more than 1% of sales and much potential remains untapped.[10]

An increasing share of profits comes from outside the headquarters country. Canadian entrepreneur John H. McCall MacBain built his business, Trader Classified Media NV, into an international success story. Based in the Netherlands and traded in Paris, his company generated 25% of its revenue in Canada with publications like *Trader Classified* and *Bargain Finder* until he sold it in 2006 and set up the McCall MacBain Foundation, funding millions of dollars of projects on health, education, and the environment.[11]

The legacy of the 2010 Vancouver Olympic Games is etched in the minds of Canadians.

International Rebranding a Nation*

Countries periodically reinvent themselves, telling new stories about their values, beliefs, and dreams. The 2008 Olympic Games allowed China to present itself to the world in new ways.

Quotations from Confucius—no longer regarded as a relic of a backward past—were featured in brochures introducing China and welcoming foreign journalists to the Olympics. Confucius is a valuable icon helping stimulate "nationalist sentiment" among Chinese people.

For Geoffrey York, the "Potemkin Olympics" hid Chinese "social and political problems" behind "a façade of spectacular architecture, cheerful volunteers and enthusiastic crowds." Lest people think that the new China is a product of power alone, Wenran Jiang of the China Institute, University of Alberta, insists that the Chinese people themselves are "agents of change" moving China forward in the direction and at the pace that they want.

When Canada hosted the Winter Olympics in 2010, Canadian Heritage invested $20 million in the opening ceremonies to "ensure that the event adequately reflects the priorities of the government and helps to achieve its domestic and international branding goals." According to Renée Smith-Valade, VANOC VP Communications, "We have spent a tremendous amount of time with the government of Canada, understanding brand Canada and what they are taking Canada out to the world and to Canadians as, and we're aligned with that."

Russia's rebranding efforts—"a blend of politics and performance"—in the Sochi Olympics was criticized more than celebrated in Western media.

*Based on Andrey Makarychev and Alexandra Yatsyk, "Sochi Olympics—the dangers of rebranding," *Open Democracy,* February 3, 2014, retrieved March 26, 2014, from http://www.opendemocracy.net/od-russia/andrey-makarychev-and-alexandra-yatsyk/sochi-olympics-%E2%80%93-dangers-of-rebranding; Diane Francis, "Winter Olympics 2014 puts Russia's corruption—and incompetence—on world stage," *Financial Post,* February 4, 2014, retrieved March 26, 2014, from http://opinion.financialpost.com/2014/02/07/winter-olympics-2014-puts-russias-corruption-and-incompetence-on-world-stage/; Peter Scowen, "Confucius says: Time to rebrand the nation," *The Globe and Mail,* August 9, 2008, F1, 8; Wenran Jiang, "Revolution from below: Chinese democracy is coming from the Chinese people, not from the rulers or from the West," *The Globe and Mail,* August 9, 2008, A15; Geoffrey York, "China's tour de force," *The Globe and Mail,* August 23, 2008; Steve Mertl, "Ottawa says it is investing, not meddling in opening ceremonies," *The Globe and Mail,* August 22, 2008; Robert Matas, "Ottawa puts its stamp on 2010 Games," *The Globe and Mail,* August 22, 2008, retrieved March 16, 2011, from http://v1.theglobeandmail.com/servlet/story/RTGAM.20080822.wolyvanoc22/REStory/National.

For executives in global companies, international experience is often essential for career advancement. Patricia Arnold (who became vice-president, Credit Suisse First Boston, Zurich) started out in financial services in Montreal and Calgary before advancing her career in Albania, Hungary, Switzerland, and Sudan. She gives a lot of credit to bilingual, multicultural Canada (and especially Quebec) for her capacity to make the most of her international experience. Arnold learns as much as she can about the history of her locale and adopts local practices and dress, refusing to be isolated in expatriate communities.[12]

Immersion in local cultures can help identify competitive advantages and opportunities that might otherwise be missed in global business. False assumptions about different cultures can obscure possibilities. Looking across the Russian border, for example, the visionary fund manager might see not a vast, empty land, but a huge new market for a Finnish tire company. With 40 offices in 20 countries, AIM Trimark Investments showed itself open to emerging markets for Finnish tires in its slick advertisements underlining the credibility of its astute manager.

Though cross-cultural training correlates with profits and two-thirds of executives experience miscommunication within global operations, resulting in 30–35% early ending of international assignments and an over 50% failure of joint ventures within two or three years, Canada still lags Australia in CEO international business experience.[13]

Whereas journalist and author Andrea Mandel-Campbell laments Canada's "global myopia" that has allowed "the corporate equivalent of the Toronto Maple Leafs, maple syrup and the Mounties" to be "snapped up by hungry foreign acquirers" and "lopped tens of billions" off the Toronto Stock Exchange, others point to Canada's knowledge-sharing and broadening global horizons. Toronto-based PharmEng International Inc. was among consultants working with Chinese exporters to ensure product safety, while Canadian International Development Agency (now Foreign Affairs, Trade and Development Canada) engaged in an initiative to improve safety, policy research, production, and internal structures for China's food safety.[14]

LO2

UNDERSTANDING CULTURES

Our cultures provide patterns of acceptable behaviours and beliefs. They shape how we see the world, understand our own and others' identities, and find meaning. Article 3 of UNESCO's Universal Declaration on Cultural Diversity underlines the benefits of cultural diversity: "Cultural diversity widens the range of options open to everyone; it is one of the roots of development, understood not simply in terms of economic growth, but also as a means to achieve a more satisfactory intellectual, emotional, moral and spiritual existence."[15] If cultural understanding and sensitivity to differences among and across cultures is a valuable asset in a global knowledge economy, barriers remain.

Generalizing about different groups is at the heart of *stereotyping* (◀◀ Chapter 1), which means imposing unfair generalizations and labelling people with unjust images. Stereotyping remains a major barrier to effective cross-cultural communication and to recognizing the true value of those we misrepresent. The result is a loss to businesses, groups, and nations that do not see or use the talents and human capital available to them. The irony is that visible minorities who have the languages and knowledge companies need often feel invisible.[16]

Stereotypes are especially hard to dislodge because of ethnocentrism and confirmation bias. **Ethnocentrism** involves the judgment of others by norms specific to one's own culture. Though the unfair generalizations are often made without awareness of the yardstick of cultural norms, they have the effect of causing hasty judgments that reinforce the belief that one's own group is superior to others. **Confirmation bias** is the process whereby the bias is confirmed when people see what they expect to see; they are blinded to the positive attributes of others.

History has some useful lessons on failures to understand those who appear different. When one Australian business consultant concluded that a developing country was "utterly unsuitable" for "work in the new economy," despite its low labour costs, it was 1915 Japan that he rejected as hopelessly undisciplined and unable "to change the habits of national heritage." Others found Germans "plodding" and undistinguished by "enterprise or activity."[17]

In Canada we have good reason to understand the cultures of our top ten source countries for immigration (Figure 5.1) and our top ten export trading partners: United States, United Kingdom, China, Japan, Mexico, South Korea, Netherlands, Germany, France, and Hong Kong.[18] (See the International box "You-Attitude with International Audiences" in ◀◀ Chapter 2.) Foreign Affairs, Trade and Development Canada's Web site (www.international.gc.ca) is a source of trade, policy, and other advice to enhance access in a global economy. Click on Countries and Regionals for an overview of conditions in selected countries. Yet Canada is short-sighted, says journalist Neil Reynolds, in excluding Mexico (fifth among trading partners) from negotiations for a North American "perimeter," an idea proposed by Mexico after 9/11. Canada's sense of superiority over Mexico and its drug war is ironic, says Reynolds, when US and Canadian laws and demand drive the trade and a US report found the Canadian border a greater threat to the United States than the Mexican one. Canada's visa requirements have added to tensions with Mexico in 2014. A Goldman Sachs report predicted Mexico would be a top five world economy by 2050.[19]

Similarly, Scotiabank is among those finding opportunity in Latin America, host to 589 million; GDP for Latin America and the Caribbean is estimated to increase 4.1% annually from 2011–2016.[20]

Understanding Asia

Economist Ha-Joon Chang challenges the popular view that culture is the source of economic failure in Africa, Latin America, and the Middle East and of success in Asia. As he shows, for instance, not only have Koreans succeeded economically but their culture can bring out the best and worst in people. Confucianism is both "a culture that values thrift, investment, hard work, education, organization and discipline" and "a culture that disparages practical pursuits, discourages entrepreneurship and retards the rule of law." When cultures operate in favourable economic circumstances, they can bring out the best in people.[21]

Claims that a Confucian work ethic explains East Asian economic success do not begin to explain the timing, scale, and differences among the different economies. Others look to different management styles, labour practices, labour market institutions, and state–corporate relations to explain behaviours and values. They find, for example, that "economic and organizational factors have a significant influence on workplace behaviours and work" in Japan as much as in North America.[22]

Although Japan had already lost to China its second place in world economies and third place among Canada's trading partners, the 2011 earthquake, tsunami, and nuclear emergency have deepened Japan's human and economic disaster.[23] Globe commentator John Doyle regrets that television reporters are failing to explain Japanese culture, the country's "insularity, the wariness of foreigners, the imperturbable surface that hides further layers of contradictions and neuroses" after centuries living under threat of such a disaster.[24]

Talk of "Asian" culture similarly obscures a diversity of cultures—and a need for cultural competence in those who would succeed there. You have to know "when to listen, when to ask for help, and when—finally—to speak," says Geneviève Hilton of Ketchum, Hong Kong. She gives examples of international journalists bemused by Chinese refusing to quote a spokesperson in press releases so as not to give undue credit, and Australian clients upsetting a Korean editor who expected the Australian boss to present "his team's unified opinion" and not to allow junior staff to speak and even contradict him.[25]

Travel can expand horizons and understanding, but not necessarily change perceptions of one's own culture. When one MBA student spent time in India as part of her program, she commented, "Culture and politics are so intertwined with business in India." This struck her as so different from the Canadian context: "Culture, politics and business are not as intertwined in Canada."[26] Australian BHP Billiton's failed takeover of PotashCorp of Saskatchewan in 2010 told a very different story of stakeholder loyalties and government involvement.[27]

Understanding the Middle East

Like Asia, the Middle East (including both Western Asia and North Africa) is home to diversities obscured by its name: 22 countries, 300 million people, and 14 religious groups. It is also home to multiple misconceptions about its peoples, only about 18% of whom are Muslim. Not only is there enormous

Female entrepreneurs in the Middle East employ a high proportion of female managers and professionals.

economic opportunity (resources, real estate, tourism, media), but also the population is youthful and dynamic (more than 50% under 15 years).[28]

It is that young and educated population (and its social media and cell phones) that precipitated the Jasmine Revolution across the region in 2011—and increased awareness around the world. Driven by high unemployment (25% compared with a world average of 14%), widening inequality, and soaring food costs, millions took to the streets and overturned regimes. Until the protests in Libya, the revolution was also remarkably peaceful, defying stereotypes of terrorism and extremism.[29] The large public city squares proved a powerful "social medium" where young and not so young men and women, in traditional and in modern dress, stood shoulder to shoulder.[30]

If Twitter and Facebook helped emancipate in Tunisia and Egypt, they have also been used to trace activists, two of whom were hanged in Iran for posting video footage from the 2009 "Twitter Revolution."[31]

While women still face many barriers and gendered norms, they also defy many expectations.[32] In Qatar and United Arab Emirates, more women than men are enrolling in university; in Egypt, women represent over half of university students.[33] Women protesters were among the leaders, reporters, and bloggers using the media to link with people. As author Naomi Wolf argues, "once you educate women, democratic agitation is likely to accompany the cultural shift that follows."[34]

In Saudi Arabia, it is estimated that 10% of businesses are run by women. If they are still forbidden to drive cars and cannot leave the country without permission of father or husband, they are also becoming increasingly educated and enterprising. A 2007 World Bank Report debunks old myths about micro enterprises and low-tech entrepreneurship among Middle Eastern women. It found little difference between male- and female-owned businesses in the Middle East and North Africa, although only 13% of surveyed firms in eight countries were owned by women.[35]

LO3

CLASSIFYING HIGH-CONTEXT AND LOW-CONTEXT CULTURES

Another response to cultural diversity is to try to manage it by classifying and categorizing. One such attempt to represent and respect cultural difference is anthropologist Edward T. Hall's distinction between high-context and low-context cultures.[36] The information, environment, and stimuli that surround an event constitute the context within which we communicate. In high-context cultures, information is inferred from the context; in low-context cultures, context is less important and information is explicitly conveyed.

Canadians may be troubled by the classification "North America" in Figure 5.2 obscuring Canadian (including Aboriginal) differences and by the implication that high-context cultures value the social aspects of communication, while low-context ones see communication's value only in terms of information.

Figure 5.2 Views of Communication in High- and Low-Context Cultures

	HIGH-CONTEXT (EXAMPLES: JAPAN, UNITED ARAB EMIRATES)	LOW-CONTEXT (EXAMPLES: GERMANY, NORTH AMERICA)
Preferred communication strategy	Indirectness, politeness, ambiguity	Directness, confrontation, clarity
Reliance on nonverbal signs to communicate	High	Low
Importance of written word	Low	High
Agreements made in writing	Not binding	Binding
Agreements made orally	Binding	Not binding

Source: VICTOR, DAVID A, INTERNATIONAL BUSINESS COMMUNICATION, 1st Edition, © 1992, pp. 148, 153, 160. Adapted by permission of Pearson Education, Inc., Upper Saddle River, NJ.

If low-context cultures seem more logical, detailed, action-oriented, and individualistic than the collectivist high-context cultures to an American anthropologist, then it may be that his cultural conditioning leads him to see what he expects to see. Perhaps it blinds him to the elaborate social rituals of his own culture.

What, for example, is the meaning of golf in the business world? Are there no rituals attached to the subtle negotiations of order of play? How many holes before business can be discussed? It's easier to be patient with one's own rituals that seem so logical than with others' strange practices.

This is why it is so important to be sensitive to our own cultural assumptions as well as those of other groups—and why we need to read Hall's classifications with great caution. If there is some truth to the distinctions he makes among cultural groups, it can be dangerous to exaggerate our differences and ignore what we share. Similarly, Hall's focus on nationality underestimates differences of class, vocation, geography, history, power, and privilege and the ways identities are negotiated through communication.[37] Communication is also influenced by the organizational culture and by personal culture (or social categories of identity), such as gender, race and ethnicity, for instance (Figure 5.3). Sometimes one kind of culture may be more important than another.

As Figure 5.2 shows, low-context cultures favour direct approaches and may see indirectness as dishonest or manipulative; high-context cultures may find the direct approach rude. A Chinese person, for instance, is more interested in relationship building than in communication as information exchange, while habits of indirection and holistic view of the business and cultural worlds make saying *no* difficult.

The Chinese understand identity as a product of interaction with others. In business that is the basis of *guanxi* (relationships), or the give and take, cooperation, and support made possible by trust and respect. Becoming known and trusted in a Chinese business context means following protocol and understanding the importance of saving face, including showing respect when handling business cards by taking time to digest contents. According to Jianwei Zhang, President of Bombardier Canada, "The culture, the background, the practices, the languages are different." That makes checking that you are on the same page critical.[38]

Figure 5.3 National Culture, Organizational Culture, and Personal Culture Overlap

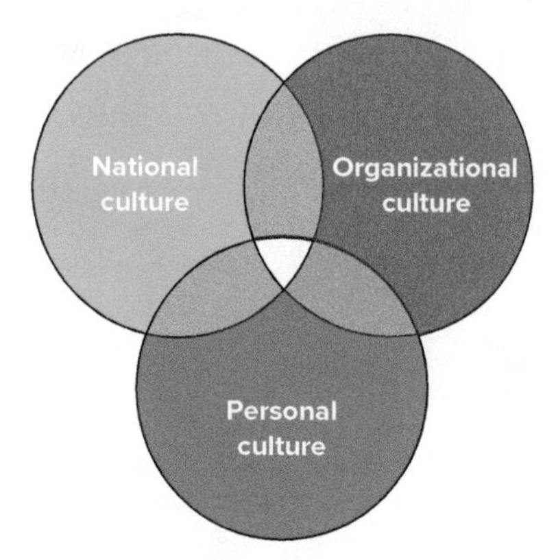

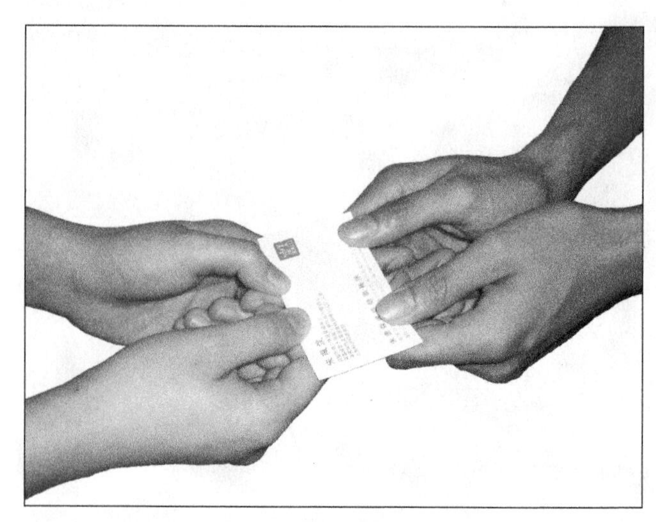

Giving or receiving a Chinese business card is a formality that takes two hands.

Still, there is change in the Year of the Rabbit: prolonged drought in the North, soaring food costs, increasing disparities between urban and rural dwellers, hundreds of millions in poverty, unprecedented strikes, aging population, increasingly educated and independent workers, pollution and air quality challenges, and rising expectations. Although media are more open than in the past, social media have been blocked to avoid events like those in the Middle East.[39]

LO4

DISTINGUISHING MONOCHRONIC AND POLYCHRONIC CULTURES

If differences in time zones complicate international communications, different views of time can create further barriers. As natural as they seem, notions of time (and space) are culturally coded and far from universal.[40]

Edward T. Hall distinguishes between **monochronic cultures,** which focus on clock time, and **polychronic cultures,** which focus on relationships. When US managers feel offended because a Latin American manager also sees other people during "their" appointments, the two kinds of time are in conflict.[41]

According to some scholars, Europeans schedule fewer events in a comparable period of time than do North Americans. Perhaps as a result, Germans and German Swiss see North Americans as too time conscious.[42]

In building business relationships in China, women can have advantages, says Carla Kearns of Toronto. If women can be better at the interpersonal and reading between the lines, Kearns suggests men and women can learn to value

The National Aboriginal Achievement Awards celebrate the accomplishments of Aboriginal people in many sectors: in this case, Dr. Marie Ann Battiste for education (2008) and James (Sakej) Youngblood Henderson for law and justice (2006).

both masculine and feminine leadership.[43] In addition to the Chinese valuing of *ren* (a sort of warm-hearted benevolence and concern for others), researchers have also noted Japanese preference for women's conversational style, "interpersonal warmth and willingness to listen."[44]

Mainstream organizations in Canada—businesses, government, and schools—keep time by the calendar and the clock. Being "on time" is seen as a sign of dependability. Other cultures may keep time by the seasons and the moon, the sun, internal "body clocks," or a personal feeling that "the time is right."

Canadians who believe that "time is money" are often frustrated in negotiations with people, including Aboriginal people, who take a much more leisurely approach.

Communicating with Aboriginal Peoples

To find "common ground between cultures" means addressing stereotypes that are the legacy of historical assaults on Aboriginal peoples, their worldview, languages, and relationship with the land, according to the Royal Commission on Aboriginal Peoples. We need to understand the importance of oral traditions and of the context of communications, such as talking circles and sweat lodges, as well as the use of humour and all the senses.[45]

Stereotypes grew when settlers failed to see the evidence of sophisticated societies living sustainably on the land with their own symbolic systems, science, spirituality, education, laws, and governance. Thus in their ignorance of different ways, settlers found the Aboriginal people lacking and in need of the "civilizing gifts" that in their minds justified the taking of the land.[46]

This history makes trust and relationship building even more important. Following protocol whenever you hold a meeting on Aboriginal territory is critical. The local community will identify what is expected in terms of visits, gifts for elders, opening and closing prayers, and other ceremonies, seating arrangements, and dress. In some communities, women will be expected to wear skirts if sitting in ceremony.

The circle (with no position of superiority) is typically preferred for meetings or problem solving to encourage free and open exchanges among participants who speak when they receive the feather or other token.[47]

International When Communication Styles Conflict*

Some cultures differ in their ideas about how business people should communicate. What if you want to close a deal with someone who expects business communications to be flowery or argumentative? If you rarely compose elegant prose, or if you dislike arguments, you may lose the business opportunity unless one of you adapts.

What if one culture is one of the fastest growing economies in the world (India) and the other is home to the highest concentration of business startups in the world? Israel's history, isolation, and economic boycotts helped make the Internet and telecommunications "a national sport" to cope with hostilities.

About two-thirds of attempts at Israeli–Indian deals fail, for example, even though the countries share a common business language (English), but very different histories and educations.

Israeli business people generally prefer communication to be simple and direct, even forceful. Israelis also value treating others as equals. Indian English emphasizes humility and politeness, as shown through long, indirect, and poetic sentences.

Indian business people often interpreted correspondence from Israelis to be rude, signalling inability to collaborate appropriately. The Israelis were confused by the indirect wording of Indian messages. They felt unsure about what to expect. However, a study by Nurit Zaidman also found examples of Israeli business people trying to choose polite and elegant language, and of Indian business people simplifying their style.

*Based on Dinesh Narayanan, Forbes, "Is the Indian economy overheating?" *Financial Post,* December 23, 2010, retrieved March 17, 2011, from http://www.financialpost.com/Indian+economy+overheating/4019159/story.html; Dan Senor and Saul Singer, "Start-up nation," *Canadian Business,* December 7, 2009, 64–67; Nurit Zaidman, "Cultural codes and language strategies in business communication," *Management Communication Quarterly* 14, no. 3 (February 2001): 408–441.

And the medicine wheel, with its emphasis on interdependence and on the mental, spiritual, physical, and emotional, may be followed in consensus decision making.

If there are many jokes about "Indian time," it means investing in time for the purpose at hand and not being late. Many an elder has scolded those who come late to meetings on that erroneous assumption.

When communicating with Aboriginal seniors, it is important to use the local language or plain language and to use these media: word of mouth, radio, and newsletters.[48]

VALUES, BELIEFS, AND PRACTICES

Values and beliefs, often unconscious, affect our response to people and situations. Most Canadians, for example, value "fairness." "You're not playing fair" is a sharp criticism calling for changed behaviour. In some countries, however, people expect certain groups to receive preferential treatment. Many Canadians accept competition and believe that it produces better performance. Others believe in the cooperation that has given us social programs, or in the cooperation and consensus building of Aboriginal peoples.

Japan's traditional culture emphasized the group, but there is evidence that this cultural value is changing in new historical conditions. According to researcher David Matsumoto, Japanese cultural norms such as the sacrifice of one's personal time for the company, avoidance of disagreements with one's boss, and the favouring of compliance over individual initiative have become part of Japan's business past. Modern business values in Japan place more emphasis on the individual person's goals and accomplishments.[49]

Values and beliefs are often influenced by religion. Christianity coexists with a view of the individual as proactive. In some Muslim and Asian countries, however, it is seen as presumptuous to predict the future by promising action by a certain date. The Protestant work ethic legitimizes wealth as a sign of divine favour. In other Christian cultures, a simpler lifestyle is considered to be closer to God.

Even everyday practices differ from culture to culture. North Americans and Europeans put the family name last; Asians put it first. North American and European printing moves from top to bottom and from left to right; Arabic reads from right to left, but still from top to bottom.

NONVERBAL COMMUNICATION

Nonverbal communication—communication that doesn't use words—takes place all the time. Smiles, frowns, who sits where at a meeting, the size of an office, how long someone keeps a visitor waiting—all these communicate pleasure or anger, friendliness or distance, power and status. We are often not conscious of interpreting those nonverbal signals.

Yet nonverbal signals can be misinterpreted just as easily as can verbal symbols (words). And the misunderstandings can be harder to clear up because people may not be aware of the nonverbal cues that led them to assume that they aren't liked, respected, or approved. An Arab student assumed that his US roommate disliked him intensely because the US student sat around the room with his feet up on the furniture, soles toward the Arab roommate. Arab culture sees the foot in general and the sole in particular as unclean; showing the sole of the foot is an insult.[50] When an Iraqi threw a shoe at then President George W. Bush, he was showing disrespect; Montrealers repeated the gesture before a scheduled Bush speech in 2009.[51]

Learning about nonverbal language can help us project the image we want to present and make us more aware of the signals we are interpreting.

However, even within a single culture, a nonverbal symbol is such a powerful source of meaning that experts claim 93% of communication is based on nonverbal signals.[52]

Body Language

Posture and body movements connote energy and openness. Canadian **open body positions** include leaning forward with uncrossed arms and legs, with the arms away from the body.

On the Job That's Not What We Meant!

If English has established itself as the language of international business, some are concerned that this is another example of North American standards imposing themselves on the rest of the world. Others see another excuse for North Americans not to learn languages. Yet others point to the many Englishes (Australian, Indian, Caribbean, Canadian, US, UK, for instance) around the world that can themselves be sources of miscommunication.

Author Oscar Wilde famously said, "We have really everything in common with America nowadays except, of course, language." Here are some examples of different words that might cause confusion for Canadians visiting the UK (or vice versa).

UK	Canadian
Bonnet	Hood (of automobile)
Boot	Trunk
Turn signals	Indicators
Petrol	Gas
Pavement	Sidewalk
Road	Pavement
Dual carriageway	Divided highway

Technology Tips Global Communication Online *

The Internet makes global communication easier via e-mail, text messaging, blogs, and chat rooms. But users also need to navigate around cultural and language barriers.

Preferences vary for media choices. Canadians give high priority to reading and responding to e-mail. Japanese and Italians tend to prefer text messaging and cell phones. In Ukraine, business people expect many matters to be handled face to face, so Ukrainians might delay acting on e-mail.

Despite low average Internet penetration of 17.3% in the Caribbean, Barbados has seen penetration rise to 63.8% with social media taking hold across the Caribbean for everything from business and non-profit applications to protesting and practising writing to challenging misconceptions and building community.

Differences in business hours can interfere with the rapid feedback that Canadians expect. But in Islamic countries, businesses may be closed on Fridays and open on Sundays. In southern Europe, many businesses close for a two-hour lunch.

Similarly, a clear, concise, and direct style may suit many Canadians and Europeans, but may cause undue "confusion and anxiety" for many Latin American, African, Asian, or Middle Eastern people who prefer a relationship-oriented style. They may read such e-mails as signs of upset or distance on the part of the sender.

*Based on Kirk St. Amant, "Communication in international virtual offices," *Intercom*, April 2003, 27–28; Karel McIntosh, "Social media swirls in the Caribbean," *Communication World*, May–June 2008, 32–35; Salvador Apud and Talis Apud-Martinex, "Effective internal communication in global organizations," *Communication World Bulletin*, April 2008; Brevard Nelson, "Adding flavor to the Caribbean marketing mix," *Communication World*, May-June 2009, 28–31.

Closed or **defensive body positions** include leaning back, sometimes with both hands behind the head, arms and legs crossed or close together, or hands in pockets. As the labels imply, open positions suggest that people are accepting and open to new ideas. Closed positions suggest that people are physically or psychologically uncomfortable, that they are defending themselves and shutting other people out.

People who cross their arms or legs often claim that they do so only because the position is more comfortable. But notice your own body the next time you're in a perfectly comfortable discussion with a good friend. You'll probably find that you naturally assume open body positions. The fact that so many people in organizational settings adopt closed positions may indicate that many people feel at least slightly uncomfortable in school and on the job.

The Chinese value the ability to sit quietly. They may see the tendency to fidget and shift as an indication of lack of mental or spiritual balance. Even in Canada, interviewers and audiences usually respond negatively to nervous gestures such as fidgeting with a tie or hair or jewellery, tapping a pencil, or swinging a foot.

It's impossible to memorize every meaning that every nonverbal sign has in every culture. And in a multicultural workforce, you can't know whether someone retains the meanings of his or her ancestors or has adopted mainstream Canadian meanings. The best solution is to state an observation: "I see you're wearing black." The other person's response will let you know whether the colour is a fashion statement or a sign of mourning.

Eye Contact

Many Canadians see **eye contact** as a sign of honesty, which can be a problem for some Aboriginal people in the justice system because they believe making eye contact shows disrespect.[53] The Japanese are taught to look at the neck.[54] In Korea, prolonged eye contact is considered rude. The lower-ranking person is expected to look down first.[55]

Eye contact is so important that Arabs dislike talking to someone wearing dark glasses or while walking side by side. It is considered impolite not to face someone directly. In Muslim countries, women and men are not supposed to have eye contact.

These differences can lead to miscommunication in the multicultural workplace. Superiors may feel that subordinates are being disrespectful when the subordinate is being respectful—according to the norms of his or her culture.

Gestures

Canadians sometimes assume that they can depend on gestures to communicate if language fails. But Birdwhistell reported that "although we have been searching for 15 years [1950–65], we have found no gesture or body motion which has the same meaning in all societies."[56] In Bulgaria, for example, people may nod their heads to signify no and shake their heads to signify yes.[57]

Gestures that mean approval in Canada may have very different meanings in other countries. The "thumbs up" sign, which means "good work" or "go ahead" in Canada, the United States, and most of Western Europe, is a vulgar insult in Greece, Italy, Afghanistan, and Iran. The circle formed with the thumb and first finger that means *OK* in Canada is obscene in Southern Italy and can mean "you're worth nothing" in France and Belgium.[58]

Space

Personal space is the distance someone wants between him- or herself and other people in ordinary, non-intimate interchanges. Observation and limited experimentation show that most North Americans, North Europeans, and Asians want a bigger personal space than do Latin Americans, French, Italians, and Arabs. People who prefer lots of personal space are often forced to accept close contact on a crowded elevator or subway.

Even within a culture, some people like more personal space. One study found that men took more personal space than women did.[59] In many cultures, people who are of the same age and sex take less personal space than do mixed-age or mixed-sex groups. Latin Americans will stand closer to people of the same sex than North Americans would, but North Americans stand closer to people of the opposite sex.[60]

Touch

Repeated studies have shown that babies need to be touched to grow and thrive and that older people are healthier both mentally and physically if they are touched. But some people are more comfortable with touch than others. Each may misinterpret the other. A person who dislikes touch may seem unfriendly to someone who's used to touching. A toucher may seem overly familiar to someone who dislikes touch.

Studies in North America have shown that touch is interpreted as power: more-powerful people touch less-powerful people. When the toucher had higher status than the recipient, both men and women liked being touched.[61]

In Asia, the Middle East, South America, and parts of Africa, male friends or female friends can hold hands or walk arm-in-arm, but it is slightly shocking for an opposite-sex couple to touch in public.[62]

In North America, a person sitting at the head of a table (like the one in the large corner office) is generally assumed to be the group's leader. However, one experiment showed that when a woman sat at the head of a mixed-sex group, observers assumed that one of the men in the group was the leader.[63]

Other Nonverbal Symbols

Many other symbols can carry nonverbal meanings: clothing, colours, age, and height, to name a few.

In Canada, certain styles and colours of clothing are considered more "professional" and more "credible." In Japan, clothing denotes not only status but also occupational group. Students wear uniforms. Company badges indicate rank within the organization. Workers wear different clothes when they are on strike than they do when they are working.[64] In Japan, government efforts in the wake of the tsunami to conserve energy with a "Super Cool Biz" campaign encouraging T-shirts and sandals for work met resistance among Japanese business people used to conservative business suits.[65]

Colours can also carry meanings in a culture (see ◂◂ "Designing Visuals" in Chapter 4). In Canada, mourners wear black to funerals, while brides wear white. In Japan, white is the colour of death. Purple flowers are given to the dead in Mexico. In Korea, red ink is used to record deaths but never to write about living people.[66] In the United States, the first-place winner gets a blue ribbon. In the United Kingdom, the first-place ribbon is usually red.

Red is sometimes used to suggest danger or *stop* in Canada; it means *go* in China and is associated with festivities. Red suggests masculinity or aristocracy in France, death in Korea, blasphemy in some African countries, and luxury in many parts of the world. Yellow suggests caution or cowardice in Canada, prosperity in Egypt, grace in Japan, and femininity in many parts of the world.[67]

Height connotes status in many parts of the world. Executive offices are usually on the top floors; the underlings work below. Even being tall can help a person succeed. Studies have shown that employers are more willing to hire men over 6 feet tall than shorter men with the same credentials. In one

International Thinking Outside the Timeline*

Negotiating styles differ across cultures, though we need to be alert to changing patterns and individual differences within groups. To organize a convincing argument, the typical European or North American will develop several points and present a case for them one by one. Negotiating a contract, this person might present a list of terms, such as price, quantity, and delivery date, expecting to discuss each one in turn, moving down the list.

The typical Chinese negotiator, in contrast, rarely thinks in terms of a sequence or timeline. Rather, the Chinese are more likely to engage in holistic thinking, considering details as part of a whole. They want to see a proposal in context and are likely to reconsider individual details repeatedly, as they review the proposal from various angles.

As a result of this difference, Americans negotiating with Chinese may make costly concessions. In a negotiation between Tandem Computers and China Telecom, the Tandem sales manager offered to reduce the price by 5% in exchange for China Telecom's commitment to sign an order for delivery within one month. The purchasing manager responded that there was no need to rush, but since the price was flexible, the price reduction would be acceptable.

Still, a 2010 study of native Chinese students fluent in English found that they were "more assertive, extroverted, and open to new experiences" when talking to an English speaker rather than a Cantonese speaker. That is, personality differs depending on the person with whom one is talking.

*Based on John L. Graham and N. Mark Lam, "The Chinese negotiation," *Harvard Business Review,* October 2003, 82–91; Michelle LeBaron, "Culture-based negotiation styles," retrieved March 19, 2011, from http://www.beyondintractability.org/essay/culture_negotiation/?nid=1287; Zhenzhong Ma, "Negotiating into China: The impact of individual perception on Chinese negotiation styles," *International Journal of Emerging Markets* 1, no. 1 (2006): 64–83; Michael Kesterton, "Social studies: Can you speak Englishly," *The Globe and Mail,* April 21, 2011, L7.

study, every extra inch of height brought in an extra $1,300 a year.[68] But being too big can be a disadvantage. One football player complained that people found him intimidating off the field and assumed that he had no brains.

LO5

ORAL COMMUNICATION

Effective oral communication requires cultural understanding. Learning at least a little of the language of the country where you hope to do business will help you in several ways. It will

- Give you a glimpse into the culture
- Help you manage the daily necessities of finding food and getting where you need to go
- Give you more time to think in business negotiations

Take advantage of the knowledge of a local translator when you travel abroad on business. Brief him or her with the technical terms you'll be using; explain as much of the context of your negotiations as possible. A good translator can also help you interpret nonverbal behaviour and negotiating strategies.

Conversational Style

Deborah Tannen uses the term **conversational style** to denote our conversational patterns and the meaning we give to them: the way we show interest, politeness, appropriateness.[69] Your answers to these questions reveal your own style:

- How long a pause tells you that it's your turn to speak?
- Do you see interruption as rude? Or do you say things while other people are still talking to show that you're interested and to encourage them to say more?
- Do you show interest by asking lots of questions? Or do you see questions as intrusive and wait for people to volunteer whatever they have to say?

One conversational style is not better or worse than another, but people with different conversational styles may feel uncomfortable without knowing why. A subordinate who talks quickly may be frustrated by a boss who speaks slowly. People who talk more slowly may feel shut out of a conversation with people who talk more quickly. Someone who has learned to make requests directly ("Please pass the salt") may be annoyed by someone who uses indirect requests ("This casserole needs some salt").

Daniel N. Maltz and Ruth A. Borker believe that differences in conversational style (Figure 5.4) may be responsible for miscommunication in male–female conversations. For example, researchers have found that women are much more likely to nod and to say "yes" or "mm hmm" than men are. Maltz and Borker hypothesize that to women, these symbols mean simply "I'm listening; go on." Men, on the other hand, may decode these symbols as "I agree" or at least "I follow what you're saying so far." A man who receives nods and *mms* from a woman may feel that she is inconsistent and unpredictable if she then disagrees with him. A woman may feel that a man who doesn't provide any feedback isn't listening to her.[70]

Those miscommunications impact women's careers. A survey completed by 250 business women at different career levels (ages 24 to 67) found that they are still waiting for a female-friendly workplace. Survey respondents believe that

Figure 5.4 Different Conversational Styles

	DEBATING	RELATING
Interpretation of questions	See questions as requests for information.	See questions as way to keep a conversation flowing.
Relation of new comment to what last speaker said	Do not require new comment to relate explicitly to last speaker's comment. Ignoring previous comment is one strategy for taking control.	Expect new comments to acknowledge the last speaker's comment and relate directly to it.
View of aggressiveness	See aggressiveness as one way to organize the flow of conversation.	See aggressiveness as directed at audience personally, as negative, and as disruptive to a conversation.
How topics are defined and changed	Tend to define topics narrowly and shift topics abruptly. Interpret statements about side issues as effort to change the topic.	Tend to define topics gradually, progressively. Interpret statements about side issues as effort to shape, expand, or limit the topic.
Response to someone who shares a problem	Offer advice, solutions.	Offer solidarity, reassurance. Share troubles to establish sense of community.

Sources: Based on Daniel N. Maltz and Ruth A. Borker, "A cultural approach to male-female miscommunication," *Language and Social Identity*, ed. John J. Gumperz (Cambridge, U.K.: Cambridge University Press, 1982), 213; and Deborah Tannen, *Talking from 9 to 5: Women and Men in the Workplace: Language, Sex and Power* (New York: William Morrow, 1995).

men still live by the numbers, while women value relationships. Most still make women feel they have to deny their femininity to fit in. Most women find a huge gap between theory and practice, and many are looking to self-employment as the answer—especially when 16% fewer women held corporate jobs in Canada in 2007.[71]

Women in the corporate world remains a hot topic in 2013–2014, with bestselling books and media responses offering different perspectives on why women remain under-represented and under-rewarded.[72] While women's representation on boards of Canada's largest companies increased from 17 to 20% in 2013, 36% of boards have no women,[73] and women continue to be judged on their appearance, dress, and hairstyle in cliché-coded business media dominated by men.[74]

Harvard's Barbara Annis thinks "gender intelligence"—"the ability to comprehend the distinguishing characteristics of each gender," including "attitudinal and behavioural distinctiveness"—is what is needed.[75]

Silence

Silence also has different meanings in different cultures and subcultures. During a period of military tension, Greek traffic controllers responded with silence when Egyptian planes requested permission to land. The Greeks intended silence as a refusal; the Egyptians interpreted silence as consent. Several people were killed when the Greeks fired on the planes as they approached the runway.[76] Similarly, men may misunderstand women who respond to offensive remarks with silence.

Voice Qualities

Tone of voice refers to the rising or falling inflection that tells you whether a group of words is a question or a statement, whether the speaker is uncertain or confident, whether a statement is sincere or sarcastic. Anyone who has written dialogue with adverbs ("he said thoughtfully") has tried to indicate tone of voice.

When tone of voice and the meaning of words conflict, people "believe" the tone of voice. One person responded to friends' "How are you?" with the words "Dying, and you?" Most of the friends responded "Fine." Because the tone of voice was cheerful, they didn't hear the content of the words.[77]

Pitch measures whether a voice uses sounds that are low (like the bass notes on a piano) or high. Low-pitched voices are usually perceived as being more authoritative, sexier, and more pleasant to listen to than are high-pitched voices. Most voices go up in pitch when the speaker is angry or excited; some people raise pitch when they increase volume. Women whose normal speaking voices are high may need to practise projecting their voices to avoid becoming shrill when they speak to large groups.

Stress is the emphasis given to one or more words in a sentence. As the following example shows, emphasizing different words can change the meaning.

I'll give you a raise.

[Implication, depending on pitch and speed: "Another supervisor wouldn't" or "I have the power to determine your salary."]

I'll **give** you a raise.

[Implication, depending on pitch and speed: "You haven't **earned** it" or "OK, all right, you win. I'm saying 'yes' to get rid of you, but I don't really agree," or "I've just this instant decided that you deserve a raise."]

I'll give **you** a raise.

[Implication: "But nobody else in this department is getting one."]

I'll give you **a** raise.

[Implication: "But just one."]

Speakers who use many changes in tone, pitch, and stress usually seem more enthusiastic, more energetic, and more

On the Job Playing by the Rules?*

- Linda Dunkin, writing on the CEO Refresher Web site (www.refresher.com), advises women to change the game and leverage the strengths of their gender: recognize that leaders don't need to be heroic, understand that information is stored in databases but knowledge resides in people, build on what is there rather than focusing on what is not there, and "make character the currency of your leadership." (Schachter)
- Fifty-seven percent of TSX-listed firms surveyed by the Ontario Securities Commission in November 2013 do not have a single female director. Only 3% of respondents had a woman chair of the board.
- "Part of the problem for women is that it is all those old guys who are the gatekeepers," says Elizabeth Watson, who has the job of finding directors for public corporations in British Columbia. (Church)
- Research is showing a "significant link" between women in top management and financial performance and hence the business case for gender equity. (McFarland)

*Based on Ontario Securities Commission, Proposed Amendments to Form 58-101F1 Corporate Governance Disclosure . . . Proposed Disclosure Requirements Regarding the Representation of Women on Boards and in Senior Management, retrieved March 29, 2014, from http://www.osc.gov.on.ca/en/SecuritiesLaw_ni_20140116_58-101_pro-amd-f1.htm; Harvey Schachter, "In a man's game, women must play by own rules," *Globe Careers*, January 18, 2005, C1; Elizabeth Church, "Women still missing at the table," *The Globe and Mail*, September 26, 2003, B1–4; Janet McFarland, "A woman's touch rewards shareholders," *The Globe and Mail*, March 8, 2011, B15.

Scriptwriters work together on a Population Media Center (PMC) radio serial drama, using old media to reach new audiences in Jamaica on HIV/AIDS, adolescent sexual and reproductive health, violence prevention, and substance abuse prevention.

intelligent. Someone who speaks in a monotone may seem apathetic or unintelligent. Non-native speakers whose first language does not use tone, pitch, and stress to convey meaning and attitude may be misunderstood.

Volume is a measure of loudness or softness. Very soft voices, especially if they are also breathy and high pitched, give the impression of youth and inexperience. People who do a lot of speaking to large groups need to practise projecting their voices so they can increase their volume without shouting.

In some cultures, it is considered rude to shout; loud voices connote anger and imminent violence. In others, everyday conversations are loud.

LO6

WRITING TO INTERNATIONAL AUDIENCES

Most cultures are more formal than Canada. When you write to international audiences,

- Use titles, not first names.
- Avoid contractions, slang (*goofed*), sports metaphors (*dropped the ball, out in left field*).
- Avoid idioms that cannot be readily translated (*by the skin of your teeth, no axe to grind, ring the changes*).
- Write in English unless you're extremely fluent in your reader's language.
- Use familiar terms (*agree*, not *concur*).
- Use specific action verbs (*buy*, not *get*).
- Replace jargon words (*win–win, buy in, benchmark, deliverables*) with familiar words (*mutually agreeable, agree to, compare, results*).[78]

The patterns of organization (⏩ Chapter 7) that work for Canadian audiences may need to be modified in international correspondence. For most cultures, buffer negative messages and make requests more indirect (⏩ Chapter 8). Make a special effort to avoid phrases that could seem cold and uncaring. Cultural mistakes made orally may be forgotten; those made

On the Job Valuing Diversity?*

While many Canadian businesses claim to value diversity, a 2007 Leger Marketing survey for Xerox Research Centre of Canada found:

- 53% have seen no increase in company diversity since 2002
- Only 56% of managers believe Canada is capitalizing on its diversity.

Despite equity legislation and diversity training, a Catalyst Canada–Diversity Institute study of 16,500 visible minority managers and executives found:

- 47% felt they were held to higher standards of performance than their peers
- 67% reported "who you know" mattered more than "what you know"
- Only 48% felt senior managers demonstrated commitment to diversity

An RBC study on the "diversity advantage" finds removal of age, gender, and culture barriers would have these results:

- 1.6 million more Canadians in the workforce
- $174 billion more in personal income

Kelly Lendsay, president and CEO of the Aboriginal Human Resource Council, underlines the benefit to Canada's GDP ($401 billion by 2026, according to the Centre for the Study of Living Standards) if Aboriginal people could reach the same level of education, employment, and social well-being as their non-Aboriginal counterparts.

*Based on Kelly Lendsay, "Aboriginal inclusion wise policy," *Saskatoon StarPhoenix*, April 7, 2011, retrieved March 29, 2014 from http://www2.canada.com/saskatoonstarphoenix/news/forum/story.html?id=07e53e4e-8fec-49c7-b298-eb1d9ab1d0da&p=2; Leger Marketing Survey for Xerox Research Centre of Canada, cit. in Wallace Immen, "Diversity of teams powers innovation, creativity, poll finds," *The Globe and Mail*, September 28, 2007; Catalyst/Diversity Institute, *Career Advancement in Corporate Canada: A Focus on Visible Minorities—Survey Findings*, Toronto, 2007, retrieved October 2, 2007, from http://www.ryerson.ca/tedrogersschool/diversityinstitute/english.pdf; RBC, "The diversity advantage: A case for Canada's 21st century economy," presented at 10th International Metropolis Conference, October 20, 2005, retrieved April 12, 2008, from http://www.rbc.com/newsroom/pdf/20051020diversity.pdf.

in writing are permanently recorded. See too ◀◀ Chapter 2 on tone.

Business people from Europe and Japan who correspond frequently with North Americans are beginning to adopt North American directness and patterns of organization. If you don't know your reader well, it may be safer to make your message less direct.

In international business correspondence, list the day before the month:

× *Not:* *April 8, 2014*
✓ *But:* *8 April 2014 (not 08 as in Microsoft)*

Dates confuse the generations.

Permission to reproduce the following cartoon image in relation to ISO 2601 was provided by Standards Council of Canada. No further reproduction is permitted without prior written approval from Standards Council of Canada. From http://www.iso.org/iso/date_and_time_format. Copyright remains with ISO.

The International Organization for Standardization ISO 8601, which is especially popular among computer software users, recommends dates be represented in the order year, month, day: 2014-04-24, for example.

In addition to attending to bias-free language and visuals (◀◀ Chapter 2), check for bias in the clip art that may complement your text. One study has shown that 22% of clip art files involving humans pictured women, and the majority portrayed women in traditional roles.[79]

LEARNING MORE ABOUT INTERCULTURAL AND INTERNATIONAL BUSINESS COMMUNICATION

Learning to communicate with people from different backgrounds shouldn't be a matter of learning rules. Instead, use the examples in this chapter to get a sense for the kinds of factors that differ from one culture to another. Test these generalizations against your experience.

If we need to be sensitive to gender differences within and across cultures, the same is true of communicating with or about people with disabilities. Disabilities are mental, physical, sensory, or emotional impairments, only 20% of which are congenital in origin (nutrition, hygiene, violence, limited access to health care, and aging are other factors). Among those of working age in Canada, 14.5% have a disability.

Just as we respect the self-naming of Aboriginal peoples in Canada, so we now adopt the names people with disabilities apply to themselves (◀◀ Chapter 2). The emphasis is on the person and not the disability: on appropriate, positive, and sensitive terms that respect people's abilities.[80]

SUMMARY OF KEY POINTS

- Cultural competence is the capacity to communicate effectively across cultural differences. It is a valuable asset in a global knowledge economy.
- The successful intercultural communicator is
  - Aware that his or her preferred values and behaviours are influenced by culture and are not necessarily "right"
  - Flexible and open to change
  - Sensitive to verbal and nonverbal behaviour
  - Aware of the values, beliefs, and practices in other cultures
  - Sensitive to differences among individuals within a culture
- *Culture* provides patterns of acceptable behaviour and beliefs. It shapes how we see the world, understand our own and others' identities, and find meaning.
- In *high-context cultures,* most of the information is inferred from the context of a message; little is explicitly conveyed. In *low-context cultures,* context is less important; most information is explicitly spelled out.
- In *monochronic* cultures, people focus on clock time. In *polychronic* cultures, people focus on relationships.
- *Conversational* style denotes our conversational patterns and the meaning we give to them: the way we show interest, politeness, and appropriateness.
- The patterns of organization that work for Canadian audiences may need to be modified in international correspondence. Use more formal and familiar language.

EXERCISES AND PROBLEMS

GETTING STARTED

5.1 LEARNING IN THE MULTICULTURAL CLASSROOM

In one of the following situations (in pairs or in groups), share your knowledge and experience of miscommunications resulting from cultural differences. Conduct an online search if you need more examples than you and your peers can gather.

1. The On the Job box "That's Not What We Meant!" gives some examples of how different versions of English around the world can lead to miscommunication. Choose any two countries represented in your class for which English is an official language and identify examples of the same words having very different meanings or very different words representing the same thing—with humorous or even unhappy results.
2. Choose two countries represented by classroom peers and share knowledge of the role that religion plays in the cultures and its effect on business communication. You might think about food, festivals, holidays, work days, for instance.
3. Choose two countries represented by classroom peers and share knowledge of their cultures (high-context or low-context, monochronic or polychronic) and their impact on business communication.

As Your Professor Directs,

a. Make a presentation to your class.

b. Post a blog on your findings on the college or department Web site.

c. Role play to illustrate your findings to the class.

5.2 ADVISING NEW STUDENTS ABOUT DEPARTMENT CULTURE

Colleges and universities and individual departments can be as different in their cultures as any other group of people. Students new to your department look to you for advice about how they can fit in and know how to behave, think, write, and speak like an insider.

As Your Professor Directs,

a. Make a group oral presentation to the class.

b. Write a group report (see ▸▸ Chapters 10 and 11) to your professor.

c. Use role-play for your advice.

d. Post advice on the department or class blog.

E-MAIL MESSAGES

5.3 SENDING A DRAFT TO CHINA

You've drafted instructions for a consumer product that will be sold in China. Before the text is translated, you want to find out if the pictures will be clear. So you send an e-mail to your Chinese counterpart, asking for a response within a week.

Write an e-mail message; assume that you will send the pictures as an attachment.

5.4 ASKING ABOUT TRAVEL ARRANGEMENTS

The CEO is planning a trip to visit colleagues in another country (you pick the country). As executive assistant to the CEO of your organization, you are responsible for the CEO's travel plans. At this stage, you don't know anything except dates and flights. (The CEO will arrive in the country at 7 a.m. local time on the 28th of next month and stay for three days.) It's your job to ask about travel and meeting plans, as well as accommodations and social events, food, holidays or festivals that may impact the CEO's visit and communicate any of the CEO's requirements.

Write an e-mail message to your contact in the other country.

Hints:

- Pick a business, non-profit organization, or government agency you know something about, making assumptions about the kinds of things its executive would want to do during an international visit.
- How much international travelling does your CEO do? Has he or she ever been to this country before? What questions will he or she want answered?

COMMUNICATING AT WORK

5.5 STUDYING INTERNATIONAL COMMUNICATION AT YOUR WORKPLACE

Does your employer buy from suppliers or sell to customers outside the country? Get a sampling of international messages, or interview managers about the problems they've encountered.

As Your Professor Directs,

a. Share your results orally with a small group of students.

b. Present your findings orally to the class.

c. Summarize your findings in a memo (see ⏩ Chapter 7 for format advice) to your professor.

d. Join with other students in your class to write a blog posting.

WEB PAGES

5.6 COMPARING COMPANY WEB PAGES FOR VARIOUS COUNTRIES

Many multinationals have separate Web pages for their operations in various countries. For example, Cadbury has Web sites for the United Kingdom, Australia, and New Zealand and its Canadian site is at www.snackworks.ca. Check out Procter & Gamble's presence in Canada, the US, Europe, and worldwide. IKEA.com has at least eight different national sites.

Analyze three of the country pages of a company of your choice.

- Is a single template used for pages in different countries, or do the basic designs differ?
- Are different images used in different countries? What do the images suggest?
- If you can read the language, analyze the links. What information is emphasized?
- To what extent are the pages similar? To what extent do they reveal national and cultural differences?

As Your Professor Directs,

a. Write a memo (see ⏩ Chapter 7 for format) analyzing the similarities and differences you find. Attach printouts of the pages to your memo.

b. Post a message to the class analyzing the pages. Include the URLs as hotlinks.

c. Make an oral presentation to the class. Paste the Web pages into PowerPoint slides.

d. Join with a small group of students to create a group report (see ⏩ Chapters 10 and 11) comparing several companies' Web pages in three specific countries. Attach printouts of the pages.

e. Make a group oral presentation to the class.

LETTER, MEMO, ORAL PRESENTATION, AND REPORT ASSIGNMENTS

5.7 PLANNING A BUSINESS TRIP

Assume that you're going to Iqaluit, or the capital city of another country, on business two months from now. (You pick the country.) Use a search engine to find out about

Holidays celebrated in that month

The climate

Current events in the news

Key features of business etiquette you should know

Kinds of gifts you should bring to your hosts

Sight-seeing you should try to include.

As Your Professor Directs,

a. Write an e-mail to your professor reporting the information you found.

b. Make an oral presentation to the class.

c. Join with a small group of students to create a group report (see ▸▸ Chapters 10 and 11) on several countries in a region.

e. Make a group oral presentation to the class.

5.8 APPLYING FOR A PLACEMENT ON AN INTERNATIONAL EXCHANGE PROGRAM

Using what you have learned about cultural competence and drawing on advice on application letters in ▸▸ Chapter 13, write a letter of application for placement on an international exchange program. Be sure to do research on your country of choice so that you are as persuasive in your letter as you will be when you get that placement interview. Be sure to demonstrate the assets you will bring (language skills, travel experience, volunteer record, for instance).

5.9 IDENTIFYING SOURCES OF MISCOMMUNICATION

In each of the following situations (in pairs or groups), identify one or more ways that cultural differences may be leading to miscommunication.

1. Alan is a Canadian sales representative in Mexico. He makes appointments and is careful to be on time. But the person he's calling on is frequently late. To save time, Alan tries to get right to business. But his hosts want to talk about sightseeing and his family. Even worse, his appointments are interrupted constantly, not only by business phone calls but also by long conversations with other people and even the customers' children who come into the office. Alan's first progress report is very negative. He hasn't yet made a sale. Perhaps Mexico just isn't the right place to sell his company's products.
2. To help her company establish a presence in Japan, Susan wants to hire a local interpreter who can advise her on business customs. Kana Tomari has superb qualifications on paper. But when Susan tries to probe about her experience, Kana just says, "I will do my best. I will try very hard." She never gives details about any of the previous positions she's held. Susan begins to wonder if the résumé is inflated, padded, or even deceptive.
3. Stan wants to negotiate a joint venture with a Chinese company. He asks Tung-Sen Lee if the Chinese people have enough discretionary income to afford his product. Mr. Lee is silent for a time, and then says, "Your product is good. People in the West must like it." Stan smiles, pleased that Mr. Lee recognizes the quality of his product, and he gives Mr. Lee a contract to sign. Weeks later, Stan still hasn't heard anything. If China is going to be so inefficient, he wonders if he really should try to do business there.
4. Elspeth is very proud of her participatory management style. On assignment in India, she is careful not to give orders but to ask for suggestions. But people rarely suggest anything. Even a formal suggestion system doesn't work. And to make matters worse, she doesn't sense the respect and camaraderie of the plant she managed in Canada. Perhaps, she decides gloomily, people in India just aren't ready for a woman boss.

As Your Professor Directs,

a. Make a presentation to your class.

b. Write an e-mail to your professor reporting your findings.

5.10 ANSWERING AN INQUIRY ABOUT PHOTOS

You've just been named vice-president for diversity, the first person in your organization to hold this position. Today, you receive this memo from Sheila Lathan, who edits the employee newsletter.

Subject: Photos in the Employee Newsletter

Please tell me what to do about photos in the monthly employee newsletter. I'm concerned that almost no single issue represents the diversity of employees we have here.

As you know, our layout allows two visuals each month. One of those is always the employee of the month (EM). In the last year, most of those have been male and all but two have been white. What makes it worse is that people want photos that make them look good. In the photo EM Ron Almos wanted me to use, you can't tell that he's in a wheelchair. Often the EM is the only photo; the other visual is often a graph of sales or something relating to quality.

Even if the second visual is another photo, it may not look balanced in terms of gender and race. After all, 62% of our employees are men, and 78% are white. Should the pictures try to represent those percentages? The leadership positions (both in management and in the union) are even more heavily male and white. Should we run pictures of people doing important things, and risk continuing the imbalance?

I guess I could use more visuals, but then there wouldn't be room for as many stories—and people really like to see their names in print. Plus, giving people information about company activities and sales is important to maintaining goodwill. A bigger newsletter would be one way to have more visuals and keep the content, but with the cost-cutting measures we're under, that doesn't look likely.

What should I do?

As Your Professor Directs,

a. Work in a small group with other students to come up with a recommendation for Sheila.

b. Write an e-mail responding to her.

c. Write an article for the employee newsletter about the photo policy you recommend and how it relates to the company's concern for diversity.

WORKING AND WRITING IN TEAMS

6

Learning Outcomes

LO1 Explain five strategies of active listening

LO2 Discuss the impact of group dynamics on team success

LO3 List the characteristics of successful and unsuccessful student teams

LO4 Identify effective conflict resolution strategies

LO5 Describe effective meeting management

LO6 Discuss the characteristics of successful collaborative writing

AN INSIDE PERSPECTIVE

In colleges, universities, and businesses, more and more projects from planning and research to proposal and report writing are accomplished by teams. Organizations invest in teams for these outcomes:

- Improved information sharing, creativity, and decision making
- Efficient preparation of documents
- Increased appreciation of others
- Enhanced morale

Born in Halifax and raised in Ottawa, Simon Pulsifer (the son of a librarian and historian) has been called "Canada's Wikipedia wonder boy." His reward is doing something he has always loved—reading and writing—and receiving a Wikipedia appreciation award in February 2011.

Open-source and user-generated, wikis have become powerful social software tools for both knowledge sharing and team or community building. While some are cautious about operating in a wiki world, where content can be edited and control shared, Simon Pulsifer was hooked from his first entry (on the Panama Canal in 2001) in Wikipedia, the largest wiki and one of the ten most popular Web sites.

More than 111,000 edits and 3,000 articles later (at January 2011), Pulsifer (a University of Toronto history graduate) is one of more than 300,000 active users, more than 39 million registered users of 25 million articles in 284 languages.

Pulsifer found a love of informal e-learning and facilitating access to "free, accurate and unbiased information." He also found celebrity that helped him land a job at Quillsoft, Toronto, researching and writing programs for children with learning disabilities.

Now that he has full-time employment, from a high of 200 posts a day, he's down to "four or five." If it was easier to write when he started, Pulsifer now finds that "an article requires days inside the University of Toronto's Robarts Library to wade through books nobody has read in 30 years." He also finds that "the scope has been getting narrower" and there is "a truly vast library of rules and policies."*

*Based on "Wikipedia—facts and figures," retrieved from http://visual.ly/wikipedia-facts-figures; Lesley Clarula Taylor, "Thousands of editors leaving Wikipedia," November 23, 2009, retrieved March 20, 2011, from http://www.thestar.com/news/sciencetech/technology/article/729552--thousands-of-editors-leaving-wikipedia; "Simon Pulsifer," retrieved March 20, 2011, from http://en.wikipedia.org/wiki/Simon_Pulsifer; Joanna Slater, "The man with all the answers," *Report on Business Weekend,* January 15, 2011, B3; Canadian Council on Learning, "Simon Pulsifer: Canada's Wikipedia wonder boy takes his talents to market," retrieved April 16, 2008, from http://www.ccl-cca.ca/CCL/Newsroom/Profiles/PILSimonPulsifer.htm; Alexandro Shimo, "Prolific Canadian is king of Wikipedia," *The Globe and Mail,* August 4, 2006, A3.

Current trends in business (see ◀◀ Chapter 1) from technology and globalization to outsourcing have made teamwork even more important. If globalization has made teamwork more necessary, technology has enabled the trend. Teleconferencing, videoconferencing, Skype, instant messaging, and electronic meetings are proving especially useful for business at a time of soaring fuel costs and fears about security. Still, they can produce embarrassing technical glitches. In the case of Web meetings pop-ups can surprise at the worst of times, or private exchanges, inadvertent actions, or bloopers can be recorded and repeated for all to see and hear.[1] A 2009 study found that 95% of professionals believed that face-to-face meetings remain "a key factor in successfully building and maintaining long-term relationships," especially in cross-cultural situations, and 89% believed they were "essential for 'sealing the deal.'"[2]

If Wikipedia is the most famous wiki today, many others around the world support group writing, project management, and research and development in colleges and universities as well as in business, non-profit, and government settings. Social media scheduling tools such as **WikiRoster, Scheedule, Koofers,** and of course Facebook and other social media help students and workers synchronize schedules, learn together, and co-ordinate work.[3]

Wikis allow contributors to create and edit text without any specialized software or information technology support. Like Simon Pulsifer (◀◀ An Inside Perspective), many celebrate an online resource that invites contributors to join in the discussion (adding, deleting, reorganizing, or correcting) and that keeps a careful archive of who has contributed what and when. Wikis, like blogs, are widely seen as encouraging students to increase and improve their writing and learning.

On the Job Leading by Listening*

According to business psychologist Debra Condren, the best way to help employees develop their skills is not to give them advice. Rather, managers should coach employees by listening to them.

When mentoring employees, the manager should talk only about one-quarter of the time.

Managers can help by listening and asking questions that lead employees through a decision-making process. For example, the manager can ask, "What would be the advantages and disadvantages of telling the customer what you're telling me? How do you think the customer would respond?" and "Would those benefits outweigh the risks?"

In the end, that decision-making skill is more significant than a supply of easy answers from the manager.

Linda Naiman of Vancouver agrees. Many companies have the "outdated notion" that "you have to be a genius to be creative." Instead, "creativity workers" want to know the company goals and "then have the freedom to figure out how to achieve it." In a study by management professor Jeffrey Dyer, the "most innovative" CEOs are the ones who "ask questions that challenge assumptions."

True engagement and innovation come not from "visible and tangible" perks and "top down initiatives" but from "management by walking around," giving "people agency"—and "a say"—and connecting skills and talents to company goals.

When managers aren't listening, they lose. When Ken Milloy pitched a plan to improve financial performance, his boss "leaned back in his big fancy chair" before responding, "You know, Ken, we hired you to do a job for us. We didn't hire you to think!" Ken quit!

*Based on Deborah Aarts, "The truth about employee engagement," *Canadian Business,* March 2014, 31–35; "Better feedback," *Sales & Marketing Management,* December 2003; Jennifer Myers, "Workplace creativity withers on the vine," *Globe Careers,* February 20, 2010, B18; Ken Milloy, "Help managers and supervisors 'do engagement,'" *CW Bulletin,* January 2011, retrieved January 24, 2011 from http://www.iabc.com/cwb/archive/2011/0111/Milloy.htm.

Whether in educational or business settings, wikis have been gaining ground. According to Richard Hammond, head of Visualwize.com, wikis depend not so much on the belief that few will damage sites as "on the idea that the community will police itself." The wiki record of contributions, IP addresses, and times of changes builds in transparency and accountability.[4] A European study found that wiki adopters reduced e-mail volume by 75% and meeting time by 50%.[5]

Although it has done much to improve collaboration and productivity, the wiki—like the e-mail before it—is proving to be a mixed blessing. Ease has translated into overload, raising concerns about storage, best practices, legal compliance, and reputation and other risks. A General Motors wiki, for example, drew challenging comments about global warming and gas-guzzling vehicles, though General Motors made the most of the situation by maintaining the wiki and getting credit for openness.[6]

Teamwork is crucial to success in an organization. Some teams produce products, provide services, or recommend solutions to problems. Other teams—perhaps in addition to providing a service or recommending a solution—produce documents.

Building the trust needed for teamwork success—whether working on problems or documents in close proximity or at opposite ends of the globe—takes careful preparation and planning, well-defined goals, clear lines of authority, cultural competence (◀◀ Chapter 5), and effective interpersonal communication. With more than 42% of its workforce remote, IBM finds Twitter, Facebook, blogging, and wikis to be effective means of keeping its workers "connected, engaged, and productive."[7]

Interpersonal communication is communication between people. Interpersonal skills such as listening and dealing with conflict are used in one-to-one interchanges, in problem-solving teams, and in writing teams. These skills will make you more successful on the job, in social groups, and in community service and volunteer work. A focus on quality and customer needs explains some of their importance to the Conference Board of Canada (◀◀ Chapter 1). In writing teams, giving careful attention to both team process and writing process (◀◀ Chapter 3) improves both the final product and members' satisfaction with the team.

LO1

LISTENING

Listening, crucial to building trust, is a learned skill that takes time and energy (◀◀ Chapter 1). However, listening on the job may be more difficult than listening in classes. Many classroom lectures are well organized, with signposts and repetition of key points to help hearers follow. But conversations usually wander, and in the workplace often assume a familiarity with the organizational culture and its norms and conventions (◀◀ Chapter 2). In exchanges with friends and co-workers, you need to listen for connotations (◀◀ Chapter 3) and voice qualities (◀◀ Chapter 5), which reflect feelings, too. Feelings of being rejected or overworked need to be dealt with as they arise. But you can't deal with a feeling unless you are aware of it. Face-to-face exchanges have the advantage over e-communications in offering a range of cues about how our words and actions are affecting others.

As Chapter 1 explains, to receive a message, the receiver must first perceive the message, then decode it (that is, translate the symbols into meaning), and then interpret it. In interpersonal communication, **hearing** denotes perceiving sounds. **Listening** means decoding and interpreting them correctly.

In other words, hearing and listening are not the same. Whereas hearing can be involuntary (overhearing a conversation among colleagues), listening requires

- A conscious choice
- A positive attitude and openness
- Attention to verbal and nonverbal cues and context

Although many associate listening with passivity and inaction, listening requires mental activity and physical energy. We learn about our culture, about ourselves, and about thinking by listening. Workers typically spend 30–45% of their communication time listening; executives spend 60–70% of theirs.[8]

People in low-context cultures (◂◂ Chapter 5) may find themselves wanting to get down to business and impatient of the demands of listening, especially when we can process what we hear (1,000–3,000 words per minute) far more quickly than people can typically speak (125–250 words per minute). These listening facts go a long way to explaining why we in Canada are not very good listeners, forgetting as much as 50% of what we hear immediately after listening.[9]

Take notes when you can. In addition, to avoid **polite listening** that is mechanical and inattentive, try these strategies:

- Make a list of the questions you have. When is the project due? What resources do you have? What is the most important aspect of this project, from the other person's point of view? During a conversation, listen for answers to your questions.
- At the end of the conversation, check your understanding with the other person. Check who does what next.
- During or immediately after the conversation, write down key points that affect deadlines or project evaluation.

Many listening errors are errors in interpretation. In 1977, when two Boeing 747 jumbo jets ran into each other on the ground in Tenerife, the pilots seemed to have heard the control tower's instructions. The KLM pilot was told to taxi to the end of the runway, turn around, and wait for clearance. But the KLM pilot didn't interpret the order to wait as an order he needed to follow. The Pan Am pilot interpreted *his* order to turn off at the "third intersection" to mean the third *unblocked* intersection. He didn't count the first blocked ramp, so he was still on the main runway when the KLM pilot ran into his plane. The planes exploded in flames; 576 people died.[10]

Listening to people is an indication that you're taking them seriously. **Acknowledgment responses**—nods, *uh huhs*, smiles, frowns—help carry the message that you're listening.

In **active listening,** receivers actively demonstrate that they've heard and understood a speaker by feeding back either the literal meaning or the emotional content or both. Five strategies create active responses (see the right-hand list in Figure 6.1):

- Paraphrase the content. Feed back the meaning in your own words.
- Mirror the speaker's feelings. Identify the feelings you think you hear.
- State your own feelings. This strategy works especially well when you are angry.
- Ask for information or clarification.
- Offer to help solve the problem.

Figure 6.1 Blocking Responses versus Active Listening

BLOCKING RESPONSE	POSSIBLE ACTIVE RESPONSE
Ordering, threatening "I don't care how you do it. Just get that report on my desk by Friday."	**Paraphrasing content** "You're saying that you don't have time to finish the report by Friday."
Preaching, criticizing "You should know better than to air the department's problems in a general meeting."	**Mirroring feelings** "It sounds as if the department's problems really bother you."
Interrogating "Why didn't you tell me that you didn't understand the instructions?"	**Stating one's own feelings** "I'm frustrated that the job isn't completed yet, and I'm worried about getting it done on time."
Minimizing the problem "You think that's bad. You should see what I have to do this week."	**Asking for information or clarification** "What parts of the problem seem most difficult to solve?"
Advising "Well, why don't you try listing everything you have to do and seeing which items are most important?"	**Offering to help solve the problem together** "Is there anything I could do that would help?"

Source: The five responses that block communication are based on a list of 12 in Thomas Gordon and Judith Gordon Sands, *P.E.T. in Action* (New York: Wyden, 1976), 117–18.

Instead of simply mirroring what the other person says, many of us immediately respond in a way that analyzes or attempts to solve or dismiss the problem. People with problems need first of all to know that we hear they're having a rough time. Figure 6.1 lists on the left some of the responses that block communication.

Active listening takes time and energy. Even people who are skilled active listeners can't do it all the time. Furthermore, active listening works only if you are genuinely receptive to the other person's ideas and feelings. Active listening can reduce the conflict that results from miscommunication, but it alone cannot reduce the conflict that comes when two people want apparently inconsistent things or when one person wants to change someone else.[11]

Active listening can find opportunity in some negative messages. When advertising account representative Beverly Jameson received a message that a client wanted to cancel ad space, instead of registering "cancel," she heard: "There's a problem here—let's get to the root of it." Jameson met with the client, asked the right questions, and discovered that the client wanted more flexibility. She changed some of the markets, kept the business, and turned the client into a repeat customer.[12]

Figure 6.2 Team Ground Rules

- Start on time; end on time.
- Come to meetings prepared.
- Focus comments on the issues.
- Avoid personal attacks.
- Listen to and respect members' opinions.
- Practise NOSTUESO (No One Speaks Twice Until Everybody Speaks Once)
- If you have a problem with another person, tell that person, not everyone else.
- Ensure that everyone is 70% comfortable with the decision and 100% committed to implementing it.
- If you agree to do something, do it.
- Communicate immediately if you think you may not be able to fulfill an agreement.

Sources: Nancy Schullery and Beth Hoger, "Business advocacy for students in small groups," Association for Business Communication Annual Convention, San Antonio, November 9–11, 1998; "An antidote to chronic cantankerousness," *Fast Company,* February/March 1998, 176; John Grossmann, "We've got to start meeting like this," *Inc.,* April 1998, 70; Gary Dessler, *Winning Commitment,* quoted in *Team Management Briefings,* preview issue (September 1998), 5; and 3M Meeting Network, "Groundrules and Agreements," www.3M.com/meetingnetwork/readingroom/meetingguide_grndrules.html (September 25, 2001).

LO2

GROUP INTERACTIONS AND TEAM FORMATION

Teams can focus on three different dimensions:

1. **Informational messages** focus on content: the problem, data, and possible solutions.
2. **Procedural messages** focus on method and process. How will the team make decisions? Who will do what? When will assignments be due?
3. **Interpersonal messages** focus on people, promoting friendliness, cooperation, and team loyalty.

Different kinds of communication dominate during the four stages of the life of a task group building team trust and loyalty: orientation, formation, coordination, and formalization.[13]

During **orientation,** when members meet and begin to define their task, groups need to develop social cohesiveness and to design procedures for meeting and acting. Interpersonal and procedural comments reduce the tension that often exists in a new group. A focus on information in this first stage can hurt the group's long-term productivity.

Teams are often most effective when they explicitly adopt ground rules (Figure 6.2).

During **formation,** conflicts may arise when the group chooses a leader and defines the problem. Successful leaders collaborate to ensure procedures are clear and agreeable to all and will be followed. Successful groups analyze the problem carefully before they begin to search for solutions.

Coordination is the longest phase and the phase during which most of the group's work is done. While procedural and interpersonal comments help maintain direction and friendliness, most of the comments need to deal with information. Good information is essential to a good decision. Conflict occurs as the group debates alternate solutions.

In **formalization,** the group seeks consensus. The success of this phase determines how well the group's decision will be implemented—and whether the group consolidates its identity as a team. It has been said that in his last year with the Vancouver Canucks, Todd Bertuzzi managed to turn a team into a mere group—without the complementary skills, cohesiveness, cooperation, commitment, and mutual accountability of a successful team.[14]

Trust in Teams

Developing trust among team members takes communication, honesty, openness, consistency, reliability, and respect. If a climate of trust is developed, teams enjoy these results:

- Problem-focused performance
- Efficient communication and coordination
- Quality outcomes[15]

When trust is high, team members can avoid stress, frustration, and resentment; focus energies on tasks; ask one another for help; openly express concerns; and rely on member roles, talents, and skills.[16]

High trust is key to the safe environment at Pixar, which makes possible the company's "collective creativity"—taking risks, sharing unfinished work, and learning from constructive feedback—and the success of their movie productions such as *A Bug's Life, Toy Story 2,* and *Finding Nemo.* All of their

Giving and getting constructive feedback is the foundation of Pixar's creative success.

stories and movies are created internally by their "community of artists," who are encouraged to problem solve and share ideas within the team. Loyalty and commitment build, releasing "everyone's creativity."[17]

Roles in Teams

Individual members can play several roles—positive or negative—in teams.

Positive Roles and Actions to Achieve Team Goals[18]

- **Seeking information and opinions**—asking questions, identifying gaps in the group's knowledge.
- **Giving information and opinions**—answering questions, providing relevant information.
- **Summarizing**—restating major points, pulling ideas together, summarizing decisions.
- **Evaluating**—comparing group processes and products to standards and goals.
- **Coordinating**—planning work, giving directions, and fitting together contributions of group members.

Positive Roles and Actions for Loyalty, Conflict Resolution, and Smooth Functioning

- **Encouraging participation**—demonstrating openness and acceptance, recognizing the contributions of members, calling on quieter group members.
- **Relieving tensions**—joking and suggesting breaks and fun activities.
- **Checking feelings**—asking members how they feel about activities and sharing one's own feelings.
- **Solving interpersonal problems**—opening discussion of interpersonal problems in the group and suggesting ways to solve them.
- **Listening actively**—showing members that they have been heard and that their ideas are taken seriously.

Negative Roles and Actions That Hurt the Team's Product and Process

- **Blocking**—disagreeing with ideas the group proposes.
- **Dominating**—trying to run the group by ordering, shutting out others, and insisting on one's own way.
- **Clowning**—making unproductive jokes and diverting the group from the task.
- **Withdrawing**—being silent in meetings, not contributing, not helping, not attending meetings.

Some actions can be positive or negative depending on how they are used. Criticizing ideas is necessary if the group is to produce the best solution, but criticizing every idea without ever suggesting solutions blocks a group. Jokes in moderation can defuse tension and make the group more fun; too many can make the work more difficult.

Leadership in Teams

You may have noted that "leader" was not one of the roles listed above. Being a leader does not mean doing all the work yourself. Indeed, someone who implies that he or she has the best ideas and can do the best work is likely playing the negative roles of blocking and dominating.

Effective teams balance three kinds of leadership:

- Informational leaders generate and evaluate ideas and text.
- Interpersonal leaders monitor the team's process, check people's feelings, and resolve conflicts.
- Procedural leaders set the agenda, ensure that everyone knows what's due for the next meeting, communicate with absent members, and check that assignments are carried out.

While it's possible for one person to perform all of these responsibilities, some teams formally or informally rotate or share these responsibilities, so that everyone—and no one—is a leader.

Several studies have shown people who talk a lot, listen effectively, and respond nonverbally to other members in the group are considered to be leaders.[19]

Decision-Making Strategies

Probably the least effective decision-making strategy is to let the person who talks first, last, loudest, or most determine the decision.

Decisions may be guided by a rational process of gathering information, assessing the evidence, and weighing advantages against disadvantages. They may be guided by intuition, by values, by ethics, or by a sense of the multiple bottom lines: social, economic, cultural, and environmental.

Democratic voting is quick but may leave people in the minority unhappy with and uncommitted to the majority's plan.

Technology Tips Conducting a Meeting*

Two examples involving orchestras show how successful meetings require thorough planning and full participation.

In the first case, a conductor addresses an audience before the performance: "Ladies and gentlemen, you'll notice there are no pieces on the program. The reason for that is that we didn't know what you'd want to hear . . . and we wanted to leave room for openness and audience participation. Therefore, if you'll shout out the pieces you want to hear we'll do our best to play them." The audience shouts out many options, until finally, after about an hour and a half of chaotic activity, the maestro announces, "Ladies and gentlemen, thank you. We have the pieces that you want to hear that we can play. However . . . I've been informed that the oboist needs to leave to catch a plane to get to her next performance. Therefore, we've asked the oboist to play all the oboe notes right now. Then, as you hear the piece, you yourself can insert them back in where they belong. Thanks for your cooperation."

In the second case, since 2009 artists and audiences have combined with technology to bring classical music to millions around the world. In 2011, 101 YouTube-auditioned musicians from 33 countries (judged by nine orchestras and online voters) came together in a week-long concert culminating in a 20 March grand finale at the Sydney Opera House in Australia. Thanks to audience mobile devices, the performance was video streamed around the world and brought millions together in a common experience.

*Based on John E. Tropman, *Making Meetings Work: Achieving High Quality Group Decisions,* 2nd ed. (Thousand Oaks, CA: Sage, 2003), 14; YouTube Symphony Orchestra 2011, retrieved March 27, 2011, from http://www.youtube.com/user/symphony; Tamara Baluja, "From the stage to the (computer) screen," *The Globe and Mail,* March 18, 2011, A19.

Coming to consensus takes time but results in speedier implementation of ideas as well as greater satisfaction and agreement. Allowing the majority view to prevail means that more people take ownership of the decision, and people are not left feeling like losers.

Two useful strategies are the standard agenda and dot planning. The **standard agenda** is a seven-step process for solving problems:

1. Understand what the group has to deliver, in what form, by what due date. Identify available resources.
2. Identify the problem. What exactly is wrong? What question(s) is the group trying to answer?
3. Gather information, share it with all group members, and examine it critically.
4. Establish criteria. What would the ideal solution include? What would be an acceptable solution? What legal, financial, moral, or other limitations might keep a solution from being implemented?
5. Generate alternate solutions. Brainstorm and record ideas for the next step.
6. Measure the alternatives against the criteria.
7. Choose the best solution.[20]

Dot planning—dot democracy or dotmocracy[21]—offers a way for large groups to choose priorities quickly. First, the group brainstorms ideas, recording each on pages that are put on the wall. Then each individual gets two strips of three to five adhesive dots in different colours. One colour represents high priority, the other lower priority. People then walk up to the pages and affix dots by the points they care most about. Some groups allow only one dot from one person on any one item; others allow someone who is really passionate about an idea to put all of his or her dots on it.

The clustering used to generate ideas (◂◂ Chapter 3) can also be a visual tool for organizing ideas and establishing priorities.

Peer Pressure and Groupthink

Teams that never express conflict may be experiencing groupthink. **Groupthink** is the tendency to put such a high premium on agreement that members directly or indirectly punish dissent.

Many people feel so much reluctance to express open disagreement that they will say they agree even when objective circumstances would suggest the first speaker cannot be right.

Teams that "go along with the crowd" and suppress conflict ignore the full range of alternatives, seek only information that supports the positions they already favour, and fail to

Dot planning or dot democracy in action.

prepare contingency plans to cope with foreseeable setbacks. A business suffering from groupthink may launch a new product that senior executives support but for which there is no demand. Student teams suffering from groupthink turn in inferior documents because they miss opportunities to rethink and revise.

The best correctives to groupthink are to search for additional alternatives, to test one's assumptions against those of other people (see ◀◀ Chapter 1 on semantic principles), and to protect team members' right to disagree.

Working in Diverse Teams

Even people who come from the same part of the country and who have the same jobs may differ in personality type (see ◀◀ Chapter 2). Savvy team members play to each other's strengths and devise strategies for dealing with differences of gender, class, race and ethnicity, religion, age, sexual orientation, and physical ability (see ◀◀ Chapter 2). A 2010 study has shown that the "collective intelligence" of teams correlates with the proportion of women members, a finding associated with their "social sensitivity." That sensitivity is invaluable to Toronto Indie band Ohbijou when it has to make decisions and write songs together.[22]

A growing body of literature addresses the complexities of intergenerational communications (see ◀◀ Chapter 5) and shows that ethnically diverse teams produce more and higher-quality ideas.[23] Despite the advantages of diverse teams, heavily recruited international students often report getting too little support to engage and to understand Canadian cultural norms, to make friends, and therefore to be fully engaged in their classes and teamwork. Training in teamwork and networking can help.[24]

One problem with our awareness of difference, however, is that when someone feels shut out, he or she can attribute the negative interaction to prejudice, when other factors may be responsible. Conversational style and nonverbal communication are two of the areas that may cause miscommunication (see ◀◀ Chapter 5).

College and university students make good use of their "collective intelligence."

LO3

SUCCESSFUL STUDENT TEAMS

Like businesses, colleges and universities turn to teamwork to teach valuable skills, although students often complain about unequal engagement in projects, unusual investments of time, and conflict and frustration. In need of "swift trust" so that they can negotiate "vulnerability, uncertainty, risk, and expectations," student teams rank effort/commitment, reliability/consistency, and open communications as key indicators of trustworthiness; secondary factors are capability, integrity, benevolence, and positive demeanour. Interdependence, mutual goals, and fairness are overarching concerns.[25]

A case study of six student teams completing class projects found that students in successful and less successful teams communicated differently in three ways: setting clear deadlines, deciding together, and engaging more members actively (Figure 6.3).[26]

Figure 6.3 Comparing Successful and Unsuccessful Student Teams

SUCCESSFUL TEAMS		UNSUCCESSFUL TEAMS
• Leader set clear deadlines. • Scheduled *frequent* meetings. • Dealt directly with conflict. • Group listened to constructive criticism. • Group decided together. • High proportion worked actively.	• Members disagreed over substance, discussed alternatives, and adopted best ideas. • Group could explain goal. • Groups spending most time meeting got highest grades on individual and team work.	• *Subgroup* made decisions. • Subgroup told others about decisions. • Small proportion worked actively. • Some members did very little. • Members performed less well on individual and group work.

Sources: Nance L. Harper and Lawrence R. Askling, "Group communication and quality of task solution in a media production organization," *Communication Monographs,* 47, no. 2 (June 1980): 77–100; Rebecca E. Burnett, "Conflict in collaborative decision-making," in *Professional Communication: The Social Perspective,* ed. Nancy Roundy Blyler and Charlotte Thralls (Newbury Park, CA: Sage, 1993), 144–162; Kimberly A. Freeman, "Attitudes toward work in project groups as predictors of academic performance," *Small Group Research,* 27, no. 2 (May 1996): 265–282.

Student teams produce better documents when they disagree over substantive issues of content and document design. The disagreement does not need to be angry: a team member can simply say, "Yes, and here's another way we could do it." Deciding among two (or more) alternatives forces the proposer to explain the rationale for an idea. Even when the team adopts the original idea, considering alternatives rather than quickly accepting the first idea produces better writing.[27]

The students who spent the most time meeting with their team had the highest grades—on their individual as well as on team assignments.[28]

LO4

CONFLICT RESOLUTION

Conflicts will arise in any group of people who care about the task. Yet many of us feel so uncomfortable with conflict that we pretend it doesn't exist. However, unacknowledged conflicts rarely go away: they fester, making the next interchange more difficult—and missing opportunities to learn from differences and innovate. Avoiding conflict can be costly (in time and money), escalate hostilities, prevent problem solving, impede creativity, discourage participation and engagement, and create conditions for groupthink.

To reduce the number of conflicts in a team,

- Make responsibilities and ground rules clear at the beginning.
- Discuss problems as they arise, rather than letting them fester until people explode.
- Realize that group members are not responsible for each other's happiness.

To resolve conflicts that do arise, teams may need to reopen discussions about responsibilities, rules, and expectations and confront a troublesome group member.[29] Focus on performance and not personality or happiness so that the team can identify what needs to be done to achieve goals.

Instead of blaming and punishing, focus on opportunities for learning and change in every mistake, disagreement, or failure.[30]

Many problems can be resolved if people respect others' contributions and advocate for their ideas in a positive way. A tactful way to advocate for the position you favour is to recognize the contributions others have made, to summarize, and then to hypothesize: "What if _____?" "Let's look six months down the road." "Let's think about *x*."[31]

Just as resolving conflict depends on identifying the needs each person is trying to meet, so dealing with criticism depends on understanding the real concern of the critic. Constructive ways to respond to criticism and get closer to the real concern include paraphrasing, checking for feelings, checking for inferences, and including you-attitude. See ◀◀ Chapter 3 on "Giving, Getting, and Using Feedback," and the ▶▶ On the Job box "Constructive Team Feedback."

Paraphrasing

To **paraphrase,** repeat in your own words the verbal content of the critic's message. The purposes of paraphrasing are (1) to be sure that you have heard the critic accurately, (2) to let the critic know what his or her statement means to you, and (3) to communicate the feeling that you are taking the critic and his or her feelings seriously.

× Criticism:	You guys are stonewalling my requests for information.
✓ Paraphrase:	You think that we don't give you the information you need quickly enough.

Checking for Feelings

Checking for feelings is an attempt to understand (1) the critic's emotions, (2) the importance of the criticism for the critic, and (3) the unspoken ideas and feelings that may actually be more important than the voiced criticism.

× Criticism:	You guys are stonewalling my requests for information.
✓ Feeling check:	You sound pretty angry.

Always *ask* the other person if you are right in your perception. Even the best reader of nonverbal cues can be wrong.

On the Job Who Does What

Working successfully on a team depends on being open about preferences, constraints, and skills and then using creative problem-solving techniques.

A person who prefers to outline the whole project in advance may be in a group with someone who expects to do the project at the last minute. Someone who likes to talk out ideas before writing may be in a group with someone who wants to work on a draft in silence and revise it before showing it to anyone. By being honest about your preferences, you make it possible for the team to find a creative solution that builds on what each person can offer.

In one team, Rob wanted to wait to start the project because he was busy with other class work. Mohammed and Natalia, however, wanted to go ahead now because their schedules would get busier later in the term. A creative solution would be for Mohammed and Natalia to do most of the work on parts of the project that had to be completed first (such as collecting data and writing the proposal) and for Rob to do work that had to be done later (such as revising, editing, and proofreading).

Checking for Inferences

When you check the inferences (◂◂ Chapter 1) you draw from criticism, you identify the implied meaning of the verbal and nonverbal content of the criticism and try to understand why the critic is bothered. The purposes of checking inferences are (1) to identify the real (as opposed to the presenting) problem and (2) to communicate the feeling that you care about resolving the conflict.

✕ Criticism:	You guys are stonewalling my requests for information.
✓ Inference:	Are you saying that you need more information from our team?

Inferences can be faulty. In the above interchange, the critic might respond, "I don't need more information. I just think you should give it to me without my having to file three forms in triplicate every time I want some data."

Including You-Attitude

You-attitude means looking at things from the audience's point of view, respecting the audience, and protecting the audience's ego (◂◂ Chapter 2). Using *you* is not the same as showing you-attitude. When the focus of angry statements, *you* attacks and judges the audience. Instead, substitute statements about your own feelings or focus on outcomes.

✕ Lacks you-attitude:	You never do your share of the work.
✓ You-attitude:	I feel that I'm doing more than my share of the work on this project.
✕ Lacks you-attitude:	Even you should be able to run the report through a spell-checker.
✓ You-attitude:	I'm not willing to have my name on a report with so many spelling errors. I did lots of the writing, and other team members can do the proofreading and spell-checking for the best results.

LO5

EFFECTIVE MEETINGS

Meetings have always taken a large part of the average manager's week. Although e-mail, wikis, and blogs have eliminated some meetings, the increased number of teams means that meetings—formal or informal (over coffee), face-to-face or virtual—are even more frequent.

Although managers can spend as much as one-quarter of their time in meetings, studies suggest that at least half of meeting time is wasted. A 2005 Microsoft online office survey of 38,000 people in 200 countries found "unclear objectives, lack of team communication and ineffective meetings" topped the list of time-wasters.[32] According to management consultant Frank Buchar, "Meeting management is the single most underdeveloped skill in North America." Buchar recommends matching meeting format and size to meeting purpose, bold leadership and member engagement, and facilitation tools (labelling, categorizing, and organizing) involving and equalizing participation.[33]

Knowing Your Purpose

Whether in the classroom or the workplace, preparation—much of which can be accomplished online—and a clear sense of purpose are key. Your purpose may be better achieved through a discussion board or wiki or blog if controversial issues are to be addressed. If you are working with a remote team on a document, spreadsheet, or presentation, Google Docs, Dropbox, or ThinkFree Office (or a **cloud computing** service offered by Google, IBM, or Amazon, for instance) may be a more efficient choice. One study reported that 67 percent of companies with revenues under $1 billion make use of cloud computing; another study found that 16 percent of users find it a useful tool to innovate.[34] Roger Johnson, Senior Vice-President of Enterprise Real Estate, Toronto-Dominion Bank, has seen cross-functional team success with their "innovation lab" of 50 internal and numerous external partners—success based on sharing "a clear vision" and "explicit objectives" in a collegial "atmosphere of respect."[35]

Or, integrated Web conferencing—WebEx, for instance—may be the answer for large and widely dispersed groups. People can even access the Web meeting from their mobile device. It can be replayed anywhere at any time.

Once you establish that a meeting is necessary, it will have one of at least six purposes:

- To share information
- To brainstorm ideas
- To evaluate ideas
- To make decisions
- To create a document
- To motivate members

When meetings combine two or more purposes, it's useful to make the purposes explicit. For example, in the meeting of a university senate or a company's board of directors, some items are presented for information. Discussion is possible, but the group will not be asked to make a decision. Other items are presented for action; the group will be asked to vote. A business meeting might specify that the first half hour will be time for brainstorming, with the second half hour devoted to evaluation.

Managing Logistics

Once you define the purpose, you can choose the time and location to suit the key participants (internal and external to your team or organization). Will you need to connect some participants by Skype, teleconference, or videoconference? Are there deadlines that narrow the scheduling options? If you are inviting guests, where might you best accommodate them on the agenda? Should they go first to present in ways that can usefully guide further decision making in the meeting? Should they go last so that they can effectively advise on your processes?

If you're planning a long meeting—for example, a training session or a conference—recognize that networking is part of the value of the meeting. Allow short breaks at least every two hours and generous breaks twice a day so participants can talk informally to each other. If participants will be strangers, include some social functions so they can get to know each other. If they will have different interests or different levels of knowledge, plan concurrent sessions on different topics or for people with different levels of expertise.

Once these logistics are determined, then you are ready to prepare the agenda and any background materials to help participants prepare.

Planning the Agenda

Planning the agenda (Figure 6.4) is the foundation of a good meeting. A good agenda indicates

- Whether each item is presented for information, for discussion, or for a decision
- Who is sponsoring or introducing each item
- How much time is allotted for each item

Many groups put first routine items on which agreement will be easy. If there's a long list of routine items, save them till the end or dispense with them in an omnibus motion. An **omnibus motion** allows a group to approve many items together rather than voting on each separately.

Taking Minutes

Formal meetings are run under strict rules, like the rules of parliamentary procedure summarized in *Robert's Rules of Order*. Motions must be made formally before a topic can be debated. Each point is settled by a vote. **Minutes** begin with a record of meeting purpose (whether for a board, subcommittee, or other group), date, time, and place, recording those present and those who are absent or have sent regrets (Figure 6.5).

Following the order of the agenda items, they record each motion and the vote on it. Formal rules help the meeting run smoothly if the group is very large or if the agenda is very long. Long minutes (organized by agenda headings) are most helpful if next steps or specific tasks are set off visually from the narrative.

Informal meetings, which are much more common in the workplace, are run more loosely. Votes may not be taken if most people seem to agree. Minutes may not be kept, although action items are typically recorded to ensure follow-up. Informal meetings are better for team building and problem solving.

If the group doesn't formally vote, the leader should summarize the group's consensus after each point. At the end of the meeting, the leader must summarize all decisions and remind the group who is responsible for implementing or following up on each item. If no other notes are taken, someone should record the decisions and assignment of tasks.

While meetings have important social functions, purposeful meetings are also eminently practical in helping groups clarify

Figure 6.4 Typical Meeting Agenda

AGENDA
Non-Profit Board Meeting, Monday, September 26, 2014, 3:30–5:30 p.m.
Conference room, business office

3:30 p.m.	1. Call to Order; attendance
3:35 p.m.	2. Approval of Agenda
3:40 p.m.	3. Minutes of Meeting of August 22, 2014
3:45 p.m.	4. Business Arising/Action Items
4:00 p.m.	5. Report of Chair (Sonja; decision)
	a. External relations
	b. Youth outreach
	c. Web presence
4:30 p.m.	6. Report of Fundraising Committee (John; information)
4:45 p.m.	7. Report of Grants Committee (Josephine; information)
5:00 p.m.	8. Report of Hiring Committee (Darren; decision)
5:20 p.m.	9. Other Business
5:25 p.m.	10. Date of next board meeting
5:30 p.m.	11. Adjournment

Figure 6.5 Typical Meeting Minutes

Minutes – Non-Profit Board Meeting
September 26, 2014, 3:30–5:30 p.m.
Conference room, business office

Present: Sonja Merasty (Chair), Joy Abrams, Josephine Duguid, Darren Findlay, James Peller, Jill McIvor, Doug Sanders, Anne Thompson, John Vieta

Regrets: Sandra Harding

3:30 p.m 1. **Call to order and attendance**

3:35 p.m. 2. **Approval of the Agenda**
- Motion to approve by Darren, seconded by Josephine. Approved unanimously.

3:40 p.m. 3. **Approval of the Minutes of August 22, 2014**
- Motion to approve by James, seconded by John. Approved unanimously.

3:45 p.m. 4. **Business Arising/Action Items**
- Sonja reported on the successful meeting with the programme coordinators. The scheduling difficulties had been resolved. The elders' programme would begin on October 1.
- Sonja had attended the poverty reduction meetings with sector and municipal representatives and listed the initiatives that were approved.

4:00 p.m. 5. **Chair's Report** (Sonja)

a. External relations
- Sonja asked for clarification of goals for upcoming activities. In particular, board members wanted to develop/clarify relationships between our membership and other affiliated or relevant organizations in order to ease communication and collaboration.
- Action Item: Joy to draft letter (Sonja to review) to our membership requesting information on their external associations, for the purpose of developing a database and building coordinated external relations.

b. Youth outreach
- Recent activities were outlined in the current newsletter. Discussion focused on youth engagement strategies related to our upcoming annual general meeting, the new youth board position, and the provincial anti-poverty conference in December.
- Action Item: Sonja to send out call for nominations from the membership for the new youth board position (deadline November 1).
- Action Item: Josephine to extend invitations to four youth to present at a youth panel at the AGM.
- Action Item: Sonja to focus this month's blog on youth opportunities to participate in the December conference.

and accomplish tasks at hand. That means beginning and ending on time and respecting business etiquette by avoiding distracting and disrespectful multitasking (checking mobile phones or updating Facebook, for instance), which is never as efficient as we like to think it in any case. If students (like those in the workplace) sometimes resist and resent the time required for careful agenda setting and minute taking, successful student groups know the value of this archive tracing who attended, who did what, and when. Like the built-in accountability mechanism of wikis, the agenda and minutes can be useful documents when it comes to evaluating the participation of different group members, identifying the slackers, and giving credit where it is due.

LO6

COLLABORATIVE WRITING

Whatever your career, it is likely that some of the documents you produce will be written with a team. Lisa Ede and Andrea Lunsford found that 87% of the 700 professionals in seven fields who responded to their survey sometimes wrote as members of a team or a group.[36] Collaboration is often prompted by one of the following situations:

1. The task is too big or the time is too short for one person to do all the work.

On the Job Constructive Team Feedback

When you are engaged in collaborative writing, getting the best out of your teamwork involves these steps:

- Focus on purpose, audience, content, and clarity
- Keep focus on performance and outcome: an effective document
- Be critical and constructive
- Be specific about changes; write example(s)
- Avoid judgmental language
- Use task checklists to keep advice impersonal
- Stress feedback as part of the writing process
- Encourage questions about and rephrasing of feedback
- Keep in mind time demands and effect on morale

2. No one person has all the knowledge required to do the task.
3. A team representing different perspectives must reach a consensus.
4. The stakes for the task are so high that the organization wants the best efforts of as many people as possible; no one person wants the sole responsibility for the success or failure of the document.

Collaborative writing can be done by two people or by a much larger team. The team can use a wiki (see the beginning of this chapter and the Technology Tips box "Collaborating on 'Remote' Teams"), Google Docs, ThinkFree Office, or other online platform. Or they can use track changes features (see the Technology Tips box "Tracking Changes" in ◀◀ Chapter 3) and exchange drafts by e-mail or in face-to-face meetings. The team can be democratic or run by a leader who makes decisions alone. The team may share or divide responsibility for each of the eight stages in the writing process (◀◀ Chapter 3).

There are several ways groups commonly divide the work. One person might do the main writing, with others providing feedback (see the On the Job box "Constructive Team Feedback"). Other groups divide the whole project into smaller tasks and assign each task (research, drafting, designing, and editing) to a different group member according to skills. This approach shares the workload more evenly but is harder to coordinate. Sometimes group members do not take turns but work together simultaneously, discussing and responding to each other's ideas.[37]

Best Practices

Research in collaborative writing indicates the strategies that produce the best writing. Rebecca Burnett found that student teams that voiced disagreements as they analyzed, planned, and wrote a document produced significantly better documents than those that suppressed disagreement, going along with whatever was first proposed.[38]

A case study of two collaborative writing teams found that the successful team followed this practice:

- Distributed power in an egalitarian way
- Worked to soothe hurt feelings

Technology Tips Collaborating on "Remote" Teams*

Members of remote—or virtual—teams who collaborate and communicate via wikis (the Hawaiian term for "quick") claim these advantages:

- Promote true collaboration and sense of common purpose
- Support effective interactivity, not "a glorified television channel"
- Seek "to influence and encourage, not control and enforce"
- Speed writing process because reading and editing are combined
- Provide open space for brainstorming
- Find "access restrictions and defined workflows anathema"
- Support meeting and conference planning
- Work by "SoftSecurity" of community culture and "self-policing"

Alan J. Porter gives examples of one company using a wiki to engage 40% of employees and secure ISO 9000 certification in nine months instead of two years. His publisher used it for editing, illustrating, and reviewing purposes.

Philippe Borremans recommends wikis for crisis communication planning and implementation, putting everyone literally on the same page, creating an archive, and allowing regular updates and "quick validations of statements, facts, and responses."

*Based on Brian Lamb, "Wide open spaces: Wikis, ready or not," *EDUCAUSE Review* 39, 5 (September/October 2004): 36–48, retrieved August 20, 2007, from http://connect.educause.edu/Library/EDUCAUSE+Review/WideOpenSpacesWikisReadyo/40498; Alan J. Porter, *Wiki: Grow Your Own for Fun and Profit* (XML Press, 2010); Matt Wilson, "The truth about wikis: A wealth of uses you may not have considered," posted January 7, 2011, retrieved January 7, 2011, from http://www.ragan.com/Main/Articles/42615.aspx?format=2; P. Borremans, "Ready for anything," *Communication World*, July–August 2010, 31–33.

- Involved all team members
- Understood the task as a response to a rhetorical situation
- Planned revisions as a team
- Saw supervisors' comments as legitimate
- Had a positive attitude toward revision.[39]

Ede and Lunsford's detailed case studies of collaborative teams in business, government, and science create an "emerging profile of effective collaborative writers": "They are flexible; respectful of others; attentive and analytical listeners; able to speak and write clearly and articulately; dependable and able to meet deadlines; able to designate and share responsibility, to lead and to follow; open to criticism but confident in their own abilities; ready to engage in creative conflict."[40]

Collaborative writing is most successful when the team explicitly discusses the best way to achieve the rhetorical goals. Businesses schedule formal planning sessions for large projects to set up a timeline specifying intermediate and final due dates (from initiation meeting to primary and secondary research to analysis, conclusions, and recommendations to draft and final report), meeting dates, who will attend each meeting, and who will do what. Putting the plan in writing reduces misunderstandings during the project.

When you plan a collaborative writing project,

- Make your analysis of the problem, the audience, and your purposes explicit so you know where you agree and where you disagree.
- Plan the organization, format, and style of the document before anyone begins to write to make it easier to blend sections written by different authors.
- Consider your work styles and other commitments.
- Build some leeway into your deadlines to allow for scheduling difficulties.

Most writers find that composing alone is faster than composing in a team. However, composing together may reduce revision time later, since the team examines every choice as it is made. Have the best writer(s) draft the document after everyone has gathered the necessary information. On the evaluation and documentation of online and print sources, see ⏩ Chapter 10.

Revising a collaborative document requires attention to content, organization, and style. The following guidelines can make the revision process more effective:

- Evaluate the content and discuss possible revisions as a team. Brainstorm ways to improve each section so the person doing the revisions has some guidance.
- Recognize that different people favour different writing styles. If the style satisfies the demands of standard English and the conventions of business writing, accept it even if you wouldn't say it that way.
- When the team is satisfied with the content of the document, one person—probably the best writer—should make any changes necessary to make the writing style consistent throughout.

A team report needs careful editing and proofreading (⏪ Chapter 3).

- Have at least one person check the whole document for correctness in grammar, mechanics, and spelling and for consistency in the way that formatting elements, names, and numbers are handled.

On the Job Diversity Matters*

- Diversity is good for team performance, especially when innovation is the goal. But diversity needs to be harnessed effectively to support collaboration:
  - Invest in maintaining social relationships through the organization.
  - Model collaborative behaviour.
  - Use coaching.
  - Train employees in collaborative skills.
  - Support a sense of community.
- Team players take many forms, but self-confidence may not be the best attribute. "Insecurity can be a good thing"—whether among parents returning to the workplace, older workers feeling compromised in "youth-valuing" organizations, women facing gender bias, or others feeling invisible or overly conspicuous.
- The needy may work harder to prove their competence and be less likely to jump to conclusions.
- The insecure may work harder at reading signals and social cues.
- Women's hesitancy or use of qualifiers should not be equated with indecision.
- Diversity is proving good for the bottom line, the payoff coming in "better workers, better results, better business." (Dib)

*Based on Tammy Erickson, "Lessons on team diversity," *Harvard Business Review,* November 26, 2007, retrieved April 15, 2008, from http://discussionleader.hbsp.com/erickson/2007/11/when_differences_become_streng.html; Lynda Gratton and Tamara J. Erickson, "Eight ways to build collaborative teams," *Harvard Business Review* 85:11 (November 2007): 100–09; Barbara Moses, "Insecurity—in all its painfully needy ways—can be strength," *The Globe and Mail,* March 16, 2007, C1; Kamal Dib, "Diversity works," *Canadian Business,* March 29–April 11, 2004, 53–54; Pamela K. Henry, *Diversity and the Bottom Line: Prospering in the Global Economy* (Turnkey Press, 2003).

Meeting rooms equipped with laptops, pagers, and cell phones help Intel employees collaborate on group projects with colleagues around the world.

- Run the document through a spell-checker if possible.
- Even if you use a computerized spell-checker, at least one human being should proofread the document too.

Like any member of the writing team, those handling the editing tasks need to consider how they express their ideas. In many situations, the editor plays the role of diplomat, careful to suggest changes in ways that do not seem to call the writer's abilities into question. Describing the reason for a change is typically more helpful than stating an opinion. Words like *could* and *should* to modify a direction can add a tone of politeness.[41]

Making the Team Process Work

All of the information in this chapter can help your collaborative writing team listen effectively, run meetings efficiently, engage technology and team members productively, and deal with conflict constructively. The following suggestions apply specifically to writing teams:

- Give yourselves plenty of time to discuss problems and find solutions. Students writing team reports spend six to seven hours a week outside class in meetings—not counting the time they spend gathering information and writing their drafts.[42]
- Take the time to get to know team members and to build trust and loyalty. Members will work harder and the final document will be better if the team is important to members.
- Be a responsible team member. Attend all the meetings; carry out your responsibilities.
- Be aware that people have different ways of experiencing reality and of expressing themselves. Use the principles of semantics discussed in ◀◀ Chapter 1 to reduce miscommunication. Attend to verbal and nonverbal cues, know that some come with no experience of teamwork, use your cultural competence, and be sensitive to gender differences in conversational style (◀◀ Chapter 5).
- Because talking is "looser" than writing, people in a team can think they agree when they don't. Don't assume that because the discussion went smoothly, a draft written by one person will necessarily be acceptable.

SUMMARY OF KEY POINTS

- In *active listening,* receivers use these five strategies:
  - Paraphrase the content. Feed back the meaning in your own words.
  - Mirror the speaker's feelings. Identify the feelings you think you hear.
  - State your own feelings. This strategy works especially well when you are angry.
  - Ask for information or clarification.
  - Offer to help solve the problem.
- Effective teams balance information leadership, interpersonal leadership, and procedural group management. They build trust and loyalty through four stages: orientation, formation, coordination, formalization. Trust depends on communication, honesty, openness, consistency, reliability, and respect.
- The *standard agenda* is a seven-step process for solving problems. In *dot planning* the team brainstorms ideas. Then each individual affixes adhesive dots by the points or proposals he or she cares most about.
- Student teams that set clear deadlines, have inclusive decision making, and comprise a high proportion of active members succeed. Students who spent the most time meeting with their teams got the highest grades.
- Constructive ways to respond to criticism include paraphrasing, checking for feelings, checking for inferences, and including you-attitude.
- To make meetings more effective,
  - State the purpose of the meeting at the beginning.
  - Manage the logistics: choose time, location, and media to connect with participants.
  - Plan and distribute an agenda that indicates whether each item is for information, for discussion, or for decision, who is responsible for each item, and how long each is expected to take.
  - Take minutes recording those present and decisions taken. If you don't take formal minutes, summarize all decisions and remind the group who is responsible for implementing or following up on each item.
- Collaborative writing means working with other writers to produce a single document. Writers producing a joint document need to pay attention not only to the basic steps in the writing process but also to the processes of team formation and conflict resolution.

EXERCISES AND PROBLEMS

GETTING STARTED

6.1 IDENTIFYING RESPONSES THAT SHOW ACTIVE LISTENING

Which of the following responses show active listening? Which responses block communication?

1. Comment: Whenever I say something, the team just ignores me.

   Responses:
   a. That's because your ideas aren't very good. Do more planning before team meetings.
   b. Nobody listens to me, either.
   c. You're saying that nobody builds on your ideas.

2. Comment: I've done more than my share of work on this project. But the people who have been freeloading are going to get the same grade I've worked so hard to earn.

   Responses:
   a. Yes, we're all going to get the same grade.
   b. Are you afraid we won't do well on the assignment?
   c. It sounds like you feel resentful.

3. Comment: My parents are going to kill me if I don't have a job lined up when I graduate.

   Responses:
   a. You know they're exaggerating. They won't really kill you.
   b. Can you blame them? I mean, it's taken you six years to get a degree. Surely you've learned something to make you employable!
   c. If you act the way in interviews that you do in our class, I'm not surprised. Companies want people with good attitudes and good work ethics.

6.2 PRACTISING ACTIVE LISTENING

Go around the room for this exercise. In turn, let each student complain about something (large or small) that really bothers him or her. Then the next student(s) will

a. Offer a statement of limited agreement that would buy time.
b. Paraphrase the statement.
c. Check for feelings that might lie behind the statement.
d. Offer inferences that might motivate the statement.

As Your Professor Directs,

- Take a listening self-assessment test (see the International Listening Association's Web site, for example, at www.listen.org) and write a blog entry on what you have learned from the class activity and the self-assessment.
- Submit a wiki based on the group's experience of and reflections on the class listening activity and self-assessment tests.

6.3 TAKING MINUTES

Have two or more people take minutes of each class or team meeting for a week. Alternatively, take minutes of a workshop, career fair, or presentation the team has attended. Compare the accounts of the same meeting.

- To what extent do they agree on what happened?
- Does one contain information missing in other accounts?
- Do any accounts disagree on a specific fact?
- How do you account for the differences you find?

6.4 KEEPING A JOURNAL OR BLOG ABOUT A TEAM

As you work in a writing team, keep a journal or post comments on a blog after each team meeting.

- What happened?
- What roles did you play in the meeting?
- What conflicts arose? How were they handled?
- What strategies could you use to make the next meeting go smoothly?
- Record one observation about each team member.

As Your Professor Directs,

(a) Give a team presentation or (b) Submit a team e-report (e-mail, wiki, or blog) on your findings.

6.5 WRITING A MEETING MANUAL

Create a manual for students next term telling them how to have effective meetings as they work on collaborative projects.

Source: Adapted from Miles McCall, Beth Stewart, and Timothy Clipson, "Teaching Communication Skills for Meeting Management," *1998 Refereed Proceedings*, Association for Business Communication Southwestern United States, ed. Marsha L. Bayless (Nacogdoches, TX), 68.

E-MESSAGES

In Problems 6.6 through 6.8, assume that your team has been asked to recommend a solution.

As Your Professor Directs,

- Send e-mail messages (or post a blog entry) to members laying out your initial point of view on the issue and discussing the various options.
- As a team, answer the message.
- Write an e-mail to your professor telling how satisfied you are with
  a. The decision your team reached.
  b. The process you used to reach it.

6.6 RECOMMENDING A POLICY ON STUDENT ENTREPRENEURS

Assume that your small team comprises the officers in student government on your campus. You receive this e-mail from the vice-president of student services:

> As you know, campus policy says that no student may use campus resources to conduct business-related activities. Students can't conduct business out of dorm rooms or use university e-mail addresses for business. They can't post business Web pages on the university server.
>
> On the other hand, a survey conducted by the Kauffman Centre for Entrepreneurial Leadership showed that 7 out of 10 teens want to become entrepreneurs.
>
> Should campus policy be changed to allow students to use dorm rooms and university e-mail addresses for business? (And then what happens when roommates complain and our network can't carry the increased e-mail traffic?) Please recommend what support (if any) should be given to student entrepreneurs.

Write a team e-report (⏩ Chapters 10 and 11) recommending what (if anything) your campus should do for student entrepreneurs and supporting your recommendation.

Hints:

- Does your campus offer other support for entrepreneurs (courses, a business plan competition, a start-up incubator)? What should be added or expanded?
- Is it realistic to ask alumni for money to fund student start-ups?

6.7 RECOMMENDING A MOBILE DEVICE/LAPTOP POLICY

Your college or university is increasingly concerned about e-distractions in the classroom and invites student input into the design of new policies on mobile device and laptop use in the classroom. Is it time for a formal policy? If so, what should it be?

Write a team response recommending standards of mobile device/laptop etiquette for students and supporting your recommendation.

6.8 RESPONDING TO AN EMPLOYEE GRIEVANCE

Assume that your small team comprises the Diversity Committee in your workplace. The vice-president for human resources contacts you for advice on generational conflict and communications. She is finding that employees (from Generation Y to boomers) are struggling with generational differences that are causing miscommunications, misunderstandings, resentments, and even formal grievances. Employees complain about feeling unappreciated, mistrusted, and even disrespected. The company is feeling the effects on productivity and profits. She asks you to recommend policies and/or workshops that might help the company address the generational communications gap and help bring people together and respect and appreciate their differences.

Write a team e-response recommending policy and/or workshop activities and supporting your recommendation.

COMMUNICATING AT WORK

6.9 ANSWERING AN ETHICS QUESTION

Assume that your small team comprises your organization's Ethics Committee. You receive the following anonymous note:

> People are routinely using the company external blog to communicate their positions on controversial issues. Making their opinions known is of course their right, but doing so on the company blog implies that they are speaking for the company, which they are not.
>
> I think that the use of the blog for anything other than official company business should be prohibited.

Determine the best solution to the problem. Then write a memo (▸▸ Chapter 7) to all employees stating your decision and building support for it.

6.10 PLANNING A GAME

Many companies are using games and contests to solve problems in an enjoyable way. One company promised to give everyone $30 a month extra if they got the error rate below 0.5%. The rate improved immediately. After several successful months, the incentive went to $40 a month for getting it under 0.3% and finally to $50 a month for getting it under 0.2%. Another company offered workers two "well hours" if they got in by 7 am every day for a month. An accounting and financial services company divided its employees into two teams. The one that got the most referrals and new accounts received a meal prepared and served by the losing team (the firm paid for the food). Games are best when the people who will play them create them. Games need to make business sense and give rewards to many people, not just a few. Rewards should be small.

Think of a game or contest that could improve productivity or quality in your classroom, on campus, or in a workplace you know well.

As Your Professor Directs,

a. Write a message to persuade your professor, boss, or other decision maker to authorize the game or contest.

b. Write a message announcing the game and persuading people to participate in it.

Source: Based on John Case, *The Open-Book Experience: Lessons from Over 100 Companies Who Successfully Transformed Themselves* (Reading, MA: Addison-Wesley, 1998), 129–201.

6.11 INTERVIEWING WORKERS ABOUT LISTENING

Interview someone who works in an organization about his or her on-the-job listening. Possible questions to ask include the following:

- Whom do you listen to as part of your job? Your superior? Subordinates? (How many levels down?) Customers or clients? Who else?

- How much time a day do you spend listening?
- What people do you talk to as part of your job? Do you feel they hear what you say? How do you tell whether or not they're listening?
- Do you know of any problems that came up because someone didn't listen? What happened?
- What do you think prevents people from listening effectively? What advice would you have for someone on how to listen more accurately?

As Your Professor Directs,

a. Share your information with a small group of students in your class.

b. Present your findings orally to the class.

c. Present your findings in an e-mail to your professor.

d. Join with other students to present your findings in a group report (⏩ Chapters 10 and 11).

6.12 ANALYZING THE DYNAMICS OF A TEAM

Analyze the dynamics of a task team of which you are a member. Answer the following questions:

1. Who was the team leader? How did the leader emerge? Were there any changes in or challenges to the original leader?
2. Describe the contribution each member made and the roles each person played.
3. Did any members officially or unofficially drop out? Did anyone join after the group had begun working? How did you deal with the loss or addition of a member, both in terms of getting the work done and in terms of helping people work together?
4. What planning did your team do at the start of the project? Did you stick to the plan or revise it? How did the team decide that revision was necessary?
5. How did your team make decisions? Did you vote? Reach decisions by consensus?
6. What problems or conflicts arose? Did the team deal with them openly? To what extent did the problems interfere with the team task?
7. Evaluate your team both in terms of its task and in terms of the satisfaction members felt. How did this team compare with other task groups you've been part of? What made it better or worse?

As you answer the questions,

- Be honest. You won't lose points for reporting that your team had problems or did something "wrong."
- Show your knowledge of good team dynamics. That is, if your team did something wrong, show that you know what should have been done. Similarly, if your team worked well, show that you know why it worked well.
- Be specific. Give examples or anecdotes to support your claims.

As Your Professor Directs,

a. Discuss these questions with the other team members.

b. Present your findings orally to the class.

c. Present your findings in an individual e-mail to your professor.

d. Join with the other members to role play your team dynamics, its highs and lows, obstacles and opportunities, and the lessons learned that will inform future team initiatives.

ROUTINE MESSAGES

7

Learning Outcomes

LO1 Distinguish audiences and formats for letters, memos, and electronic media

LO2 Explain three messages sent to readers by document format

LO3 Explain how to organize routine messages

LO4 List three characteristics of a good subject line

LO5 Describe when reader benefits are needed in routine messages

LO6 Distinguish varieties of routine messages

AN INSIDE PERSPECTIVE

Mayor, blogger, and Twitter personality Naheed Nenshi became celebrated as a superhero for his leadership during the 2013 Calgary floods.

Naheed Nenshi has become famous for his use of social media to engage Calgarians and to turn municipal politics from boring to compelling and citizen-focused. His is a remarkable feat at a time of widespread citizen disengagement. With his ability to connect with accessible and authentic communications, Nenshi went from a "virtual unknown" to mayor in 2010—and to re-election in 2013 with approval ratings over 80%. From everyday issues such as parks and parking to transit, taxes, roads, policing, and disaster management, Mayor Nenshi listens to and learns from his wide consultations and everyday conversations with Calgarians and responds promptly and productively.

"It is important for mayors to not only do the hard work that we do every day to keep the city going, but also to embody the spirit of the city," says Nenshi. During the 2013 Calgary floods, Nenshi became "clearly the voice of all Calgarians" and a superhero to many when he worked 43 hours without a break to tweet updates, encourage, direct, console, and cheer on. If many of his messages were positive and informative, Nenshi was also quick to denounce those who risked lives canoeing on the dangerous Bow River and to remind people that they "do have a larger responsibility."

His messages inspired Calgarians to coin new terms and celebrate their own potential to "Keep Calm and Nenshi On." According to political strategist Stephen Carter, "Nenshi is a master of social media, forging relationships and trust one tweet at a time. . . . He uses the medium as it was designed to be used—as an interactive communications technique." Nenshi loves his "dream job" that allows him "just to make it easy for those people to be amazing."

*Based on Jason Markusoff, "Liberal leader? Infrastructure minister? No thanks: Nenshi's year-end interview transcript," *Calgary Herald*, December 17, 2013, retrieved May 8, 2014, from http://blogs.calgaryherald.com/2013/12/17/liberal-leader-infrastructure-minister-no-thanks-nenshis-year-end-interview-transcript-part-2/; Colin Ellis, "Calgary's Mayor Naheed Nenshi re-elected," TVO, October 22, 2013, retrieved May 8, 2014, from http://theagenda.tvo.org/blog/agenda-blogs/calgarys-mayor-naheed-nenshi-re-elected; Gary Mason, "Dull, staid Alberta boring no more," *The Globe and Mail*, September 27, 2013, A11; Dean Bennett, "'The voice of all Calgarians': Flood leaves Mayor Naheed Nenshi with Superman status," *National Post*, June 28, 2013, retrieved May 8, 2014, from http://news.nationalpost.com/2013/06/28/the-voice-of-all-calgarians-flood-leaves-mayor-naheed-nenshi-with-superman-status/; Suzy Thompson, "Apparently our mayor is sexy, beloved and good at Twitter," *FFWD Weekly*, June 13, 2013, retrieved May 8, 2014, from http://www.ffwdweekly.com/article/life-style/best-calgary/apparently-our-mayor-is-sexy-beloved-and-good-at-twitter-10884/; Rosella Chibambo, "Mayor Nenshi weighs in on city budget," *The City Blog*, November 21, 2011, retrieved May 8, 2014, from http://theagenda.tvo.org/blog/agenda-blogs/calgarys-mayor-naheed-nenshi-re-elected.

In an environment where customers and other stakeholders have the tools to engage actively, regularly, and publicly with business, business messages must meet the needs of the writer (and the writer's organization), be sensitive to the audience, accurately reflect the topic being addressed, and be appropriate to the situation. Asking the five questions listed in ◀◀ Chapter 1 is a useful guide.

Routine messages are the bread-and-butter correspondence in organizations: acceptances; positive answers to requests; announcements of policy changes that are neutral or positive; routine requests and orders; transmittals; confirmations and updates; summaries; fact sheets and news releases; thank-you and congratulatory notes; and responses to complaints. Understanding the conventions and formats of each kind of document will help you adapt to different audiences and situations and achieve your purpose. If all messages are **informative** to the extent that they explain or tell readers something, all professional messages also involve some persuasion. Anticipating audience reaction will help you determine how persuasive your message needs to be—and hence how to organize your message.

When we convey information that the reader will receive positively, the message is a **positive** or **good-news message.** ▶▶ Chapter 8 discusses messages where the reader will respond negatively; ▶▶ Chapter 9 discusses messages where you will need to persuade a resistant or even hostile reader to act.

Even a routine or good-news message usually has several purposes. Primary purposes:

- To give information or good news to the reader or to reassure the reader
- To have the reader read the message, understand it, and view the information positively
- To de-emphasize any negative elements

On the Job The (Earning) Power of Good Writing*

Communications skills offer the highest return on investment in Canada and the U.S., where there is high demand for these skills. A 2001 Canadian study based on a seven-country International Adult Literacy Survey connects labour market success and earning power to literacy skills—the ability to understand and use information in textual form—which account for one-third of the "return on education," each additional year of education raising earnings by 8.3%.

A 2010 Canadian government research study to measure the impact of Literacy and Essential Skills (LES) training among 110 firms and 1,500 workers in 8 provinces found "improved skills and performance," "increased worker productivity," an 8% increase in worker retention, a 25% return on employer investment, and an overall return on investment of 130% when government funding is included. In a 2011 study comparing education and earning levels of men and women, economist Eric Howe finds that Aboriginal students are an untapped economic resource that would yield "a total social benefit" of $90 billion in Saskatchewan alone if it invested in their education and closed the education gap between Aboriginal and non-Aboriginal people.

*Based on David A. Green and W. Craig Riddell, *Literacy, Numeracy and Labour Market Outcomes in Canada*, Cat. No. 89-552-MPE (Ottawa: Minister of Industry, 2001); David Gyarmati, "Making the Business Case for Workplace Essential Skills Training: Evidence from UPSKILL," April 22, 2014, retrieved May 17, 2014, from http://www.centreforliteracy.qc.ca/sites/default/files/UPSKILL_CFL_Webinar_April_22_2014.pdf; Eric Howe, *Bridging the Aboriginal Education Gap in Saskatchewan*. Saskatoon: Gabriel Dumont Institute; retrieved May 18, 2014, from http://www.nwtopportunities.com/sites/default/files/educationemployment.pdf.

Secondary purposes:

- To build the credibility of the writer
- To enhance the reputation of the writer's organization
- To cement a good relationship between the writer and reader
- To ensure the message doesn't require more messages and create more work for the writer

Routine messages are not necessarily short. Instead, the length of a message depends on your purposes, the audience's needs, and the complexity of the situation. A public health inspector got a lot of teasing from his colleagues because he wrote ten-page inspection reports; the other inspectors rarely wrote more than four pages. He got the last laugh, however, when the lawyers complimented him on his reports—they were getting enough information to win cases against companies and individuals charged with violating public health legislation. The shorter reports didn't give enough information.

LO1

WRITING LETTERS, MEMOS, AND ELECTRONIC MEDIA

Routine messages can be delivered in a variety of print and electronic media, including letters, memos, e-mails, text messaging, instant messaging, blogs, podcasts, as well as social media such as Twitter, Facebook, and LinkedIn. If electronic media are taking over from print and allow fast, cost-effective reach across distance, print messages can stand out from the e-crowd when the situation requires a higher level of formality (congratulatory message to CEO) or print is a legal requirement (of government regulation, for instance).

Letters go to someone outside your organization; **memos** go to someone in your own organization. E-mails (with features of letters and memos) as well as instant and text messages, tweets, and other social media, go to those inside and outside your organization. In large organizations where each unit is autonomous, however, the organization's culture determines whether people in different units exchange letters or memos or use texts and instant messages or social media. In some universities and colleges, for example, faculty send letters if they need to write to faculty in other departments. Like businesses, universities and colleges are also concerned about overuse and abuse of electronic media and the information overload and work–life imbalance they can cause (see ◂◂ "Balancing Work and Family" in Chapter 1).

Letters and memos have different formats, using and arranging document parts to meet the needs of their different audiences.

Both letters and memos can be

- Long or short, depending on the complexity of the message or situation
- Formal or informal, depending on whether you know your audience or not, or are writing for the record
- Simple responses that you can dash off in 15 minutes or difficult ones that take hours of analysis and revision when the situation is new or when the stakes are high

Although e-mail feels informal and private, it is both public and permanent. Writers welcomed the early informality of e-mail until hasty, careless, or casual words came back to haunt them. Ottawa career coach Alan Kearns underlines the risks of e-mail's "digital shadow": lost credibility, lost clients, lost time and opportunities—and even cabinet minister resignations and legal liability.[1] The use and overuse of e-mail has led to new business risks and remedies:

- Developing e-mail policies and procedures
- Safeguarding access and controls

Ethics and Legal Information, Please*

Information is power, yet some managers hoard that power for fear of weakening "their authority—their 'edge.'"

New-style managers disagree. "It's better to overcommunicate," says Anu Shukla, whose Web startup, Rubric, made 65 of her 85 employees millionaires. Rather than dispensing information on a need-to-know basis, she made sure information was shared with all of her employees. She also created the CEO lunch, inviting six to eight employees at a time to discuss the business with her.

High-trust organizations reap the multiple benefits (productivity, performance, innovation, and low turnover) of open, timely sharing of information; withholding information can be costly when employees share their views on social media.

*Based on Toni Cascio, "Creating a high-trust organization," *CW Bulletin*, February 2009, retrieved April 2, 2011, from http://www.iabc.com/cwb/archive/2009/0209/Rewers.htm; Jim Gray, "A visionary entrepreneur . . . and lousy communicator," *The Globe and Mail*, April 2, 2008, C3; Rochelle Sharpe, "As leaders, women rule," *BusinessWeek*, November 20, 2000, 80.

- Monitoring e-mail use by employees
- Limiting or prohibiting personal use
- Training employees to treat e-mail appropriately

Text and instant messaging have followed a similar pattern in becoming increasingly used for professional purposes with the same need for appropriate etiquette. In these cases, it is important to attend to both organizational and receiver needs and expectations of these channels for short and fast messages. They may well save time and money, support multitasking, and reduce telephone tagging, but they may also add legal liabilities and risks to security while reducing face-to-face interactions and increasing the socio-economic and health burden of e-distractions in the workplace.[2]

All the principles of good business writing still apply in e-mail or other electronic media: from attending to purpose and audience needs and benefits to checking for grammatical accuracy and completeness of information. Mayor Nenshi (◀◀ An Inside Perspective) is clear that "there's no point in . . . spinning stuff. . . . I just try to be honest with people," which is why people keep coming back "to talk about the future of their city."[3]

Young Africans using Google Earth, the Ushahidi (Swahili for testimony) Web site, and cell phones to share information about conflict zones, fatalities, and displaced people have also increased political participation.

Goodwill building on good you-attitude, positive emphasis, and bias-free language remains important (◀◀ Chapter 2).

Language and tone choices should be made carefully in a digital environment where readers have no access to reassuring nonverbal cues (see ◀◀ "Tone, Power, and Politeness" in Chapter 2). As a result, Canadian entrepreneur Matt Eldridge has developed ToneCheck for Outlook, a program that assesses tone according to message context.[4]

Jennifer Chandrawinata, a Canadian tax specialist, found out the hard way that neither long-winded academic writing nor text talk was adequate to professional needs. One buried her point, while the other did not give enough information for colleagues to act.[5]

See the ◀◀ On the Job box "Straight Talk with Professors?" in Chapter 2 for examples of casual e-mails that may set the tone for how people are perceived. Just as some organizations require writers to be concise and limit memos to one page, many insist that e-mails be kept to one screen. See also the ▶▶ Ethics and Legal box "Minding Your Texts and Tweets" later in this chapter.

LO2

FORMATTING LETTERS, MEMOS, AND E-MAILS

Whatever the message—routine, negative, or persuasive—document format plays its part in getting the message across, in building writer and organization credibility, and in solidifying a good relationship between writer and reader. How a document looks tells the reader how caring, careful, and professional the writer is. See also ◀◀ Chapter 4.

Knowing business community standards (and the standards of your own organization) helps you ensure that your letters, memos, and e-mails will send appropriate messages.

Technology Tips E-mail Etiquette*

Learn from the 35% of Canadians that have sent e-mails in haste:

- Ensure the message is necessary.
- Keep to one topic or purpose per e-mail.
- Use an accurate, concise, and specific subject line.
- Choose appropriate language, tone, and organization.
- Never send angry or emotional messages.
- Limit use of block capitals, enhanced text, or special formatting.
- Use the high-priority feature only for urgent messages.
- Retain only enough of the original message to aid your reader.
- Insert attachments only for long, heavily formatted, or non-text files (Excel, PowerPoint slides).
- Tell your reader what attachment program you have used.
- Open attachments only when you are confident about the source.
- Forward e-mails only when (a) they are not confidential and (b) you are confident about the source.
- Use "reply to all" function cautiously.
- Schedule e-mails in batches; limit expectations of response time.
- Carefully revise, edit, and proofread before sending.

*Adapted from Erin Anderssen, "Inbox of burden," *The Globe and Mail,* March 31, 2014, I1-4;"Thirty-five per cent of Canadians send e-mails they might rue," *National Post,* June 25, 2008; Keith Woolhouse, "Reclaim your e-mail," *Saskatoon StarPhoenix,* April 10, 2004, E1–2; Kitty O. Locker, Stephen Kyo Kaczmarek, and Kathryn Braun, *Business Communication: Building Critical Skills* (Toronto: McGraw-Hill Ryerson, 2005), 268–269.

Formatting Letters

Block format with inside address, date, and signature block aligned at the left margin (Figure 7.1) is now the standard in business, although organizations may make minor changes from the examples in margins or spacing.

Use the same level of formality in the **salutation,** or greeting, as you would in talking to someone on the phone: *Dear Glenn* if you're on a first-name basis, *Dear Mr. Helms* if you don't know the reader well enough to use the first name. For advice on courteous, unbiased options, see ◂◂ Chapter 2. Remember too that readers like to see their names—something merge functions in word processing programs allow you to do even in a form letter.

Sincerely and *Yours truly* are standard **complimentary closes.** When you are writing to people in special groups or to someone who is a friend as well as a business acquaintance, you may want to use a less formal close. Depending on the circumstances, the following informal closes might be acceptable: *Yours for a better environment* or *Cordially.*

In **mixed punctuation,** a colon follows the salutation and a comma follows the close. In a sales or fundraising letter, it is acceptable to use a comma after the salutation to make the letter look like a personal letter rather than like a business letter. Subject lines are required in memos; they are optional in letters (where they follow the salutation or, in some organizations, the inside address). Good subject lines are specific, concise, and appropriate for your purposes and the response you expect from your reader. For examples of subject lines in negative and persuasive messages, see ▸▸ Chapters 8 and 9.

A **reference line** (keyed two lines below the date line) refers the reader to the number used on the previous correspondence this letter replies to, or the order or invoice number this letter is about. Very large organizations, like Canada Revenue Agency, use numbers on every piece of correspondence they send out so that they may quickly find the earlier document to which an incoming letter refers.

Letterhead is preprinted stationery with the organization's name, logo, address, and phone number (see Figures 7.1, 7.5, 7.6, and 7.7). (It is also acceptable to use block format without letterhead.)

When your letter runs two or more pages, use a heading on the second page to identify it. Using the reader's name helps the writer, who may be printing out many letters at a time, to make sure the correct second page gets in the envelope. For the remaining pages, use plain paper that matches the letterhead in weight, texture, and colour.

A common format is shown in Figure 7.1. Even when the signature block is on the second page, it is still lined up with the date on the first page.

To eliminate keying the reader's name and address on an envelope, some organizations use envelopes with cut-outs or windows so that the **inside address** (the reader's name and address) on the letter can be used for delivery. If your organization does this, adjust your margins, if necessary, so that the whole inside address is visible.

Many letters are accompanied by other documents called **enclosures,** because they are enclosed in the envelope. The writer should refer to the enclosures in the body of the letter: "As you can see from my résumé. . . ." The enclosure line reminds the person who seals the letter to include the enclosures.

Sometimes you write to one person but send copies of your letter to other people. If you want the reader to know that other people are getting copies, list their names on the last page. The abbreviation *cc* originally meant *carbon copy* but

Figure 7.1 Block Format on Letterhead (mixed punctuation; collection letter)

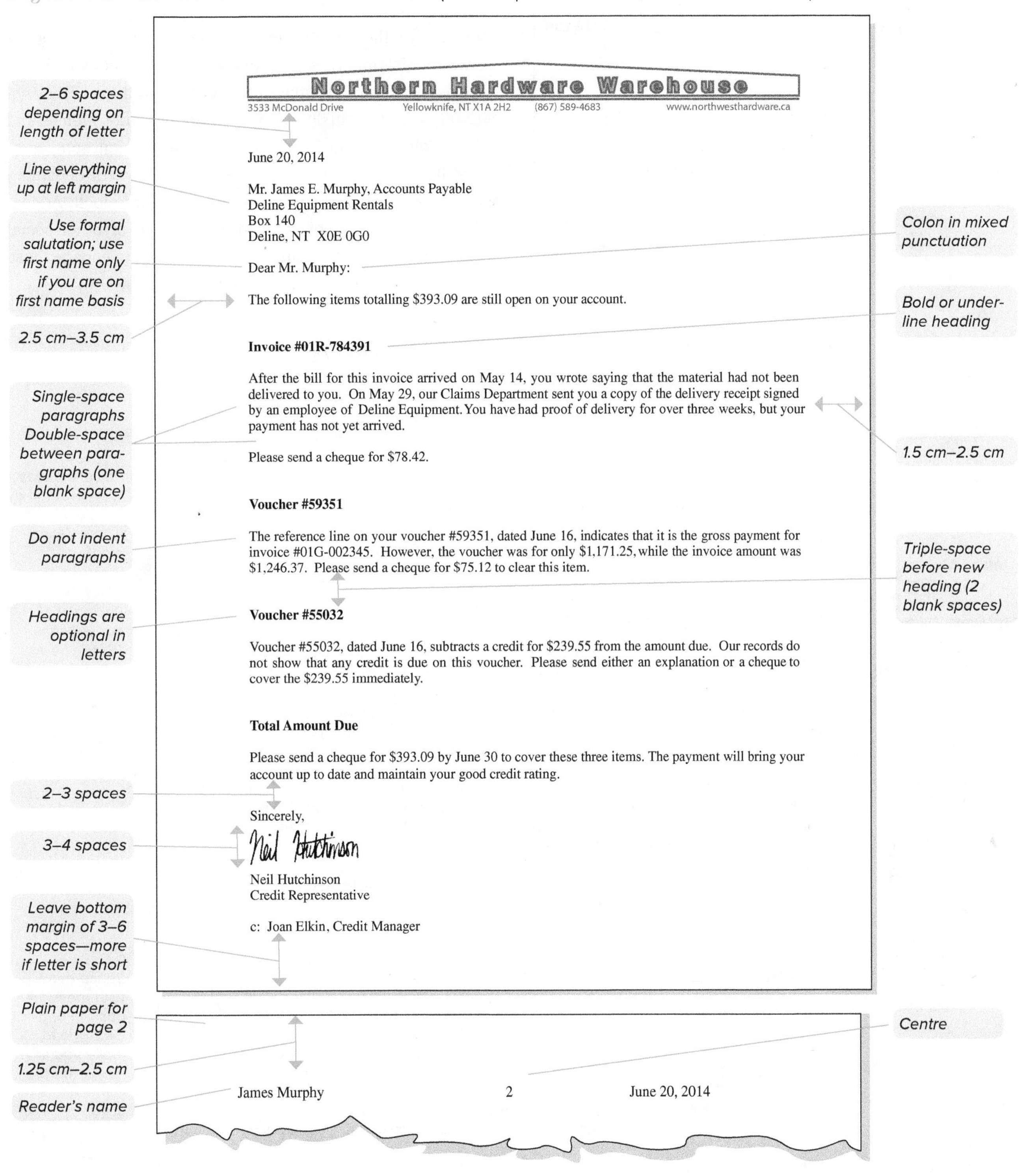
Northern Hardware Warehouse
3533 McDonald Drive Yellowknife, NT X1A 2H2 (867) 589-4683 www.northwesthardware.ca

June 20, 2014

Mr. James E. Murphy, Accounts Payable
Deline Equipment Rentals
Box 140
Deline, NT X0E 0G0

Dear Mr. Murphy:

The following items totalling $393.09 are still open on your account.

Invoice #01R-784391

After the bill for this invoice arrived on May 14, you wrote saying that the material had not been delivered to you. On May 29, our Claims Department sent you a copy of the delivery receipt signed by an employee of Deline Equipment. You have had proof of delivery for over three weeks, but your payment has not yet arrived.

Please send a cheque for $78.42.

Voucher #59351

The reference line on your voucher #59351, dated June 16, indicates that it is the gross payment for invoice #01G-002345. However, the voucher was for only $1,171.25, while the invoice amount was $1,246.37. Please send a cheque for $75.12 to clear this item.

Voucher #55032

Voucher #55032, dated June 16, subtracts a credit for $239.55 from the amount due. Our records do not show that any credit is due on this voucher. Please send either an explanation or a cheque to cover the $239.55 immediately.

Total Amount Due

Please send a cheque for $393.09 by June 30 to cover these three items. The payment will bring your account up to date and maintain your good credit rating.

Sincerely,

Neil Hutchinson

Neil Hutchinson
Credit Representative

c: Joan Elkin, Credit Manager

James Murphy 2 June 20, 2014

now means *computer copy*. Other acceptable abbreviations include *pc* for *photocopy* or simply *c* for *copy*. You can also send copies called **blind copies** to other people without telling the reader. Blind copies are listed only on the copy saved for the file with the abbreviation *bc* preceding the names of people getting these copies.

Formatting Envelopes

Canada Post Corporation requires consistency for efficient handling of business envelopes.[6] For more detailed advice, see the Postal Guide on the Canada Post Web site at www.canadapost.ca.

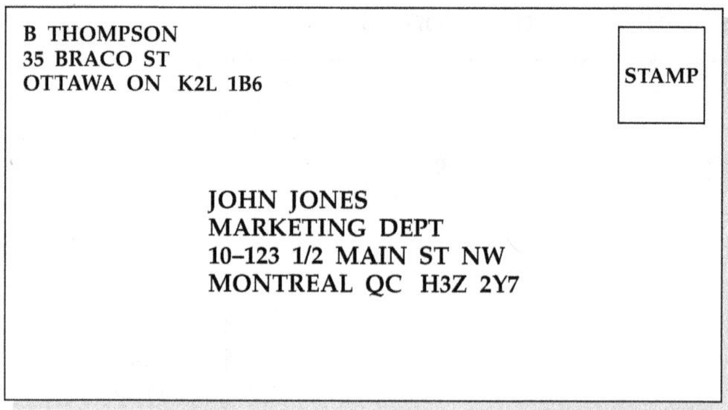

B THOMPSON
35 BRACO ST
OTTAWA ON K2L 1B6

STAMP

JOHN JONES
MARKETING DEPT
10–123 1/2 MAIN ST NW
MONTREAL QC H3Z 2Y7

Source: Copied with permission of the Canada Post Corporation.

Formatting Memos and E-Mails

Memos—whether electronic or paper—are standard means of communicating. E-mail programs prompt you to supply the various parts of the format in the **guide headings** (*To/From/Subject*); they supply date and time automatically. Memos and e-mails follow similar format and structure, though some writers still treat e-mail messages as informal letters beginning with a salutation and closing with a signature block. Adding your Twitter, Facebook, LinkedIn, Pinterest, or other social media profiles to your signature is a good way to engage those who don't already know you.[7] See Figure 7.2.

Figure 7.2 An E-Mail Reply with Copies (response to a complaint)

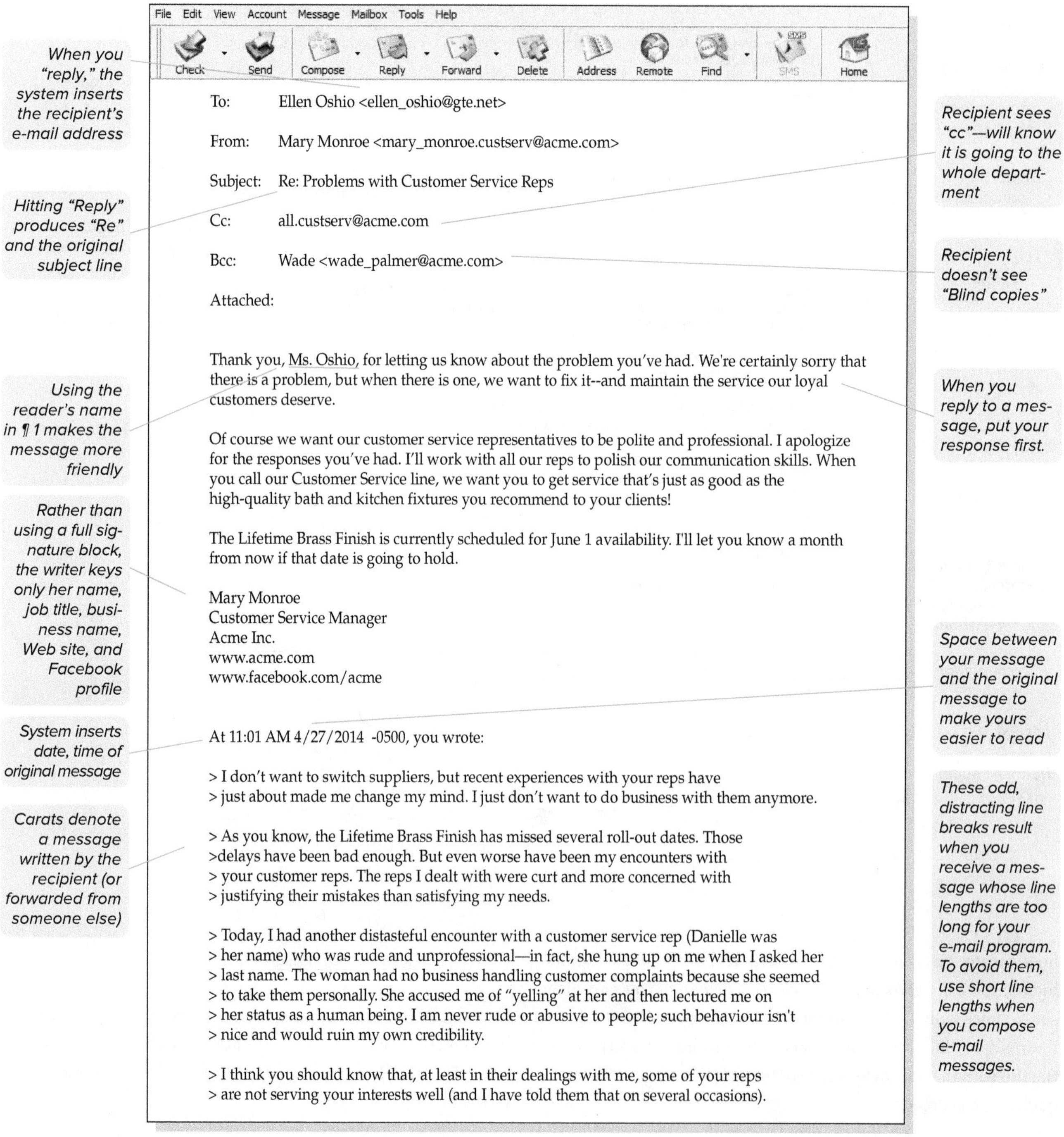

File Edit View Account Message Mailbox Tools Help

Check Send Compose Reply Forward Delete Address Remote Find SMS Home

When you "reply," the system inserts the recipient's e-mail address

Hitting "Reply" produces "Re" and the original subject line

Recipient sees "cc"—will know it is going to the whole department

Recipient doesn't see "Blind copies"

To: Ellen Oshio <ellen_oshio@gte.net>

From: Mary Monroe <mary_monroe.custserv@acme.com>

Subject: Re: Problems with Customer Service Reps

Cc: all.custserv@acme.com

Bcc: Wade <wade_palmer@acme.com>

Attached:

Using the reader's name in ¶ 1 makes the message more friendly

When you reply to a message, put your response first.

Thank you, Ms. Oshio, for letting us know about the problem you've had. We're certainly sorry that there is a problem, but when there is one, we want to fix it--and maintain the service our loyal customers deserve.

Of course we want our customer service representatives to be polite and professional. I apologize for the responses you've had. I'll work with all our reps to polish our communication skills. When you call our Customer Service line, we want you to get service that's just as good as the high-quality bath and kitchen fixtures you recommend to your clients!

The Lifetime Brass Finish is currently scheduled for June 1 availability. I'll let you know a month from now if that date is going to hold.

Rather than using a full signature block, the writer keys only her name, job title, business name, Web site, and Facebook profile

Mary Monroe
Customer Service Manager
Acme Inc.
www.acme.com
www.facebook.com/acme

Space between your message and the original message to make yours easier to read

System inserts date, time of original message

At 11:01 AM 4/27/2014 -0500, you wrote:

Carats denote a message written by the recipient (or forwarded from someone else)

These odd, distracting line breaks result when you receive a message whose line lengths are too long for your e-mail program. To avoid them, use short line lengths when you compose e-mail messages.

\> I don't want to switch suppliers, but recent experiences with your reps have
\> just about made me change my mind. I just don't want to do business with them anymore.

\> As you know, the Lifetime Brass Finish has missed several roll-out dates. Those
\>delays have been bad enough. But even worse have been my encounters with
\> your customer reps. The reps I dealt with were curt and more concerned with
\> justifying their mistakes than satisfying my needs.

\> Today, I had another distasteful encounter with a customer service rep (Danielle was
\> her name) who was rude and unprofessional—in fact, she hung up on me when I asked her
\> last name. The woman had no business handling customer complaints because she seemed
\> to take them personally. She accused me of "yelling" at her and then lectured me on
\> her status as a human being. I am never rude or abusive to people; such behaviour isn't
\> nice and would ruin my own credibility.

\> I think you should know that, at least in their dealings with me, some of your reps
\> are not serving your interests well (and I have told them that on several occasions).

E-mail expert Dawn-Michelle Baude cautions, "The signoff is, in fact, where the emotional tenor of the message is registered as neutral, friendly, respectful, endearing, chilly." Instead of relying on the same signoff, she argues that audience and context matter. Europeans appreciate "Cheers"; "Regards" is acceptable internationally.[8]

Memos never use indented paragraphs. Subject lines are required; headings are optional. Never use a separate heading for the first paragraph.

Figure 7.3 illustrates the standard memo format keyed on a plain sheet of paper. Note that the first letters of the writer's name, the reader's name, the date, and the subject phrase are lined up vertically. Note also that memos are usually initialled by the *To/From* block. Initialling tells the reader that you have proofread the memo and prevents someone sending a memo you did not in fact write.

Some organizations have special letterhead for memos. When *To/From/Date/Subject* are already printed on the form, writers' and readers' names, date, and subject are set at the main margin to save keying time.

Some organizations alter the order of items in the *To/From/Date/Subject* block. Some use word-processing templates. Some organizations ask employees to sign memos rather than simply initialling them. The signature goes below the last line of the memo, starting halfway over on the page, and prevents anyone's adding unauthorized information.

If the memo runs two pages or more, set up the second and subsequent plain pages in one of the following ways.

Brief Subject Line or Reader's Name
Date
Page Number

or

Brief Subject Line or Reader's Name	Page Number	Date

LO3

ORGANIZING ROUTINE MESSAGES

The patterns of organization in this chapter and the chapters that follow will work for 70% to 90% of the writing situations most people in business and government face. Understanding

Figure 7.3 A Good-News Policy Memo

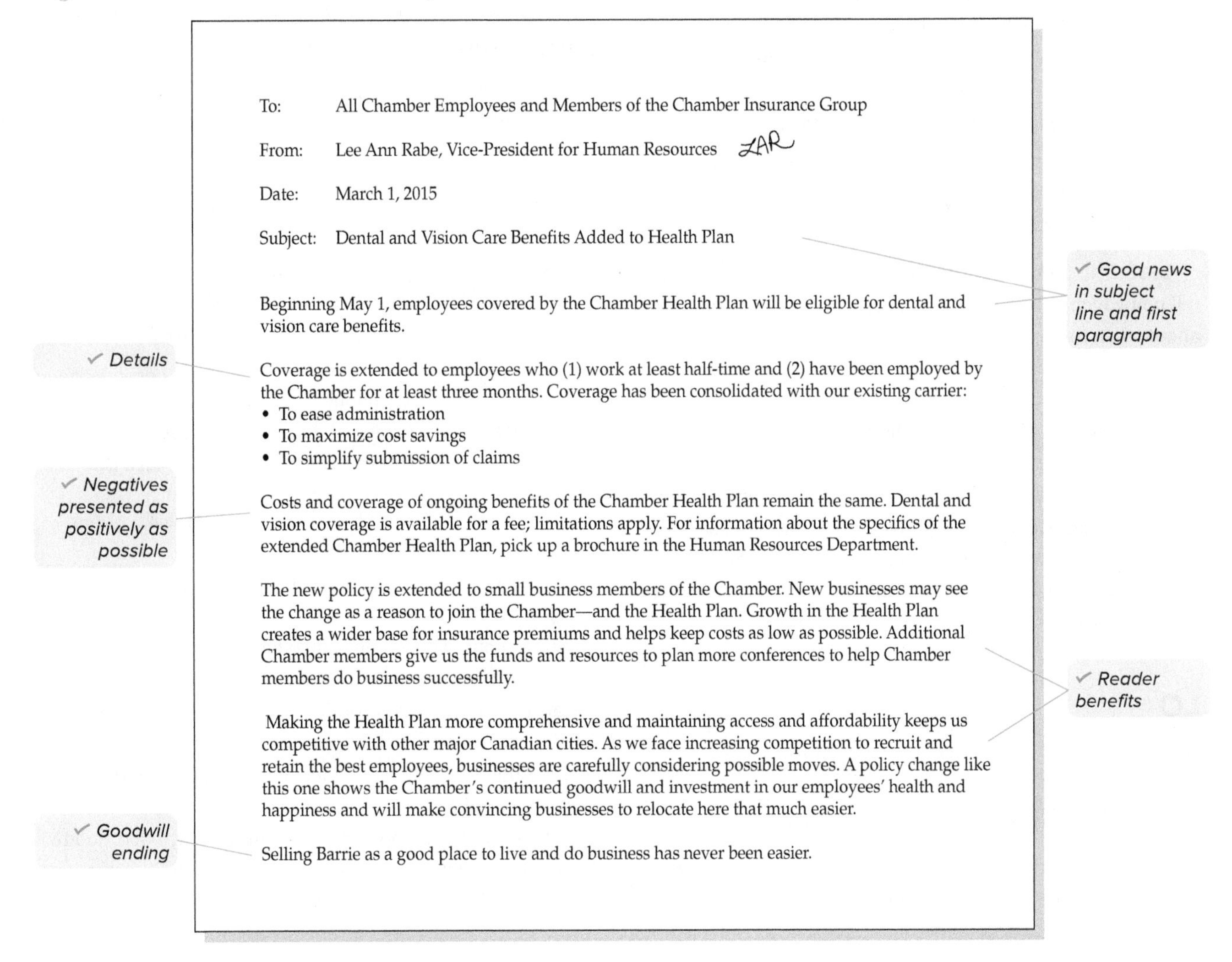

To: All Chamber Employees and Members of the Chamber Insurance Group

From: Lee Ann Rabe, Vice-President for Human Resources LAR

Date: March 1, 2015

Subject: Dental and Vision Care Benefits Added to Health Plan

Beginning May 1, employees covered by the Chamber Health Plan will be eligible for dental and vision care benefits.

Coverage is extended to employees who (1) work at least half-time and (2) have been employed by the Chamber for at least three months. Coverage has been consolidated with our existing carrier:

- To ease administration
- To maximize cost savings
- To simplify submission of claims

Costs and coverage of ongoing benefits of the Chamber Health Plan remain the same. Dental and vision coverage is available for a fee; limitations apply. For information about the specifics of the extended Chamber Health Plan, pick up a brochure in the Human Resources Department.

The new policy is extended to small business members of the Chamber. New businesses may see the change as a reason to join the Chamber—and the Health Plan. Growth in the Health Plan creates a wider base for insurance premiums and helps keep costs as low as possible. Additional Chamber members give us the funds and resources to plan more conferences to help Chamber members do business successfully.

Making the Health Plan more comprehensive and maintaining access and affordability keeps us competitive with other major Canadian cities. As we face increasing competition to recruit and retain the best employees, businesses are carefully considering possible moves. A policy change like this one shows the Chamber's continued goodwill and investment in our employees' health and happiness and will make convincing businesses to relocate here that much easier.

Selling Barrie as a good place to live and do business has never been easier.

Figure 7.4 Direct Pattern for Organizing Routine Messages

1. **Give any good news and summarize the main points.** Include the date policies begin and the amount of a discount. If the reader has already raised the issue, make it clear that you're responding. Share good news immediately.
2. **Give details, clarification, background.** Don't repeat information you've already given. Do answer all the questions your reader is likely to have; provide all the information necessary to achieve your purposes. Present details in the order of importance to the reader.
3. **Present any negative elements as positively as possible.** A policy may have limits; information may be incomplete; the reader may have to satisfy requirements to get a discount or benefit. Make these negatives clear, but present them as positively as possible.
4. **Explain any reader benefits.** Most informative memos need reader benefits. Show that the policy or procedure helps readers, not just the company. Give enough detail to make the benefits clear and convincing. It's often possible to combine a short reader benefit with a goodwill ending in the last paragraph.
5. **Use a goodwill ending: positive, personal, and forward looking.** Shifting your emphasis away from the message to the specific reader suggests that serving the reader is your real concern.

and using the appropriate pattern can help you compose more quickly and create a better final product—with better first and last impressions.

- Understanding the reason behind each pattern will help you change the pattern if necessary. (For example, if you write instructions, any warnings should go up front, not in the middle of the message.)
- Not every message that uses the direct pattern for good-news messages will have all the elements listed. Any elements will go in the order presented in the pattern.
- Sometimes you can present several elements in one paragraph. Sometimes you'll need several paragraphs for just one element.

In real life, writing problems don't come with labels that tell you which pattern to use. ▸▸ Chapters 8 and 9 offer advice about when to use each pattern.

Figure 7.4 shows how to organize routine messages in a direct pattern.

The letter in Figure 7.5 authorizes a one-year appointment that the reader and writer have already discussed and describes the organization's priorities. Since the writer knows that the reader wants to accept the job, the letter doesn't need to persuade. The opportunity to study records that aren't available to the public is an implicit reader benefit; the concern for the reader's needs builds goodwill.

LO4

CHOOSING SUBJECT LINES FOR ROUTINE MESSAGES

A subject line is the title of a document. It creates important first impressions, aids in filing and retrieving the document, tells readers why they need to read the document, and provides a framework for what you say.

A good subject line meets three criteria: it is specific, concise, and appropriate to the kind of message (routine, negative, persuasive).

The subject line needs to be specific enough to differentiate that message from others on the same subject, but broad enough to cover everything in the message.

✗ Too general:	Training Sessions
✓ Better:	Dates for 2015 Training Sessions
✓ or:	Evaluation of Training Sessions on Conducting Interviews
✓ or:	Should We Schedule a Short Course on Proposal Writing?

Most subject lines are relatively short (typically not a sentence and with no punctuation at the end)—usually no more than ten words, often only three to seven words.[9]

✗ Wordy:	Survey of Student Preferences in Regards to Various Pizza Factors
✓ Better:	Students' Pizza Preferences
✓ or:	The Feasibility of a Family Pizza Branch on Campus
✓ or:	What Students Like and Dislike about Giovanni Pizza

If you can't make the subject both specific and short, be specific.

Since your subject line introduces your reader to your message, it must satisfy the psychological demands of the situation; it must be appropriate to your purposes and to the immediate response you expect from your reader. In general, do the same thing in your subject line that you would do in the first paragraph.

When you have good news for the reader, build goodwill by highlighting it in the subject line. When your information is neutral, summarize it concisely for the subject line.

Figure 7.5 A Letter Confirming Appointment

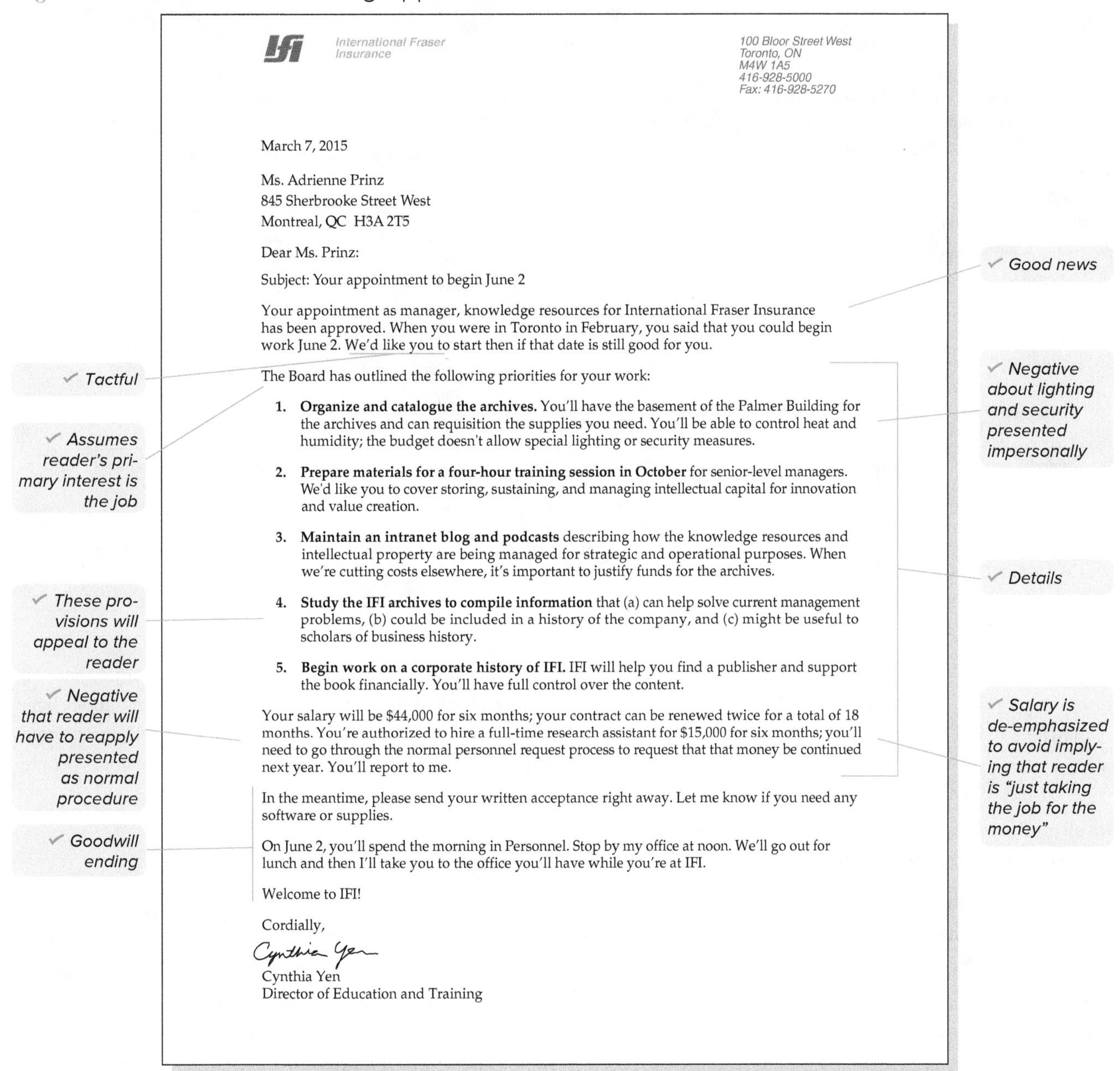
IFI International Fraser Insurance

100 Bloor Street West
Toronto, ON
M4W 1A5
416-928-5000
Fax: 416-928-5270

March 7, 2015

Ms. Adrienne Prinz
845 Sherbrooke Street West
Montreal, QC H3A 2T5

Dear Ms. Prinz:

Subject: Your appointment to begin June 2

Your appointment as manager, knowledge resources for International Fraser Insurance has been approved. When you were in Toronto in February, you said that you could begin work June 2. We'd like you to start then if that date is still good for you.

The Board has outlined the following priorities for your work:

1. **Organize and catalogue the archives.** You'll have the basement of the Palmer Building for the archives and can requisition the supplies you need. You'll be able to control heat and humidity; the budget doesn't allow special lighting or security measures.
2. **Prepare materials for a four-hour training session in October** for senior-level managers. We'd like you to cover storing, sustaining, and managing intellectual capital for innovation and value creation.
3. **Maintain an intranet blog and podcasts** describing how the knowledge resources and intellectual property are being managed for strategic and operational purposes. When we're cutting costs elsewhere, it's important to justify funds for the archives.
4. **Study the IFI archives to compile information** that (a) can help solve current management problems, (b) could be included in a history of the company, and (c) might be useful to scholars of business history.
5. **Begin work on a corporate history of IFI.** IFI will help you find a publisher and support the book financially. You'll have full control over the content.

Your salary will be $44,000 for six months; your contract can be renewed twice for a total of 18 months. You're authorized to hire a full-time research assistant for $15,000 for six months; you'll need to go through the normal personnel request process to request that that money be continued next year. You'll report to me.

In the meantime, please send your written acceptance right away. Let me know if you need any software or supplies.

On June 2, you'll spend the morning in Personnel. Stop by my office at noon. We'll go out for lunch and then I'll take you to the office you'll have while you're at IFI.

Welcome to IFI!

Cordially,

Cynthia Yen
Director of Education and Training

Subject: Discount on Rental Cars Effective January 2

Starting January 2, as an employee of Amalgamated Industries you can get a 15% discount on cars you rent for business or personal use from Roadway Rent-a-Car.

Subject: Update on Arrangements for Videoconference with France

In the last month, we have chosen the participants and developed a tentative agenda for the videoconference with France scheduled for March 21.

Subject lines in e-mail are even more important than those in letters and memos.[10] Subject lines must be specific, concise, and catchy. Some e-mail users get so many messages that they don't bother reading messages if they don't recognize the sender or if the subject doesn't catch their interest. The good news for e-mail marketers is that e-mail still outperforms social media in driving sales, according to a report by e-commerce software firm Monetate.[11] Some e-mail default options, however, mean that 57% of e-mail recipients see only 38–47 characters of the subject line.[12]

If you have good news to convey, put it in the subject line. The following subject lines would be acceptable for good-news e-mail messages:

- Travel Plans for Sales Meeting
- Your Proposal Accepted
- Reduced Prices during February
- Your Funding Request Approved

Technology Tips Spam Costs*

In 2002, spam accounted for 38% of all e-mail; in 2003, 60%; in January and February 2004, 75%; in January 2005, 83.11%. By 2010, e-security company Symantec recorded 1 in 455.2 e-mails was phishing and 1 in 1.11 e-mails was spam. In 2013 Industry Canada estimated that spam and phishing cost the Canadian economy $3 billion each year.

- Spam in Canada in 2010 was exceeded only by that in Italy, Germany, Netherlands, Hong Kong, the United States, the United Kingdom, and Australia.
- Phishing scams (e-mails that appear to come from legitimate sources) collecting data for marketing and ad campaigns reached 35 million a week in the second half of 2004 (up from 9 million in the first half of 2004).
- 53% of users in 2005 said spam has made them less trusting of e-mail.
- Filtering can block legitimate e-communications, such as service notices, invoices, and newsletters.
- When Bill C-28 (The Fighting Internet and Wireless Spam Act) received Royal Assent on December 15, 2010, Canada became the last of the G-8 countries to implement such legislation. New regulations around consent and options to unsubscribe are effective July 1, 2014.
- For updates on Internet and e-commerce law and regulation, check out Professor Michael Geist's multimedia site at www.michaelgeist.ca

*Adapted from Susan Krashinsky, "Tired of unsolicited spam? Relief is on the way," *The Globe and Mail*, December 3, 2013, retrieved May 18, 2014, from http://www.theglobeandmail.com/report-on-business/industry-news/marketing/unsolicited-spam-is-history-thanks-to-new-law-in-effect-july-1/article15774176/; "Global spam statistics," retrieved April 3, 2011, from http://www.internetekg.com/?p=66; Keith Woolhouse, "Reclaim your e-mail," *Saskatoon StarPhoenix*, April 10, 2004, E1–2; Simon Avery, "Hacker alert: Report finds surge in on-line attacks," *The Globe and Mail*, March 21, 2005, B1–5; Industry Canada, "What is spam?" retrieved April 18, 2008, from http://e-com.ic.gc.ca/epic/site/ecic-ceac.nsf/en/h_gv00170e.html#cost; Industry Canada, "The digital economy in Canada," retrieved April 3, 2011, from http://www.ic.gc.ca/eic/site/ecic-ceac.nsf/eng/h_gv00567.html.

LO5

USING READER BENEFITS IN ROUTINE MESSAGES

Not all routine messages need reader benefits (see ◂◂ Chapter 2). You do not need reader benefits when

- You are presenting factual information only.
- The reader's attitude toward the information does not matter.
- Stressing benefits may make the reader sound selfish.
- The benefits are so obvious that to restate them insults the reader's intelligence.

You do need reader benefits when

- You are presenting policies.
- You want to shape readers' attitudes toward the information or toward your organization.
- Stressing benefits presents readers' motives positively.
- Some of the benefits may not be obvious to readers.

Messages to customers or potential customers sometimes include a sales paragraph promoting products or services you offer in addition to the product or service the reader has asked about. Sales promotion in a routine message should be low-key, not "hard sell."

Reader benefits are hardest to develop when you are announcing policies. The organization probably decided to adopt the policy because it appeared to help the organization. Yet reader benefits are essential in this kind of message so readers see the reason for the change and support it (see ◂◂ Figure 2.6).

To develop reader benefits for routine messages, use the steps suggested in ◂◂ Chapter 2. Be sure to think about benefits that come from the activity or policy itself, apart from any financial benefits. Does a policy improve the hours people spend at work?

Ending Routine Messages

Ending a letter, memo, e-mail, text, or instant message gracefully can be a problem in short routine messages. In a one-page memo where you have omitted details and proof, you can tell readers where to get more information. In long messages, you can summarize your basic point. In persuasive messages, as you'll learn in ▸▸ Chapter 9, you can tell readers what you want them to do. In a short message containing all the information readers need, either write a goodwill paragraph that refers directly to the reader or the reader's organization, or just stop.

Goodwill endings should focus on the business relationship you share with your reader. When you write to one person or organization, a good last paragraph fits that audience so specifically that it would not work with any other.

Use a paragraph that shows you see your reader as an individual. Possibilities include complimenting the reader for a job well done, describing a reader benefit, or looking forward to something positive that relates to the subject of the message.

In the following examples, a letter answers the question "When a patient leaves the hospital and returns, should we count it as a new stay?" The company answers that if a patient was gone from the hospital overnight or longer, the hospital should start a new claim when the patient was readmitted.

× Weak closing paragraph:

Should you have any questions regarding this matter, please feel free to call me.

✓ Goodwill paragraph:

Many employee-patients appreciate the freedom to leave the hospital for a few hours. It's nice working with a hospital that is flexible enough to offer that option.

✓ Also acceptable:

Omit the paragraph; stop after the explanation.

Some writers end every message with a standard invitation:

If you have questions, please do not hesitate to ask.

That sentence lacks positive emphasis. But revising it to say "feel free to call" still leaves the impression of a clichéd (and insincere) ending. It also invites extra work unnecessarily. Most of the time, the writer should omit the sentence entirely.

The memo in ◂◂ Figure 7.3 announcing a new employee benefit follows the direct pattern:

1. The first paragraph summarizes the policy.
2. Paragraphs 2 to 3 give details. Negative elements in paragraph 3 are stated as positively as possible.
3. The last section of the memo gives reader benefits and a goodwill ending.

LO6

DISTINGUISHING VARIETIES OF ROUTINE MESSAGES

Some messages are clearly positive—acceptances, positive answers to requests, and positive policy changes (◂◂ Figure 7.3). Other messages can be informative, negative, or persuasive depending on what you have to say. A transmittal, for example, can be positive when you're sending glowing sales figures or persuasive when you want the reader to act on the information. A collection letter is persuasive; it becomes negative in the last stage when you threaten legal action.

Understanding the conventions and formats will help you change the pattern if necessary to adapt to different audiences and situations and achieve your purpose.

Writing Routine Requests

Routine requests for information, products, services, or options (see Figure 7.6) that expect the reader to be receptive follow the direct pattern of organizing, matching tone and content to audience needs:

1. The opening makes the request precisely, concisely, and courteously.
2. The body adds detail (specific needs) to enable the reader to act on the request.
3. The ending links the request to a specific deadline, expresses appreciation, and/or anticipates a future business relationship.

Technology Tips Welcome News*

Many companies, profit and non-profit, maintain ties with customers by sending out a regular newsletter via e-mail. Customers welcome this type of communication if it is interesting and easy to read. According to the Direct Marketing Association (2014), e-newsletters still deliver "the best return on investment" in face of competition from social media. The open rate for the Hunter Public Relations monthly one-page e-newsletter is 29% (compared to an industry average of 9.4%).

Here are pointers for a successful electronic newsletter:

- **Be relevant.** Everyone gets plenty of cute humour online. The newsletter should be limited to information recipients can use.
- **Be brief.**
- **Be consistent.** Set up a regular schedule for the newsletter, and get it out on time. This conveys an image of dependability.
- **Be engaging.** Use an enticing, informative subject line (not "June issue") and give readers a forum for feedback.
- **Be simple.** Skip the embedded photos and audio or video clips unless they are essential to your message. They tend to be distracting, and they slow down the process of opening e-mail.
- **Be considerate.** Set yourself apart from spammers by making it easy to unsubscribe as well as to subscribe. Lead off each mailing with an explanation like "ABC Digest is a monthly newsletter with hints for alphabet soup lovers, sent to subscribers who have requested it. If you would like to be removed from our mailing list, click on this link."

*Based on Barb Sawyers, "10 simple ways to revive your newsletter," Ragan.com, March 24, 2014, retrieved May 19, 2014, from http://www.ragan.com/Main/Articles/48117.aspx; John M. Cowan, "Winning email newsletter focuses on just 'five things'," Ragan.com, March 8, 2013, retrieved May 19, 2014, from http://www.ragan.com/Main/Articles/46342.aspx; Natalie Canavor and Claire Meirowitz, "E-newsletters: A smart way to market," *CW Bulletin*, May 2009, retrieved April 2, 2011, from http://www.iabc.com/cwb/archive/2009/0509/WorkingWords.htm; Ellen Neuborne, "Making e-mail work," *Sales & Marketing Management*, February 2004, p. 18, downloaded from http://www.salesandmarketing.com; and Rebecca Rohan, "The messenger," *Black Enterprise*, July 2000, 55–56.

Figure 7.6 Routine Request Letter

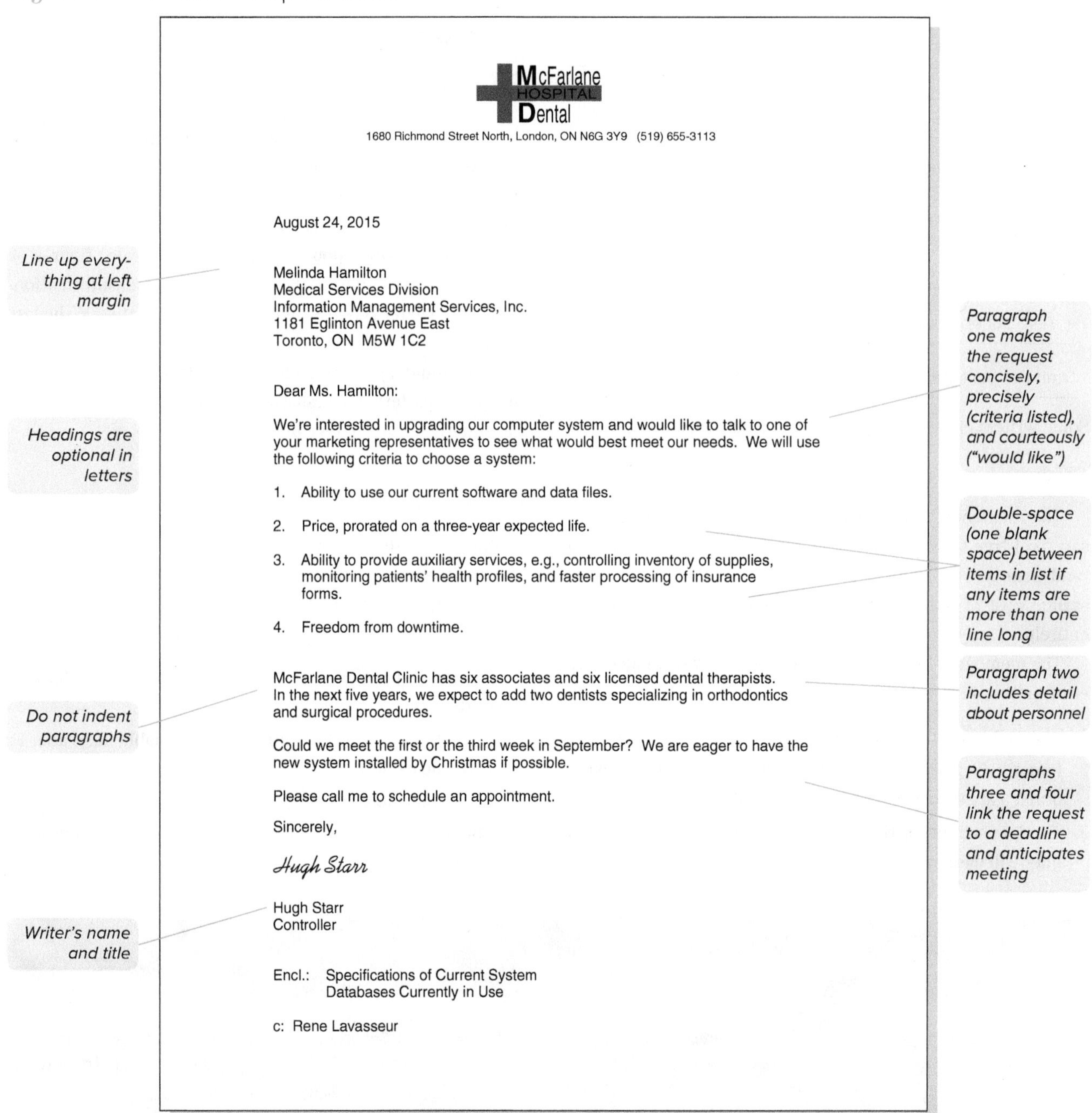

McFarlane HOSPITAL Dental
1680 Richmond Street North, London, ON N6G 3Y9 (519) 655-3113

August 24, 2015

Melinda Hamilton
Medical Services Division
Information Management Services, Inc.
1181 Eglinton Avenue East
Toronto, ON M5W 1C2

Dear Ms. Hamilton:

We're interested in upgrading our computer system and would like to talk to one of your marketing representatives to see what would best meet our needs. We will use the following criteria to choose a system:

1. Ability to use our current software and data files.

2. Price, prorated on a three-year expected life.

3. Ability to provide auxiliary services, e.g., controlling inventory of supplies, monitoring patients' health profiles, and faster processing of insurance forms.

4. Freedom from downtime.

McFarlane Dental Clinic has six associates and six licensed dental therapists. In the next five years, we expect to add two dentists specializing in orthodontics and surgical procedures.

Could we meet the first or the third week in September? We are eager to have the new system installed by Christmas if possible.

Please call me to schedule an appointment.

Sincerely,

Hugh Starr

Hugh Starr
Controller

Encl.: Specifications of Current System
Databases Currently in Use

c: Rene Lavasseur

For more complicated requests requiring persuasion to achieve written purposes, see ⏩ Chapter 9.

Writing Transmittals

When you send someone something in an organization, attach a memo, letter, or e-transmittal explaining what you're sending. A transmittal can be as simple as a business card or sticky note with "FYI" ("for your information") written on it, or it can be a separate keyed document.

Organize your transmittal in this order:

1. Tell the reader what you're sending.
2. Summarize the main point(s) of the document.
3. Indicate any special circumstances or information that would help the reader understand the document. Is it a draft? Is it a partial document that will be completed later?
4. Tell the reader what will happen next. Will you do something? Do you want a response? If you do want the reader to act, specify exactly what you want the reader to do and give a deadline.

Frequently, transmittals have important secondary purposes. Consider the writer's purpose in Figure 7.7, a transmittal from a lawyer to her client. The primary purpose of this transmittal is to give the client a chance to affirm that his story and the lawyer's understanding of it are correct. If there's anything wrong, the lawyer wants to know before she files the brief.

Figure 7.7 A Transmittal

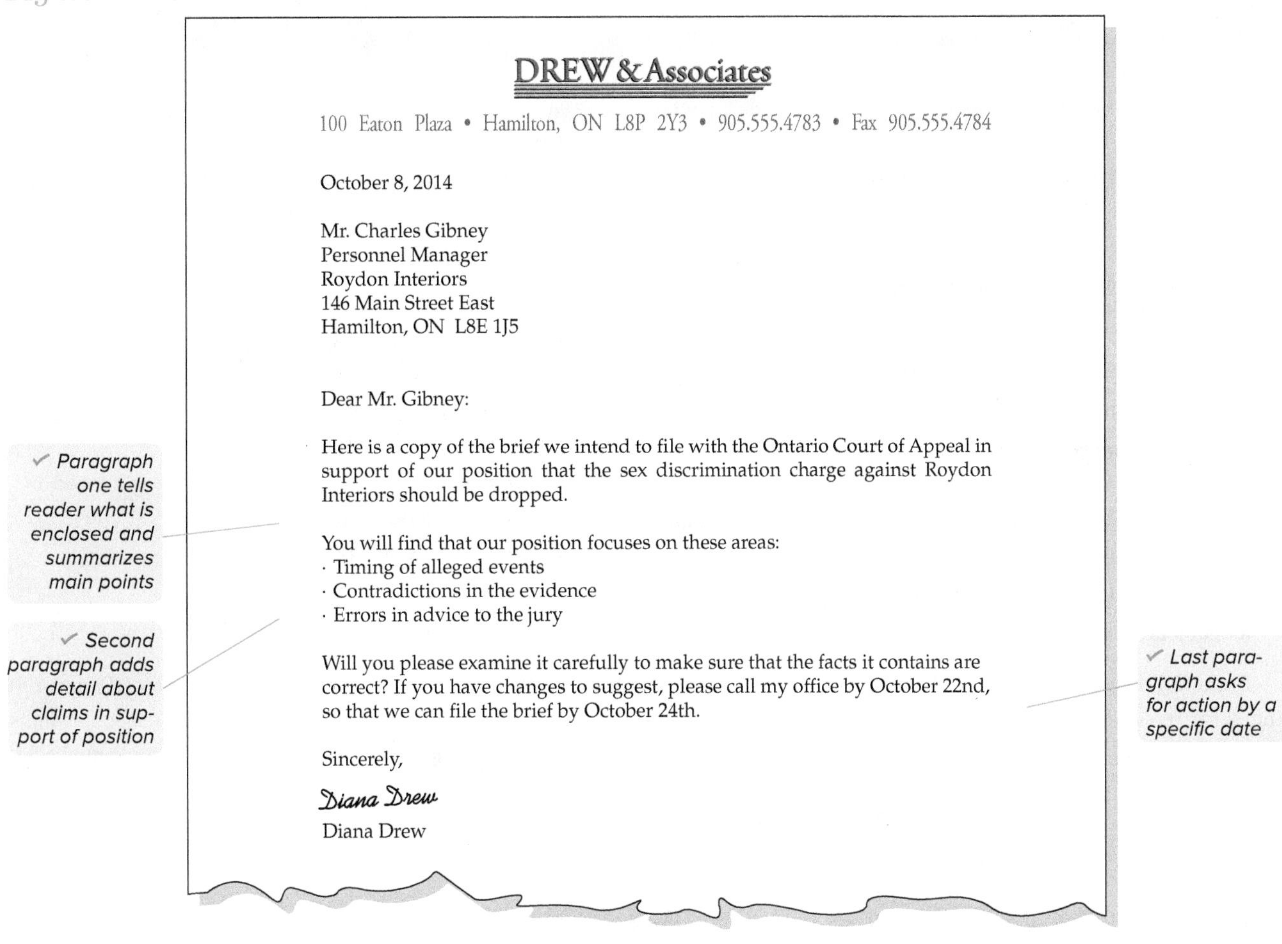

DREW & Associates

100 Eaton Plaza • Hamilton, ON L8P 2Y3 • 905.555.4783 • Fax 905.555.4784

October 8, 2014

Mr. Charles Gibney
Personnel Manager
Roydon Interiors
146 Main Street East
Hamilton, ON L8E 1J5

Dear Mr. Gibney:

Here is a copy of the brief we intend to file with the Ontario Court of Appeal in support of our position that the sex discrimination charge against Roydon Interiors should be dropped.

You will find that our position focuses on these areas:
· Timing of alleged events
· Contradictions in the evidence
· Errors in advice to the jury

Will you please examine it carefully to make sure that the facts it contains are correct? If you have changes to suggest, please call my office by October 22nd, so that we can file the brief by October 24th.

Sincerely,

Diana Drew

Diana Drew

But an important secondary purpose is to build goodwill: "I'm working on your case; I'm earning my fee." The greatest number of complaints officially lodged against lawyers are for the lawyer's neglect—or what the client perceives as neglect—of the client's case.

Sending Confirmations and Updates

Many routine messages confirm actions (as in financial trades), events, understandings, and agreements. ◀◀ Figure 7.5 confirms approval for an appointment, adding detail about roles and responsibilities. Other messages update on progress or timelines or confirm and record oral conversations. These messages are generally short and give only the information shared orally; they go to the other party in the conversation. Start the message by indicating that it is an update or confirmation, not a new message:

> As we discussed on the phone today, . . .
> As I told you yesterday, . . .
> Here is the meeting schedule we discussed earlier today.

Summarizing

You may be asked to summarize a conversation, document, or outside meeting for colleagues or superiors. (Minutes of an internal meeting are usually more detailed. See ◀◀ Chapter 6 for advice on writing minutes of meetings.) See ▶▶ Chapters 10 and 11 for advice on summarizing and repeating with style in reports.

In a summary of a conversation for internal use, identify

- People present
- Topics of discussion
- Decisions made
- Actions needed

To summarize a document

- Start with the main point.
- Give supporting evidence or details.
- Evaluate the document, if desired. Should others in the company read this book? Should someone in the company write a letter to the editor responding to this newspaper article?

When you visit a client or go to a conference your company needs to know what it should do as a result of the meeting.

Technology Tips Voice-Mail Information

Before you make a phone call, think of the information you'll need if you must leave a voice-mail message.

- Summarize the purpose of your message in a sentence or two.
- Give your name and phone number early in the message. Speak slowly and distinctly.
- Give the recipient enough information to act.
- Tell when you'll be at your desk to receive a return call.

Summarize a visit with a client or customer in this way:

1. Put the main point from your organization's point of view—the action to be taken, the perceptions to be changed—in the first paragraph.
2. Provide an **umbrella paragraph** to list in order and foreshadow the points you will make in the report.
3. Provide necessary detail to support your conclusions and cover each point.
4. Use lists and headings to make the structure of the document clear.

In the following example, the first paragraph summarizes the sales representative's conclusions after a call on a prospective client:

> Consolidated Tool Works (CTW) is an excellent prospect for purchasing a Matrix-Churchill grinding machine. To get the order, we should
>
> 1. Set up a visit for CTW personnel to see the Matrix-Churchill machine in Saskatoon.
> 2. Guarantee 60-day delivery if the order is placed by the end of the quarter.
> 3. Extend credit terms to CTW.

Writing Fact Sheets and News Releases

Summarizing is the foundation of **fact sheets** (see Figure 7.8). To keep stakeholders informed, fact sheets have become indispensable tools. Typically part of an organization's media kit,

Figure 7.8 Fact Sheet: Young Canadians in a Wired World

Young Canadians in a Wired World Phase III: Life Online
Fact Sheet

Initiated in 2000 by MediaSmarts, *Young Canadians in a Wired World* (YCWW) is the most comprehensive and wide-ranging study of children's and teens' Internet use in Canada. Through this research, MediaSmarts has harvested a wealth of information on the impact of networked technologies on young Canadians.

Our latest *YCWW* findings from a survey conducted in 2013 provide new insights on the Internet behaviours and attitudes of students across the country. *Life Online* focuses on what youth are doing online, what sites they're going to, and their attitudes towards online safety, household rules, and unplugging from digital technology. This report is the first in a series that will examine several themes which are emerging from the survey findings, including: privacy, cyberbullying, digital literacy, online relationships and offensive content.

Methodology
In total, 5,436 students in grades 4 through 11, representing every province and territory, were surveyed. The research was conducted from February to June 2013 and was administered by teachers in 140 schools to both English- and French-speaking students.

Key Findings

Online access
- Students are highly connected, with over 99% having access to the Internet outside of school.
- Portable devices are used more than desktop computers to access the Internet.
- **Cell phones and smartphones** are among the primary devices for going online and 39% of students with a cell phone report sleeping with it in case they get calls or messages at night.

Online activities
- Digital media are important sources for **finding information** but students primarily go online **for entertainment and communicating with friends and family**, with Facebook being the second most popular site for students in grades 7 to 11.
- A large number of students in grades 4 to 6 are on Facebook and Twitter despite user agreements that restrict people under the age of 13 from using these sites.

Favourite Sites
- 7 of the 10 top favourite sites for all students focus on posting and sharing information and content, **illustrating the need to teach young people digital skills** so they understand privacy, digital permanence, ethical decision-making and how to protect their personal information.
- **YouTube (75%) topped the list of ten favourite sites for all students**, while Facebook, Google and Twitter also appeared in the overall top 10 list.

Boys and girls have different experiences online
- A surprising number of girls (82%) agree with the sentence "I could be hurt if I talk to someone I don't know online", compared to 63% of boys. Girls are also less likely to see the Internet as a safe place (51% compared to 61% of boys).
- **Girls were more likely than boys to have household rules** in place regarding online activities. This suggests that girls are more regulated than boys and may carry additional burdens with respect to their own online safety and the tone of their online interactions, **despite the fact that boys are more likely to engage in risky online behaviours.**

Parental Involvement
- Parents have fewer rules in place compared to 2005, even though having household rules reduces risky online behaviours.

Importance of life balance with digital media
- One third of students **worry that they spend too much time online,** but the majority choose to go offline to do other things, like spending time with friends and family, going outside, or enjoying quiet time alone. Almost half wouldn't care if they couldn't use the Internet for anything other than school for a week.

Young Canadians in a Wired World – Phase III: Life Online **was made possible by financial contributions from Canadian Internet Registration Authority, Office of the Privacy Commissioner of Canada and The Alberta Teachers' Association.**

fact sheets give a brief introduction to the organization and its expertise, present data in digestible chunks, and answer questions the public may have.

Writing effective fact sheets calls for the careful planning discussed in ◀◀ Chapter 3 and meets the criteria for effective messages (◀◀ Chapter 1). It makes good use of facts and figures to support claims, provides well-chosen visuals, and guides readers through the facts with good page design and informative headings (◀◀ Chapter 4). Fact sheets may also include links to social media and YouTube videos.

Depending on topic, purpose, and audience, fact sheets can be organized in these ways:

- Question and answer
- Who, what, where, when, why, and how
- Step by step
- Chronologically

A **news release** complements the fact sheet that may serve as a backgrounder to the news event. A news release (also called a press or media release) is sent to the media by fax, e-mail, or via a wire service to ensure search engine and database access. The news release may announce a press conference or product recall; a promotion, partnership, or product name change; a major sponsorship or philanthropic event; or a new business, product, or service. The release succeeds to the extent that it persuades a journalist that the story is newsworthy.

Carefully designed following conventional format, the release is typically no more than one to two pages concluding with contact information (Figure 7.9). It begins with a well-chosen headline that grabs attention and continues with a lead paragraph that answers clearly and concisely the journalist's questions: who, what, where, when, why, and how.

Succeeding paragraphs organized from the most to least important give supporting facts and incorporate brief quotations to humanize the story. Using the direct pattern to get the meat of the story in the opening paragraphs is especially important when an editor starts cutting from the end to fit stories into available news space.

Social media press releases are designed to bypass the reporters, targeting bloggers, Web sites, and social media that will post the releases—which come with visual as well as verbal, audio, and video content, links, and tags that make reuse easy.[13]

Writing Thank-You and Congratulatory Notes

Sending a **thank-you note** will make people more willing to help you again in the future. Thank-you letters can be short but must be prompt. They need to be specific to sound sincere.

Congratulating someone can cement good feelings between you and the reader and enhance your own visibility. Again, specifics help.

Avoid language that may seem condescending or patronizing. A journalism professor was offended when a former student wrote to congratulate her for a feature article that appeared in a major newspaper. As the professor pointed out, the letter's language implied that the writer had more status than the person being praised. The praiser was "quite impressed," congratulated the professor on reaching a conclusion that she had already reached, and assumed that the professor would have wanted to discuss matters with the praiser. To the professor, "Keep up the good work!" implied that the one cheering her on had been waiting for ages at the finish line.[14]

Granting Adjustments and Responding to Complaints

A study sponsored by Travelers Insurance showed that when people had gripes but didn't complain, only 9% would buy from the company again. But when people did complain—and their

Ethics and Legal Minding Your Texts and Tweets*

Texting abbreviations are migrating into everyday communications, according to Calgary researcher Maria Bakardjieva, and with both humorous and harmful results. If texting can increase productivity, it can also distract in meetings. Vibrating devices can add to distractions; multitasking means people "actually perform all [tasks] poorly"; and 42% of executives report mobile devices contribute to workplace etiquette breaches.

Fake tweets purvey false information without the transparency and accountability associated with independent sources: "if you pose as an unbiased source and then promote for personal gain . . . you have definitely crossed the line," says consultant Ann Latham. But online deception will ultimately harm brands (and Twitter's democratizing potential) if writers try "to pull the 'tweet' over their publics' eyes."

As writer Oscar Wilde argued, "Be yourself. Everyone else is already taken." Keeping it personal draws people in, but a CNN senior editor, Octavia Nasr, lost her job when she tweeted regret at the passing of one "of Hezbollah's giants I respect a lot" and compromised her credibility in CNN's eyes. Others lament CNN's "disregard for free speech" and "a sweeping bureaucratic gesture meant to appease the angry masses."

*Based on Derek Sanbkey, "Techie talk hampers communication: Etiquette at work suffers from text lingo, study finds," *Calgary Herald*, March 2, 2010; Linda Pophal, "Tweet ethics: Trust and transparency in a Web 2.0 world," *CW Bulletin*, September 2009, retrieved April 2, 2011, from http://www.iabc.com/cwb/archive/2009/0909/Pophal.htm; Elena Verlee, "Twitter: 15 ways you can stay interesting," posted January 4, 2011, retrieved January 4, 2011, from http://www.ragan.com/Main/Articles/42605.aspx?format=2; Chris Lake, "Garnering retweets: A 10-step guide," posted February 21, 2011, retrieved March 7, 2011, from http://www.ragan.com/Main/Articles/42714.aspx?format=2; Lisan Jutras, "Opinions are a risky business," *The Globe and Mail*, July 19, 2010, L4.

Figure 7.9 Canadian Football League News Release Announcing Coaches' Community Contributions

CFL.ca - Official Site of the Canadian Football League

http://www.cfl.ca/article/cfl-coaches-give-back-to-football-community

aged 12 years GIBSON'S FINEST CANADIAN WHISKY

AFTER 3 YEARS IT'S WHISKY. AFTER 12 YEARS IT'S GIBSON'S FINEST.

VISIT NOW

CFL Network | Search | Login | Login I Register

THIS IS OUR LEAGUE

SINGLE GAME > Buy Tickets Now

News | Video | Schedule | Standings | Stats | Players | Events | Tickets | Shop | Fanzone

Schedule Full Schedule

Montreal at Edmonton
September 23, 2011
at 9:00 PM ET
Tickets >

BC at Saskatchewan
September 24, 2011
at 4:00 PM ET
Tickets >

Winnipeg at Toronto
September 24, 2011
at 7:00 PM ET
Tickets >

Calgary at Hamilton
September 25, 2011
at 1:00 PM ET
Tickets > Stamps Arrive >

Related Thoughts

To this story

> Nye: Changes necessary on road to redemption

> Can they do it? Als enter 2011 wanting more

> CFL Coach of the Year finalists named

> Meet the 2009 Ticats coaching staff

Related Media

Related Videos

> Stampeders Arrive in Moncton

> Purolator Sack Attack #12

Related Photo Galleries

> Huddle for Haiti

> 98GC: Meet the Coaches

CFL coaches give back to football community

March 24, 2011

Share | Tweet | 8 | 1

CFL.ca Staff

OTTAWA -- The Football Canada Coaches Association (FCCA) and the Canadian Football League are proud to announce that three current CFL head coaches, Greg Marshall (Saskatchewan Roughriders), Marcel Bellefeuille (Hamilton Tiger-Cats) and Marc Trestman (Montreal Alouettes) will present at the 2011 FCCA convention which runs April 2nd and 3rd in Burlington, ON at Corpus Christi Secondary School.

The FCCA Convention is a two day coaching development opportunity which will include coaches from high school and minor football, USA Football, the NFL, the CFL and more.

Trestman will present two sessions on the topic "developing young quarterbacks". The 2009 CFL Coach of the Year is excited to give back to the minor league football community.

"I am honoured and privileged to assist in the promotion and growth of Football in Canada," said Trestman when asked about presenting at the FCCA Convention.

Bellefeuille will present the topic "offensive systems" while Marshall will present on "defensive line pass rush".

In addition, newly appointed Hamilton Tiger-Cats defensive coordinator and defensive backs coach Corey Chamblin will also be presenting two topics at the FCCA Convention: defensive systems and defensive backs.

"The CFL and its coaches are proud to be playing a leadership role at this year's FCCA convention," said Kevin McDonald, CFL Director of Football Operations and Development. "While more and more young athletes are enrolling to play football at all levels across Canada, it's important that we are also developing young coaches."

"Football Canada is extremely excited in launching the first annual coaches convention supported by an incredible line up of coaches as presenters," added Rick Sowieta, Football Canada Director of Sport. "This is a continuation of our mandate to provide our coaches with professional development and resources."

For more information regarding the convention please visit http://www.footballcanada.com or www.canadafootballchat.com.

aged 12 years GIBSON'S FINEST CANADIAN WHISKY

AFTER 3 YEARS IT'S WHISKY. AFTER 12 YEARS IT'S GIBSON'S FINEST.

VISIT NOW

Most Popular Articles View All >

> Saskatcha-win! Three in a row for Riders

> Still the beasts: Bombers remain first in the East

> Lions claw to victory in Hall of Fame Game

> Nye: Riders' brass on the money with draft picks

> CFL.ca Power Rankings for Week #12

Video

00:00 00:00

Stampeders Arrive In Moncton

http://www.cfl.ca/article/cfl-coaches-give-back-to-football-community.

problems were resolved quickly—82% would buy again.[15] (For an e-mail response to a complaint, see ◀◀ Figure 7.2.)

When you grant a customer's request for an adjusted price, discount, replacement, or other benefit to resolve a complaint, do so in the very first sentence.

> Your Visa bill for a night's lodging has been adjusted to $63. Next month a credit of $37 will appear on your bill to reimburse you for the extra amount you were originally asked to pay.

Don't talk about your own process in making the decision, or sound grudging. Give the reason for the original mistake only if it reflects credit on the company. (In most cases it doesn't, so the reason should be omitted.)

Ruth King, who coaches building contractors, recommends avoiding the following in handling customer complaints:

- *We're busy.* These words focus on your organization; you should focus on the customer and the earliest possible time you can give your attention to the problem.
- *No.* When a customer is angry, the word no is like "gasoline on a fire." Instead, offer reasonable alternatives to choose from.
- *We can't.* Instead, specify what you can offer.
- *It's our policy.* Writing about the organization's policy takes the focus off the customer and is yet another way to say what you will not do. Focus on alternatives that are available.[16]

See Figure 7.10 for a checklist for handling routine messages.

Figure 7.10 Checklist for Routine Messages

- ☐ In routine messages, does the subject line give the good news? Is the subject line specific enough?
- ☐ Does the first paragraph summarize the information or good news?
- ☐ Is all the information given in the message? [Information about dates, places, times, and anything related to money is usual.]
- ☐ In messages announcing policies, is there at least one reader benefit for each segment of the audience? Are all reader benefits relevant to this organization?
- ☐ Does each reader benefit show that the benefit will come from the policy and why the benefit matters to this organization?
- ☐ Does the message end with a positive paragraph—preferably one that is specific to the readers, not a general one that could fit any organization or policy?
- ☐ Does the message use you-attitude and positive emphasis?
- ☐ Is the style easy to read and friendly?
- ☐ Is the visual design of the message inviting?
- ☐ Is the format correct?
- ☐ Does the message use standard grammar? Is it free from typos?

SUMMARY OF KEY POINTS

- Letters go to people outside your organization. Memos go to people within your own organization.
- Letters and memos use different formats for their different audiences.
- E-mails, text and instant messaging, podcasts, and social media are good choices for internal and external communications. In professional situations, all the principles of good business writing apply: from attending to purpose and audience needs and benefits to checking grammar and completeness of information.
- Document format tells your reader how caring, careful, and professional the writer is.
- Routine messages normally use the following direct pattern of organization:
  1. Give any good news and summarize the main points.
  2. Give details, clarification, background.
  3. Present any negative elements—as positively as possible.
  4. Explain any reader benefits.
  5. Use a goodwill ending: positive, personal, and forward looking.
- The title of a document, a good subject line meets three criteria: it's specific, short, and adapted to the kind of message (routine, negative, persuasive).
- Use reader benefits in routine messages when
  - You are presenting policies.
  - You want to shape readers' attitudes toward the information or toward your organization.
  - Stressing benefits addresses readers' motives positively.
  - Some of the benefits may not be obvious to readers.
- Routine messages include acceptances; positive answers to requests; announcements of policy changes that are neutral or positive; routine requests and orders; transmittals; confirmations and updates; summaries; fact sheets and news releases; thank-you and congratulatory notes; and responses to complaints. Understanding the conventions and formats will help you change the pattern if necessary to adapt to different audiences and situations and achieve your purpose.

EXERCISES AND PROBLEMS

GETTING STARTED

7.1 MEMOS FOR DISCUSSION—INTRODUCING A SUGGESTION SYSTEM

Your organization has decided to institute a suggestion system. Employees on hourly pay scales will be asked to submit suggestions. (Managers and other employees on salary are not eligible for this program; they are supposed to be continually suggesting ways to improve things as part of their regular jobs.) If the evaluating committee thinks that the suggestion would save money, the employee will receive 10% of the first year's estimated annual savings. If the suggestion won't save money but will improve work conditions, service, or morale, the employee will get a cheque for $50.

The following memos are possible approaches. How well does each message meet the criteria in the checklist for routine messages?

1.

Subject: Suggestions Unlimited (SU)

I want to introduce you to Suggestions Unlimited (SU). This program enables the production worker to offer ideas about improving his job description, working conditions, and general company procedures. The plan can operate as a finely tuned machine, with great ideas as its product.

Operation will begin November 1. Once a week, a designate of SU will collect the ideas and turn them over to the SU Committee. This committee will evaluate and judge the proposed changes.

Only employees listed as factory workers are eligible. This excludes foremen and the rest of supervisory personnel. Awards are as follows:

1. Awards of $50 will be given to those ideas judged operational. These are awarded monthly.
2. There will be grand prizes given for the best suggestions over the six-month span.

Ideas are judged on feasibility, originality, operational simplicity, and degree of benefit to the worker and company. Evaluation made by the SU Committee is final. Your questions should be channelled to my office.

2.

Subject: Establishment of Suggestions Unlimited

We announce the establishment of Suggestions Unlimited. This new program is designed to provide a means for hourly employees to submit suggestions to company management concerning operations and safety. The program will also provide an award system to compensate non-management employees for implemented suggestions.

Here is how the program will work: beginning October 1, suggestions can be submitted by hourly workers to the company on Form 292, which will be furnished to all plants and their departments by October 1. On the form, the submitting employee should include the suggestion, his or her name, and the department number. The form can be deposited in a suggestion drop box, which will be located near the personnel office in each plant.

Any suggestion dealing with the improvement of operations, safety, working conditions, or morale is eligible for consideration. The award structure for the program will be as follows:

1. For an implemented suggestion that improves safety or efficiency with no associated monetary benefits or cost reduction: $50.
2. For an implemented suggestion that makes or saves the company money: 10% of the first year's estimated annual savings or additional revenue.

It is hoped that we will have a good initial and continuous response from all hourly employees. This year, we are out to try to cut production costs, and this program may be the vehicle through which we will realize new savings and increased revenues. New ideas that can truly increase operational efficiency or cut safety problems will make the company a nicer place for all employees. A safer work environment is a better work environment. If department operations can be made more efficient, this will eventually make everyone's job just a little easier, and give that department and its employees a sense of pride.

3.

Subject: New Employee Suggestion System

Beginning October 1, all of you who are hourly employees of Video Adventures will be able to get cash awards when your suggestions for improving the company are implemented.

Ideas about any aspect of Video Adventures are eligible: streamlining behind-the-counter operations, handling schedule problems, increasing the life of videotapes.

- If your idea cuts costs or increases income (e.g., increasing membership sales, increasing the number of movie rentals per customer), you'll receive 10% of the first year's estimated annual savings.
- If the idea doesn't save money but does improve service, work conditions, or morale, you'll receive a cheque for $50.

To submit a suggestion, just pick up a form from your manager. On the form, explain your suggestion, describe briefly how it could be implemented, and show how it will affect Video Adventures. Return the completed form in the new suggestion box behind the back counter. Suggestions will be evaluated at the end of each month. Turn in as many ideas as you like!

Think about ways to solve the problems you face every day. Can we speed up the check-in process? Cut paperwork? Give customers faster service? Increase the percentage of customers who bring back their tapes on time? As you serve people at the counter, ask them what they'd like to see at Video Adventures.

Your ideas will keep Video Adventures competitive. Ten years ago, Video Adventures was the only video store on the west side of town. Now there are six other video stores within a two-kilometre radius, and even the grocery stores rent videotapes. Efficiency, creativity, and service can keep Video Adventures ahead.

Employees whose ideas are implemented will be recognized in the regional Video Adventures newsletter. The award will also be a nice accomplishment to add to any university or community college application or résumé. By suggesting ways to improve Video Adventures, you'll demonstrate your creativity and problem-solving abilities. And you'll be able to share the credit for keeping Video Adventures' reputation as the best video store in town.

7.2 E-MAILS FOR DISCUSSION—SAYING YES TO A SUBORDINATE

Today, you get this request from a subordinate.

Subject: Request for Leave

You know that I've been feeling burned out. I've decided that I want to take a three-month leave of absence this summer to travel abroad. I've got five weeks of vacation time saved up; I would take the rest as unpaid leave. Just guarantee that my job will be waiting when I come back!

You decide to grant the request. The following messages are possible responses. How well does each message meet the criteria in the checklist for routine messages?

As Your Professor Directs,

Discuss answers within your group or write a group report on your findings.

1.

Subject: Re: Request for Leave

I highly recommend Italy. Spend a full week in Florence, if you can. Be sure to visit the Brancacci Chapel—it's been restored, and the frescoes are breathtaking. And I can give you the names of some great restaurants. You may never want to come back!

2.

Subject: Your Request for Leave

As you know, we are in a very competitive position right now. Your job is important, and there is no one who can easily replace you. However, because you are a valued employee, I will permit you to take the leave you request, as long as you train a replacement before you leave.

3.

Subject: Your Request for Leave Granted

Yes, you may take a three-month leave of absence next summer using your five weeks of accumulated vacation time and taking the rest as unpaid leave. And yes, your job will be waiting for you when you return!

I'm appointing Garrick to take over your duties while you're gone. Talk with him to determine how much training time he'll need, and let me know when the training is scheduled.

Have a great summer! Let us know every now and then how you're doing!

E-MAIL MESSAGES

7.3 ANNOUNCING AN ELECTRONIC NEWSLETTER

Your organization has decided to create an electronic newsletter to build goodwill with its customers. You have created a mailing list of customers' e-mail addresses and plan to send them monthly messages with information related to your industry. The goal is that customers will think of your organization as a valuable source of expertise, so they will prefer to do business with you.

Think about the qualities customers are likely to value in a monthly electronic newsletter: clean and consistent design; well-chosen graphics; clear, concise writing; and relevant content. Keep in mind that many people like to review their e-mail quickly and are annoyed by spam.

Working in your group, write an e-mail to your customers, announcing the electronic newsletter. Include an overview of the benefits and the kinds of information that will be included.

Hints:

- Pick a business, government, or non-profit organization that you know something about.
- Identify who your customers are and what will interest them. What information do you have that might be harder for your customers to learn? Will you provide hyperlinks to other information on the Web?
- Be sure the subject line is clear and appealing.
- What can customers do if they are not interested in receiving your newsletter?

COMMUNICATING AT WORK

7.4 PRAISING WORK DONE WELL

Write a memo to a co-worker (with a copy to the person's supervisor) thanking him or her for helping you or complimenting him or her on a job well done. Be sure to be specific enough to convey sincerity and to make clear what actions deserve praise.

7.5 GIVING GOOD NEWS

Individually or in groups, write in an appropriate channel to a customer, to a vendor, or to your boss announcing good news (using what you have learned here about communicating good news). Possibilities include a product improvement, a price cut or special, an addition to your management team, or a new contract.

LETTER AND MEMO ASSIGNMENTS

7.6 REMINDING GUESTS ABOUT THE TIME CHANGE

Twice a year most of Canada (Saskatchewan is an exception) switches to daylight saving time and back again. The time change can be disruptive for hotel guests, who may lose track of the date, forget to change the clocks in their rooms, and miss appointments as a result.

Prepare a form letter to leave in each hotel room reminding guests of the impending time change. What should guests do? How do they change the clock?

Write the letter.

Hints:

- Use an attention-getting page layout so readers don't ignore the message.
- Pick a specific hotel or motel chain you know something about.
- Use the letter to build goodwill for your hotel or motel chain. Use specific references to services or features the hotel offers, focusing not on what the hotel does for the reader, but on what the reader can do at the hotel.

7.7 ANSWERING AN INTERNATIONAL INQUIRY

Your business, government, or non-profit organization has received the following inquiries from international correspondents. (You choose the country the inquiry is from.)

1. Please tell us about a new product, service, or trend so that we can decide whether we want to buy, license, or imitate it in our country.
2. We have heard about a problem [technical, social, political, or ethical] that occurred in your organization. Could you please tell us what really happened and estimate how it is likely to affect the long-term success of the organization?
3. Please tell us about college or university programs in this field. We are interested in sending some of our managers to your country to complete a degree or diploma.
4. We are considering setting up a plant in your city. We have already received adequate business information. However, we would also like to know how comfortable our nationals will feel. Do people in your city speak our language? How many? What opportunities exist for our nationals to improve their English? Does your town already have people from a wide mix of nations? Which are the largest groups?
5. Our organization would like to subscribe to an English-language trade journal. Which one would you recommend? Why? How much does it cost? How can we order it?

As Your Professor Directs,

a. Answer one or more of the inquiries. Assume that your reader either reads English or can have your message translated. Consider the level of formality.

b. Write a memo to your professor explaining how you've adapted the message for your audience.

Hints:

- Even though you can write in English, English may not be your reader's native language. Write a letter that can be translated easily.
- In some cases, you may need to spell out background information that might not be clear to someone from another country.

7.8 PROVIDING INFORMATION TO JOB APPLICANTS

Your company is in a prime vacation spot, and as personnel manager you get many letters from students asking about summer jobs. Company policy is to send everyone an application for employment, a list of the jobs you expect to have open that summer with the rate of pay for each, a description of benefits for seasonal employees, and an interview schedule. Candidates must come for an interview at their own expense and should call to schedule a time in advance. Competition is keen: only a small percentage of those interviewed will be hired.

Write a form letter to students who have written to you asking about summer jobs. Give them the basic information about the hiring procedure and tell them what to do next. Be realistic about their chances, but maintain their interest in working for you.

Discuss your letters in your group and, as your professor instructs, peer grade.

7.9 SUMMARIZING *THE GLOBE AND MAIL: REPORT ON BUSINESS*

Today, your in-basket contains this message from your boss:

> As you know, I'm leaving tomorrow for a vacation in Egypt. While I'm gone, will you please scan *The Globe and Mail: Report On Business* every day and summarize any articles that are relevant to our business? I'd like your summary in hard copy on my desk when I return.

As Your Professor Directs,

a. Scan *The Globe and Mail: Report on Business* for one week, two weeks, or until you find three to five relevant articles for the company you have chosen.

b. Summarize the articles in a memo.

c. Compare summaries with a small group of students. Do summaries of the same article for different organizations focus on different points?

d. Present one of your summaries to the class.

Hints:

- Pick an organization you know something about. If the organization is large, focus on one division or department.
- Provide an overview to let your boss know whether the articles you've summarized are on a single topic or on several topics.
- Show how each article relates to the organization.
- Give the full citation (see ▸▸ Chapter 10) so that it's easy to track down articles if the boss wants to see the original.

7.10 SUMMARIZING INFORMATION

Summarize one or more of the following:

1. Richard B. Chase and Sriram Dasu, "Want to Perfect Your Company's Service? Use Behavioral Science," *Harvard Business Review*, June 2001, 79–84; reprint R0106D.
2. One of Jakob Nielsen's Alertboxes (www.useit.com/alertbox).
3. An article or Web page published by Adbusters Media Foundation (www.adbusters.org).
4. The criticisms of a company on an "anticorporate activism" Web site (in a search engine, key in the company name and "customer opinion").
5. An article assigned by your professor.
6. An article or Web page of your choice.

As Your Professor Directs,

a. Write a summary of no more than 100 words.

b. Write a 250- to 300-word summary.

c. Write a one-page fact sheet or press release.

d. Write a series of tweets.

e. Compare your summary, fact sheet, press release, or tweets to those of a small group of students. Did everyone agree on what information to include? How do you account for any differences?

7.11 SOLVING A SAMPLE PROBLEM

Real-life problems are richer and less well defined than textbook problems and cases. But even textbook problems require analysis before you begin to write. Examine the following problem. See how the analysis questions probe the basic points required for a solution. Study the two sample solutions to see what makes one unacceptable and the other one good. Note the recommendations for revision that could make the good solution excellent.[17] The checklist at the end of the chapter can help you evaluate a draft.

Hints:

In Sentinel Insurance's computerized handling of payments and billings, there is often a time lag between receiving and recording a payment from a customer. Sometimes, while the payment is in line to be processed, the computerized system sends out additional notices: past-due notices, collection letters, even threats to sue. Customers are frightened or angry and write asking for an explanation. In most cases, if they just waited a little while, the situation would be straightened out. But policyholders are afraid that they'll be without insurance because the company thinks the bill has not been paid.

Sentinel doesn't have the time to check each individual situation to see if the cheque did arrive and has been processed. It wants you to write a letter that will persuade customers to wait. If something is wrong and the payment never reached Sentinel, the company would send a legal notice to that effect saying the policy would be cancelled by a certain date (which the notice would specify) at least 30 days after the date on the original premium bill. Continuing customers always get this legal notice as a third chance (after the original bill and the past-due notice).

Prepare a form letter that can go out to every policyholder who claims to have paid a premium for automobile insurance and resents getting a past-due notice. The letter should reassure readers and build goodwill for Sentinel.

ANALYSIS OF THE PROBLEM

1. **Who is your audience? What audience characteristics are relevant to this particular message?**

Automobile insurance customers who say they've paid but have still received a past-due notice. They're afraid they're no longer insured. Because it's a form letter, different readers will have different situations: in some cases payments did arrive late, in some cases the company made a mistake, in some the reader never paid (cheque was lost in mail, unsigned, bounced, etc.).

2. **What are your purposes in writing?**

To reassure readers that they're covered for 30 days. To inform them that they can assume everything is OK *unless* they receive a second notice. To avoid further correspondence on this subject. To build goodwill for Sentinel: (a) we don't want to suggest Sentinel is error prone or too cheap to hire enough people to do the necessary work; (b) we don't want readers to switch companies; (c) we do want readers to buy from Sentinel when they're ready for more insurance.

3. **What information must your message include?**

Readers are still insured. We cannot say whether their cheques have now been processed (company doesn't want to check individual accounts). Their insurance will be cancelled if they do not pay after receiving the second past-due notice (the legal notice).

4. **What reasons or reader benefits will your reader find convincing?**

Computers help us provide personal service to policyholders. We offer policies to meet all their needs. Both of these points would need specifics to be interesting and convincing.

5. **What objection(s) can you expect your reader(s) to have? What negative elements of your message must you de-emphasize or overcome?**

Computers appear to cause errors. We don't know if the cheques have been processed. We will cancel policies if their cheques don't arrive.

6. How will the context affect reader response? The economy? The time of year? Morale in the organization? The relationship between the reader and writer? Any special circumstances?

The insurance business is highly competitive—other companies offer similar rates and policies. The customer could get a similar policy for about the same money from someone else. Most people find that money is tight, so they'll want to keep insurance costs low. Many insurance companies are refusing to renew policies (car, liability, malpractice insurance). These refusals to renew have received lots of publicity, and many people have heard horror stories about companies and individuals whose insurance has been cancelled or not renewed after a small number of claims. Readers don't feel very kindly toward insurance companies. Drivers have a legitimate worry when laws everywhere in Canada require basic coverage for all vehicles driven on public roads, and the provinces of British Columbia, Saskatchewan, and Manitoba require the purchase of insurance when drivers obtain vehicle registration.

DISCUSSION OF THE SAMPLE SOLUTIONS

The solution in Figure 7.11 is unacceptable. The blue marginal comments show problem spots. Since this is a form letter, we cannot tell customers we have their cheques; in some cases, we may not. The letter is far too negative. The explanation in paragraph 2 makes Sentinel look irresponsible and uncaring. Paragraph 3 is far too negative. Paragraph 4 is too vague; there are no reader benefits; the ending sounds selfish.

A major weakness with the solution is that it lifts phrases straight out of the problem; the writer does not seem to have thought about the problem or about the words he or she is using. Measuring the draft against the answers to the questions for analysis suggests that this writer should start over.

The solution in Figure 7.12 is much better. The blue marginal comments show the letter's strong points. The letter is dated, the salutation is personalized, and the message opens with the good news that is true for all readers. (Whenever possible, one should use the good-news pattern of organization.) Paragraph 2 explains Sentinel's policy. It avoids assigning blame and ends on a positive note. The negative information is buried in paragraph 3 and is presented positively: the notice is information, not a threat; the 30-day extension is a "grace period." Telling the reader now what to do if a second notice arrives eliminates the need for a second exchange of letters. Paragraph 4 offers benefits for using computers, since some readers may blame the notice on computers, and offers benefits for being insured by Sentinel. Paragraph 5 promotes other policies the company sells and prepares for the last paragraph.

Figure 7.11 An Unacceptable Solution to the Sample Problem

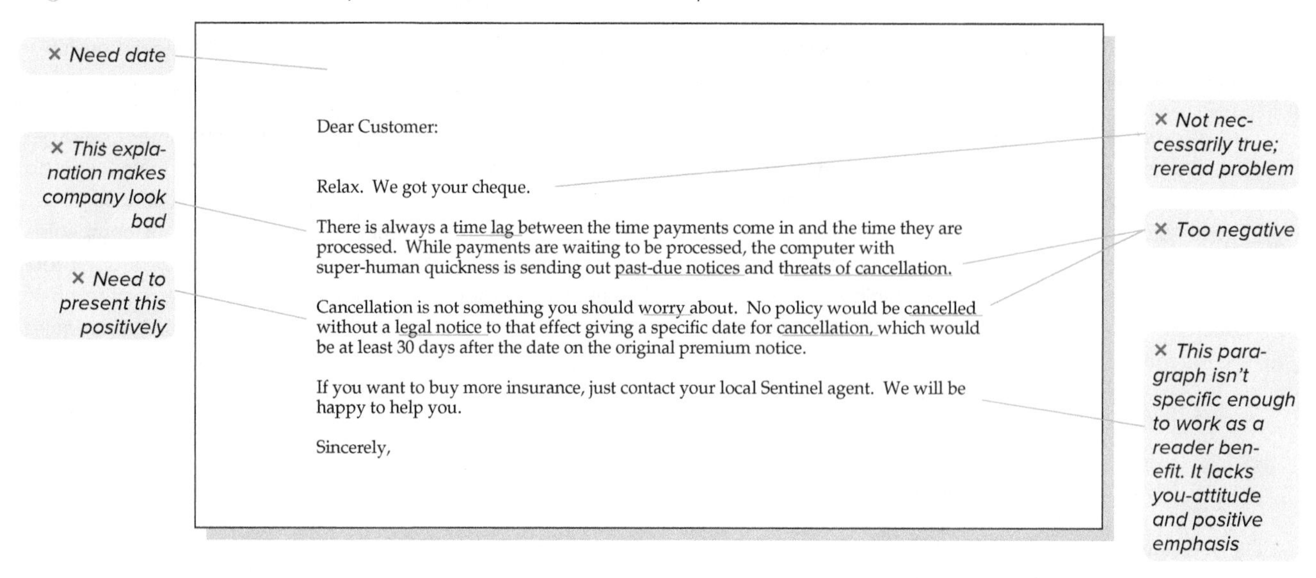

Dear Customer:

Relax. We got your cheque.

There is always a time lag between the time payments come in and the time they are processed. While payments are waiting to be processed, the computer with super-human quickness is sending out past-due notices and threats of cancellation.

Cancellation is not something you should worry about. No policy would be cancelled without a legal notice to that effect giving a specific date for cancellation, which would be at least 30 days after the date on the original premium notice.

If you want to buy more insurance, just contact your local Sentinel agent. We will be happy to help you.

Sincerely,

Figure 7.12 A Good Solution to the Sample Problem

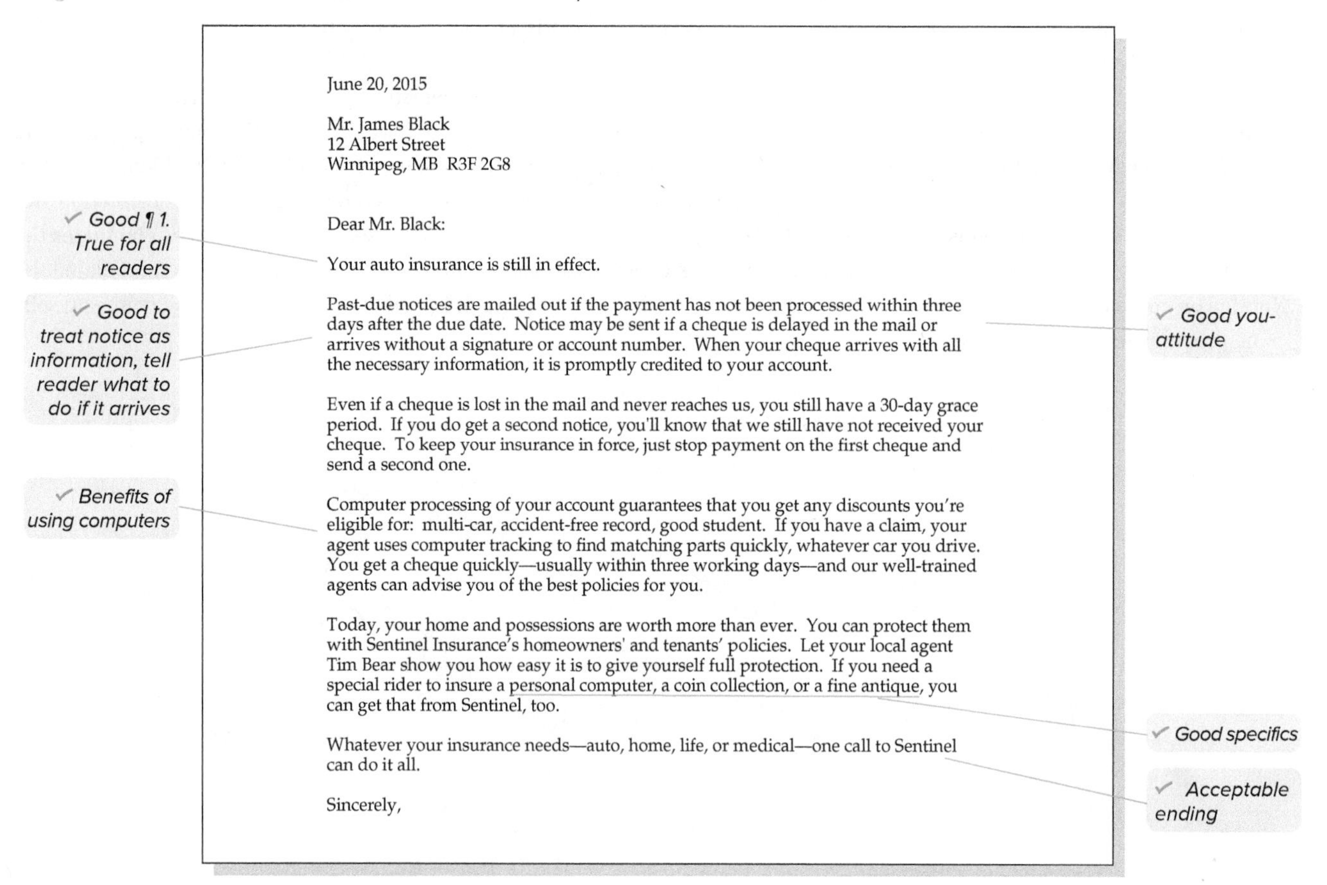

June 20, 2015

Mr. James Black
12 Albert Street
Winnipeg, MB R3F 2G8

Dear Mr. Black:

Your auto insurance is still in effect.

Past-due notices are mailed out if the payment has not been processed within three days after the due date. Notice may be sent if a cheque is delayed in the mail or arrives without a signature or account number. When your cheque arrives with all the necessary information, it is promptly credited to your account.

Even if a cheque is lost in the mail and never reaches us, you still have a 30-day grace period. If you do get a second notice, you'll know that we still have not received your cheque. To keep your insurance in force, just stop payment on the first cheque and send a second one.

Computer processing of your account guarantees that you get any discounts you're eligible for: multi-car, accident-free record, good student. If you have a claim, your agent uses computer tracking to find matching parts quickly, whatever car you drive. You get a cheque quickly—usually within three working days—and our well-trained agents can advise you of the best policies for you.

Today, your home and possessions are worth more than ever. You can protect them with Sentinel Insurance's homeowners' and tenants' policies. Let your local agent Tim Bear show you how easy it is to give yourself full protection. If you need a special rider to insure a personal computer, a coin collection, or a fine antique, you can get that from Sentinel, too.

Whatever your insurance needs—auto, home, life, or medical—one call to Sentinel can do it all.

Sincerely,

NEGATIVE MESSAGES

8

Learning Outcomes

LO1 Explain how to organize negative messages

LO2 Discuss effective subject lines for different audiences

LO3 Describe how to word the parts of a negative message

LO4 Check the tone in a negative message

LO5 Explain how to handle apologies

LO6 Discuss alternative strategies for negative messages

AN INSIDE PERSPECTIVE

Delivering bad news for internal or external audiences is one of the most difficult tasks you may be asked to perform. To reduce the potential for dysfunctional behaviour, bad news should be communicated openly and honestly.

Preparation is required to effectively communicate bad news so that people understand the reasons for a decision and how it affects them. Be able to answer the following key questions:

Maple Leaf Foods CEO Michael McCain has drawn praise for his direct and open handling of the 2008 listeria outbreak.

- What is the big picture? Why is the change needed?
- What is the purpose of the change?
- How does the bad news relate to business objectives?
- How will the bad news affect employees, customers, shareholders, and other stakeholders?

In expressing sympathy, apologizing, and taking responsibility for the 2008 listeriosis outbreak at Maple Leaf Foods, CEO Michael McCain was "doing all the right things" so that he would "be in a position to re-establish the brand," argues lawyer Purdy Crawford. Far in advance of the crisis, Maple Leaf was ready with a crisis plan.

McCain not only delivered bad news honestly and openly, but also used the opportunity to enhance commitment to food safety. Showcasing improved protocols at Maple Leaf plants, he established a food safety advisory council and hired the first chief food safety officer in North America. It's been a long-term commitment: "We have spent seven years fundamentally rebuilding our business and we're on the home stretch," said McCain in February 2014.

On television and YouTube, in newsprint and press conferences, McCain came across as "the human face of a company that cared." It was not for McCain a matter of crisis management, but of acting on the company's "ingrained values."

*Based on Eric Atkins, "Maple Leaf restructuring heats up with sale of Canada Bread," *The Globe and Mail,* February 12, 2014, retrieved from http://www.theglobeandmail.com/report-on-business/maple-leaf-selling-canada-bread-to-mexicos-grupo-bimbo-for-183-billion/article16823614/; Gordon Pitts, "Man under fire," *The Globe and Mail,* August 30, 2008, B1–B6; Gordon Pitts, "The testing of Michael McCain," *Report on Business,* December 2008, 60–66; Sarah Schmidt, "Food inspection agency trims staff as Maple Leaf hires safety officer," Canwest News Service, December 12, 2008, retrieved December 16, 2008, from http://www.canada.com/topics/news/national/story.html?id=1069371; Niraj Dawar, "Can your brands withstand the shock of recall?" *The Globe and Mail,* September 15, 2008, B2.

In a **negative message,** the basic information we have to convey is bad news; we expect the reader to be disappointed or angry. To reduce negative impact on your reader, your organization, and you, negative messages require your problem-solving skills. This chapter focuses on purposes, audiences, direct and indirect strategies, and tone for reader-friendly results. Keeping your purpose and your audience's needs in mind will help you choose the right medium, organization, language, and tone. Delivered promptly and sensitively in the right medium, negative messages can minimize conflict and renew goodwill.

Negative messages include

- Rejections and refusals
- Layoffs and firings
- Announcements of policy changes that do not benefit customers or consumers
- Requests the reader may see as insulting or intrusive
- Negative performance appraisals
- Disciplinary notices
- Product recalls or notices of defects

A negative message always has several purposes:

Primary purposes:

- To give the reader the bad news
- To have the reader read, understand, and accept the message
- To maintain as much goodwill as possible

Secondary purposes:

- To maintain a good image of the writer
- To maintain a good image of the writer's organization
- To reduce or eliminate future correspondence on the same subject
- To reduce risk and avoid legal liability

Even when it is not possible to make the reader happy with the news we must convey, we still want readers to feel that

- They have been taken seriously.
- Our decision is fair and reasonable.
- If they were in our shoes, they would make the same decision.

On the Job The Awful News*

Although the company took a beating on the markets, Maple Leaf Foods and its CEO Michael McCain won praise for the promptness and forthrightness of the recall of 220 products as a result of deaths and illnesses associated with listeria-contaminated meat products.

Announcing an expanded recall and escalating costs, CEO McCain claimed to have paid no attention to "two advisers": "The first are the lawyers, and the second are the accountants. It's not about the money or the legal liability; this is about being accountable for providing consumers with safe food."

Professor Daniel Diermeier, Kellogg School of Management, Chicago, praised Maple Leaf for having "stepped forward and accepted responsibility," for showing it cared, and thus rebuilding public trust.

CEO McCain has drawn as much praise for the amount of information released as for the low production of the television spots on which he and his fatigue come across so compellingly.

Communication consultant John Lute has liked what he has seen: "Get it out there, apologize, tell people what you're doing to fix it and then move on, doing what you say you'd do."

*Based on Steve Ladurantaye, "Maple Leaf recalls 220 products," *Report On Business,* August 24, 2008; Steve Ladurantaye, "Maple Leaf moves into crisis mode," *Report On Business,* August 22, 2008; Oliver Moore, "For companies, surviving a recall crisis takes forthrightness," *The Globe and Mail,* August 26, 2008, A7.

In other words, negative messages always require a level of persuasion (▸▸ Chapter 9).

LO1

ORGANIZING NEGATIVE LETTERS, MEMOS, AND ELECTRONIC MEDIA

Although negative messages are typically associated with the extremes of discipline, rejections, and refusals, even minor negatives (a small rate increase, for example) and potentially positive messages (a congratulatory note) can qualify as bad news if writers do not adopt the appropriate tone and tactics.

The direct approach illustrated in ◂◂ Chapter 7 is appropriate for negative messages when

- Announcing bad news to subordinates
- Announcing policy decisions
- Dealing with clients who prefer a direct approach
- Demonstrating firmness is necessary and maintaining goodwill is not (discontinuing clients, sending a final collections letter)

The first pattern in Figure 8.1 helps writers maintain goodwill.

Figure 8.2 illustrates how the basic pattern for negative messages can be used. This letter omits the reason, probably because the change benefits the company, not the customer. Putting the bad news first (though pairing it immediately with an alternative) makes it more likely that the recipient will read the letter. Although the option not to replace the old liability coverage is available to the customer ("unless you select"), the letter explains the new Assurance Plan before emphasizing reader choice in the last paragraph.

If this letter seemed to be just a routine renewal, or if it opened with the good news that the premium was lower, few recipients would read the letter carefully, and many would not read it at all. Then, if they had accidents and found that their coverage was reduced, they'd blame the company for not communicating clearly. Emphasizing the negative here is both good ethics and good business.

The best way to organize a negative memo depends on whether you're writing to a superior, peer, or subordinate, and on the severity of the negative information.

In the context of a global financial crisis, bad news for tourism can be good news for tourists. The Canadian Tourism Commission's strategy for 2009–2013 was intent on "seizing the opportunity: inspiring the world to explore Canada."

Used with the permission of Canadian Tourism Commission.

Figure 8.1 How to Organize Negative Messages

NEGATIVE LETTERS

1. When you have a reason that readers will understand and accept, give the reason before the refusal. A good reason prepares the reader to expect the refusal.
2. Give the negative information or refusal just once, clearly. Inconspicuous refusals can be missed altogether, making it necessary to say no a second time.
3. Present an alternative or compromise, if one is available. An alternative not only gives readers another way to get what they want but also suggests that you care about readers and helping them meet their needs.
4. End with a positive, forward-looking statement.

NEGATIVE MEMOS TO SUPERIORS

1. Describe the problem. Tell what's wrong, clearly and unemotionally.
2. Tell how it happened. Provide the background. What underlying factors led to this specific problem?
3. Describe the options for fixing it. If one option is clearly best, you may need to discuss only one. But if the reader will think of other options, or if different people will judge the options differently, describe all the options, giving their advantages and disadvantages.
4. Recommend a solution and ask for action. Ask for approval so that you can go ahead to make the necessary changes to fix the problem.

NEGATIVE MEMOS TO PEERS AND SUBORDINATES

1. Describe the problem. Tell what's wrong, clearly and unemotionally.
2. Present an alternative or compromise, if one is available. An alternative not only gives readers another way to get what they want but also suggests that you care about readers and helping them meet their needs.
3. If possible, ask for input or action. People in the audience may be able to suggest solutions. And workers who help make a decision are far more likely to accept the consequences.

Your superior expects you to solve minor problems by yourself. But sometimes, solving a problem requires more authority or resources than you have. When you give bad news to a superior, also recommend a way to deal with the problem. Turn the negative message into a persuasive one (➧ Chapter 9). See the middle column in Figure 8.1.

When you must pass along serious bad news to peers and subordinates, use the variation in the last column in Figure 8.1.

No serious negative (such as being downsized or laid off) should come as a complete surprise. Managers can prepare for possible negatives by giving full information as it becomes available. It is also possible to let the people who will be affected by a decision participate in setting the criteria. Someone who has bought into the criteria for awarding cash for suggestions or retaining workers is more likely to accept decisions using such criteria.

Montreal-based airline Jetsgo's founder Michel Leblanc faced widespread criticism when he abruptly announced in the middle of winter holidays (March 2005) the grounding of the airline. Neither the 17,000 travellers left in limbo nor the 1,200 employees who discovered themselves unemployed overnight had been prepared for the announcement.

Employees learned the news via 1:00 a.m. telephone calls and via an e-mail in which Leblanc blamed an unnamed creditor for the situation. Employees had been kept in the dark when Jetsgo instructed pilots to fly aircraft to Quebec "for air worthiness checks" that were not in fact ordered. The Jetsgo fleet was, however, safe from creditors in Quebec. Although Leblanc apologized to travellers, he remained unapologetic about his little "white lie" to employees. "You can't tell them, or the job won't get done," Leblanc argued. Conceding that "the name Jetsgo has been blemished badly," Leblanc acknowledged a name change was a possibility.[1]

Delays marked another Canadian crisis in 2012. Despite regulatory requirements to disclose, the Nilsson family, owners of Canada's second largest meat processing plant, XL Foods in Brooks, Alberta, proved "virtually invisible through the crisis" precipitated by routine tests finding *E. coli* that sickened 18 people and caused the largest Canadian Food Inspection Agency (CFIA) meat recall ever.[2] An independent review found that the $16- to $27-million crisis "was all preventable": "issues persisted" despite government commitment to change in the wake of the 2008 listeriosis outbreak, "a relaxed attitude toward applying mandatory procedures" persisted among CFIA and plant staff, and "poor communication with both CFIA and the public" contributed.[3] Wild Rose party leader Danielle Smith learned a lesson about the limits of 140 characters when she was widely criticized for her tweet seeming to suggest feeding the hungry with tainted meat.[4]

Columnist Gary Mason argues that the RCMP could also learn much from Maple Leaf's Michael McCain (⏪ An Inside Perspective), who not only accepted responsibility, apologized sincerely, and managed the recall process, but also compensated victims without engaging in costly litigation. Faced with cases claiming police brutality, including the Robert

Danielle Smith was quick to apologize and admit that Twitter might not have been the best medium for her message.

Figure 8.2 A Negative Letter

Vickers
Insurance Company

3373 Forbes Avenue
Markham, ON L3R 2L8
(416) 572-0100

Liability Coverage Is Being Discontinued— Here's How to Replace It!

June 2, 2015

Dear Policyholder:

When your homeowner's insurance is renewed, it will no longer include liability coverage unless you select the new Assurance Plan. Here's why.

Liability coverage is being discontinued. It, and the part of the premium that paid for it, will be dropped from all policies when they are renewed.

This change could leave a gap in your protection. But you can replace the old Liability Coverage with Vickers' new Assurance Plan.

With the new Assurance Plan, you receive benefits for litigation or awards arising from an accident or injury. The cost for the Assurance Plan at any level is based on the age of homeowners, where you live, your claims record, and other factors. If these change before your policy is renewed, the cost of your Assurance Plan may also change. The actual cost will be listed in your renewal statement.

To sign up for the Assurance Plan, just check the level of coverage you want on the enclosed form and return it in the postage-paid envelope within 14 days. You'll be assured of the coverage you select.

Sincerely,

C. J. Morgan

C. J. Morgan
President

P.S. The Assurance Plan protects you against possible legal costs arising from homeowners' liability. Sign up for the Plan today and receive full coverage from Vickers.

✓ Negative information highlighted so reader won't ignore message

Negative

✓ Alternative

Negative

✓ Alternative

✓ No reason is given. The change probably benefits the company rather than the reader, so it is omitted.

✓ Positive information underlined for emphasis

✓ Forward-looking ending emphasizes reader's choice

✓ Alternative

Technology Tips A Blogger's World*

Blogs allow just about anyone to publish information—negative or positive—that can quickly influence public opinion. While some see threats in online communities, others embrace the potential to respond to the most negative of messages.

- Mom bloggers are fuelling "ferocious viral campaigns around diapers, pain killers and other products." In March 2011 they forced Abercrombie Kids to delete the "push-up" in its marketing campaign to promote bikinis to tweens.
- *BusinessWeek* exposed the blog "Wal-Marting across America" as a "flog" (fake blog) in October 2006.
- PR firm Edelman set up the "grassroots" blogs Working Families for Wal-Mart and Paid Critics, designed to expose Walmart critics.
- Vancity sees benefits in internal and external blogs: in building culture, sharing successes and learning, and engaging diverse employees, "your true brand ambassadors." Vancity's William Azaroff recommends building to include—and not avoid—controversy. While external blogs carry anonymous comments, people "need to stand behind what they say" on internal blogs.
- When Toronto CEO Richard Cooper found an online complaint, far from burying it, he highlighted it in a blog post that explained the reasons for the complaint and the actions to address it: "If you're transparent about what the complaint is and what you're doing to resolve it, it's really effective," says Cooper.

*Adapted from Deborah Aarts, "Make angry customers love you," *Canadian Business*, Summer 2014, 18; Tralee Pearce, "Momming the barricades," *The Globe and Mail*, April 15, 2011, L1–2; Angelo Fernando, "Transparency under attack," *Communication World*, March–April 2007, 9–11; Andrea Southcott, "Give your brand a human touch—Enter the blogosphere," *Report On Business*, March 31, 2008, B10.

Figure 8.3 An Open Letter from Michael H. McCain, President and CEO, Maple Leaf Foods

MAPLE LEAF FOODS

Dear fellow Canadians,

It was a year ago that some of our products were linked to a listeriosis outbreak that caused the death of 22 Canadians.

The friends and family of these people will never forget and neither will we.

As a result, we have a deep commitment to becoming a global leader in food safety to prevent this kind of tragedy from ever happening again.

On behalf of our 24,000 employees, we promise to never forget.

Michael H. McCain
President and CEO

Maple Leaf Foods, Inc.

Dziekanski case, and concerns around the then commissioner's management style, the Mounties "circle the wagons" and resort to "disparaging the victim" to "rationalize" officer actions. Instead of cleaving to an outmoded "paramilitary" model, the RCMP needs to "become a 21st-century company whose job it is to provide services across the country." Only then, Mason argues, will the RCMP renew the trust of the Canadian public so necessary to staying in business.[5]

Knowing the importance of public trust, McCain promises never to forget and to continue to invest in public safety (see Figure 8.3).

When the bad news is less serious, as in Figure 8.4, use the pattern for negative letters unless your knowledge of the reader(s) suggests that another pattern will be more effective. Then you might want to delay the negative by using a buffer (a neutral or positive sentence), even though the organization's discourse community (see ◀◀ Chapter 2) as a whole favours directness.

For memos, the context of communication is crucial. The reader's reaction is influenced by the following factors:

- Do you and the reader have a good relationship?
- Does the organization treat people well?
- Have readers been warned of possible negatives?
- Have readers bought into the criteria for the decision?
- Do communications after the negative build goodwill?

Tiburon, a company that provides public safety systems and services, used "open book management"—sharing all its financial information with employees. When the company had to lay off 80 of its 320 employees, the layoffs weren't a surprise, and people understood that the layoffs were necessary.

Figure 8.4 A Negative Memo to Subordinates

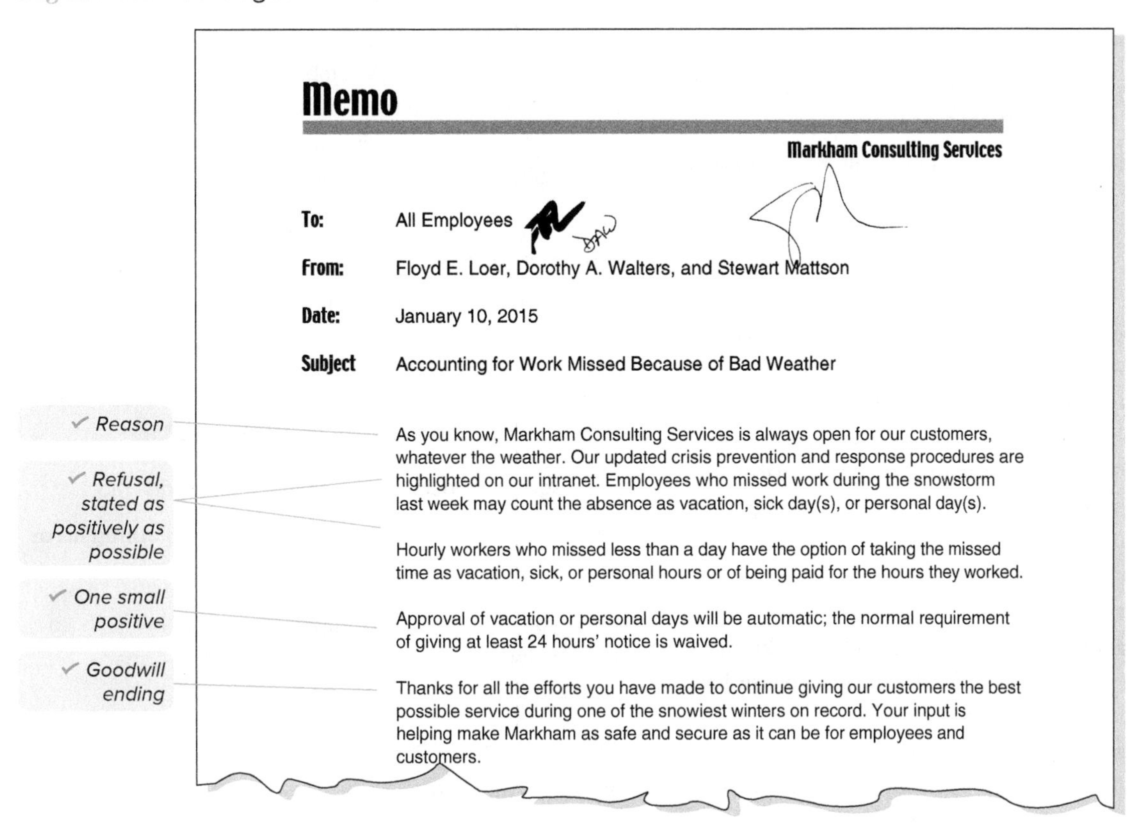

Memo

Markham Consulting Services

To: All Employees

From: Floyd E. Loer, Dorothy A. Walters, and Stewart Mattson

Date: January 10, 2015

Subject Accounting for Work Missed Because of Bad Weather

As you know, Markham Consulting Services is always open for our customers, whatever the weather. Our updated crisis prevention and response procedures are highlighted on our intranet. Employees who missed work during the snowstorm last week may count the absence as vacation, sick day(s), or personal day(s).

Hourly workers who missed less than a day have the option of taking the missed time as vacation, sick, or personal hours or of being paid for the hours they worked.

Approval of vacation or personal days will be automatic; the normal requirement of giving at least 24 hours' notice is waived.

Thanks for all the efforts you have made to continue giving our customers the best possible service during one of the snowiest winters on record. Your input is helping make Markham as safe and secure as it can be for employees and customers.

Says founder and CEO Bruce Kelling, "I even received calls and in one case a letter from terminated employees, offering condolences, knowing how difficult it was for the company and that we did the right thing." Cuts to the rank-and-file hurt less when it's clear that senior managers are also taking cuts.[6]

LO2

CHOOSING SUBJECT LINES FOR NEGATIVE MESSAGES

When you write to superiors, use a subject line (see ◀◀ Chapter 7) that focuses on solving the problem.

Subject: Improving Our Subscription Letter

When you write to peers and subordinates, put the topic (but not your action on it) in the subject line.

Subject: Status of Conversion Table Program

Owing to heavy demands on our time, we have not yet been able to write programs for the conversion tables you asked for.

Use a negative subject line in e-mail messages.

Subject: Delay in Converting Tables

Use a negative subject line in letters and memos when you think readers may ignore what they think is a routine message. Major negatives, like firing someone, should be delivered in person, not by e-mail.

The best subject line for negative e-mail messages depends on whether you're refusing a request or initiating the negative. When you say no to an e-mail request, just hit "reply" and use "Re:" plus whatever the original subject line was for your response. When you initiate the negative, you will have to decide whether to use the negative in the subject line. The subject line should contain the negative when

- The negative is serious. Many people do not read all their e-mail messages. A neutral subject line may lead the reader to ignore the message.
- The reader needs the information to make a decision or act.
- You report your own errors (as opposed to the reader's).

Thus the following would be acceptable subject lines in e-mail messages:

Subject: We Lost The Bay's Account

Subject: Power to Be Out Sunday, March 8

Subject: Error in Survey Data Summary

When you write to people whom you know well, exaggerated subject lines are acceptable:

Subject: Gloom, Despair, and Agony

In other situations, a neutral subject line is acceptable.

Subject: Results of 360° Performance Appraisals

LO3

WORDING THE PARTS OF A NEGATIVE MESSAGE

This section provides more information about wording each part of a negative message.

Buffers

Traditionally, textbooks recommended that negative messages open with buffers. A **buffer** is a neutral or positive statement that allows you to delay the negative and prepare the reader. Research in the United States suggests that buffers do not make readers respond more positively,[7] and good buffers are very hard to write.

Even though buffers are hard to write, they remain important signals of tact and diplomacy for many audiences. That includes Canadians, many of whom value their history of treaty making with First Nations, their experience with negotiation, and association with diplomacy and peacekeeping under the auspices of the United Nations. Compromise has even been described as "the Canadian way."[8] A direct no-nonsense style may be preferred in the United States, but many Canadians appreciate indirection and the art of tactful, careful preparation for negative messages.

To be effective, a buffer must put the reader in a good frame of mind, without implying a positive answer, and provide a natural transition to the body of the letter. The kinds of statements most often used as buffers are good news, facts and chronologies of events, references to enclosures, thanks, and statements of principle.

1. **Start with any good news or positive elements the letter contains.**

   Starting Thursday, June 26, you'll have access to your money 24 hours a day at First Nations Bank of Canada.

   Message announcing that the drive-up windows will be closed for two days while new automated teller machines are installed

2. **State a fact or provide a chronology of events.**

   As a result of the new graduated dues schedule—determined by vote of the Delegate Assembly last December and subsequently endorsed by the Executive Council—members are now asked to establish their own dues rate and to calculate the total amount of their remittance.

   Announcement of a new dues structure that will raise most members' dues

3. **Refer to enclosures in the letter.**

   Enclosed is a new sticker for your car. You may pick up additional ones in the office if needed. Please *destroy* old stickers bearing the signature of "L.S. LaVoie."

   Message announcing increase in parking rental rates

4. **Thank (or compliment) the reader for something he or she has done.**

   Thank you for scheduling appointments for me with so many senior people at First Nations Bank of Canada. My visit there March 14 was very informative.

   Letter refusing a job offer

5. **State a general principle.**

   Good drivers should pay substantially less for their auto insurance. The Good Driver Plan was created to reward good drivers (those with five-year accident-free records) with our lowest available rates. A change in the plan, effective January 1, will help keep those rates low.

   Message announcing that the company will now count traffic tickets, not just accidents, in calculating insurance rates—a change that will raise many people's premiums

Some readers will feel betrayed by messages whose positive openers delay the central negative point. Therefore, use a buffer only when the reader (individually or culturally) values harmony or when the buffer serves another purpose (e.g., "thank you" for a letter).

International To Say Or Not to Say No*

Saying no can be hard in any situation, but it is taboo in some cultures. Building relationships and negotiating in these contexts requires sensitivity to cultural indirections to avoid serious misunderstanding and to save face.

Chinese culture's nonconfrontational style means that "no" is avoided in favour of indirect refusals (a need to consult, for instance) that avoid offence.

According to Masaaki Imai, Japanese have "16 ways to avoid saying 'no.'" Philippine investment in harmony likewise means avoiding "no" as too blunt and impolite. Altering the facts may be a preferred alternative.

Avoiding "no" in Mexico where it is felt as hurtful and wounding may leave Canadians questioning the ethical implications of resorting to mañana (another time; in the future) to avoid "no."

*Based on Yuh-Fang Chang, "How to say 'no': An analysis of cross-cultural difference and pragmatic transfer," *Language Sciences*, 31, no. 4 (July 2009): 477–493; Masaaki Imai, *16 Ways to Avoid Saying No: An Invitation to Experience Japanese Management from the Inside* (Nihon Keizai Shimbun, 1982); Larry A. Samovar, Richard E. Porter, & Edwin R. McDaniel, *Communication between Cultures* (Wadsworth Publishing, 2009); International Business Centre's Blog, retrieved April 16, 2011, from http://www.lavaltechnopole.org/cailt/en/tag/mexico/.

Reasons

Research shows that readers who described themselves as "totally surprised" had much more negative feelings than did those who expected the refusal.[9] A clear and convincing reason prepares the reader to accept the negative.

The following reason is inadequate.

✕ WEAK REASON:

The goal of the Lennoxville CHARGE-ALL Centre is to provide our customers faster, more personalized service. Since you now live outside the Lennoxville CHARGE-ALL service area, we can no longer offer you the advantages of a local CHARGE-ALL Centre.

If the reader says, "I don't care if my bills are slow and impersonal," will the company let the reader keep the card? No. The real reason for the negative is that the bank's franchise allows it to have cardholders only in a given geographical region.

✓ REAL REASON:

Each local CHARGE-ALL centre is permitted to offer accounts to customers within our region. The Lennoxville CHARGE-ALL centre serves customers east of Montreal. You can continue to use your current card until it expires. When that happens, you'll need to open an account with a CHARGE-ALL centre that serves your region of Quebec.

Don't hide behind "company policy": readers will assume the policy is designed to benefit you at their expense. If possible, show how readers benefit from the policy. If they do not benefit, don't mention policy at all.

✕ WEAK REASON:

I cannot write an insurance policy for you because company policy does not allow me to do so.

✓ BETTER REASON:

Gorham insures cars only when they are normally garaged at night. Standard insurance policies cover a wider variety of risks and charge higher fees. Limiting the policies we write gives Gorham customers the lowest possible rates for auto insurance.

Avoid saying that you *cannot* do something. Most negative messages exist because the writer or company has chosen certain policies or cutoff points. In the example above, the company could choose to insure a wider variety of customers if it wanted to do so.

If you have several reasons for saying no, use only those that are strong and watertight. If you give five reasons and readers dismiss two of them, readers may feel that they've won and should get the request.

✕ WEAK REASON:

You cannot store large bulky items in residence over the summer because moving them into and out of storage would tie up the stairs and the elevators just at the busiest times when people are moving in and out.

WAY TO DISMISS THE REASON:

We'll move large items before or after the two days when most people are moving in or out.

If you do not have a good reason, omit the reason rather than use a weak one. Even if you have a strong reason, omit it if it makes the company look bad.

✕ REASON THAT HURTS COMPANY:

Our company is not hiring at the present time because profits are down. In fact, the downturn has prompted top management to reduce the salaried staff by 5% just this month, with perhaps more reductions to come.

✓ BETTER:

Our company does not have any openings now.

Negatives

De-emphasize the negative (in this case a refusal) by putting it in the same paragraph as the reason, rather than in a paragraph by itself.

Sometimes you may be able to imply the refusal rather than stating it directly.

✕ Direct refusal:	You cannot get insurance for just one month.
✓ Implied refusal:	The shortest term for an insurance policy is six months.

Be sure the implication is crystal clear. Any message can be misunderstood, but an optimistic or desperate reader is particularly unlikely to understand a negative message. One of your purposes in a negative message is to close the door on the subject. You do not want to have to write a second message saying that the real answer is *no*. You want to maintain company credibility while incurring no legal liability.

Alternatives

Giving the reader an alternative or a compromise, if one is available, is a good idea for several reasons:

- It offers the reader another way to get what he or she wants.
- It suggests that you really care about the reader and about helping to meet his or her needs.
- It enables the reader to re-establish the psychological freedom you limited when you said no.
- It allows you to end on a positive note and to present yourself and your organization as positive, friendly, and helpful.

When you give an alternative, give readers all the information they need to act on it. Let readers decide whether to try the alternative.

Negative messages limit the reader's freedom. People may respond to a limitation of freedom by asserting their freedom in some other arena. Jack W. Brehm calls this phenomenon **psychological reactance.**[10] Psychological reactance is at work when a customer who has been denied credit no

Figure 8.5 A Refusal with an Alternative

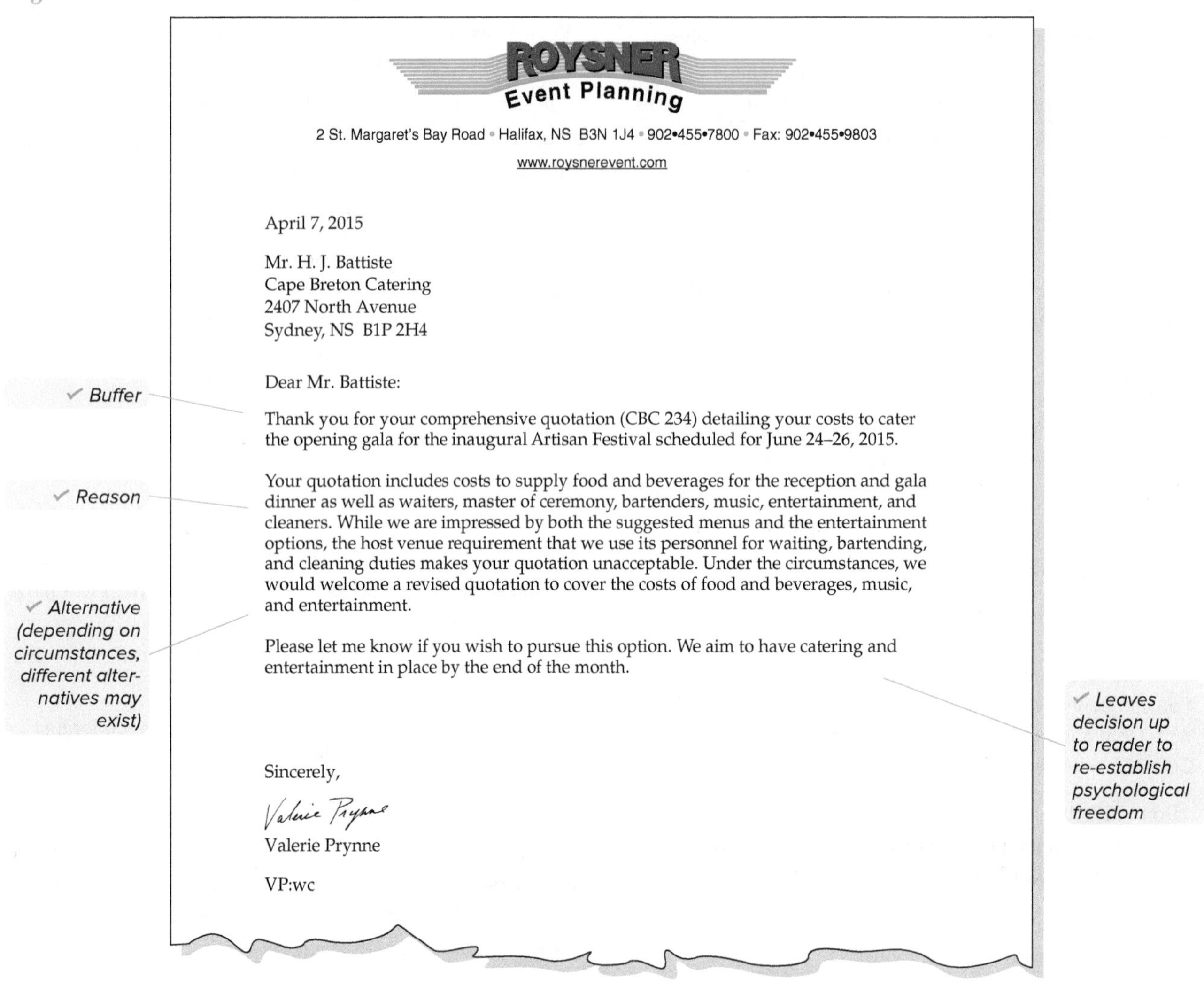

ROYSNER
Event Planning

2 St. Margaret's Bay Road • Halifax, NS B3N 1J4 • 902•455•7800 • Fax: 902•455•9803
www.roysnerevent.com

April 7, 2015

Mr. H. J. Battiste
Cape Breton Catering
2407 North Avenue
Sydney, NS B1P 2H4

Dear Mr. Battiste:

Thank you for your comprehensive quotation (CBC 234) detailing your costs to cater the opening gala for the inaugural Artisan Festival scheduled for June 24–26, 2015.

Your quotation includes costs to supply food and beverages for the reception and gala dinner as well as waiters, master of ceremony, bartenders, music, entertainment, and cleaners. While we are impressed by both the suggested menus and the entertainment options, the host venue requirement that we use its personnel for waiting, bartending, and cleaning duties makes your quotation unacceptable. Under the circumstances, we would welcome a revised quotation to cover the costs of food and beverages, music, and entertainment.

Please let me know if you wish to pursue this option. We aim to have catering and entertainment in place by the end of the month.

Sincerely,

Valerie Prynne

Valerie Prynne

VP:wc

longer buys even on a cash basis, or a subordinate who has been passed over for a promotion gets back at the company by deliberately doing a poor job.

An alternative allows the reader to react in a way that doesn't hurt you. By letting readers decide for themselves whether they want the alternative, you allow them to re-establish their sense of psychological freedom.

The specific alternative will vary depending on the circumstances. In Figure 8.5, the company rejects a quotation on account of host venue rules but offers an alternative that leaves the caterer some freedom.

Endings

If you have a good alternative, refer to it in your ending: "Please let me know if you wish to pursue this option."

The best endings look to the future.

> Wherever you have your account, you'll continue to get all the service you've learned to expect from CHARGE-ALL, and the convenience of charging items at over a million stores, restaurants, and hotels in Canada—and in Lennoxville, too, whenever you come back to visit!

Letter refusing to continue charge account for a customer who has moved

Avoid endings that seem insincere.

> We are happy to have been of service, and should we be able to assist you in the future, please contact us.

This ending lacks you-attitude and would not be good even in a positive message. In a situation where the company has just refused to help, it's likely to sound sarcastic or sadistic.

LO4

CHECKING TONE IN NEGATIVE MESSAGES

Tone—the implied attitude of the author toward the reader and the subject—is particularly important when you want readers to feel that you have taken their requests seriously. Check your draft carefully for positive emphasis and you-attitude (see ◀◀ Chapter 2), both at the level of individual words and at the level of ideas.

If poor language and tone can turn a congratulatory letter into an insult (see ◀◀ "Organizing Negative Letters, Memos, and Electronic Media" earlier in this chapter), an apology for lateness at an interview that suggests the interviewer's directions were unclear is also likely to be heard as a negative message.

Similarly, when Tim Hortons promoted its 2005 "Get Mugged with Tim Hortons" campaign (punning on its famous mugs), the company was forced to withdraw and apologize to the family of Erin Sperrey, who had been murdered while working the night shift at a Tim Hortons in Caribou, Maine.[11]

Writing in electronic formats has added to some writers' difficulties in communicating negative messages. Whether they are high school students chatting on MSN, employees responding too hastily or too angrily to colleagues, or business leaders musing in e-mail or text or instant messaging, many are finding that their "private" messages are creating serious conflict as well as public liabilities. "Flaming" among employees, for example, can lead to dismissal.

Dr. Liss Jeffrey, director of the McLuhan Global Research Network, University of Toronto, warns, "There is no childhood in cyberspace." Young people face suspension or expulsion from school, while others face humiliating exposure on Web sites or in chat rooms. Others share the fate of business leaders whose e-mail musings have become evidence in legal cases. Their e-mails leave "a permanent record" of CEO "deep cynicism . . . toward investors," says Michael Useem, ethics and leadership professor, Wharton School of Business. Conrad Black, for one, would not "re-enact the French Revolutionary renunciation of the rights of nobility." He relied on his sense of the rights of proprietors. As in the case of Enron, his words returned to haunt him.[12] Figure 8.6 lists some of the phrases to avoid in negative messages.

Even the physical appearance and timing of a message can convey tone. An obvious form rejection letter, for example, suggests that the writer has not given much consideration to the reader's application. An immediate negative suggests that the rejection didn't need any thought; an e-mail rejection based on "not being qualified" to someone who had held the position in question seems as offensive as it is ill considered. A negative delivered just before a major holiday seems especially unfeeling.

Communicating negative messages in a financial crisis has added to organizational challenges. Whether reassuring employees, customers, or investors, communicators need to share and explain information in a timely and tactful way to restore trust after a crisis that even former US Federal Reserve Board Chair Alan Greenspan said that he did not see coming. Still, few were persuaded by his argument that global forces entirely beyond Federal control—"There's really nothing we could have done about it"—fed the US mortgage bubble.[13]

Nova Scotia high school students David Shepherd and Travis Price used the Internet to say no to bullying and spread the word about their "sea of pink" campaign. Now the Day of Pink is the International Day against Bullying, Discrimination and Homophobia in schools and communities.

When Gerhild Somann received from her mutual fund company a "dear investor" letter highlighting investor opportunities rather than the financial meltdown of the last year which cut her portfolio by 25%, she was so upset at the clichés that she wrote the president (and copied it to *The Globe and Mail*). When the Franklin Templeton president wrote about lessons learned for the future, Ms. Somann countered, "Obviously, the valuable lessons of the past have not taught our investment community prudence, watchfulness and responsibility."[14] She would have preferred to be told about the industry taking responsibility and taking action to avoid a repetition of the financial meltdown.[15]

A 2008 survey of the impact of the economic climate on the workplace found that 54% of respondents said that employers had not addressed concerns. Nor had they received information in a timely way, "leading to panic and a sense of powerlessness."[16] Roy Briggs of the Royal Bank of Canada, UK, recommended against such an information "vacuum" and for communicating "regularly and proactively." Unfortunately, during trying economic times, communications departments can be the first to

Figure 8.6 Avoid These Phrases in Negative Messages

PHRASE	BECAUSE
I am afraid that we cannot	You aren't fearful. Don't hide behind empty phrases.
I am sorry that we are unable	You probably are able to grant the request; you simply choose not to. If you are so sorry about saying no, why don't you change your policy and say yes?
I am sure you will agree that	Don't assume that you can read the reader's mind.
Unfortunately	Unfortunately is negative in itself. It also signals that a refusal is coming.

For Buckley's cough syrup, leading with the bad news—"It tastes awful. And it works"—has been good for the bottom line.

Courtesy of Novartis Consumer Health Canada, Inc.

face cuts. Unfortunately too, in the United States communications often focused on the impact on companies rather than on the people who were the focus in Europe and the Caribbean.[17]

An International Association of Business Communicators survey found that 75% of respondents felt the impact of the financial crisis in their organizations, although only 56% agreed that their organizations were communicating proactively, 30% said their organizations responded only to specific inquiries, and 14% had organizations without any communication response. Only 49% had active and visible leaders in communicating information.[18]

LO5

HANDLING APOLOGIES

If accountants and lawyers once advised against apologies as a way of reducing legal and other risk, Michael McCain (◂◂ An Inside Perspective and ◂◂ On the Job) is not alone in thinking that sincere apologies are at the heart of doing the right thing. Eastern Regional Health Authority in Newfoundland and Labrador learned that apologies are good for organizational as well as individual health (see the ▸▸ Ethics and Legal feature "Medical Apologies").

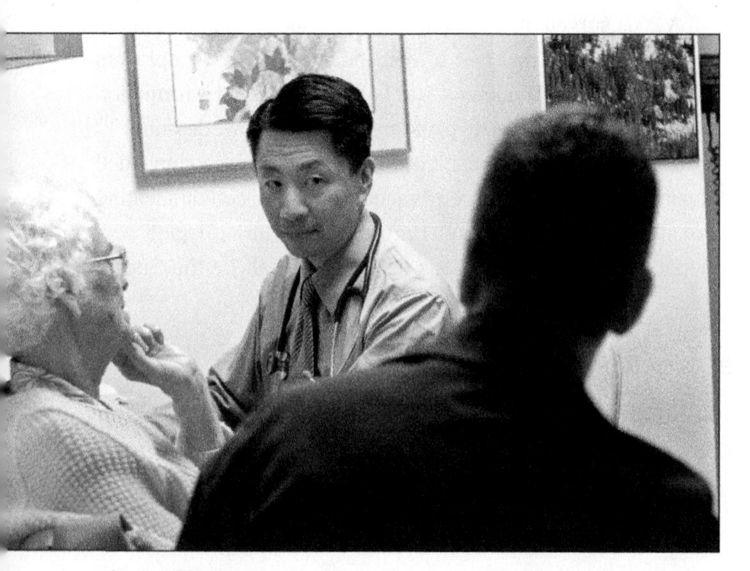

Saying "I'm sorry" can be good for the health of the patient as well as the health care system.

Even if an error is small and you are correcting it, an apology can be in order. Showing respect for customer feelings is the basis of sensitive customer service.

Still, not all negative messages need to include apologies.

- **Do not apologize when you are not at fault.** When you have done everything you can and when a delay or problem is due to circumstances beyond your control, you aren't at fault and don't need to apologize. It may be appropriate to include an explanation so the reader knows you weren't negligent. If the news is bad, put the explanation first. If you have good news for the reader, put it before your explanation.

✕ NEGATIVE:

I'm sorry that I could not answer your question sooner. I had to wait until the sales figures for the second quarter were in.

✓ BETTER (NEUTRAL OR BAD NEWS):

We needed the sales figures for the second quarter to answer your question. Now that they're in, I can tell you that . . .

✓ BETTER (GOOD NEWS):

The new advertising campaign is a success. The sales figures for the second quarter are in, and they show that . . .

- **If you apologize, do it early, briefly, and sincerely.** Apologize only once, early in the message. Let the reader move on to other, more positive information. Focus, for example, on what you have done to correct the situation.

If you don't know whether any inconvenience has resulted, don't raise the issue at all.

Ethics and Legal Medical Apologies*

Long advised not to apologize for fear of medical malpractice suits, doctors in some major medical centres are learning to say they are sorry. The move is being seen as "a promising step toward improving the quality" of health care.

Understanding that lawsuits are not the best way to deter potentially deadly medical errors, some medical centres have adopted a policy of quickly admitting errors, apologizing, and ensuring reasonable compensation.

Results so far suggest that patients are satisfied, while legal costs and even insurance premiums are reduced.

To increase candid disclosure, 30 U.S. states have enacted laws making medical apologies inadmissible in court.

In Newfoundland and Labrador, Eastern Regional Health Authority's failure to disclose errors in the reading of breast cancer test results between 1997 and 2005 led to a Commission of Inquiry on Hormone Receptor Testing and 60 recommendations, including one to adopt apology legislation. Eastern informed patients only when the media broke the story five months after the errors were uncovered. Eastern's response was "defensive and reactive." Forty-two percent of test results were wrong and 108 patients died.

In responding to what Justice Margaret Cameron called "a failure of both accountability and oversight at all levels," then Premier Danny Williams' public apology was "well received." The 2009 *Apology Act* recognized "the importance of apologies to both the care provider and the patient."

*Based on "Editorial: Doctors who say they're sorry," *New York Times*, May 22, 2008, retrieved August 25, 2008, from http://www.nytimes.com/2008/05/22/opinion/22thu2.html?_r=1&oref=slogin; "Considerable progress continues to be made in implementing Cameron Report recommendations," April 7, 2011 news release, retrieved April 16, 2011, from http://www.releases.gov.nl.ca/releases/2011/health/0407n02.htm; Heather Pullen and Terry Flynn, "Eastern Health: A case study on the need for public trust in health care communities," retrieved April 16, 2011, from http://www.awpagesociety.com/images/uploads/EasternHealth_CaseStudy.pdf; "Lab mistakes, poor oversight flagged in NL breast cancer inquiry," CBC News, retrieved April 16, 2011, from http://www.cbc.ca/news/health/story/2009/03/03/cameron-report.html.

× Negative:	I'm sorry I didn't answer your letter sooner. I hope that my delay hasn't inconvenienced you.
✓ Better:	I'm sorry I didn't answer your letter sooner.

According to linguist Deborah Tannen, North American women use "I'm sorry" both to mean "I'm responsible for the error or problem" and "It's too bad that this situation happened." She claims that North American men interpret "I'm sorry" as admitting guilt and avoid using the words to avoid being put down in a conversation.[19] Canadians show no such reluctance, having, by one account, 12 ways to say "I'm sorry."[20] Although generalizations should be handled with care, be aware that "I'm sorry" may be interpreted as an admission of error, and avoid overusing the phrase.

LO6

CONSIDERING ALTERNATIVE STRATEGIES FOR NEGATIVE SITUATIONS

Whenever you face a negative situation, consider recasting it as a positive or persuasive message.

If the negative information will directly lead to a benefit that you know readers want, use the pattern of organization for informative and positive messages:

SITUATION:

You're raising parking rates to pay for lot maintenance, ice and snow removal, and signs so tenants can have cars that park in their spots towed away—all services tenants have asked for.

× NEGATIVE:

Effective May 1, parking rentals will go up $5 a month.

✓ POSITIVE EMPHASIS:

Effective May 1, if someone parks in your spot, you can have the car towed away. Signs are being put up announcing that all spaces in the lot are rented. Lot maintenance is also being improved. The lot will be resurfaced this summer, and arrangements have been made for ice and snow removal next winter.

Often a negative situation can be recast as a persuasive message (see ⏩ Chapter 9). If your organization has a problem, ask readers to help solve it. A solution that workers have created will be much easier to implement.

When one association raised dues, the executive director wrote a persuasive message urging members to send in renewals early so they could beat the increase: using an attention-getting opener, offsetting the negative by setting it against the benefits of membership, telling the reader what to do, and ending with a picture of the benefit the reader received by acting. Its recent increases, however, have been announced directly.

Schwinn needed a new product line to attract sophisticated cyclists. This apology for its old, boring line moves quickly to a discussion of its new technology. By evoking an experience every cyclist has had, the headline also suggests that falling is a minor event.

Humour can defuse negative messages. Kathryn McGrath, head of the Securities and Exchange Commission's division of investment management, needed to tell an investment firm that its ad was illegal. The ad showed an index finger pointing up and large bold letters saying that performance was "up," too. Tiny print at the bottom of the page admitted that performance figures hadn't been adjusted to include front-end sales charges. Rather than writing a heavy-handed letter, McGrath sent the firm a photocopy of a thumb pointing down. The ad never ran again.[21]

Humour works best when it's closely related to the specific situation and the message. Humour that seems tacked on is less likely to work. Never use humour that belittles readers.

DISTINGUISHING VARIETIES OF NEGATIVE MESSAGES

Among the most difficult kinds of negative messages to write are rejections and refusals, and layoffs and firings.

Rejections and Refusals

When you refuse requests from people outside your organization, try to use a buffer. Give an alternative if one is available. For example, if you are denying credit, it may still be possible for the reader to put an expensive item on layaway.

Politeness and length help. In two studies, job applicants preferred rejection letters that addressed them as *Mr./Ms.* rather than calling them by their first names, that said something specific about their good qualities, that phrased the refusal itself indirectly, that offered alternatives (such as another position the applicant might be qualified for), and that were longer.[22]

Double-check the words in the draft to be sure the reason can't backfire if it is applied to other contexts. The statement that a plant is "too noisy and dangerous" for a group tour could be used as evidence against the company in a worker's compensation claim.[23]

Researcher Catherine Schryer asked writers at an insurance company to evaluate the firm's letters denying claims. She found four differences between the letters judged effective and those judged ineffective:

1. Good letters were easier to read. Poor letters contained jargon, longer words and sentences, and awkward phrasing.
2. Good letters gave fuller reasons for the rejection. Poor letters often used cut and paste text without explaining terms.

Technology Tips Benefits of a Mobile Blackout?*

Being obsessed with your mobile phone can get you in trouble—and increase stress, while reducing efficiency and quality of life. Whether mobile distraction causes you to bump into something, to follow someone into a washroom, not to follow meeting or presentation etiquette, or to inadvertently dial an emergency line, more organizations are trying to put mobile devices in their place.

With 60% of a global survey of 20,000 professionals confessing to compulsions to check their BlackBerry at all hours, organizations from Pfizer to Citizenship and Immigration Canada have called for overnight BlackBerry blackouts in the interests of work–life balance.

A 2014 Ipsos online poll found that mobile phone users "spend 86 percent of their time staring at one screen or another."

While some argue that you are not "your best at 2 a.m." or you are not productive when you are constantly checking e-mail, others fear missing clients—especially new ones you want to impress.

Xerox Canada's Sacha Fraser's "Take Back the Hour" e-mail campaign is credited with teaching employees "how to use rather than abuse e-mail." Instead of getting kudos for unusual-hour e-mails, employees now find themselves in talks with managers to find "a deeper issue" behind the practice.

*Based on Erin Anderssen, "Crushed," *The Globe and Mail,* March 29, 2014, F1-7; Wallace Immen, "Mind your BlackBerry manners, or risk your career," *The Globe and Mail,* June 24, 2009, B14; Trevor Melanson, "Accidental pocket dialers hang up emergency line," *The Globe and Mail,* January 8, 2011, A6; Gillian Shaw, "Weaning ourselves away from technology," *Vancouver Sun,* January 16, 2010; Kira Vermond, "Time for a BlackBerry blackout," *The Globe and Mail,* February 9, 2008, B18.

3. Good letters were less likely to talk about the reader's emotions ("angry," "disappointed").
4. Good letters were more likely to portray the writer and reader as active agents.[24]

When you refuse requests within your organization, use your knowledge of the organization's culture and of the specific individual to craft your message. In some organizations, it may be appropriate to use company slogans, offer whatever help already-established departments can give, and refer to the individual's good work (if you know that it is good). In other, less personal organizations, a simple negative without embellishment may be more appropriate.

Layoffs and Firings

Information about layoffs and firings is normally delivered orally but accompanied by a written statement explaining severance pay or unemployment benefits that may be available.

If a company is in financial trouble, management needs to communicate the problem clearly. Sharing information and enlisting everyone's help in finding solutions may make it possible to save jobs. Sharing information also means that layoff notices, if they become necessary, will be a formality; they should not be new information to employees.

Give the employee the real reason for the firing. Offering a face-saving reason unrelated to poor performance can create legal liabilities. But avoid broadcasting the reason: to do so can leave the company liable to a defamation suit.[25]

Figure 8.7 provides a checklist for negative messages.

Figure 8.7 Checklist for Negative Messages

- ☐ Is the subject line appropriate?
- ☐ If a buffer is used, does it avoid suggesting either a positive or a negative response?
- ☐ Is the reason, if it is given, presented before the refusal? Is the reason watertight, with no loopholes?
- ☐ Is the negative information clear?
- ☐ Is an alternative given if a good one is available? Does the message provide the information needed to act on the alternative? Does it leave the choice up to the reader?
- ☐ Does the last paragraph avoid repeating the negative information?
- ☐ Is the tone acceptable—not defensive, but not cold, preachy, or arrogant either?

And, for all messages, not just negative ones,

- ☐ Does the message use you-attitude and positive emphasis?
- ☐ Is the style easy to read and friendly?
- ☐ Is the visual design of the message inviting?
- ☐ Is the format correct?
- ☐ Does the message use standard grammar? Is it free from typos?

SUMMARY OF KEY POINTS

- Organize negative letters in this way:
  1. Give the reason for the refusal before the negative or refusal itself when you have a reason that readers will understand and accept.
  2. Give the negative just once, clearly.
  3. Present an alternative or compromise, if one is available.
  4. End with a positive, forward-looking statement.
- Organize negative memos to superiors in this way:
  1. Describe the problem.
  2. Tell how it happened.
  3. Describe the options for fixing it.
  4. Recommend a solution and ask for action.
- Organize negative messages to peers and subordinates in this way:
  1. Describe the problem.
  2. Present an alternative or compromise, if one is available.
  3. If possible, ask for input or action.
- When you write to superiors, use a subject line focused on solving the problem. When you write to peers and subordinates, put the topic (but not your action on it) in the subject line.
- Use a negative subject line in e-mail messages. Use a negative subject line in letters and memos when you think readers may ignore what they think is a routine message. The best subject line for negative e-mail messages depends on whether you're refusing a request or initiating the negative.
- A *buffer* is a neutral or positive statement that allows you to delay the negative message and prepare the reader. Buffers include good news, facts and chronologies of events, references to enclosures, thanks, and statements of principle.
- A clear and convincing reason prepares the reader to accept the negative. Omit the reason if it is weak or makes the business look bad.
- Make the negative or refusal crystal clear.
- Give the reader an alternative or a compromise, if one is available. Give readers the information they need to act. If you have a good alternative, refer to it in the ending.
- Tone—the implied attitude of the author toward the reader and subject—is important when you want readers to feel that you have taken their requests seriously. Use positive emphasis and you-attitude. Even the appearance and timing of communications can convey tone.
- Sincere apologies are good for business. Even if an error is small and you are correcting it, an apology can be in order. Apologize early, briefly, and sincerely.
- Do not apologize when you are not at fault.
- Many negative situations can be redefined to use the patterns of organization for routine or for persuasive messages. Humour sometimes works to defuse negative situations.

EXERCISES AND PROBLEMS

GETTING STARTED

8.1 LETTERS FOR DISCUSSION—CREDIT REFUSAL

As director of customer service at C'est Bon, an upscale furniture store, you manage the store's credit. Today you will reject an application from Francine Devereux. Although her income is fairly high, her last two payments on her student loans were late, and she has three bank credit cards, all charged to the upper limit, on which she's made just the minimum payment for the last three months.

The following letters are possible approaches to giving her the news. How well does each message meet the criteria in the checklist for negative messages?

1.

Dear Ms. Devereux:

Your request to have a C'est Bon charge account shows that you are a discriminating shopper. C'est Bon sells the finest merchandise available.

Although your income is acceptable, records indicate that you carry the maximum allowable balances on three bank credit cards. Moreover, two recent payments on your student loans have not been made in a timely fashion. If you were given a C'est Bon charge account, and if you charged a large amount on it, you might have difficulty paying the bill, particularly if you had other unforeseen expenses (car repair, moving, medical emergency) or if your income dropped suddenly. If you were unable to repay, with your other debt you would be in serious difficulty. We would not want you to be in such a situation, nor would you yourself desire it.

Please reapply in six months.

Sincerely,

2.

Dear Francine:

No, you can't have a C'est Bon credit card—at least not right now. Get your financial house in order and try again.

Fortunately for you, there's an alternative. Put what you want on layaway. The furniture you want will be held for you, and paying a bit each week or month will be good self-discipline.

Enjoy your C'est Bon furniture!

Sincerely,

3.

Dear Ms. Devereux:

Over the years, we've found that the best credit risks are people who pay their bills promptly. Since two of your student loan payments have been late, we won't extend store credit to you right now. Come back with a record of six months of on-time payments of all bills, and you'll get a different answer.

You might like to put the furniture you want on layaway. A $50 deposit holds any item you want. You have six months to pay, and you save interest charges.

You might also want to take advantage of one of our Saturday Seminars. On the first Saturday of each month at 11 a.m., our associates explain one topic related to furniture and interior decorating. Upcoming topics are

How to Wallpaper a Room	February 5
Drapery Options	March 6
Persian Carpets	April 1

Sincerely,

8.2 E-MAILS FOR DISCUSSION—SAYING NO TO A COLLEAGUE

A colleague in another provincial agency has e-mailed you asking if you would like to use the payroll software her agency developed. You wouldn't. Switching to a new program would take a lot of time, and what you have works well for you.

The following messages are possible approaches to giving her the news. How well does each message meet the criteria in the checklist for negative messages?

As Your Professor Directs,

1. Discuss your findings as a group and present to the class.
2. Post your group findings on the class blog.

1.

Subject: Re: Use Our Software?

No.

2.

Subject: Re: Use Our Software?

Thanks for telling me about the payroll software your team developed. What we have works well for us. Like every other agency, we're operating on a bare-bones budget, and no one here wants to put time (that we really don't have) into learning a new program. So we'll say, no, thanks!

3.

Subject: Re: Use Our Software?

The payroll software your team developed sounds very good.

I might like to use it, but the people here are computer phobic. They HATE learning new programs. So, being a good little computer support person, I soldier on with the current stuff. (And people wonder why the provincial government is SO INEFFICIENT! Boy, the stories I could tell!)

Anyway, thanks for the offer. Keep me posted on the next development—maybe it will be something so obviously superior that even the Neanderthals here can see its advantages!

8.3 REVISING A NEGATIVE MESSAGE

Rewrite and reorganize the following negative message to make it more positive. Eliminate any sentences that are not needed.

As Your Instructor Directs, peer grade your answers.

Dear Tenant:

Effective March 1, the rent for your parking space will go up $10 a month. However, our parking lot is still not the most expensive in town.

Many of you have asked us to provide better snow and ice removal and to post signs saying that all spaces are rented so that a car can be towed if it parks in your space. Signs will be posted by March 1, and, if we get any more snow, Acme Company will have the lot cleared by 7 a.m.

Enclosed is a new parking sticker. Please hang it on your rearview mirror.

Sincerely,

A. E. Jackson

E-MAIL MESSAGES

8.4 NOTIFYING STUDENTS THAT THEY MAY NOT GRADUATE

The University of Regina asks students to file an application to graduate one term before they plan to graduate. The application lists the courses the student has already had and those he or she will take in the last two terms. Your office reviews the lists to see that the student will meet the requirements for total number of hours, hours in the major, and general education requirements. Some students have forgotten a requirement or not taken enough courses and cannot graduate unless they take more courses than those they have listed.

As Your Professor Directs,

Write form e-mail messages to the following audiences. Leave blanks for the proposed date of graduation and specific information that must be merged into the message:

a. Students who have not taken enough total hours.

b. Students who have not fulfilled all the requirements for their majors.

c. Students who are missing one or more general education courses.

d. Advisers of students who do not meet the requirements for graduation.

8.5 CORRECTING A MISTAKE

Today, as you reviewed some cost figures, you realized they didn't fit with the last monthly report you filed. You had pulled the numbers together from several sources, and you're not sure what happened. Maybe you miscopied, or didn't save the final version after you'd checked all the numbers. But whatever the cause, you've found errors in three categories. You gave your boss the following totals:

Personnel	$2,843,490
Office supplies	$43,500
Telephone	$186,240

E-mail your boss to correct the information.

As Your Professor Directs,

Write e-mail messages for the following situations:

a. The correct numbers are

Personnel	$2,845,490
Office supplies	$34,500
Telephone	$186,420

b. The correct numbers are

Personnel	$2,845,490
Office supplies	$84,500
Telephone	$468,240

Variations for each situation:

i. Your boss has been out of the office; you know she hasn't seen the data yet.

ii. Your boss gave a report to the executive committee this morning using your data.

Hints:

- How serious is the mistake in each situation?
- In which situations, if any, should you apologize?
- Should you give the reason for the mistake? Why or why not?
- How do your options vary depending on whether your job title gives you responsibility for numbers and accounting?

8.6 TELLING EMPLOYEES TO REMOVE PERSONAL WEB PAGES

You're director of management and information systems (MIS) in your organization. At your monthly briefing for management, a vice-president complained that some employees have posted personal Web pages on the company's Web server.

"It looks really unprofessional to have stuff about cats and children and musical instruments. How can people do this?"

You took the question literally. "Well, some people have authorization to post material—price changes, job listings, marketing information. Someone who has authorization could put up anything."

Another manager said, "I don't think it's so terrible—after all, there aren't any links from our official pages to these personal pages."

A third person said, "But we're paying for what's posted—so we pay for server space and connect time. Maybe it's not much right now, but as more and more people become Web-literate, the number of people putting up unauthorized pages could spread. We should put a stop to this now."

The vice-president agreed. "The Web site is carefully designed to present an image of our organization. Personal pages are dangerous. Can you imagine the flak we'd get if someone posted links to pornography?"

You said, "I don't think that's very likely. If it did happen, as system administrator, I could remove the page."

The third speaker said, "I think we should remove all the pages. Having any at all suggests that our people have so much extra time that they're playing on the Web. That suggests our prices are too high and may make some people worry about quality. In fact, I think we need a new policy prohibiting personal pages on the company's Web server. And any pages that are already up should be removed."

A majority of the managers agreed and told you to write a message to all employees. Create an e-mail message to tell employees that you will remove the personal pages already posted and that no more will be allowed.

Hints:

- Suggest other ways that people can post personal Web pages. Commercial services are possibilities. (Check to be sure that the groups you recommend are still offering Web sites. If possible, get current prices.)
- Give only reasons that are watertight and make the company look good.

COMMUNICATING AT WORK

8.7 TELLING THE BOSS ABOUT A PROBLEM

In any organization, things sometimes go wrong. Tell your supervisor (or professor) about a problem in your unit (or class group) and recommend what should be done.

8.8 REFUSING A CUSTOMER REQUEST

The customer isn't always right. Sometimes customers ask for things you're truly unable to provide. Even more frequently, you say no because the refusal serves your organization's needs. Think of a situation where a customer asked for something your organization could not provide or felt was unreasonable. Write a response refusing the request.

As Your Professor Directs in 8.7 and 8.8,

a. Prepare notes for a meeting with or phone call to the person to whom you must give the bad news.

b. Write a paper or e-mail document to achieve the goal.

c. Write a blog post or make a presentation describing the situation and culture at your workplace and explaining your rhetorical choices (medium, strategy, tone, wording, graphics or document design, and so forth).

8.9 PERSONALIZING BAD NEWS

Your financial services company is tasked with communicating with investors in a year in which most have faced 25% losses on their portfolios. Knowing that clients can feel insulted by form letters that try to turn bad financial news into an investment opportunity for some (see ◀◀ "Checking Tone in Negative Messages" earlier in this chapter), your manager asks you to personalize letters addressing clients' portfolio losses.

Prepare a personalized letter to go to a customer explaining the portfolio losses.

8.10 HANDLING NEGATIVE MESSAGES IN A CRISIS SITUATION

A number of businesses, organizations, and governments have had to handle natural, environmental, and other crisis situations in recent years. In addition to examples outlined in this chapter, you might consider the cases of oil spills, pipeline ruptures, mining spills, airline disruptions and tragedies, cruise ship or railway disasters, toy or car recalls, tsunami, or nuclear disasters. Choose one such crisis situation and research and assess how well a business, organization, or government handled negative messages. For advice on documenting your sources, see ▸▸ Chapter 10.

As Your Professor Directs,

a. Post your findings on the class blog.

b. Prepare a presentation to report your findings.

c. Prepare a fact sheet on best practices for communicating negative messages in a crisis.

d. Present your findings in a short video.

8.11 HANDLING NEGATIVE MESSAGES ETHICALLY

Research and assess the ethics of claims and counterclaims about a topic such as "ethical oil," "clean energy," or "natural products." For advice on documenting your sources, see ◂◂ Chapter 10.

As Your Professor Directs,

a. Post your findings on the class blog.

b. Prepare a presentation to report your findings.

c. Prepare a fact sheet on best practices for communicating negative messages in a crisis.

d. Present your findings in a short video.

8.12 SOLVING A SAMPLE PROBLEM

Solving negative problems requires careful analysis. The checklist in ◂◂ Figure 8.7 can help you discuss the analysis of the problem and evaluate Figures 8.8 and 8.9.

The Problem

You're director of employee benefits for a Fortune 500 company. Today, you received the following memo:

From: Michelle Jagtiani

Subject: Getting My Retirement Benefits

Next Friday will be my last day here. I am leaving [name of company] to take a position at another firm.

Please process a cheque for my retirement benefits, including both the deductions from my salary and the company's contributions for the last six and a half years. I would like to receive the cheque by next Friday if possible.

You have bad news for Michelle. Although the company does contribute an amount to the retirement fund equal to the amount deducted for retirement from the employee's paycheque, employees who leave with fewer than seven years of employment get only their own contributions. Michelle will get back only the money that has been deducted from her own pay, plus 4% interest compounded quarterly. Her payments and interest come to just over $17,200; the amount could be higher depending on the amount of her last paycheque, which will include compensation for any unused vacation days and sick leave. Furthermore, since the amounts deducted were not considered taxable income, she will have to pay income tax on the money she will receive.

You cannot process the cheque until after her resignation is effective, so you will mail it to her. You have her home address on file; if she's moving, she needs to let you know where to send the cheque. Processing the cheque may take two to three weeks.

Analysis of the Problem

1. *Who is your audience? What characteristics are relevant to this particular message? If you are writing to more than one reader, how do the readers differ?*

   Michelle Jagtiani is your audience. Unless she's a personal friend, you probably wouldn't know why she's leaving and where she's going.

   There's a lot you don't know. She may not know much about taxes; she may not be able to take advantage of tax-reduction strategies. You can't assume the answers because you wouldn't have them in real life.

2. *What are your purposes in writing?*

- To tell her that she will get only her own contributions, plus 4% interest compounded quarterly; that the cheque will be mailed to her home address two to three weeks after her last day on the job; and that the money will be taxable as income
- To build goodwill so that she feels that she has been treated fairly and consistently
- To minimize negative feelings she may have
- To close the door on this subject

3. *What information must your message include?*

   Your message must tell her when the cheque will come; the fact that her cheque will be based on her contributions, not the employer's; that the money will be taxable income; how lump-sum retirement benefits are calculated; the fact that you have her current address on file but need a new address if she's moving.

4. *How can you build support for your position? What reasons or reader benefits will your reader find convincing?*

   Giving the amount currently in her account may make her feel that she is getting a significant sum of money. Suggesting someone who can give free tax advice (if the company offers this as a fringe benefit) reminds her of the benefits of working with the company. Wishing her luck with her new job is a nice touch.

5. *What objection(s) can you expect your reader(s) to have? What negative elements of your message must you de-emphasize or overcome?*

   She is getting about half the amount she expected, since she gets no matching funds. She might have been able to earn more than 4% interest if she had invested the money in the stock market. Depending on her personal tax situation she may pay more tax on the money as a lump sum than would have been due had she paid it each year as she earned the money.

Discussion of the Sample Solutions

The solution in Figure 8.8 is not acceptable. The subject line gives a bald negative with no reason or alternative. The first sentence has a condescending tone that is particularly offensive in negative messages. The last sentence focuses on what is being taken away rather than what remains. Paragraph 2 lacks you-attitude and is vague. The memo ends with a negative. There is nothing anywhere in the memo to build goodwill.

The solution in Figure 8.9, in contrast, is very good. The policy serves as a buffer and explanation. The negative is stated clearly but is buried in the paragraph to avoid overemphasizing it. The second paragraph begins on a positive note by specifying the amount in the account and the fact that the sum might be even higher.

Paragraph 3 contains the additional negative information that the amount will be taxable but offers the alternative that it may be possible to reduce taxes. The writer builds goodwill by suggesting a specific person the reader could contact.

Paragraph 4 tells the reader what address is in the company files (Michelle may not know whether the files are up to date), asks that she update it if necessary, and ends with the reader's concern: getting her cheque promptly.

The final paragraph ends on a positive note. This generalized goodwill is appropriate when the writer does not know the reader well.

Figure 8.8 An Unacceptable Solution to the Sample Problem

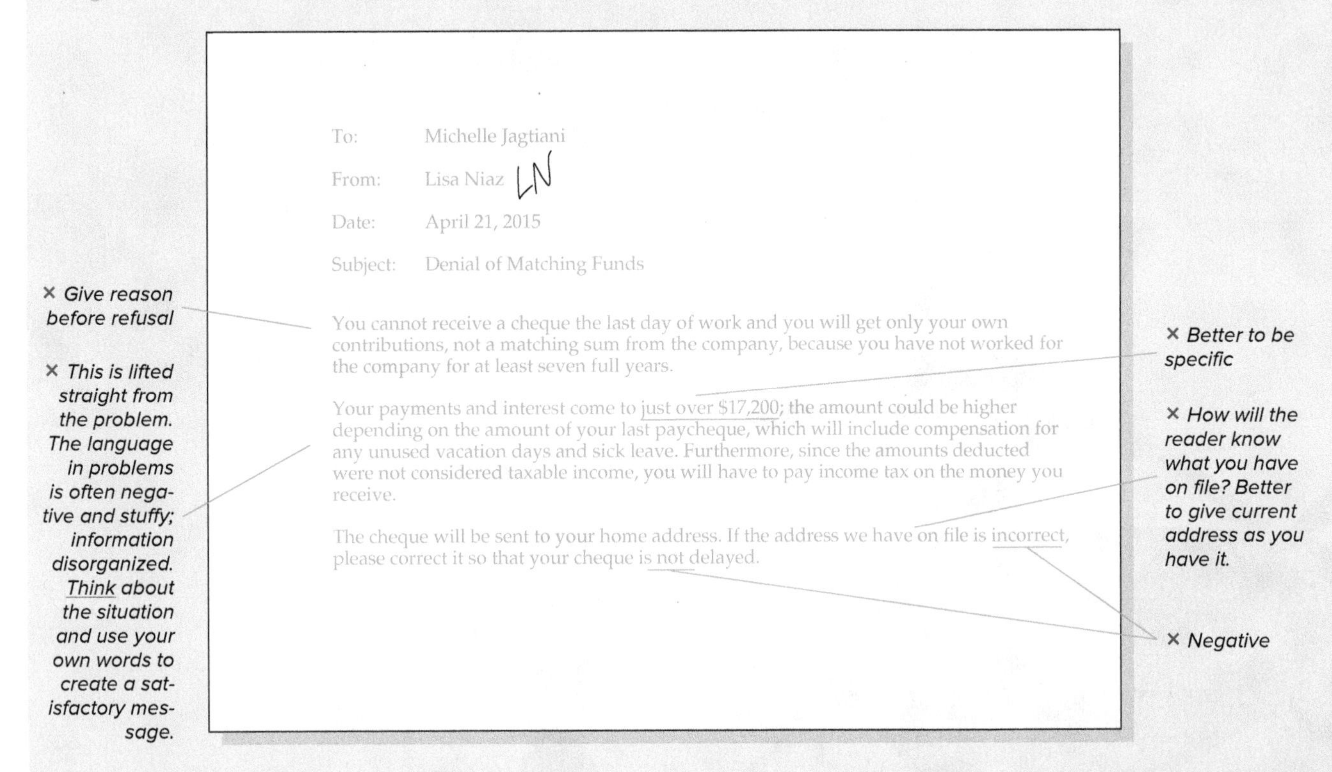
To: Michelle Jagtiani

From: Lisa Niaz LN

Date: April 21, 2015

Subject: Denial of Matching Funds

You cannot receive a cheque the last day of work and you will get only your own contributions, not a matching sum from the company, because you have not worked for the company for at least seven full years.

Your payments and interest come to just over $17,200; the amount could be higher depending on the amount of your last paycheque, which will include compensation for any unused vacation days and sick leave. Furthermore, since the amounts deducted were not considered taxable income, you will have to pay income tax on the money you receive.

The cheque will be sent to your home address. If the address we have on file is incorrect, please correct it so that your cheque is not delayed.

Figure 8.9 A Good Solution to the Sample Problem

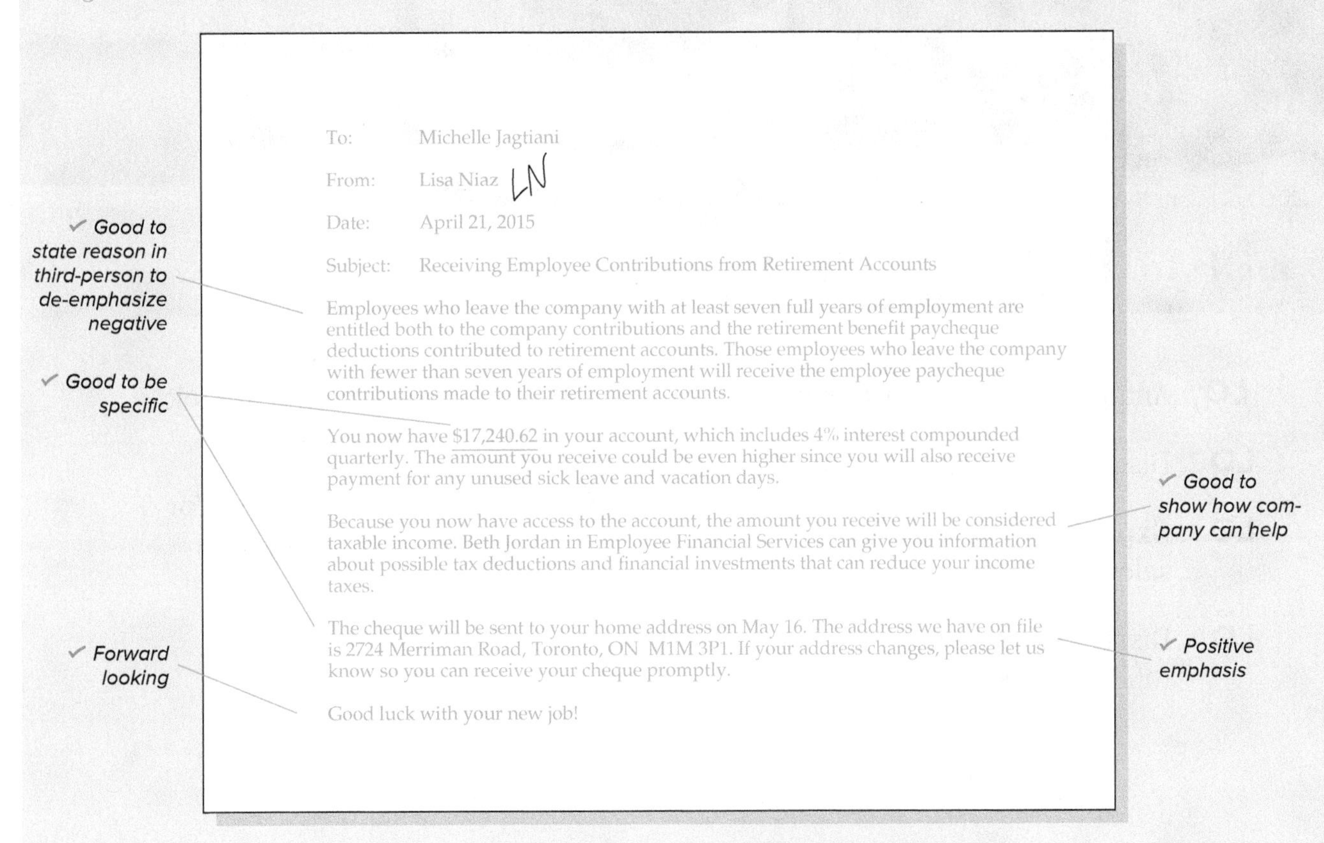
To: Michelle Jagtiani

From: Lisa Niaz LN

Date: April 21, 2015

Subject: Receiving Employee Contributions from Retirement Accounts

Employees who leave the company with at least seven full years of employment are entitled both to the company contributions and the retirement benefit paycheque deductions contributed to retirement accounts. Those employees who leave the company with fewer than seven years of employment will receive the employee paycheque contributions made to their retirement accounts.

You now have $17,240.62 in your account, which includes 4% interest compounded quarterly. The amount you receive could be even higher since you will also receive payment for any unused sick leave and vacation days.

Because you now have access to the account, the amount you receive will be considered taxable income. Beth Jordan in Employee Financial Services can give you information about possible tax deductions and financial investments that can reduce your income taxes.

The cheque will be sent to your home address on May 16. The address we have on file is 2724 Merriman Road, Toronto, ON M1M 3P1. If your address changes, please let us know so you can receive your cheque promptly.

Good luck with your new job!

PERSUASIVE AND SALES MESSAGES

9

Learning Outcomes

LO1 Analyze a persuasive situation

LO2 Discuss persuasive strategies

LO3 Explain how to organize sales messages

LO4 Discuss sales and fundraising strategy

LO5 Describe strategy in rack cards and brochures

LO6 Devise a writing style for sales and fundraising

AN INSIDE PERSPECTIVE

Winner of awards for Aboriginal Business Leader of the Year, CANDO Economic Developer of the Year, and National Aboriginal Achievement, Chief Clarence Louie is a powerful motivator behind the Osoyoos Indian Band success story. Seen here shaking hands with Donald Triggs, former president and CEO of Vincor Canada, who fostered the joint venture winery with Louie.

To achieve his dream of generating wealth for his people "to see us take our rightful place in the economy," Chief Clarence Louie had to build a powerful case based on compelling logic and powerful emotional appeals. Chief Louie called on statistics and stories, testimonials, and expert advice underlining direct and indirect benefits to overcome resistance, build support, motivate action, and realize his vision for the Osoyoos Indian Band near Penticton, B.C.

Chief since 1985, Louie has been the driving force taking the band from bankruptcy to annual revenues in excess of $13 million from businesses including a resort and spa, golf course, and the Nk'Mip Cellars, the first Aboriginal-owned winery in North America. And he achieved as much not with oil riches but on a desert—"hardly an auspicious starting point for an aboriginal economic revolution."

Having long spoken out against dependency and government's misdirected priorities, Chief Louie challenges his own people to be self-reliant and take responsibility for their futures. "We need no strings attached by government," he says. "In the 1800s, the government took away the Natives' economic development by removing their ability to support themselves."

If his views are controversial, he's also changed a lot of thinking within and beyond his community, bringing well-deserved attention to Aboriginal economic achievement, which is, he says, "the horse that pulls the social cart." And a critical part of this success story has been Chief Louie's persuasive promotion of education and invitation to "Join a Band on the Move."

*Based on Alex Rose, "How capitalism can save Canadian natives from poverty," *Canadian Business,* February 22, 2013, retrieved from http://www.canadianbusiness.com/economy/people-cant-protect-their-culture-when-theyre-on-welfare/; Tom Brodbeck, "A splendid role model: BC chief gives leadership, inspiration," *Winnipeg Sun,* January 19, 2011, retrieved April 17, 2011, from http://www.winnipegsun.com/news/columnists/tom_brodbeck/2011/01/18/16941746.html; Geoff Johnson, "The challenge to improve First Nations' education," *Vancouver Sun,* April 15, 2011, retrieved April 17, 2011, from http://www.vancouversun.com/opinion/challenge+improve+First+Nations+education/4613568/story.html; Rachel Pulfer, "Band on a run," *Canadian Business,* February 26, 2007, 18–20; "Chief Clarence Louie," retrieved April 18, 2008, from http://www.newrelationshiptrust.ca/about/2006-regional-engagement-process/chief-clarence-louie.

Whether you're selling safety equipment or ideas, effective persuasion is based on accurate logic (◂◂ Chapter 1), effective emotional appeal, and credibility or trust. Reasons have to be reasons the audience finds important; emotional appeal is based on values the audience cares about; credibility is in the eye of the beholder. In other words, persuasive strategies and messages cannot be separated from their cultural situations, ethical choices, and the genres or kinds of documents that shape and are shaped by those strategies.

In Classical Greece, Aristotle's *Rhetoric* promoted these same elements in elaborating the art of rhetoric or persuasion:

- *Pathos:* appeal to values, needs, and beliefs shared with audience
- *Logos:* appeal to sound reasoning or logic
- *Ethos:* audience perception of speaker's/writer's good character or credibility

In the 21st century, businesses depend more and more on persuasion and buy-in to get quality work done. You can command people to make widgets, but you can't command people to be creative. Even if you're making widgets, just going through the motions isn't enough. You want people to make high-quality widgets, while reducing scrap and other costs. Internal commitment is needed to make that happen.

External motivation doesn't last. Some people will buy a certain brand of pizza if they have a "2 for 1" coupon. But if the coupon expires, or if another company offers the same deal, customers may leave. In contrast, if customers like your pizza better, if they are motivated internally to choose it, then you may keep your customers even if another company comes in with a lower price.

Although all good communications involve some persuasion to motivate readers to read and respond, the focus in this chapter is on the following persuasive messages:

- Orders and requests
- Collection letters
- Sales and fundraising letters
- Promotional materials (rack cards and brochures)

On the Job Persuasion and Emotional Intelligence*

Emotional intelligence (EI) is what enables people to succeed in the workplace. Psychologist Daniel Goleman studied 181 jobs in 121 companies worldwide, separating technical skills from emotional competencies. The latter "competencies like trustworthiness, adaptability, and a talent for collaboration" were twice as important.

For high-level executive jobs, Goleman asks, "How persuasive are you? Can you get 'buy-in' for your ideas from the people around you? . . . Can you . . . communicate with people in terms they can understand and embrace?" Such "great leadership. . . . takes huge social intelligence, including a strongly developed sense of empathy." When team work and social media are changing "the internal environment" of businesses, "fluency in people skills is essential."

Canadian researchers Steven Stein and Howard Book show EI at work in survival stories, sports, health, business, and law enforcement. According to their Emotional Quotient Inventory (developed by Dr. Reuven Bar-On) findings, "emotional intelligence cuts across the gender gap," although women score better on social responsibility and empathy while men score better on stress tolerance.

And while they find that "core elements of emotional intelligence" are relevant to leadership, Yvonne Stys and Shelley Brown call for further research on the legitimacy of EI, its teachability and applicability to the Public Service of Canada.

*Based on Guy Dixon, "Today's leader needs EQ as much as IQ," *Report on Business*, May 13, 2014, B12; "About EQ," EQ Web site, retrieved April 20, 2011, from http://www.eqedge.com/AboutTheBook.aspx; Steven J. Stein & Howard E. Book, *EQ Edge: Emotional Intelligence and Your Success* (Mississauga: John Wiley & Sons Canada, 2006); Yvonne Stys & Shelley L. Brown, "A review of the emotional intelligence literature and implications for corrections," Research Branch, Correctional Service of Canada, March 2004, retrieved April 20, 2011, from http://www.csc-scc.gc.ca/text/rsrch/reports/r150/r150_e.pdf; Anne Fisher, "Success secret: A high emotional IQ," *Fortune*, October 26, 1998, 293–294.

For proposals and reports recommending action, see ⏩Chapters 10 and 11; for oral presentations, see ⏩Chapter 12; for employment communications, see ⏩Chapter 13.

All persuasive messages have several purposes:

Primary purposes:

- To motivate the reader to read the message
- To have the reader act
- To provide enough information so that the reader knows exactly what to do
- To overcome any objections that might prevent or delay action

Secondary purposes:

- To build a good image of the writer
- To enhance the reputation of the writer's organization
- To cement a good relationship between the writer and reader
- To reduce or eliminate future correspondence on the same subject (or to make readers more likely to respond positively next time)

LO1

ANALYZING A PERSUASIVE SITUATION

Choose a persuasive strategy based on your answers to four questions:

- What do you want people to do?
- What objections, if any, will the audience have?
- How strong is your case?
- What kind of persuasion is best for the organization and the culture?

1. What Do You Want People to Do?

Identify the specific action you want and the person who has the power to do it. If your goal requires several steps, specify what you want your audience to do *now*. For instance, your immediate goal may be to have people come to a meeting or let you make a presentation, even though your long-term goal is a major sale or a change in policy.

2. What Objections, If Any, Will the Audience Have?

If you're asking for something that requires little time, money, or physical effort and for an action that's part of the person's regular duties, the audience is likely to have few objections. For example, when you order a product, the firm is happy to supply it.

Often, however, you'll encounter some resistance. People may be busy and may have other uses for their time and money. To be persuasive, you need to show your audience that your proposal meets their needs; you need to overcome any objections.

People are likely to be most aware of and willing to share objective concerns such as time and money. They will be less willing to tell you that their real objection is emotional. Readers have a **vested interest** in something if they benefit directly from keeping things as they are. People who are in power have a vested interest in retaining the system that gives them their power.

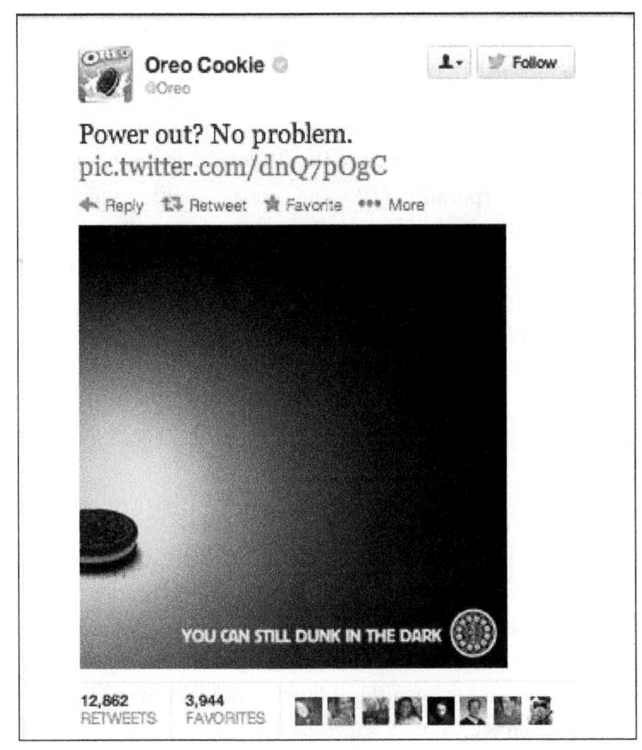

A well-planned Oreo social media strategy was ready when the lights went out at the 2012 Super Bowl.

Both individuals and organizations have self-images. It's easier for readers to say yes when you ask for something that is consistent with that self-image. For example, Aramis persuaded men to buy its over-the-counter skin peel, Lift Off, by linking it to shaving: men who exfoliated with the product could reduce their shaving time by one-third.[1]

When Old Spice launched its YouTube viral video campaign featuring former NFL footballer Isaiah Mustafa, or "The Man That Your Man Could Smell Like," the video struck a chord. Sales jumped 55% in three months (70% in the last four weeks). The responses segment of the campaign was a three-day initiative collecting and answering fan responses on social media and attracting 35.7 million views—and imitators and parodies around the world.[2] Humour added to the urge to share the clip with others.

Humour came to the rescue when the lights went out at the 2012 Super Bowl. Getting in on the online conversation was the Oreo social media team, well prepared with its timely tweet: "Power out? No problem. You can still dunk in the dark."[3] But Motrin discovered how risky humour can be when its online ad claiming mothers looked "more official" wearing baby slings backfired. Mothers felt belittled and let the company know.[4]

3. How Strong Is Your Case?

The strength of your case is based on three aspects of persuasion: argument, credibility, and emotional appeal.

Argument refers to the reasons or logic you offer. Sometimes you may be able to prove conclusively that your solution is best. Sometimes your reasons may not be as strong, the benefits may not be as certain, and obstacles may be difficult or impossible to overcome. For example, suppose that you wanted to persuade your organization to offer a tuition reimbursement plan for employees. You'd have a strong argument if you could show that tuition reimbursement would improve the performance of marginal workers or that reimbursement would be an attractive recruiting tool in a tight job market. However, if dozens of fully qualified workers apply for every opening, your argument would be weaker. The program might be nice for workers, but you'd have a hard job proving that it would help the company.

You can strengthen your argument and your credibility by accurately documenting sources in building your case. See ⏩ Chapter 10.

Credibility is the audience's response to you as the source of the message. Credibility in the workplace has three sources: knowledge, image, and relationships.[5] Citing experts can make your argument more credible. In some organizations, workers build credibility by getting assigned to high-profile teams. You build credibility by your track record. The more reliable you've been in the past, the more likely people are to trust you now.

Building a relationship with someone—even if the relationship is based on an outside interest, like sports or children—makes it easier for that person to see you as an individual and to trust you.

When you don't yet have the credibility that comes from being an expert or being powerful, build credibility by the language and strategy you use:

- **Be factual.** Don't exaggerate. Use concrete language and reliable statistics.
- **Be specific.** If you say "X is better," show in detail *how* it is better. Show the reader exactly where the savings or other benefits come from.
- **Be reliable.** If you suspect that a project will take longer to complete, cost more money, or be less effective than you originally thought, tell your audience *immediately*. Negotiate a new schedule that you can meet.

Emotional appeal means making the reader *want* to do what you ask. People don't make decisions—even business decisions—based on logic alone. Consumers, for instance, don't make purchasing decisions on logical grounds. They care about relationships with the products and services, according to marketer Marie Germain. The Four Ps of marketing—product, place, price, and promotion—are simple "left-brain" models, she says. Conscious memory explains only about 5% of the reasons people buy. And they have a habit of focusing attention on the competition, so that everyone ends up emulating the competition or working too hard to be different. "It's better to be better than to be different," says Germain.

She is supported by the findings of Joe Calloway, author of *Becoming a Category of One,* who claims, "The place to differentiate is in that very personal sensory-emotional realm of what the customer feels." Consider Krispy Kreme's ability to sell fatty food because it frees us from those who would tell us what not to eat.[6]

Loblaw CEO Galen Weston draws on his own credibility and the logical and emotional appeals associated with supporting Canadian farmers by purchasing locally grown food.

Or consider McCain Foods' success after trying to persuade parents that their pizza product was as good as delivery and better than Kraft's Delissio. Although first to market in Canada, McCain's lost market share. Then the company targeted teens in a campaign that saw sales increase 25% in January 2005.[7]

A 2014 study presents evidence that early impressions on children by food marketing mascots and characters persist into adulthood. Biases created in children under 13 years of age by the emotional appeals of loveable characters survived well into adulthood in positive images of the product and its nutrition value.[8]

Faced with millennial mothers representing a 13% reduction in peanut butter purchasing in Canada, Kraft is "humanizing" its peanut butter brand to reach an audience that resists the push of marketing messages. Instead Kraft is relying on moms responding to an "emotional story" in which the teddy bears and not the product are "central."[9]

In tourism and hospitality industries trying to satisfy experienced and educated travellers eager to find new territory, Newfoundland and Labrador Tourism makes the most of its unique culture, unspoiled land, and rich natural environment in inviting tourists "to break away from the pack," "journey off the beaten path," and "learn the language."[10]

4. What Kind of Persuasion Is Best for the Organization and the Culture?

A strategy that works in one organization may not work somewhere else. James Suchan and Ron Dulek point out that Digital Equipment Corporation (DEC)'s corporate culture values no-holds-barred aggressiveness. "Even if opposition is expected, a subordinate should write a proposal in a forceful, direct manner."[11] In another organization with different cultural values, an employee who used a hard-sell strategy for a request antagonized the boss.[12]

LO2

USING YOUR ANALYSIS TO CHOOSE A PERSUASIVE STRATEGY

If your organization prefers a specific approach, use it. If your organization has no preference, or if you do not know your readers' preference, use the following guidelines to choose a strategy (see ◂◂ Chapter 7 for routine requests):

- Use the persuasive **direct request (good news) pattern** (Figure 9.1) when
  - You need responses only from people who will find it easy to do as you ask.
  - Busy readers may not read all the messages they receive.
- Use the indirect problem-solving (bad news) pattern (▸▸ Figure 9.3) when
  - The audience may resist doing as you ask.
  - You expect logic to be more important than emotion in the decision.
- Use the indirect **AIDA** (or AIRA) persuasive plan (▸▸ Figure 9.10) when you may have to overcome resistance (R). The AIDA model focuses on attracting attention (A), arousing interest (I) and desire (D) to elicit action (A). It is as relevant to persuasive as to sales messages (see ▸▸ "How to Organize a Sales or Fundraising Letter" later in this chapter).

WRITING PERSUASIVE DIRECT REQUESTS

When you expect quick agreement, save the reader's time by presenting the request directly (refer to Figure 9.1). One study found that executives were most likely to pay attention to messages that

- Were personalized
- Evoked an emotional response
- Came from a credible sender
- Were concise[13]

Figure 9.1 Pattern for a Persuasive Direct Request

1. **Consider asking immediately for the information or service you want.** Delay the request if it seems too abrupt or if you have several purposes in the message.
2. **Give readers all the information they will need to act on your request.** Number your questions or set them off with bullets so the reader can check that all have been answered.

   In a claim (where a product is under guarantee or a shipment was defective), explain what happened. Be sure to include date of purchase, model or invoice number, and so on.

   In more complicated direct requests, anticipate possible responses. Suppose you're asking for information about equipment meeting certain specifications. Explain which criteria are most important so that the reader can recommend an alternative if no single product meets all your needs. You may also mention your price constraints and ask whether the item is in stock or must be special-ordered.
3. **Ask for the action you want.** Do you want a cheque? A replacement? A catalogue? Answers to your questions? If you need an answer by a certain time, say so. If possible, show the reader why the time limit is necessary.

The direct request does not contain reader benefits and does not need to overcome objections: it simply asks for what is needed (see Figure 9.2).

Direct requests should be direct. Don't make the reader guess what you want.

Indirect request:	Is there a newer version of the 2010 *Accounting Reference Manual?*
Direct request:	If there is a newer version of the 2010 *Accounting Reference Manual,* please send it to me.

In a direct request, put the request, the topic, or a question in the subject line (Request for Updated Software).

In some direct requests, your combination of purposes may suggest a different pattern of organization. For example, in an e-mail asking an employer to reimburse you for expenses after a job interview, you'd want to thank your hosts for their hospitality and cement the good impression you made at the interview. To do that, you'd spend the first several paragraphs talking about the trip and the interview. Only in the last third of the letter would you put your request for reimbursement.

WRITING PERSUASIVE PROBLEM-SOLVING MESSAGES

Use an **indirect approach** and the **problem-solving pattern** of organization when you expect resistance from your reader but can show that doing what you want will solve a problem you and your reader share. The pattern in Figure 9.3 allows you to disarm opposition by showing reasons in favour of your position before you give your readers a chance to say no.

Figure 9.4 uses the problem-solving pattern of organization. Reader benefits can be brief in this kind of message since the biggest benefit comes from solving the problem.

When you have a reluctant reader, putting the request in the subject line just gets a quick no before you've had a chance to give all your arguments. One option is to use a **directed subject line** that makes your purpose and stance on the issue clear.[14] In the following examples, the first is the most neutral. The remaining two increasingly reveal the writer's preference.

International Persuading across Cultures*

Even if its combination of cheap and chic is seductive, IKEA does not rest on its laurels. It invests in Canadian-specific photography for ads, well aware that Scandinavian interiors look very different from Canadian ones. Plain white paperbacks on European shelves don't resonate in Canada. Nor do the native light woods that help maximize space in Europe work in Canada, where larger homes and dark woods are in order.

Tim Hortons is learning about the cross-cultural challenge of its persuasive appeals in connecting with new markets. When it ran a TV spot during the Vancouver 2010 Olympics opening ceremonies featuring an African immigrant being welcomed to Canada with a Tim Hortons coffee and winter clothes, it was criticized for exploiting the immigrant experience. Communications professor Robert Seiler felt the spot risked misrepresenting "our treatment of immigrants" and the obstacles they face in becoming part of Canadian society.

Tim Hortons' Canadian identity resonates for its exoticism in Taiwan, but not in the United States, where it needs to rebuild the brand for an American market.

Loblaw is counting on the international expertise of its president Vicente Trius to help target new Canadians and become "the No. 1 ethnic player in Canada." Visible minorities are predicted to be the source of 70% of growth within 10 years.

Based on *Marina Strauss, "How does IKEA seduce us?" *Report on Business,* June 2010, 56–61; Simon Houpt, "Tim Hortons: At the intersection of commerce and culture," *The Globe and Mail,* March 5, 2010, B5; Marina Strauss, "Loblaw taps leader with global flavor," *The Globe and Mail,* January 25, 2011, B5.

Figure 9.2 A Persuasive Direct Request

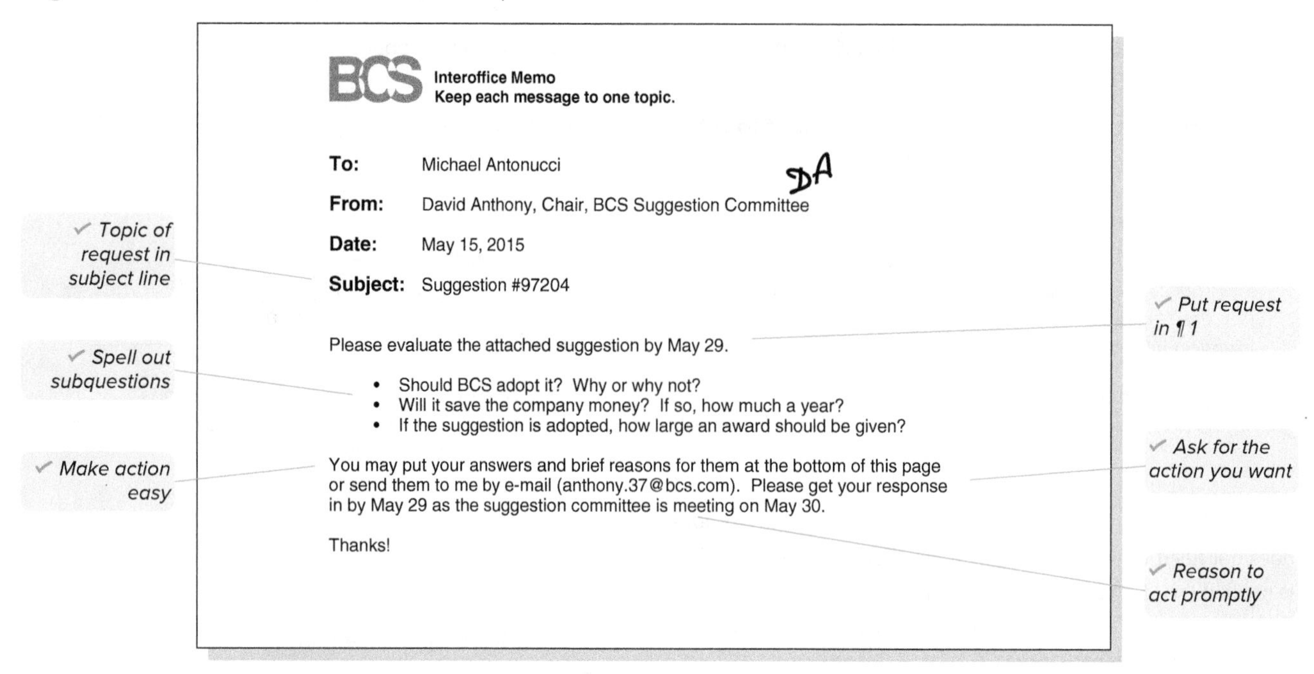
BCS Interoffice Memo
Keep each message to one topic.

To: Michael Antonucci

From: David Anthony, Chair, BCS Suggestion Committee DA

Date: May 15, 2015

Subject: Suggestion #97204

Please evaluate the attached suggestion by May 29.

- Should BCS adopt it? Why or why not?
- Will it save the company money? If so, how much a year?
- If the suggestion is adopted, how large an award should be given?

You may put your answers and brief reasons for them at the bottom of this page or send them to me by e-mail (anthony.37@bcs.com). Please get your response in by May 29 as the suggestion committee is meeting on May 30.

Thanks!

Subject: A Proposal to Change the Formula for Calculating Retirees' Benefits

Subject: Why Cassano's Should Close Its Westside Store

Subject: Arguments for Expanding the Wolfville Plant

Catching Attention and Developing a Common Ground

In order to persuade, you need first to catch attention by beginning with a startling fact or statistic, engaging question, thoughtful compliment, striking headline, or quotation. For example, instead of making a general claim about the costs of poverty, mention that "every single day 30,000 children are dying as a result of extreme poverty."

A common ground avoids the me-against-you of some persuasive situations and suggests that both you and your audience have a mutual interest in solving the problems you face.

The best common grounds are specific. Often a negative—a problem the reader will want to solve—makes a good common ground.

✗ WEAK COMMON GROUND:

This program has had some difficulty finding enough individuals to volunteer their services for the children. As a result, we are sometimes unable to provide the one-on-one mentoring that is our goal.

✓ IMPROVED COMMON GROUND:

On five Sundays in the last three months, we've had too few volunteers to provide one-on-one mentoring. Last Sunday, we had just two students to take eight children to the Museum of Science and Industry.

Figure 9.3 Indirect Persuasive Problem-Solving Message

1. **Catch the reader's interest by mentioning a common ground.** Show that your message will be interesting or beneficial. You may want to catch attention with a negative (which you will show can be solved).
2. **Define the problem you share (which your request will solve).** Present the problem objectively: don't assign blame or mention personalities. Be specific about the cost in money, time, and lost goodwill. Once you have convinced readers that something has to be done, you can convince them that your solution is the best one.
3. **Explain the solution to the problem.** If you know that the reader will favour another solution, start with that solution and show why it won't work before you present your solution. Present your solution without using the words I or my. Don't let personalities enter the picture.
4. **Show that positives outweigh any negative elements (cost, time, etc.).**
5. **Summarize any additional benefits of the solution.** The main benefit—solving the problem—can be presented briefly since you described the problem in detail. Mention any additional benefits.
6. **Request and motivate the action you want.** Often your reader will authorize or approve something; other people will implement the action. Give your reader a reason to act promptly, perhaps offering a new reader benefit. ("By buying now, we can avoid the next quarter's price hikes.")

Figure 9.4 A Problem-Solving Persuasive Message

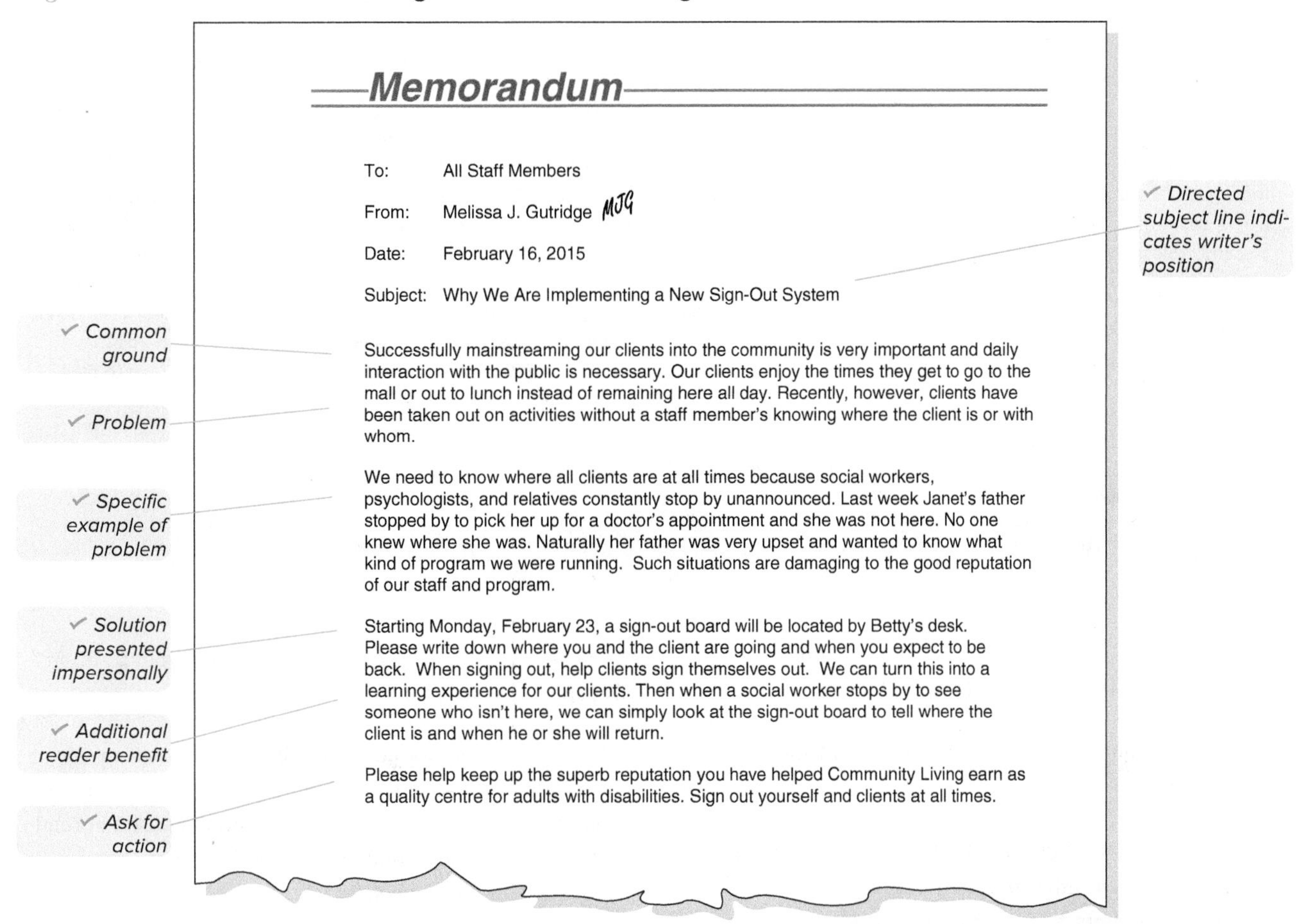
Memorandum

To: All Staff Members

From: Melissa J. Gutridge MJG

Date: February 16, 2015

Subject: Why We Are Implementing a New Sign-Out System

Successfully mainstreaming our clients into the community is very important and daily interaction with the public is necessary. Our clients enjoy the times they get to go to the mall or out to lunch instead of remaining here all day. Recently, however, clients have been taken out on activities without a staff member's knowing where the client is or with whom.

We need to know where all clients are at all times because social workers, psychologists, and relatives constantly stop by unannounced. Last week Janet's father stopped by to pick her up for a doctor's appointment and she was not here. No one knew where she was. Naturally her father was very upset and wanted to know what kind of program we were running. Such situations are damaging to the good reputation of our staff and program.

Starting Monday, February 23, a sign-out board will be located by Betty's desk. Please write down where you and the client are going and when you expect to be back. When signing out, help clients sign themselves out. We can turn this into a learning experience for our clients. Then when a social worker stops by to see someone who isn't here, we can simply look at the sign-out board to tell where the client is and when he or she will return.

Please help keep up the superb reputation you have helped Community Living earn as a quality centre for adults with disabilities. Sign out yourself and clients at all times.

Defining the Problem

Include a problem description that is concise, concrete, and carefully targeted to your audience. In recommending a new wellness program, the following might arouse management interest: With job stress creating 60% of absenteeism, reducing productivity, and sucking the profits out of the business, a wellness program is an investment that returns $3 in cost benefits for every $1 spent.

Explaining the Solution to the Problem

Avoiding judgmental language or personal references (*I, me*), present your solution in factual, reliable, impersonal terms. For example, supply figures to support your claim about profits being sucked out of the business: According to the Conference Board of Canada, absenteeism costs in Canada are estimated at $16.6 billion annually.[15] Vancouver Airport Authority experienced a drop in absenteeism among participants in its Workplace Wellness Program from 4.07% to 2.56%.[16] When employee retention is becoming an issue, survey results on employee satisfaction would add to the logical appeals.

If you know that your readers will hear other points of view, or if your audience's initial position is negative, you have to deal with their objections to persuade them. The stronger the objection is, the earlier in your message you should deal with it.

The best way to deal with an objection is to eliminate it. One dealer keeps frequently ordered items in stock to eliminate the objection "I don't want to wait." In 2008 Toyota added to its strategies to entice young people to buy cars: it took the cars to the shoppers. It set up its showrooms in the walkways of a shopping centre it owns and operates in Yokohama.[17]

If an objection is false and is based on misinformation, give the response to the objection without naming the objection (as in a "question/answer" format in a brochure). For example, health economist Robert Evans of the University of British Columbia debunks the myth that aging boomers are going to cause a health care crisis—a myth repeated by the media as well as policymakers and pundits. Instead of responding directly to the objection, Professor Evans focuses attention on the inflationary effects of increased drug costs and health care provider salaries, on the increasing good health of boomers and the reduced time "between decline and death," and on more aggressive medical interventions for all groups. Some even argue that the focus on boomer costs is a "red herring" designed to cover ideological interests in privatizing health care.[18]

Showing That Positives Outweigh Negatives

If real objections remain, try one or more of the following strategies to counter objections:

1. Specify how much time and/or money is required—it may not be as much as the reader fears.

On the Job The Art and Science of Persuasion*

Published in the UK as *Flipnosis*, the book *Split-Second Persuasion* disarms its readers with case studies of the art and science of persuasion. Although some have more talent than others, author Kevin Dutton argues, "it's largely trial and error." From babies to advertisers and airline stewards to health care workers, con men, police, sales people, and professional negotiators, the best follow the SPICE formula:

- **S**implicity
- **P**erceived self-interest
- **I**ncongruity (often disarming humour)
- **C**onfidence
- **E**mpathy

Knowing that formula can help protect against its seductive power, although Dutton warns about "the brain's hard-wired preference to be part of a group" as a survival mechanism.

Professor Dante Pirouz of the Richard Ivey School of Business studies the brain's response to advertising encouraging people to do risky things. Cigarette ads stimulated cravings not only among smokers but also among non-smokers. And adults are as susceptible as children. Her findings are relevant to alcohol industry defences such as the self-regulatory Advertising Standards Canada's that they persuade people to change brands and not to take up risky behaviours.

*Based on Kevin Dutton, *Split-Second Persuasion: The Ancient Art and New Science of Changing Minds* (Doubleday Canada, 2010); Simon Houpt, "A master of persuasion reveals his secrets," *The Globe and Mail*, December 3, 2010, B9; Susan Krashinsky, "One more reason for those constant cravings," *The Globe and Mail*, April 8, 2011, B6; Jordan Timm, "The art of 'Flipnosis': changing people's minds on the sly," *Canadian Business*, Winter 2010/2011, 92–93.

> Distributing flyers to each house or apartment in your neighbourhood will probably take two afternoons.

2. Put the time and/or money in the context of the benefits they bring.

> The additional $152,500 will (1) allow the Open Shelter to remain open 24 rather than 16 hours a day, (2) pay for three social workers to help men find work and homes, and (3) keep the neighbourhood bank open, so that men don't have to cash cheques in bars and so that they can save up the $800 they need to rent an apartment.

3. Show that money spent now will save money in the long run.

> By buying a $100 safety product, you can avoid $500 in Occupational Health and Safety fines.

4. Show that doing as you ask will benefit some group or cause the reader supports, even though the action may not help the reader directly. This is the strategy used in fundraising letters, discussed in detail in ▸▸ "How to Organize a Sales or Fundraising Letter" later in this chapter.

> By being a Big Brother or a Big Sister, you'll give a child the adult attention he or she needs to become a well-adjusted, productive adult.

5. Show the reader that the sacrifice is necessary to achieve a more important goal to which he or she is committed.

Ethics and Legal In the Public Good?*

Concerned both to defend the integrity of the PR profession and to ensure climate change debates are based on credible evidence, James Hoggan, president of Vancouver-based James Hoggan and Associates, launched his DeSmogBlog.com. Its mission is to "clear the PR pollution that is clouding the science on climate change." Hoggan is targeting "a well-funded and highly organized public relations campaign" that is "poisoning" the debate.

A Canadian survey Hoggan commissioned showed that 72% of 1,000+ respondents understand that PR professionals help companies report their environmental performance; 81% think they misrepresent performance.

Similarly, scientists with the Professional Institute of the Public Service of Canada responded to government communications policies constraining their access to media by launching in October 2010 PublicScience.ca to open up "the world of science for the public good."

Ninety percent of 4,000 federal scientists surveyed in 2013 "feel that they are not allowed to speak to the media."

Scientists are also raising concerns about politics rather than peer review driving a shift in funding strategy of the National Research Council, from "basic research" to "programmes designed to attract industry partners and generate revenue."

*Based on Bob Holmes, "How Canada's green credentials fell apart," *New Scientist*, October 22, 2013, retrieved from http://www.newscientist.com/article/mg21328585.900-how-canadas-green-credentials-fell-apart.html#.U4z6bm39xEM; Chris Freimond, "Global warming reaches the boardroom," *Communication World*, November–December 2007, 22–24; Professional Institute of the Public Service of Canada, homepage, retrieved April 21, 2011, from http://www.publicscience.ca/portal/page/portal/science; Hannah Hoag, "Canadian research shift makes waves," posted online April 18, 2011, *Nature* 472 (2011), 269; Sheila Pratt, "Funding shift puts scientists on edge," *Edmonton Journal*, December 5, 2010.

These changes will mean more work for all of us. But we've got to cut our costs 25% to keep the plant open and to keep our jobs.

6. Show that the advantages as a group outnumber or outweigh the disadvantages as a group.

No location is perfect. But the Burnaby location gives us the most advantages and the fewest disadvantages.

7. Turn a disadvantage into an opportunity.

With the hiring freeze, every department will need more lead time to complete its own work. By hiring another person, the planning department could provide that lead time.

The draft in Figure 9.5 makes the mistake of attacking readers in a negative message. Making the memo less accusatory would help, but the message doesn't need to be negative at all. Instead, the writer can take the information in paragraph 3 and use it as the attention-getter and common ground for a problem-solving persuasive message. Figure 9.6 shows a possible revision, changing the language and tone.

Sense impressions—what the reader sees, hears, smells, tastes, feels—evoke a strong emotional response. **Psychological description** (Figure 9.7) means creating a scenario rich with sense impressions so readers can picture themselves using your product or service and enjoying its benefits. You can also use psychological description to describe the problem your product will solve. Psychological description works best early in the message to catch readers' attention. Häagen-Dazs has used psychological description so effectively that it has grown from its Bronx beginnings to include franchises around the world (Figure 9.8).

Figure 9.5 Ineffective Persuasive Memo

BIERNAT LABORATORIES

Inter-office Memorandum

To: Todd Neumann

From: Heather Johnson HJ

Date: May 24, 2015

Subject: Problems with Instrument Lab Results

The Instrument Technicians Lab again seems to believe that if a result is printed out, it is the correct answer. It doesn't seem to matter that the chromatogram is terribly noisy, the calibration standards are over a month old, or the area of the internal standards is about half what it should be. I'm aware that the conditions in the lab have contributed to the discouraged atmosphere, but I don't feel it's an excuse for the shape of the lab and the equipment. The G.C. columns are in bad shape just from abuse. I've lost count of the number of 10 ml syringes the lab has buried (at least $20 each) mainly because they were not properly rinsed.

During the last six months, I have either reminded the technician of such things or written reminders in the log book. Isn't it time for our responsible lab technicians to have fresh standards made up? Granted, we've had many false starts, but I am still uncomfortable that the technicians will be ready when the time comes.

I don't feel that I should have to go over the chromatograms, printouts, and G.C. book every time we submit samples for analysis. However, just two weeks ago I sent out results without doing this and immediately received a call that the results were impossible—and they were because unacceptable KF was used, the result of an old calibration standard.

One other item bothers me. I don't know how to get the technicians interested in the way the Autolab integrates each peak when they don't seem to look at anything other than the answer.

I think it's time they either take hold and run the lab themselves or they be treated as if they were children. I also would like to see them read the Autolab I Instruction Manual and take the tape courses on the gas chromatograph and the Autolab I.

The morale of the lab must be raised and a step in that direction is to give them the responsibility and expect them to accept it. These people are being called technicians but they are actually classed as chemists and should be assuming more initative and responsibility.

× Accusatory tone makes this writer look unprofessional

× Makes reader feel incompetent

× Negative

× Lacks you-attitude (YA)

× Accusatory tone

× Attacks reader

× Lacks YA

× Insults and attacks reader

× Lacks YA

× Problem presented as reader's fault, not a common problem that both share

× Lacks YA

× Whole ¶ lacks YA

× Attacks and insults reader

× Attacks reader

Figure 9.6 Effective Persuasive Memo

BIERNAT LABORATORIES

Inter-office Memorandum

To: Todd Neumann

From: Heather Johnson HJ

Date: May 24, 2015

Subject: Cutting Requests for Rework

Two weeks ago a customer called to tell me that the results we'd sent out were impossible. I checked, and the results were wrong because we'd used an old calibration standard.

Redoing work for outside customers and for in-house projects doubles our workload. Yet because people don't trust our results, we're getting an increasing number of requests for rework.

Part of the problem is that we've had so many false starts. Customers and especially in-house engineers say they'll need a run but then don't have the materials for another day or even a week. Paul Liu has told me that these schedule glitches are inevitable. We'll just have to prepare fresh calibration standards every time a run is scheduled—and again when the run is ready.

You've told me that the equipment in the lab is unreliable. The Capital Expenditures Request includes a line item for G.C. columns and a new gas chromatograph. We'll be able to be more persuasive at the Board meeting if we can show that we're taking good care of the equipment. Please remind your staff to

- Rinse the 10-ml syringes every day.
- Check the glass insert in the B column every week.
- Check the filter on the Autolab I every week.

Do workers find the Autolab I instruction manual and the tape courses on the gas chromatograph and the Autolab I helpful? If not, perhaps we should ask the manufacturer to redo them and, in the meantime, to offer a short course for our workers. How do you think the technical expertise of our staff can be increased?

By getting our results right the first time, we can eliminate the rework and give both customers and in-house clients better service.

✓ Straightforward problem-solving approach is the mark of a professional manager

✓ Positive subject line

✓ Common ground
✓ Problem writer and reader share

✓ Writer shows understanding of reader's problems

✓ List emphasizes what reader needs to do

✓ Treats reader as an equal who can help solve the problem

✓ Links desired action to benefit and picture of the problem being solved

Summarizing Benefits and Building Emotional Appeal

Stories and psychological description are effective ways of building emotional appeal and underlining benefits. Emotional appeal works best when people want to be persuaded.

Even when you need to provide statistics or numbers to convince the careful reader that your anecdote is a representative example, telling a story first makes your message more persuasive. Stories alone are more effective than a combination of stories and statistics; the combination was more effective than statistics alone. Research suggests that stories are more persuasive because people remember them.[19]

Requesting and Motivating Action

The longer people delay, the less likely they are to carry through with the action they had decided to take. In addition, you want a fast response so you can go ahead with your own plans.

Request action by a specific date. Try to give people at least a week or two: they have other things to do besides respond to your requests. Set deadlines in the middle of the month, if possible. If you say, "Please return this by March 1," people will think, "I don't need to do this till March." Ask for the response by February 28 instead. If you can use a response even after the deadline, say so. Otherwise, people who can't make the deadline may not respond.

Show why you need a quick response:

- **Show that the time limit is real.** Perhaps you need information to use it in a report with an early due date.
- **Show that acting now will save time or money.** If business is slow and your industry isn't doing well, then your company needs to act now (to economize, to better serve customers) in order to be competitive. If business is booming

Figure 9.7 Using Psychological Description to Develop Reader Benefits

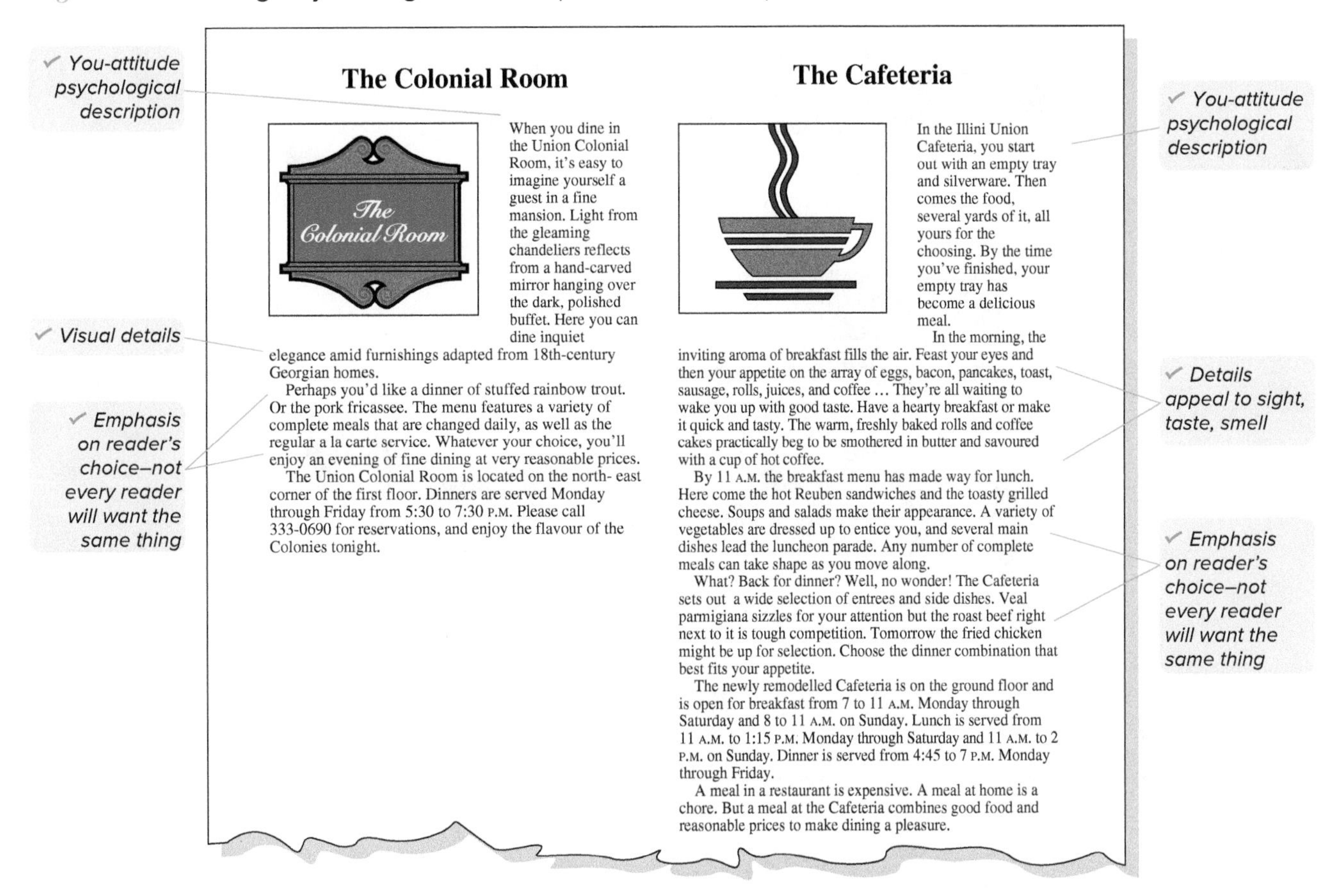

The Colonial Room

When you dine in the Union Colonial Room, it's easy to imagine yourself a guest in a fine mansion. Light from the gleaming chandeliers reflects from a hand-carved mirror hanging over the dark, polished buffet. Here you can dine inquiet elegance amid furnishings adapted from 18th-century Georgian homes.

Perhaps you'd like a dinner of stuffed rainbow trout. Or the pork fricassee. The menu features a variety of complete meals that are changed daily, as well as the regular a la carte service. Whatever your choice, you'll enjoy an evening of fine dining at very reasonable prices.

The Union Colonial Room is located on the north- east corner of the first floor. Dinners are served Monday through Friday from 5:30 to 7:30 P.M. Please call 333-0690 for reservations, and enjoy the flavour of the Colonies tonight.

The Cafeteria

In the Illini Union Cafeteria, you start out with an empty tray and silverware. Then comes the food, several yards of it, all yours for the choosing. By the time you've finished, your empty tray has become a delicious meal.

In the morning, the inviting aroma of breakfast fills the air. Feast your eyes and then your appetite on the array of eggs, bacon, pancakes, toast, sausage, rolls, juices, and coffee ... They're all waiting to wake you up with good taste. Have a hearty breakfast or make it quick and tasty. The warm, freshly baked rolls and coffee cakes practically beg to be smothered in butter and savoured with a cup of hot coffee.

By 11 A.M. the breakfast menu has made way for lunch. Here come the hot Reuben sandwiches and the toasty grilled cheese. Soups and salads make their appearance. A variety of vegetables are dressed up to entice you, and several main dishes lead the luncheon parade. Any number of complete meals can take shape as you move along.

What? Back for dinner? Well, no wonder! The Cafeteria sets out a wide selection of entrees and side dishes. Veal parmigiana sizzles for your attention but the roast beef right next to it is tough competition. Tomorrow the fried chicken might be up for selection. Choose the dinner combination that best fits your appetite.

The newly remodelled Cafeteria is on the ground floor and is open for breakfast from 7 to 11 A.M. Monday through Saturday and 8 to 11 A.M. on Sunday. Lunch is served from 11 A.M. to 1:15 P.M. Monday through Saturday and 11 A.M. to 2 P.M. on Sunday. Dinner is served from 4:45 to 7 P.M. Monday through Friday.

A meal in a restaurant is expensive. A meal at home is a chore. But a meal at the Cafeteria combines good food and reasonable prices to make dining a pleasure.

and everyone is making a profit, then your company needs to act now to get its fair share of the available profits.

- **Show the cost of delaying action.** Will labour or material costs be higher in the future? Will delay mean more money spent on repairing something that will still need to be replaced?

CHECKING TONE IN PERSUASIVE MESSAGES

The best phrasing depends on your relationship to the reader. When you ask for action from people who report directly to you, orders ("Get me the Ervin file") and questions ("Do we have the third-quarter numbers yet?") will work. When you need action from co-workers, superiors, or people outside the organization, you need to be both more forceful and more polite.

Avoiding messages that sound parental or preachy is often a matter of tone. Saying "Please" is essential, especially to people on your level or outside the organization. Tone will also be better when you give reasons for your request or reasons to act promptly.

× Parental: Everyone is expected to comply with these regulations. I'm sure you can see that they are common-sense rules needed for our business.

✓ Better: Even on casual days, visitors expect us to be professional. So leave the gym clothes at home!

Writing to superiors is trickier. You may want to tone down your request by using subjunctive verbs and explicit disclaimers that show you aren't taking a *yes* for granted.

× Arrogant: Based on this evidence, I expect you to give me a new computer.

✓ Better: If department funds permit, I would like a new computer.

It can be particularly tricky to control tone in e-mail and text messages, which tend to sound less friendly than paper documents or conversations. For important requests, compose your message offline and revise it carefully before you send it.

The subject line of a persuasive e-mail message should make it clear that you're asking for something. To be sure that the reader will read the message, be specific.

Subject: Move Meeting to Tuesday?

Subject: Provide Story for Newsletter?

Subject: Want You for United Way Campaign

Major requests that require changes in values, culture, or lifestyles should not be made in e-mail or text messages.

COLLECTION LETTERS

Collection letters are among the most common persuasive messages.

Figure 9.8 Häagen-Dazs Knows the Power of Psychological Description

HÄAGEN-DAZS® is a registered trademark used under licence in Canada by Nestlé Canada Inc.

Most businesses find that phoning rather than writing results in faster payment. But you will need to write letters when leaving messages doesn't work (see ◀◀ Figure 7.1 in Chapter 7).

Collection letters ask customers to pay (as they have already agreed to do) for the goods and services they have already received. Good credit departments send a series of letters a week apart.

Early letters are gentle, assuming that the reader intends to pay but has forgotten or has met with temporary reverses. Early letters can be obvious form letters or even just a second copy of the bill with the words "Second Notice" or "Past Due" stamped on it.

A student who had not yet been reimbursed by a company for a visit to the company's office put the second request in the P.S. of a letter refusing a job offer:

> P.S. The cheque to cover my expenses when I visited your office in March hasn't come yet. Could you check to see whether you can find a record of it? The amount was $490 (airfare $290, hotel room $185, taxi $15).

If one or two early letters don't result in payment, call the customer to ask if your company has created a problem. It's possible that the invoice arrived before the product and was filed and forgotten. If any of these situations apply, you'll build goodwill by solving the problem rather than arrogantly asking for payment.[20]

Middle letters are more assertive in asking for payment. Figure 9.9 gives an example of a middle letter. This form letter is merged with database information about the customer's name, the amount due, and the magazine the customer is receiving. Other middle letters offer to negotiate a schedule for repayment if the reader is not able to pay the whole bill immediately, may remind the reader of the importance of a good credit rating, educate the reader about credit, and explain why the creditor must have prompt payment.

Late letters threaten legal action if the bill is not paid. At this point, you must assume that only serious consequences will change the behaviour. Short of legal action, you may threaten turning the account over to a collection agency.

Still, expressions of reluctance are in order—combined with a promise to act if the customer does not pay the amount due within a specified time limit (say, 10 days).

Many small businesses find that establishing personal relationships with customers is the best way to speed payment. The most serious collection letters typically require legal review before being sent.

Technology Tips Migrating to Social Media*

Although television is still the number one medium for advertising, the Web and mobile devices were predicted to overtake print as number two in 2012. In fact, Internet advertising is predicted to produce 37% of industry growth.

Rhett McLaughlin and Link Neal share their community-building keys to successful viral videos:

- Take time to build your audience through Facebook and Twitter
- Find the tribal leaders or influencers
- Interact with your fans
- Embrace the medium
- Be subtle about the plug
- Be flexible

Corning's "A Day Made of Glass" drew more than 14 million YouTube views even though, at six minutes, it had neither humour nor celebrities. Wanting to let people know about its core business—LCD glass and not cookware (divested in 1998)—it commissioned a video to showcase Corning's problem-solving talents and ended up engaging the "Technorati/Gizmodo crowd."

Mobile devices are predicted to generate $119 billion in spending by 2015 (from $1.2 billion in 2009). Google's Shopper app adds to Facebook Deals and Amazon's Price Check, Scandit, and Shopsavvy and other apps to locate outlets and malls and even to pay using cell phones—a technology already available in Japan and Korea.

*Based on Simon Houpt, "Web ads may surpass print, ending an era," *The Globe and Mail*, December 7, 2010, B8; Russell Working, "6 ways to make your video campaign a success," retrieved February 8, 2011, from http://www.ragan.com/Main/Articles/42686.aspx?format52; Matt Wilson, "Corning 'breaks all the rules' of viral videos, draws millions of views," retrieved April 11, 2011, from http://www.ragan.com/Main/Articles/42835.aspx; Simon Houpt, "There could be a deal right where you are standing," *The Globe and Mail*, February 1, 2011, B9; Jeff Beer, "The future is mobile," *Canadian Business*, March 14, 2011, 40.

SALES AND FUNDRAISING LETTERS

Douglas & McIntyre Publishing Group, Chrysler Canada, and FedEx are only a few of the companies that use letters to persuade customers to buy their products, visit their showrooms, or use their services. Rethink Breast Cancer, Canadian Cancer Society, McGill University, and George Brown College are only a few of the organizations that use letters—as well as proposals (⏩ Chapter 11) and grant applications—to persuade people to donate time or money to their causes.

Sales and fundraising letters are a special category of persuasive messages known as **direct mail** because they ask for an order, inquiry, or contribution directly from the reader. In 2002, direct mail accounted for $1.51 billion or 13.8% of

Figure 9.9 A Middle Collection Letter

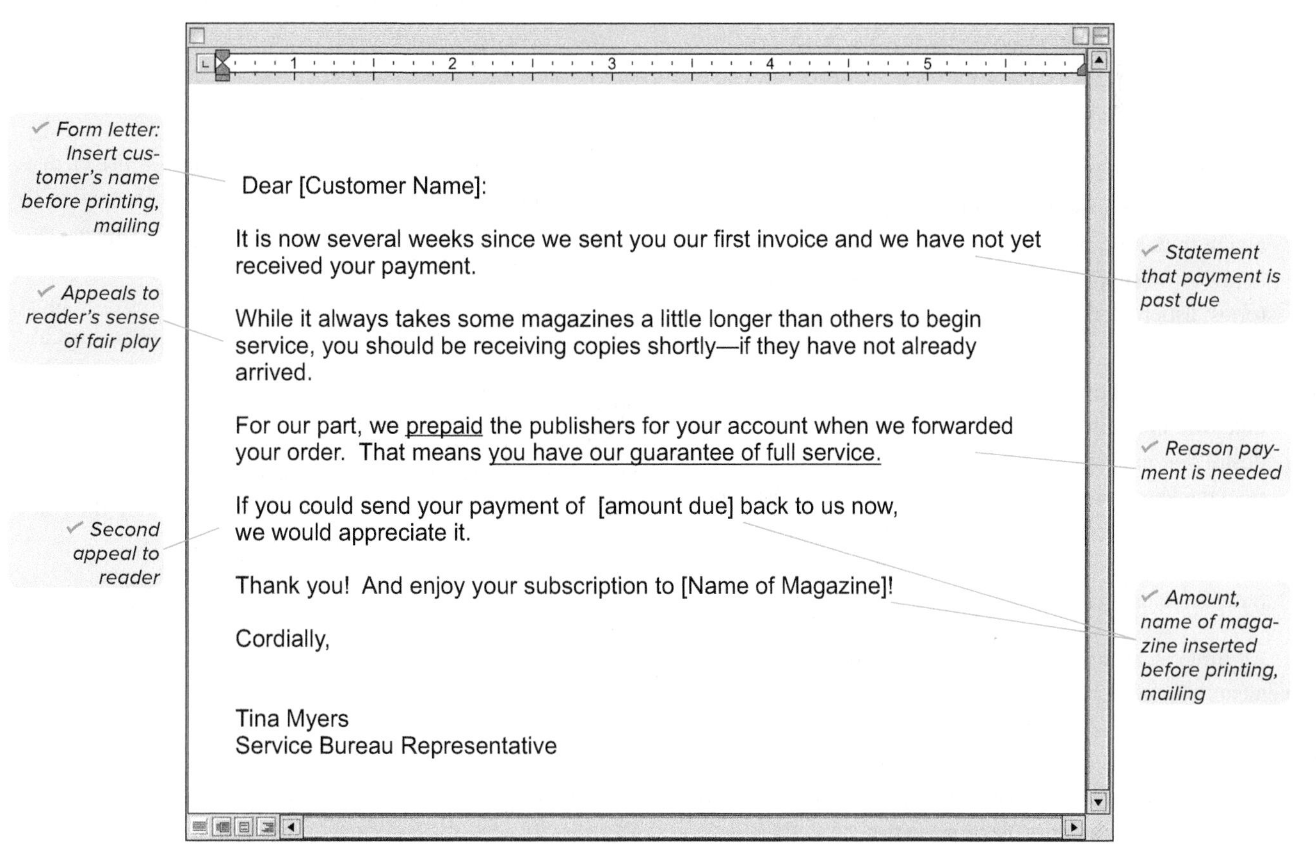

Dear [Customer Name]:

It is now several weeks since we sent you our first invoice and we have not yet received your payment.

While it always takes some magazines a little longer than others to begin service, you should be receiving copies shortly—if they have not already arrived.

For our part, we prepaid the publishers for your account when we forwarded your order. That means you have our guarantee of full service.

If you could send your payment of [amount due] back to us now, we would appreciate it.

Thank you! And enjoy your subscription to [Name of Magazine]!

Cordially,

Tina Myers
Service Bureau Representative

Ethics and Legal Greening or Greenwashing?*

Distinguishing between those that are greening their companies and those that are greenwashing (or merely marketing a semblance of environmentally friendly action) can be challenging for consumers.

When ISL Engineering of Edmonton launched its sustainability program, it gave 25 "green-minded" staff 10% of each day to develop projects such as recycling, energy reduction, car-sharing, and waste diversion to the city's compost. According to CEO Rodney Peacock, aligning "with your employees' values, you get happy people who do great work."

Taking on big-brand detergents, Method co-founders Adam Lowry and Eric Ryan rely on "an army of advocates" or "People Against Dirty" to spread the word. By 2014 Tide was attracting 147K followers compared to Method's 17.7K. Instead of depicting cleaning as "drudgery," the company exudes energy and promotes products with phrases such as "floor love." Its mix of style and environmentalism appeals to those who want to be credited with doing the right thing.

Responding to U.S. efforts to boycott the oil sands, then Environment Minister Peter Kent's "ethical oil" marketing strategy promoted Canadian democracy's superiority to resource-rich but democracy-poor alternatives. "It is a regulated product. . . . The proceeds are used to better society," Kent claimed.

*Based on Jennifer Myers, "The greening of workplaces," *The Globe and Mail*, May 22, 2010, B15; Simon Houpt, "Taking on Big Soaps: There's Method in their madness," *The Globe and Mail*, January 8, 2010, B1–6; Steven Chase, "Peter Kent's plan to clean up the oil sands' dirty reputation," *The Globe and Mail*, January 7, 2011, A8–9.

yearly Canadian advertising. By 2009, Canada Post's average 334 pieces to 14.9 million addresses was down 13%.[21] After years of profits until 2011, Canada Post reported a $193 million operating loss in 2013; a Conference Board of Canada study predicts $1 billion annual shortfalls within ten years. Yet online shopping has added to parcel revenue (7.2% revenue increase in 2013) and charities and others remain significant direct mail senders.[22]

Good direct mail has three components: a good product, service, or cause; a good mailing list; and a good appeal. A **good product** appeals to a specific segment of people, can be mailed, and provides an adequate profit margin.

- A **good service or cause** fills an identifiable need.
- A **good mailing list** has accurate addresses and is a good match to the product. In-house lists of customers or members can be supplemented with prospects from city directories, lists rented from specialist companies, or exchange lists with similar organizations.
- A **good appeal** offers a believable description of benefits, links the benefits of the product or service to a need or desire that motivates the reader, makes the reader want to read the letter, and motivates the reader to act. The appeal is made up of the words in the letter, the pictures in the brochure or rack card, and all the parts of the package, from outer envelope to reply card.

All three elements are crucial. This section focuses on the elements of a good appeal: how to create a message that will motivate a reader to act, assuming that you already have a good product to sell or a worthy cause to raise funds for and that you already have a good list of people who might be interested in that product, cause, or organization.

Successful sales and fundraising messages depend on three steps:

- Understanding your product, service, or organization.
- Knowing your **target audience** (people likely to be interested in your product, service, or cause).
- Choosing a **central selling point** (a reader benefit that could motivate your readers and that can act as an umbrella under which all the other benefits can fit).

Writing an effective e-mail message rather than a letter has been estimated to cut costs to about one-fifth of a print mailing.[23]

Industry wisdom suggests that a **cold list**—a list of people with no prior connection to your group—will have a 2% response rate. Good timing, a good list, and a good appeal can double or even triple that percentage.

For people who open some of their mail, the three most important factors in deciding whether to open a specific envelope were timing, personalization, and an attractive appearance.[24]

Companies that want people to continue opening direct mail have to be careful that what they send is *not* junk. People today receive so many marketing messages that they are impatient when the messages seem irrelevant.

LO3

HOW TO ORGANIZE A SALES OR FUNDRAISING LETTER

Use the AIDA persuasive plan to organize your letter (see Figure 9.10).

Figure 9.10 AIDA Persuasive Plan

1. Gain **A**ttention: opening with a provocative headline, startling statements or facts, audience benefit, compliment, quotation, question, summary of problem/action, stories, or point of agreement.
2. Create **I**nterest: supporting argument in concrete and specific terms (facts, figures, examples, experts), underlining benefits, and appealing to fairness.
3. Build **D**esire while reducing **R**esistance: imagining and anticipating scenarios, underlining credibility, and citing testimonials and test results.
4. Motivate **A**ction: reinforcing benefits, asking for specific response, and giving deadlines linked to incentives.

Note that sales or fundraising letters omit date (a campaign may last months), inside address, and even salutation, although some open with Dear Reader, for instance. This strategy allows for maximum flexibility as organizations target their mailing lists.

Opener (Attention)

The opener of your letter gives you 30 to 60 seconds to motivate readers to read the rest of the letter.

A good opener will make readers want to read the letter and provides a reasonable transition to the body of the letter (see Figure 9.11). A very successful subscription letter for *Psychology Today* started out,

> Do you still close the bathroom door when there's no one in the house?

The question is both intriguing in itself and a good transition into the content of *Psychology Today:* practical psychology applied to the quirks and questions we come across in everyday life.

It's essential that the opener not only get the reader's attention but also be something that can be linked logically to the body of the letter. A sales letter started,

> Can you use $50 this week?

Certainly that gets attention. But the letter offered the reader only the chance to save $50 on a product. Readers may feel disappointed or even cheated when they learn that instead of getting $50, they have to spend money to save $50.

It's hard to write a brilliant opener the minute you sit down. To brainstorm possible openers, use the four basic modes: startling statements, quotations, questions, and narration.

1. Startling Statements

> Dear Membership Candidate:
>
> I'm writing to offer you a job.
>
> It's not a permanent job, understand. You'll be working for only as much time as you find it rewarding and fun.
>
> It's not even a paying job. On the contrary, it will cost *you* money.

This fundraising letter from Earthwatch invites readers to participate in its expeditions, subscribe to its journal, and donate to its programs. Earthwatch's volunteers help scientists and scholars dig for ruins, count bighorns, and monitor changes in water; they can work as long as they like; they pay their own (tax-deductible) expenses.

2. Quotations

> "I never tell my partner that my ankle is sore or my back hurts. You can't give in to pain and still perform."
>
> —Jill Murphy
> Soloist

Quotations sell season tickets to the Royal Winnipeg Ballet by focusing on the people who work to create the season. The letters encourage readers to see the artists as individuals, to appreciate their hard work, and to share their excitement about each performance.

3. Questions

> Dear Writer:
>
> What is the best way to start writing?

This letter selling subscriptions to *Writer's Digest* goes on to discuss Hemingway's strategy for getting started on his novels and short stories. *Writer's Digest* offers practical advice to writers who want to be published so the recipient keeps reading.

4. Narration, Stories, Anecdotes

> Dear Reader:
>
> She hoisted herself up noiselessly so as not to disturb the rattlesnakes snoozing there in the sun.

Figure 9.11 A Form Letter Whose Attention-Getter Mimics an Inside Address

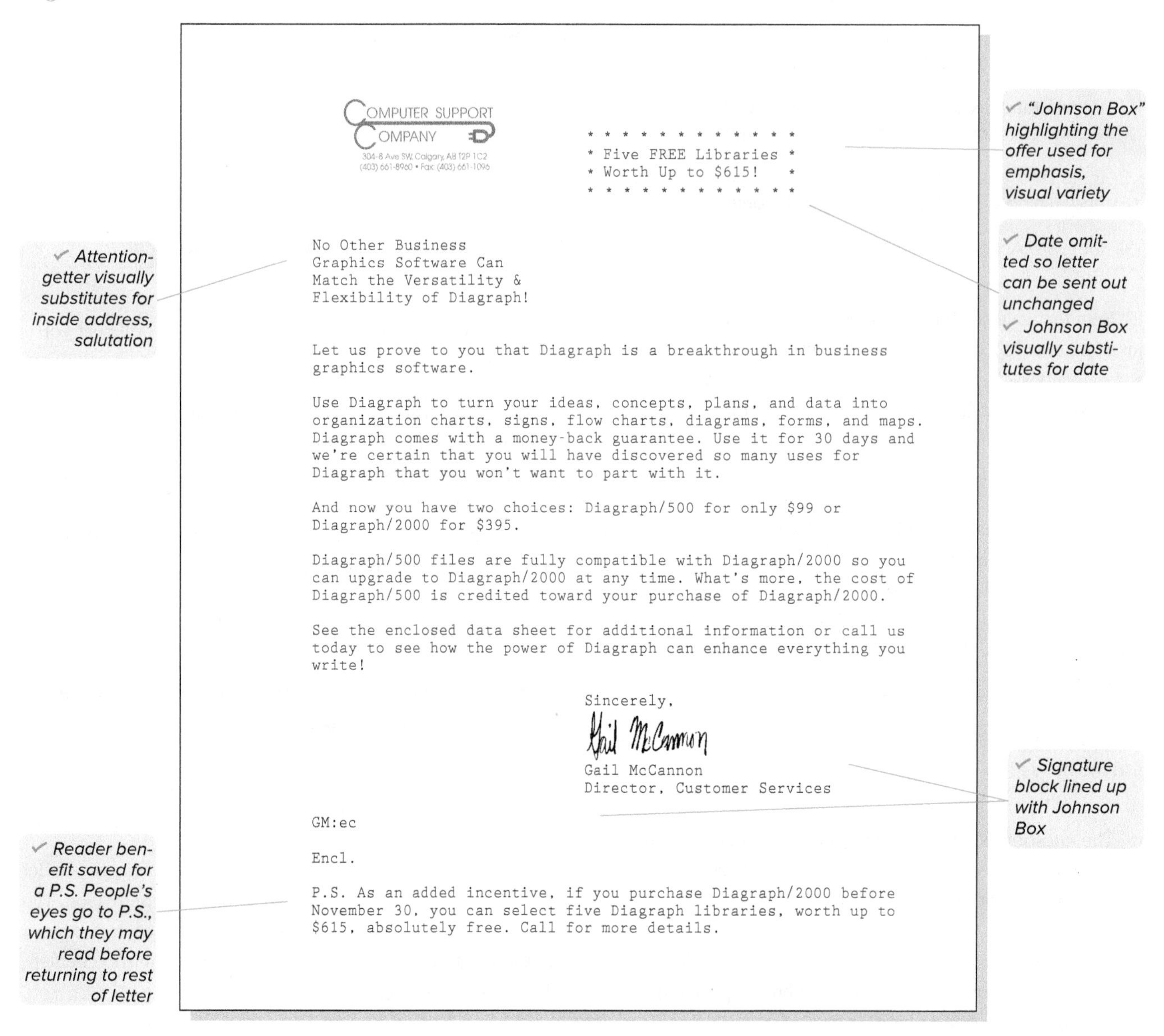
COMPUTER SUPPORT COMPANY

* * * * * * * * * * * * *
* Five FREE Libraries *
* Worth Up to $615! *
* * * * * * * * * * * * *

No Other Business
Graphics Software Can
Match the Versatility &
Flexibility of Diagraph!

Let us prove to you that Diagraph is a breakthrough in business graphics software.

Use Diagraph to turn your ideas, concepts, plans, and data into organization charts, signs, flow charts, diagrams, forms, and maps. Diagraph comes with a money-back guarantee. Use it for 30 days and we're certain that you will have discovered so many uses for Diagraph that you won't want to part with it.

And now you have two choices: Diagraph/500 for only $99 or Diagraph/2000 for $395.

Diagraph/500 files are fully compatible with Diagraph/2000 so you can upgrade to Diagraph/2000 at any time. What's more, the cost of Diagraph/500 is credited toward your purchase of Diagraph/2000.

See the enclosed data sheet for additional information or call us today to see how the power of Diagraph can enhance everything you write!

Sincerely,

Gail McCannon
Director, Customer Services

GM:ec

Encl.

P.S. As an added incentive, if you purchase Diagraph/2000 before November 30, you can select five Diagraph libraries, worth up to $615, absolutely free. Call for more details.

To her left, the high desert of New Mexico. Indian country. To her right, the rock carvings she had photographed the day before. Stick people. Primitive animals.

Up ahead, three sandstone slabs stood stacked against the face of the cliff. In their shadow, another carving. A spiral consisting of rings. Curious, the young woman drew closer. Instinctively, she glanced at her watch. It was almost noon. Then just at that moment, a most unusual thing happened.

Suddenly, as if out of nowhere, an eerie dagger of light appeared to stab at the topmost ring of the spiral. It next began to plunge downwards—shimmering, laser-like.

It pierced the eighth ring. The seventh. The sixth. It punctured the innermost and last. Then just as suddenly as it had appeared, the dagger of light was gone. The young woman glanced at her watch again. Exactly twelve minutes had elapsed.

Coincidence? Accident? Fluke? No. What she may have stumbled across that midsummer morning three years ago is an ancient solar calendar. . . .

The opener of this *Science84* subscription letter both builds suspense so that the reader reads the subscription letter and suggests that the magazine will be as interesting as the letter and as easy to read.

Body (Interest)

The body of the letter provides the logical and emotional links that move readers from their first flicker of interest to the desired action. A good interest-building section underlines benefits, overcomes their objections, and involves them emotionally.

All this takes space. One of the industry truisms is "The more you tell, the more you sell." Tests show that longer letters bring in more new customers or new donors than do shorter letters.

Can short letters work? Yes, when you're writing to old customers or when the mailing is supported by other media (see ▸▸ Figure 9.12). One study showed that a one-page letter was just as effective as a two-page letter in persuading recent purchasers of a product to buy a service contract.[25] E-mail direct mail is also short—generally just one screen. The shortest letter on record may be the two-word postcard that a fishing lake resort sent its customers: "They're biting!"

Content for the body of the letter can include

- Information readers will find useful even if they do not buy or give.
- Stories about how the product was developed or what the organization has done.
- Stories about people who have used the product or who need the organization's help.
- Word pictures of readers using the product and enjoying its benefits.

Body (Desire)

Build desire while reducing resistance by adding detail that answers reader questions. What concerns might they have about products or services? What reassurances do they need? Promote your credibility by citing evidence and authorities to support your claims. Preparing your readers for the call to action in the close, this section can usefully cite from these sources:

- Survey results
- Testimonials from satisfied consumers
- Test results
- Expert/celebrity endorsements

Close (Action)

The action close in the letter must do four things:

1. **Tell the reader what to do:** Respond. Avoid *if* ("If you'd like to try. . .") and *why not* ("Why not send in a cheque?"). They lack positive emphasis and encourage your reader to say *no.*
2. **Make the action sound easy:** Fill in the information on the reply card, sign the card (for credit sales), put the card and cheque (if payment is to accompany the order) in the envelope (if postage-paid, stress it), and mail the envelope. Outline online options.
3. **Offer a reason for acting promptly.** Readers who wait to act are less likely to buy or contribute. Reasons for acting promptly are easy to identify when a product is seasonal or there is a genuine limit on the offer—time limit, price rise scheduled, or limited supply. Sometimes you can offer a premium or a discount if the reader acts quickly. Otherwise, remind readers that the sooner they get the product, the sooner they can benefit from it; the sooner they contribute funds, the sooner their dollars can go to work to solve the problem.
4. **End with a positive picture** of the reader enjoying the product (sales letter) or of the reader's money working to solve the problem (fundraising letter). The last sentence should never be a selfish request for money.

The action close can also remind readers of the central selling point, stress the guarantee, and mention when the customer will get the product.

Using a P.S.

Studies of eye movement show that people often look to see who a letter is from before they read the letter. Ray Jutkins cites a study showing that 79% of the people who open direct mail read the P.S. first.[26] Therefore, direct mail often uses a deliberate P.S. after the signature block. It may restate the central selling point, preferably in different words so that it won't sound repetitive.

Here are two of the many kinds of effective P.S.s.

- Reason to act promptly:

> P.S. Once I finish the limited harvest, that's it! I do not store any SpringSweet Onions for late orders. I will ship all orders on a first-come, first-served basis and when they are gone they are gone. Drop your order in the mail today . . . or give me a call toll free at 800-531-7470!

- Restatement of central selling point:

> P.S. It is not easy to be a hungry child in the Third World. If your parents' crops fail or if your parents cannot find work, there [are] . . . no free government-provided cafeteria lunches.
>
> Millions of hungry schoolchildren will be depending on CARE Canada this fall. Your gift today will ensure that we will be there—that CARE Canada won't let them down.

LO4

STRATEGY IN SALES LETTERS

The basic strategy in sales letters is satisfying a need. Your letter must remind people of the need your product meets, prove that the product will satisfy that need, show why your product is better than similar products, and make readers *want* to have the product. Use psychological description (◂◂ Figure 9.7) to show readers how the product will help them. Testimonials from other buyers can help persuade them that the product works; details about how the product is made can carry the message of quality.

Many sales letters make the offer early in the letter—even on the envelope. The exact price, however, is not mentioned until the last quarter of the letter, after the copy makes the reader *want* the product (◂◂ Figure 9.11). The only exception occurs when you're selling something that has a reputation for being expensive (a luxury car, *Encyclopaedia Britannica*). Then you may want to deal with the price issue early in the letter.

You can make the price more palatable with the following techniques:

1. **Link the price to the benefit the product provides.** "Your piece of history is just $39.95."
2. **Show how much the product costs each day, each week, or each month.** "You can have all this for less than the cost of a cup of coffee a day."
3. **Allow customers to charge sales or pay in instalments.** Your bookkeeping costs will rise, and some sales may be uncollectible, but the total number of sales will increase.

Always offer a guarantee, usually right after the price. The best guarantees are short, convincing, and positive.

× Negative: If the magazine fails to meet your expectations, you can cancel at any time and receive a refund on any unmailed copies.

✓ Better: You'll be satisfied or we'll refund your money. I guarantee that.

STRATEGY IN FUNDRAISING APPEALS

In a fundraising letter, the basic emotional strategy is **vicarious participation.** By donating money, readers participate vicariously in work they are not able to do personally. This strategy affects the pronouns you use. Throughout the letter, use *we* to talk about your group. However, at the end, talk about what *you* the reader will be doing. End positively, with a picture of the reader's dollars helping to solve the problem.

To achieve fundraising letter purposes, providing extensive information achieves these results:

1. Helps to persuade readers
2. Gives supporters evidence to use in conversations with others
3. Gives readers who are not yet supporters evidence to see the group as worthwhile.

In your close, in addition to asking for money, suggest other ways the reader can help: doing volunteer work, scheduling a meeting on the subject, writing letters to Parliament, the provincial legislature, or the leaders of other countries, and so on. By suggesting other ways to participate, you not only involve readers but also avoid one of the traps of fundraising letters: sounding as though you are selfish, interested in readers only for their money.

Deciding How Much to Ask For

Most letters to new donors suggest a range of amounts, from $25 or $50 (for employed people) up to perhaps double what you *really* expect to get from a single donor. A second strategy is to ask for a small, set amount that nearly everyone can afford ($10 or $15).

One of the several reasons people give for not contributing is that a gift of $25 or $100 seems too small to matter. It's not. Small gifts are important both in themselves and to establish a habit of giving. Some of the people who can give only $25 or even $5 today will someday have more money.[27]

Annual letters to past donors often use the amount of the last donation as the lowest suggested gift, with other gifts 25%, 50%, or even 100% higher.

Always send a thank-you letter to people who respond to your letter, whatever the size of their gifts. By telling about the group's recent work, a thank-you letter can help reinforce donors' commitment to your cause.

Logical Proof in Fundraising Letters

The body of a fundraising letter must prove

1. The problem deserves the reader's attention.
2. The problem can be solved or at least alleviated.
3. Your organization is helping to solve it.
4. Private funds are needed.
5. Your organization will use the funds wisely. (See Figure 9.12.)

1. The Problem Deserves the Reader's Attention

If your problem is life threatening, give some statistics: Tell how many people are killed in Canada every year by drunk drivers. Also tell about one individual who is affected.

2. The Problem Can Be Solved or Alleviated

People will not give money if they see the problem as hopeless. Sometimes you can reason by analogy. Cures have been found for other deadly diseases, so it's reasonable to hope that research can find a cure for cancer and AIDS. Sometimes you can show that short-term or partial solutions exist. For example, a UNICEF letter showed that four simple changes could save the lives of millions of children: oral rehydration, immunization, promoting breastfeeding, and giving mothers cardboard growth charts so they'll know if their children are malnourished. Those solutions keep children alive while we work on long-term solutions to poverty.

Figure 9.12 A Fundraising Letter

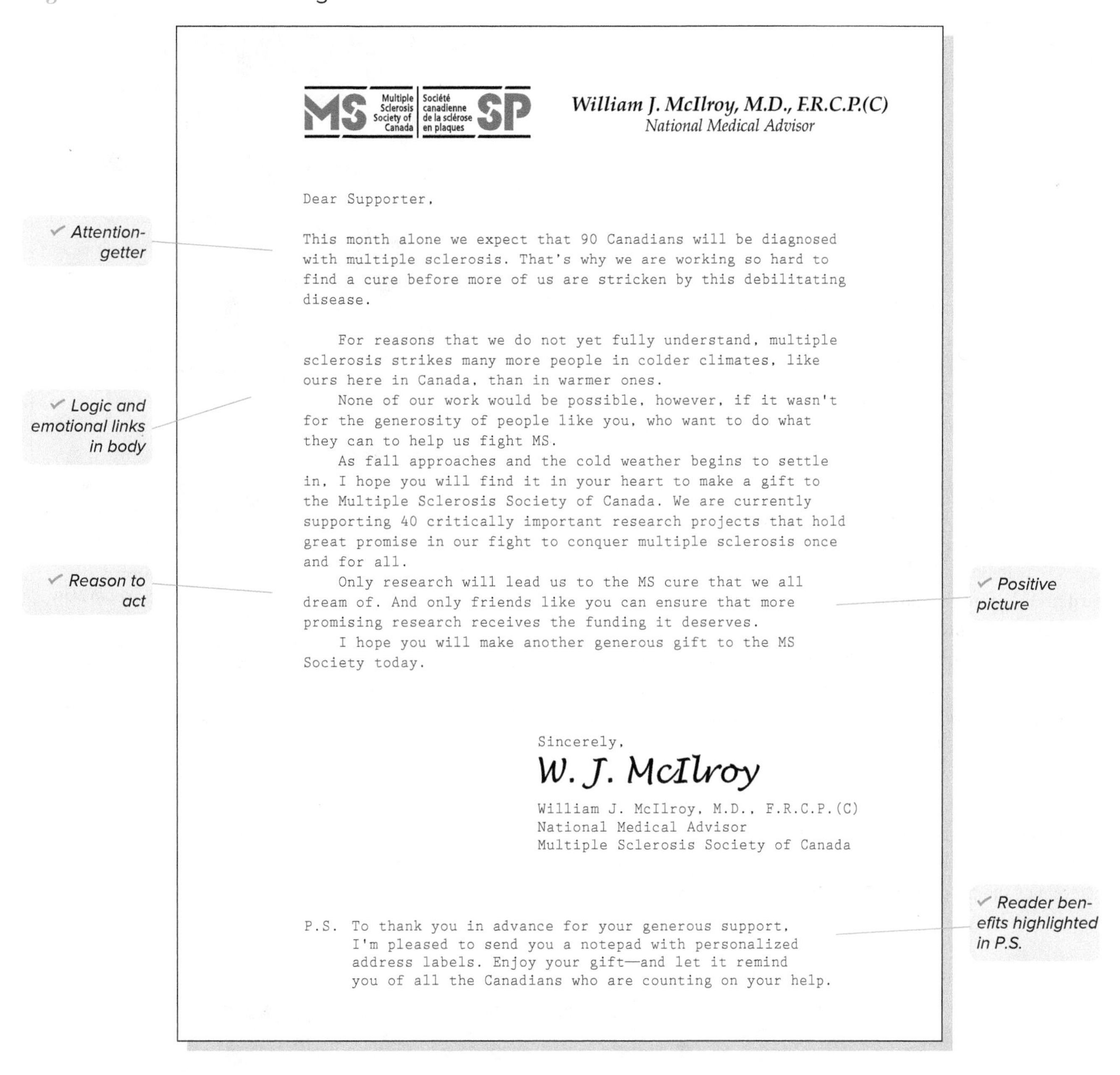

MS Multiple Sclerosis Society of Canada | Société canadienne de la sclérose en plaques SP

William J. McIlroy, M.D., F.R.C.P.(C)
National Medical Advisor

Dear Supporter,

This month alone we expect that 90 Canadians will be diagnosed with multiple sclerosis. That's why we are working so hard to find a cure before more of us are stricken by this debilitating disease.

For reasons that we do not yet fully understand, multiple sclerosis strikes many more people in colder climates, like ours here in Canada, than in warmer ones.

None of our work would be possible, however, if it wasn't for the generosity of people like you, who want to do what they can to help us fight MS.

As fall approaches and the cold weather begins to settle in, I hope you will find it in your heart to make a gift to the Multiple Sclerosis Society of Canada. We are currently supporting 40 critically important research projects that hold great promise in our fight to conquer multiple sclerosis once and for all.

Only research will lead us to the MS cure that we all dream of. And only friends like you can ensure that more promising research receives the funding it deserves.

I hope you will make another generous gift to the MS Society today.

Sincerely,

W. J. McIlroy

William J. McIlroy, M.D., F.R.C.P.(C)
National Medical Advisor
Multiple Sclerosis Society of Canada

P.S. To thank you in advance for your generous support, I'm pleased to send you a notepad with personalized address labels. Enjoy your gift—and let it remind you of all the Canadians who are counting on your help.

Courtesy of Multiple Sclerosis Society of Canada

3. Your Organization Is Helping to Solve or Alleviate the Problem

Talking about specific successes in the past helps readers believe that you can accomplish your goals.

4. Private Funds Are Needed

If your group does get some tax or foundation money, show why more money is needed. If the organization helps people who might be expected to pay for the service, show why they cannot pay, or why they cannot pay enough to cover the full cost. If some of the funds have been raised by the people who will benefit, make that clear.

5. Your Organization Will Use the Funds Wisely

Prove that the money goes to the cause, not just to the cost of fundraising.

Emotional Appeal in Fundraising Letters

Emotional appeal is needed to make people pull out their chequebooks. A mild appeal is unlikely to sway any reader who is not already committed, but readers will feel manipulated by appeals they find too strong and reject them. If you don't know your audience well, use the strongest emotional appeal *you* feel comfortable with.

Emotional appeal is created by specifics. It is hard to care about, or even to imagine, a million people; it is easier to care about one specific person. Details and quotes help us see that person as real and yield greater responses.

Coast Capital Savings and Volunteer Richmond Information Services proudly present their Leadership Richmond–Youth Now, designed to harness the leadership potential found in their community by training young adults who are high school graduates and under the age of 26 to serve as board members for local non-profit organizations. These volunteers are among the 65% of Canadian teenagers who volunteer (the highest participation of any group).

LO5

STRATEGY IN RACK CARDS AND BROCHURES

Rack cards (Figure 9.13) and brochures can serve several purposes: they can build general support for an organization or candidate, give specific information ("How to Cope with Chemotherapy"), or even have a reply coupon that readers can return to buy a book, register for a conference, or donate to a cause.

Popular in the hospitality and tourism sectors, the rack card is a cost-effective, colourful, and portable way of getting your message out. Strategy is based on clean design and clear messages that make audience action easy. The front of the rack card grabs attention and communicates key messages; a back panel can add details about the organization, such as products and services, discounts and other benefits, and a locator map.

To create a brochure, determine your purpose(s) and your audience(s). Think about where and how your brochure will be distributed. Think about visual constraints and clutter that your brochure needs to overcome: other brochures, a holder that will block the bottom portion of the cover, and so forth. Plan photos and other visual elements.

To keep a brochure size manageable, you might focus on just one of the programs or products you offer. For example, the Heifer Project brochure (Figure 9.14) focuses on the Kids 2 Kids program and doesn't mention any of its other programs. Choose a central selling point or theme. See « Chapter 4 on designing brochures.

Figure 9.13 Rack Card Displays Introduce Area Amenities

Figure 9.14 Inside Panels of a Brochure

✓ Inside Panels

✓ Quotation

✓ Startling statement

× Most paragraphs should be 7 lines or less

✓ Details explain, "Why goats?"

✓ Banners unify panels

✓ What money buys

✓ Logo banner separates stories

"Foster Mother to the Human Race"

In a world in which hunger seems to defy large-scale solutions, the answer may well lie with a much smaller one, the goat.

For most of the world's people, goat's milk is the only milk they have ever known. However, in many countries even goat's milk is in short supply. When children — at the most nutritionally vulnerable point in their lives — are deprived of milk, the consequences are disastrous. An absence of milk in their diet makes children easy targets for malnutrition and disease.

Goats offer an ideal solution to this grave situation. Goat's milk is as highly nutritious as that of any dairy animal. In fact, if children drink only one liter of goat's milk per day, they will be consuming all of the protein required for the first six years of life, and more than half of what they need to become teenagers and grow into adulthood. Even more impressive is the fact that this same single liter provides all the calcium required at almost every stage of life.

Just as important, goats require an extremely low investment and are very easy to keep. They will eat almost any kind of forage, need very little space, and are comfortable in a wide range of climates. They can also go longer without water than most other farm animals and reproduce quickly, allowing families to build their herds while producing extra milk to sell for income. Moreover, goat manure makes excellent fertilizer.

Finally, goats and children appear to have a natural affinity for one another. Even young children are able to raise and take care of their family's goats. Such responsibility helps children gain the self-esteem that comes from playing a significant role in their family's economic life.

At a cost of only $120 for a goat and the training in its care — or $10 for a share of a goat — Heifer Project's **Kids-2-Kids Campaign** makes it possible for us to send this four-footed economic miracle to needy children and their families all over the world. We invite you to take a glimpse into just some of the places where this miracle is taking place.

KIDS·2·KIDS

In Nepal

Ten years ago, when she got the idea that would change her life, Gyandhari Basel could not even write her own name. Forced as a young girl to migrate from her native hill country to Nepal's southern plains, Gyandhari helped her family eke out a bare living as subsistence farmers. She was typical of many women in her situation, impoverished and soon married with four children of her own.

Gyandhari and several of her friends made the decision to band together to do what had previously been considered impossible. In a land

LO6

WRITING STYLE

Direct mail is one kind of business writing where elegance and beauty of language matter. Direct mail imitates the word choice and rhythm of conversation; its language shimmers with images, echoes with sound, and vibrates with energy.

Humour is used sparingly because sales letters and brochures are focused on a direct response—say, subscribing to a magazine or contributing to a cause. Humour can actually distract the audience from that purpose.

Still, some use humour in their direct mail, perhaps because humour is part of what they are known for. One of the most successful mailings by *The Nation* magazine featured a caricature of President George W. Bush wearing a crown, along with the words "Don't you just love this guy? If your answer is yes, don't open this envelope."[28]

1. Make Your Writing Interesting

If the style is long-winded and boring, the reader will stop reading. Eliminating wordiness (◀◀ Chapter 3) is crucial. You've already seen ways to tighten your writing in Chapter 3. Direct mail goes further, breaking some of the rules of grammar for specific effects. Note how sentence fragments are used in parallel structure to move the reader along:

> So tiny, it fits virtually unnoticed in your pocket. So meticulously hand-assembled by unhurried craftsmen in Switzerland, that production may never exceed demand. So everyday useful, that you'll wonder how you ever got along without it.

Letter asking for inquiries about a mobile phone.

2. Use Sound Patterns to Emphasize Words

When you repeat sounds, you create patterns that catch the reader's attention, please the ear, and emphasize the words. **Alliteration** occurs when several syllables begin with the same sound (see the *Science84* opener under "Narration, Stories, Anecdotes" in this chapter). **Rhyme** is the repetition of the final vowel sounds and, if the words end with consonants, the final consonant sounds. **Rhythm** is the repetition of a pattern of accented and unaccented syllables. Rhyme, rhythm, and the **rule of three** explain some of the lasting power of The Three Bears and Three Blind Mice! The rule of three explains that when you have a series of three items that are logically parallel, the last receives the most emphasis:

> Nightcalls, pratfalls, and jungle shrieks . . . a scattering of wings, a chattering of monkeys, and big, yellow eyes in my headlights!

Headline, sales letter for an all-terrain vehicle.

On the Job Canadian Giving: Facts and Figures*

Canada is home to the second largest non-profit sector in the world; the Netherlands is in the top spot, although the World Giving Index cautions that what "is considered charitable in one country may be seen as a regular, everyday activity in another." Being happy (not wealthy) correlates strongly with giving.

The Canadian non-profit and voluntary sector represents

- 8.1% of the Canadian GDP
- More than the entire retail trade sector and three times the size of the motor vehicle industry
- 2 million employees
- $106 billion in revenues and 170,000 non-profit and charitable organizations
- 54% of organizations run exclusively by volunteer staff
- Over 13 million volunteers
- 45.6% of income comes from sales of goods and services

*Adapted from Imagine Canada, "Charities and nonprofit organizations," retrieved June 1, 2014, from http://www.imaginecanada.ca/node/32; Imagine Canada, "Sector impact," retrieved from http://sectorsource.ca/research-and-impact/sector-impact; Sarah Boesveld, "In Canada, charity begins at home," *The Globe and Mail*, September 9, 2010, A3; "Canada has world's second largest nonprofit sector," Association of Fundraising Professionals, http://www.afpnet.org/tier3_cd.cfm?folder_id52345&content_item_i, retrieved May 8, 2005; Georgina Steinsky-Schwartz, Canadian Centre for Philanthropy and Coalition of National Voluntary Organizations, Speech to the Empire Club of Canada, Toronto, November 16, 2004; Julia Howell, "The business of community," retrieved August 26, 2008, from http://www.imaginecanada.ca/files/en/publications/macleans_supplement_20080409.pdf.

3. Use Psychological Description

In a sales letter, you can use psychological description (◀◀ Figure 9.7) to create a scenario so readers can picture themselves using your product or service and enjoying its benefits. You can also use psychological description to describe the problem your product will solve.

4. Make Your Letter Sound Like a Letter, Not an Ad

Maintain the image of one person writing to another person—that is the foundation of all letters. Use an informal style with short words and sentences, and even slang.

You can also create a **persona**—the character who allegedly writes the letter—to make the letter interesting and keep us reading. Use the rhythms of speech, vivid images, and conversational words to create the effect that the author is a "character."

The following opening creates a persona who fits the product:

> Dear Friend:
>
> There's no use trying. I've tried and tried to tell people about my fish. But I wasn't rigged out to be a letter writer, and I can't do it. I can close-haul a sail with the best of them. I know how to pick out the best fish of the catch, I know just which fish will make the tastiest mouthfuls, but I'll never learn the knack of writing a letter that will tell people why my kind of fish—fresh-caught prime-grades, right off the fishing boats with the deep-sea tang still in it—is lots better than the ordinary store kind.
>
> Sales letter, Frank Davis Fish Company

This letter, with its "Aw, shucks, I can't sell" persona, with language designed to make you see an unassuming fisherman ("rigged out," "close-haul"), was written by a professional advertiser.[29]

Figures 9.15, 9.16, and 9.17 provide checklists for writing persuasive direct requests, indirect problem-solving persuasive messages, and AIDA persuasive plans, respectively.

Figure 9.15 Checklist for Persuasive Direct Requests

- ☐ If the message is a memo, does the subject line indicate the request? Is the subject line specific enough to differentiate this message from others on the same subject?
- ☐ Does the first paragraph summarize the request or the specific topic of the message?
- ☐ Does the message give all of the relevant information? Is there enough detail?
- ☐ Does the message answer questions or overcome objections that readers may have without introducing unnecessary negatives?
- ☐ Does the last paragraph tell the reader exactly what to do? Does it give a deadline if one exists and a reason for acting promptly?

And, for all messages, not just direct requests,

- ☐ Does the message use you-attitude and positive emphasis?
- ☐ Is the style easy to read and friendly?
- ☐ Is the visual design of the message inviting?
- ☐ Is the format correct?
- ☐ Does the message use standard grammar? Is it free from typos?

Figure 9.16 Checklist for Indirect Problem-Solving Persuasive Messages

- ☐ If the message is a memo or e-mail, does the subject line indicate the writer's purpose or offer a reader benefit? Does the subject line avoid making the request?
- ☐ Does the first sentence interest the reader?
- ☐ Is the problem presented as a joint problem both writer and reader have an interest in solving, rather than as something the reader is being asked to do for the writer?
- ☐ Does the message give all of the relevant information? Is there enough detail?
- ☐ Does the message overcome objections that readers may have?
- ☐ Does the message avoid phrases that sound dictatorial, condescending, or arrogant?
- ☐ Does the last paragraph tell the reader exactly what to do? Does it give a deadline and a reason for acting promptly?

Figure 9.17 Checklist for AIDA Persuasive Plan

- ☐ Does the opener catch the reader's attention and prepare for the body?
- ☐ Does the body provide a chain of reasons and logic?
- ☐ Does the body provide emotional links? Word pictures?
- ☐ Does the message give all of the relevant information? Is there enough detail?
- ☐ Does the message overcome reader objections and increase desire?
- ☐ Does the last paragraph tell the reader exactly what to do? Does it make it easy to act promptly? Does it include positive emphasis?

SUMMARY OF KEY POINTS

- Analyze a persuasive situation by answering these four questions:
  - What do you want people to do?
  - What objections, if any, will the audience have?
  - How strong is your case?
  - What kind of persuasion is best for the organization and culture?
- Use the persuasive strategy your organization prefers.
- Use the *persuasive direct request pattern* when the audience will find it easy to do as you ask. Also use the direct request pattern for busy readers who may not read all the messages they receive.
- Use the *indirect problem-solving pattern* when the audience may resist doing what you ask and you expect logic to be more important than emotion in the decision.
- To organize sales messages, use the indirect AIDA persuasive plan. The AIDA pattern focuses on attracting attention (A), and arousing interest (I) and desire (D) to elicit action (A). It is as relevant to persuasive as to sales messages.
- The basic strategy in sales appeals is satisfying a need. You must remind people of the need your product meets, prove that the product will satisfy that need, show why your product is better than similar products, and make readers *want* to have the product.
- In a fundraising appeal, the basic strategy is *vicarious participation.* By donating money, readers participate vicariously in work they are not able to do personally.
- The body of a fundraising request must prove that (1) the problem deserves the reader's attention, (2) the problem can be solved or alleviated, (3) your organization is helping to solve it, (4) private funds are needed, and (5) your organization will use the funds wisely.
- Rack cards are cost-effective, colourful, and portable ways of getting your message out. Strategy is based on clean design and clear messages that make audience action easy. The front grabs attention with key messages; a back panel can add details about the organization, its products and services, discounts and other benefits, and a locator map.
- Brochure strategy depends on your purpose(s) and audience(s). Think about where and how your brochure will be distributed. Think about visual constraints and clutter that your brochure needs to overcome. Plan photos and other visual elements around a central selling point.
- Good writing for sales and fundraising is interesting, specific, and conversational, uses sound patterns to emphasize words, and uses psychological description.

EXERCISES AND PROBLEMS

GETTING STARTED

9.1 WRITING PSYCHOLOGICAL DESCRIPTION

Choose one of the following five topics and write two or three paragraphs of psychological description that could be used in a brochure, news release, or direct mail letter. In choosing your words, consider what will appeal to your audience (some audiences are suggested in the first three cases).

1. Having a personal trainer

   Audiences: Professional athletes

   Busy managers

   Someone trying to lose weight

   Someone making a major lifestyle change after a heart attack

2. Buying a cell phone

   Audiences: People who do a lot of big-city driving

   People who do a lot of driving in rural areas

   People who do a lot of flying

3. Buying a laptop computer

   Audiences: University and community college students

   Financial planners who visit clients at home

   Sales representatives who travel constantly

   People who make PowerPoint presentations

4. Attending a fantasy sports camp (you pick the sport), playing with and against retired players who provide coaching and advice.
5. Attending a health spa where clients get low-fat and low-calorie meals, massages, beauty treatments, and guidance in nutrition and exercise.

Hints:

- For this assignment, you can combine benefits or programs as if a single source offered them all.
- Add specific details about particular sports, activities, and so on, as material for your description.
- Be sure to move beyond reader benefits to vivid details and sense impressions.
- Put your benefits in you-attitude.

9.2 EVALUATING SUBJECT LINES

Evaluate the following subject lines. Is one subject line in each group clearly best? Or does the "best" line depend on company culture, whether the message is a paper memo or an e-mail message, or on some other factor?

As your professor directs, peer grade answers

1. Subject: Request

   Subject: Why I Need a New Computer

   Subject: Increasing My Productivity

2. Subject: Who Wants Extra Hours?

   Subject: Holiday Work Schedule

   Subject: Working Extra Hours during the Holiday Season

3. Subject: Student Mentors

   Subject: Can You Be an E-Mail Mentor?

   Subject: Volunteers Needed

4. Subject: More Wine and Cheese

   Subject: Today's Reception for Japanese Visitors

   Subject: Reminder

5. Subject: Reducing Absenteeism

   Subject: Opening a Day Care Centre for Sick Children of Employees

   Subject: Why We Need Expanded Day Care Facilities

9.3 EVALUATING OPENER DRAFTS

The following are the results of a session brainstorming openers for a letter raising funds for a community college that has suffered budget cuts. Suggest ways to improve each opener. Which seems the most promising? Why?

1. Do you realize that there are students who are getting a poorer education than you got from the same program you attended?
2. We are in danger of losing our accreditation.
3. Engineering students using dial calipers of only 10% the accuracy needed . . . cancelled library subscriptions . . . bigger classes . . . closed courses . . . obsolete equipment. . . . Budget cuts have made it harder for XYZ students to get a good education.

EVALUATION AND ETHICS ASSIGNMENTS

9.4 EVALUATING SALES AND FUNDRAISING LETTERS

Collect the sales and fundraising letters that come to you, your co-workers, landlord, neighbours, or family. Use the following questions to evaluate each package:

- What mode does the opener use? Is it related to the rest of the letter? How good is the opener?
- What central selling point or common ground does the letter use?
- What kinds of proof does the letter use? Is the logic valid? What questions or objections are not answered?
- How does the letter create emotional appeal?
- Is the style effective? Where does the letter use sound to emphasize points?
- Does the close tell readers what to do, make action easy, give a reason for acting promptly, and end with a positive picture?
- Does the letter use a P.S.? How good is it?
- Is the letter visually attractive? Why or why not?
- What other items besides the letter are in the package?

As Your Professor Directs,

a. Share your analysis of one or more letters with a small group of your classmates.

b. Analyze one letter in a presentation to the class. Make slides or photocopies of the letter to use as a visual aid in your presentation.

c. Analyze one letter in a memo to your professor. Provide a copy or photocopy of the letter along with your memo.

d. With several other students, write an e-report analyzing one part of the letter (e.g., openers) or one kind of letter (e.g., political letters, organizations fighting hunger, etc.). Use at least six letters for your analysis if you look at only one part; use at least four letters if you analyze one kind of letter. Provide copies or photocopies as an appendix to your report.

9.5 THE ETHICS OF "UP TO"*

*This exercise based on Herschell Gordon Lewis, "Up to No Good," *Direct*, January 2004.

As companies struggle to be noticed in direct mail and on the Internet, many are tempted to exaggerate. A phrase that is easy to misuse is *up to*. This phrase suggests the offer approaches the upper limit, but it does not really promise anything. Consumers learn to distrust such unethical appeals—and the companies that make them.

The following e-mail offers contain "up to" promises. Rewrite each offer so that it is both ethical and appealing. As your professor directs, discuss and grade answers in pairs.

1. Save up to $22,000 on latest SUV models! Visit dealer for details.
2. You're pre-approved for up to 10,000 bonus miles! We've reserved up to 10,000 bonus miles. You get 1,000 miles each time you rent a car from selected merchants. You get 200 bonus miles for phone services from selected providers. See reverse for credit card disclosures regarding rates and fees.
3. Get up to $100 cash back on your telephone service. Eligible customers will receive a $25 coupon for each qualifying service: Long Distance, Privacy Features, DSL Connection, and Wireless Deluxe.

9.6 ANSWERING AN ETHICS QUESTION

You're a senior staffer in a charitable organization. Today, you get this message from your boss:

Subject: Using "Handwritten" Messages

I'd like your feedback on the suggestion from our direct mail consultant to use a mailing with handwritten notes. I understand the argument that this will increase response. But the idea of hiring people who don't have any relation to us to write notes—and implying that the notes are by loyal donors—seems unethical. And frankly, I worry about the image we'd create if our real donors learned that we'd done this.

What do you think?

As Your Professor Directs,

a. Answer the question, using a charitable organization that you know something about.

b. Answer the question, assuming that it comes from a federal candidate.

c. Answer the question, assuming that the strategy has been recommended for a sales rather than for a fundraising letter.

d. Write an e-mail message to your professor justifying your answer.

COMMUNICATING AT WORK

9.7 WRITING COLLECTION LETTERS

You have a small desktop publishing firm. Unfortunately, not all your clients pay promptly.

As Your Professor Directs,

Write letters for one or more of the following situations:

a. A $450 bill for designing and printing a brochure for Juggles Inc., a company that provides clowns and jugglers for parties, is now five weeks overdue. You've phoned twice, and each time the person who answered the phone promised to send you a cheque, but nothing has happened.

b. A $2,000 bill for creating a series of handouts for a veterinarian to distribute to clients. This one is really embarrassing: somehow you lost track of the invoice, so you never followed up on the original (and only) bill. The bill is now 72 days overdue.

c. A $3,750 bill for designing and printing a series of 10 brochures for Creative Interiors, a local interior decorating shop, is three weeks past due. When you billed Creative Interiors, you got a note saying that the design was not acceptable and that you would not be paid until you redesigned it (at no extra charge) to the owner's satisfaction. The owner had approved the preliminary design on which the brochures were based; she did not explain in the note what was wrong with the final product. She's never free when you are; indeed, when you call to try to schedule an appointment, you're told the owner will call you back—but she never does. At this point, the delay is not your fault; you want to be paid.

d. A $100 bill for designing (but not actually creating) a brochure for a cleaning company that, according to its owner, planned to expand into your city. You got the order and instructions by mail and talked to the person on the phone but never met him. You tried to call once since then (as much to try to talk him into having the brochures printed as to collect the $100); the number was no longer in service. You suspect the owner may no longer be in business, but you'd like to get your money if possible.

9.8 PERSUADING PEOPLE TO USE BETTER PASSWORDS

Your computer system requires each employee to change his or her password every three months. But many people choose passwords that are easy to guess. According to Deloitte & Touche's fraud unit, the 10 most commonly used passwords are (1) the employee's name or child's name, (2) "secret," (3) stress-related words ("deadline," "work"), (4) sports teams or terms, (5) "payday," (6) "bonkers," (7) the current season ("autumn," "spring"), (8) the employee's ethnic group, (9) repeated characters ("AAAAA"), (10) obscenities and sexual terms ("Hackers' Delight," *BusinessWeek*, February 10, 1997, p. 4).

As director of management information systems (MIS), you want employees to choose passwords that hackers can't guess based on knowing an employee's background. The best passwords contain numbers as well as letters, use more characters (at least five; preferably eight), and aren't real words.

Write an e-mail message to all employees, urging them to choose better passwords.

9.9 PERSUADING GUESTS TO ALLOW EXTRA TIME FOR CHECKOUT

Your hotel has been the headquarters for a convention, and on Sunday morning you're expecting 5,000 people to check out before noon. You're staffing the checkout desk to capacity, but if everyone waits till 11:30 a.m. to check out, things will be a disaster.

So you want to encourage people to allow extra time. And they don't have to stand in line at all: by 4:00 a.m., you'll put a statement of current charges under each guest's door. If that statement is correct and the guest is leaving the bill on the credit card used at check-in, the guest can just leave the key in the room and leave. You'll mail a copy of the final bill together with any morning charges by the end of the week.

Write a one-page message that can be put on pillows when the rooms are made up Friday and Saturday night.

9.10 REQUESTING MORE FUNDS FOR THE WRITING CENTRE

Your university is facing major budget cuts. A popular idea is to reduce or eliminate funding for the Writing Centre. As the Centre's director, you're horrified by these ideas.

The Writing Centre offers free tutoring in writing to any student or faculty member on campus. Your emphasis is not on fixing an individual paper, but on helping the writer develop strategies that he or she can use not only in this paper but in everything he or she writes.

The services you offer help students do better in classes. Your help is particularly important when budget cuts are leading to larger classes, so that faculty spend less time with each student. Furthermore, your operation is really quite efficient. You have only one paid regular faculty member on your staff; the rest are graduate teaching assistants (who are paid much less than faculty receive) or undergraduate peer tutors. Finally, the dollars involved aren't that great. Cutting the Centre's budget in half would mean you would have to turn away most students. Yet the dollars are small in comparison with the budgets of large departments.

As Your Professor Directs,

a. Write a memo to all faculty urging them to support full funding for the Writing Centre.

b. Write a news release for the campus newspaper about the problem.

c. Identify the person or group on your campus with the power to make budget decisions, and write to that group urging that it support a Writing Centre on your campus. Use information about the centre and the fiscal situation that fits your community college or university.

Hints:

- Visit the Writing Centre on campus to get information about its hours and policies. Sign up for an appointment. What happens in a session? What parts are especially helpful?
- Be sure to prove and limit your claims. Even if the Centre is fully funded, some students will be turned away. Even if its funding is increased, not everyone will write well.
- Be sure to use you-attitude and to make sure that the writing in your message is a good advertisement for your own writing skills.

9.11 CREATING A BROCHURE OR RACK CARD

In pairs or groups, create a brochure or rack card for a campus group or a non-profit organization. Turn in two copies of your brochure and a memo to your professor or post to the class blog explaining your choices for strategy, content, and design. Would this brochure or rack card be part of a series? What are the purposes? Who are the audiences? Where will the brochure or rack card be physically available? Why did you choose your central selling point? Why did you choose to be more or less formal, more or less complete, and so forth? Explain your choices for strategy, content, wording, layout, visuals (if any), and colour (if any).

9.12 WRITING A SALES OR FUNDRAISING LETTER

a. Write a sales letter to promote a product that has just been launched in your area or one that you have created/imagined—one that you are eager to share with the world.

   OR

b. Write a 2.5-page letter to raise money from new donors for an organization you support. You must use a real organization, but it does not have to be conducting a fundraising drive now. Assume that your letter would have a reply card and postage-paid envelope. You do NOT have to write these, but DO refer to them in your letter.

   Options for organizations include

   - Tax-deductible charitable organizations—churches; synagogues; hospitals; groups working to feed, clothe, and house poor people.
   - Lobbying groups—Mothers Against Drunk Driving, groups working against nuclear weapons, etc.
   - Groups raising money to fight a disease or fund research.
   - Universities and colleges trying to raise money for endowments, buildings, scholarships, faculty salaries.
   - Athletic associations raising money for scholarships, equipment, buildings, facilities.

   For this assignment, you may also use groups that do not regularly have fundraising drives but that may have special needs. Perhaps a school needs new uniforms for its band or an automatic timing device for its swimming pool.

PLANNING, RESEARCHING, AND DOCUMENTING REPORTS

10

Learning Outcomes

LO1 Explain how to define a report problem

LO2 Distinguish primary and secondary research

LO3 Explain how to evaluate research sources

LO4 Discuss how to create a survey and conduct interviews

LO5 List ways to analyze data effectively and ethically

LO6 Illustrate how to document sources

AN INSIDE PERSPECTIVE

Strong research and powerful writing reside behind many a business or organizational initiative. In problem solving, policy development, and strategic planning, well-written proposals and reports are invaluable.

At the age of 12, Craig Kielburger discovered the power of research and writing when he read a newspaper headline, "Battled Child Labour, Boy, 12, Murdered." It was the story of Iqbal Masih, sold into debt slavery at four and "chained to a carpet-weaving loom" for six years before being freed, speaking out about children's rights, and being killed for his courage.

Craig Kielburger and his brother Marc Kielburger return half the profits from their social enterprise Me to We to support Free the Children and continue their research and writing to inspire change.

This story marked the beginning of Craig's journey into the world of research—and social change. He researched child labour before travelling to South Asia to interview children on the topic—"I had a million questions." He wanted to know "how did they get up each morning knowing this was what they were going to do. . . I wanted to put myself in their life for a day." Like all good researchers Keilburger wanted to understand; he wanted to learn about their thoughts, hopes, and fears—and bring that knowledge back to Canada.

Beginning with a letter-writing campaign and presentations to his class, 12-year-old Craig founded Free the Children in 1995: Free children from poverty. Free children from exploitation. Free children from the idea that they are powerless to change the world.

Still 60% funded by children's fundraising, today it is the "world's largest network of children helping children through education," engaging more than a million children in 40 countries, building over 650 schools, delivering over $16 million of medical supplies, and winning awards (World's Children's Prize for the Rights of the Child and Human Rights Award).

Sustaining a charitable organization working in remote areas requires ongoing research, assessments, and proposals and reports. For Craig and brother Marc, his co-founder, it also means engagement with social media, book writing, running a social enterprise (Me to We), and keeping up a strenuous schedule of public presentations and research and writing for weekly and biweekly newspaper columns.

*Based on Free the Children, Our Founders, retrieved June 3, 2014, from http://www.freethechildren.com/about-us/our-team/our-founders/; Free the Children, About Us, retrieved April 28, 2011, from http://www.freethechildren.com/aboutus/history.php; "Craig Kielburger: Children's rights crusader," CBC News, April 18, 2006, retrieved April 28, 2011, from http://www.cbc.ca/news/background/kielburger/; Josh Wingrove, "The Right Brothers," *The Globe and Mail*, March 20, 2010, F1–7.

Many kinds of documents are called *reports*. In some organizations, a report is a long document or a document that contains numerical data. In others, one- and two-page memos are called *reports*. A short report to a client may use letter format; a report to your manager may use memo format. *Formal reports* contain formal elements such as a title page, a transmittal, and a table of contents. *Informal reports* may be letters and memos, fill-in-the-blank forms for regular routine reports (progress, for instance), electronic documents, or even computer printouts of production or sales figures. But all reports, whatever their length or degree of formality, provide the information that people in organizations such as Free the Children (◂◂ An Inside Perspective) need to solve problems and make plans.

Proposals suggest a method for finding information or solving a problem[1] and help organizations make decisions. They are as informative as they are persuasive.

Proposals and reports depend on research. The research may be as simple as pulling up data online or as complicated as calling many different people, conducting focus groups and surveys, or even planning and conducting experiments. Care in planning and researching reports is needed to produce reliable data.

In writing any report, there are five basic steps:

1. Define the problem.
2. Gather the necessary data and information.
3. Analyze the data and information.
4. Organize the information.
5. Write the report.

This chapter reviews report writing timelines and discusses the first four steps in writing any report. Chapter 11 discusses the last step, illustrating how to organize different kinds of reports and guiding you through the process of writing proposals and the progress and trip reports that often support proposal (and report) writing.

On the Job The Long and Short of Report Writing*

World War II Britain's Prime Minister Winston Churchill's concern that too much time was being wasted with masses of "far too long" reports resonates in business today. He asked for reports that "set out the main points in a series of short, crisp paragraphs." Any "detailed analysis of some complicated factors" could be relegated to an appendix.

To meet the intense competition of marketing consumer products, Procter & Gamble depends on well-reasoned ideas presented in well-organized memos.

Employees are expected to present their ideas in memos that summarize the main point in the first paragraph and then develop it in about one page of supporting information. New employees even complete a memo-writing course in P&G's training program.

According to Marketing Director Ed Burghard, memo writing at P&G is "a means to an end": the development of a clear idea. Putting the idea into a memo helps employee and manager evaluate the logic behind the idea. Burghard says, "Writing is a more cost-effective medium [than an oral presentation] because it allows identification and correction of problems before we spend money to implement an idea in the form of a P&G product or service."

When GE Plastics found it took too long to get updated reports on sales and operations, it developed a digital dashboard—the continuously updated online display of a company's vital stats. GE's new "digital cockpits" give 300 managers access to the company's essential data—on desktop PCs and smartphones. Involving several senior managers, the project "wasn't just an IT feat," says the chief information officer. "It was about changing the culture so everyone has a common way to look at the business."

*Based on John Bowden, *Writing a Report: How to Prepare, Write and Present Effective Reports* (Oxford: How to Books, 2004); Kevin Ryan, *Write Up the Corporate Ladder* (New York: Amacom, 2003), 216–222 (interview with Ed Burghard); Bob Tedeschi, "End of the paper chase," *Business 2.0*, March 2003, 64.

A TIMELINE FOR WRITING REPORTS

Writing reports—formal or informal, individual or team—calls for good project management. It involves the careful planning and managing of resources to achieve project purposes and meet audience needs within time, personnel, financial, legal, ethical, generic, or other constraints.

Once you define the report purposes and assess your resources, you can define the scope of the report (what it will and will not consider) and therefore what information you need, where and how you might access and analyze data, who is responsible for what tasks, according to what timelines and what monitoring and controls. To ensure timely, objective, quality, and cost-effective results, you may follow your work plan in order, but you may also find yourself reassessing and redefining in the light of new information. Once your report is submitted, it is time to review what worked, what issues you faced, and what lessons you learned to guide future report writing projects.

When you are writing a report for a class project, your professor will likely help design the project management, listing the steps and identifying progress reports (⏩ Chapter 11) to keep the team on task.

When you write a report, plan to spend approximately half your time analyzing your data, writing and revising the draft, and preparing visuals and slides. When you write a report for a class project:

- Plan to complete about one-quarter of your research before you write the proposal to solve the problem.
- Begin analyzing your data as you collect them.
- Prepare your list of sources and drafts of visuals as you go along.
- Save at least one-quarter of your time to think and write after all your data are collected. For a collaborative report, you will need even more time to write and revise.

Upfront planning helps you use your time efficiently.

- Read the sample proposal and reports in Chapter 11 even before you write your proposal.
- Talk to your readers to understand how much detail and formality they want.
- Review earlier company (or class) reports.
- List all the parts of the report you will need to prepare.
- Articulate the purposes, audiences, and generic constraints for each part. The fuller an idea you have of the final product when you start, the fewer drafts you will need to write and the better your final product will be.

LO1

DEFINING PROBLEMS TO BE SOLVED

When you write a report as part of your job, the organization may define the topic. To think of problems for class reports, think about problems that face your college or university; campus housing units; social, religious, and professional groups; local businesses; and municipal, provincial, and federal governments and their agencies. Read print or online campus and local papers and newsmagazines; watch the news on TV, or listen to it on CBC or a local radio station.

A well-defined report problem in business meets the following criteria:

1. The problem is
   - Real
   - Important enough to be worth solving
   - Narrow but challenging
2. The audience for the report is
   - Real
   - Interested in the problem
   - Able to implement the recommended action
3. The data, evidence, and facts are
   - Sufficient to document the severity of the problem
   - Sufficient to prove that the recommendation will solve the problem
   - Available to *you*
   - Comprehensible to *you*

Alissa Kozuh analyzes the words customers key in on the search feature at www.nordstrom.com. She's found five patterns: customers key in particular items ("shoes"), trends ("leopard prints"), departments from the bricks-and-mortar stores ("Brass Plum," the juniors department), designer names, and special occasions ("prom"). The changes she suggested for the site based on her research increased Web sales 32%.

Often you need to narrow the problem statement. For example, "improving the post-secondary experiences of international students studying in Canada" is too broad. First, choose one college or university. Second, identify the specific problem. Do you want to increase the social interaction between Canadian and international students? Increase language instruction? Help international students find housing? Third, identify the specific audience with the power to implement your recommendations. Depending on the topic, the audience might be the Office of International Studies, the residence counsellors, a service organization on campus or in town, a store, or a group of investors.

Define the problem in terms of the time available to solve it. Six months of full-time (and overtime) work and a team of colleagues might allow you to assess all the ways to make a store more profitable. If you're doing a report in 6 to 12 weeks for a class that is only one of your responsibilities, limit the scope of the topic. You could choose to examine the store's prices and product, its inventory procedures, its overhead costs, its layout and decor, or its advertising budget.

How you define the problem shapes the solutions you find. For example, suppose that a manufacturer of frozen foods isn't making money. If you define the problem as a marketing problem, you may analyze the product's price, image, advertising,

On the Job Access to Information?*

"Democracy cannot be maintained," the Supreme Court of Canada argues, "without its foundation in free public opinion and free discussion throughout the nation of all matters affecting the state within the limits of the criminal code and the common law."

The Information Age has raised expectations of free access, of information a simple click away. But a study published in *Government Information Quarterly* of freedom-of-access information in five parliamentary democracies placed New Zealand first and Canada last! Canada, the report claims, "has continually suffered from a combination of low use, low political support and a weak Information Commissioner since its inception."

Discouraging electronic requests and requiring paper cheques, Canada has gone from being in the vanguard and advising other countries on legislation to being "a laggard," say authors Robert Hazell and Ben Worthy.

Information Commissioner Suzanne Legault concedes, "We have fallen behind." Government statistics for 2009–2010 show full disclosure in only 16% of 35,000 requests compared to 40% 10 years earlier. Delays and "excessive censorship" have been issues.

The 2012 National Freedom of Information Audit found that the federal government performance compared to other levels of government "was again among the worst" with a D grade, 50% completion rate within the statutory 30 days, and a continued reliance on 1970s technology: "paper or unreadable copies of electronic data."

The loss of the long-form census and five other surveys (in business, the environment, and health) to $7 million cuts to Statistics Canada further compromises information access.

*Based on Supreme Court of Canada, Reference re: Alberta Legislation [1938] SCR 100; Dean Beeby, "Canada hits bottom on freedom-of-information ranking, new study finds," Canadian Press, January 9, 2011, retrieved from http://www.cbc.ca/cp/media/GT1103.html; Fred Vallance-Jones, *National Freedom of Information Audit 2012,* retrieved June 3, 2014, from http://www.newspaperscanada.ca/sites/default/files/Freedom-of-Information-Audit-2012-FINAL.pdf; André Picard, "Ottawa should come to its Census," *The Globe and Mail,* July 8, 2010, L1–2; Dean Beeby, "Ordered to find $7 million in savings, Statscan cuts five more surveys," *The Globe and Mail,* October 12, 2010, A8.

and position in the market. But perhaps the problem is really that poor inventory management makes overhead costs too high. Defining the problem accurately is essential to defining your report purpose and finding an effective solution.

Once you've defined your problem, you're ready to write at least a tentative *purpose statement*. The purpose statement goes in your proposal and in your final report. A good purpose statement makes three things clear:

- The organizational problem (or challenge or opportunity)
- The specific technical questions that must be answered to solve the problem
- The rhetorical purpose (to explain, to recommend, to request, to propose) in terms of audience benefits

The following purpose statement has all three elements:

> When banner ads on Web pages first appeared in 1994, the initial reponse, or "click-through" rate, was about 10%. However, as ads have proliferated on Web pages, the click-through rate has dropped sharply. Rather than assuming that any banner ad will be successful, we need to ask, What characteristics do successful banner ads share? Are ads for certain kinds of products and services or for certain kinds of audiences more likely to be successful on the Web? The purpose of this report is to summarize the available research and anecdotal evidence and to recommend what Rethink Advertising Agency should tell its clients about whether and how to use banner ads.

LO2

RESEARCH STRATEGIES FOR REPORTS

Research for a report may be as simple as getting a computer printout of sales for the last month; it may involve finding published material or surveying or interviewing people as Craig Kielburger did (◀◀ An Inside Perspective). Having a research plan before gathering data and information will strengthen your findings. It will also strengthen the reliability and cogency of the proposal or report, adding to your credibility while testing your core idea and identifying where revision is required to incorporate new information.

Knowing your topic, articulating your problem statement and report purpose, and identifying your information gaps and reliable resources will help you better target your search and keep it ethical. To avoid bias in your findings and to test your own assumptions, you will want to research with an open mind, ready to represent reliable and relevant research sources.

Nicholas Carr has famously asked if Google is making us stupid. As a researcher and author, Carr acknowledges that Google has been a rich resource of "immediate access," but he worries that it is "chipping away my capacity for concentration and contemplation." It encourages skimming before "bounc[ing] out to another site." We tend, he thinks, to become "decoders of information" rather than critical or deep thinkers.[2]

Others worry about the unevenness of Google search results. Demand Media and Answers.com, for example, are said to be exploiting freelancers to produce low-quality content that gets prominence by manipulating keyword and search engine optimization. Algorithm and ranking formulae changes to address these problems collide with "skyrocketing expectations of Google." Also, columnist Jeff Beer points to Google's "conflict of interest in any large campaign against content farms" and the ongoing challenge of social searches including Facebook's partnership with Microsoft's Bing search engine.[3]

Others complain about the high placing of Wikipedia entries and explain why professors don't like to see research results reduced to Google (which searches Web sites without the ability to evaluate content) and Wikipedia, whose entries can be informative but can also be changed by anyone. Some professors deduct marks or even fail assignments based on Wikipedia, About.com, Answers.com, and other such sources.

While company and industry association Web sites can be useful sources on company and industry history, products, and services, they are marketing tools and not credible research sources.

Also blurring the line between reliable research sources and marketing are advertorials or infomercials now known as "native advertising," "branded content," or "sponsored content" made to look like editorial content.[4] While some in the news publishing industry see the growing phenomenon as a dangerous "Faustian pact," others are "confident that . . . readers will appreciate what is sponsor-generated content and what is content from our global staff." And social media users add to the mix with 10% claiming to have posted news videos they produced themselves and 11% having posted material to news sites and blogs, while 50% repost news stories.[5] So read carefully and critically.

Although it can be a helpful place to start (especially if you follow links to reliable sources), Wikipedia is not the best place to end a search if reliability and your credibility matter. That's where the library's databases of peer-reviewed resources can save the day!

Even Google Scholar, heralded as a free search engine for peer-reviewed content, "exhibits limitations in accuracy and timeliness" compared to such free search engines as PubMed, according to librarian Marian Burright.[6]

Being open to possibilities can help avoid what Peter Nicholson, president of the Council of Canadian Academies, calls a "just-in-time approach" to research "narrowing peripheral intellectual vision" to the point of "reducing the serendipity that has been the source of most radical innovation."[7]

Secondary research retrieves information that someone else gathered. Library research and online searches are the best-known kinds of secondary research. **Primary research** gathers new information. Surveys, interviews, and observations are common methods for business reports.

LO3

FINDING INFORMATION ONLINE AND IN PRINT

You can save time and money by checking online and published sources of data before you gather new information.

Although there has been much talk of a paperless society, print sources—books, magazines, and journals—remain valuable. Not all published research is available online or is appropriate for online delivery. When you want an in-depth treatment of a subject, you may still want to read a book and access other library resources (catalogues, directories, databases, indexes, newspapers and periodicals, government publications), even if online.

To evaluate research, consider:

- **Validity.** Is the research accurate, important, and original? Is it widely cited in the field? Independently verified?
- **Reliability.** Are the data consistent? Does research design test the hypothesis? Is the author credible? Are the sources unbiased?
- **Currency.** Do findings remain accurate? Have they been overtaken by events? Some studies from the 1970s remain relevant (for example, studies by Henry Mintzberg cited in Chapter 1), while others from four years ago may fail to take into account the latest census results.

To use an online database efficiently, identify the concepts you're interested in and choose keywords that will help you find relevant sources. *Keywords* or *descriptors* are the terms that the computer searches for. If you're not sure what terms to use, check the ABI/Inform Thesaurus online for synonyms and the hierarchies in which information is arranged in various databases.

Specific commands allow you to narrow your search. For example, to study the effect of the minimum wage on employment in the restaurant industry, you might use a Boolean search (see Figure 10.1):

(minimum wage) *and* (restaurant *or* fast and food) and (employment *or* unemployment).

This descriptor would give you the titles of articles that treat all three of the topics in parentheses. Without *and,* you'd get articles that discuss the minimum wage in general, articles about every aspect of *restaurants,* and every article that refers to *unemployment,* even though many of these would not be relevant to your topic. The *or* descriptor calls up articles that use the term *fast food* but not the term *restaurant.* An article that used the phrase *food service industry* would be eliminated unless it also used the term *restaurant.* Google and some other Web search engines allow you to specify words that cannot appear in a source.

Figure 10.1 Example of a Boolean Search

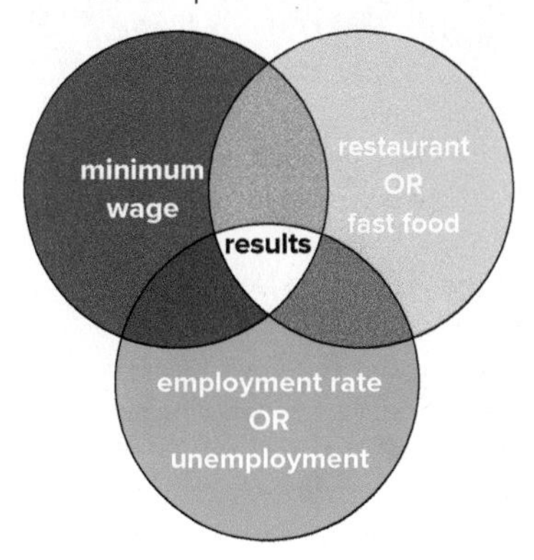

Many words can appear in related forms. To catch all of them, use the database's **wild card** or **truncated code** for shortened terms and root words.

Figures 10.2 and 10.3 list a few of the specialized sources available.

Evaluating Web Sources

Some of the material on the Web is excellent, but some of it is wholly unreliable (see the Technology Tips boxes in this

Michael Frank, former CEO of Toronto's Sprylogics, developer of Cluuz.com, shows what its innovative search engine offers. Cluuz.com uses semantics to search for and get results that rely on the meanings of words and not only matched keywords.

Technology Tips More of the Same Information*

At a time of proliferating sources of information, we might presume that we have access to more and better information. Right? Not necessarily.

A study "The State of the News Media" by Columbia University's Project for Excellence in Journalism, reporting on proliferating news Web sites and citizen news blogs, concludes that possibly even less news is being reported. The same news uncovered by "conventional media" is simply being "repackaged" and recirculated as news: "with . . . a million sources reporting the same story."

These trends help explain "why celebrity news and trivia" abound. Newer media tend to trivialize and polarize, with the 24-hour TV news channels "stretch[ing] out to fill an entire cycle."

The latest entrant on the Canadian news scene—Sun News—is reportedly doing little to change the scene. Even in the context of a federal election, it is attracting audiences as small as 4,000–5,000. In 2012 it was still "lagging behind its competitors."

Meanwhile, a study by UBC Professor Alfred Hermida finds that almost 60% of Canadians report visiting social network sites, with a majority claiming those sites give them better access to "a broader range of news and information than traditional media." Although they still consider traditional media important and reliable, they are likely to get their news "personalized"; that is, "selected and filtered by family, friends and acquaintances." While 25% consider social networks "reliable," 90% trust traditional media.

*Based on Russell Smith, "Way more news sites, way less news," *The Globe and Mail,* March 27, 2008, R1–2; Bill Brioux, "Sun News drawing as few as 4,000 viewers," Canadian Press, retrieved April 28, 2011, from http://www.thestar.com/entertainment/article/981673--sun-news-drawing-as-few-as-4-000-viewers; Diana Mehta, "Sun News turns one, but who's watching?" retrieved June 3, 2014, from http://metronews.ca/news/canada/109029/sun-news-turns-one-but-whos-watching/; "Social media transforming how Canadians get the news, study finds," retrieved April 28, 2011, from http://www.publicaffairs.ubc.ca/2011/04/27/social-media-transforming-how-canadians-get-the-news-study-finds/.

Figure 10.2 Sources for Electronic Research

Online databases are available in many university libraries. Check your college or university library to find additional sources.

ABI/Inform Global (indexes and abstracts over 3,000 publications in management and business)
Business Index ASAP
Canadian Business & Current Affairs (CBCA) Complete
Canadian Newsstand
Communication and Mass Media Complete
EBSCOhost
Emerald & Emerald Backfile
Factiva
Gender Studies Database
Google Scholar
Governments Canada Database
LEXIS/NEXIS Canada
LGBT Life
McGraw-Hill Encyclopedia of Science
PAIS International—Public Affairs Information Service
Social Sciences Citation Index
Wilson Business Abstracts
Women's Studies International

Technology Tips Not Necessarily True*

Information on the Web is not necessarily true. Scambusters.org exposes popular scams; the RCMP advises on identity theft and fraud.

Even skeptical Web surfers are being taken in by those buying domain names in advance of disasters. Criminals set up legitimate sounding Web sites that turn up in a standard Web search for a charity after disaster hits. Generous Canadians are vulnerable to such scams.

According to Cpl. Louis Robertson of Phonebusters, an RCMP anti-fraud call centre, 63 victims reported charitable donation scams in Canada between January 2007 and mid-2008.

Press releases from "Independent Financial Reports" touted an Internet stock. "Independent Financial Reports" did not exist; the press releases were fakes, designed to boost the price of the stock. (The U.S. SEC filed suit.)

The satirical newspaper *The Onion* (www.theonion.com) posted an "interview" in which Harry Potter author J. K. Rowling "admitted" that she worshipped Satan. The interview was a spoof but was taken seriously by some readers.

*Based on Scambusters.org, retrieved April 29, 2011, from http://www.scambusters.org/; RCMP, "Identity theft and identity fraud," retrieved April 29, 2011, from http://www.rcmp-grc.gc.ca/scams-fraudes/id-theft-vol-eng.htm; Darcy Keith, "Don't be fooled by fake charities," CanWest, August 29, 2008, retrieved August 30, 2008, from http://www.canada.com/topics/technology/story.html?id=ec4bf8ce-2446-4e30-a6d6-e25b3d93036b; "Beware the press release," *BusinessWeek,* April 24, 2000, 153; "You said it," *Reader's Digest,* April 2001, 18.

Figure 10.3 Sources for Web Research

Subject Matter Directories

Canada Business: canadabusiness.ca

Canadiana Discovery Portal: search.canadiana.ca

Education Index: www.educationindex.com

Financial Web: www.finweb.com

GlobalEdge: http://globaledge.msu.edu/reference-desk

Industry Canada: www.ic.gc.ca

KnowThis.com: www.knowthis.com

Management and Entrepreneurship—LSU Libraries: http://www.lib.lsu.edu/sp/subjects/management

Marketing Resources—LSU Libraries: www.lib.lsu.edu/sp/subjects/marketing

Questia: Human Resource Management: www.questia.com

Resources for Economists on the Internet: www.aeaweb.org/rfe

SmartPros Accounting: accounting.smartpros.com

News Sites

BusinessWeek: www.businessweek.com/

Canadian Business: www.canadianbusiness.com/

CBC: www.cbc.ca/

CNN/CNNMoney: www.cnn.com/ (news); http://money.cnn.com/ (financial news)

CTV: www.ctv.ca/

Global TV: www.globaltv.com/

The Globe and Mail: www.globeandmail.ca/

Maclean's: www.macleans.ca/

National Post: www.nationalpost.com/

National Public Radio: www.npr.org/

NewsLink (links to U.S., Canadian, and international newspapers, magazines, and resources online): newslink.org/

New York Times: www.nytimes.com/

The Wall Street Journal: online.wsj.com/

Washington Post: www.washingtonpost.com/

Canadian Government Information

Census of Population and Census of Agriculture: www12.statcan.ca/English/census01/home/index.cfm

Consumer Price Index: www23.statcan.gc.ca/imdb/p2SV.pl?Function=getSurvey&SDDS=2301

Historical Statistics of Canada: http://www5.statcan.gc.ca/olc-cel/olc.action?ObjId=11-516-X&ObjType=2&lang=en&limit=0

Statistics Canada: www.statcan.gc.ca/start-debut-eng.html

The Daily: www.statcan.gc.ca/dai-quo/index-eng.htm?MM

Print Research Sources

Accountants' Index

Business Periodicals Index

Canadian Business Index

Personnel Management Abstracts

Reader's Guide to Periodical Literature

chapter). With print sources, the editor or publisher serves as a gatekeeper, so you can trust the material in good journals. To put up a Web page, all one needs is access to a server.

Use four criteria to decide whether a Web site is good enough to use for a research project:

1. **Authors.** What person or organization sponsors the site? What credentials do the authors have?
2. **Objectivity.** Does the site give evidence to support its claims? Does it give both sides of controversial issues? Is the tone professional?
3. **Information.** How complete is the information? What is it based on?
4. **Revision date.** When was the site last updated?

Answers to these questions may lead you to discard some of the relevant sites you find. For example, if you find five different Web pages about cell phones and car accidents that all cite the same Toronto study, you have one source, not five. Choose the most complete for your project.

See Figure 10.4 for further resources for evaluating Web sources.

Figure 10.4 Further Resources for Evaluating Web Sources

Purdue Online Writing Lab, "Evaluating Sources: Overview," February 22, 2013: http://owl.english.purdue.edu/owl/resource/553/01/

Ryerson University Library & Archives, "Evaluating Internet Resources," April 2011: http://library.ryerson.ca/guides/toolbox/web_resources/

University of Albany Libraries, "Evaluating Web Content," March 2009: https://library.albany.edu/usered/eval/evalweb/

University of Alberta Libraries, "Critical Evaluation of Resources on the Internet," November 29, 2013: guides.library.ualberta.ca/eval_internet

University of British Columbia Library, "Evaluating Information Sources," August 20, 2013: http://help.library.ubc.ca/evaluating-and-citing-sources/evaluating-information-sources/

LO4

DESIGNING QUESTIONS FOR SURVEYS AND INTERVIEWS

A **survey** questions a large group of people, called *respondents* or *subjects*. The easiest way to ask many questions is to create a **questionnaire,** a written list of questions that people fill out. An **interview** is a structured conversation with someone able to give you useful information. Surveys and interviews can be useful only if the questions are well designed.

Good questions ask only one thing, are phrased neutrally, avoid making assumptions about the respondent, and mean essentially the same thing to different people. Learn from the experts on CBC, CTV, and Global.

Phrase questions in a way that won't bias the response or lead the respondent. Words like *often* and *important* mean different things to different people. Whenever possible, use more objective measures:

× Vague: Do you study in the library frequently?
✓ Better: How many hours a week do you study in the library?

In two decades of writing and using surveys, psychologist Palmer Morrel-Samuels has seen that the wording of a survey question can affect responses. In a survey to learn about the leadership skills of a photo equipment maker's managers, a question asked employees whether their manager "takes bold strides" and "has a strong grasp" of complicated issues. Male managers tended to outscore female managers.

Morrel-Samuels noted that, in a literal sense, males on average take longer strides and have more muscle strength than females. The company changed the wording of the survey. "Has a strong grasp of complex problems" became "discusses complex problems with precision and clarity." After this change, the difference in ratings of female and male managers disappeared.[8]

Another word-related bias is that respondents tend to agree more than disagree with statements. If a survey about managers asks employees whether their manager is fair, ethical, intelligent, knowledgeable, and so on, they are likely to assign all of these qualities to the manager—and to agree more and more as the survey goes along. To correct for this, some questions should be worded to generate the opposite response. For example, a statement about ethics can be balanced by a statement about corruption, and a statement about fairness can be balanced by a statement about bias or stereotypes.[9]

Questions can be categorized in several ways. *Closed questions* have a limited number of possible responses. *Open questions* do not lock the subject into any sort of response. See Figure 10.5. Closed questions are faster for subjects to answer and easier for researchers to score. However, since all answers must fit into pre-chosen categories, they cannot probe the complexities of a subject.

Use an "Other, Please Specify" category when you want the convenience of a closed question but cannot foresee all the possible responses:

What is the single most important reason that you ride the bus?
______ I don't have a car.
______ I don't want to fight rush-hour traffic.
______ Riding the bus is cheaper than driving my car.
______ Riding the bus conserves fuel and reduces pollution.
______ Other (Please specify) ______________

Technology Tips Polling Then and Now*

In some of the first Gallup polls, 82% of Canadians in 1936 supported capital punishment and 86% in 1939 believed in life after death. Since many had no phones, conducting thousands of interviews with demographically diverse people was challenging. Still, in 1936, Gallup predicted the re-election of Franklin D. Roosevelt.

Today, pollsters face a technological "reality check." They can no longer rely on phones (down from 70% 20 years ago to 20% response rate) if they want to reach young people. They have to spend time and money tracking cell phones. Online polling depending on market research databases is problematic because participants are "self-selected" and omit the less connected.

Instead of getting at underlying social issues, the media are often content with "horse-race" online polls that are cheaper than random phone surveys. Wildly different calculations of the "undecided" further undermine polling reliability.

When 60% of Canadians in the north and 52% in the south reported that the Arctic was under threat, a view not shared by the Department of Defence that commissioned the poll, University of Calgary Professor Ron Huebert suggested that Conservative Party rhetoric and media reports were shaping public conclusions.

Others worry that polling increases voter apathy in the face of seemingly preordained outcomes. Yet others worry that polls "encourage a pragmatism that looks devious to purists."

Pollsters' claim "to know Canada's collective will" is belied by the variability of poll results by up to 15%. John Allemang concludes that polling seems "as much like sorcery as like science," although he identifies a public good in giving "the entire body politic a collective voice."

*Based on Neil Reynolds, "Life then and now: We're polls apart," *The Globe and Mail*, April 6, 2007, B2; John Allemang, "To poll or not to poll, that is the question," *The Globe and Mail*, April 9, 2011, A4; Murray Brewster, "Tories play to misconceptions on Arctic, poll suggests," *The Globe and Mail*, March 8, 2011, A5.

Figure 10.5 Closed and Open Questions

CLOSED QUESTIONS

Are you satisfied with the city bus service? (yes/no)

How good is the city bus service?
Excellent 5 4 3 2 1 Terrible

Indicate whether you agree or disagree with each of the following statements about city bus service:

A D The schedule is convenient for me.

A D The routes are convenient for me.

A D The drivers are courteous.

A D The buses are clean.

Rate each of the following improvements in the order of their importance to you (1 = most important, 6 = least important)

_____ Buy new buses.

_____ Increase non-rush-hour service on weekdays.

_____ Increase service on weekdays.

_____ Provide earlier and later service on weekdays.

_____ Buy more buses with wheelchair access.

_____ Provide unlimited free transfers.

OPEN QUESTIONS

How do you feel about the city bus service?

Tell me about the city bus service.

Why do you ride the bus? (or, Why don't you ride the bus?)

What do you like and dislike about the city bus service?

How could the city bus service be improved?

When you use multiple-choice questions, make sure that one answer fits only in one category. In the following example of overlapping categories, a person who worked for a company with exactly 25 employees could check either *a* or *b*. The resulting data would be unreliable.

✕ OVERLAPPING CATEGORIES:

Indicate the number of full-time employees in your company on May 16:

_____ a. 0–25
_____ b. 25–100
_____ c. 100–500
_____ d. over 500

✓ DISCRETE CATEGORIES:

Indicate the number of full-time employees on your payroll on May 16:

_____ a. 0–25
_____ b. 26–100
_____ c. 101–500
_____ d. more than 500

Giving several options is more important the older your respondents are. Psychologist Cynthia Adams notes that older people are uncomfortable choosing between only two options. When asked "Are discounts important to you," more mature people want to answer, "It depends."[10] A good survey will specify the context or allow the respondent to do so.

Branching questions direct different respondents to different parts of the questionnaire based on their answers to earlier questions.

> 10. Have you talked to an academic adviser this year?
> _____ Yes _____ No (If "no," skip to question 14.)

Generally, early in the questionnaire put questions that will be easy to answer. Put questions that are harder to answer or that people may be less willing to answer (e.g., age and income) near the end of the questionnaire. Even people who choose not to answer such questions fill out the rest of the survey.

If subjects will fill out the questionnaire themselves, pay careful attention to the physical design of the document. Pretest the questionnaire to make sure the directions are clear. One researcher mailed a two-page questionnaire without pretesting it. Twenty-five respondents didn't answer the questions on the back of the first page.[11]

Conducting Surveys and Interviews

Face-to-face surveys are convenient when you are surveying a fairly small number of people in a specific location. In a face-to-face survey, the interviewer's sex, race, and nonverbal cues can bias results. Most people prefer not to say things they think their audience will find unacceptable. For that reason, women will be more likely to agree that sexual harassment is a problem if the interviewer is also a woman. Members of a minority group are more likely to admit that they suffer discrimination if the interviewer is a member of the same minority.

Telephone surveys are popular because they can be closely supervised. Interviewers can read the questions from a computer screen and key in answers as the respondent gives them. The results can then be available just a few minutes after the last call is completed.

The major limitation of phone surveys is that they reach only people who have phones and thus underrepresent poor and young people. To include people with unlisted numbers, professional survey-takers use automatic random-digit dialling. Since women are more likely to answer the phone than men are,[12] decide in advance to whom you want to speak, and ask for that person rather than surveying whoever answers the phone.

Mail surveys can reach anyone who has an address. Some people may be more willing to fill out an anonymous questionnaire than to give sensitive information to a stranger over the phone.

Online surveys deliver questions over the Internet. The researcher can contact respondents with e-mail containing a link to a Web page with the survey or can ask people by mail or in person to log on and visit the Web site with the survey.

A survey posted on a Web site inviting the site's visitors to complete the survey does not generate a random sample, so the results probably do not reflect the opinions of the entire population.

Interactive technology makes it easy to use branching questions; the survey can automatically send respondents to the next question on a branch. However, many people worry about the privacy of online surveys, so they may be reluctant to participate. Researchers have found that a lower percentage of people are willing to complete online surveys than other kinds. To encourage participation, researchers should make online surveys as short as possible.[13]

A major concern with any kind of survey is the **response rate,** the percentage of people who respond. People who refuse to answer may differ from those who respond quickly, and you need information from both groups to be able to generalize to the whole population. To get as high a response rate as possible, good researchers contact non-respondents at least once to try to persuade them to participate in the survey. Still, they face significant survey fatigue as people are receiving more and more requests for their opinion on everything from internal organizational matters to major public issues.

Selecting a Sample for Surveys and Interviews

To keep research costs reasonable, only a sample of the total population is polled. How that sample is chosen and the attempts made to get responses from non-respondents will determine whether you can infer that what is true of your sample is also true of the population as a whole. The *population* is the group you want to make statements about. Depending on the purpose of your research, your population might be all Top 1000 companies from the *Report on Business* annual listing, all business students at your college or university, or all consumers.

A *convenience sample* is a group of subjects who are easy to get: students who walk through the students' union, people at a shopping mall, workers in your own unit. Convenience samples are useful for a rough pretest of a questionnaire and may be acceptable for some class research projects. However, you cannot generalize from a convenience sample to a larger group.

A *judgment sample* is a group of people whose views seem useful. Someone interested in surveying the kinds of writing done on campus might ask each department for the name of a faculty member who cared about writing, and then send surveys to those people.

In a *random sample,* each person in the population theoretically has an equal chance of being chosen.

True random samples rely on random digit tables, published in statistics texts and books such as *A Million Random Digits* or computer-generated random numbers.

Conducting Research Interviews

Schedule interviews in advance; tell the interviewee about how long you expect the interview to take.

Interviews can be structured or unstructured. In a **structured interview,** the interviewer uses a detailed list of questions to guide the interview. Indeed, a structured interview may use a questionnaire just as a survey does. In an **unstructured interview,** the interviewer has three or four main questions. Other questions build on what the interviewee says. To prepare for an unstructured interview, learn as much as possible about the interviewee and the topic. Go into the interview with three or four main topics you want to cover.

Interviewers sometimes use closed questions to start the interview and set the interviewee at ease. The strength of an interview, however, is getting at a person's attitudes, feelings, and experiences. Situational questions let you probe what someone would do in a specific circumstance. Hypothetical questions that ask people to imagine what they would do generally yield less reliable answers than questions about *critical incidents* or key past events.

> Hypothetical question: What would you say if you had to tell an employee that his or her performance was unsatisfactory?
> Critical incident question: You've probably been in a situation where someone who was working with you wasn't carrying his or her share of the work. What did you do the last time that happened?

A **mirror question** paraphrases the content of the last answer: "So you confronted him directly?" "You think that this product costs too much?" Mirror questions check that the

Ethics and Legal Ethical Issues in Interviewing

If you're trying to get sensitive information, interviewees may give useful information when the interview is "over" and the tape recorder has been turned off. Is it ethical to use that information?

If you're interviewing a hostile or very reluctant interviewee, you may get more information if you agree with everything you can legitimately agree to, and keep silent on the rest. Is it ethical to imply acceptance even when you know you'll criticize the interviewee's ideas in your report?

Most people would say that whatever public figures say is fair game: they're supposed to know enough to defend themselves. Many people would say that different rules apply when you cite someone by name than when you use the information as background or use a pseudonym so that the interviewee cannot be identified.

As a practical matter, if someone feels you've misrepresented him or her, that person will be less willing to talk to you in the future. But quite apart from practical considerations, interview strategies raise ethical issues as well.

Ethnographic research closely observes how people choose and use products. Videotapes showed that many customers bought only a few cuts of meat because they didn't know how to cook other cuts. As a result, many grocers are now rearranging meat products by cooking methods and offering simple, three-step instructions on packages.

interviewer understands what the interviewee has said and prompt the interviewee to continue talking. **Probes** follow up an original question to get at specific aspects of a topic:

Question: What do you think about the fees for campus parking?
Probes: Would you be willing to pay more for a reserved space? How much more?
Should the fines for vehicles parked illegally be increased?
Do you think fees should be based on income?

Observing Customers and Users

Answers to surveys and interviews may differ from actual behaviour—sometimes greatly. To get more accurate consumer information, many marketers observe users.

When she introduced Growing Healthy, a line of frozen baby foods, founder Julia Knight enlisted friends with kids to join her on research shopping trips. She quickly realized that the frozen food section wasn't a good location. Kids didn't like the cold, and parents sped through as quickly as possible. So she persuaded supermarket managers to place cutaway freezers in the baby food section, and her company succeeded. Her observations also showed Knight why survey and interview data can be so unreliable: "What mother, especially in front of other mothers, would really tell you that she spent more on cat food than on baby food?"[14]

When a 60-ish woman announced to her husband, "We beat the . . . out of the front desk and got a terrific room!" they were taking part in marketing research "to figure out what consumers really think" about Best Western International products. Tapes of 25 couples who had agreed to tape themselves on their travels proved to the hotel that "it didn't need to boost its standard 10% senior citizen discount." The couples got more out of "the thrill of the deal." So the hotel concluded that bigger discounts would do "absolutely nothing for Best Western."[15]

International Targeting Ethnic Audiences*

Kraft Canada is among companies competing for the spending power of a growing immigrant community. Chef Smita Chandra has been sharing recipes that use Kraft products and fit new lifestyles in Canada without the help of home—while appealing still to South Asian tastes. Kraft has now added chef Susur Lee to target Chinese consumers.

Campbell's Canada is among others positioning themselves to compete with specialty grocers and benefit from immigration over the next 15 years, when 75% are predicted to be visible minorities. Joel Gregoire, industry analyst with NDP Group in Toronto, warns that South Asians represent very different cultures: "To target the ethnic consumer? Well, good luck."

Loblaws has already blundered when it aired, during Muslim Ramadan, an ad in Punjabi during a Hindi movie. They are not alone in such language lapses and others have been guilty of predictable, token ads.

Politicians too have been targeting the ethnic, even "very ethnic" vote to try to shift traditional patterns of voting out of loyalty to Liberal immigration policies of the past. The Tories, says Bernard Simon, banked on "the ethnic vote to help convert their five-year minority government into a majority." Toronto lawyer Avvy Go resents being treated as "homogeneous groups." He finds it "insulting" that people think they can understand others on the basis of "what we wear and what we eat."

*Based on Wency Leung, "Will ethnic market follow Susur to Kraft?" *The Globe and Mail,* April 13, 2011, L4; Marina Strauss, "A worldly ad approach," *The Globe and Mail,* September 24, 2010, B1–7; Bernard Simon, "Canada's parties target big ethnic vote," FT.com April 1, 2011, retrieved April 29, 2011, from http://www.ft.com/cms/s/0/f00c165a-5bd2-11e0-b8e7-00144feab49a.html#axzz1L3BZ4qKE; Joe Friesen, "From 'ethnic' dress to political distress for the Tories," *The Globe and Mail,* April 14, 2011, A5.

LO5

ANALYZING DATA AND INFORMATION FOR REPORTS

Analyzing the data you have gathered is essential to produce the tight logic needed for a good report. Analyze your data with healthy skepticism. Professor Raymond Panko found that 30% of spreadsheets had errors, such as misplaced decimal points, transposed digits, and wrong signs, built into their rules.[16]

Check to be sure that your data come from a reliable source. Use the strategies outlined in this chapter to evaluate Web sources. When the source has a *vested interest* (◀◀ Chapter 9) in the results, scrutinize them with special care. To analyze a company's financial prospects, use independent information as well as the company's annual report and press releases.

If your report is based upon secondary data from library and online research, look at the sample, the sample size, and the exact wording of questions to see what the data actually measure. According to Web guru Jakob Nielsen's research, a sample of just five people is enough to test the usability of a Web site. That conclusion is surprising, because for many kinds of research, a large sample is important for giving significant results. But other tests have led to similar conclusions.[17]

Identify exactly what the data measure. For example, using a Dun & Bradstreet database, many people claim that only 28% of small businesses survive for eight years. But that database counts a small business as "surviving" only if it remains under the same ownership. Researcher Bruce Kirchoff found that another 26% survive with ownership changes, for a total survival rate of 54%.[18]

In 2014 the federal government was widely criticized for its claims about job skills shortages based not on Statistics Canada data but on Kijiji job listings found to be "overly volatile" by the Conference Board of Canada.[19] Even Statistics Canada data can be insufficiently specific on where exactly within provinces job vacancies are an issue[20]—with profound implications for policy on temporary foreign worker and employment insurance programs.[21]

If your data include words, try to find out what the words mean to the people who said them. Respondents to appliance manufacturer Whirlpool's survey of 180,000 households said they wanted "clean refrigerators." After asking more questions, Whirlpool found that what people really wanted were refrigerators that *looked* clean, so the company developed models with textured fronts and sides to hide fingerprints.[22] Also try to measure words against numbers. When he researched possible investments, one analyst found that people in mature industries were pessimistic. People in immature industries were optimistic, even when the numbers weren't great.[23]

Look for patterns. If you have library sources, on which points do experts agree? Which disagreements can be explained by theories or numbers that have now changed? Which are the result of having different values and criteria? In your interviews and surveys, what patterns do you see?

State accurately what your data show. Don't confuse causation with correlation. *Causation* means that one thing causes or produces another. *Correlation* means that two things happen at the same time. Both might be caused by a third.

For example, suppose you're considering whether to buy tablets instead of PCs for everyone in your company, and suppose your surveys show that the people who currently have tablets are, in general, more productive than people who don't. Does having a tablet lead to higher productivity? Perhaps. But perhaps productive people are more likely to push to get tablets from company funds, while less productive people are more passive. Perhaps some other factor—experience in the company, education, or social background—leads both to increased productivity and to acquiring tablets.

Consciously search for at least three possible causes for each phenomenon you've observed and at least three possible solutions for each problem. The more possibilities you brainstorm, the more likely you are to find good options. In your report, mention all of the possibilities; discuss in detail only those that you think are the real reasons and the best solutions.

When you have identified patterns that seem to represent the causes of the problem or the best solutions, check these ideas against the evidence. Can you find support in the quotations or in the numbers? Can you answer counterarguments? If you can, you will be able to present evidence for your argument in a convincing way.

Make the nature of your evidence clear to your reader. Do you have observations that you yourself have made? Or do you have inferences based on observations or data collected by others?

If you can't prove the claim you originally hoped to make, modify your conclusions to fit your data. Even when your market test is a failure or your experiment disproves your hypothesis, you can still write a useful—and ethical—report.

- Identify changes that might yield a different result. For example, selling the product at a lower price might enable the company to sell enough units.
- Divide the discussion to show what part of the test succeeded.
- Discuss circumstances that may have affected the results.
- Summarize your negative findings in progress reports to let readers down gradually and to give them a chance to modify the research design.
- Remember that negative results aren't always disappointing to the audience. For example, the people who commissioned a feasibility report may be relieved to have an impartial outsider confirm their suspicions that a project isn't feasible.[24]

ORGANIZING INFORMATION IN REPORTS

Do not put information in reports just because you have it or just because it took you a long time to find it. Instead, choose the information that your reader needs to make a decision.

How much information you need to include depends on whether your audience is likely to be supportive, neutral, or skeptical.

You must also decide whether to put information in the body of the report or in appendixes. Put material in the body of the report if it is crucial to your proof or if it is short. (Something less than half a page won't interrupt the reader.)

Anything that a careful reader will want but that is not crucial to your proof can go in an appendix.

Most sets of data can be organized in several logical ways. The following three guidelines will help you choose the arrangement that will be the most useful for your reader:

1. **Process your information before you present it to your reader.** The order in which you found information usually is not the best order to present it to your reader.
2. **When you have lots of information, group it into three to seven categories.** The average person's short-term memory can hold only seven chunks, though the chunks can be of any size.[25] By grouping your information into seven categories (or fewer), you make your report easier to read.
3. **Work with the reader's expectations, not against them.** Use a direct pattern if your reader is likely to be supportive, or indirect (◂◂ Chapter 9) if likely to be skeptical. Introduce ideas in the overview in the order in which you will discuss them.

Basic Patterns for Organizing Information

When you are organizing information, you are creating relationships with readers, ideas, outcomes, and actions, creating frameworks within which readers will access information and use your document (see ◂◂ Chapter 3). You are clarifying order and emphasis, making clear the logical connections among ideas.

Seven basic patterns for organizing information are useful in whole reports or in parts.

1. Comparison/Contrast

Many reports use comparison/contrast sections within a larger report pattern. Comparison/contrast can also be the purpose of the whole report. Feasibility studies usually use this pattern. You can focus either on the alternatives you are evaluating or on the criteria you use. See Figure 10.6 for examples of these two patterns in a report.

Focus on the alternatives when:

- One alternative is clearly superior.
- The criteria are hard to separate.
- The reader will intuitively grasp the alternative as a whole rather than as the sum of its parts.

Focus on the criteria when:

- The superiority of one alternative to another depends on the relative weight assigned to various criteria. Perhaps Alternative A is better if we are most concerned about Criterion 1, cost, but worse if we are most concerned about Criterion 2, proximity to target market.
- The criteria are easy to separate.
- The reader wants to compare and contrast the options independently of your recommendation.

A variation of the divided pattern is the **pro-and-con pattern.** In this pattern, under each specific heading, give the arguments for and against that alternative. Whatever information comes second will carry more psychological weight. This pattern is least effective when you want to de-emphasize the disadvantages of a proposed solution, for it does not permit you to bury the disadvantages between neutral or positive material.

Figure 10.6 Two Ways to Organize a Comparison/Contrast Report

FOCUS ON *ALTERNATIVES*

Alternative A	**Opening a New Store on Campus**
Criterion 1	Cost of Renting Space
Criterion 2	Proximity to Target Market
Criterion 3	Competition from Similar Stores
Alternative B	**Opening a New Store in the Suburban Mall**
Criterion 1	Cost of Renting Space
Criterion 2	Proximity to Target Market
Criterion 3	Competition from Similar Stores

FOCUS ON *CRITERIA*

Criterion 1	**Cost of Renting Space for the New Store**
Alternative A	Cost of Campus Locations
Alternative B	Cost of Locations in the Suburban Mall
Criterion 2	**Proximity to Target Market**
Alternative A	Proximity on Campus
Alternative B	Proximity in the Suburban Mall
Criterion 3	**Competition from Similar Stores**
Alternative A	Competing Stores on Campus
Alternative B	Competing Stores in the Suburban Mall

2. Problem–Solution

Identify the problem, explain its background or history, discuss its extent and seriousness, and identify its causes. Discuss the factors (criteria) that affect the decision. Analyze the advantages and disadvantages of possible solutions. Conclusions and recommendations can go either first or last, depending on reader preferences. This pattern works well when the reader is neutral.

3. Elimination of Alternatives

After discussing the problem and its causes, discuss the *impractical* solutions first, showing why they will not work. End with the most practical solution. This pattern works well when the solutions the reader is likely to favour will not work, while the solution you recommend is likely to be perceived as expensive, intrusive, or radical.

4. General to Particular or Particular to General

General to particular starts with the problem as it affects the organization or as it manifests itself in general and then moves to a discussion of the parts of the problem and solutions to each of these parts. Particular to general starts with the problem as the audience defines it and moves to larger issues of which the problem is a part. Both are good patterns when you need to redefine the reader's perception of the problem to solve it effectively.

5. Geographic or Spatial

In a geographic or spatial pattern, you discuss problems and solutions in units by their physical arrangement. Move from office to office, building to building, factory to factory, province to province, region to region, and so on.

6. Functional

In functional patterns, discuss the problems and solutions of each functional unit. For example, a report on a new plant might divide data into sections on the costs of land and building, on the availability of personnel, on the convenience of raw materials, and so on. A government report might divide data into the different functions an office performed, taking each in turn.

7. Chronological

A chronological report records events in the order in which they happened or are planned to happen. Many progress reports (▸▸ Chapter 11) are organized chronologically.

LO6

USING AND DOCUMENTING SOURCES

Good writing is the result of good research—and a major source of credibility. Consider the original (Figure 10.7) and revised version (Figure 10.8) of the introductory paragraph to a student proposal to write a report for a client business recommending ways to increase the business's visibility in a competitive market. Which do you find persuasive? Do you believe the claims in Figure 10.7? Would you be willing to risk investing in the team's work? Does the team persuade that they have the qualifications and resources to complete the task? Does the research add credibility to Figure 10.8? Would citing Wikipedia work as well?

Ethics of Secondary Source Use

In a good report, sources are cited and documented smoothly and unobtrusively. **Citation** means attributing an idea or fact to its source *in the body of the report:* "According to the 2011 Census. . ."; "Jane Bryant Quinn argues that. . . ." Citing sources enhances your credibility and helps you avoid **plagiarism** charges. **Documentation** means providing the bibliographic

Figure 10.7 An Unacceptable Introduction to a Student Proposal

Introduction

Retail clothing outlets need public recognition. The main problem that we will address is that the business is not getting its message across. Our team of communications consultants aims to increase your visibility by ten percent.

Communications are essential to the effectiveness of any firm. In this day and age, you cannot afford not to improve your external communications. Research has enabled us to locate your problem and to identify solutions. Your lack of communications means that people don't know they have the best retail clothing outlet right here in the heart of London. Our team can beat out any competitors. You can rely on us.

× *Direct organization is too abrupt*

× *Tone is unnecessarily negative*

× *Positive emphasis is lost in negatives*

× *Claim to increase visibility unsupported by evidence*

× *Claim about research is unsupported*

× *Clichéd phrasing undermines credibility*

Figure 10.8 A Good Introduction to a Student Proposal

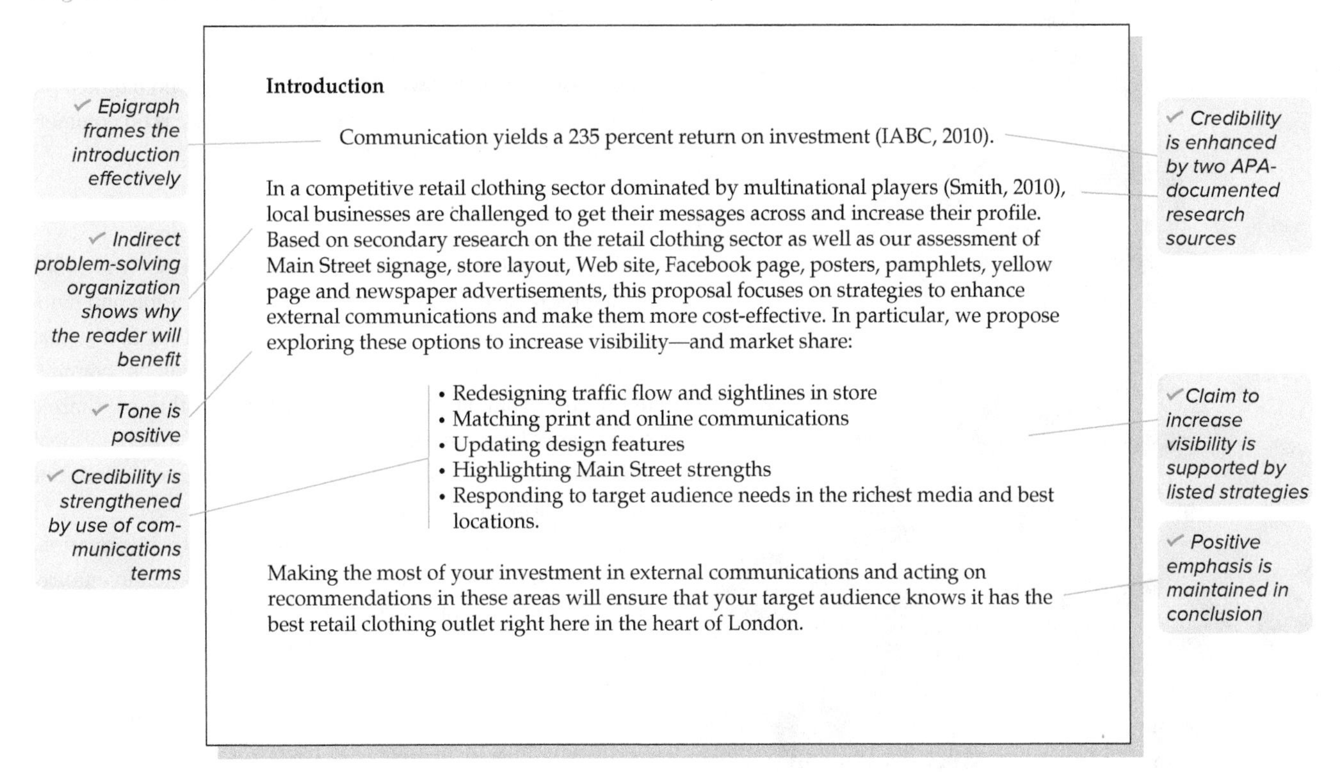

information readers would need to go back to the original source. In other words, documenting your sources has these benefits:

- Gives credit for intellectual debts
- Reinforces and supports your line of argument
- Adds credibility of supporting authorities
- Protects your reputation and reassures readers of your honesty
- Gives readers access to further sources on a particular topic

Plagiarism

While plagiarism, the unacknowledged use of another's ideas and/or expression, can be a deliberate act by desperate, cynical, or lazy people (concealing sources, handing in a report written by someone else), it is also often an act of omission. When students or professionals unintentionally recall and repeat exact wording from a source, forget to ensure quotation marks around exact quotations, use online material they thought was copyright free, or paraphrase or summarize a source's ideas without acknowledgment, they are guilty of plagiarism.

High-profile cases like the 2002 suspension of 44 students at Simon Fraser University and a CBC survey of 42 universities finding more than 7,000 students guilty of academic dishonesty (though many more go undetected)[26] have kept plagiarism at the forefront and have caused many post-secondary institutions to develop programs and to use Turnitin.com, a site with over 1 million previously submitted papers. University of Toronto is one of a number of Canadian universities using Turnitin.com services, though the majority of students remain honest and "recognize that plagiarism threatens the value of their hard work."[27]

Journalistic plagiarism and firings have also made the news: reporter Jayson Blair admitted that he had faked or stolen material for 36 stories for *The New York Times;* a *Los Angeles Times* photographer acknowledged that in 2003 he had combined two pictures to make "a more dramatic image" of the war in Iraq; a *Toronto Star* reporter conceded that she had copied almost a third of a story about a U.S. Army deserter from *The Village Voice;* and *National Post* medical reporter Brad Evenson was fired for faking quotations in nine stories.[28]

Although she faced disciplinary action but was not fired, *Globe and Mail* columnist Margaret Wente similarly faced accusations of plagiarism of an *Ottawa Citizen* article by Dan Gardner in a July 2009 article that her editor found "unacceptable."[29] Wente denied she was a "serial plagiarist" and claimed that she was more often "a target for people who don't like what I write." Still, she apologized for being "extremely careless,"[30] and in a subsequent article responding to print and

Facing accusations of plagiarism, columnist Margaret Wente learned the value of "respect and trust" to the good name of writers.

online outrage apologized to those she had "let down," conceding that she had "learned that respect and trust are the most important currencies any writer has."[31]

Although poor training and inadequate resources have caused many plagiarism problems, the Internet has added to the challenges. At the University of Toronto, plagiarism related to the Internet increased from 50% to 99% of cases between 2000–2001 and 2001–2002; official plagiarism cases increased from 92 to 403 cases in 12 years to 2005–2006. Managing Editor Kirk LaPointe of the *Vancouver Sun* warns of Internet enticements "to this exciting information that a reporter can steal," while cautioning that the same source leaves "a record of it and anybody who steals can be caught."[32]

A 2006–2010 study of 14,000 undergraduates found that 40% confessed to copying from the Internet, and 29% did not regard such copying as "serious cheating." The majority of 196 plagiarism cases at the University of California, Davis, acted unethically while "knowing it was wrong." The disciplinary office concluded that the students "were unwilling to engage the writing process. Writing is difficult, and doing it well takes time and practice." Others agree that "students leave high school unprepared for the intellectual rigors of college writing."[33]

Fair Dealing

The *Copyright Act* spells out what constitutes fair dealing in Canada (fair use in the United States is more permissive); that is, what are exceptions to exclusive copyrights. For purposes of "research or private study," "criticism or review," and "news reporting," there is no infringement of copyright so long as the source is acknowledged. In these cases, no payment to the copyright holder is required so long as there is no commercial purpose to the dealing.[34]

Shared Use

Consistent with the philosophy of open source software (see ▸▸ Chapter 6) shared in the interests of collaboration and innovation, Creative Commons is re-establishing itself in Canada. A non-profit organization, Creative Commons is committed to the "legal and technical infrastructure that maximizes digital creativity, sharing, and innovation." Its commitment is to grant access outside the "all rights reserved" model of copyright laws in different jurisdictions.

It acts out of a belief that free access to information, education, and science, as well as full participation in culture, is key to "a new era of development, growth, and productivity." Creative Commons does not abandon the duty to acknowledge sources, but it does limit the cost of doing so. The approach is that "some rights [are] reserved." Creative Commons licences permit creators to define what users may and may not do without express permission.[35]

Quoting

Whether you are dealing with an online or print source, you will have to decide whether to quote or put it into your own words. You will choose to quote when

- The source's expression is especially effective, vivid, or original.
- The source depends on specialized or technical terms.
- You want to dispute the terms of the source's argument.

Be sure to integrate quotations into your own grammar/developing argument, varying introductory words (*Jennifer Barton agrees, argues, claims, responds, notes, suggests; from Jennifer Barton's point of view; according to Jennifer Barton*). Quote only those words necessary for document purposes and reader needs; mark omissions with ellipses (spaced dots) and changes with square brackets.

Long quotations (four typed lines or more) are used sparingly in business reports. Since many readers skip quotations, always summarize the main point of the quotation in a single sentence before the quotation itself. End the sentence with a colon, not a period, since it introduces the quotation. Indented quotations do not need quotation marks; the indentation shows the reader that the passage is a quotation.

Summarizing, or Paraphrasing

When quotation is not necessary, put the source ideas in your own words (a summary or paraphrase) and follow regular documentation style (shown in Figures 10.9 to 10.12).

Figure 10.9 Report Paragraphs with APA Documentation

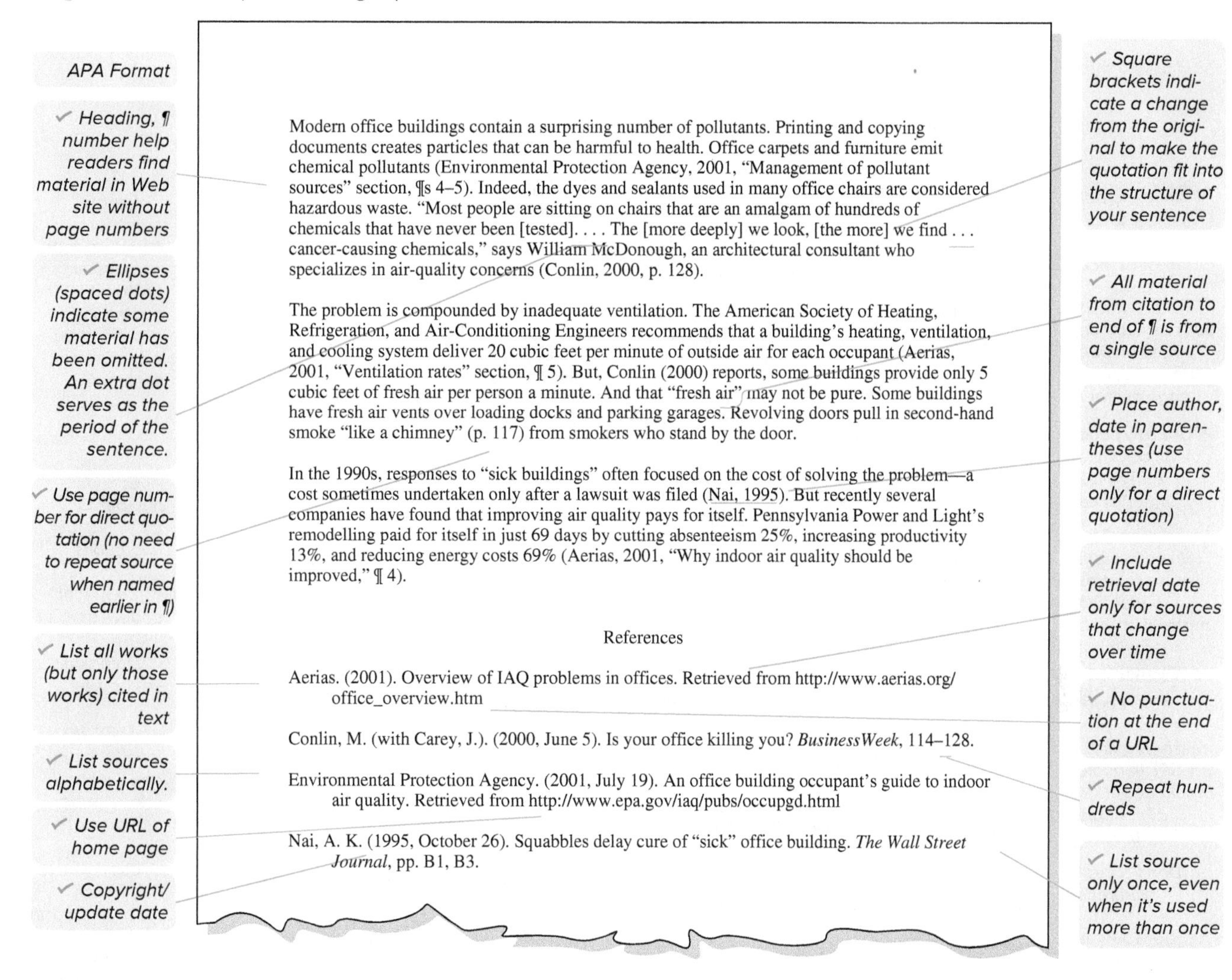

Modern office buildings contain a surprising number of pollutants. Printing and copying documents creates particles that can be harmful to health. Office carpets and furniture emit chemical pollutants (Environmental Protection Agency, 2001, "Management of pollutant sources" section, ¶s 4–5). Indeed, the dyes and sealants used in many office chairs are considered hazardous waste. "Most people are sitting on chairs that are an amalgam of hundreds of chemicals that have never been [tested]. . . . The [more deeply] we look, [the more] we find . . . cancer-causing chemicals," says William McDonough, an architectural consultant who specializes in air-quality concerns (Conlin, 2000, p. 128).

The problem is compounded by inadequate ventilation. The American Society of Heating, Refrigeration, and Air-Conditioning Engineers recommends that a building's heating, ventilation, and cooling system deliver 20 cubic feet per minute of outside air for each occupant (Aerias, 2001, "Ventilation rates" section, ¶ 5). But, Conlin (2000) reports, some buildings provide only 5 cubic feet of fresh air per person a minute. And that "fresh air" may not be pure. Some buildings have fresh air vents over loading docks and parking garages. Revolving doors pull in second-hand smoke "like a chimney" (p. 117) from smokers who stand by the door.

In the 1990s, responses to "sick buildings" often focused on the cost of solving the problem—a cost sometimes undertaken only after a lawsuit was filed (Nai, 1995). But recently several companies have found that improving air quality pays for itself. Pennsylvania Power and Light's remodelling paid for itself in just 69 days by cutting absenteeism 25%, increasing productivity 13%, and reducing energy costs 69% (Aerias, 2001, "Why indoor air quality should be improved," ¶ 4).

References

Aerias. (2001). Overview of IAQ problems in offices. Retrieved from http://www.aerias.org/office_overview.htm

Conlin, M. (with Carey, J.). (2000, June 5). Is your office killing you? *BusinessWeek*, 114–128.

Environmental Protection Agency. (2001, July 19). An office building occupant's guide to indoor air quality. Retrieved from http://www.epa.gov/iaq/pubs/occupgd.html

Nai, A. K. (1995, October 26). Squabbles delay cure of "sick" office building. *The Wall Street Journal*, pp. B1, B3.

Summarizing (see ➤➤ Chapter 7) involves condensing in your own words the argument/information in your source. You will summarize when you want to give the gist of the source without supplying details of the developing argument.

Paraphrasing involves rephrasing in your own words and generally following the source's line of reasoning without any concern to reduce the number of words in the source. To avoid charges of plagiarism, you need to be careful that you do not simply substitute synonyms while retaining the source's grammar. If words from the source are important in your paraphrase, be sure to put quotation marks around those particular words.

Whether summarizing or paraphrasing, be careful not to inadvertently repeat words or sentence structure from your source. For example:

ORIGINAL:

According to Kirk LaPointe, the Internet is a source of "exciting information that a reporter can steal, but on the other hand, there's a record of it and anybody who steals can be caught" (4).

✕ PLAGIARISM:

The Internet is a great gateway to information that a reporter can borrow, but the record means that anybody who borrows can be found.

✓ ACCEPTABLE PARAPHRASES:

If it gives access to information that reporters may use without credit, the Internet also supplies the evidence that will prove their theft (LaPointe 4).

According to Kirk LaPointe, the Internet is both a rich source of information for reporters and the source of evidence to catch them if they take without credit.

Note that citation and documentation are used in addition to quotation marks. If you use the source's exact words, you'll use the name of the person you're citing and quotation marks in the body of the report; you'll indicate the source in parentheses and a list of references, or works cited, or in a footnote or endnote. If you put the source's idea into your own words,

Figure 10.10 Report Paragraphs with MLA Documentation

MLA Format

Modern office buildings contain a surprising number of pollutants. Printing and copying documents creates particles that can be harmful to health. Office carpets and furniture emit chemical pollutants (Environmental Protection Agency, "Management of Pollutant Sources" section, pars. 4–5). Indeed, the dyes and sealants used in many office chairs are considered hazardous waste. "Most people are sitting on chairs that are an amalgam of hundreds of chemicals that have never been [tested]. . . . The [more deeply] we look, [the more] we find . . . cancer-causing chemicals," says William McDonough, an architectural consultant who specializes in air-quality concerns (Conlin 128).

The problem is compounded by inadequate ventilation. The American Society of Heating, Refrigeration, and Air-Conditioning Engineers recommends that a building's heating, ventilation, and cooling system deliver 20 cubic feet per minute of outside air for each occupant (Aerias, "Ventilation Rates" section, par. 5). But, Michelle Conlin reports, some buildings provide only 5 cubic feet of fresh air per person a minute. And that "fresh air" may not be pure. Some buildings have fresh air vents over loading docks and parking garages. Revolving doors pull in second-hand smoke "like a chimney' (117) from smokers who stand by the door.

In the 1990s, responses to "sick buildings" often focused on the cost of solving the problem—a cost sometimes undertaken only after a lawsuit was filed (Nai B1). But recently, several companies have found that improving air quality pays for itself. Pennsylvania Power and Light's remodelling paid for itself in just 69 days by cutting absenteeism 25%, increasing productivity 13%, and reducing energy costs 69% (Aerias, "Why Indoor Air Quality Should Be Improved," par. 4).

Works Cited

Aerias. "Overview of IAQ Problems in Offices." 2001. Web. 24 Sept. 2005 <http://www.aerias.org/office_overview.htm>.

Conlin, Michelle with John Carey. "Is Your Office Killing You?" *BusinessWeek* 5 June 2000: 114–28. Print.

Environmental Protection Agency. "An Office Building Occupant's Guide to Indoor Air Quality." Web. 19 July 2001. 19 Sept. 2005 <http://www.epa.gov/iaq/pubs/occupgd.html>.

Nai, Amal Kumar. "Squabbles Delay Cure of 'Sick' Office Building." *The Wall Street Journal* 26 October 1995: B1+. Print.

✓ An extra dot serves as the period of the sentence

✓ No comma between author, page number; no "p." before page number

✓ Use only page number since author identified in sentence

✓ Heading, paragraph number helps reader find material in Web sites without page numbers

✓ If reader needs or professor requires, list URL in angle brackets; period after angle bracket

✓ Don't repeat hundreds

✓ List sources alphabetically

✓ Square brackets indicate a change from the original to make the quotation fit into the structure of your sentence

✓ Give page number for facts, not just quotations

✓ Copyright/ update date

✓ Date you visited site

✓ If URL is too long to fit on one line, break after a punctuation mark

✓ Use day month year; abbreviate month

✓ "+" indicates article continues

or if you condense or synthesize information, you don't need quotation marks, but you still need to tell whose idea it is and where you found it.

Documenting Sources

The three most widely used formats for footnotes, endnotes, and bibliographies in reports are those of the American Psychological Association (APA), the Modern Language Association (MLA), and the University of Chicago *Manual of Style* format, which this book uses.

The APA format is a two-part system that uses internal documentation with a list of references; it does not use footnotes or endnotes to document sources. **Internal documentation** provides in parentheses in the text the author's name (if it isn't already in the sentence) and date of publication (Smith, 2011, for instance); APA includes the page number where the reference was found only in the case of quotation. The full bibliographical citation appears in a list of references at the end of the report.

MLA format similarly uses internal documentation in the text, in this case listing author's last name and page number (Smith 234, for instance). The full bibliographic citation appears in a list of works cited at the end of the report.

Figures 10.9 and 10.10 show a portion of a report in APA and MLA formats, respectively, with the list of references (APA) or works cited (MLA). Figures 10.11 and 10.12 show the APA and MLA formats for sources used most often in reports. See ▸▸ Figure 11.8 for APA format.

It is also important to be clear when you do not need to credit sources. You do not need to cite your own original observations, although you need to explain the basis of your thinking. Whereas there is no need to cite a source for

Figure 10.11 APA Format for Sources Used Most Often in Reports

APA Format

APA internal documentation gives the author's last name and the date of the work in parentheses in the text. A comma separates the author's name from the date (Gilsdorf & Leonard, 2001). The page number is given only for direct quotations (Cross, 2001, p. 74). If the author's name is used in the sentence, only the date is given in parentheses. (See Figure 10.9.) A list of References gives the full bibliographic citation, arranging the entries alphabetically by the first author's last name.

Anonymous Authorship

Anonymous. (1993). Social learning theory. *Journal of Personality and Social Psychology, 65*(6), 1154-1166. doi: 10.1037/a0018581/

Social learning theory. (1993). *Journal of Personality and Social Psychology, 65*(6), 1154-1166. doi: 10.1037/a0018581/

Article in a Periodical

Gilsdorf, J., & Leonard, D. (2001). Big stuff, little stuff: A decennial measurement of executives' and academics' reactions to questionable usage elements. *The Journal of Business Communication, 38*, 439–475. doi: 1177/002194361036451 0/

McCartney, S. (2000, December 27). Why a baseball superstar's megacontract can be less than it seems. *The Wall Street Journal*, p. B1, B3.

Article in an Edited Book

Killingsworth, M. J., & Jacobsen, M. (1999). The rhetorical construction of environmental risk narratives in government and activist websites: A critique. In J. M. Perkins & N. Blyler (Eds.), *Narrative and professional communication* (pp. 167-177). Stamford, CT: Ablex.

Article from a Publication on the Web

Greengard, S. (2001, May). Scoring web wins. *Business Finance Magazine*. p. 37. Retrieved from http://www.businessfinancemag.com/archives/appfiles/Article.cfm?IssueID=348&ArticleID=13750

Book

Cross, G. A. (2001). *Forming the collective mind: A contextual exploration of large-scale collaborative writing in industry*. Creskill, NJ: Hampton Press.

Book or Pamphlet with a Corporate Author

Citibank. (1994). *Indonesia: An investment guide*. [Jakarta:] Author.

E-Mail Message

[Identify e-mail messages in the text as personal communications (without mentioning e-mail addresses). Give name of author (surname followed by initials) and as specific a date as possible. Do not include references.

✓ In titles of articles and books capitalize only (1) First word, (2) First word of subtitle, and (3) Proper nouns

✓ Where source is signed anonymous

✓ Where there is no author

✓ last name first

✓ comma

✓ Year (period outside parentheses)

✓ Italicize volume

✓ Editors before book title

✓ Ampersands join names of co-authors, co-editors

✓ Include URL if no doi available

✓ No punctuation after URL

✓ Initials only

✓ Italicize title of book

✓ No quotation marks around title of article

✓ Capitalize all major words in title of journal, magazine, or newspaper

✓ List digital object identifier (doi) if assigned

✓ No "pp." when journal has a volume number

✓ Separate discontinuous pages with comma and space

✓ Editors' names have last names last

✓ Give state or province when city is not well known

✓ Repeat "1" in 177

✓ Indicates organization authoring document also published it

✓ Put in square brackets information known to you but not printed in document

(continued)

facts such as the dates of tenure of a particular prime minister, you do need to cite a source for statistics relating to his/her increasing or waning support during that tenure or for a particular perspective on the success or failure of the prime minister. In general, you do not need to credit sources for proverbial sayings ("People in glass houses should not throw stones"), familiar quotations ("We shall overcome"), or common knowledge (the dates of World War II, the name of the first prime minister of Canada). When in doubt, cite your source.

If you have used many sources that you have not cited, you may want to list both works cited and works consulted. The term *bibliography* covers all sources on a topic.

If you use a printed source that is not readily available, consider including it as an appendix in your report. For example, you could copy an ad or include an organization's promotional brochure.

Figure 10.11 APA Format for Sources Used Most Often in Reports *(concluded)*

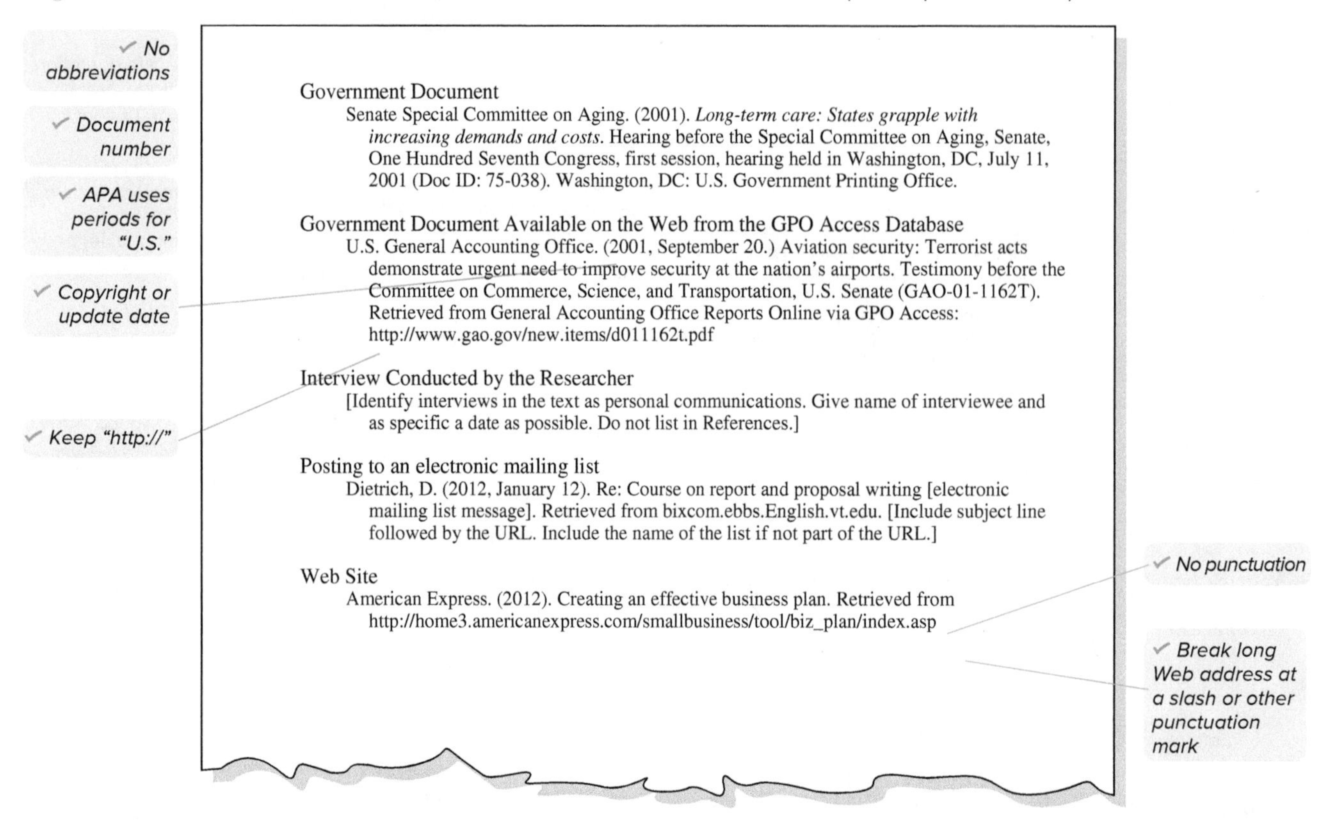

Figure 10.12 MLA Format for Sources Used Most Often in Reports

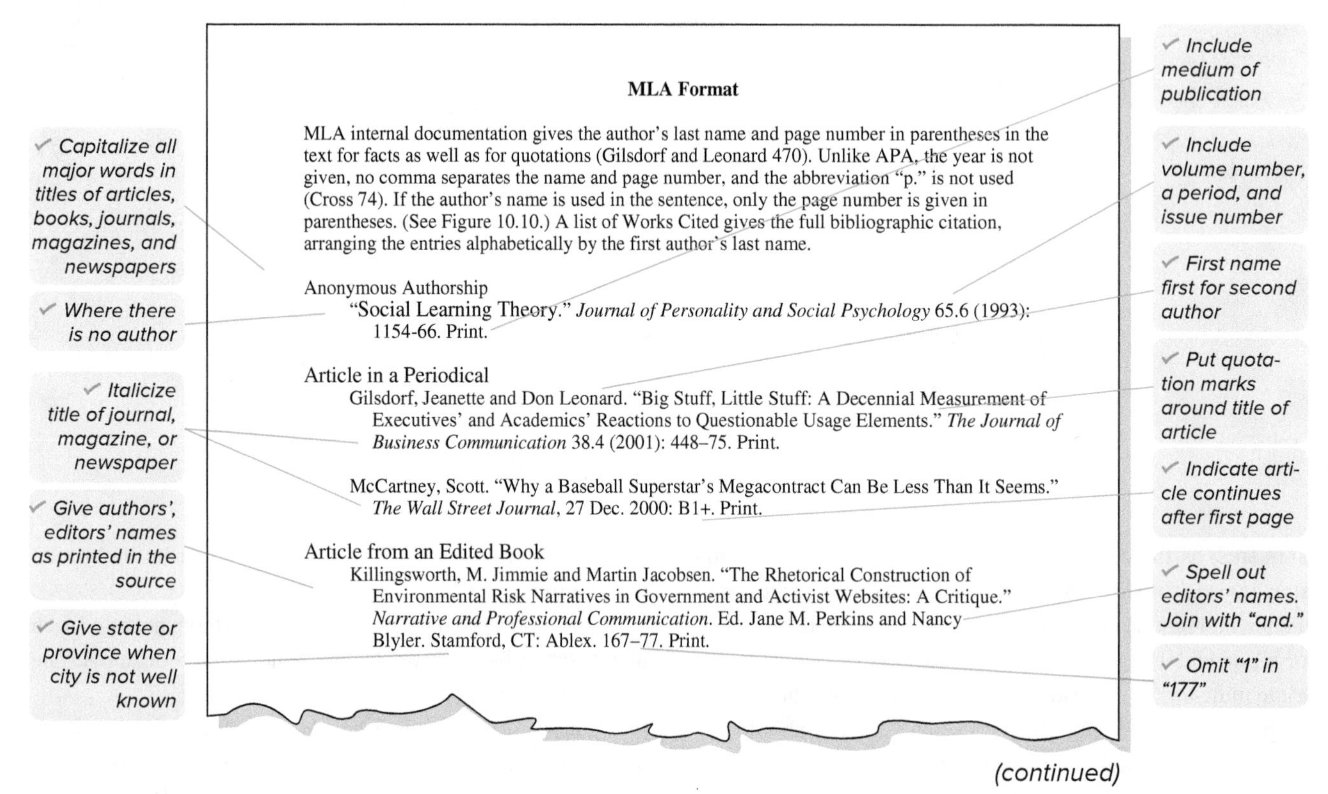

(continued)

Figure 10.12 MLA Format for Sources Used Most Often in Reports *(concluded)*

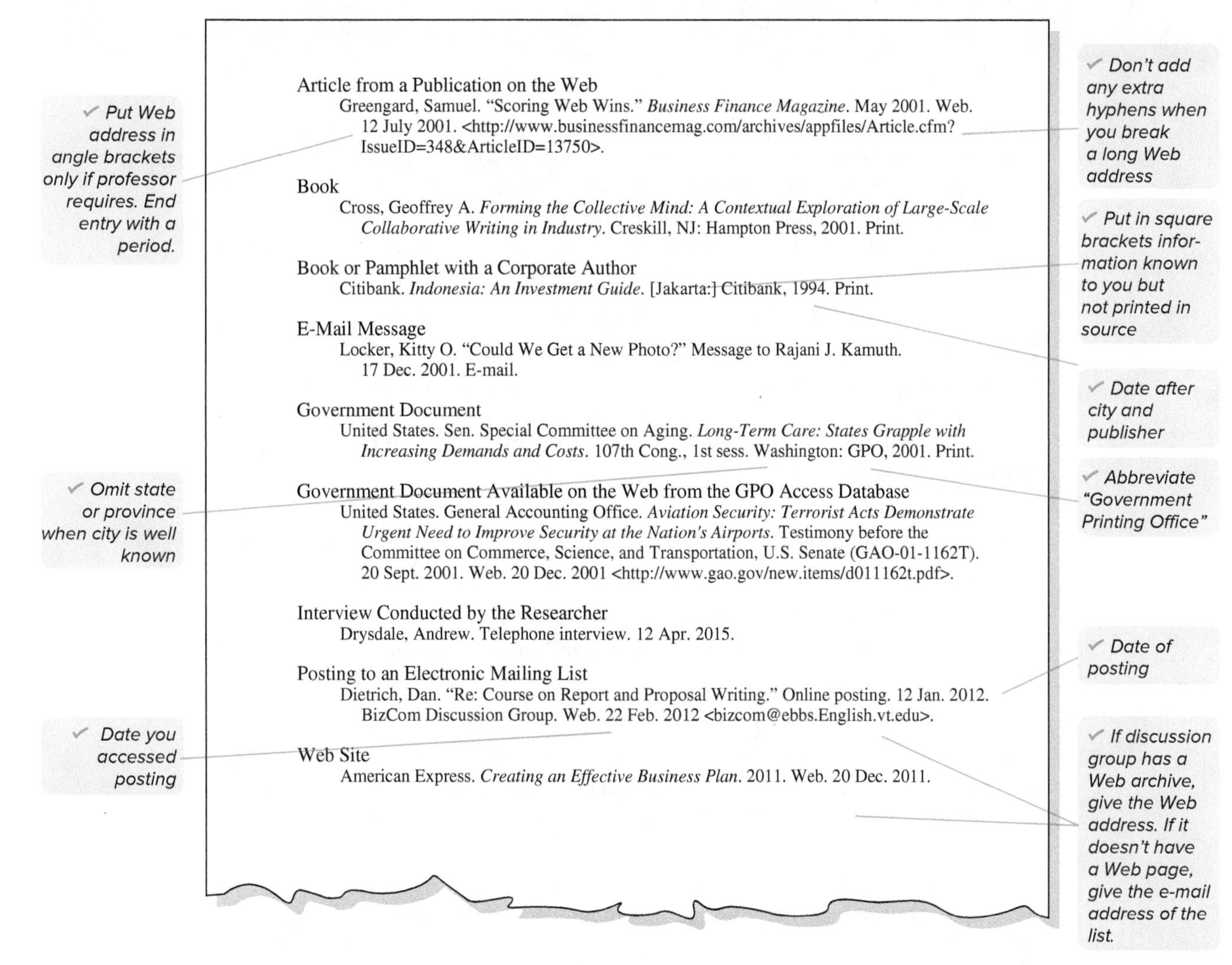

Article from a Publication on the Web

Greengard, Samuel. "Scoring Web Wins." *Business Finance Magazine*. May 2001. Web. 12 July 2001. <http://www.businessfinancemag.com/archives/appfiles/Article.cfm?IssueID=348&ArticleID=13750>.

Book

Cross, Geoffrey A. *Forming the Collective Mind: A Contextual Exploration of Large-Scale Collaborative Writing in Industry*. Creskill, NJ: Hampton Press, 2001. Print.

Book or Pamphlet with a Corporate Author

Citibank. *Indonesia: An Investment Guide*. [Jakarta:] Citibank, 1994. Print.

E-Mail Message

Locker, Kitty O. "Could We Get a New Photo?" Message to Rajani J. Kamuth. 17 Dec. 2001. E-mail.

Government Document

United States. Sen. Special Committee on Aging. *Long-Term Care: States Grapple with Increasing Demands and Costs*. 107th Cong., 1st sess. Washington: GPO, 2001. Print.

Government Document Available on the Web from the GPO Access Database

United States. General Accounting Office. *Aviation Security: Terrorist Acts Demonstrate Urgent Need to Improve Security at the Nation's Airports*. Testimony before the Committee on Commerce, Science, and Transportation, U.S. Senate (GAO-01-1162T). 20 Sept. 2001. Web. 20 Dec. 2001 <http://www.gao.gov/new.items/d011162t.pdf>.

Interview Conducted by the Researcher

Drysdale, Andrew. Telephone interview. 12 Apr. 2015.

Posting to an Electronic Mailing List

Dietrich, Dan. "Re: Course on Report and Proposal Writing." Online posting. 12 Jan. 2012. BizCom Discussion Group. Web. 22 Feb. 2012 <bizcom@ebbs.English.vt.edu>.

Web Site

American Express. *Creating an Effective Business Plan*. 2011. Web. 20 Dec. 2011.

SUMMARY OF KEY POINTS

- For a well-defined report problem, check that it meets these three criteria: (1) The problem is real, important enough to be worth solving, and narrow but challenging; (2) The report audience is real, interested in the problem, and able to implement the recommended action; and (3) The data, evidence, and facts are sufficient to document the problem, sufficient to prove that the recommendation will solve the problem, and available and comprehensible to you.
- Limit the scope of the problem depending on time and resources.
- Having a research plan will strengthen your findings. Knowing your topic, articulating your problem statement and report purpose, and identifying your information gaps and reliable resources will help you better target your search and keep it ethical. Research with an open mind and represent reliable and relevant research.
- Secondary research retrieves information that someone else gathered. Library research and online searches are the best-known kinds of secondary research.
- Primary research gathers new information. Surveys, interviews, and observations are common methods for business reports.
- To evaluate research, consider validity, reliability, and currency.
- To decide whether to use a Web site as a source in a research project, evaluate the site's authors, objectivity, information, and revision date.
- A survey questions a large group of people, called respondents or subjects. A questionnaire is a written list of questions that people fill out. An interview is a structured conversation with someone who will be able to give you useful information.
- Good questions ask just one thing, are phrased neutrally, avoid making assumptions about the respondent, and mean essentially the same thing to different people.
- Analyze data with healthy skepticism. Check for data accuracy, source reliability, sample size, and wording bias. Search for patterns, distinguish causation and correlation, and make the nature of your evidence clear.
- Citation means attributing an idea or fact to its source in the body of the report. Documentation means providing the bibliographic information readers would need to go back to the original source. Plagiarism is the unacknowledged use of another's ideas and/or expression.
- The APA format uses internal documentation with a list of references giving full bibliographic citation at the end of the report. Internal documentation provides in parentheses in the text the author's name (if it isn't already in the sentence) and date of publication; APA includes the page number where the reference was found only in the case of quotation.
- MLA format uses internal documentation in the text, listing author's last name (if it isn't already in the sentence) and page number. The full bibliographic citation appears in a list of works cited at the end of the report.

EXERCISES AND PROBLEMS

GETTING STARTED

10.1 IDENTIFYING THE WEAKNESSES IN PROBLEM STATEMENTS

Identify the weaknesses in the problem statements below. Discuss in your collaborative group and present your group findings to the class. Use these criteria:

- Is the problem narrow enough?
- Can a solution be found in a term?
- What organization could implement any recommendations to solve the problem?
- Could the topic be limited or refocused to yield an acceptable problem statement?

1. One possible report topic I would like to investigate would be the differences in women's intercollegiate sports in our athletic conference.
2. How to market products effectively to university students.
3. Should Web banners be part of a company's advertising?
4. How can Canadian students get jobs in Europe?
5. We want to explore ways our company can help raise funds for the Open Shelter. We will investigate whether collecting and recycling glass, aluminum, and paper products will raise enough money to help.
6. How can XYZ university better serve students from traditionally underrepresented groups?
7. What are the best investments for the next year?

10.2 WRITING A PRELIMINARY PURPOSE STATEMENT

Answer the following questions about a topic on which you could write a formal report. (Refer to Problems 11.4, 11.11, 11.12, 11.13, and 11.14 in the next chapter.)

As Your Professor Directs,

a. Be prepared to answer the questions orally in a conference.

b. Bring written answers to a conference.

c. Submit written answers in class.

d. Give your professor a photocopy of your statement after it is approved.

1. What problem will you investigate or solve?

a. What is the name of the organization facing the problem?

b. What is the technical problem or difficulty?

c. Why is it important to the organization that this problem be solved?

d. What solution or action might you recommend to solve the problem?

e. List the name and title of the person in the organization who would have the power to accept or reject your recommendation.

2. Will this report use information from other classes or from work experiences? If so, give the name and topic of the class and/or briefly describe the job. If you will need additional information (that you do not already have from other classes or from a job), how do you expect to find it?
3. List the name, title, and business phone number of a professor who can testify to your ability to handle the expertise needed for this report.

4. List the name, title, and business phone number of someone in the organization who can testify that you have access to enough information about that organization to write this report.

COMMUNICATING AT WORK

10.3 CHOOSING RESEARCH STRATEGIES

For each of the following reports, indicate the kinds of research that might be useful. If a survey is called for, indicate the most efficient kind of sample to use. As your professor directs, peer grade answers.

a. How can XYZ store increase sales?

b. What is it like to live and work in [name of country]?

c. Should our organization have a dress code?

d. Is it feasible to start a monthly newsletter for students in your major?

e. How can we best market to mature adults?

f. Can compensation programs increase productivity?

g. What skills are in demand in our area? Of these, which could the local community college offer courses in?

10.4 IDENTIFYING KEYWORDS FOR COMPUTER SEARCHES

As Your Professor Directs,

Identify the keyword combinations that you could use in researching one or more of the following topics:

a. Ways to evaluate whether recycling is working.

b. Safety of pension funds.

c. Ethical issues in accounting.

d. Effects of advertising on sales of automobiles.

e. What can be done to increase the privacy of personal data.

f. Accounting for intellectual capital.

g. Advantages and problems of Web advertising.

10.5 COMPARING WEB SEARCH ENGINES

Using at least three different search engines, search for sources on a topic on which you could write a formal report. (Refer to Problems 11.4, 11.11, 11.12, 11.13, and 11.14 in the next chapter.) Compare the top 30 sources. Which sites turn up on all three search engines? Which search engine appears to be most useful for your project?

As Your Professor Directs,

a. Share your results orally with a small group of students.

b. Present your results to the class documenting your sources.

c. Write a memo to your professor summarizing your results. Be sure to document sources.

d. With a small group of students, write a report recommending guidelines for using search engines and documenting your sources.

10.6 EVALUATING WEB SITES

Evaluate 10 Web sites related to the topic of your report. For each, consider

- Authors.
- Objectivity.

- Information.
- Revision date.

Based on these criteria, which sites are best for your report? Which are unacceptable? Why?

As Your Professor Directs,

a. Share your results with a small group of students.

b. Present your results in a memo to your professor documenting sources carefully.

c. Present your results to the class in an oral presentation or class blog posting that documents your sources.

10.7 EXPLAINING PLAGIARISM AND HOW TO AVOID IT

In the face of some high-profile cases of plagiarism resulting in firings and scandal, your manager asks you to give advice to your staff on plagiarism, explaining why it has become a major business concern and giving specific advice on how the organization can protect itself by documenting its sources accurately. Be sure to include examples of MLA or APA documentation.

As Your Professor Directs,

a. Share your results in a blog posting.

b. Present your results in a two-page memo-report.

c. Present your results in a Web page with links to relevant and reliable resources.

WRITING PROPOSALS AND REPORTS

11

Learning Outcomes

LO1 List different kinds of reports

LO2 Explain how to organize different kinds of reports

LO3 Identify seven questions a proposal must answer

LO4 Discuss report style

LO5 Explain the functions of the different parts of formal reports

AN INSIDE PERSPECTIVE

Trends in business (◂◂ Chapter 1) have impacted not only how workplaces are organized, but also how organizations communicate everything from routine messages to reports, including annual reports. In the early days of corporate reporting, annual reports were as short as one page and were targeted almost exclusively to analysts and regulators. Facts and figures were their stock in trade. In addressing the needs and knowledge of a much broader audience today, annual reports are much longer, packed with stories, and visually dramatic. In short, they have taken on a much more human face (refer to ◂◂ Figure 3.5).

Tamara Vrooman relishes opportunities for creativity, leadership, and innovation in her position as president and CEO of Vancity, the largest community credit union in Canada and one of the largest Canadian organizations to be certified as a Living Wage Employer. In 2011 she was named to Canada's Most Powerful Women: Top 100 Hall of Fame.

At a time when employee satisfaction is as important as client and investor satisfaction, and accountability and transparency are expected, new forms of reporting—triple bottom line, corporate social responsibility (CSR), and sustainable development reports—are addressing new audiences and needs. (See the corporate social responsibility and reputation management sections in ◂◂ Chapter 1.)

For Vancity president and CEO Tamara Vrooman, the triple bottom line is an important measure of success. CSR is more than donating and volunteering: "It's about operating in a way that is respectful of the environment and that is supportive of the communities in which we live and work." Vrooman's leadership is focused on using Vancity's $17.5 billion in assets to help improve the financial well-being of its members while at the same time helping to develop healthy communities that are socially, economically, and environmentally sustainable.

If consumer and employee interests are better served by new reporting measures, they are also bringing companies new rewards. Vancity was the first financial institution in North America to win the Ceres-ACCA North American Award for Sustainability Reporting in 2006 and more recently received a Corporate Register Reporting Award in 2013. Ranked one of *Maclean's* Top 50 Socially Responsible Corporations and *Corporate Knights* Best 50 Corporate Citizens in Canada in 2014, Vancity now has 2,500 employees in 57 branches serving more than 500,000 members. In 2014, Vancity was recognized as one of Canada's Greenest Employers for the seventh year in a row, as well as one of Canada's Top 100 Employers and Top Family-Friendly Employers.

*Based on "Tamara Vrooman," retrieved June 8, 2014, from https://www.vancity.com/AboutVancity/GovernanceAndLeadership/LeadershipTeam/CEOBiography/; Vancity, About Us, retrieved June 8, 2014, from https://www.vancity.com/AboutVancity/; Q&A, *Canadian Business,* November 19, 2007, p. 9; David Jordan, "Tamara Vrooman," *Crossroads,* October 1, 2007, retrieved August 30, 2008, from http://www.bcbusinessonline.ca/bcb/people/2007/10/01/tamara-vrooman; Bruce Constantineau, "Shakeup at Vancity," *Vancouver Sun,* November 6, 2007, retrieved August 30, 2008, from http://www.canada.com/vancouversun/news/business/story.html?id=81986ef4-c983-4986-8aaa-3276b4927886.

Careful research and analysis, smooth writing, and effective document design (◂◂ Chapter 4) work together to make effective reports, whether you're writing a 2.5-page memo report or a 250-page formal report complete with all the report components.

◂◂ Chapter 10 covered the first four steps in writing a report:

1. Define the problem
2. Gather the necessary data and information
3. Analyze the data and information
4. Organize the information

This chapter covers the last step:

5. Write the report

It guides you through the process of writing proposals and defines and explains how to organize different kinds of reports.

Other chapters that are especially useful for reports are ◂◂ Chapters 4, 6, 9, and ▸▸ 12.

LO1

VARIETIES OF REPORTS

Reports can provide information, provide information and analyze it, or provide information and analysis to support a recommendation (Figure 11.1). Reports can be called *information reports* if they collect data for the reader (Figure 11.2), *analytical reports* if they interpret data but do not recommend action, and *recommendation reports* (▸▸ Figure 11.8) if they recommend action or a solution.

Ethics and Legal Tripling the Bottom Line*

Since its one-page beginnings in 1823, the annual report has changed. In response to increasing expectations of corporate social responsibility (CSR), more and more businesses are reporting in ways variously titled:

- Social reports
- Green reports
- Environmental and social reports
- Sustainable development reports
- Corporate citizenship reports
- People, planet, profit
- Triple-bottom-line reports

The triple bottom line measures corporate or organizational performance in terms of social, environmental, and economic impacts.

While some commentators are skeptical about business motivation—detecting public relations rather than commitment to sustainability—a 2013 PricewaterhouseCoopers Global Corporate Responsibility Reporting Survey of 4,100 companies in 41 countries is itself a measure of how the reporting has become "a mainstream business practice" since the survey started 20 years ago. The survey found that 71% overall reported: 71% in Asia Pacific, 73% in Europe, and 76% in the Americas now publish CR reports; 93% of the world's largest 250 companies report.

The triple bottom line is integrated into the design and development of Victoria's Dockside Green as a key element of its sustainability initiative.

*Based on Robert Colapinto, "Worth reporting," *CA Magazine*, January/February 2005, 30–34; Alison Arnot, "The triple bottom line," *CGA Magazine*, January/February 2004, retrieved from http://www.cga-canada.org/eng/magazine/jan-feb04/triple_line_e.htm; KPMG, *The KPMG Survey of Corporate Responsibility Reporting* 2013, retrieved June 8, 2014, from http://www.kpmg.com/Global/en/IssuesAndInsights/ArticlesPublications/corporate-responsibility/Documents/corporate-responsibility-reporting-survey-2013.pdf; Paul Hawken, "McDonald's and corporate social responsibility?" April 25, 2002, retrieved January 25, 2005, from http://www.foodfirst.org/media; Dockside Green, "Triple bottom line," retrieved September 1, 2008, from http://docksidegreen.com/sustainability/triple-bottom-line/triple-bottom-line.html.

The following can be information, analytical, or recommendation reports, depending on what they provide:

- *Progress* and *interim reports* can simply record the work done so far and the work remaining on a project. These reports can also recommend that a project be stopped, continued, or restructured.
- *Trip reports* can simply share what the author learned at a conference or during a visit to a customer or supplier. These reports can also recommend action based on that information.

Figure 11.1 Three Levels of Reports

REPORTS CAN PROVIDE:

Information only

- *Sales reports* (sales figures for the week or month).
- *Quarterly reports* (figures showing a plant's productivity and profits for the quarter).

Information plus analysis

- *Annual reports* (financial data and an organization's accomplishments during the past year).
- *Audit reports* (interpretations of the facts revealed during an audit).
- *Make-good or payback reports* (calculations of the point at which a new capital investment will pay for itself).

Information plus analysis plus a recommendation

- *Feasibility reports* evaluate two or more alternatives and recommend which alternative the organization should choose.
- *Justification reports* justify the need for a purchase, an investment, a new personnel line, or a change in procedure.
- *Problem-solving reports* identify the causes of an organizational problem and recommend a solution.

LO2

HOW TO ORGANIZE DIFFERENT KINDS OF REPORTS

Information, feasibility, and justification reports will be more successful when you work with the readers' needs (see "Writing or Speaking to Multiple Audiences with Different Needs" in ◀◀ Chapter 2) and expectations for that kind of report.

Information and Closure Reports

Information and **closure reports** summarize completed work or research that does not typically result in action or recommendation.

Information reports often include the following elements:

- Introductory paragraph summarizing the problems or successes of the project
- Purpose and scope section(s) giving the purpose of the report and indicating what aspects of the topic it covers
- Chronological account of how the problem was discovered, what was done, and what the results were
- Concluding paragraph with suggestions for later action. In a recommendation report, the recommendations would be based on proof. In contrast, the suggestions in a closure report are not proved in detail.

Figure 11.2 presents this kind of information or closure report.

Figure 11.2 An Information Report Describing How a Company Solved a Problem

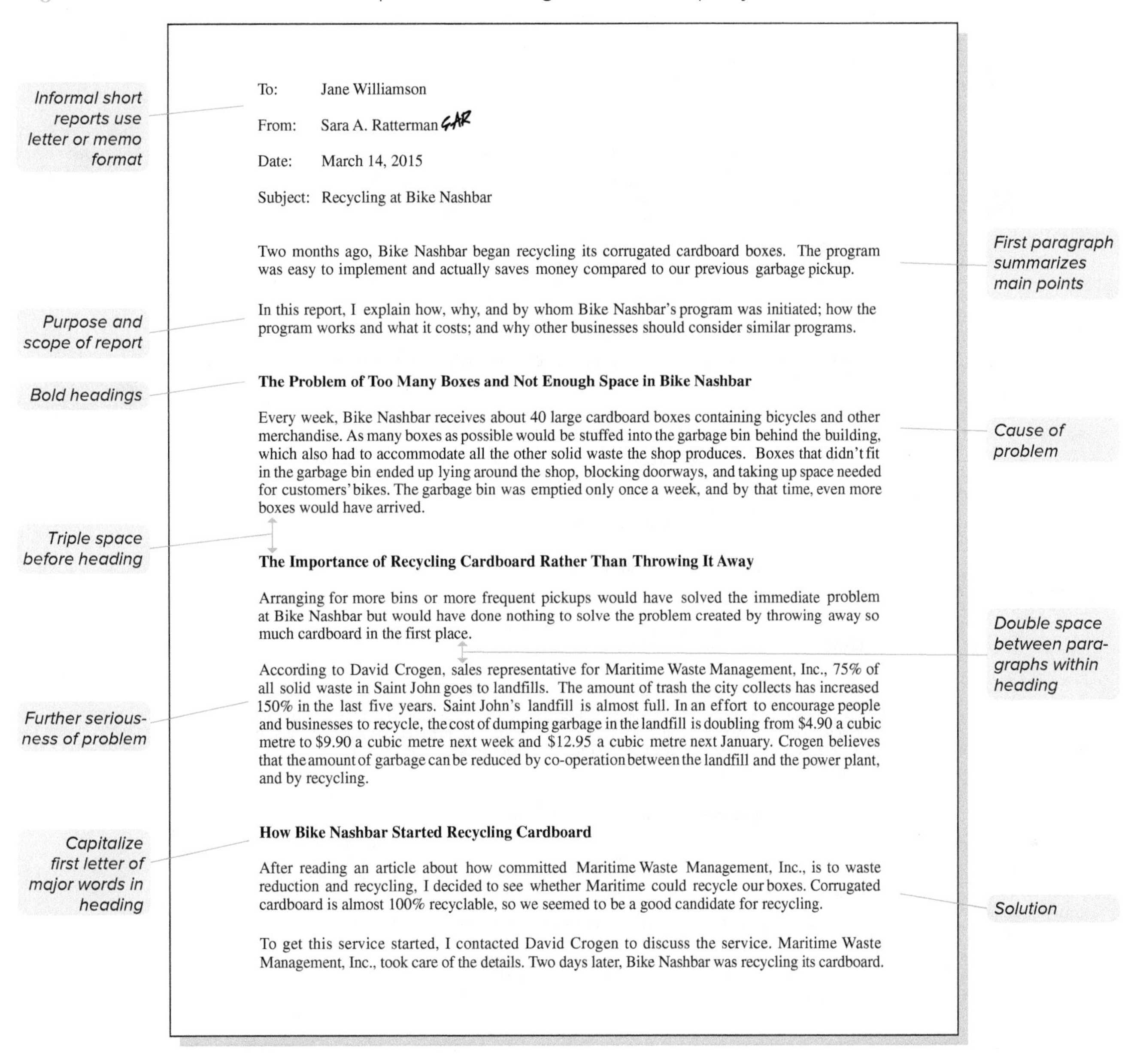

To: Jane Williamson

From: Sara A. Ratterman SAR

Date: March 14, 2015

Subject: Recycling at Bike Nashbar

Two months ago, Bike Nashbar began recycling its corrugated cardboard boxes. The program was easy to implement and actually saves money compared to our previous garbage pickup.

In this report, I explain how, why, and by whom Bike Nashbar's program was initiated; how the program works and what it costs; and why other businesses should consider similar programs.

The Problem of Too Many Boxes and Not Enough Space in Bike Nashbar

Every week, Bike Nashbar receives about 40 large cardboard boxes containing bicycles and other merchandise. As many boxes as possible would be stuffed into the garbage bin behind the building, which also had to accommodate all the other solid waste the shop produces. Boxes that didn't fit in the garbage bin ended up lying around the shop, blocking doorways, and taking up space needed for customers' bikes. The garbage bin was emptied only once a week, and by that time, even more boxes would have arrived.

The Importance of Recycling Cardboard Rather Than Throwing It Away

Arranging for more bins or more frequent pickups would have solved the immediate problem at Bike Nashbar but would have done nothing to solve the problem created by throwing away so much cardboard in the first place.

According to David Crogen, sales representative for Maritime Waste Management, Inc., 75% of all solid waste in Saint John goes to landfills. The amount of trash the city collects has increased 150% in the last five years. Saint John's landfill is almost full. In an effort to encourage people and businesses to recycle, the cost of dumping garbage in the landfill is doubling from $4.90 a cubic metre to $9.90 a cubic metre next week and $12.95 a cubic metre next January. Crogen believes that the amount of garbage can be reduced by co-operation between the landfill and the power plant, and by recycling.

How Bike Nashbar Started Recycling Cardboard

After reading an article about how committed Maritime Waste Management, Inc., is to waste reduction and recycling, I decided to see whether Maritime could recycle our boxes. Corrugated cardboard is almost 100% recyclable, so we seemed to be a good candidate for recycling.

To get this service started, I contacted David Crogen to discuss the service. Maritime Waste Management, Inc., took care of the details. Two days later, Bike Nashbar was recycling its cardboard.

(continued)

Feasibility Reports

Feasibility reports evaluate two or more alternatives and recommend one of them. (Doing nothing or delaying action can be one of the alternatives.)

Feasibility reports normally open by explaining the decision to be made, listing the alternatives, and explaining the criteria. In the body of the report, each alternative is evaluated according to the criteria using one of the two comparison/contrast patterns. Discussing each alternative separately is better when one alternative is clearly superior, when the criteria interact, and when each alternative is indivisible. If the choice depends on the weight given to each criterion, you may want to discuss each alternative under each criterion.

Whether your recommendation should come at the beginning or the end of the report depends on your reader and the culture of your organization. Most readers want the "bottom line" upfront. However, if the reader will find your recommendation hard to accept, you may want to delay your recommendation until the end of the report when you have given all your evidence.

Justification Reports

Justification reports recommend or justify a purchase, investment, hiring, or change in policy. If your organization has a standard format for justification reports, follow that format. If you can choose your headings and organization, use this direct pattern when your recommendation will be easy for your reader to accept:

1. **Indicate what you are asking for and why it is needed.** Since the reader has not asked for the report, you must link your request to the organization's goals.

Figure 11.2 An Information Report Describing How a Company Solved a Problem *(concluded)*

Reader's name, page number, and date

Jane Williamson 2 March 14, 2015

Talking heads tell reader what to expect in each section

How the Service Works and What it Costs

Details of solution

Maritime replaced our existing bin with two 4-metre bins picked up once a week: the contents of the white one marked "cardboard only" go to the recycling plant; those of the brown one for all other solid waste go to the landfill or power plant.

Since Bike Nashbar was already paying more than $60 a week for garbage pickup, our basic cost stayed the same. (Maritime can absorb the extra overhead only if the current charge is at least $60 a week). The cost is divided 80/20 between the two bins: 80% for landfill and powerplant bin; 20% for the cardboard pickup. Bike Nashbar actually receieves $5.00 for each ton of cardboard it recycles.

Double space between paragraphs

Employees must follow these rules when putting boxes in the recycling bin:

- The cardboard must have the word "corrugated" printed on it, along with the universal recycling symbol.
- The boxes must be broken down to their flattest form. More boxes means more money and space.
- Only corrugated cardboard can be put in the recycling bin. Other materials could break the recycling machinery or contaminate the new cardboard.
- The recycling bin is to be kept locked with a padlock provided by Maritime so that theft does not lose money for Maritime and Bike Nashbar.

Indented lists provide visual variety

Minor Problems with Running the Recycling Program

Disadvantages of solution

The only problems have been minor violations of the rules. Sometimes employees at the shop forget to flatten boxes; sometimes people forget to lock the recycling bin. Cardboard has been stolen, and plastic cups and other solid waste dumped in the cardboard bin. I've posted signs reminding employees to empty and fold boxes and relock the bin.

Advantages of the Recycling Program

Advantages of solution

The program is a great success. Our company depends on a clean, safe environment for people to ride their bikes in. Now we have become part of the solution. By choosing to recycle and reduce the amount of solid waste our company generates, we can also save money while gaining a reputation as a socially responsible business.

Why Other Companies Should Adopt Similar Programs

Argues that her company's experience is relevant to other companies

Businesses and institutions in the region currently recycle less than 4% of their solid waste. David Crogen tells me he has over 8,000 clients in Saint John alone, and he acquires new ones every day. Many of these businesses can recycle a large portion of their solid waste at no additional cost. Depending on what they recycle, they may even get money back.

The environmental and economic benefits of recycling as part of a comprehensive waste reduction program are numerous. Recycling helps preserve our environment. We can use the same materials over and over again, saving natural resources such as trees, fuel, and metals, and decreasing the amount of solid waste in landfills. Crogen predicts that Saint John will be on a 100% recycling system by the year 2020. I hope he is right.

2. **Briefly give the background of the problem or need.**
3. **Explain each of the possible solutions.** For each, give the cost and the advantages and disadvantages.
4. **Summarize the action needed to implement your recommendation.** If several people will be involved, indicate who will do what and how long each step will take.
5. **Ask for the action you want.**

If the reader will be reluctant to grant your request, use this variation of the indirect problem-solving pattern described in ◂◂ Chapter 9:

1. **Describe the organizational problem (which your request will solve).** Use specific examples to prove the seriousness of the problem.
2. **Show why easier or less expensive solutions will not solve the problem.**
3. **Present your solution impersonally.**
4. **Show that the disadvantages of your solution are outweighed by the advantages.**
5. **Summarize the action needed to implement your recommendation.** If several people will be involved, indicate who will do what and how long each step will take.
6. **Ask for the action you want.**

How much detail you give in a justification report depends on the corporate culture and on your reader's knowledge of and attitude toward your recommendation.

Progress Reports

When you are assigned to a single project that will take a month or more, you will probably be asked to file one or more progress reports. A progress report (Figure 11.3) reassures

Figure 11.3 A Student Chronological Progress Report

To: Isobel M. Findlay

From: David G. Bunnel DGB

Date: November 10, 2014

Subject: Progress on Software Feasibility Study for the Architecture Firm Patrick and Associates, Inc.

✓ ¶ 1: Summarize results in terms of purpose, schedule

I have obtained most of the information necessary to recommend whether CADAM or CATIA is better for Patrick and Associates, Inc. (P&A). I am currently analyzing and organizing this information and am on schedule.

✓ Underline headings or bold

Background

To learn how computer literate P&A employees are, I interviewed a judgment sample of five employees. My interview with Bruce Ratekin, the director of P&A's Computer-Aided Design (CAD) Department, on November 3 enabled me to determine the architectural drafting needs of the firm. Mr. Ratekin also gave me a basic drawing of a building showing both two- and three-dimensional views so that I could replicate the drawing with both software packages.

Work Completed

✓ Be very specific about what you've done and how you've overcome problems

I obtained tutorials for both packages to use as a reference while making the drawings. First I drew the building using CADAM, the package designed primarily for two-dimensional architectural drawings. I encountered problems with the isometric drawing because there was a mistake in the manual I was using; I fixed the problem by trying alternatives and finally getting help from another CADAM user. Next, I used CATIA, the package whose strength is three-dimensional drawings, to construct the drawing.

✓ Show how you've overcome minor problems and solutions to potential problems

✓ Indicate changes in purpose, scope, or recommendations. Progress report is a low-risk way to bring the readers on board.

I am in the process of comparing the two packages based on these criteria: quality of drawing, ease of data entry (lines, points, surfaces, etc.) for computer experts and novices, and ease of making changes in the completed drawings. Based on my experience with the packages, I have analyzed the training people with and without experience in CAD would need to learn to use each of these packages.

Work to Be Completed

Making the drawings has shown that neither of the packages can do everything that P&A needs. Therefore, I want to investigate the feasibility of P&A's buying both packages.

✓ Specify the work that remains

As soon as he comes back from an unexpected illness that has kept him out of the office, I will meet with Tom Merrick, the CAD systems programmer for Mount Royal University, to learn about software expansion flexibility for both packages as well as the costs for initial purchase, installation, maintenance, and software updates. After this meeting, I will be ready to begin the first draft of my report.

✓ End on a positive note

Whether I am able to meet my deadline will depend on when I am able to meet with Mr. Merrick. Right now, I am on schedule and plan to submit my report by the December 10 deadline.

that you are making progress and allows for problems to be resolved as they arise. Different readers may have different concerns. A professor may want to know whether you will meet your deadline. A client may be more interested in what you are learning about the problem. Adapt your progress report and its headings to the audience.

A study of the progress reports in a large research and development organization found that poor writers tended to focus on what they had done and said very little about the value of their work. Good writers, in contrast, spent less space on details and much more space explaining the value of their work for the organization.[1]

Subject lines for progress reports are straightforward. Specify the project on which you are reporting your progress.

Subject: Progress on Group Survey on Campus Parking

You may need to include a heading "Background" if the reader needs reminding of or educating on the background to the report.

Make your progress report as positive as you honestly can. You'll build a better image of yourself if you show that you can take minor problems in stride and that you're confident of your own abilities.

× Negative: I have not deviated markedly from my schedule, and I feel that I will have very little trouble completing this report by the due date.

✓ Positive: I am back on schedule and expect to complete my report by the due date.

Progress reports can be organized in three ways: by chronology, by task, and in support of a recommendation.

The *chronological* pattern of organization focuses on what you have done and what work remains.

1. **Summarize your progress in terms of your goals and your original schedule.** Use measurable statements.

   × Poor: My progress has been slow.

   ✓ Better: The research for my report is about one-third complete.

2. **Under the heading "Work Completed," describe what you have done.** Be specific, both to support your claims in the first paragraph and to allow the reader to appreciate your hard work. Acknowledge the people who have helped you. Describe any serious obstacles you've encountered and tell how you've dealt with them.

   × Poor: I have found many articles about Procter & Gamble on the Web. I have had a few problems finding how the company keeps employees safe from chemical fumes.

   ✓ Better: On the Web, I found Procter & Gamble's home page, its annual report, and mission statement. No one whom I interviewed could tell me about safety programs specifically at P&G. I have found seven articles about ways to protect workers against pollution in factories, but none mentions P&G.

3. **Under the heading "Work to Be Completed," describe the work that remains.** If you're more than three days late (for school projects) or two weeks late (for business projects) submit a new schedule, showing how you will be able to meet the original deadline. Depending on the length and complexity of the report, you may use a heading "Potential Problems and Solutions." You may want to discuss "Preliminary Conclusions" if you want feedback before writing the final report or if your reader has asked for substantive interim reports.

4. **Either express your confidence in having the report ready by the due date or request a conference to discuss extending the due date or limiting the project.** If you are behind your original schedule, show why you think you can still finish the project on time.

In a task progress report, organize information under the various tasks you have worked on during the period. For example, a task progress report for a group report project might use these headings:

Finding Background Information on the Web and in Print

Analyzing Our Survey Data

Working on the Introduction of the Report and the Appendices

Under each heading, the group could discuss the tasks it has completed and those that remain.

Recommendation progress reports recommend action: increasing the funding for a project, changing its direction, cancelling a project that isn't working out. When the recommendation will be easy for the reader to accept, use the persuasive direct request pattern of organization from ◂◂ Chapter 9. If the recommendation is likely to meet strong resistance, the indirect problem-solving pattern may be more effective.

Trip, Conference, and Workshop Reports

Businesses want to know the benefits of business trips or conference or workshop participation they have supported. Typically submitted to supervisors on return to the office, these reports clarify the value to the participant and the business of the learning (about new procedures, regulations, software, equipment) and other opportunities (networking, potential or completed deals, for instance).

Trip reports (Figure 11.4) should be organized with the audience in mind to evaluate what the writer accomplished on the trip. They should avoid merely enumerating a chronological list of activities and/or listing activities, times, and expenses.

Using a direct pattern of organization, trip reports include these parts:

- **Introduction:** Where you went, when you went, why you went there, and report overview.
- **Body:** What you achieved, how you and the business benefit, and what the trip cost (expenses may be listed separately).

  × Poor: After registration at 8:30 a.m., the first speaker at 9:00 a.m. started the seminar with a talk on evidence-based management.

  ✓ Better: The highlight of the morning was keynote speaker Joan Reynolds, who engaged her audience with examples of evidence-based management in action: sharing decision making, learning from mistakes, and saving lives in the process.

On the Job The Political Uses of Progress Reports

Progress reports can do more than just report progress. You can use progress reports to

- **Enhance your image.** Details about the number of documents you've read, people you've surveyed, or experiments you've conducted create a picture of a hardworking person doing a thorough job.
- **Float trial balloons.** Explain, "I could continue to do X [what you approved]; I could do Y instead [what I'd like to do now]." The detail in the progress report can help back up your claim. Even if the idea is rejected, you don't lose face because you haven't made a separate issue of the alternative.
- **Minimize potential problems.** As you do the work, it may become clear that implementing your recommendations will be difficult. In your regular progress reports, you can alert your boss or the funding agency to the challenges that lie ahead, enabling them to prepare psychologically and physically to act on your recommendations.

Figure 11.4 A Student Trip Report

To: Dean Susan J. Andrews, Wilson Business School

From: Joanne Lachance

Date: February 20, 2015

Subject: Connections 2015: A Valuable investment in Learning

Attending the February 18 business seminar Connections 2015 sponsored by the Wilson Business School at the Trade Centre taught me more than I had expected. Networking with business leaders, gathering information from the trade show, and listening to keynote speakers and the panel of Wilson graduates led me to revalue connections and my own diverse experience. Although I also saw impressive oral presentation skills, got advice on social networking etiquette, and gained crucial contacts, my report focuses on what I learned about how my classes and extracurricular experience can help me get an interview and land my dream job in human resource management.

Connecting Work, Educational, and Extracurricular Experience

Before the seminar I looked forward to learning from contacts in the real world, but I underestimated the experience of the classroom and the sports arena. When I listened to Jesse Steeves, Wilson graduate and Olympic rower, talk about returning from the Olympics with "absolutely nothing to put on his résumé," his assessment made sense at first. Focused on training, travelling to competition, and winning medals, he had left room only for his academic commitments. He had no "real" experience for the human resources positions he wanted. But a mentor helped him see how for years he had been putting theory into practice in class and extracurricular settings. Only then did he redesign his strategy, make visible his assets, and land his job as HR Manager.

Making Visible the Value of Diverse Experience

Just as Steeves learned to reassess the leadership, teamwork, time management, interpersonal, and communication skills he had refined over his years in sports and school, so I am now rethinking (a) how I benefit from my classes and my commitment to intercollegiate soccer and (b) how I can present that experience as business assets.

I now recognize benefit in both the topic and process of class group work, adapting to different perspectives, learning styles, and work schedules. Instead of thinking of class projects as make-work, I am now determined to make them work for me in my professional development strategy. My soccer too is no longer just about keeping fit but about keeping prepared for my professional future.

Getting a Good Return on Investment

In conclusion, I did learn from the real world, although not in the ways I had expected. In addition to making some good contacts and acquiring some useful professional tips, I learned how work, school, and sports can complement rather than compete with one another and help build the well-rounded candidate businesses seek today. I am grateful for this opportunity. Continuing to sponsor the annual Connections seminar is an important investment in the professional development of all our students.

- **Conclusion:** Expresses thanks for the opportunity and summarizes value. Close may also include recommendations on future trips.

Refer to ◂◂ Figure 3.3 for a planning guide for a trip report.

LO3

WRITING PROPOSALS

By suggesting a method for finding information or solving a problem, proposals help an organization decide whether to change, how to change, or how to implement a change that is agreed on. (See Figure 11.5.)

Proposals have two goals: to get the project accepted and to get you accepted to do the job. In defining the problem and purpose, you already consider audience needs. Depending on proposal content and reader expectations, you will choose your organizational strategy—direct or indirect. When the reader may be receptive to your findings, use the direct pattern (◂◂ Figure 9.1). When the reader is unfamiliar with the content or may be reluctant to accept the proposal, use the indirect pattern (◂◂ Figure 9.3) to prepare the reader for your findings.

Proposals must stress reader benefits and provide specific supporting details. Attention to details—including good visual impact and proofreading—helps establish your professional image and suggests that you'd give the same care to the project if your proposal is accepted. See ◂◂ Figures 10.7 and 10.8 for unacceptable and good examples of proposal introductions.

To write a good proposal, you need to have a clear view of the problem and the kind of research or other action needed to solve it. A proposal must answer the following questions convincingly:

- **What problem will you solve?** Define the problem as the audience sees it, even if you believe that the presenting problem is part of a larger problem that must first be solved.

Figure 11.5 Relationship among Situation, Proposal, and Final Report

COMPANY'S CURRENT SITUATION	THE PROPOSAL OFFERS TO	THE FINAL REPORT WILL PROVIDE
We don't know whether we should change.	Assess whether change is a good idea.	Insight, recommending whether change is desirable.
We need to/want to change, but we don't know exactly what we need to do.	Develop a plan to achieve the desired goal.	A plan for achieving the desired change.
We need to/want to change, and we know what to do, but we need help doing it.	Implement the plan, increase (or decrease) measurable outcomes.	A record of the implementation and evaluation process.

Source: Adapted from Richard C. Freed, Shervin Freed, and Joseph D. Romano, *Writing Winning Proposals: Your Guide to Landing the Client, Making the Sale, Persuading the Boss* (New York: McGraw-Hill, 1995), 21.

- **How will you solve it?** Prove that your methods and timelines are feasible and that your solution is economic and efficient. Specify the topics you'll investigate. Explain how you'll gather data.
- **What exactly will you provide?** Specify the tangible products you'll produce; explain how you'll evaluate them.
- **Can you deliver what you promise?** Show that you have the knowledge, the staff, and the facilities to do what you say you will. Describe your previous work in this area, your other qualifications, and the qualifications of any people who will be helping you.
- **What benefits can you offer?** Show why the company should hire you. Discuss the benefits—direct and indirect—that your firm can provide.
- **When will you complete the work?** Provide a detailed schedule showing when each phase of the work will be completed.
- **How much will you charge?** Provide a detailed budget that includes costs for materials, salaries, and overhead.

Government agencies and companies often issue **requests for proposals,** known as **RFPs.** Follow the RFP exactly when you respond to a proposal. Evaluators look only under the heads specified in the RFP. If information isn't there, the proposal gets no points in that category.

Proposals for Class Research Projects

A proposal for a student report usually has the following sections:

1. In your first paragraph (no heading), summarize in a few sentences the topic and purposes of your report, explaining its benefits and giving an overview of its contents.
2. **Problem.** What organizational problem (or challenge or opportunity) exists? What is at issue? Why does it need to be solved? Is there a history or background that is relevant?
3. **Feasibility.** Can a solution be found in the time available? How do you know?
4. **Audience.** Who in the organization would have the power to implement your recommendation? What secondary audiences might be asked to evaluate your report? What audiences would be affected by your recommendation? Will anyone in the organization serve as a gatekeeper, determining whether your report is sent to decision makers? What watchdog audiences might read the report?

   For each of these audiences and for your initial audience (your professor), give the person's name, job title, and business address and answer the following questions:

   - What is the audience's major concern or priority?
   - What will the audience see as advantages of your proposal?
   - What objections, if any, is the reader likely to have?
   - How interested is the audience in the topic of your report?
   - How much does the audience know about the topic of your report?
   - What terms, concepts, equations, or assumptions may need to be explained?
   - How do your audiences affect the content, organization, or style of the report?
5. **Topics to investigate.** List the questions and subquestions you will answer in your report, the topics or concepts you will explain, and the aspects of the problem you will discuss. Indicate how deeply you will examine each and explain your rationale.
6. **Methods/procedure.** How will you get answers to your questions? Whom will you interview or survey? Provide a draft of your questions. What published sources will you use? Give the full bibliographic references.
7. **Qualifications/facilities/resources.** Do you have the knowledge and skills needed to conduct this study? Do you have adequate access to the organization? Do you have access to equipment to conduct your research (computer, books, etc.)? Where will you get help if you hit an unexpected snag? You will be more convincing if you have already scheduled an interview, checked out books, or printed out online sources.
8. **Work schedule.** List the date when you expect to finish each of the following activities:

   - Gathering information
   - Analyzing information
   - Preparing the progress report

Figure 11.6 Proposal for a Student Report Using Survey, Online, and Library Research

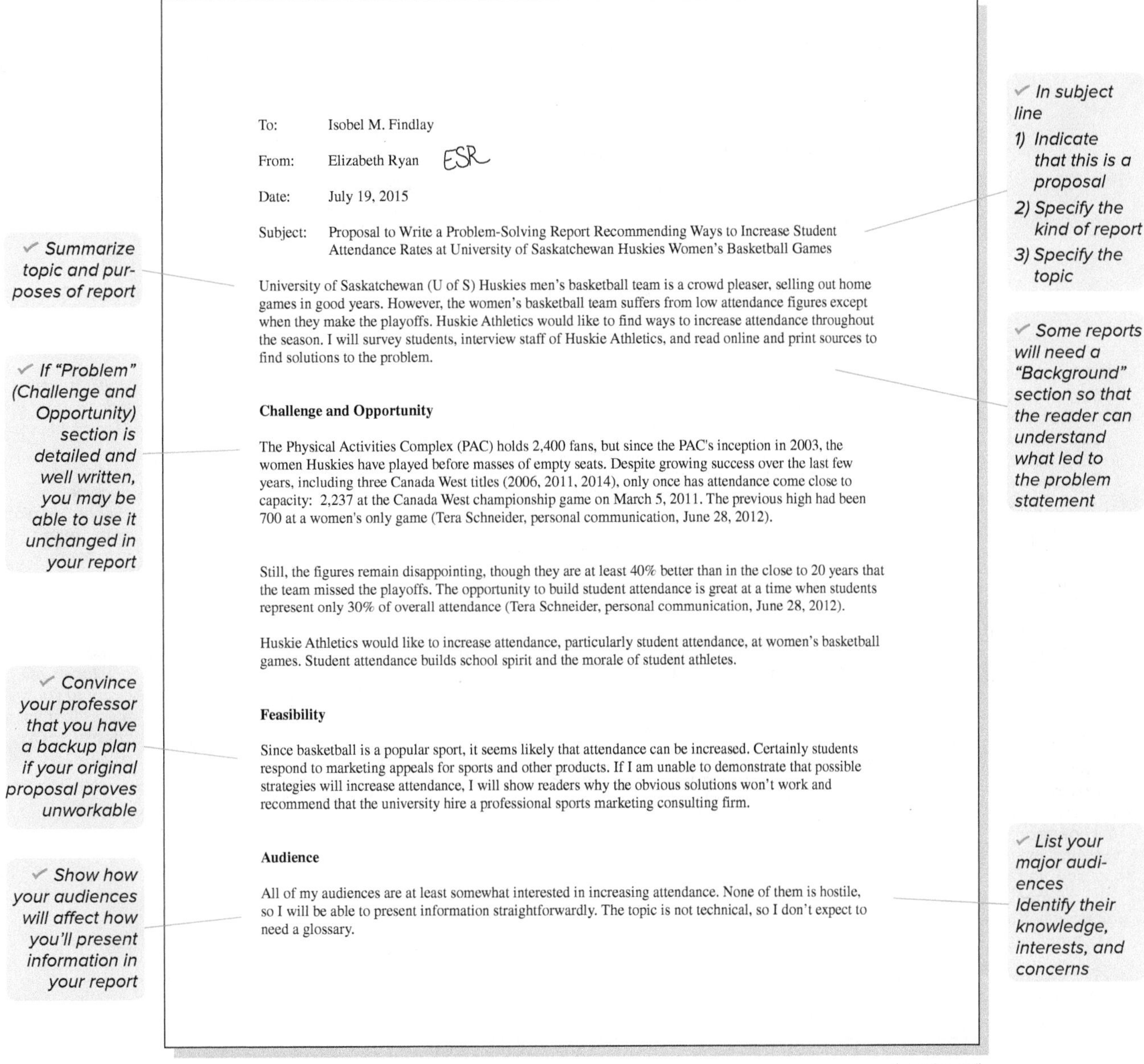
To: Isobel M. Findlay

From: Elizabeth Ryan ESR

Date: July 19, 2015

Subject: Proposal to Write a Problem-Solving Report Recommending Ways to Increase Student Attendance Rates at University of Saskatchewan Huskies Women's Basketball Games

University of Saskatchewan (U of S) Huskies men's basketball team is a crowd pleaser, selling out home games in good years. However, the women's basketball team suffers from low attendance figures except when they make the playoffs. Huskie Athletics would like to find ways to increase attendance throughout the season. I will survey students, interview staff of Huskie Athletics, and read online and print sources to find solutions to the problem.

Challenge and Opportunity

The Physical Activities Complex (PAC) holds 2,400 fans, but since the PAC's inception in 2003, the women Huskies have played before masses of empty seats. Despite growing success over the last few years, including three Canada West titles (2006, 2011, 2014), only once has attendance come close to capacity: 2,237 at the Canada West championship game on March 5, 2011. The previous high had been 700 at a women's only game (Tera Schneider, personal communication, June 28, 2012).

Still, the figures remain disappointing, though they are at least 40% better than in the close to 20 years that the team missed the playoffs. The opportunity to build student attendance is great at a time when students represent only 30% of overall attendance (Tera Schneider, personal communication, June 28, 2012).

Huskie Athletics would like to increase attendance, particularly student attendance, at women's basketball games. Student attendance builds school spirit and the morale of student athletes.

Feasibility

Since basketball is a popular sport, it seems likely that attendance can be increased. Certainly students respond to marketing appeals for sports and other products. If I am unable to demonstrate that possible strategies will increase attendance, I will show readers why the obvious solutions won't work and recommend that the university hire a professional sports marketing consulting firm.

Audience

All of my audiences are at least somewhat interested in increasing attendance. None of them is hostile, so I will be able to present information straightforwardly. The topic is not technical, so I don't expect to need a glossary.

(continued)

- Organizing information
- Writing the draft
- Revising the draft
- Preparing the visuals
- Editing the draft
- Proofreading the report

Organize your work schedule either in a chart or in a calendar. A good schedule provides realistic estimates for each activity, allows time for unexpected snags, and shows that you can complete the work on time.

9. **Call to action.** In your final section, invite any suggestions your professor may have for improving the research plan. Ask your professor to approve your proposal so that you can begin work on your report.

Figure 11.6 shows a student proposal for a long report.

Proposals for Action

You can write a proposal for action or change in your organization. Normally, proposals for action recommend new programs or ways to solve organizational problems.

Organize a proposal for action as a direct request (◀◀ Chapter 9). Explain in detail how your idea could be implemented. Be sure to answer your readers' questions and to overcome objections.

Sales Proposals

To sell goods, ideas, or services, you may be asked to submit a proposal.

Be sure that you understand the buyer's priorities. Do not assume that the buyer will understand why your product or system is good. Show the reader benefits (◀◀ Chapter 2) and

Figure 11.6 Proposal for a Student Report Using Survey, Online, and Library Research *(continued)*

Proposal to Write a Recommendation Report on Attendance at U of S Huskies Women's Basketball Games
July 19, 2015
Page 2

My primary audience will be Athletic Director Basil Hughton, who can accept or reject my recommendations. He is interested in women's basketball and is knowledgeable about sports marketing.

Secondary audiences to this report include staffers in Huskie Athletics who will implement the recommendations. The coaching staff of the basketball team may be asked to evaluate the report. Finally, players and students are part of the secondary audience. Players benefit from student support at games, and the students are the people being targeted for increased attendance. Only a few of these secondary audiences will be very interested in my report.

You will be my initial audience. You've told me that you like men's basketball but have never been to a women's basketball game, even though several of your friends have season tickets.

Topics to Investigate

I plan to answer these questions in detail:

1. What factors affect student attendance?
   - Why do the students who attend women's basketball games do so?
   - Why do the students who don't attend stay away?
   - What promotions or publicity could make students more likely to attend?
2. How can student awareness of the team be increased?
   - What short-term strategies exist?
   - What long-term strategies exist?
   - Does it make sense to market the team to female audiences?
3. Would a loyalty program help?
   - What programs are available, and what is involved?
   - What are some university examples of programs?

I will briefly discuss how attendance and newspaper publicity correlate to the win/loss record. I will not discuss the cost or the return on investment of my recommendations. I will not discuss how changes in coaching or recruiting might affect attendance.

Methods

I expect to get data from four sources: (1) surveys (draft attached) of a convenience sample of 50 to 100 students at the Students' Union, (2) interviews with members of Huskie Athletics, (3) my observations of marketing tactics on campus and in Saskatchewan, and (4) library and online sources about attendance at basketball games.

✓ Indicate what you'll discuss briefly and what you'll discuss in more detail. This list should match your audience's concerns

✓ All items in list must be grammatically parallel. Here, all are questions.

✓ If you'll administer a survey or conduct interviews, tell how many subjects you'll have, how you'll choose them, and what you'll ask them.

✓ If it is well written, the "Topics to Investigate" section will become the "Scope" section of the report—with minor revisions

✓ Indicate any topics relevant to your report that you choose not to discuss

(continued)

present the benefits using you-attitude (◂◂ Chapter 2). Consider using psychological description (◂◂ Chapter 9) to make the benefits vivid.

Use language appropriate for your audience. Even if the buyers want a state-of-the-art system, they may not want the level of detail that your staff could provide; they may not understand or appreciate technical jargon (◂◂ Chapter 3).

In the case of long proposals, provide a one-page cover letter in a modified version of the sales pattern in ◂◂ Chapter 9:

1. Catch the reader's attention and summarize up to three major benefits.
2. Discuss each of the major benefits in the order they are listed in the first paragraph.
3. Deal with any objections or concerns the reader may have.
4. Mention other benefits briefly.
5. Ask the reader to approve your proposal; provide a reason for acting promptly.

Proposals for Funding

Proposals for funding include both **business plans** (documents written to raise capital for new business ventures) and proposals submitted to a foundation, a corporation, a government agency, or a religious agency. In a proposal for funding, stress the needs your project will meet and show how your project helps fulfill the goals of the organization you are asking for funds.

Every funding source has certain priorities; some have detailed lists of the kind of projects they fund. The Voluntary Sector Initiative's *Canadian Directory to Foundations and Corporations* is a bilingual online directory listing funding resources relevant to those working in the voluntary sector.

Figure 11.6 Proposal for a Student Report Using Survey, Online, and Library Research *(continued)*

Proposal to Write a Recommendation Report on Attendance at U of S Huskies Women's Basketball Games
July 19, 2015
Page 3

I have already identified the following useful Web sites with additional links:

Canadian Association for the Advancement of Women and Sport and Physical Activity. (2012). Web site. Retrieved from http://www.caaws.ca/

Canadian Interuniversity Sport. (2012) Web site. Retrieved from http://www.universitysport.ca

Qualifications

I am a student majoring in Marketing at the University of Saskatchewan and a sports fan. I would like to see the student community offer more support to the Huskies. My friend Tera Schneider of Huskie Sports Information can give me access to key personnel.

Work Schedule

The following schedule will enable me to finish this report by the end of the summer term.

Activity	Total Time	Completion Date
Gathering information	15 hours	July 6
Analyzing information	10 hours	July 19
Organizing information	7 hours	July 25
Preparing the progress report	3 hours	July 30
Writing the draft/creating visuals	15 hours	August 6
Revising the draft/visuals	12 hours	August 10
Editing the draft	5 hours	August 13
Proofreading the report	3 hours	August 20
Preparing PowerPoint slides	5 hours	August 20

Call to Action

Could we schedule a conference to discuss my draft proposal? I would appreciate your suggestions to strengthen it. Please approve my draft so I may complete my research and report.

✓ *If you're using library or Web research, list sources you hope to use. Use full bibliographic citations.*

✓ *This list uses APA format*

✓ *Cite knowledge and skills from other classes, jobs, and activities that will enable you to conduct the research and interpret your data. If you've already done some of the work, say so*

✓ *Allow plenty of time! Good reports need good revision, editing, and proofreading as well as good research.*

✓ *Time needed will depend on the length and topic of the report, your knowledge of the topic, and your writing skills*

✓ *It's tactful to indicate you'll accept suggestions. End on a positive note.*

(continued)

Figuring the Budget and Costs

For a class research project, you may not be asked to prepare a budget. However, a good budget is crucial to making the winning bid for many proposals. Ask for everything you need to do a quality job. Asking for too little may lead the funder to think you don't understand the project scope.

Read the RFP to find out what is and isn't fundable. Talk to the program officer and read successful past proposals to find answers to these questions:

- What size projects will the organization fund in theory?
- Does the funder prefer making a few big grants or many smaller grants?
- Does the funder expect you to provide in-kind or cost-sharing funds from other sources?

Think about exactly what needs to be done and who will do it. What supplies or materials will be needed? Also think about indirect costs for office space, retirement and health benefits, salaries, office supplies, administration, and infrastructure.

Make the basis of your estimates specific.

× Weak:	75 hours of transcribing interviews	$1,500
✓ Better:	25 hours of interviews; a skilled transcriber can complete 1 hour of interviews in 3 hours; 75 hours @ $20/hour	$1,500

Figure your numbers conservatively. For example, even if you might be able to train someone and pay only $12 an hour, use the going rate of $20 an hour. Then, even if your grant is cut, you still will be able to do the project well.

Figure 11.6 Proposal for a Student Report Using Survey, Online, and Library Research *(concluded)*

Survey: Why Do Students Attend Athletic Events?

The purpose of this survey is to determine why students attend sports events, and what might increase attendance. All information is to be used solely for a student research paper. Please return completed surveys to Elizabeth or Vicki in the Students' Union. Thank you for your assistance!

1. Gender (Please circle one) M F

2. What is your rank? (Please circle) 1 2 3 4 Grad Other

3. How do you feel about women's sports? (Please circle)

1	2	3	4	5
I enjoy watching women's sports		I'll watch, but it doesn't really matter		Women's sports are boring/ I'd rather watch men's sports

4. Do you like to attend U of S men's basketball games or listen on the radio? (Please circle)

Y N

5. How often do you attend U of S women's basketball games? (Please circle)

1	2	3	4	5
All/most games	Few games a season	Once a season	Less than once ayear	Never

6. If you do not attend all of the women's basketball games, why not? (Please check all that apply. If you attend all the games, skip to #7.)

__I've never thought to go.
__I don't like basketball.
__I don't like sporting events.
__The team isn't good enough.
__My friends are not interested in going.
__I want to go, I just haven't had the opportunity.
__Game time (6:15 P.M.) is less convenient than for men's play (8:00 P.M.)
__The tickets cost too much for friends without U of S ID cards ($8).
__Other (please specify) ____________________

7. To what extent would each of the following make you more likely to attend a U of S women's basketball game? (please rank all)

1	2	3
Much more likely to attend	Possibly more likely	No effect

__Increased awareness on campus (flyers, bulletin boards, more articles in *The Sheaf*)
__Marketing to students (giveaways, days for residence halls or student societies)
__Student loyalty program (awarding points towards free tickets, clothing, food for attending games)
__Education (pocket guide explaining the rules of the game provided at the gate)
__Other (please specify) ____________________

Thank you!
Please return this survey to Elizabeth or Vicki.

✓ Start with easy-to-answer questions

✓ The words below each number anchor responses, while still allowing you to average the data numerically

✓ Think about factors that affect the problem you're studying, and write survey questions to get information about them.

✓ In your introductory ¶,
1) Tell how to return the survey
2) Tell how the information will be used.

✓ Seeing a response in a survey can make respondents more willing to admit to feelings they may be embarrassed to admit

✓ Repeat where to turn in or mail completed surveys

On the Job The Bulletproof Business Plan*

Business plans are themselves compilations of other reports—sales and marketing, operations, human resources, and financials, for instance—and include conventional parts from the transmittal document, cover, table of contents, executive summary, and introduction (idea history and background, mission, vision, values, goals) to environment (including social, economic, and political trends), operations, human resources, marketing, financial plans, and references to persuade the reader that it is a viable plan.

Emily Barker recommends that your plan:

- "Be crystal clear about how your own offering is different [from the competition] and why it gives customers a better value."
- Provide "evidence that customers will buy your product—and buy it at the price you're charging."
- Ensure the "path to profitability" is "both clear and short—a year to 18 months. . . . Savvy entrepreneurs will also want to include the slowing economy in their assumptions."

When students compete for real money, the stakes are high and the learning curve steep. And the opportunities are increasing. The Venture Forward Business Plan Competition, a $100,000 competition modelled on such plans as the MIT Entrepreneurship Competition and the Munich Business Plan Competition, has been one more economic development and academic tool to add to the competition mix.

*Based on Canada Business, *Developing Your Business Plan,* retrieved April 29, 2011, from http://www.canadabusiness.ca/eng/125/138/; Emily Barker, "The bullet-proof business plan," *Inc.,* October 2001, 102–104; Venture Forward Homepage, retrieved April 28, 2011, from www.ventureforward.ca.

LO4

PRESENTING INFORMATION EFFECTIVELY IN REPORTS

Careful writing is as critical to effective reports as the careful planning, research, and analysis discussed in ◀◀Chapter 10. Effective writing is effective revision. Careful revision changes organization, argument, and wording to meet purposes and audience needs while ensuring report accuracy, clarity, and credibility.

Careful revision clarifies the key messages as well as the headings and other design elements (◀◀ Chapter 4) that will make your document reader friendly and action oriented. As Bertolt Brecht has argued, "You cannot just write the truth; you have to write it *for* and *to* somebody, somebody who can do something with it."

In sum, investment in careful planning, research, and revision yields significant returns, and helps reports highlight profitable initiatives and shape business futures.

The advice about style in ◀◀ Chapter 3 also applies to reports, with three exceptions:

1. **Use a fairly formal style, without contractions or slang.** In the interests of objectivity, avoid the word *I* and such phrases as "I/we think/believe. . . ." Report credibility depends on the use of you-attitude, positive emphasis, and bias-free language (◀◀ Chapter 2).
2. **Avoid the word *you*.** In a document with multiple audiences, it will not be clear who *you* is. Instead, use the company name.
3. **Include in the report all the information, definitions, and documents needed to understand the conclusions and recommendations.** The multiple audiences for reports include readers who may consult the document months or years from now; they will not share your special knowledge. Explain acronyms and abbreviations the first time they appear. Explain the history or background of the problem. Add as appendices previous documents on which you are building.

The following four points apply to any kind of writing, but they are particularly important in reports whether you submit paper copy or online (i.e., PDF attached).

1. Say What You Mean

Not-quite-right word choices are particularly damaging in reports, which may be skimmed by readers who know very little about the subject. Occasionally you can simply substitute a word.

× Incorrect: With these recommendations, we can overcome the solutions to our problem.

✓ Correct: With these recommendations, we can overcome our problem.

✓ Also correct: With these recommendations, we can solve our problem.

Putting the meaning of your sentence in the verbs will help you say what you mean.

× Vague: My report revolves around the checkout lines and the methods used to get price checks when they arise.

✓ Better: The report shows how price checks slow checkout lines and recommends ways to reduce the number of price checks needed.

2. Tighten Your Writing

Eliminate unnecessary words, use gerunds and infinitives, combine sentences, and reword sentences to cut the number of words.

× Wordy: Campus Jewellers' main objective is to increase sales. Specifically, the objective is to double sales in the next five years by becoming a more successful business.

✓ Better: Campus Jewellers' objective is to double sales in the next five years.

No reader wants length for the sake of length. In a class report, the page requirement is an indication of the complexity of analysis that the professor expects.

Some repetition in reports is legitimate (see the ▶▶ On the Job box "Repeating with Style" later in this chapter). The conclusion restates points made in the body of the report; the recommendations appear in the transmittal, the executive summary, and the recommendations sections of the report. However, repetitive references to earlier material ("As we have already seen") may indicate that the document needs to be reorganized.

Read the document through at a single sitting to make sure that any repetition serves a useful purpose. For example, general readers will focus on the executive summary, professional readers will appreciate the detail of the body, and experts will turn to the technical information in appendices. If the repetition does not appeal to a specific group of readers or add meaningfully to a particular section, eliminate it.

3. Introduce Sources and Visuals Gracefully

The first time you cite an author's work, use his or her full name except in *APA* style (Kanter, 2008 found): "Rosabeth Moss Kanter points out. . . ." In subsequent citations, use only the last name: "Kanter shows. . . ." Use active rather than passive verbs.

The verb you use indicates your attitude toward the source. *Says* and *writes* are neutral. *Points out, shows, suggests, discovers,* and *notes* suggest that you agree with the source. Words such as *claims, argues, contends that, believes,* and *alleges* distance you from the source. At a minimum, they suggest that you know that not everyone agrees with the source; they are also appropriate to report the views of someone with whom you disagree.

Use active verbs to refer to visuals, too:

As Table 1 shows, . .
See Figure 4

For a fuller discussion of when and how to integrate good visuals, see ◂◂ Chapter 4.

4. Use Blueprints, Transitions, Topic Sentences, and Headings

Blueprints are overviews or forecasts that tell the reader what you will discuss in a section or in the entire report. Make your blueprint easy to read by telling the reader how many points there are and using bullets or numbers. In the following example, the first sentence in the revised paragraph tells the reader to look for four points; the numbers separate the four points clearly. This overview paragraph also makes a contract with readers, who now expect to read about tax benefits first and employee benefits last.

✗ PARAGRAPH WITHOUT NUMBERS:

Employee stock ownership programs (ESOPs) have several advantages. They provide tax benefits for the company. ESOPs also create tax benefits for employees and for lenders. They provide a defence against takeovers. In some organizations, productivity increases because workers now have a financial stake in the company's profits. ESOPs are an attractive employee benefit and help the company hire and retain good employees.

✓ REVISED PARAGRAPH WITH NUMBERS:

Employee stock ownership programs (ESOPs) provide four benefits. First, ESOPs provide tax benefits for the company, its employees, and lenders to the plan. Second, ESOPs help create a defence against takeovers. Third, ESOPs may increase productivity by giving workers a financial stake in the company's profits. Fourth, as an attractive employee benefit, ESOPs help the company hire and retain good employees.

Transitions (◂◂ Chapter 3) are words, phrases, or sentences that tell the reader whether the discussion is continuing on the same point or shifting points:

There are economic advantages, too

(Tells the reader that we are still discussing advantages but that we have now moved to economic advantages.)

An alternative to this plan is . . .

(Tells the reader that a second option follows.)

These advantages, however, are found only in A, not in B or C

(Prepares the reader for a shift from A to B and C.)

A *topic sentence* (◂◂ Chapter 3) introduces or summarizes the main idea of a sentence. Readers who skim reports can follow your ideas more easily if each paragraph begins with a clear topic sentence.

✗ HARD TO READ (NO TOPIC SENTENCE):

Another main use of ice is to keep the fish fresh. Each of the seven kinds of fish served at the restaurant requires 3.78 litres twice a day, for a total of 52.92 litres. An additional 22.68 litres a day are required for the salad bar.

✓ BETTER (BEGINS WITH TOPIC SENTENCE):

Seventy-six litres of ice a day are needed to keep food fresh. Of this, the biggest portion (52.92 litres) is used to keep the fish fresh. Each of the seven kinds of fish served at the restaurant requires 3.78 litres twice a day ($7 \times 7.56 = 52.92$ L). An additional 22.68 litres a day are required for the salad bar.

Headings (see ◂◂ Chapter 4) are single words, short phrases, or complete sentences that indicate the topic in each section. A heading must cover all of the material under it until the next heading. For example, *Cost of Tuition* cannot include the cost of books or of room and board. You can have one paragraph under a heading or several pages. If you do have several pages between headings you may want to consider using subheadings. Use subheadings only when you have two or more divisions within a main heading.

Topic (or functional) headings focus on the structure of the report. As you can see from the following example, topic headings give very little information.

Topic Headings Are Vague

Recommendation

Problem
- Situation 1
- Situation 2

Causes of the Problem
- Background
  - Cause 1
  - Cause 2

Recommended Solution

Talking heads (or informative headings), in contrast, tell the reader what to expect. Talking heads, like those in the examples in this chapter, provide an overview of each section and of the entire report.

Talking Heads Are Specific

Recommended Reformulation for Vibe Bleach

Problems in Maintaining Vibe's Granular Structure
- Solidifying During Storage and Transportation
- Customer Complaints about "Blocks" of Vibe in Boxes

Why Vibe Bleach "Cakes"
- Vibe's Formula
- The Manufacturing Process
- The Chemical Process of Solidification

Modifications Needed to Keep Vibe Flowing Freely

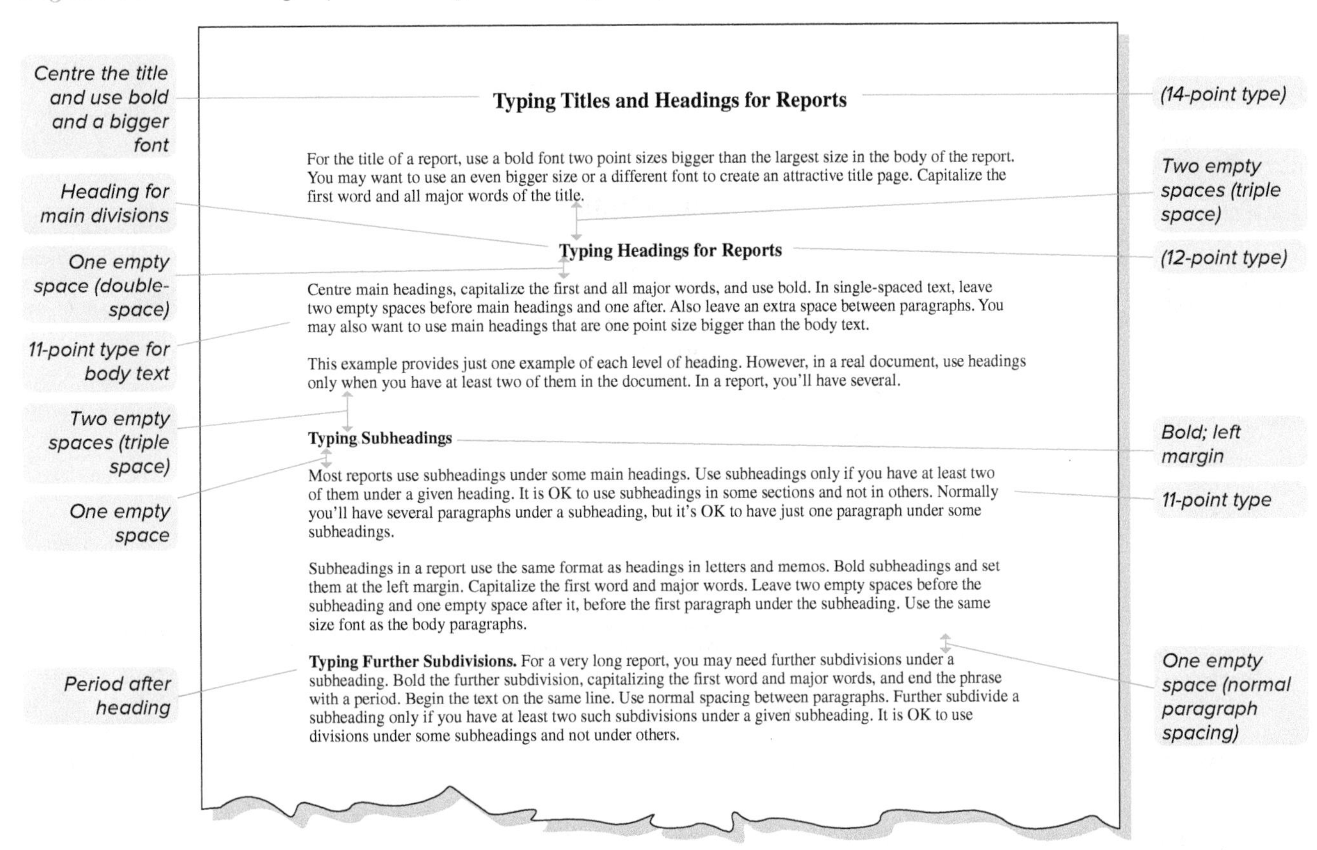

Typing Titles and Headings for Reports

For the title of a report, use a bold font two point sizes bigger than the largest size in the body of the report. You may want to use an even bigger size or a different font to create an attractive title page. Capitalize the first word and all major words of the title.

Typing Headings for Reports

Centre main headings, capitalize the first and all major words, and use bold. In single-spaced text, leave two empty spaces before main headings and one after. Also leave an extra space between paragraphs. You may also want to use main headings that are one point size bigger than the body text.

This example provides just one example of each level of heading. However, in a real document, use headings only when you have at least two of them in the document. In a report, you'll have several.

Typing Subheadings

Most reports use subheadings under some main headings. Use subheadings only if you have at least two of them under a given heading. It is OK to use subheadings in some sections and not in others. Normally you'll have several paragraphs under a subheading, but it's OK to have just one paragraph under some subheadings.

Subheadings in a report use the same format as headings in letters and memos. Bold subheadings and set them at the left margin. Capitalize the first word and major words. Leave two empty spaces before the subheading and one empty space after it, before the first paragraph under the subheading. Use the same size font as the body paragraphs.

Typing Further Subdivisions. For a very long report, you may need further subdivisions under a subheading. Bold the further subdivision, capitalizing the first word and major words, and end the phrase with a period. Begin the text on the same line. Use normal spacing between paragraphs. Further subdivide a subheading only if you have at least two such subdivisions under a given subheading. It is OK to use divisions under some subheadings and not under others.

Figure 11.7 Setting Up Headings in a Single-Spaced Document

In a very complicated report, you may need up to three levels of headings. Figure 11.7 illustrates one way to set up headings. Although the figure shows only one example of each level of headings, in an actual report you would not use a subheading unless you had at least two subsections under the next higher heading.

Avoid having a heading or subheading all by itself at the bottom of the page. Instead, have at least one line (preferably two) of type. If there isn't room for a line of type under it, put the heading on the next page. Don't use a heading as the antecedent for a pronoun. Instead, repeat the noun. Maintain parallelism (◀◀ Chapter 3) when writing headings. Each of the numbered talking heads in this section begins with a verb, for instance (Say, Tighten, Introduce, Use).

LO5

WRITING FORMAL REPORTS

Formal reports are distinguished from informal letter and memo reports by their length and by their components. A full formal report may contain the following components (see Figure 11.8):

Cover
Title Page
Letter or Memo of Transmittal
Table of Contents
List of Illustrations
Executive Summary
Body
Introduction (Orients the reader to the report.)
Background or History of the Problem (Orients the reader to the topic of the report.)
Body (Presents and interprets data in words and visuals.)
Conclusions (Summarizes main points of report.)
Recommendations (Recommends actions to solve the problem. May be combined with Conclusions; may be put at beginning of body rather than at the end.)
Notes, References, or Works Cited (Document sources cited in the report.)
Appendices (Provide additional materials that the careful reader may want: transcript of an interview, copies of questionnaires, tallies of all the questions, computer printouts, previous reports.)

Not every formal report necessarily has all these components. In addition, some organizations call for additional components or arrange these components in a different order.

Using Your Time and Proposal Efficiently

To use your time efficiently, think about your audience, purpose, and the parts of the report before you begin writing. Remember that much of the introduction comes from your proposal, with only minor revisions. You can write six sections even before you've finished your research: Purpose, Scope, Assumptions, Methods, Criteria, and Definitions.

Figure 11.8 A Formal Report: Title Page

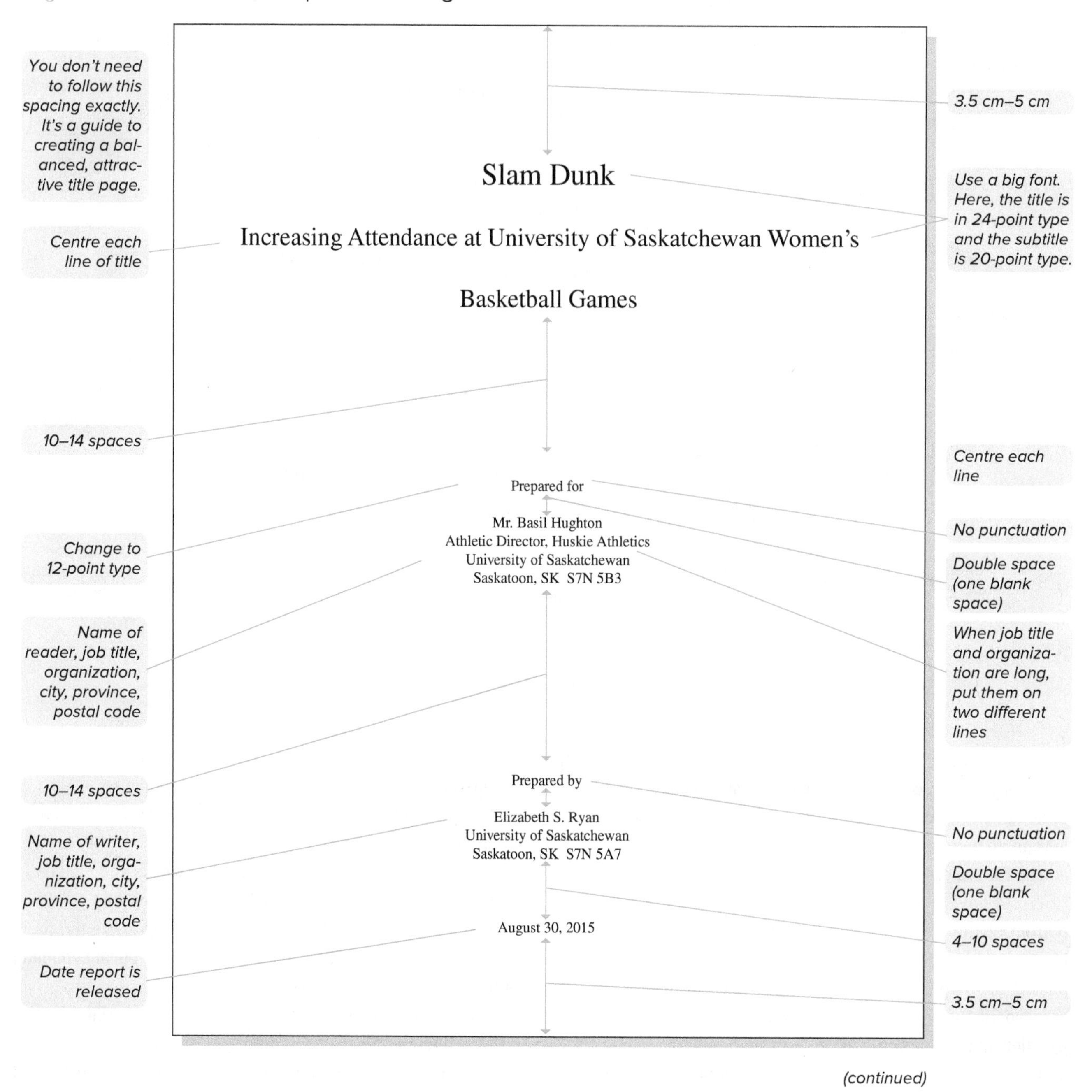

(continued)

You can write the title page and the transmittal as soon as you know what your recommendation will be.

Save a copy of your questionnaire or interview questions to use as an appendix. As you tally and analyze the data, prepare an appendix summarizing all the responses to your questionnaire, your figures and tables, and a complete list of references from your background reading. You can print appendices before the final report is ready if you number their pages separately. (Appendix A pages would be A-1, A-2, and so forth.)

After you've analyzed your data, write the body, the conclusions, and recommendations. Prepare a draft of the table of contents and the list of illustrations. Write the executive summary last when you have clarified your core ideas.

When you write a long report, list all the sections (headings) that your report will have. Mark those that are most important to your readers and your logic, and spend most of your time on them.

Title Page

The title page of a report usually contains four items: the title of the report, for whom the report is prepared, by whom it is prepared, and the release date.

The title of the report should be as informative as possible. Like subject lines, report titles are typically straightforward.

✕ Poor title: New Plant Site

✓ Better title: Why Woodstock, Ontario, Is the Best Site for the New Toyota Plant

Figure 11.8 A Formal Report: Letter of Transmittal

You may also design a letterhead for yourself, especially if you're assuming that you are doing the report as a consultant

2315 Lorne Avenue
Saskatoon, SK S7J 0S4

August 30, 2015

This letter uses block format.

Basil Hughton, Athletic Director
Huskie Athletics
University of Saskatchewan
87 Campus Drive
Saskatoon, SK S7N 5B3

Dear Mr. Hughton:

In paragraph 1, record the submission of the report. Note when and by whom the report was authorized. Note report's purpose.

Here is the report you authorized in July identifying why attendance at women's Huskies basketball games is low and recommending ways to increase student attendance at the games.

As you know, even though the team has been doing well, attendance at women's home games has not increased to expected levels. When I surveyed a convenience sample of students, I found no season ticket holders and only two people who said they attended "a few" games each season. Fully 34% had never been to a Huskies women's basketball game.

Give recommendations or thesis

Because most students do like basketball (62% follow the men's team), it's reasonable to think that some students could be persuaded to attend women's games as well. The two biggest reasons for not attending, according to my survey, were "I never thought to go" and "my friends aren't interested in going." I therefore recommend strategies that would remind students that the women's team exists and is playing, and would encourage groups of people to go to the games together.

Short-term solutions that could be implemented this year include having team members visit the Memorial Union Building, Place Riel, or the Bowl to drum up support, posting an abundance of signs about upcoming games around campus, and ensuring regular Twitter and Facebook updates. Longer-term strategies include creating a calendar of special days for specific groups, offering giveaways, and cultivating sports writers. Because further research is needed, you might want to put a staff member in charge of marketing the women's basketball team and hire a student intern to do the legwork for this research.

Acknowledge people who helped you

The information in this report came from print and online sources, a survey of U of S students, and interviews with several members of Huskie Athletics. Tera Schneider of Huskie Athletics' Sports Information office was particularly helpful.

Use a goodwill ending: positive, personal, and forward looking.

Thank the reader for the opportunity to do the research

Thank you for the opportunity to conduct this research. I've enjoyed learning more about the basketball team, the workings of Huskie Athletics, and sports marketing strategies. I look forward to presenting my report findings to you and your staff at the Physical Activities Complex at 3:00 p.m. on September 6.

Sincerely,

Elizabeth Ryan

Elizabeth Ryan

If used, centre page number at the bottom of the page. Use a lowercase Roman numeral.

i

(continued)

Large organizations that issue many reports may use two-part titles to make it easier to search for reports electronically.

Small Business Administration: Steps Taken to Better Manage Its Human Capital, But More Needs to Be Done

In many cases, the title will state the recommendation in the report: "Why the United Nations Should Establish a Seed Bank." However, the title should omit recommendations in these cases:

- The reader will find the recommendations hard to accept
- Putting all the recommendations in the title would make it too long
- The report does not offer recommendations

If the title does not contain the recommendation, it normally indicates what problem the report tries to solve.

Eliminate unnecessary words:

✕ Wordy: Report of a Study on Ways to Market Life Insurance to Urban Professional People Who Are in Their Mid-40s

✓ Better: Ways to Market Life Insurance to the Mid-40s Urban Professional

The *prepared for* section normally includes the name of the person who will make a decision based on the report, his or her job title, the organization's name, and its location.

The *prepared by* section will have the author's name, his or her title, the organization, and its location.

Figure 11.8 A Formal Report: Table of Contents

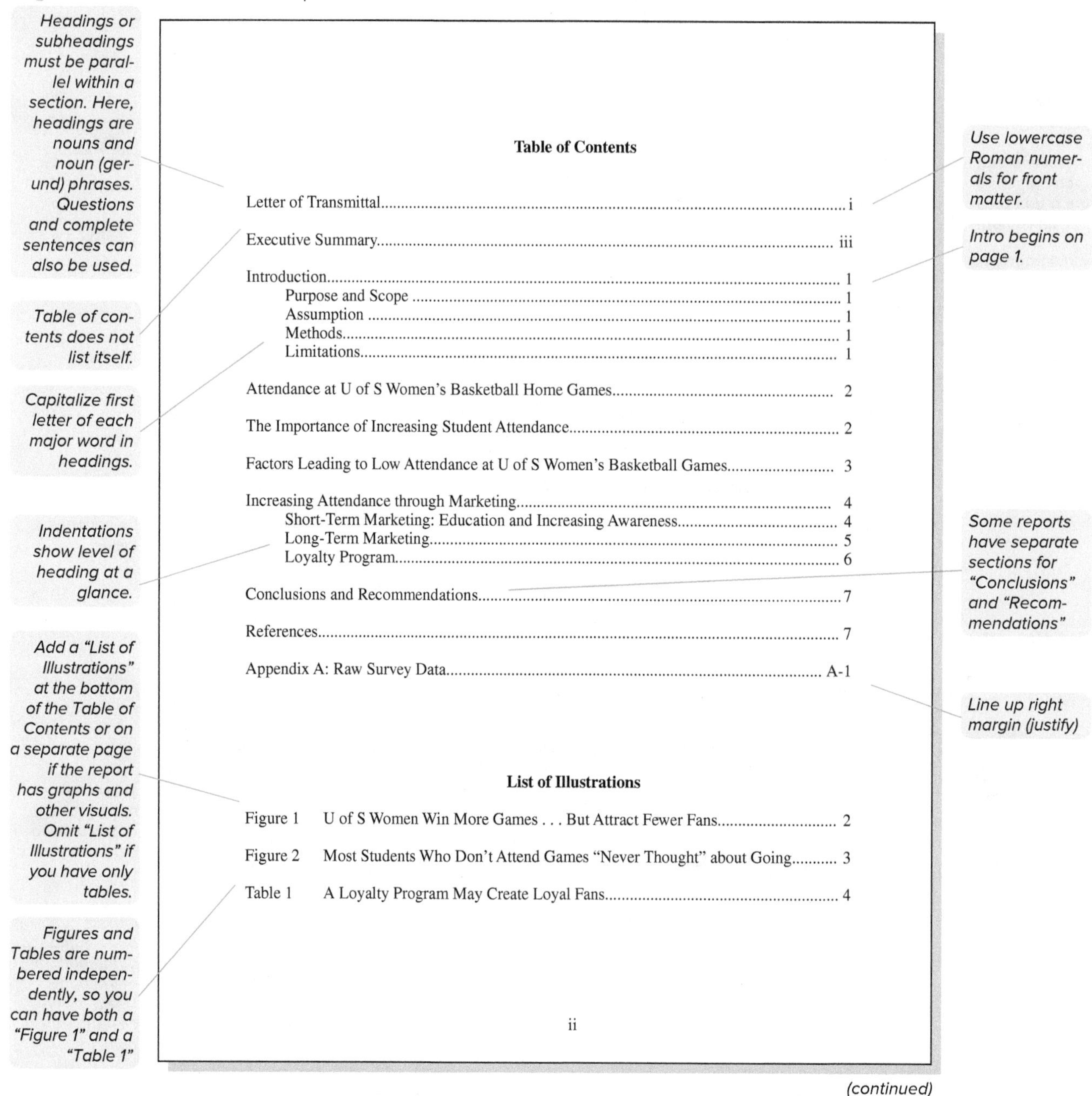
Table of Contents

Letter of Transmittal	i
Executive Summary	iii
Introduction	1
Purpose and Scope	1
Assumption	1
Methods	1
Limitations	1
Attendance at U of S Women's Basketball Home Games	2
The Importance of Increasing Student Attendance	2
Factors Leading to Low Attendance at U of S Women's Basketball Games	3
Increasing Attendance through Marketing	4
Short-Term Marketing: Education and Increasing Awareness	4
Long-Term Marketing	5
Loyalty Program	6
Conclusions and Recommendations	7
References	7
Appendix A: Raw Survey Data	A-1

List of Illustrations

Figure 1	U of S Women Win More Games . . . But Attract Fewer Fans	2
Figure 2	Most Students Who Don't Attend Games "Never Thought" about Going	3
Table 1	A Loyalty Program May Create Loyal Fans	4

ii

(continued)

The **release date,** the date the report will be released to the public, is usually the date the report is scheduled for discussion by the decision makers. The report is due four to six weeks before the release date so that the decision makers can review the report before the meeting.

If you have the facilities and the time, try using different sizes and styles of type, colour, and artwork to create a visually attractive and impressive title page. However, a plain typed page is acceptable. See Figure 11.8.

Letter or Memo of Transmittal

Use a letter of transmittal (see page i of Figure 11.8) if you are not a regular employee of the organization for which you prepare the report; use a memo if you are a regular employee.

The transmittal has several purposes: to transmit or record the submission of the report, to orient the reader to the report, and to build a good image of the report and of the writer. An informal writing style is appropriate for a transmittal even when the style of the report is more formal.

Organize the transmittal in this way:

1. **Transmit the report.** Record the transmission (*Here is. . .*). Tell when and by whom it was authorized and the purpose it was to fulfill.
2. **Summarize your conclusions and recommendations.** If the recommendations will be easy for the reader to accept, put them early in the transmittal. If they will be difficult, summarize the findings and conclusions before the recommendations.

Figure 11.8 A Formal Report: Executive Summary

Report title

Start with recommendations or thesis

Provide brief support for recommendations

Language in executive summary can come from report. Make sure any repeated language is well written!

Many readers read only the executive summary, not the report. Include enough information to give the reader the key points you make.

The abstract or executive summary contains the logical skeleton of the report: the recommendation(s) and evidence supporting them.

Slam Dunk
Increasing Attendance at University of Saskatchewan Women's Basketball Games

Executive Summary

To increase student attendance at University of Saskatchewan women's basketball games, this report recommends that Huskie Athletics implement short- and long-term marketing strategies and consider implementing a loyalty program.

Even though the team has been doing well, attendance at women's home games has failed to meet expectations. Student attendance at games is especially important because there are close to 20,000 students; attending games is fun, promotes bonding with other students, and creates school spirit; and athletes do better when other students cheer them on.

Because most students do like basketball (62% follow the men's team), it's reasonable to think that some students could be persuaded to attend women's games as well. The two biggest reasons for not attending, according to my survey, were "I never thought to go" and "My friends aren't interested in going." Students might be interested in going to the Huskies women's games if it occurred to them to go or if their friends went, too.

To increase attendance, the Athletic Department should do the following:

1. **Implement short-term marketing this fall.** Capitalize on the Huskies' winning streak last year to attract a higher attendance this year. Since basketball season is only weeks away, it might be smart to focus on increased awareness for the upcoming season.
   - Chalk and poster the Bowl before each home game.
   - Ask the women basketball players to host impromptu meet-and-greets at the Memorial Union Building or Place Riel or pickup games in the Bowl.
   - Implement short-term marketing this fall. Post regular Twitter and Facebook updates.
2. **Use students to develop a long-term marketing program and a formal publicity campaign.** Changing perceptions takes time and many messages.
   - Designate days for specific groups.
   - Offer deals and freebies. Ask sponsors to donate freebies or items to be raffled or auctioned.
   - Create an advertising campaign focusing on women students in student societies, women's floors in residence halls, and Women's Studies classes.
   - Buy more advertising space in *The Sheaf* and *The Saskatoon StarPhoenix*.
   - Try to persuade more reporters to write more stories about the women's team.
3. **Consider adopting a loyalty program.** A loyalty program rewards students for behaviour Huskie Athletics wants to encourage. Further research is needed on the financial implications.

iii

(continued)

3. **Mention any points of special interest in the report.** Indicate minor problems you encountered in your investigation and show how you surmounted them. Thank people who helped you. These optional items can build goodwill and enhance your credibility.
4. **Point out additional research that is necessary, if any.** Sometimes your recommendation cannot be implemented until further work is done. If you'd be interested in doing that research, or if you'd like to implement the recommendations, say so.
5. **Thank the reader for the opportunity to do the work and offer to answer questions.** Even if the report has not been fun to do, expressing satisfaction in doing the project is expected.

Table of Contents

The table of contents gives an overview of the report structure and is a useful resource for the busy professional. In the table of contents (page ii of Figure 11.8), list the headings exactly as they appear in the body of the report. If the report is fewer than 25 pages, you'll probably list all the levels of headings. In a very long report, pick a level and put all the headings at that level and above in the table of contents.

List of Illustrations

A list of illustrations enables readers to refer to your visuals.

Report visuals comprise both **tables** and **figures.** *Tables* are words or numbers arranged in rows and columns. *Figures*

Figure 11.8 A Formal Report: Introduction

A running header is optional

Here, the running heads and page numbers are one point size smaller than body

Spell out term the first time; put abbreviation in parentheses

"Purpose" and "Scope" can also be separate sections if either is long

"Scope" section should match report. You may need to revise "Topics to Investigate" from the proposal.

Assumptions cannot be proved. But if they are wrong, the report's recommendation may no longer be valid.

If your report has limitations, state them. Giving the number makes it easier for the reader to read the paragraph.

Slam Dunk: Increasing Attendance at U of S Women's Basketball Games Page 1

Introduction

University of Saskatchewan's (U of S) men's basketball team is a crowd pleaser, selling out home games at the Physical Activities Complex (PAC) in good years. However, the U of S Huskies women's basketball team suffers from low attendance figures, filling less than a quarter of the PAC for the regular-season games.

Purpose and Scope

The purpose of this report is to recommend ways to increase student attendance at Huskies women's basketball games.

In this report, I will focus on three topics: the factors that affect student attendance, ways that student awareness of the women's team can be increased, and loyalty programs as a way of increasing attendance. I will briefly discuss how attendance and newspaper publicity correlate to the win/loss record.

I will not discuss the cost of or the return on investment of my recommendations. I will not discuss how changes in coaching or recruiting might affect attendance.

Assumption

My recommendations are based on the assumption that reasons for U of S student attendance at games are similar to those of students at other universities.

Methods

My information for this report comes from library and online sources, interviews with Huskies Athletics staff, and a survey of 50 U of S students, using a convenience sample. I surveyed students during the lunch hour in Louis' in the Memorial Union Building dining area on July 27, 2015. I walked around the room and asked everyone if he or she would be willing to answer the survey, until I had 50 people.

The students filling out my survey represent all academic ranks from undergraduate students (including incoming first-year students) to graduate students. Sixty percent of the respondents are male, and 40% are female. Sixty-eight percent of the people surveyed have never attended a women's basketball game, although 62% watch men's games. (See Appendix A for the raw data.)

Limitations

My research has four limitations. First, because I used a convenience survey, I cannot generalize from the people I surveyed to all U of S students. Second, the timing of the survey was a problem. In the summer, many of the people in Louis' are international students and incoming first-year students

Also OK to omit "Page"

Start with "Introduction"

Centre main headings. This head uses bold (one point larger than body).

rhetorical purpose

Tell what you discuss and how thoroughly you discuss each topic

Give topics in the order in which you'll discuss them

List any relevant topics you don't discuss

Tell how and when you collected original data (surveys, interviews, or observations)

Summarize respondent demographic information

Refer to your Appendices in the text of your report

(continued)

are everything else: bar graphs, pie charts, flow charts, maps, drawings, photographs, computer printouts, and so on (see "Designing Visuals" in ◀◀ Chapter 4). Tables and figures may be numbered independently, so you may have both a Table 1 and a Figure 1. In a report with maps and graphs but no other visuals, the visuals are sometimes called Map 1 and Graph 1. Whatever you call the illustrations, list them in the order in which they appear in the report; give the name of each visual as well as its number.

Executive Summary

An **executive summary** tells the reader what the document is about. It summarizes the recommendation of the report and the reasons for the recommendation or describes the topics the report discusses and indicates the depth of the discussion.

A good executive summary is easy to read, concise, and clear. Edit carefully to tighten your writing and eliminate any unnecessary words.

✕ Wordy: The author describes two types of business jargon, *businessese* and *reverse gobbledygook*. He gives many examples of each of these and points out how their use can be harmful.

✓ Tight: The author describes and gives examples of two harmful types of business jargon, *businessese* and *reverse gobbledygook*.

Executive summaries generally use a more formal style than other forms of business writing. Avoid contractions. Use

Figure 11.8 A Formal Report: Background

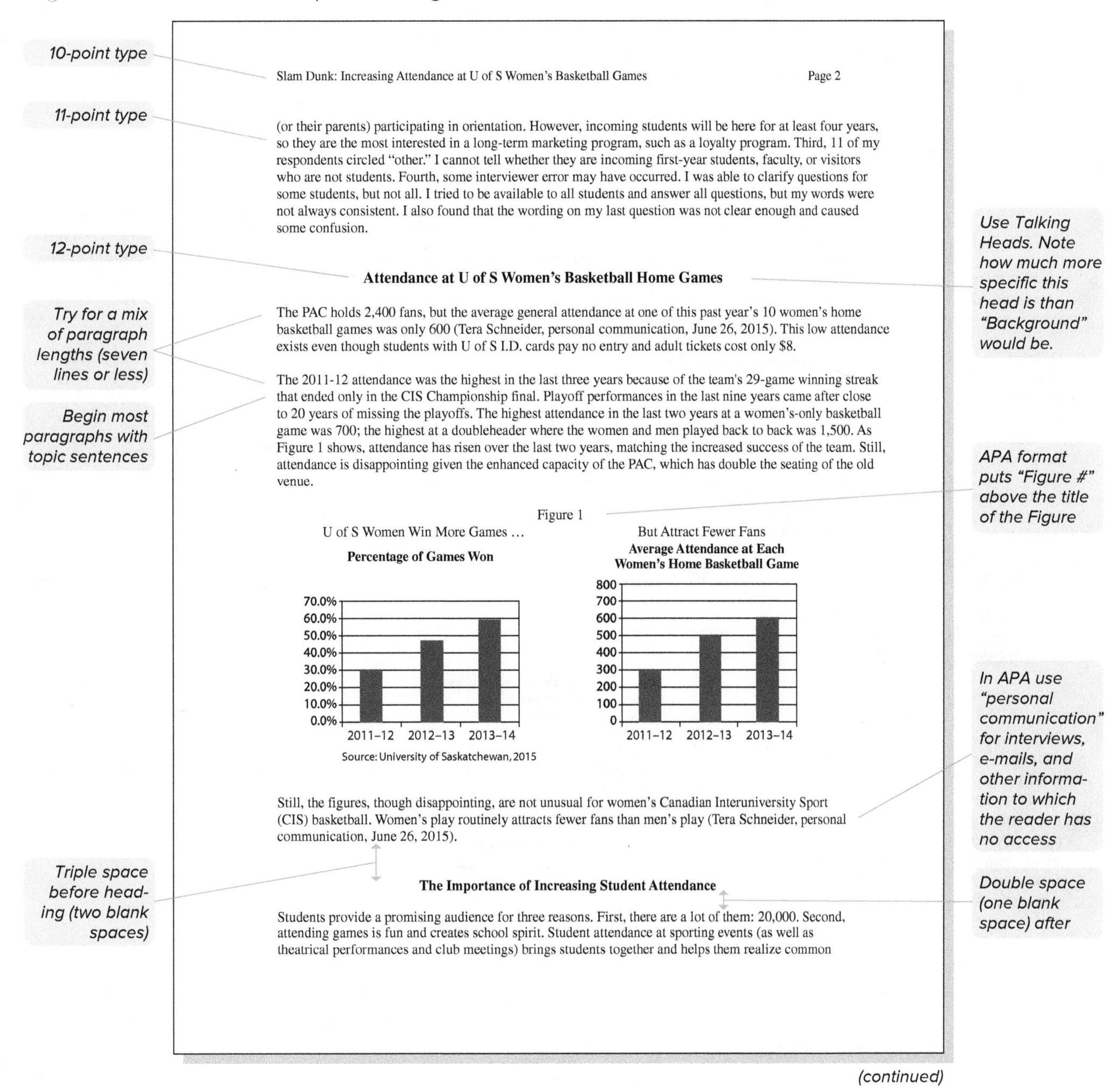

Slam Dunk: Increasing Attendance at U of S Women's Basketball Games Page 2

(or their parents) participating in orientation. However, incoming students will be here for at least four years, so they are the most interested in a long-term marketing program, such as a loyalty program. Third, 11 of my respondents circled "other." I cannot tell whether they are incoming first-year students, faculty, or visitors who are not students. Fourth, some interviewer error may have occurred. I was able to clarify questions for some students, but not all. I tried to be available to all students and answer all questions, but my words were not always consistent. I also found that the wording on my last question was not clear enough and caused some confusion.

Attendance at U of S Women's Basketball Home Games

The PAC holds 2,400 fans, but the average general attendance at one of this past year's 10 women's home basketball games was only 600 (Tera Schneider, personal communication, June 26, 2015). This low attendance exists even though students with U of S I.D. cards pay no entry and adult tickets cost only $8.

The 2011-12 attendance was the highest in the last three years because of the team's 29-game winning streak that ended only in the CIS Championship final. Playoff performances in the last nine years came after close to 20 years of missing the playoffs. The highest attendance in the last two years at a women's-only basketball game was 700; the highest at a doubleheader where the women and men played back to back was 1,500. As Figure 1 shows, attendance has risen over the last two years, matching the increased success of the team. Still, attendance is disappointing given the enhanced capacity of the PAC, which has double the seating of the old venue.

Figure 1

Still, the figures, though disappointing, are not unusual for women's Canadian Interuniversity Sport (CIS) basketball. Women's play routinely attracts fewer fans than men's play (Tera Schneider, personal communication, June 26, 2015).

The Importance of Increasing Student Attendance

Students provide a promising audience for three reasons. First, there are a lot of them: 20,000. Second, attending games is fun and creates school spirit. Student attendance at sporting events (as well as theatrical performances and club meetings) brings students together and helps them realize common

(continued)

second-person "you" only if the article uses the second person; even then, use "you" sparingly.

Informative executive summaries present the logical skeleton of the article: the thesis or recommendation and its proof. Use an informative summary to give the most useful information in the shortest space.

To market life insurance to mid-40s urban professionals, Fidelity Insurance should advertise in upscale publications and use social media.

Network TV and radio are not cost efficient for reaching this market. This group comprises a small percentage of the prime-time network TV audience and a minority of most radio station listeners. They tend to discard newspapers and general-interest magazines quickly, but many of them keep upscale periodicals for months or years. Magazines with high percentages of readers in this group include *Architectural Digest, Bon Appetit, BusinessWeek, Canadian Gardening, Golf Digest,* and *Smithsonian.* Most urban professionals in their mid-40s are already used to shopping online and respond positively to well-conceived and well-executed social media appeals.

Any advertising campaign needs to overcome this group's feeling that they already have the insurance they need. One way to do this would be to encourage them to check the coverage their employers provide and to calculate the cost

Figure 11.8 A Formal Report: Body

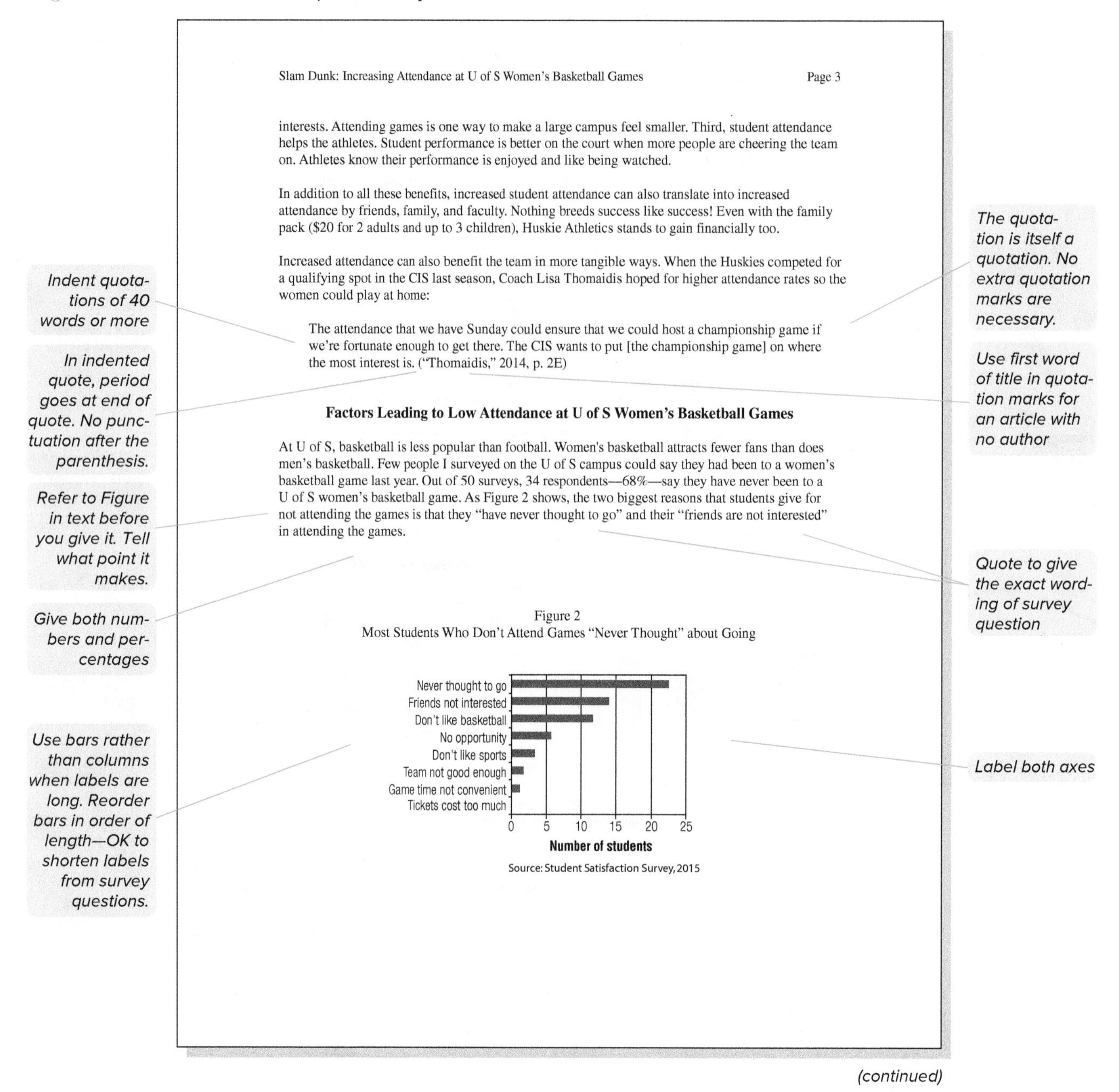

Slam Dunk: Increasing Attendance at U of S Women's Basketball Games Page 3

interests. Attending games is one way to make a large campus feel smaller. Third, student attendance helps the athletes. Student performance is better on the court when more people are cheering the team on. Athletes know their performance is enjoyed and like being watched.

In addition to all these benefits, increased student attendance can also translate into increased attendance by friends, family, and faculty. Nothing breeds success like success! Even with the family pack ($20 for 2 adults and up to 3 children), Huskie Athletics stands to gain financially too.

Increased attendance can also benefit the team in more tangible ways. When the Huskies competed for a qualifying spot in the CIS last season, Coach Lisa Thomaidis hoped for higher attendance rates so the women could play at home:

> The attendance that we have Sunday could ensure that we could host a championship game if we're fortunate enough to get there. The CIS wants to put [the championship game] on where the most interest is. ("Thomaidis," 2014, p. 2E)

Factors Leading to Low Attendance at U of S Women's Basketball Games

At U of S, basketball is less popular than football. Women's basketball attracts fewer fans than does men's basketball. Few people I surveyed on the U of S campus could say they had been to a women's basketball game last year. Out of 50 surveys, 34 respondents—68%—say they have never been to a U of S women's basketball game. As Figure 2 shows, the two biggest reasons that students give for not attending the games is that they "have never thought to go" and their "friends are not interested" in attending the games.

Figure 2
Most Students Who Don't Attend Games "Never Thought" about Going

Source: Student Satisfaction Survey, 2015

(continued)

> of their children's expenses through college or university graduation. Insurance plans that provide savings and tax benefits as well as death benefits might also be appealing.

To write executive summaries of business and government reports, conference papers, and published articles, write a sentence outline. A sentence outline not only uses complete sentences rather than words or phrases but also contains the thesis sentence or recommendation and the points that prove that point. Combine the sentences into paragraphs, adding transitions if necessary, and you'll have your summary.

Descriptive executive summaries indicate what topics the report covers and how deeply it goes into each topic, but they do not summarize what the report says about each topic. Phrases that describe the report ("this paper includes," "it summarizes," "it concludes") are marks of a descriptive summary. An additional mark of a descriptive executive summary is that the reader can't tell what the report says about the topics it covers. Descriptive summaries are like elaborated tables of contents, are typically shorter than informative executive summaries, and explain the report in terms of its purpose and scope.

> This report recommends ways Fidelity Insurance could market insurance to mid-40s urban professionals. It examines demographic and psychographic profiles of the target market. Survey results are used to show attitudes toward insurance. The report suggests some appeals that might be successful with this market.

Figure 11.8 A Formal Report: Body

Slam Dunk: Increasing Attendance at U of S Women's Basketball Games Page 4

It's true that almost one-quarter of the respondents don't like basketball. But most do, and indeed, 62% watch men's games. Two people felt that the team wasn't "good enough." However, this past year, the team again made the CIS playoffs. It seems that perception, not reality, is likely the issue for these students. No one in my sample felt that the tickets cost too much. However, 2% found the game time of 6:15 P.M. inconvenient. It is obvious that the eight-dollar ticket price for those without U of S I.D. cards is not an issue.

Increasing Attendance through Marketing

Marketing sports events can increase attendance, as Daughtrey and Gillentine (2000) found in their research about marketing swim meets:

> Marketing techniques such as advertising, posters, word of mouth, and expanded ticket distribution were all identified as effective in increasing attendance. Making the meet more enjoyable for fans was also seen as imperative to increase fan attendance. This [goal] was achieved through music, giveaways, promotions, and fan participation exercises. Results could be useful to other Olympic or youth sport organizations that are attempting to market, increase public interest and generate funds for their sport. (p. A-118)

The three most promising options for U of S are short-term marketing to educate and increase awareness of games, long-term marketing programs, and loyalty programs. All of these methods should be used, but, as Table 1 shows, long-term marketing and a loyalty program are likely to have the greatest effect.

Table 1
A Loyalty Program May Create Loyal Fans

"To what extent would each of the following make you more likely to attend an U of S women's basketball game?"

Rank	Option	Average; N=50 (3 = Much more likely, 2 = Possibly more likely, 1 = No effect)
1	Loyalty Program	1.88
2	Long-Term Marketing	1.76
3	Increased Awareness	1.56
4	Education	1.28

Short-Term Marketing: Education and Increasing Awareness

Just walking across the U of S campus each day is a learning experience. Daily, groups pass out flyers, chalk the sidewalks, and set up booths with messages about credit cards, club meetings, textbook and class notes deals, Web sites, clothing sales, and parties. Most of this "publicity" takes place in the Bowl, the centre of campus.

Short-term marketing can be as simple as chalking messages on the sidewalk or tacking posters on the information poles near the library or posting Twitter and Facebook updates about upcoming games and when and where they will be held. If the team is not playing at home, the messages can remind students to listen to the radio for game coverage, to watch the nightly sports wrap-up on the local news, or to look for a game report on social media or in the university newspaper, *The Sheaf*, or the local *StarPhoenix*. Many of the

10-point type

11-point type

12-point type

Summarize the point of a quotation before you give the quotation

Tables and Figures are numbered independently, so you can have both a "Figure 1" and "Table 1"

Reorder from high to low

Not every idea needs a source. Use your knowledge of people and of business.

Heading must cover everything under that heading until the next head or subhead at that level

Use square brackets around words you add

Don't need authors' names in parentheses when they're in the sentence introducing the quote.

Give question from survey

Tell what numbers in a Likert-type scale mean

"N" is the total number of people responding to the question. Use "n" to give the number of people giving a particular response.

Italicize newspaper titles

(continued)

A **mixed executive summary** is a hybrid: part summary, part description. Mixed summaries enable you to comment about the kind of information and present the thesis and its proof.

Body

The **introduction** of the report always contains a statement of purpose and scope and may include all the parts in the following list. As in Figure 11.8, include only those parts relevant to your report.

- **Purpose.** The purpose statement (◂◂ Chapter 10) identifies the organizational problem the report addresses, the technical investigations it summarizes, and the rhetorical purpose (to explain, to recommend).
- **Scope.** The scope statement identifies how broad an area the report surveys. For example, Company XYZ is losing money on its line of cell phones. Does the report investigate the quality of the cell phones? The advertising campaign? The cost of manufacturing? The demand for cell phones? A scope statement allows the reader to evaluate the report on appropriate grounds. If the person who approved the proposal accepted a focus on advertising, then one cannot fault a report that considers only that factor.
- **Assumptions.** Assumptions in a report are like assumptions in geometry: statements whose truth you assume, and which you use to prove your final point. If they are wrong, the conclusion will be wrong too.

Figure 11.8 A Formal Report: Body

Slam Dunk: Increasing Attendance at U of S Women's Basketball Games Page 5

students surveyed say they've never thought to go to a game; maybe a friendly reminder in rather busy schedules would work.

A visit from the female basketball players in the Bowl is another way to attract fans. The Huskies could set up a booth to sell tickets in advance for a game, erect a temporary basketball hoop and play a pickup game, or host a shooting contest against interested students walking across the Bowl. Players might also visit the Memorial Union Building (MUB) or Place Riel and meet with students. Some respondents said they do not attend games because they do not know any players.

A lesson in the rules of the game may be in order. When the Western Hockey League (WHL) Saskatoon Blades wanted to increase attendance and bring in new fans, one of the sponsors, Credit Union Centre, provided pocket-size pamphlets that unfolded into a cheat sheet with facts about the playing surface and players and explanations of the rules of the game. A pocket guide for women's basketball may be helpful to students who are new to women's CIS basketball, or in fact new to the game of basketball.

Long-Term Marketing

People like to do things in groups. The fact that U of S football games are "events" means that students want to go to the games whether they like football or not. Huskie Athletics needs to work to increase interest in women's basketball in general. As Figure 2 showed, the second most-common reason that students do not attend games is that their friends aren't interested.

Huskie Athletics could designate days for specific groups: student societies, residential halls, and student organizations. Invite these groups to a game, seat them together in a certain spot in the arena, recognize them, and offer them a price break on food or merchandise for the game. Some of the students will invite friends from outside of the group to join in the fun. People who come just to be with their friends may enjoy the experience and return for other games.

Offering freebies to the first so many fans attending a game will attract students. Besides shirts, other giveaways could include hats (which have been given away at a Huskies football game), ear coverings for the winter, drink and food coupons, promotional music CDs, signed posters of the team, or key chains. Fans also like raffles. The Orientation Days at the beginning of the year attract students because everyone hopes his or her ticket will be pulled for the term of free tuition. The campus bookstore could give away a gift certificate to be used towards textbooks, as most students know how expensive books are each term. Campus travel agents could donate a plane ticket to fly home or to be used for February Break travel.

Men's basketball attracts many students, and men may always identify with the men's sport first. Therefore, it might make sense for Huskie Athletics to launch a campaign appealing to women students. Huskie Athletics could work with student societies, the advisers on women's residence hallfloors, and Women's Studies classes to find out what the students would like to see at games. It can create an advertising campaign for women, posting information on the floor bulletin boards, holding informational sessions throughout the year in the dorms with basketball players as speakers, and holding "Women's Nights" at the games. Once women students are recognized and catered to at games, they may attend more often and bring their male friends and classmates to games. Increasing women students' attendance will increase men's attendance.

Limit claims you cannot prove with certainty

Begin most paragraphs with topic sentences

Divide a heading only when you have two or more subheads.

APA does not capitalize words after a colon when the words are not a complete sentence

Limit claims you cannot prove with certainty

Limit claims you cannot prove with certainty

(continued)

For example, to plan cars that will be built five years from now, an automobile manufacturer commissions a report on young adults' attitudes toward cars. The recommendations would be based on assumptions both about gas prices and about the economy. If gas prices radically rose or fell, the kinds of cars young adults wanted would change. If there were a major recession, people wouldn't be able to buy new cars.

- **Methods.** If you conducted surveys, focus groups, or interviews, you need to tell how you chose your subjects, and how, when, and where they were interviewed.

  If your report is based solely on library or online research, you may simply cite your sources in the text and document them in notes or references. See ◀◀ Chapter 10 on how to cite and document sources. Still, you might see a Methods section as an opportunity to enhance your credibility by highlighting the range of research resources you have used: print and online, government publications as well as industry and business reports, for example.

- **Limitations.** Limitations make your recommendations less valid or valid only under certain conditions. Limitations usually arise because time or money constraints haven't permitted full research. For example, a campus pizza restaurant considering expanding its menu may ask for a report but not have enough money to take a random sample of students and non-students. Without a random sample, the writer cannot generalize from the sample to the larger population.

Figure 11.8 A Formal Report: Body

Slam Dunk: Increasing Attendance at U of S Women's Basketball Games Page 6

Last, Huskie Athletics could launch a formal publicity campaign: Buy more advertising space in *The Sheaf* and *The StarPhoenix*, and push for more articles to be written. In a search for articles over the past year about the women's basketball team in *The StarPhoenix,* I found approximately 50 articles. With an average of 537 words an article, a majority of the articles rehash the statistics of games or discuss injuries that plagued the team last season. Only 26% of the articles appeared on the front or inside front page of the Sports section. After the playoff win last season several Saskatoon residents wrote to the Sports editor to complain about the coverage of the team, or lack thereof:

> I understand that women's basketball usually doesn't produce the same crowds and therefore the same revenue that men's basketball produces. But one would think that they would deserve the same respect and praise that comes along with winning a championship. However, all that was awarded them was a passing mention on the TV news, and a small mention on the bottom of the front page of this newspaper and one article in the sports section compared with the multiple mentions that the men's team receives. . . . One of my co-workers didn't even know that the women's team was in a tournament. (Adams, 2014, p. 3D)

Although the men's team was not as successful as the women's this past season, it had more and longer articles (averaging 603 words). Most of the articles built interest in the team, rather than simply rehashing the game. Almost twice as many articles about the men's team (49%) appeared on the front or inside front page of the Sports section. Several reporters wrote articles about the men's team, while one reporter wrote almost all the articles about women. Inviting more reporters for more interviews with the women's team and encouraging more reports on the front page would boost awareness of the team.

Reporters will write more stories if they know the team better. Daughtrey and Gillentine (2000) found "the most effective method used to generate media attention was to create a personal relationship with members of the media. Sponsorship was increased most when signage, hospitality, recognition through plaques/ announcements, newspaper articles, and personal thank-you notes were offered" (p. A-118).

Hire an Edwards School of Business student on an hourly salary to do the legwork for a long-term marketing program, contacting other university marketing programs, evaluating the financial expectations, and presenting a business plan to Huskie Athletics. In return, the student gains real-world experience that serves him or her well when interviewing for jobs later on.

Loyalty Program

Most Canadians today have at least one "club card" for the local grocery store. Many have three or four cards ranging from the supermarket to the drugstore and the video store that award points and give discounts on certain items each time the cards are swiped (as an ATM card is) and a purchase is made.

In recent years, professional and collegiate athletic teams have joined the phenomenon. Raymond (2001) explains, "Each time fans use their card, they rack up attendance points redeemable for promotional coupons or items such as food, drinks, and souvenirs. The more points they compile, the more 'rewards' they receive" (p. 35). When fans sign up for the club cards, they provide basic information that the teams can use to tailor their offerings to the target audience. Customer relationship marketing (CRM) uses databases to track fan attendance and identify those most likely to buy season tickets.

U of S can use the information that students give to create e-mail updates about the basketball team, give advance notice for tickets and giveaways, and attract more season ticket holders. The information can also clue the PAC in on what kind of concessions students want and what kind of merchandise penny-pinching university students will spend their money on.

APA calls for a capital letter after a colon when the words after the colon form a complete sentence

Use ellipses (3 spaced dots) when you omit part of a quote

Use author's name in parentheses when it isn't in the sentence introducing quote

When quote is part of your sentence, period goes after the parenthesis

When author's name is in the sentence, it isn't repeated in the parentheses

Short quotations (fewer than 40 words) go in your sentence

When the original has a word in quotation marks, use single quotation marks (and double quotation marks for the whole quotation)

(continued)

Many recommendations are valid only for a limited time. For instance, a report on campus clothing recommendations will remain in force only for a short time: Three years from now, styles and tastes may have changed.

A good report spells out its assumptions so that readers can make decisions more confidently.

- **Criteria.** The criteria section outlines the factors or standards that you are considering and the relative importance of each. If a company is choosing a city for a new office, is the cost of office space more or less important than the availability of skilled workers? Check with your audience before you write the draft to make sure that your criteria match those of your readers.
- **Definitions.** When you know that some members of your primary, secondary, or immediate audience will not understand technical terms, define them. If you have only a few definitions, you can put them in the Introduction. If you have many terms to define, use a **glossary** either early in the report or at the end. If the glossary is at the end, refer to it in the introduction so that readers know you've provided it.

Formal reports usually have a section that gives the **background** of the situation or the *history of the problem.* Even though the current audience for the report probably knows the situation, reports are filed and consulted years later. These later audiences will probably not know the background, although it may be crucial for understanding the options that are possible.

Figure 11.8 A Formal Report: Conclusions, Recommendations, and References

Conclusions repeat points made in the report. Recommendations are actions the readers should take.

Numbering points makes it easy for readers

Make sure items in a list are parallel

APA format

Use "p." when you don't have volume number

Italicize volume number

Start with the title of the article when no author is given

Copyright/ update date

Month follows year. Period outside parentheses.

Slam Dunk: Increasing Attendance at U of S Women's Basketball Games Page 7

Conclusions and Recommendations

A majority of students like basketball and might be interested in going to the U of S women's games if it occurred to them to go or if their friends went, too. To increase attendance, the Athletic Department should

1. **Implement short-term marketing this fall.** Capitalize on the Huskies' winning streak last year to attract a higher attendance this year. Since basketball season is only weeks away, it might be smart to focus on increased awareness for the upcoming season.
   - Chalk and poster the Bowl before each home game.
   - Ask the women basketball players to host impromptu meet-and-greets at the MUB or Place Riel, or pickup games in the Bowl.
   - Post regular Twitter and Facebook updates.
2. **Use U of S students to develop a long-term marketing program and a formal publicity campaign.** Changing perceptions takes time and many messages.
   - Designate days for specific groups.
   - Offer deals and freebies. Ask sponsors to donate freebies or items to be raffled or auctioned.
   - Create an advertising campaign focusing on women students in student societies, women's floors in residence halls, and Women's Studies classes.
   - Buy more advertising space in *The Sheaf* and *The StarPhoenix*.
   - Try to persuade more reporters to write more stories about the women's team.
3. **Consider adopting a loyalty program.** A loyalty program rewards students for behaviour Huskie Athletics wants to encourage. Further research is needed on the financial implications.

References

Adams, E. (2014, April 8). U of S women deserved more attention from the media. *The StarPhoenix*, p. 3D.

Daughtrey, C., & Gillentine, A. (2000, March). The marketing of swim meets. *Research Quarterly for Exercise and Sport, 71*, A-118.

Raymond, J. (2001, April). Home field advantage. *American Demographics*, 34–36.

Thomaidis looks for U of S victory, big crowd. (2014, March 24). *The StarPhoenix*, p. 2E.

University of Saskatchewan. (2015). Huskie Women's Basketball Retrieved from http://huskiebasketball.com

Some companies ask for Conclusions and Recommendations at the beginning of reports

Because many readers turn to the "Recommendations" first, provide enough information so that the reason is clear all by itself. The ideas in the section must be logical extensions of the points made and supported in the body of the report.

No "p." when you give volume number

List all the printed and online sources cited in your report. Do not list sources you used for background but did not cite. Do not list interviews, phone calls, or other information to which the reader has no access.

(continued)

On the Job Repeating with Style

The different parts of a formal report are designed to convey the same overall message, although they do not all include the same level of detail. The title page, transmittal document, table of contents, and executive summary, for instance, prepare readers (who rarely read the report in its entirety) for what is to follow.

As a result, the parts often repeat key terms and concepts. Although some exact repetition is useful to reinforce important messages, too much cut-and-paste can give the impression of too much haste and insufficient attention to the needs of different readers.

To make your report as readable, memorable, and credible as possible, do the following:

- Quote sources when the phrasing is especially vivid or original.
- Learn the art of paraphrase.
- Increase level of detail in the body of the report.
- Include previews as well as reviews.
- Reinforce visually key verbal messages.

Figure 11.8 A Formal Report: Appendix

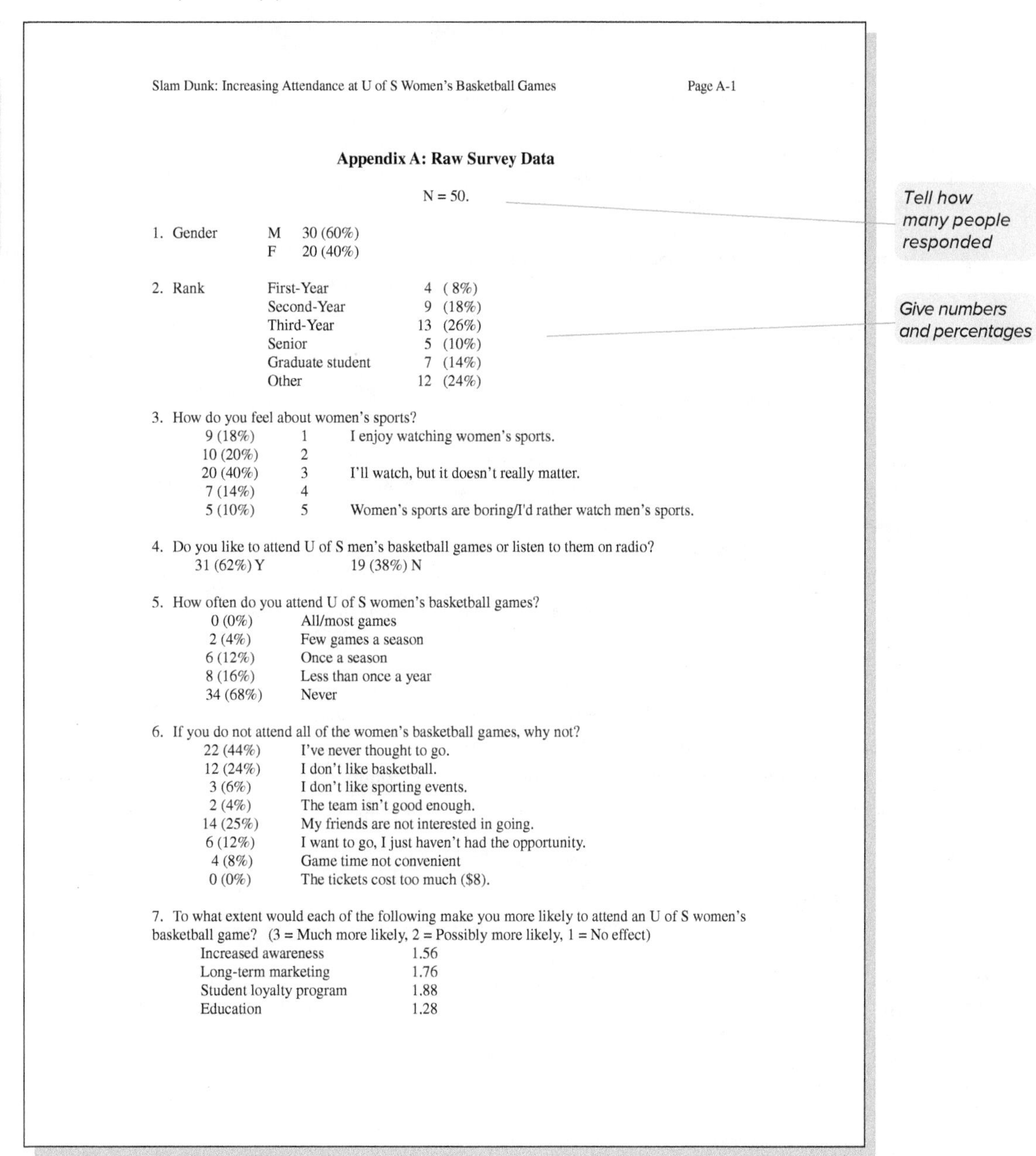

Slam Dunk: Increasing Attendance at U of S Women's Basketball Games — Page A-1

Appendix A: Raw Survey Data

N = 50.

1. Gender
   - M 30 (60%)
   - F 20 (40%)

2. Rank

First-Year	4 (8%)
Second-Year	9 (18%)
Third-Year	13 (26%)
Senior	5 (10%)
Graduate student	7 (14%)
Other	12 (24%)

3. How do you feel about women's sports?

9 (18%)	1	I enjoy watching women's sports.
10 (20%)	2	
20 (40%)	3	I'll watch, but it doesn't really matter.
7 (14%)	4	
5 (10%)	5	Women's sports are boring/I'd rather watch men's sports.

4. Do you like to attend U of S men's basketball games or listen to them on radio?
   31 (62%) Y   19 (38%) N

5. How often do you attend U of S women's basketball games?

0 (0%)	All/most games
2 (4%)	Few games a season
6 (12%)	Once a season
8 (16%)	Less than once a year
34 (68%)	Never

6. If you do not attend all of the women's basketball games, why not?

22 (44%)	I've never thought to go.
12 (24%)	I don't like basketball.
3 (6%)	I don't like sporting events.
2 (4%)	The team isn't good enough.
14 (25%)	My friends are not interested in going.
6 (12%)	I want to go, I just haven't had the opportunity.
4 (8%)	Game time not convenient
0 (0%)	The tickets cost too much ($8).

7. To what extent would each of the following make you more likely to attend an U of S women's basketball game? (3 = Much more likely, 2 = Possibly more likely, 1 = No effect)

Increased awareness	1.56
Long-term marketing	1.76
Student loyalty program	1.88
Education	1.28

In some cases, the history section may cover many years. For example, a report recommending that a Canadian hotel chain open hotels in Ukraine will probably give the history of that country for at least the last hundred years. In other cases, the history section is much briefer, covering only a few years or even just the immediate situation.

The rest of the **body** presents and interprets data in words and visuals. It analyzes causes of the problem and evaluates possible solutions, demonstrating the evidence that will support your conclusions and recommendations. Specific headings depend on the topic of the report and the organization that you have adopted to suit your purpose and audience.

Conclusions and Recommendations

Conclusions summarize main points you have made in the body of the report in the order of their presentation, clarify the meaning of findings in relation to report purpose and scope, and avoid jargon and abbreviations. **Recommendations** emerging from the findings and conclusions are action items that would solve or ameliorate the problem. Recommendations use action verbs and explain their rationale. These sections are often combined if they are short: *Conclusions and Recommendations.*

No new information should be included in the conclusions.

Technology Tips — Best Practices in Sustainability Reporting*

Tools to "change external perceptions and to instigate dialogue with stakeholders," sustainability reports are increasingly integrated into interactive, Web-based corporate communications. CSR Europe identifies best practices across five dimensions: report formats, topical updates, multimedia features, interactive dialogue, and personalization.

Avoiding technical jargon, acknowledging impact of industry trends and competition, making online disclosure user-friendly (HTML rather than PDF downloading), educating the board, and matching graphic design and report content are some of the ways of meeting best practice objectives:

- Clear, concise articulation of key business risks and sustainability issues
- Communication of corporate vision for sustainability in terms of business strategy and decision making
- Communication of corporate governance structure and management systems
- Comprehensive performance indicators for environment, regulatory compliance, product stewardship, community impacts, health and safety, and economic development

Deloitte offers six tips for best practice reporting:

1. Adopt appropriate key performance indicators (KPIs).
2. Involve numerous stakeholders.
3. Obtain third-party verification of non-financial information.
4. Leverage reporting efforts to further embed corporate responsibility across the organization.
5. Cross-reference hard copy reports to corporate Web sites.
6. Keep abreast of reporting innovations.

*Based on CSR Europe, "Trends and best practice in online CSR/sustainability reporting," September 2009, retrieved May 2, 2011, from http://ec.europa.eu/enterprise/policies/sustainable-business/corporate-social-responsibility/reporting-disclosure/swedish-presidency/files/surveys_and_reports/trends_and_best_practice_in_online_csr_and_sustainability_rep_en.pdf; Robert Colapinto, "Worth reporting," *CA Magazine*, January/February 2005, 30–34, retrieved June 30, 2005, from http://www.camagazine.com/index.cfm/ci_id/24114/la_id/1.htm; Deloitte, "Best practices in corporate responsibility reporting," retrieved September 1, 2008, from http://www.deloitte.com/dtt/article/0,1002,cid%253D153081,00.html.

Many readers turn to the recommendations section first. Number the recommendations to make it easy for people to discuss them. If the recommendations will seem difficult or controversial, give a brief paragraph of rationale after each recommendation. If they'll be easy for the audience to accept, you can simply list them without comments or reasons. The recommendations will also be in the executive summary and perhaps in the title and the transmittal.

On the Job — Why the Numbers Don't Add Up*

How many people work at home in Canada? That depends on who collected the data and how.

According to Statistics Canada, there was a decline from 8.2% in 1996 to 8.0% reporting the home as the workplace in the 2001 Census. But a 2001 survey (also by StatsCan) shows that the home workforce increased from 16% to 17% between 1995 and 2000. That survey used different wording. A 2007 update finds "virtually no increase" in work at home since 2000 despite information and telecommunications technology and lobbying. Factors include increased employer daycare, improved transportation, extended mobile telecommunications permitting work from multiple sites, and increased security concerns.

A 2010 update notes employees working from home (largely part-time and highly educated) increased from 1,425,700 in 2000 to 1,748,600 in 2008 (only a 1% increase). Yet managerial "reluctance" and employee discontent (feeling isolated, forgotten, or misunderstood and finding work-life separations difficult) remain issues.

Statistics Canada warns that "users should be aware of [data] inaccuracies":

- Census returns are self-administered and depend on respondents understanding questions
- Persons who did not check the Place of Work question could not be coded
- Results differ from business and establishment surveys that report all workers as if they worked in one location
- Census collects information on only one job; those with multiple jobs can report only the main one
- Results may reflect two trends: increased working at home and decreased agricultural sector

The replacement of the mandatory long-form census by the voluntary National Household Survey has increased non-response error and made comparison over time difficult. The 2011 Survey based on a sample covering one third of households found that "1.1 million worked at home most of the time." The census included "usual residents in collective dwellings and persons living abroad," while the survey did not.

*Based on National Household Survey, 2011, "Commuting to Work," Statistics Canada Catalogue No. 99-012-2011003, retrieved June 19, 2014, from http://www12.statcan.gc.ca/nhs-enm/2011/as-sa/99-012-x/99-012-x2011003_1-eng.pdf; Martin Turcotte, "Working at home: An update," *Canadian Social Trends*, December 7, 2010, retrieved May 2, 2011, from http://www.statcan.gc.ca/pub/11-008-x/2011001/article/11366-eng.pdf; Statistics Canada, "Data quality measurement," retrieved July 2, 2005, from http://www12.statcan.ca/english/census01/release/release6.cfm; E. Akyeampong and R. Nadwodny, "Evolution of the Canadian workplace: Work from home," *Perspectives on Labour and Income* 2.9 (September 2001): 31; Ernest B. Akyeampong, "Working at home: An update," *Perspectives on Labour and Income* 8.6 (June 2007).

SUMMARY OF KEY POINTS

- Reports can provide information, provide information and analysis, or provide information and analysis to support a recommendation. *Information reports* collect data for the reader, *analytical reports* interpret data but do not recommend action, and *recommendation reports* (including feasibility and justification reports) recommend action or a solution.
- Information, feasibility, and justification reports will be more successful when you work with the readers' needs and expectations for that kind of report.
- Whether you use direct or indirect problem-solving organization depends on your reader's receptivity (or not) and the culture of your organization.
- Progress reports may be organized chronologically, by task, or in support of a recommendation.
- Trip, conference, or workshop reports typically follow the direct pattern of organization; they may include recommendations.
- A proposal must answer the following questions:
  - What problem will you solve?
  - How will you solve it?
  - What exactly will you provide?
  - Can you deliver what you promise?
  - What benefits can you offer?
  - When will you complete the work?
  - How much will you charge?
- Reports use the same style as other business documents, with three exceptions:
  1. Reports use a fairly formal style.
  2. Reports rarely use the word *you.*
  3. Reports should include all the information, definitions, and documents needed to understand the conclusions and recommendations.
- To create good report style,
  1. Say what you mean.
  2. Tighten your writing.
  3. Introduce sources and visuals gracefully.
  4. Use blueprints, transitions, topic sentences, and headings.
- *Summary* or *informative executive summaries* present the logical skeleton of the report: the thesis or recommendation and its proof. *Descriptive executive summaries* indicate what topics the report covers and how deeply it goes into each topic, but do not summarize what the report says about each topic. *Mixed executive summaries* have some characteristics of both summary and descriptive ones.
- The introduction of the report always contains a statement of purpose and scope. The introduction may also include *assumptions, methods, limitations, criteria,* and *definitions.*
- A *background* or *history* section is included in the *body* because reports are filed and may be consulted years later.
- *Conclusions* summarize points made in the body of the report; *recommendations* are action items that would solve or ameliorate the problem. These sections are often combined if they are short.

EXERCISES AND PROBLEMS

GETTING STARTED

11.1 IDENTIFYING ASSUMPTIONS AND LIMITATIONS

Indicate whether each of the following would be an assumption or a limitation in a formal report. Discuss in pairs or groups and present findings to the class.

a. Report on Ways to Encourage More Students to Join XYZ Organization

1. I surveyed a judgment sample rather than a random sample.
2. These recommendations are based on the attitudes of current students. Presumably, students in the next several years will have the same attitudes and interests.

b. Report on Car-Buying Preferences of Young Adults

1. These recommendations may change if the cost of gasoline increases dramatically or if there is another deep recession.
2. This report is based on a survey of adults ages 20 to 24 in Alberta, Newfoundland, British Columbia, Ontario, and Yukon.
3. These preferences are based on the cars now available. If a major technical or styling innovation occurs, preferences may change.

11.2 REVISING AN EXECUTIVE SUMMARY

The following executive summary is poorly organized and too long. Rearrange information to make it more effective. Cut information that does not belong in the summary. You may use different words as you revise. As your professor directs, peer grade answers.

In this report I will discuss the communication problems that exist at Rolling Meadows Golf Club. The problems discussed will deal with channels of communication. The areas that are causing problems are internal. Mobile phones would solve these internal problems.

Taking a 15-minute drive on a golf cart in order to find the superintendent is a common occurrence. Starters and rangers need to keep in touch with the clubhouse to maintain a smooth flow of players around the course. The rangers have expressed an interest in being able to call the clubhouse for advice and support.

Purchasing mobile phones for personnel would provide three advantages. First, mobile phones would make the golf course safer by providing a means of notifying someone in the event of an emergency. Second, they would make the staff more efficient by providing a faster channel of communication. Third, they would enable clubhouse personnel to keep in touch with the superintendent, the rangers, and the starters.

During the week, mobile phones can be carried by the superintendent, the golf pro, and another course worker. On weekends and during tournaments, one will be used by the golf professional. The other two will be used by one starter and one ranger. Three mobile phones is the minimum needed to meet basic communication needs. A fourth would provide more flexibility for busy weekends and during tournaments.

Mobile phones can be purchased now from Page-Com for $129 each as part of a special professional package. They are durable and easy to service. It is possible that another brand might be even less expensive.

Rolling Meadows Golf Club should purchase four mobile phones. They will cost under $600 and can be paid for from the current equipment budget.

11.3 CHOOSING SUBJECT LINES FOR MEMO REPORTS

Identify the strengths and weaknesses of each subject line, and choose the best subject line(s) from each group. As your professor directs, peer grade answers.

1. A proposal to conduct research.

    a. Membership Survey

    b. Proposal to Survey Former Members to Learn Their Reasons for Not Rejoining

    c. Proposal to Investigate Former Members' Reasons for Not Rejoining

2. A survey to find out why former members did not renew their memberships.

    a. 2014 Delinquency Survey

    b. Results of 2014 Former Member Survey

    c. Why Members Did Not Renew Their Memberships in 2014

3. A progress report.

    a. Progress Report

    b. Work Completed, October 15–November 5

    c. Status of the Survey of Former Members

COMMUNICATING AT WORK

11.4 RECOMMENDING ACTION

Write a report recommending an action that your unit or organization should take. Possibilities include

- Buying more equipment for your department
- Hiring an additional worker for your department
- Making your organization more family friendly
- Making a change that will make the organization more efficient
- Making changes to improve accessibility for customers or employees with disabilities

Address your report to the person who would have the power to approve your recommendation.

11.5 EVALUATING A REPORT FROM YOUR WORKPLACE

Consider the following aspects of a report from your workplace:

- How much information is included? How is it presented?
- Visuals and layout. Are visuals used effectively? Are they accurate and free from chartjunk (see ◀◀ Chapter 4)? What image do the pictures and visuals create? Are colour and white space used effectively?
- Emphasis. What points are emphasized? What points are de-emphasized? What verbal and visual techniques are used to highlight or minimize information?

As Your Professor Directs,

a. Write an e-mail to your professor analyzing the report.

b. Join with a small group of students to compare and contrast several reports. Present your evaluation in an informal group report.

c. Present your evaluation orally to the class.

As Your Professor Directs in Problems 11.6 and 11.7,

a. Create a document or presentation to achieve the goal.

b. Write a memo to your professor describing the situation at your workplace and explaining your rhetorical choices (medium, strategy, tone, wording, graphics or document design, and so forth).

c. Plan, research, and write a report based on the proposal.

d. Present your report findings in an oral presentation.

11.6 PROPOSING A CHANGE

No organization is perfect. Propose a change that would improve your organization (refer to Problem 11.4). The change can affect only your unit or the whole organization; it can relate to productivity and profits, to quality of life, or to any other aspect your organization can control. Direct your proposal to the person or committee with the power to authorize the change.

11.7 PROPOSING TO UNDERTAKE A RESEARCH PROJECT

Pick a project you would like to study whose results could be used by your organization. (See Problem 11.4.) Write a proposal to your supervisor requesting time away from other duties to do the research. Show how your research (whatever its outcome) will be useful to the organization.

11.8 WRITING A SALES PROPOSAL

Pick a project that you could do for a local company, non-profit, or government office. Examples include

- Creating a brochure, Facebook, or Web page.
- Revising form letters.
- Conducting a training program.
- Writing a newsletter or an annual report.
- Developing a marketing plan.
- Providing plant care, catering, or janitorial services.

Write a proposal specifying what you could do and providing a detailed budget and work schedule.

As Your Professor Directs,

a. Phone someone in the organization to talk about its needs and what you could offer.

b. Write an individual proposal.

c. Join with other students in the class to create a group proposal.

d. Present your proposal orally.

REPORT ASSIGNMENTS

11.9 WRITING A REPORT BASED ON A SURVEY

As Your Professor Directs,

a. Survey 40 to 50 people on some subject of your choice.

b. Team up with your classmates to conduct a survey and write it up as a group. Survey 50 to 80 people if your group has two members, 75 to 120 people if it has three members, 100 to 150 people if it has four members, and 125 to 200 people if it has five members.

c. Keep a journal during your group meetings and submit it to your professor.

d. Write a memo to your professor describing and evaluating your group's process for designing, conducting, and writing up the survey. (See ◀◀ Chapter 6 on working and writing in groups.)

For this assignment, you do **not** have to take a random sample. Do, however, survey at least two different groups so that you can see if they differ in some way. Possible groups are men and women, business majors and English majors, first-year students and seniors, students and non-students.

As you conduct your survey, make careful notes about what you do so that you can use this information when you write up your survey. If you work with a group, record who does what. Use complete memo format. Your subject line should be clear and reasonably complete. Omit unnecessary words such as "Survey of." Your first paragraph serves as an introduction, but it needs no heading. The rest of the body of your memo will be divided into four sections with the following headings: Purpose, Procedure, Results, and Discussion.

In your first paragraph, briefly summarize (not necessarily in this order) who conducted the experiment or survey, when it was conducted, where it was conducted, who the subjects were, what your purpose was, and what you found out. You will discuss all of these topics in more detail in the body of your memo.

In your **Purpose** section, explain why you conducted the survey. What were you trying to learn? What hypothesis were you testing? Why did this subject seem interesting or important?

In your **Procedure** section, describe in detail *exactly* what you did. "The first 50 people who came through the Students' Union on Wed., Feb. 2" is not the same as "The first 50 people who came through the south entrance of the Students' Union on Wed., Feb. 2, and agreed to answer my questions." Explain any steps you took to overcome possible sources of bias.

In your **Results** section, first tell whether your results supported your hypothesis. Use both visuals and words to explain what your numbers show. (See Chapter 4 on how to design visuals.) Process your raw data in a way that will be useful to your reader.

In your **Discussion** section, evaluate your survey and discuss the implications of your results. Consider these questions:

1. What are the limitations of your survey and your results?
2. Do you think a scientifically valid survey would have produced the same results? Why or why not?
3. Were there any sources of bias either in the way the questions were phrased or in the way the subjects were chosen? If you were running the survey again, what changes would you make to eliminate or reduce these sources of bias?
4. Do you think your subjects answered honestly and completely? What factors may have intruded? Is the fact that you did or didn't know them, were or weren't of the same sex relevant? If your results seem to contradict other evidence, how do you account for the discrepancy? Were your subjects shading the truth? Was your sample's unrepresentativeness the culprit? Or have things changed since earlier data were collected?
5. What causes the phenomenon your results reveal? If several causes together account for the phenomenon, or if it is impossible to be sure of the cause, admit this. Identify possible causes and assess the likelihood of each.
6. What action should be taken?

The discussion section gives you the opportunity to analyze the significance of your survey. Its insight and originality lift the otherwise well-written memo from the ranks of the merely satisfactory to the ranks of the above-average and the excellent.

The whole assignment will be more interesting if you choose a question that interests you. It does not need to be "significant" in terms of major political or philosophic problems; a quirk of human behaviour that fascinates you will do nicely.

11.10 WRITING A PROGRESS REPORT FOR A GROUP REPORT

Write a memo to your professor summarizing your group's progress and adding appropriate headings.

In the introductory paragraph, summarize the group's progress in terms of its goals and its schedule, your own progress on the tasks for which you are responsible, and your feelings about the group's work thus far.

Under a heading titled *Work Completed,* list what has already been done. Be most specific about what you yourself have done. Describe briefly the chronology of group activities: number, time, and length of meetings; topics discussed; and decisions made at meetings.

If you have solved problems creatively, say so. You can also describe obstacles you've encountered that you have not yet solved. In this section, you can also comment on problems that the group has faced and whether or not they've been solved. You can comment on things that have gone well and have contributed to the smooth functioning of the group.

Under *Work to Be Completed,* list what you personally and other group members still have to do. Indicate the schedule for completing the work.

In your last paragraph, either indicate your confidence in completing the report by the due date or ask for a conference to resolve the problems you are encountering.

11.11 WRITING A FEASIBILITY STUDY

Write a report evaluating the feasibility of two or more alternatives. Possible topics include the following:

1. Is it feasible for a local restaurant to open another branch? Where should it be?
2. Is it feasible to create a program to mentor women and minorities in your organization?
3. Is it feasible to produce a video yearbook in addition to or instead of a paper yearbook at your community college or university?

4. Is it feasible to create or enlarge a day care centre for the children of students?
5. Could your college or university host a regional meeting of the Association for Business Communication on or off campus?

Pick a limited number of alternatives, explain your criteria clearly, evaluate each alternative, and recommend the best course of action.

11.12 WRITING AN INFORMATION OR CLOSURE REPORT

In pairs or groups, write an information report on one of the following topics:

1. What should a Canadian manager know about dealing with workers from __________ [you fill in the country or culture]? What factors do and do not motivate people in this group? How do they show respect and deference? Are they used to a strong hierarchy or to an egalitarian setting? Do they normally do one thing at once or many things? How important is clock time and being on time? What factors lead them to respect someone? Age? Experience? Education? Technical knowledge? Wealth? Or what else? What conflicts or miscommunications may arise between workers from this culture and other workers due to cultural differences? Are people from this culture similar in these beliefs and behaviours, or is there lots of variation?
2. What benefits do companies offer? To get information, check the Web pages of three companies in the same industry. Information about benefits is usually on the page about working for the company. For example, Eddie Bauer's Associate Benefits page is www.eddiebauer.com/career/career-in-store.jsp.
3. Describe an ethical dilemma encountered by workers in a specific organization. What is the background of the situation? What competing loyalties exist? In the past, how have workers responded? How has the organization responded? Have whistleblowers been rewarded or punished? What could the organization do to foster ethical behaviour?
4. Describe a problem or challenge encountered by an organization where you've worked. Describe the problem, show why it needed to be solved, tell who did what to try to solve it, and tell how successful the efforts were. Possibilities include
   - How the organization is implementing work teams, downsizing, or a change in organizational culture
   - How the organization uses e-mail or voice mail, social media, statistical process control, or telecommuting
   - How managers deal with stress, make ethical choices, or evaluate subordinates
   - How the organization is responding to changing Canadian demographics or international competition and opportunities

11.13 WRITING A LIBRARY RESEARCH REPORT

In groups, (a) write a library research report; (b) present your findings in an oral presentation.

As Your Professor Directs,

Turn in the following documents:

a. The approved proposal

b. Two copies of the report, including

   Cover

   Title Page

   Letter or Memo of Transmittal

   Table of Contents

   List of Illustrations

   Executive Summary or Abstract

   Body (Introduction, all information, recommendations). Your professor may specify a minimum length, a minimum number or kind of sources, and a minimum number of visuals

   References or Works Cited

c. Your notes and rough drafts

Choose one of the following topics:

1. **Making Money from Football.** Your boss, the athletic director at your college or university, is interested in increasing revenue. "CFL teams make money in lots of ways—and some of the teams that are successful financially don't have good teams. Look at what they're doing, and recommend whether we could copy any of their strategies. Also recommend ways to ensure that students aren't priced out of attending the games." You might start by reading Cam Cole, "CFL Players Hoping for Boost in Pay with League in Rare Position of Strength," *National Post*, March 28, 2014, retrieved from http://sports.nationalpost.com/2014/03/28/cfl-players-hoping-for-boost-in-pay-with-league-in-rare-position-of-strength/.
2. **Recommending a Dress Policy.** Your boss asks you to look into "business casual" dress. "Is it time to retire it? And what is 'business casual'? Recommend how our employees should dress, and why. Include some photos of what is and isn't appropriate." To start, read Leah Eichler, "Mastering Work Wear Etiquette," *Globe and Mail*, September 7, 2013, B16.

   Hint: Choose a business, non-profit, or government agency you know well and recommend a dress policy for it.
3. **Accounting for Intellectual Capital.** You work for the Ontario Securities Commission. Your boss hands you a copy of Thomas A. Stewart, "Accounting Gets Radical," *Fortune*, April 1, 2001, 184–194. "Many experts believe that traditional, generally accepted accounting principles don't work well now that knowledge and intellectual property can be a firm's most important assets. Write a report summarizing proposals for alternate accounting schemes and explain the advantages and disadvantages of each."
4. **Evaluating Online Voting.** As an aide to a member of Parliament, you frequently research topics for legislation. You have been told, "Look into online voting. I want to know what the problems are and whether it's feasible for the next election." Start with Stephen H. Wildstrom, "Click and Be Counted," *BusinessWeek*, April 24, 2000, 22; and Thomas E. Weber, "'Scalable' Ballot Fraud: Why One Tech Maven Fears Computer Voting," *The Wall Street Journal*, March 19, 2001, B1. Or read Elections Canada, "A Comparative Assessment of Electronic Voting," retrieved June 20, 2014, from http://www.elections.ca/content.aspx?section=res&dir=rec/tech/ivote/comp&document=benefit&lang=e.
5. **Evaluating the Ethics of "Weblining."** You're an aide to a member of Parliament. You've been told, "I'm concerned that information on the Web allows companies to 'rank' customers and then charge rates and provide customer service based on how 'good' a customer is. Poor people and small businesses will be hurt. Find out how widespread the practice is. Especially consider the ethical implications. Should the federal government outlaw the practice?" Start with Marcia Stepanek, "Weblining," *BusinessWeek e.biz*, April 3, 2000, EB26–E34.
6. **Understanding Demographic Changes.** You work for a major political party. Your boss says, "As you know, the number of so-called minorities is growing. Moreover, they're increasingly middle class. I want you to analyze one ethnic group in our province. What issues are they interested in? Which party do they favour? What appeals might persuade them to vote for a candidate of the other party?" "Canadians of Colour Don't Want 'Costumes,' They Want Change," The Nudge Report Political Blog, *Huffington Post*, March 10, 2014, retrieved June 20, 2014, from http://www.huffingtonpost.ca/the-nudge-report/multiculturalism-canada_b_4922419.html; Kamal Dib, "Diversity Works," *Canadian Business*, March 29–April 11, 2004, 53–54; Jill Mahoney, "Visible Majority by 2017," *The Globe and Mail*, March 23, 2005, A1 to A7.
7. **Improving Laptop Security.** Your boss hands you a copy of Charles C. Mann, "Where the Hell Is My Laptop?" www.ecompany.com, March 2001, 84–90. She says, "This article is frightening. If laptop theft is still rising, my concern is not just the cost of the computers stolen, but the danger of data theft as well. Put together a report on how we can protect our data and our computers."
8. With your professor's permission, investigate a topic of your choice.

11.14 WRITING A RECOMMENDATION REPORT

(a) Write an individual or a group report. (b) Present your findings in an oral presentation.

As Your Professor Directs,

Turn in the following documents:

1. The approved proposal
2. Two copies of the report, including

Cover

Title Page

Letter or Memo of Transmittal

Table of Contents

List of Illustrations

Executive Summary or Abstract

Body (Introduction, all information, recommendations). Your professor may specify a minimum length, a minimum number or kind of sources, and a minimum number of visuals

Appendices if useful or relevant

3. Your notes and rough drafts.

Pick one of the following topics.

1. **Improving Customer Service.** Many customers find that service is getting poorer and workers are getting ruder. Evaluate the service in a local store, restaurant, or other organization. Are customers made to feel comfortable? Is workers' communication helpful, friendly, and respectful? Are workers knowledgeable about products and services? Do they sell them effectively? Write a report analyzing the quality of service and recommending what the organization should do to improve.
2. **Recommending Courses for the Local College or University.** Businesses want to be able to send workers to local colleges or universities to upgrade their skills; colleges and universities want to prepare students to enter the local workforce. What skills are in demand in your community? What courses at what levels should be offered?
3. **Improving Sales and Profits.** Recommend ways a small business in your community can increase sales and profits. Focus on one or more of the following: the products or services it offers, its advertising, its decor, its location, its accounting methods, its cash management, or any other aspect that may be keeping the company from achieving its potential. Address your report to the owner of the business.
4. **Increasing Student Involvement.** How could an organization on campus persuade more of the students who are eligible to join or to become active in its programs? Do students know that it exists? Is it offering programs that interest students? Is it retaining current members? What changes should the organization make? Address your report to the officers of the organization.
5. **Evaluating a Potential Employer.** What training is available to new employees? How soon is the average entry-level person promoted? How much travel and weekend work are expected? Is there a "busy season," or is the workload consistent year-round? What fringe benefits are offered? What is the corporate culture? Is the climate non-racist and non-sexist? How strong is the company economically? How is it likely to be affected by current economic, demographic, and political trends? Address your report to the Placement Office on campus; recommend whether it should encourage students to work at this company.
6. With your professor's permission, choose your own topic.

MAKING ORAL PRESENTATIONS

12

Learning Outcomes

LO1 Explain the purposes of oral presentations

LO2 Discuss presentation strategy

LO3 List five ways to organize information

LO4 Discuss delivery techniques for effective presentations

LO5 Illustrate how to handle questions

LO6 Identify the characteristics of the best group presentations

AN INSIDE PERSPECTIVE

Canadian Stephen Lewis, as his Massey Lectures suggest, is in a Race Against Time—feeling an urgency and conviction that his audiences are compelled to share. "I have spent the last four years watching people die"—the words with which the Massey Lectures begin—speak to his powerful need to bear witness and to speak plainly about what he has seen. Whether he is talking about HIV/AIDS in Africa, violence against women, literacy, or making poverty history, he commands attention and inspires action.

When many presenters feel naked without PowerPoint, Lewis is driven to tell his story simply and plainly, to focus attention on people—the people who suffer from and battle injustice, the people responsible, the powerful people and institutions that could make a difference, and the people in the audience who can demand and promote change.

Without a script, often without even an outline, Lewis speaks from the heart, from the images traced in his memory, from the anecdotes that won't be forgotten, from the facts and figures that cannot—should not—be ignored. With all the credibility of his immense experience and powerful presence, with logic and emotion on his side, he takes his audiences to global theatres of devastation, helping them hear the voices and see the faces of those for whom inequality, violence, disease, and war are daily companions. Instead of euphemisms that cloud and conceal or protect the guilty, his impassioned phrasing and clear vision persuade people to care and to take action.

Check out his presentations on YouTube. You can get a flavour of the Stephen Lewis style from his May 2012 Sixth Annual June Callwood Lecture, The Power of Advocacy: Fighting for Social Justice, at http://www.youtube.com/watch?v=VCnNkEJkqBQ.

He has been an academic, author, activist, leader of the Ontario New Democratic party, Canada's Ambassador to the United Nations, Deputy Executive Director of UNICEF, United Nations Special Envoy for HIV/AIDS in Africa, one of the 100 Most Influential People in the World (TIME), a Distinguished Visiting Professor at Ryerson University, Toronto, board chair of the Stephen Lewis Foundation, and recipient of multiple awards and honorary degrees. In whatever capacity, Stephen Lewis is a passionate and tireless spokesperson for and defender of human rights and social justice.

Whether you are selling a budget, a proposal, a mission, an idea, or yourself, the power to persuade people to care about something you believe in is crucial to business and career success. But that power does not come naturally to all. Although some rank presenting in public as their number one fear, it is possible to reduce those fears and use anxiety to advantage.

According to blogger and advertising professional Steffan Postaer, your nerves can send strong signals about your respect for your audience, endear you to them, and energize you into a powerful performance.[1]

Making a good oral presentation is more than just good delivery: it also involves careful planning, preparation, and practice to build the confidence that marks the best presenters. It involves developing a strategy that fits your audience and purpose, having good content, and organizing material effectively. The choices you make in each of these areas are affected by your purposes, the audience, and the situation.

LO1

UNDERSTANDING PURPOSES IN ORAL PRESENTATIONS

Oral presentations, whether delivered in person or online, have the same three basic purposes that written documents have: to inform, to persuade, and to build goodwill. Like written messages, most oral presentations have to persuade to achieve their purposes. To gain and retain your audience's attention, the AIDA persuasive plan (◂◂ Chapter 9) can be helpful.

Informative presentations inform or teach the audience. Training sessions in an organization are primarily informative. Secondary purposes may be to persuade new employees to follow organizational procedures, rather than doing something their own way, and to help them appreciate the organizational culture (◂◂ Chapter 2).

A flight attendant leader motivates CUPE members protesting Air Canada plans to cut jobs, Halifax, July 28, 2008.

Persuasive presentations motivate the audience to act or to believe. Giving information and evidence is an important means of persuasion. Stories, visuals, and self-disclosure are also effective. In addition, the speaker must build goodwill by appearing to be credible and sympathetic to the audience's needs. Presentations can persuade the audience to approve proposals, adopt ideas, buy products, change behaviour or attitudes, or reinforce existing attitudes. For example, a speaker at a meeting of factory workers may stress the importance of following safety procedures. **Goodwill presentations** entertain and validate the audience. In an after-dinner speech, the audience wants to be entertained. Presentations at sales meetings may be designed to stroke the audience's egos and to validate their commitment to organizational goals.

Make your purpose as specific as possible.

× Weak:	The purpose of my presentation is to discuss saving for retirement.
✓ Better:	My presentation will explain how to calculate how much money you need to save in order to maintain a specific lifestyle after retirement.

Note that the purpose is *not* the introduction of your talk; it is the principle that guides your choice of strategy and content.

LO2

PLANNING A STRATEGY FOR YOUR PRESENTATION

A **strategy** is your plan for reaching your specific goals with a specific audience. See ◀◀ Figure 2.1 on oral and written channels and messages, the strengths of each, and shared concerns with audience needs, expectations, and potential objections.

In all oral presentations, identify the one idea you want the audience to take away. Simplify your supporting detail so it's easy to follow. Simplify visuals so they can be taken in at a glance. Simplify your words and sentences, simplifying the written form so it is easy to understand in oral delivery.

× Too complicated:	Information Storage Devices provide voice solutions using the company's unique, patented multilevel storage technique.
✓ Simple:	We make voice chips. They're extremely easy to use. They have unlimited applications. And they last forever.[2]

An oral presentation needs to be simpler than a written message to the same audience. If readers forget a point, they can turn back to it and reread the paragraph. Headings, paragraph indentation, and punctuation provide visual cues to help readers understand the message. Listeners, in contrast, must remember what the speaker says. And good presenters allow for listening that is typically several times faster than talking (◀◀ Chapter 6) in order to stress key messages by repetition and emphasis.[3]

Winston Churchill, for instance, knew that subtlety is not the best approach in the circumstances: "If you have an important point to make, don't try to be subtle or clever. Use a pile driver. Hit the point once. Then come back and hit it again. Then hit it a third time—a tremendous whack." In driving home his messages, Stephen Lewis is a master of repetition, rephrasing, and pointed restatement. He also knows the power of parallelism (◀◀ Chapter 3) to mimic the natural rhythms of the speaking voice and embed messages in audience memories (◀◀ An Inside Perspective).

Analyze your audience for an oral presentation just as you do for a written message. If you'll be speaking to co-workers, talk to them about your topic or proposal to find out what questions or objections they have and therefore what they need to know and in what order. For audiences inside the organization, the biggest questions are often practical ones: Will it work? How much will it cost? How long will it take?

Think about where and when you'll be speaking. Is the room large or small, brightly lit or dark? Will the audience be tired at the end of a long day of listening? Sleepy after a big meal? Will the group be large or small? The more you know about your audience and setting, the better you can adapt your message to them.

Choosing the Kind of Presentation

Although it is important to understand that presentation types (even online ones) are never as discrete as their titles suggest (monologues have interactive elements), most speakers choose one of three basic kinds: monologue, guided discussion, or interactive.

In a **monologue presentation,** the speaker speaks without interruption; questions are held until the end of the

Technology Tips Sharing the Stage with Visuals*

The audience can look at the speaker or the visual, but not both at the same time. An effective speaker directs the audience's attention to the visual and then back to the speaker, rather than trying to compete with the visual. Artist and designer Christopher Fahey argues that when visuals make the point better than words, or when words on the slides help the audience understand the point, then the slides properly "under*line*, not under*mine*."

When Steve Mandel coaches clients on public speaking, he teaches them to use brief silences for visuals, so the audience has time to pay attention. For example, a speaker might say, "I've just talked to you about several problems you might experience. Now I'd like you to see a possible solution." Then the speaker shows the slide without talking for several seconds. This gives the audience time to absorb the contents of the slide. The presenter can regain attention by stepping toward the audience as he or she begins to speak again.

At its sales workshops, Communispond teaches a technique called "think-turn-talk." The presenter stands next to the visual and points to it with an open hand, thinking of what he or she intends to say. Then the presenter turns and makes eye contact with a person in the audience. Finally, the presenter talks. Communispond also teaches presenters to walk toward the audience when giving details from a visual. The connection is between presenter and audience, not presenter and slide.

*Based on Michael Fahey, "In defense of PowerPointism," posted April 29, 2007, retrieved May 2, 2011, from http://www.graphpaper.com/2007/04-29_in-defense-of-powerpointism; Dave Zielinski, "Perfect practice," *Presentations*, May 2003; and "Back to school," *Sales & Marketing Management*, July 2004, both downloaded from http://www.findarticles.com.

presentation, where the speaker functions as an expert. The speaker plans the presentation in advance and delivers it without deviation. This kind of presentation is often boring for the audience. Good delivery skills are crucial, since the audience is comparatively uninvolved.

Guided discussions offer a better way to present material and help an audience find a solution it can "buy into." Rather than functioning as an expert with all the answers, the speaker serves as a facilitator to help the audience tap its own knowledge of questions or issues agreed on in advance. This kind of presentation is excellent for presenting the results of consulting projects, when the speaker has specialized knowledge, but the audience must implement the solution if it is to succeed. Guided discussions need more time than monologue presentations, but produce more audience response, more responses involving analysis, and more commitment to the result.[4]

An **interactive presentation** is a conversation, even if the speaker stands up in front of a group and uses charts, chalkboard or whiteboard, or presentation software. Most sales presentations are interactive presentations. The sales representative uses questions to determine the buyer's needs, probe objections, and gain provisional and then final commitment to the purchase. Even in a memorized sales presentation, the buyer will talk at least 30% of the time. In a problem-solving sales presentation, the buyer may do 70% of the talking up until the action close (◀◀ Chapter 9).[5]

Preparing Your Presentation Outline

Preparing your outline is as important to planning a presentation as it is to planning a piece of writing (◀◀ Chapter 3). For an oral presentation, you might try creating a **storyboard,** with a rectangle representing each page or unit (see Figure 12.1). Draw a box with a visual for each main point. Below the box, write a short caption or label.

The outline helps you organize material, distinguishing your purpose and core idea, the outcome you want, as well as the major and minor points to support your presentation. An outline helps you see if you have included all the necessary parts and in the order that will support your purpose. Do the introduction, body, and close perform their functions? Do the points follow logically? Are there gaps in the argument? Is it clear how you connect the dots?

An outline is your guide or map to help you carry your audience with you and help them (and you) know where you are going and why, avoid unnecessary obstacles or distractions, and keep on track without losing direction. Remember the words of Dale Carnegie: "A talk is a voyage with a purpose, and it must be charted. The man [sic] who starts out going nowhere, generally gets there."

An outline also serves as a basis for your speaker's notes (see ▶▶ "Using Notes and Visuals" later in this chapter). An outline (like your speaker's notes) can include complete sentences or key words that act as useful prompts to keep the larger story in view.

An outline of Al Gore's *An Inconvenient Truth* begins to explain how he was so successful in achieving his purpose: to warn about the threats of global warming.

1. A clear statement of the problem
2. Evidence for and implications of the problem
3. Causes of the problem
4. Responses to counter-arguments
5. Solution with specific action steps[6]

An outline for a five- or ten-minute presentation reporting on progress on a class project might be as simple as this:

- Purpose: to review progress on our communication plan for Habitat for Humanity

Figure 12.1 Storyboards Help Clarify Outlines

C2SC Fun With Storyboards © Stanford University, Stanford, California 94305. Used with permission.

- Introduction: review project purpose, scope, methods, and timelines
- Work completed
- Obstacles and solutions
- Work to be completed
- Revised timelines
- Next steps

See Figure 12.2 for an outline for a 30-minute student presentation on the advantages and disadvantages of business blogs. The outline may be even more detailed to include specific examples you will use to illustrate points and/or identify who will present what in a group presentation.

Adapting Your Ideas to the Audience

Measure the message you'd like to send against where your audience is now. If your audience is indifferent, skeptical, or hostile, focus on the part of your message the audience will find most interesting and easiest to accept.

Don't seek a major opinion change in a single oral presentation. If the audience has already decided to hire an advertising agency, then a good presentation can convince them that your agency is the one to hire. But if you're talking to a small business that has always done its own ads, limit your purpose. You may be able to prove that an agency can earn its fees by doing what the owner can't do and by freeing the owner's time for other activities. A second presentation may be needed to prove that an ad agency can do a *better* job than the small business could do on its own. Only after the audience is receptive should you try to persuade the audience to hire your agency rather than a competitor.

Make your ideas relevant to your audience by linking what you have to say to their experiences and interests. Showing your audience that the topic affects them directly is the most effective strategy. Environmental activist Simon Jackson, who founded the Spirit Bear Youth Coalition when he was only 13, has motivated people with his talk of the "power of one" to see how each person can make a difference and support his efforts "to give a voice" to the spirit bear. The result of this British Columbian's motivational speeches is that his coalition is the largest youth-run environmental organization in the world, and two-thirds of the habitat of the spirit bear is already protected.[7]

Planning a Strong Opening and Close

The beginning and the end of a presentation, like the beginning and the end of a written document, are positions of emphasis. Use those key positions to connect with and interest the audience, emphasize your key point, and establish your credibility. You'll sound more natural and more effective if you talk without notes, but write out your opener and close in advance and memorize them. (They'll be short: just a sentence or two.)

One of TIME magazine's 60 Heroes for the Planet, motivational speaker Simon Jackson challenges us all "to give voice to a creature that did not have one."

Figure 12.2 Outline: The Advantages and Disadvantages of Business Blogs

Purpose: To explain the advantages and disadvantages of blogging for business purposes.

Introduction

1. Getting attention and establishing credibility
   - Questions and answers related to facts and figures on blogging in business
   - How many, who uses, for what purposes?
2. Defining terms (blogging from "Web log")
3. Previewing the parts of the presentation

Body

1. Types and uses of business blogs
   - internal and external uses
   - information archive
   - community building
   - project management tool
2. Promise/advantages of business blogging
   - cost-effectiveness and efficiency
   - immediacy and openness of communications
   - interactivity and stakeholder engagement
   - source of learning and innovation
3. Disadvantages/costs of business blogging
   - training and monitoring costs
   - reputation management, liability, and litigation
   - privacy, security, intellectual property issues
   - productivity losses to employee blogging/reading blogs

Close

Summary, opener revisited, call to action

Once you grab audience attention, you can develop three to five points in the body of your presentation, presenting evidence, citing authorities, and following conventional organization (see ▸▸ "Organizing Your Information" later in this chapter) before an equally compelling close.

Consider using one of the four modes for openers that appeared in ◂◂ Chapter 9: startling statement, quotation, question, or narration or anecdote. The more you can do to personalize your opener for your audience, the better. Recent events are better than those that happened long ago; local events are better than events at a distance; people your readers know are better than people who are only names.

Startling Statement

> Twelve of our customers have cancelled orders in the past month.

This presentation to a company's executive committee went on to show that the company's distribution system was inadequate and to recommend a third warehouse located in the Atlantic provinces.

Quotation

> According to Towers Perrin, the profits of Fortune 100 companies would be 25% lower—they'd go down $17 billion—if their earnings statements listed the future costs companies are obligated to pay for retirees' health care.

This presentation on options for health care for retired employees urges executives to start now to investigate options to cut the future costs.

Your opener should interest the audience and establish a rapport with them. Some speakers use humour to achieve those goals. However, an inappropriate joke can turn the audience against the speaker. Rory McAlpine, vice-president of government and industry relations for Maple Leaf Foods, had to apologize for his opening joke about listeria and the Stanley Cup at an Orillia, Ontario, conference. Even though he went on to make serious points about the outbreak and his own son had been affected, his remarks made it to YouTube—where many did not find it a joking matter.[8]

Never use humour that's directed against the audience. In contrast, confident speakers who can make fun of themselves almost always succeed:

> It's both a privilege and a pressure to be here.[9]

Humour isn't the only way to set an audience at ease. Smile at your audience before you begin; let them see that you're a real person—and a nice one.

Question

> Are you going to have enough money to do the things you want to when you retire?

This presentation to a group of potential clients discusses the value of using the services of a professional financial planner to achieve one's goals for retirement.

Narration or Anecdote

> A mother was having difficulty getting her son up for school. He pulled the covers over his head.
>
> "I'm not going to school," he said. "I'm not ever going again."
>
> "Are you sick?" his mother asked.
>
> "No," he answered. "I'm sick of school. They hate me. They call me names. They make fun of me. Why should I go?"
>
> "I can give you two good reasons," the mother replied. "The first is that you're 42 years old. And the second is *you're the school principal.*"[10]

This speech to a seminar for educators went on to discuss "the three knottiest problems in education today." Educators had to face those problems; they couldn't hide under the covers.

Even better than canned stories are anecdotes that happened to you and that contain the point of your talk.

The end of your presentation should be as strong as the opener. For your close, you could do one or more of the following:

- Restate your main point.
- Refer to your opener to create a frame for your presentation.
- End with a vivid, positive picture.
- Tell the audience exactly what to do to solve the problem you've discussed.

The following close from a fundraising speech combines a restatement of the main point with a call for action, telling the audience what to do.

> Plain and simple, we need money to run the foundation, just like you need money to develop new products. We need money to make this work. We need money from you. Pick up that pledge card. Fill it out. Turn it in at the door as you leave. Make it a statement about your commitment . . . make it a big statement.[11]

When you write out your opener and close, be sure to use oral rather than written style. As you can see in the example close above, oral style uses shorter sentences and shorter, simpler words than writing does. Oral style can even sound a bit choppy when it is read by eye. Oral style uses more personal pronouns, a less varied vocabulary, and more repetition.

Planning Visuals and Other Devices to Involve the Audience

Visuals can give your presentation a professional image. One study showed that presenters using visuals were perceived as "better prepared, more professional, more persuasive, more credible, and more interesting" than speakers who did not use visuals. They were also more likely to persuade a group to adopt their recommendations.[12]

Another study found that in an informative presentation, multimedia (PowerPoint slides with graphics and animation) produced 5% more learning than overheads made from the slides and 16% more learning than text alone.

In sales presentations by two different banks, one bank's use of multimedia (PowerPoint slides with graphics, animation, and video) motivated 58% more students to choose that bank over the bank that used overheads only, and 50% more than text alone. Although the two banks offered identical fees and services, students said that the bank represented by the multimedia presentation "was more credible, was more professional, and offered better services and fees."[13]

Designing Visuals

To enhance visibility and readability, use at least 18-point type for visuals you prepare with a word processor. When you prepare slides with PowerPoint, Prezi, Corel, or another presentation program, use at least 24-point type for the smallest words. You should be able to read the smallest words easily when you print a handout version of your slides.

Well-designed visuals can serve as an outline for your talk (see Figure 12.3), eliminating the need for additional notes. Visuals should highlight your main points, not give every detail. If detail is important—if research statistics support your main points, for example—then consider including them in a supplementary handout. A handout with value-added information can allow you to keep to your storyline.[14]

Use these guidelines to create and show visuals for presentations:

- Make only one point with each visual. Break a complicated point down into several visuals.
- Substitute visuals for text when possible.
- Give each visual a title that makes a point.
- Limit the amount of information on a visual. Use 35 words or less on seven lines or less; use simple graphs, not complex ones.
- Put your visual up when you're ready to talk about it.
- Leave it up until your next point.

See ◀◀ Chapter 4 for information on designing slides and on how to present numerical data through visuals. And consider that not every speech needs visuals. As Peter Norvig shows, Lincoln's Gettysburg Address is hurt, not helped, by adding bland PowerPoint slides.[15] Visuals work only if the technology they depend on works. When you give presentations in your own office, check the equipment in advance. When you make a presentation in another location or for another organization,

PowerPoint slides aren't the only or even necessarily the best way to involve the audience. Dan Leeber persuaded UPS to switch to Valeo clutches by completely disassembling the competitor's clutch and showing part by part why Valeo's product was better.

Figure 12.3 PowerPoint Slides for an Informative Presentation

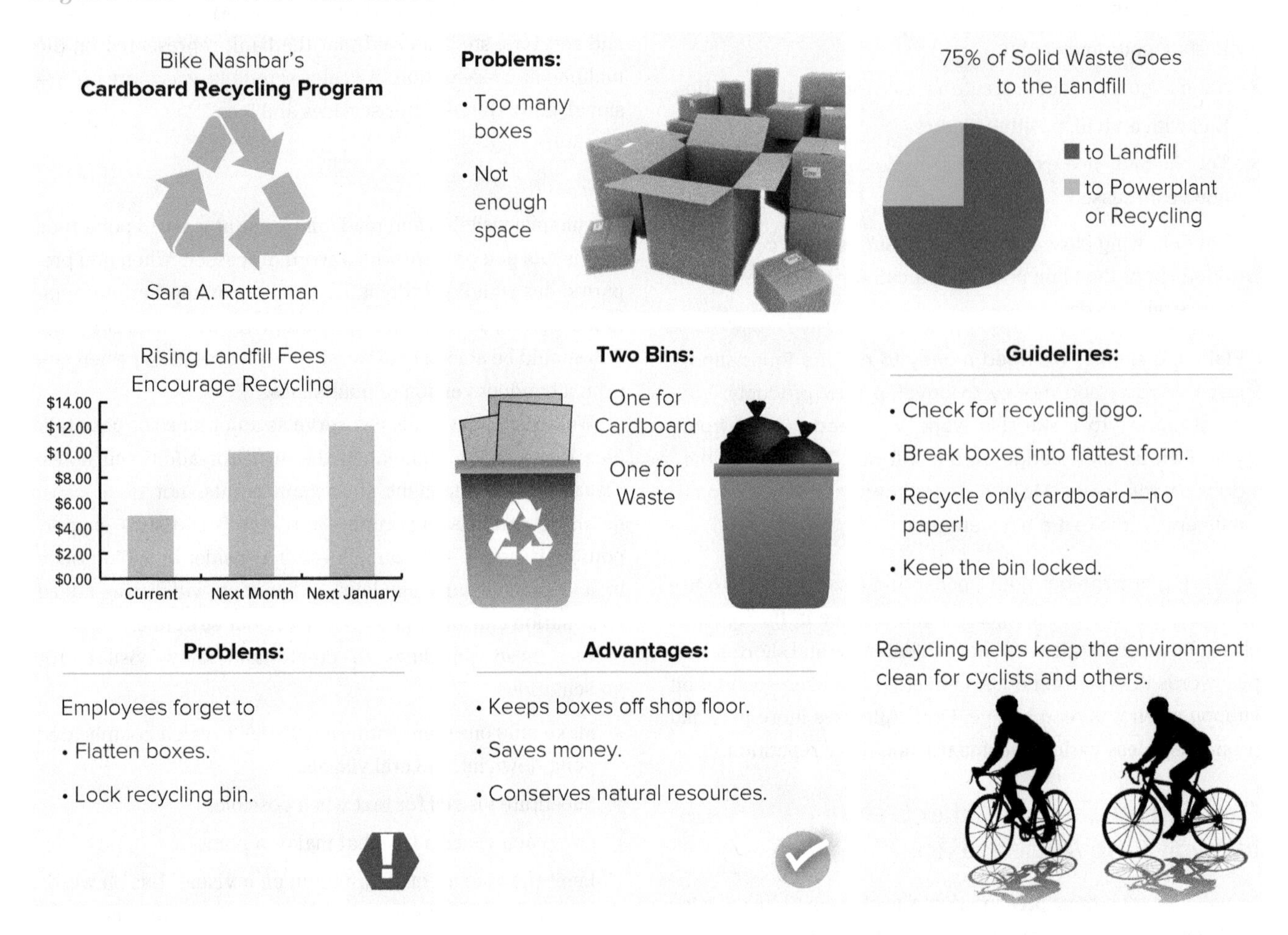

arrive early so that you'll have time not only to check the equipment but also to track down a service worker if the equipment isn't working. Be prepared with a backup plan to use if you're unable to show your slides or videotape.

Choosing PowerPoint—Or Not

Although students claim to be motivated by PowerPoint, 20 years after it appeared on the scene a PowerPoint presentation may prove all too predictable for many professional audiences. Especially if it was written on the plane or in the airport! It can turn the most exciting initiative into a series of bulleted points, turning presenters into "bullet-point dandies" required to fit "an oddly pedantic, prescriptive opinion . . . about the way we should think." After e-mail, PowerPoint is the second most used communication tool, with an estimated 30 million presentations daily. An audience's number one peeve is being read to. Still, it is important to remember that "PowerPoint doesn't kill presentations: people kill presentations."[16]

Toronto presentations coach Jim Gray worries about the reasoning that led many to an addiction to PowerPoint: the belief that it offers protection from "the oppressive scrutiny of audiences by diverting at least some attention to visuals, away from the speaker." From his point of view, wrongly used PowerPoint "isolates and diminishes" the speaker.[17] Yale professor Edward Tufte agrees, arguing that presentation programs can turn "everyone into bores" and prove "punishing to both content and audience," while turning "everything into a sales pitch" and reducing student writing to "infomercials."[18] Some even argue that there is no competition between speaker and screen: the screen always wins.

Just as PowerPoint has had its detractors and supporters, so Prezi, an online presentation tool, is attracting much discussion on the Internet. Some commentators praise Prezi as a non-linear, highly visual, and collaborative response to PowerPoint's predictability. Others wonder if the novelty will last and if the cost of use beyond the basic package is worth it. For many, too, the key factors in choosing a presentation format remain your audience and situation.[19]

Depending on your audience, purpose, setting, and budget, the right visual aids may still be low-tech options such as flipcharts and whiteboards, skits, or demonstrations. Skits can be a powerful means of presenting and involving the audience in a sales meeting or a classroom. Here are some other ways presenters have got their points across:

- A student giving a presentation on English–French business communication demonstrated the differences in Canadian and French handshakes by asking a fellow class member to come up to shake hands with her.

- A student discussing the need for low-salt products brought in a container of salt, a measuring cup, a measuring spoon, and two plates. As he discussed the body's need for salt, he measured out three teaspoons onto one plate: the amount the body needs in a month. As he discussed the amount of salt the average diet provides, he continued to measure out salt onto the other plate, stopping only when he had 567 grams of salt—the amount in the average diet. The demonstration made the discrepancy clear in a way words or even a chart could not have done.[20]
- Another speaker who was trying to raise funds used the simple act of asking people to stand to involve them, to create emotional appeal, and to make a statistic vivid:

> [A speaker] was talking to a luncheon club about contributing to the relief of an area that had been hit by a tornado. The news report said that 70% of the people had been killed or disabled. The room was set up [with] ten people at each round table. He asked three persons at each table to stand. Then he said, ". . . You people sitting are dead or disabled. You three standing have to take care of the mess. You'd need help, wouldn't you?"[21]

Planning Web Presentations

If your purpose, audience, setting, and budget can favour low-tech options, they can also dictate high-tech multimedia investments. If you are working with a small internal audience or you are intent on building interpersonal skills, face-to-face will remain the best medium. When your audience is large and widely dispersed, however, multimedia presentations may be the right choice for training, meetings, information sharing, or product or program promotion. Whether you are in the profit or not-for-profit sector, Skype, YouTube, and online seminars or **webinars** may fill the bill.[22]

With weather challenges, travel disruptions, environmental issues, cost, and collaboration needs, Web conferencing can be "a great productivity and cost-saving tool for a business of any size," says CEO Michael Ball of Victoria's GenoLogics, whose company uses WebEx 15 to 20 times a day. The record and replay features increase access and convenience. Delivering webinars instead of in-person seminars, BizLaunch reduced training costs by 75% while managing to "reach more people anywhere, anytime," according to co-founder Roger Pierce.[23]

Planning a webinar typically involves teamwork: organizer or facilitator, presenter(s), and assistants. Although experienced presenters may also act as organizers, organizers are usually needed to set the topic, identify the speaker(s), promote the event, handle registration and logistics, and moderate the event. Assistance with technical and logistical issues leaves the presenter(s) able to focus on content, audience, and relevant visuals. A clear agenda, rehearsal, and equipment check are as critical to online as to offline presentations. Breaking a day-long event into two-hour sections shows sensitivity to audience needs.[24] Sensitivity to "Sharing the Stage with Visuals" (see the ◂◂ Technology Tips feature earlier in this chapter) likewise remains critical if you want to maintain your relationship with your audience and keep the focus on you and your key messages.

Still, Dr. Leslie Roberts, president of Calgary-based entrepreneur school GoForth Institute, claims that nothing beats "the 'eyeball-to-eyeball' exchange." Although Internet technology can maintain relations, "it's the initial 'handshake' that makes a lasting impression." Marketing Professor Alan Middleton of York University agrees that face time is the "single most powerful marketing medium."[25]

CHOOSING INFORMATION TO INCLUDE IN A PRESENTATION

Choose the information that is most interesting to your audience and that answers the questions your audience will have. Limit your talk to three main points. In a long presentation (20 minutes or more) each main point can have subpoints. Your content will be easier to understand if you clearly show the relationship between each of the main points. Turning your information into a story also helps.

For example, a presentation about a plan to reduce scrap rates on the second shift can begin by setting the scene and defining the problem: Production expenses have cut profits in half. The plot unfolds as the speaker describes the facts that helped her trace the problem to scrap rates on the second shift. The resolution to the story is her group's proposal. One way to keep the choice of supporting information focused on

Donovan Bailey, former World and Olympic Champion sprinter, is a powerful and passionate motivational speaker dedicated to charitable causes and to his foundation in support of Canada's most talented amateur athletes.

what the audience needs to know is to start by writing the conclusion. Then move backward, identifying the main points that led to this conclusion.

As part of choosing what to say, you should determine what data to present, including what to show in visuals (◀◀ Chapter 4). Any data you mention should be related to the points you are making. Databases and presentation software (such as PowerPoint, Prezi, or Flypaper) have given employees direct access to ready-made and easy-to-create slides. The temptation is to choose these and sprinkle them throughout the presentation, rather than starting with decisions about what the audience needs to know. Corporate trainer Pam Gregory observes, "What presentations are supposed to do is save the audience time in sifting through data themselves. But often presentations are overloaded with data; there may be an argument but it is buried."[26]

Statistics and numbers can be convincing if you present them in ways that are easy to hear. Simplify numbers by reducing them to two significant digits.

× Hard to hear:	If the national debt were in pennies, it would take 17,006,802,720 people, each carrying 100 pounds of pennies, to carry all of our debt.
✓ Easier to hear:	If the national debt were in pennies, it would take 17 billion people, each carrying 100 pounds of pennies, to carry all of our debt.[27]

In an informative presentation, link the points you make to the knowledge your audience has. Show the audience members that your information answers their questions, solves their problems, or helps them do their jobs. When you explain the effect of a new law or the techniques for using a new machine, use specific examples that apply to the decisions they make and the work they do. If your content is detailed or complicated, give people a written outline or handouts. The written material both helps the audience keep track of your points during the presentation and serves as a reference after the talk is over.

Quotations work well as long as you cite authorities whom your audience genuinely respects. Often you'll need to paraphrase a quote to put it into simple language that's easy to understand. Be sure to tell whom you're citing: "According to Jack Layton," "An article in *BusinessWeek* points out that," and so forth.

To be convincing, you must answer the audience's questions and objections.

> Some people think that women are less reliable than men. But the facts show that women take fewer sick days than men do.

However, don't bring up negatives or inconsistencies unless you're sure that the audience will think of them. If you aren't sure, save your evidence for the question phase. If someone does ask, you'll have the answer.

LO3

ORGANIZING YOUR INFORMATION

Most presentations use a direct pattern of organization, even when the goal is to persuade a reluctant audience. If you are presenting to a multicultural audience, a more indirect approach might be in order (◀◀ Chapter 9).

In a Canadian business setting, the audience is in a hurry and knows that you want to persuade them. Be honest about your goal, and then prove that your goal meets the audience's needs too.

In a persuasive presentation, start with your strongest point, your best reason. If time permits, give other reasons as well and respond to possible objections. Put your weakest point in the middle so that you can end on a strong note.

Often one of five standard patterns of organization will work:

- **Chronological.** Start with the past, move to the present, and end by looking ahead.
- **Problem–causes–solution.** Explain the symptoms of the problem, identify its causes, and suggest a solution. This pattern works best when the audience will find your solution easy to accept.

On the Job Thanking a Speaker

Thanking a speaker can be even more challenging than introducing one, when you usually have time—and resources—on your side. The task of building interest and expectation is often made easier by bios and handouts received in advance. If clichés, colloquialisms, jargon, and negative words can kill presentations, they can also undermine efforts to thank (and introduce) a speaker.

Never begin with the overused "I would like to thank you for a wonderful presentation." Instead actually thank the speaker—and make it sincere by being specific about what you and the rest of the audience have learned. Listen carefully for key messages and watch for audience reaction. What moved or motivated the audience to engage? What examples resonated with their local concerns? Instead of rehearsing the presenter's points, explain what they meant to the audience. And never end with a pronoun error: Your participation here means so much to the members and I!

- **Exclude alternatives.** Explain the symptoms of the problem. Explain the obvious solutions first and show why they won't solve the problem. End by discussing a solution that will work. This pattern may be necessary when the audience will find the solution hard to accept.
- **Pro–con.** Give all the reasons in favour of something, then those against it. This pattern works well when you want the audience to see the weaknesses in its position.
- **1–2–3.** Discuss three aspects of a topic. This pattern works well to organize short informative briefings. "Today I'll review our sales, production, and profits for the last quarter."

First, I'd like to talk about who the homeless in Winnipeg are. Second, I'll talk about the services The Open Shelter provides. Finally, I'll talk about what you—either individually or as a group—can do to help.

Make your organization clear to your audience. Early in your talk—perhaps immediately after your opener—provide an overview of the main points you will make.

An overview provides a mental peg that hearers can hang each point on. It also can prevent someone from missing what you are saying because he or she wonders why you aren't covering a major point that you've saved for later.[28]

Offer a clear signpost as you come to each new point. A **signpost** is an explicit statement of the point you have reached. Choose wording that fits your style. The following statements are four different ways that a speaker could use to introduce the last of three points:

Now we come to the third point: what you can do as a group or as individuals to help homeless people in Winnipeg.

So much for what we're doing. Now let's talk about what you can do to help.

You may be wondering, what can I do to help?

As you can see, the Shelter is trying to do many things. We could do more things with your help.

LO4

DELIVERING AN EFFECTIVE PRESENTATION

Audiences want the sense that you're talking directly to them and that you care that they understand and are interested. They'll forgive you if you get tangled up in a sentence and end it ungrammatically. They won't forgive you if you seem to have a "canned" talk that you're going to deliver no matter who the audience is or how they respond. You can convey a sense of caring to your audience by making direct eye contact with them and by using a conversational style.

Dealing with Fear

Feeling nervous is normal. But you can harness that nervous energy to help you do your best work. As Ralph Waldo Emerson said, "All the great speakers were bad speakers at first." And as one student said, "You don't need to get rid of your butterflies. All you need to do is make them fly in formation." Relabel your nerves. Instead of saying, "I'm scared," try saying, "My adrenaline is up." Adrenaline sharpens our reflexes and helps us do our best.

Toastmasters International reassures us that "our chances of dying of stage fright are extremely slim" and that few will "even notice our wobbly knees."[29] They recommend preparing for what can go wrong and being ready with some "clever lines." For example, if the microphone goes dead, you might comment, "Evidently, someone has heard this speech before."[30]

If presentation nerves get the better of you, the "antidote is simple." Redirect attention from yourself to the audience with these six rules:

To calm your nerves before you give an oral presentation,

- **Be prepared.** Analyze your audience, organize your thoughts, prepare visual aids, and practise your opener and close.
- **Check out the venue.** Instead of fearing the unknown, you'll "luxuriate in the known."
- **Connect with your audience.** Connect with those you know, get to know "those you don't," and smile (except when you are delivering bad news).
- **Avoid stimulants.** Use only the amount of caffeine you normally use. More or less may make you jumpy. Avoid alcohol.
- **Have a backup.** Bring a handout in case of technology failures. Be ready to adapt or reduce to fit allotted time.
- **Start slowly.** Take your time so that your audience remains connected throughout.[31]

Just before your presentation,

- Consciously contract and then relax your muscles, starting with your feet and calves and going up to your shoulders, arms, and hands.
- Take several deep breaths from your diaphragm.

During your presentation,

- Pause and look at the audience before you begin speaking.
- Concentrate on communicating well.
- Use body energy in strong gestures and movement.

Using Eye Contact

Look directly at the people you're talking to. In one study, speakers who looked more at the audience during a seven-minute informative speech were judged to be better informed, more experienced, more honest, and friendlier than speakers who delivered the same information with less eye contact.[32] An earlier study found that speakers judged sincere looked at the audience 63% of the time, while those judged insincere looked at the audience only 21% of the time.[33]

The point in making eye contact is to establish one-on-one contact with the individual members of your audience. People want to feel that you're talking to them. Looking directly at individuals also enables you to be more conscious of feedback from the audience, so that you can modify your approach if necessary.

If you lose eye contact, audience members might wonder why you are not looking their way. They might question your honesty: *Why did the speaker look down when announcing the last quarter figures? Why is she looking over my shoulder? Is she searching for someone more important?*

Building and maintaining respect and trust means mastering "the curriculum of eye contact." The best speakers know how to use "visual connectivity." They know when to combine eye contact with a pause, the phrasing, and pacing that signals and supports a major message. But they also know that "unbroken eye contact" can be as ineffective or even as offensive as too little.[34]

Developing a Good Speaking Voice

One of the important lessons of the award-winning movie *The King's Speech* is that even those who feel least equipped (and mortified by the merciless teasing of a stutter) can deliver if they practise, use language with which they are comfortable, and turn their challenges into strengths. For example, by the end of the movie, "King George VI's pauses lend gravitas to his speech."[35] As actor Colin Firth commented, "Rhetoric was important in that job. When he spoke, the nation felt he spoke to and for them. Yet he felt that he couldn't speak."[36]

People will enjoy your presentation more if your voice is easy to listen to. To find out what your voice sounds like, record it. Also record the voices of people on TV or on campus whose voices you like and imitate them. In a few weeks, record yourself again.

To find your best speaking voice, close your ears with your fingers and hum up and down the scale until you find the pitch where the hum sounds loudest or most vibrant to you. This pitch will be near your optimum pitch.[37]

When you speak to a group, talk loudly enough so that people can hear you easily. If you're using a microphone, adjust your volume so you aren't shouting. As you move, turn, and engage your audience, take care to keep speaking into the microphone so that all can hear. When you speak in an unfamiliar location, try to get to the room early so you can check the size of the room and the power of the amplification equipment. If you can't do that, ask early in your talk, "Can you hear me in the back of the room?"

The bigger the group is, the more carefully you need to **enunciate**—that is, voice all the sounds of each word. Words starting or ending with *f, t, k, v,* and *d* are especially hard to hear. "Our informed and competent image" can sound like "Our informed, incompetent image."

To enunciate, use your tongue and lips. Researchers have identified 38 different sounds, of which 31 are made with your tongue and 7 with your lips. None is made with the jaw, so how wide you open your mouth really doesn't matter. If the tongue isn't active enough, muscles in the throat try to compensate, producing sore throats and strained voices.[38]

Tongue twisters can help you exercise your tongue and enunciate more clearly. Stephen Lucas, author of *The Art of Public Speaking,* suggests the following:

- Sid said to tell him that Benny hid the penny many years ago.
- Fetch me the finest French-fried freshest fish that Finney fries.
- Three grey geese in the green grass grazed.[39]

You can also reduce pressure on your throat by fitting phrases to your ideas. If you cut your sentences into bits, you'll emphasize words beginning with vowels, making the vocal cords hit each other. Instead, run past words beginning with vowels to emphasize later syllables or later words[40]:

✗ Choppiness hurts vocal cords:	*We must take more* *responsibility not* *Only for Ourselves* *And Our families* *but for* *Our communities* *And* *Our country.*
✓ Smooth phrasing protects throat:	*We must take more* *Responsibility* *Not only for our* *Selves and our* *Families but for our* *Communities and our* *Country.*

You can reduce the number of *uhs* you use by practising your talk several times. Filler sounds aren't signs of nervousness. Instead, say psychologists, they occur when speakers pause searching for the next word. Searching takes longer when people have big vocabularies or talk about topics where many word choices are possible. Practising your talk makes your word choices automatic, and you'll use fewer *uhs.*[41]

On the Job Words to Embrace/ Words to Avoid*

A proven way to connect with your audience is to use words such as "you" and "we" to make your listeners feel "valued and included." Know and show what interests and engages them and they will reward you by helping you succeed. Consultant Tanja Parsley recommends "easy," "money," and "you" as "language that's compelling."

The wrong words in a presentation can equally undermine your success. They can clutter, distract, obscure—and alienate your audience. Taping yourself or getting feedback from a coach can help identify the problem words.

Prune these words and phrases:

- Negative words: *never, can't, ineffective*
- Sarcastic words: *clearly, in reality, nobody can think that*
- Vague statements: *I believe*
- Confusing constructions: *I wouldn't hesitate to agree—agree!*
- Filler: *umm, O.K., right?*
- Clichés: *To tell the truth, in this day and age*
- Technical jargon: *geek, total sunk costs*
- Colloquialisms: *you guys, like*

*Based on Jacqueline Nelson, "Public speaking need not be an ordeal," *Canadian Business,* March 14, 2011, 67; Jim Gray, "Orator Obama: Lessons for leaders," *The Globe and Mail,* August 29, 2008, B13; Wallace Immen, "Hone the message, trim out the confusing jargon," *The Globe and Mail,* November 4, 2006, B11.

Vary your volume, pitch, and speed. Inexperienced speakers are inclined to rush to the end. Like King George VI, President Barack Obama knows the power of pauses to impress audiences that the speaker is relaxed, confident, and credible.[42] Sound energetic and enthusiastic. If your ideas don't excite you, why should your audience find them exciting?

Standing and Gesturing

Stand with your feet far enough apart for good balance, with your knees flexed. Some speakers like to come in front of the lectern to remove that barrier between themselves and the audience. If you use slides or transparencies, stand beside the screen so that you don't block it.

Unless the presentation is very formal or you are on camera (in an online presentation, for instance), movement will add to the energy and effectiveness of your presentation. We have the technology (wireless microphones and remote controls) to free us to engage our audiences through choreographed movement and gesture.

The best presenters know when to move and mesmerize their audiences and how to "move in tandem with their narrative." Indeed, the effect is to "communicate poise, panache and personality." Even though movement has the power to enhance credibility and persuasion, you need to understand when it won't work for you. Politicians announcing electrical power crises or CEOs announcing layoffs do not want to be seen to be restless and meandering. In short, the "more serious the situation, the less you should move."[43]

Since as much as 65% of our communication depends on body language, it's important to make the most of our gestures. Hand gestures can tell your story graphically and economically, "signal your conviction and confidence, and add texture and dimension to your material and ideas."[44]

Videotaping your presentation can help you see where gestures enhance your power and where they signal stage fright (clutching, clenching, fidgeting). Build on your natural style for gestures. Gestures usually work best when they're confident.

Using Notes and Visuals

Even experts use speaker's or speaking notes or cards to keep their presentations focused and to avoid too many digressions. Put your notes on cards or on sturdy pieces of paper and number them. Most speakers like to use 10 × 15cm or 12 × 17cm cards. Your notes need to be complete enough to help you if you go blank, so use long phrases or complete sentences. Under each main point, jot down the evidence or illustration you'll use. Indicate where you'll refer to visuals.

Look at your notes infrequently. Most of your gaze time should be directed to members of the audience. Hold your notes high enough so that your head doesn't bob up and down as you look from the audience to your notes and back again.

If you have lots of visuals and know your topic well, you won't need notes. Face the audience, not the screen. You can use the presentation software or laser pointer to call attention to your points as you talk. Show the entire visual at once: don't cover up part of it. If you don't want the audience to read ahead, prepare several visuals that build up. In your overview, for example, the first visual could list your first point, the second the first and second, and the third all three points.

Keep the room lights on if possible; turning them off makes it easier for people to fall asleep and harder for them to concentrate on you.

International Presenting across Cultures*

President Barack Obama has been hailed as a great orator who has shown that powerful words can make a difference. Adept at "politics as theatre," Obama has "played his role to perfection," according to communications coach Jim Gray. Yet President Obama received mixed reviews when he addressed the Indian Parliament in the House's Central Hall, November 2010. While some hailed the speech as "vintage Obama," others wondered about his reliance on a teleprompter—a first in this setting. So unfamiliar was it that some commented that it looked "like a podium," but "Where do they put the paper?"

The confusion was caused by the fact that Indian politicians typically give "long, impromptu speeches." One anonymous official explained that people "thought Obama is a trained orator and skilled in the art of mass address with his continuous eye contact."

Hence the surprise at what some call the use of "idiot cards"—and an offence to "a parliamentary tradition in an important ally." According to lawmaker Sanjay Nirupam of Mumbai, "the really good speakers don't need to have a text in front of them."

*Jim Gray, "Orator Obama: Lessons for leaders," *The Globe and Mail*, August 29, 2008, B13; Rama Lakshmi, "Obama's speech, his teleprompter, the reaction," November 8, 2010, retrieved May 19, 2011, from http://voices.washingtonpost.com/44/2010/11/by-rama-lakshmi-in-his.html; "Obama to use teleprompter for Hindi speech," November 9, 2010, retrieved May 19, 2011, from http://www.hindustantimes.com/Obama-to-use-teleprompter-for-Hindi-speech/Article1-622605.aspx; Thomas Lifson, "Obama's teleprompter embarrassment in India," posted October 22, 2010, retrieved from http://www.americanthinker.com/blog/2010/10/obamas_teleprompter_embarrassm.html.

LO5

HANDLING QUESTIONS

Prepare for questions by listing every fact or opinion you can think of that challenges your position. Treat each objection seriously and try to think of a way to deal with it. If you're talking about a controversial issue, you may want to save one point for the question period, rather than making it during the presentation. Speakers who have visuals to answer questions seem especially well prepared.

During your presentation, tell the audience how you'll handle questions. If you have a choice, save questions for the end. In your talk, answer the questions or objections that you expect your audience to have. Don't exaggerate your claims so that you won't have to back down in response to questions later.

During the question period, don't nod your head to indicate that you understand a question as it is asked. Audiences will interpret nods as signs that you agree with the questioner. Instead, look directly at the questioner. As you answer the question, expand your focus to take in the entire group. Don't say, "That's a good question." That response implies that the other questions have been poor ones.

If the audience may not have heard the question or if you want more time to think, repeat the question before you answer it. Link your answers to the points you made in your presentation. Keep the purpose of your presentation in mind, and select information that advances your goals.

If a question is hostile or biased, rephrase it before you answer it: "You're asking whether. . . ." Or suggest an alternative question: "I think there are problems with both the positions you describe. It seems to me that a third solution that is better than either of them is. . . ."

Canadian presentation skills coach James Gray gives this advice for handling "the audience bully":

- Engage and make an ally of the know-it-all.
- Ask for his or her views, make the bully a co-presenter, and then re-establish your expertise.
- Freeze out if the bully persists in intervening (limit eye contact and your responses).
- Involve the whole group if interruption persists ("How should we handle this problem?").
- Establish ground rules (no shouting or insults) when you anticipate controversy.[45]

Occasionally someone will ask a question that is really designed to state the speaker's own position. Respond to the question if you choose. Another option is to say, "That's a clear statement of your position. Let's move to the next question now." If someone asks about something that you already explained in your presentation, simply answer the question without embarrassing the questioner. No audience will understand and remember 100% of what you say.

If you don't know the answer to a question, say so. If your purpose is to inform, write down the question so that you can look up the answer before the next session. If it's a question to which you think there is no answer, ask if anyone in the room knows. When no one does, your "ignorance" is vindicated. If an expert is in the room, you may want to refer questions of fact to him or her. Answer questions of interpretation yourself.

At the end of the question period, take two minutes to summarize your main point once more. (This can be a restatement of your close.) Questions may or may not focus on the key point of your talk. Take advantage of having the floor to repeat your message briefly and forcefully.

On the Job Avoid Ten Common Presentation Errors

- Failing to test equipment before the presentation
- Rushing the introduction
- Failing to give clear overview
- Reading from slides
- Talking in a monotone
- Walking/standing in front of the screen
- Creating hard-to-read slides (too small font, too much text)
- Using text and background colours with poor contrast
- Incorporating clip art to fill space rather than clarify point
- Ignoring time limits

LO6

MAKING GROUP PRESENTATIONS

Group presentations are a key part of the teamwork our economies and organizations now demand (see ◂◂ Chapter 6). Plan carefully to involve as many members of the group as possible in speaking roles. Group presentations can benefit not only from diverse perspectives and talents, voices, styles, and paces, but also from team building activities that nurture cohesion. Learning to appreciate one another's style is as much a valued outcome as the ability to sway your audience.

The easiest way to make a group presentation is to outline the presentation and then divide the topics, giving one to each group member. Another member can be responsible for the opener and the close. During the question period, each member answers questions that relate to his or her topic.

In this kind of divided presentation, be sure to

- Plan transitions.
- Establish seating or standing arrangements to minimize disruption and audience distractions.
- Enforce time limits strictly.
- Coordinate your visuals so that the presentation seems a coherent whole.
- Practise the presentation as a group at least once; more is better.

The best group presentations are much more fully integrated: the group problem solves, writes a detailed outline, chooses points and examples, consolidates key messages, creates visuals together—and becomes a team.

Then, within each point, voices trade off. This presentation is most effective because each voice speaks only a minute or two before a new voice comes in. However, it works only when all group members know the subject well and when the group plans carefully and practises extensively.

Practice helps you anticipate audience needs and decide who will handle technology, how you will arrange yourselves, what you will wear, what formality is required, where transitions are needed, and how to handle questions. You will agree who will answer what sorts of questions, knowing who feels confident with details, the big picture, research sources, personal experience, or exemplary anecdotes (see also "Handling Questions" earlier in this chapter). Whatever form of group presentation you use, be sure to introduce each member of the team to the audience and use the opportunity to reinforce names, topics, and messages: "Next, Raquel will discuss the project timelines." By taking your time with introductions and transitions, you are personalizing your presentation, increasing the audience comfort level, and helping them engage with you. It is easier to ask a question when you are confident that you have the speaker's name right, for example.

Pay close attention to each other, and model behaviour for the audience. Smile at a play on words, for instance. If other members of the team seem uninterested in the speaker, the audience gets the sense that that speaker isn't worth listening to. With this kind of planning, preparation, and practice, you will look and sound like a thoroughly professional team.

A group presentation aims to show how Hong Kong can help Canadian companies doing business in China.

EVALUATING PRESENTATIONS

Whether presenting individually or in groups, giving and receiving feedback is critical to improvement and presentation success. Invite as much feedback when you are practising as when you present in formal situations. Learn from audiotapes and videotapes of your presentations. Learn from the informal and formal feedback, from the body language as well as the verbal feedback. Even if a listener has misheard or misunderstood your point, focus on the opportunity to be even clearer next time. Figure 12.4 provides a checklist for oral presentations.

If you are assessing your own, your group's, or others' presentations, these criteria can be useful guides to success (see also ⏩ problems 12.6, 12.7, and 12.8):

- Verbal skills (enunciation, phrasing, pitch, projection, speed)
- Nonverbal skills (body language, eye contact, movement, gesture, dress)
- Readable, relevant, professional visuals
- Clear purpose, logical organization, appropriate evidence
- Engaging opener and compelling conclusion
- Signposts, transitions, previews, reviews, reinforcements
- Team identity, participation, cohesion, timing, enthusiasm
- Creativity, coherence, responsiveness, professionalism

Figure 12.4 Checklist for Oral Presentations

Strategy

- ☐ Choosing an effective kind of presentation for the situation
- ☐ Adapting ideas to audience's beliefs, experiences, and interests
- ☐ Using a strong opening and close
- ☐ Using visual aids or other devices to involve the audience

Content

- ☐ Using specific, vivid supporting material and language
- ☐ Providing rebuttals to counterclaims or objections
- ☐ Strengthening credibility by making research visible

Organization

- ☐ Providing an overview of main points
- ☐ Signposting main points in body of talk
- ☐ Providing adequate transitions between points and speakers

Visuals

- ☐ Using an appropriate design or template
- ☐ Using standard edited English
- ☐ Being creative

Delivery

- ☐ Making direct eye contact with audience
- ☐ Using voice and gestures effectively
- ☐ Handling questions effectively
- ☐ Maintaining appropriate stance, position (not blocking screen)

SUMMARY OF KEY POINTS

- *Informative presentations* inform or teach the audience. *Persuasive presentations* motivate the audience to act or to believe. *Goodwill presentations* entertain and validate the audience. Most oral presentations have more than one purpose.
- A strategy is your plan for reaching your specific goals with a specific audience.
- An oral presentation needs to be simpler than a written message to the same audience.
- In a *monologue presentation,* the speaker plans the presentation in advance and delivers it without deviation. In a *guided discussion,* the speaker serves as a facilitator to help the audience tap its own knowledge. An *interactive presentation* is a conversation using questions to determine the buyer's needs, probe objections, and gain provisional and then final commitment to the purchase.
- Preparing an outline is as important to planning a presentation as it is to planning a piece of writing. An outline is your guide or map to help you carry your audience with you and help them (and you) know where you are going and why. It can also be the basis of your speaker's notes.
- Make your ideas relevant to your audience by linking what you have to say to their experiences and interests.
- Use the beginning and end of the presentation to interest the audience, emphasize your key point, and establish your credibility.
- Plan visuals to involve your audience. For large and dispersed audiences, a webinar or seminar delivered over the Web may be the right choice.
- Five ways to organize your presentation include chronological, problem-causes-solution, exclude alternatives, pro-con, and 1-2-3.
- Convey a sense that you're talking directly to the audience and that you care that they understand and are interested. Use nerves to advantage, make eye contact, develop a good speaking voice, move to mesmerize your audience, and use visuals to seem more prepared and persuasive.
- Treat questions as opportunities to give more detailed information than you had time to give in your presentation. Link your answers to the points you made in your presentation.
- The best group presentations result when the group problem solves, writes a very detailed outline, chooses points and examples, consolidates key messages, and creates visuals together. Then, within each point, voices trade off.
- Ongoing evaluation is critical to improvement and presentation success.

EXERCISES AND PROBLEMS

GETTING STARTED

12.1 ANALYZING OPENERS AND CLOSES

The following openers and closes came from class presentations on information interviews. As your professor directs, peer grade answers.

- Does each opener make you interested in hearing the rest of the presentation?
- Does each opener provide a transition to the overview?
- Does the close end the presentation in a satisfying way?

a. Opener: I interviewed Mark Perry at CIBC.
   Close: Well, that's my report.

b. Opener: How many of you know what you want to do when you graduate?
   Close: So, if you like numbers and want to travel, think about being a CMA. Ernst & Young can take you all over the world.

c. Opener: You don't have to know anything about computer programming to get a job as a technical writer at SaskTel.
   Close: After talking to Raj, I decided technical writing isn't for me. But it is a good career if you work well under pressure and like learning new things all the time.

d. Opener: My report is about what it's like to work in an advertising agency.
   Middle: They keep really tight security; I had to wear a badge and be escorted to Susan's desk.
   Close: Susan gave me samples of the agency's ads and even a sample of a new soft drink she's developing a campaign for. But she didn't let me keep the badge.

12.2 DEVELOPING STORIES

Think of personal anecdotes that you could use to open or illustrate presentations on the following topics:

1. Why people need to plan.
2. Dealing with change.
3. The importance of lifelong learning.
4. The value of good customer service.
5. The culture of an organization you know well.

As Your Professor Directs,

a. Share your stories with a small group of students.
b. Include your stories in a blog posted to the class.
c. Make an oral presentation using one of the stories.

PRESENTATION ASSIGNMENTS

12.3 MAKING A SHORT ORAL PRESENTATION

As Your Professor Directs,

In pairs or individually, make a short (three- to five-minute) presentation with PowerPoint slides on one of the following topics:

a. Explain how what you've learned in classes, in campus activities, or at work will be useful to the employer who hires you after graduation.

b. Profile someone who is successful in the field you hope to enter and explain what makes him or her successful.

c. Describe a specific situation in an organization in which communication was handled well or badly.

d. Make a short presentation based on another problem in this book:

1.5 Explain the role of communication in your organization.

5.1 Tell the class about your learning in the multicultural classroom.

6.7 Share your recommendations for a mobile device/laptop policy.

13.1 Tell the class in detail about one of your accomplishments.

12.4 MAKING A LONGER ORAL PRESENTATION

As Your Professor Directs,

In pairs or groups, make a 5- to 12-minute presentation on one of the following. Use visuals to make your talk effective.

a. Show why your unit is important to the organization and either should be exempt from downsizing or should receive additional resources.

b. Persuade your supervisor to make a change that will benefit the organization.

c. Persuade your organization to make a change that will improve the organization's image in the community.

d. Persuade classmates to donate time or money to a charitable organization. (Read Chapter 9.)

e. Persuade an employer that you are the best person for the job.

f. Use another problem in this book as the basis for your presentation:

3.1 Describe the composing process(es) of a writer you've interviewed.

4.1 Evaluate the page design of one or more documents.

4.6 Evaluate the design of a Web page.

5.5 Analyze international messages that your workplace has created or received.

9.4 Analyze one or more sales or fundraising letters.

9.10 Persuade your campus to fund the Writing Centre.

11.9 Summarize the results of a survey you have conducted.

11.14 Summarize the results of your research.

12.5 MAKING A GROUP ORAL PRESENTATION

As Your Professor Directs,

Make a 5- to 12-minute presentation on one of the following. Or present findings for Problem 12.7 or 12.8. Use visuals to make your talk effective.

a. Explain the role of communication in one or more organizations.

b. Report on another country.

c. Present brochures you have designed to the class.

d. Describe the listening strategies of workers you have interviewed.

EVALUATION ASSIGNMENTS

12.6 EVALUATING ORAL PRESENTATIONS

Evaluate an oral presentation given by a classmate or given by a speaker on your campus. Use the categories listed in the Checklist for Oral Presentations (◂◂ Figure 12.4):

As Your Professor Directs,

a. Fill out a form indicating your evaluation in each of the areas.

b. Share your evaluation orally with the speaker.

c. Write an e-mail to the speaker evaluating the presentation. Send a copy of your e-mail to your professor.

12.7 EVALUATING TEAM PRESENTATIONS

Evaluate team presentations using the following questions:

1. How thoroughly were all team members involved?
2. Did members of the team introduce themselves or each other?
3. Did team members seem interested in what their teammates said?
4. How well was the material organized?
5. How well did the material hold your interest?
6. How clear did the material seem to you?
7. How effective were the visuals?
8. How well did the team handle questions?
9. What could be done to improve the presentation?
10. What were the strong points of the presentation?

As Your Professor Directs,

a. Fill out a form indicating your evaluation in each of the areas.

b. Share your evaluation orally with the team.

c. Write an e-mail to the team evaluating the presentation. Send a copy of your e-mail to your professor.

12.8 EVALUATING THE WAY A SPEAKER HANDLES QUESTIONS

Listen to a speaker talking about a controversial subject. (Go to a talk on campus or in town, or watch a speaker on a TV show such as *Dragons' Den* or *Marketplace.*) Observe the way he or she handles questions.

- About how many questions does the speaker answer?
- What is the format for asking and answering questions?
- Are the answers clear? Responsive to the question? Something that could be quoted without embarrassing the speaker and the organization he or she represents?
- How does the speaker handle hostile questions? Does the speaker avoid getting angry? Does the speaker retain control of the meeting? If so, how?
- If some questions were not answered well, what (if anything) could the speaker have done to leave a better impression?
- Did the answers leave the audience with a more or less positive impression of the speaker? Why?

As Your Professor Directs,

a. Share your evaluation with a small group of students.

b. Present your evaluation formally to the class.

c. Summarize your evaluation in an e-mail to your professor.

EMPLOYMENT COMMUNICATIONS

13

Learning Outcomes

LO1 Explain the complementary parts of the job search process

LO2 List the advantages and disadvantages of different kinds of résumés

LO3 Distinguish the conventional parts of résumés

LO4 Explain how job letters differ from résumés

LO5 Describe how to organize a job application letter

LO6 Explain how to develop an interview strategy

LO7 Distinguish kinds of interviews

LO8 Discuss performance appraisals

AN INSIDE PERSPECTIVE

When she applied to become Marketing Manager at Bravado! Designs, Toronto, Alina Szober Morkin was interested in the company's work–life balance policy. When she discovered its green practices, she was sold: "If a company is responsible to their community and environment, then that really tells you something about them. It's a reflection of their bigger corporate value system." Szober Morkin is now Senior Marketing Manager at CarProof, London, ON, one of Canada's 50 Best Managed Companies.

Learning how to manage and market yourself is not as natural or self-evident as it sounds. In fact, you may find yourself overlooking the meaning and value of who you are and what you have achieved! Yet developing the complementary parts of the job search is a critical professional skill that we all need to nourish so that we can land our dream job.

Know Yourself

Career consultant Niels Lindhard advises that "until you know who you are, you cannot know what you can become." The basis of any good job search strategy is therefore to know yourself, to identify your strengths and weaknesses, values and goals, skills and abilities, education and experience. You can get help from career counsellors, business seminars and networking connections, and online and print resources.

Know Job Trends

Understand the major trends in the business world (◂◂ Chapter 1) and the range of skills and competencies that employers are looking for. Know that communications skills remain number one (see Conference Board of Canada Employability Skills, ◂◂ Figure 1.7). Research the industry or profession as well as the particular businesses and organizations that you target. Know the trends, learn the language and culture, show your value by speaking in their terms. Nothing, not even your degree, speaks for itself.

Know the Job Search Process

The process is less sequential than simultaneous—repeated efforts at self-evaluation, targeting careers, researching, networking, calling, answering ads, writing résumés and cover letters—a set of complementary strategies designed to secure an interview for your job target. Learn how to access the hidden job market, how to make opportunities happen for you. Don't rely on luck: be proactive and get the information that will translate into opportunities—and the outcomes you want.

Informal preparation for a job search should start soon after you arrive on campus. Join extracurricular organizations on campus and in the community to increase your knowledge and provide a network for learning. Find a job that gives you experience. Note which courses you like—and why you like them. If you like thinking and learning about a subject, you're more likely to enjoy a job in that field.

Formal preparation for job hunting should begin a full year *before you begin interviewing*. Visit the campus placement office to see what services it provides. Attend job fairs—or virtual fairs such as the Monster.ca one. Ask friends who are in the job market about their interview experiences and job offers. Check into the possibility of an internship or a co-op job that will give you relevant experience before you interview.

Try to have a job offer lined up *before* you get the degree. People who don't need jobs immediately are more confident in interviews and usually get better job offers. If you have to job-hunt after graduation, plan to spend at least 30 hours a week on your job search. The time will pay off in a better job that you find more quickly.

This chapter guides you through the job search process, from knowing your own worth and the needs of the market to making strategic use of paper, Web, and scannable résumés, job application letters (cover letters), interviews, and communications after the interview and on the job. The focus is on the job search in Canada. Conventions, expectations, and criteria differ from culture to culture: different norms apply in different countries.

All job communications must be tailored to your unique qualifications. Adopt the wording or layout of an example if it's relevant to your own situation, but don't be locked in to the forms in this book. You've got different strengths; your application will be different, too.

LO1

EVALUATING YOUR STRENGTHS AND INTERESTS

A self-assessment is the first step in producing a good job search strategy. It is at the heart of defining your "career brand" or identity so that you can position yourself in social and other media.[1] Each person could do several jobs happily. Personality and aptitude tests can tell you what your strengths are, but they won't say, "You should be a _____." You'll still need to answer questions like those listed in Figure 13.1.

You may find that workplace culture is as valuable to you as to Alina Szober Morkin (◀◀ An Inside Perspective). If so, you are like many of the 33,000 students in Canada surveyed in 2013, although business students rated high earnings and advancement more highly than people and culture.[2]

Once you uncover what is most important to you, analyze the job market to see where you could find what you want. For example, your greatest interest is athletics, but you aren't good enough for the pros. Studying the job market might suggest several alternatives. You could teach sports and physical fitness as a high school coach or a corporate fitness director. You could cover sports for a newspaper, a magazine, or a TV station. You could go into management or sales for a professional sports team, a health club, or a company that sells sports equipment.

DEALING WITH DIFFICULTIES

This section gives advice on how to highlight the positives of experience job hunters often overlook or undervalue. The examples here (and in ▶▶ "Putting Motherhood on Your Résumé" later in this chapter) demonstrate the importance of portable or transferable skills. Although not in your job title, you may well have built valuable communication, time management, conflict resolution, problem solving, or other relevant skills.

Figure 13.1 Self-assessment Checklist

- ☐ What achievements have given you the most satisfaction? *Why* did you enjoy them?
- ☐ Do you prefer working alone or with other people?
- ☐ Do you prefer specific instructions and standards for evaluation or freedom and uncertainty? How comfortable are you with pressure? Would you rather have firm deadlines or a flexible schedule?
- ☐ How confident are you in your communications abilities? Writing, presenting, social media?
- ☐ Are you willing to take work home? To relocate? To travel? To take contract or part-time work?
- ☐ Are you willing to pay your dues for several years before you are promoted? How much challenge do you want?
- ☐ How important is money to you? Prestige? Time to spend with family and friends?
- ☐ Where do you want to live? What weather, geography, cultural, and social life do you see as ideal?
- ☐ Do you see work as just a way to make a living? Or is it about values? Are the organization's culture and ethical standards important to you?

"All My Experience Is in My Family's Business"

In your résumé, simply list the company you worked for. For a reference, instead of a family member, list a supervisor, client, or vendor who can talk about your work. Since the reader may wonder whether "Jim Clarke" is any relation to the owner of "Clarke Construction Company," be ready to answer interview questions about why you're looking at other companies. Prepare an answer that stresses the broader opportunities you seek but doesn't criticize your family or the family business. Remember too that those who work in the family business often amass a valuable range of experience.

"I've Been Out of the Job Market for a While"

You need to prove to a potential employer that you're up to date and motivated:

- Be active in professional organizations. Attend meetings; read trade journals.
- Learn the computer programs that professionals in your field use.
- Find out your prospective employer's immediate priorities. If you can show you'll contribute from day one, you'll have a much easier sell.
- Show how your at-home experience relates to the workplace. Dealing with unpredictable situations, building consensus, listening, raising money, and making presentations are transferable skills.
- Create a portfolio of your work (see ▶▶ "What's in Your E-Portfolio?" later in this chapter)—even if it's for imaginary clients—to demonstrate your expertise.[3] It may also get you Prior Learning Assessment and Recognition (PLAR) for post-secondary credits.

"I Want to Change Fields"

Have a good reason for choosing the field in which you're looking for work.

Think about how your experience relates to the job you want—and the benefits to the employer. Jack is an older-than-average student who wants to be a pharmaceutical sales representative. He has sold woodstoves, served subpoenas, and worked on an oil rig. A chronological résumé makes his work history look directionless. But a skills résumé could focus on persuasive ability (selling stoves), initiative and persistence (serving subpoenas), and technical knowledge (courses in biology and chemistry).[4]

"I Was Fired"

First, deal with the emotional baggage before you're ready to job-hunt.

Second, try to learn from the experience. You'll be a much more attractive job candidate if you can show that you've improved work habits, for example.

Third, suggests Phil Elder, an interviewer for an insurance company, call the person who fired you and say something like this: "Look, I know you weren't pleased with the job I did at _____. I'm applying for a job at _____ now and the personnel director may call you to ask about me. Would you be willing to give me the chance to get this job so that I can try to do things right this time?" All but the hardest of heart, says Elder, will give you one more chance. You won't get a glowing reference, but neither will the statement be so damning that no one is willing to hire you.[5]

"I Don't Have Any Experience"

If you have a year or more before you job-hunt, you can get experience in several ways:

- **Take a fast-food job—and keep it.** If you do well, you'll be promoted to a supervisor within a year. Use every opportunity to learn about the management and financial aspects of the business.
- **Volunteer.** If you work hard, you'll quickly get an opportunity to do more: manage a budget, write fundraising materials, and supervise other volunteers.
- **Freelance.** Design brochures, create Web pages, blog, do tax returns for small businesses. Use your skills—for free, if you have to at first.[6]
- **Write.** Create a portfolio of ads, instructions, or whatever documents are relevant for the field you want to enter. Volunteer social media expertise—Twitter, Facebook, LinkedIn, blogging—to promote your favourite non-profit.

Pick something where you interact with other people, so that you can show you can work well in an organization.

Identify your transferable skills. If you are in the job market now, think carefully about what you have really done and see your value from the perspective of employers, avoiding underestimating your worth (see the relevant student learning in ◀◀Figure 11.4). Consider the action verbs in Figure 13.5 (later in this chapter). Think about what you have done in courses, in volunteer work, in unpaid activities. Focus on skills in problem solving, critical thinking, teamwork, cultural competence (◀◀Chapter 5) as well as communication. Solving a problem for a hypothetical firm in an accounting class, thinking critically about a report problem in business communication, working with a group in a marketing class, and communicating with people at the senior centre where you volunteer are experience, even if no one paid you.

FINDING OUT ABOUT EMPLOYERS AND JOBS

Knowing job trends and researching industries, professions, and businesses helps you match your skills and strategy to the needs of employers. If arts graduates were inclined to focus on what they didn't have—a business degree—they are learning to sell what they can do. Toronto recruitment consultant Greg Arbitman points to a "general shift" among his clients, who feel arts grads "have the ability to think outside the box." Arts grads "can present, do research, interact with peers, articulate messaging"—skills especially important in the context of social media. Still, like others, they need to sell their skills, not just their degrees.[7]

Dean Roger Martin of Toronto's Rotman School of Management agrees that students need "to learn how to think critically and creatively" as much as "to learn finance or accounting." The financial crisis has increased demand for flexible, critical thinkers and is reshaping MBA programs focused on "leadership and social responsibility and, yes, learning how to think critically."[8]

In their 2012 book, Lee Rainie, director of Pew Research Center Internet and American Life Project, and Barry Wellman, director of NetLab, University of Toronto, give new meaning to networking in the context of social media. The quantity and quality of people's social networks are a critical business resource whereby the best become invaluable "information brokers" representing a significant return on investment.[9]

The trend to "employer brands" to attract and retain the best gives access to broad company information. PepsiCo, for instance, focuses less on its consumer brands and more on videos of employees on its careers page and iPad application. It has revised its LinkedIn, Facebook, and Twitter profiles accordingly. Employer branding may not attract more applications (although AT&T noted a 20% increase), but its focus is on attracting the best candidates.[10]

Interested in both recruitment and retention, Deloitte invested in a Deloitte Film Festival asking 40,000 dispersed employees to make three-minute films on "What's Your Deloitte?" Seventy-five percent participated in "filmmaking, viewing, rating and/or voting" and 76.4% claimed "deeper connections to their local office."[11]

Another Deloitte strategy to recruit those that can navigate a fast-changing world of ambiguity is its pilot, Deloitte Distinction, with the Rotman School of Management at the University of Toronto. Of 25 selected students participating in workshops and career coaching, Deloitte hired two.[12]

Google's chief financial officer is actively engaged in its "recruitment pitch" telling Canadians "to send their CVs in" and relying on their new offices, bonuses, and stock options to attract candidates to "an unconventional company": "And we are looking for unconventional people."[13]

The Internet is an invaluable source of advice and information on companies and on meeting *their* needs in your applications (see Figure 13.2). To adapt your job search strategy to a specific organization, you need information both about the employer and about the job itself (check Web sites, Twitter, Facebook, and LinkedIn profiles, and talk to your contacts). Social media and your network of contacts are critical when 24% of companies are relying less on "third-party employment

Figure 13.2 Comprehensive Web Job Sites Covering the Entire Job Search Process

Aboriginal Affairs and Northern Development Canada: https://www.aadnc-aandc.gc.ca/eng/1100100033784/1100100033788

AboriginalCareers.ca: http://www.aboriginalcareers.ca/

Canadian Association of Career Educators and Employers: www.cacee.com/

Canadian Careers: www.canadiancareers.com/

Career Beacon: www.careerbeacon.com/

Career Edge: https://www.careeredge.ca/

Employment and Social Development Canada: www.esdc.gc.ca/eng/home.shtml

Job Bank: www.jobbank.gc.ca/

Job Hunters Bible: www.jobhuntersbible.com/

Monster: www.monster.ca/

National Educational Association of Disabled Students (NEADS) Online Work System: www.neads.ca/

Public Service Commission of Canada: http://www.psc-cfp.gc.ca/index-eng.htm

Working: www.working.com/life/story.html

Workopolis: www.workopolis.com/

websites and job boards" and 80% are turning to employee referrals and Facebook or LinkedIn to avoid being overwhelmed by online applications.[14]

A 2013 study by CareerXroads found that 42 percent of hirings involved current employees and that those with referrals were "three to four times more likely to be hired." So cultivating your brand online and off remains key. According to Toronto *Get the Job* author, Pamela Paterson, "It's never just about the résumé—never."[15]

If summer employment is your goal, don't neglect traditional venues, especially when Statistics Canada recorded only a 51.8% full-time employment rate for students in 2010. Dominica Whittaker of Toronto's Youth Employment Services says that online searches are least effective for summer jobs: "many employers don't post openings on the web, opting for . . . internal postings, responding to cold calls."[16]

Whatever platform you use, you'll need to know the following:

- **The name and address of the person you should address.** Check the ad, call the organization, or visit its Web site. An advantage of calling is that you can find out what courtesy title (◂◂ Chapter 2) a woman prefers and get current information.
- **What the organization does, and at least four or five facts about it.** Knowing the organization's larger goals enables you to show how your specific work will help the company meet its goals. Useful facts can include
- Market share
- New products, services, or promotions
- Plans for growth or downsizing
- Challenges and opportunities the organization faces
- The corporate culture (◂◂ Chapter 2).

To learn about new products, plans for growth, or solutions to industry challenges, keep connected to your networks (via social and other media), and read business newspapers such as *The Globe and Mail*, *The Wall Street Journal*, the *National Post*, or the *Financial Post;* business magazines such as *Canadian Business*, *Report on Business*, *Fortune*, and *BusinessWeek;* and trade journals. (See Figure 13.2.)

In an **information interview** you talk to someone who works in the field you hope to enter to find out what the day-to-day work involves and how you can best prepare. Here is what an information interview can do for you:

- Give you specific information that you can use to present yourself effectively in your résumé and letter
- Create a good image of you in the mind of the interviewer who may remember you when openings arise

In an information interview, you might ask these questions:

- What are you working on right now?
- How do you spend your typical day?
- Have your duties changed much since you started working here?
- What do you like best about your job? What do you like least?
- What do you think the future holds for this kind of work?
- How did you get this job?
- What courses, activities, or jobs would you recommend to someone who wanted to do this kind of work?

To set up an information interview, you can phone, e-mail, or write a letter like the one in Figure 13.3. If you do write, phone the following week to set up a specific time.

Many jobs are never advertised—and the number rises the higher on the job ladder you go. More than 60% of all new jobs come not from responding to an ad but from networking with personal contacts.[17] Some of these jobs are created especially for a specific person. According to Steven Rothberg, founder of CollegeRecruiter.com, 80% of jobs are unlisted.[18] These unadvertised jobs are called the **hidden job market.** Referral interviews, an organized method of networking, offer the most systematic way to tap into these jobs.

Referral interviews are interviews you schedule to learn about current job opportunities in your field. Sometimes an interview that starts out as an information interview turns into a referral interview.

A **referral interview** should refer you to other people who can tell you about job opportunities, and enable the interviewer to see that you could make a contribution to his or her organization. Therefore, the goal of a referral interview is to put you face to face with someone who has the power to hire you.

Figure 13.3 Letter Requesting an Information Interview

Use the courtesy title the reader prefers

Refer to any previous contact with reader

Ask about ways to enter the field

Even though you shouldn't depend on the reader to call you, it's polite to give your phone number under your name

If starting with the request seems too abrupt, work up to it more gradually

Mentioning your qualifications and including a sample of your work may help persuade the reader to take time to see you

72 E. 13th Avenue
Windsor, ON N9B 2P1

April 4, 2015

Mrs. Kam Yuricich
Clary Communications
372 Sunset Avenue
Windsor, ON N9B 3P4

Dear Mrs. Yuricich:

May I schedule an information interview with you to learn more about how public relations consultants interact with their clients?

Your talk at the University of Windsor last month about the differences between working for a PR firm and being a PR staff person within an organization was inspiring. Last summer I had the chance to work as an intern at Management Horizons. While many of my assignments were "gofer" jobs, my supervisor gave me the chance to work on several brochures and to draft blogs and two speeches for managers. I enjoyed this variety and would like to learn more about the possibility of working in a PR firm.

Perhaps we could also talk about courses that would best prepare me for PR work. I have a year and a half left before I graduate, and I have room for several free electives in my schedule. I'd like to use them as productively as possible.

I'll call you early next week to set up an appointment. I look forward to your advice as I attempt to find my niche in the workforce.

Sincerely,

Lee Tan

Lee Tan
555-5932

Encl.: Marketing Brochure for the Cleary International Centre

Technology Tips Ten Deadly Job Search Sins*

You may think you are ready for the job market, but you may have overlooked communications that could return to haunt you. If you want to be taken seriously, take yourself seriously. Invest in the careful preparation needed to sell your skills throughout the job search.

- Avoid postings on Facebook, MySpace, YouTube, Twitter, or other social networking sites that you would not want potential employers to see.
- Do not use the scatter-gun approach blasting your résumé across cyberspace.
- Do not rely on generic cover letters and résumés that give little sense of what makes you the best qualified candidate.
- Eliminate from letters and résumés typographical, spelling, and grammar errors that mark you as unprofessional—or worse.
- Avoid textspeak that works for friends better than for hiring managers.
- Jettison emoticons that might be read as immature.
- Do not just rely on academic achievements to win the day in interviews.
- Do not forget to bring specific evidence of your invaluable soft skills, such as communications, leadership, and organizational abilities.
- Avoid hasty cell phone messages too soon after interviews to have digested the experience.
- Never fail to respect personal space. Do not presume to call an interviewer's cell phone or send an invitation to your personal Facebook page—unless the company itself uses social networking sites for recruitment.

*Based on Amanda Ash, "Reputation on the line," Saskatoon *StarPhoenix*, September 26, 2009, E1; Darcy Keith, "Job application should be customized: Focus on job," *National Post*, April 30, 2008, WK5; Brian Morton, "A typo that could ruin your career: Resume must be error free," *National Post*, November 15, 2006, WK4; Sarah E. Needleman, "Thx 4 cing me. Wud luv a job!" *The Globe and Mail*, August 15, 2008, C3.

Technology Tips The Accidental Job Hunter*

Jennifer Beardsley found her job as marketing manager for Starbucks almost by accident. Checking her business school alumni page for news of friends, she found a link to Career Central for MBAs (www.mbacentral.com). Bored, she typed in her profile one night in about 20 minutes. "I wasn't really looking for a job," she said.

Six weeks later, she got an e-mail asking her if she wanted to send her résumé to Starbucks, where the Web page had found a match. She did, and she got the job.

Digital profiles matter more than ever, according to Gord Brandt, a Toronto-based consultant: "Companies are using social media as a convenient way to approach people indirectly" in the event that they are open to a new job.

A tweet about a social media communications job in Ottawa found Mark Buell, who until then had no interest in a new position. Three weeks after submitting his cover letter and résumé, he was interviewed and his own Twitter record landed him the job.

According to one study, 48% of Canadians found jobs through informal networks. A 2011 survey of U.S. and Canadian employers found that 32% were using employee referrals.

*Based on "The accidental job seeker," *Fast Company,* August 1998, 198; Virginia Galt, "Networking tops Web in CEO job search," *The Globe and Mail,* April 4, 2001, M1; Wallace Immen, "Why the race for a job just got slower," *Report on Business,* May 6, 2011, B18; Wallace Immen, "Tweet your way to a job," *The Globe and Mail,* May 19, 2010, B16.

Then, armed with a referral from someone you know, you call Mr. or Ms. Big and say, "So-and-so suggested I talk with you about job-hunting strategy." If the person says, "We aren't hiring," you say, "Oh, I'm not asking *you* for a job. I'd just like some advice from a knowledgeable person about the opportunities in banking [or desktop publishing, or whatever] in this city." If this person doesn't have the power to create a position, you seek more referrals at the end of *this* interview. (You can also polish your résumé, if you get good suggestions.)

Some business people are cynical about information and referral interviewing. Prepare carefully for these interviews just as some resist networking that is too evidently just about looking for a job. Think in advance of good questions; know something about the general field or industry; try to learn at least a little bit about the specific company.

Always follow up information and referral interviews with personal thank-you cards or letters. Use specifics to show that you paid attention during the interview, and enclose a copy of your revised résumé.

Be aware too that you may be the object of "stealth recruiting." In the current job market, employers are actively searching out potential employees and are turning to LinkedIn, Facebook, and other social networking sites to identify likely candidates who may be ready to consider new opportunities. In this context it is important to consider how you are coming across on these sites. You never know who is watching.[19] A 2013 study reported that 43 percent of managers (up from 34 percent in 2012) found evidence on social media that caused them not to hire job candidates.[20]

While some applicants can be indiscreet or unprofessional in their social media presence, companies have also been found to act unprofessionally or worse. A Carnegie Mellon University study reported that Facebook posts revealing religious affiliation resulted in Muslims being less likely to receive interviews than Christians. Screening based on illegal factors such as religion, age, or sexuality is "an example of unintended consequences of information sharing online."[21]

On the Job Putting Motherhood on Your Résumé*

When Barbara Mossberg was a candidate for president of Goddard College, Vermont, she listed as her greatest accomplishment "creating a nurturing structure in which to witness and guide the growth of unique human beings." She not only got the job but also had her answer posted on the college Web site.

Many professionals agree that parenting has made them better professionals. In a 2010 survey, 38% of women said that "being mothers actually made them better employees." Employers found too that they are "our best and most efficient staff." Yet few list parenting among their credentials. And they still face bias that is "unjustified." says Professor Jennifer Berdahl, Rotman School of Management, Toronto.

Anne Crittenden says it is time to see parenting as one more career of many in our lifetime. And her interviews suggest the time is right and attitudes are changing.

In an advertising profession desperate for talent, women face real employment opportunities. Still dominated by men at the top by a ratio of 2.77 to 1, the profession produces ads that 58% of women claim annoy them. So in advertising, as in many other professions, those parenting skills—people, organizational, and financial planning skills—are in high demand.

*Based on Zosia Bielski, "In: Baby care; Out: Job care," *The Globe and Mail,* March 9, 2010, L1-2; Ann Crittenden, "Time to put motherhood on your résumé," *Globe Careers,* March 25, 2005, B16; Keith McArthur, "Got itchy feet? You must be in the ad biz," *Globe Careers,* April 6, 2005, C1.

LO2

UNDERSTANDING KINDS OF RÉSUMÉS

A **résumé** is a persuasive summary of your qualifications for employment. If you're in the job market, having a résumé makes you look well organized and prepared. Posting it on LinkedIn tells employers you are available. When you're employed, having an up-to-date résumé makes it easier to take advantage of opportunities that may come up for an even better job. If you're several years away from job hunting, preparing a résumé now will help you become more conscious of what to do to make yourself an attractive candidate.

Although the job market has seen a proliferation of kinds and names, there are two broad kinds of résumés: chronological and skills. A **chronological résumé** summarizes what you did in a timeline (starting with the most recent events, and going backward in **reverse chronology**). It emphasizes degrees, job titles, and dates. It is the traditional résumé format (Figure 13.4).

Use a chronological résumé in these circumstances:

- Your education and experience are a logical preparation for the position for which you're applying.
- You have impressive job titles, offices, or honours.
- You have shown good and steady progress to your current position.

Figure 13.4 Chronological Résumé

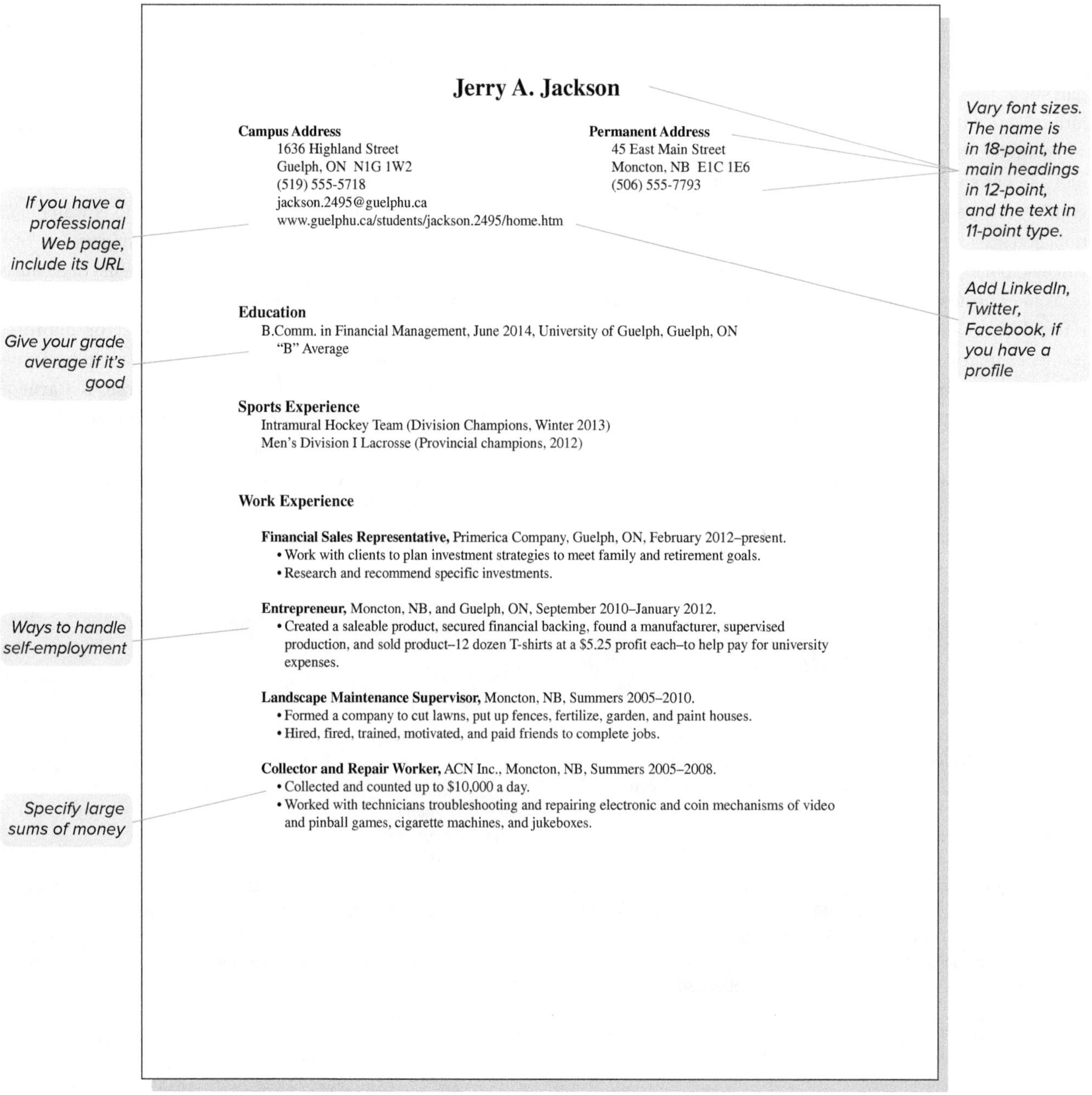

Jerry A. Jackson

Campus Address
1636 Highland Street
Guelph, ON N1G 1W2
(519) 555-5718
jackson.2495@guelphu.ca
www.guelphu.ca/students/jackson.2495/home.htm

Permanent Address
45 East Main Street
Moncton, NB E1C 1E6
(506) 555-7793

Education
B.Comm. in Financial Management, June 2014, University of Guelph, Guelph, ON
"B" Average

Sports Experience
Intramural Hockey Team (Division Champions, Winter 2013)
Men's Division I Lacrosse (Provincial champions, 2012)

Work Experience

Financial Sales Representative, Primerica Company, Guelph, ON, February 2012–present.
- Work with clients to plan investment strategies to meet family and retirement goals.
- Research and recommend specific investments.

Entrepreneur, Moncton, NB, and Guelph, ON, September 2010–January 2012.
- Created a saleable product, secured financial backing, found a manufacturer, supervised production, and sold product–12 dozen T-shirts at a $5.25 profit each–to help pay for university expenses.

Landscape Maintenance Supervisor, Moncton, NB, Summers 2005–2010.
- Formed a company to cut lawns, put up fences, fertilize, garden, and paint houses.
- Hired, fired, trained, motivated, and paid friends to complete jobs.

Collector and Repair Worker, ACN Inc., Moncton, NB, Summers 2005–2008.
- Collected and counted up to $10,000 a day.
- Worked with technicians troubleshooting and repairing electronic and coin mechanisms of video and pinball games, cigarette machines, and jukeboxes.

If you have a professional Web page, include its URL

Give your grade average if it's good

Ways to handle self-employment

Specify large sums of money

Vary font sizes. The name is in 18-point, the main headings in 12-point, and the text in 11-point type.

Add LinkedIn, Twitter, Facebook, if you have a profile

A **skills résumé** (or functional résumé) emphasizes the skills you've developed and used rather than the job you did or the dates when you used the skills. Figures 13.6 and 13.7 later in this chapter show examples of functional or skills résumés. A **functional résumé** stresses individual areas of competence and accomplishment, while subordinating work and educational experience.

A version of the skills résumé, a **targeted résumé** highlights abilities and achievements that relate to a specific job target. Like the functional or skills résumé, it puts the emphasis on what you can do, and it supplies evidence in the form of concrete achievements described in action verbs (see ⏩ Figure 13.5 later in this chapter). This kind of résumé shows that you know one size résumé does not fit all and have taken the care to adjust your strategy to meet the particular job requirements specified in a posting. A targeted résumé signals the value you attach to the job because you tailor the information to one position and employer.

Use a skills résumé when the following apply:

- Your education and experience are not the usual route to the position for which you're applying.
- You're changing fields.
- You want to combine experience from paid jobs, activities or volunteer work, and courses to show the extent of your experience in administration, finance, speaking, social media, and so on.
- Your recent work history may create the wrong impression (gaps, demotions, frequent changes).

The two kinds—chronological and skills/targeted—differ in what information is included and how that information is organized. The advice in this chapter applies to both kinds of résumés unless there is an explicit statement that the two kinds of résumés would handle a category differently.

KNOWING HOW EMPLOYERS USE RÉSUMÉS

Understanding how employers use résumés will help you create a résumé that works for you.

1. **Employers use résumés to decide whom to interview.** (The major exceptions are on-campus interviews, where the campus placement office has policies that determine who meets with the interviewer.) Since résumés are used to screen out applicants, omit anything that may create a negative impression.
2. **Résumés are scanned or skimmed.** At many companies, résumés are requested in electronic form or scanned into an electronic job applicant tracking system. Only résumés that match keywords are skimmed by a human being. A human may give a résumé 3 to 30 seconds before deciding to keep or toss it. You must design your résumé to pass both the "scan test" and the "skim test."

Some job candidates go to great lengths to grab attention to their résumés—and not always successfully. Misjudgments can be costly!

3. **Employers assume that your letter and résumé represent your best work.** Ensure neatness, accuracy, and freedom from typographical, spelling, and grammatical errors.
4. **Interviewers usually reread your résumé before the interview to refresh their memories.** Be ready to offer fuller details about everything on your résumé.
5. **After the search committee has chosen an applicant, it submits the applicant's résumé to people in the organization who must approve the appointment.** These people may have different backgrounds and areas of expertise. Spell out acronyms and explain unusual job titles or organizations that may be unfamiliar to the reader.

LO3

GUIDELINES FOR RÉSUMÉS

Writing a résumé is not an exact science. If your skills are in great demand, you can violate every guideline here and still get a good job. But when you must compete against many applicants, these guidelines will help you look as good on paper as you are in person. You want a résumé with eye appeal!

If you have little experience, a one-page résumé can be sufficient, but do fill the page. Less than a full page suggests that you do not have very much to say for yourself.

The average résumé is now two pages. An experiment that mailed one- or two-page résumés to recruiters at accounting firms showed that even readers who said they preferred short résumés were more likely to want to interview the candidate with the longer résumé.[22]

Emphasize the things you've done that (a) are most relevant to the position for which you're applying, (b) show your superiority to other applicants, and (c) are recent (last three to five years):

- Emphasize problem-solving, organizational, interpersonal, and communications skills.
- Use action verbs (see ▸▸ Figure 13.5 later in this chapter) to emphasize your contributions ("planned major trade show" or "trained five employees").
- Give details to support claims: "increased sales by 15% in first six months."
- List relevant technical skills and knowledge.
- List relevant course projects, activities, and jobs where you have done similar work. Marketing recruiters favoured résumés giving details about course projects, especially in the absence of work experience.[23]
- Emphasize promotions, honours and achievements, experience with computers or other technology, other languages, and so on.

Once you are pursuing a degree, omit high school jobs, activities, and honours unless you need them to fill the page. Briefly mention low-level jobs to show dependability.

Include full-time work after high school and during college or university. Present low-level jobs briefly or combine them.

You can emphasize material by putting it at the top or the bottom of a page, by giving it more space, and by setting it off with white space. The beginning and end—of a document, a page, a list—are positions of emphasis.

× Weak order:	Coordinated weekly schedules, assigned projects to five staff members, evaluated their performance, and submitted weekly time sheets.
✓ Emphatic order:	Coordinated weekly schedules and submitted weekly time sheets. Assigned projects to five staff members and evaluated their performance.

You can also emphasize material by presenting it in a bulleted list, using a phrase in a heading, and providing details.

Without sacrificing content, be as concise and concrete as possible.

× Wordy:	Member, Meat Judging Team, 2011–12 Member, Meat Judging Team, 2012–13 Member, Meat Judging Team, 2013–14 Captain, Meat Judging Team, 2014–15
✓ Tight:	Meat Judging Team, 2011–14; Captain 2014–15

Résumés normally use phrases and sentence fragments. Complete sentences are acceptable if they are the briefest way to present information. To save space and to avoid sounding arrogant, never use *I* in a résumé. *Me* and *my* are acceptable if they are unavoidable or if using them reduces wordiness.

Verbs or gerunds (the *-ing* form of verbs) create a more dynamic image than do nouns. In the following revisions, nouns, verbs, and gerunds are in bold type:

Nouns:	Chair, Income Tax Assistance Committee, Winnipeg, MB, 2014–15. Responsibilities: **recruitment** of volunteers; flyer **design, writing,** and **distribution** for **promotion** of program; **speeches** to various community groups and nursing homes to advertise the service.
Verbs:	Chair, Income Tax Assistance Committee, Winnipeg, MB, 2014–15. **Recruited** volunteers for the program. **Designed, wrote,** and **distributed** a flyer to promote the program; **spoke** to various community groups and nursing homes to advertise the service.
Gerunds:	Chair, Income Tax Assistance Committee, Winnipeg, MB, 2014–15. Responsibilities included **recruiting** volunteers for the program; **designing, writing,** and **distributing** a flyer to promote the program; and **speaking** to various community groups and nursing homes to advertise the service.

Note that the items in the list must be in parallel structure (◂◂ Chapter 3).

Experiment with layout, fonts, and spacing to get an attractive and readable résumé. Consider creating a letterhead that you use for both your résumé and your application letter. Use enough white space to make your résumé and its blocks of information easy to read.

Even if you pay someone else to produce your résumé, you must specify the exact layout: you cannot expect a professional to care as much about your résumé as you do or to understand what needs emphasis.

Laser print your résumé on standard white (or grey or cream) paper. Take advantage of different sizes of type and perhaps of rules (thin lines) to make your résumé look professional.

Technology Tips Templates: Use Caution

Many Web sites have templates for paper and online résumés. If you choose to use one of them, print out a copy before you submit your résumé. Less sophisticated programs use fixed spacing before headings. If you skip the objective, or have less experience than the template allows, you may get blank space—hardly a way to build a good impression.

Almost certainly, you can create a better résumé by adapting a basic style you like to your own unique qualifications.

Ethics and Legal Honesty in the Résumé*

Never lie in a résumé. As many as 53 percent of résumés have some falsified content, according to the Statistic Brain Research Institute. Tang Jun, past president of Microsoft China, for instance, got people talking about integrity when he was discovered to have exaggerated his academic achievements in his résumé. He had not earned the PhD he claimed.

It's OK to omit negative information (such as a low grade point average). If you were an officer in an organization, it's OK to list the title even if you didn't do much. It's OK to provide details when you did more than the job title indicates, or to give the job title alone if you had an inflated official title (e.g., Assistant Manager) but didn't really do much.

But it isn't OK to lie. Grant Cooper argues, "if you cannot be trusted to provide accurate information about your past, how can you be trusted with their business, money, or customers?"

Interviewers will ask you about items in the résumé. If you have to back down, you destroy your credibility. And if lies are discovered after you are hired, you will be fired.

Workopolis has partnered with BackCheck, a Canadian company that checks out candidates, because 18% misrepresent work experience and 9% misrepresent their education.

*Based on Statistic Brain Research Institute, "Resume falsification statistics," retrieved June 21, 2014, from http://www.statisticbrain.com/resume-falsification-statistics/; Jesse Juang, "A shady resume sparks debate over honesty in China," *Time*, July 30, 2010, retrieved from http://www.time.com/time/world/article/0,8599,2007297,00.html; Grant Cooper, "Honesty in your resume," *International Business Times*, September 8, 2011, retrieved from http://www.ibtimes.com/contents/20090908/honesty-your-resume.htm; "Workopolis to offer background checks," *The Globe and Mail*, February 4, 2005, C2.

ORGANIZING THE PARTS OF A RÉSUMÉ

Although the résumé is a factual document, its purpose is to persuade. In a job application form or an application for graduate or professional school, you answer every question even if the answer is not to your credit. In a résumé, you cannot lie, but you can omit anything that does not work in your favour.

Résumés commonly contain the following information. The categories marked with an asterisk are essential.

* Name and Contact Information
Career Objective
Summary of Qualifications
* Education
Honours
* Experience
Activities
References

You may choose other titles for these categories and add categories that are relevant for your qualifications: COMPUTER SKILLS, FOREIGN LANGUAGES.

EDUCATION and EXPERIENCE always stand as separate categories, even if you have only one item under each head. Combine other headings so that you have at least two long or three short items under each heading. For example, if you're in one honour society and two social clubs, and on one athletic team, combine them all under ACTIVITIES AND HONOURS.

If you have more than seven items under a heading, consider using subheadings. For example, a student who had a great many activities might divide them into STUDENT GOVERNMENT, OTHER CAMPUS ACTIVITIES, and COMMUNITY SERVICE.

Put your strongest categories near the top and at the bottom of the first page. If you have impressive work experience, you might want to put that category first after your name and contact information.

Name and Contact Information

Put your full name in big type. You may use an initial rather than spelling out your first or middle name. Omit your age, marital status, race, gender, and health. Questions about these topics are illegal. Know your rights and read resources on employment equity and on screening and employment selection.[24]

If you use only one address, consider centring it under your name. If you use two addresses (office and home, campus and permanent, until _____ / after _____) set them up side by side to balance the page visually.

Include an e-mail address, Web page URL, and a complete phone and/or cell number, including the area code in parentheses, or separate the area code by a hyphen.

(250) 555-1212
or 250-555-1212

If you don't have a phone, try to make arrangements with someone to take messages for you—employers usually call to schedule interviews and make job offers. Add links to your social media profiles to show your facility with the media and to showcase what distinguishes you from other candidates. Avoid buzzwords. A 2010 LinkedIn study found that most Canadians "are using the same 10 words in their profiles": extensive experience, innovative, dynamic, motivated, team player, results-oriented, fast-paced, proven track record, multitasker, and entrepreneurial.[25]

Career Objective

CAREER OBJECTIVE statements (immediately after your contact information) should sound like the job descriptions an employer might use in a job listing. Keep your statement brief—two or three lines at most. Tell what you want to do, what level of responsibility you want to hold.

✕ Ineffective career objective:	To offer a company my excellent academic foundation in hospital technology and my outstanding skills in oral and written communication
✓ Better career objective:	Selling state-of-the-art medical equipment

Good CAREER OBJECTIVES are hard to write. If you talk about entry-level work, you won't sound ambitious; if you talk about where you hope to be in 5 or 10 years, you won't sound as though you're willing to do entry-level work. You may omit this category and specify the job you want in your cover letter.

Summary of Qualifications

A section summarizing the candidate's qualifications seems to have first appeared in scannable résumés, where its keywords helped to increase the number of matches a résumé produced. But the section proved useful for human readers as well and now is a standard part of most résumés. The best summaries show your knowledge of the specialized terminology of your field and offer specific quantifiable achievements.

✕ Weak:	Reliable
✓ Better:	Achieved zero sick days in four years with Pacific Products.
✕ Weak:	Presentation skills
✓ Better:	Gave 20 individual and 7 team presentations to groups ranging from 5 to 100 people.

Your real accomplishments should go in the SUMMARY section. Include as many keywords as you legitimately can.

The relevant section of a *targeted résumé* (following name and contact information) typically uses present-tense verbs to describe CAPABILITIES and past-tense verbs to demonstrate the evidence of what the writer has achieved to support the claims for the job target.

JOB TARGET	Communications assistant, King Associates.
CAPABILITIES	Write, edit, design publishable work
	Solicit articles and negotiate effectively
	Master Microsoft Office 2013
	Use Twitter and blog
	Succeed in independent and team settings
	Meet deadlines and organize production
ACHIEVEMENTS	Wrote eight feature articles for student newspaper *The Sheaf.*
	Designed and implemented new production procedures at *The Sheaf*
	Designed *The Sheaf* anti-racist supplement
	Solicited, edited, and designed three issues of the community newsletter, *NutanaNews*
	Tweeted and blogged twelve times a week on campus issues from tuition to service learning
	Strengthened communication skills in customer service at The Bay

After the summary section of capabilities and achievements, the targeted résumé chooses the categories that best suit the job target. Education may well be the next most important category, for instance.

Education

EDUCATION can be your first major category if you've just earned (or are about to earn) a degree, if you have a degree that is essential or desirable for the position you're seeking, or if you lack work experience. Put EDUCATION later if you need all of page 1 for skills and experience or if you lack a degree that other applicants may have.

Under EDUCATION, include information about your undergraduate and graduate degrees as well as certificate programs. You may also include selected courses and grades related to the career objective.

To punctuate your degrees, do not space between letters and periods:

B.B.A. in Office Administration

B.Comm in Accountancy

Current usage also permits you to omit the periods:

MBA

PhD in Finance

There are two basic options for presenting your educational information.

Option I: List in reverse chronological order each degree earned, field of study, date, school, city, province of any graduate work, short courses and professional certification courses, university, community college, or school from which you transferred.

MSc in Management, May 2014, University of Manitoba, Winnipeg, MB

Bachelor of Commerce in Finance, May 2014, Saint Mary's University, Halifax, NS

Plan to sit for the CMA exam November 2015

BComm in Business Management, June 2014, University of Calgary, Calgary, AB

BUIS in Business-Information Systems, June 2014, Georgian Community College, Barrie, ON

Option II: After giving the basic information (degree, field of study, date, school, city, province) about your degree, list courses, using short descriptive titles rather than course numbers. Use a subhead like "Courses Related to Major" or "Courses Related to Financial Management" that will allow you to list all the courses (including psychology, speech, and business communication) that will help you in the job for which you're applying. Don't say "Relevant Courses," as that implies your other courses were irrelevant.

Bachelor of Business Administration in Management, May 2014, St. Francis Xavier, Antigonish, NS

Courses Related to Management:

Personnel Administration
Finance
Management I and II
Accounting I and II
Business Communications
Business Decision Making
International Business
Marketing
Legal Environment of Business

Valedictorian, Westmount High School, June 2010, Montreal, QC

Honours and Awards

It's nice to have the word HONOURS in a heading where it will be obvious even when the reader skims the résumé.

Include the following kinds of entries in this category:

- Listings in recognition books (e.g., *Who's Who in Advertising*).
- Academic honour societies. Make clear that honour societies aren't just social clubs.
- Fellowships and scholarships, including honorary scholarships for which you received no money and fellowships you could not hold because you received another fellowship at the same time.
- Awards given by professional societies or civic groups.
- Selection to provincial or national teams; finishes in provincial, national, or Olympic meets; drama or music awards. (These could also go under ACTIVITIES but may look more impressive under HONOURS. Put them under one category or the other—not both.)

Figure 13.5 Action Verbs for Résumés

analyzed	evaluated	recruited
budgeted	helped	reported
built	hired	researched
chaired	improved	reviewed
coached	increased	revised
collected	interviewed	saved
conducted	introduced	scheduled
coordinated	investigated	simplified
counselled	led	sold
created	managed	solved
demonstrated	motivated	spoke
designed	negotiated	started
developed	observed	supervised
directed	organized	trained
earned	persuaded	translated
edited	planned	wrote
established	presented	
examined	produced	

Experience

Under this section include the following information for each job you list: position or job title, organization, city and province (no postal code), dates of employment, and other details, such as full- or part-time status, job duties, special responsibilities, or the fact that you started at an entry-level position and were promoted. Use the verbs in Figure 13.5 to brainstorm what you've done. Include unpaid jobs and self-employment if they provided relevant skills (e.g., supervising people, budgeting, planning, persuading).

In a functional or skills résumé the subheadings under EXPERIENCE will be the *skills* used in or the *aspects* of the job you are applying for, rather than the title or the dates of the jobs you've held (as in a chronological résumé). For entries under each skill, combine experience from paid jobs, unpaid work, classes, activities, and community service.

Use headings that reflect the jargon of the job for which you're applying: *logistics* rather than *planning* for a technical job. Figure 13.6 shows a functional résumé for someone who is changing fields. The functions you perform produce the headings.

A job description can give you ideas for headings. Possible headings and subheadings for functional or skills résumés include

Figure 13.6 A Functional Résumé for Someone Changing Fields

On the first page of a functional résumé, put skills directly related to the job for which you're applying

An extra half space creates good visual impact

Put company's name in objective

Computer experience is crucial for almost every job. Specify the hardware and software you've worked with

Marcella G. Cope

370 49th Avenue
Yellowknife, NT X1A 2R3
867-555-1997
mcope@shaw.ca

Objective

To help create high quality social media content in Metatec's New Media Solutions Division

Editing and Proofreading Experience

- **Edited** a textbook published by Simon and Schuster, revising with attention to format, consistency, coherence, document integrity, and document design.
- **Proofed** training and instructor's manuals, policy statements, student essays and research papers, internal documents, and promotional materials.
- **Worked with authors** in a variety of fields including English, communication, business, marketing, economics, education, history, sociology, biology, agriculture, computer science, law, and medicine to revise their prose and improve their writing skills by giving them oral and written feedback.

Writing Experience

- **Wrote** training and instructor's manuals, professional papers, and letters, memos, and reports.
- **Authored** biweekly blog on northern issues.
- **Contributed** to a forthcoming textbook (Fall 2015) from Bedford Books/St. Martin's Press.

Computer Experience

- **Designed** a Web page using Dreamweaver (www.unbc.ca/english/People/Bracken.1/Sedgwick/)
- **Learned and used** a variety of programs on both Macintosh and PC platforms:
  - Word Processing and Spreadsheets — Dreamweaver
  - Microsoft Project — PageMaker
  - E-Mail — PowerPoint
  - Blackboard (a forum for online asynchronous discussion)
  - Storyspace (a hypertext writing environment)

Other Business and Management Experience

- **Developed** policies, procedures, and vision statements.
- **Supervised** new staff members in a mentoring program.
- **Coordinated** program and individual schedules, planned work and estimated costs, set goals, and evaluated progress and results.
- **Directed** (with team members) the largest first-year writing program in Western Canada.

(continued)

ADMINISTRATION	COMMUNICATION
Alternates or Subheadings:	*Alternates or Subheadings:*
Budgeting	Conducting Meetings
Coordinating	Editing
Evaluating	Fundraising
Implementing	Interviewing
Keeping Records	Negotiating
Negotiating	Persuading
Planning	Presenting
Scheduling	Proposal Writing
Solving Problems	Report Writing
Supervising	Social Networking

Many jobs require a mix of skills. Try to include the skills that you know will be needed in the job you want. For example, one study identified the six top communication skills for jobs in finance and in management.[26] Applicants who had experience in some of these areas could list them as well as subject-related skills and knowledge.

You need at least three subheadings in a skills résumé. Give enough detail under each subheading so the reader will know what you did. Put the most important category from the reader's point of view first.

In a skills résumé, list your paid jobs under WORK HISTORY or EMPLOYMENT RECORD near the end of the résumé (see Figure 13.6). List only job title, employer, city, province, and dates. Omit details that you have already used under EXPERIENCE.

Figure 13.6 A Functional Résumé for Someone Changing Fields *(concluded)*

Marcella G. Cope

Page 2

Employment History

Graduate Teaching Associate, Department of English, University of Northern British Columbia (UNBC), September 2014–Present. Taught Intermediate and First-Year Composition.
Writing Consultant, University Writing Centre, UNBC, January–April 2014
Program Administrator, First-Year Writing Program, UNBC, September 2013–January 2014

Honours

Phi Kappa Phi Honour Society, inducted 2013. Membership based upon performance in top 10% of graduate students nationwide.
Letters of Commendation, 2011–2012. Issued by the Director of Graduate Studies in recognition of outstanding achievement.
Dean's List, University of Alberta, Edmonton, AB

Education

Master of Arts, June 2014, University of Northern British Columbia, Prince George, BC. Cumulative GPA: 4.0/4.0
Bachelor of Arts, June 2010, University of Alberta, Edmonton, AB. Graduated with Honours.

References

Marilyn Duffey
Director, UNBC University Writing Program
3333 University Way
Prince George, BC V2N 4Z9
205-960-5555
duffeymc@unbc.ca

James Bracken
Associate Professor, English and Library Science
University of Northern British Columbia
3333 University Way
Prince George, BC V2N 4Z9
205-960-6300
bracken@unbc.ca

Kitty O. Locker
Associate Professor, Business and Administrative Communication
The Ohio State University
421 Denney Hall, 164 W. 17th Ave.
Columbus, OH 43210
614-555-6556
locker.1@osu.edu

If you use two pages be sure to put your name and "Page 2" on the second page. The reader may remove a staple.

Most recent job first

Explain honour societies that the reader may not know

Choose references who can speak about your skills for the job for which you're applying

Activities

Employers are interested in your activities if you're a new graduate. If you've worked for several years or have an advanced degree (MBA, MSc), you can omit ACTIVITIES and include PROFESSIONAL ACTIVITIES AND AFFILIATIONS or COMMUNITY AND PUBLIC SERVICE.

Include the following kinds of items under ACTIVITIES:

- Volunteer work. Include important committees and leadership roles.
- Membership in organized student activities. Include important subcommittees, leadership roles.
- Membership in professional associations.
- Participation in organized activities that require talent or responsibility (e.g., sports, choir, new-student orientation).

Major leadership roles may look more impressive if they're listed under EXPERIENCE instead of under ACTIVITIES.

References

Including references (with full contact information) anticipates the employer's needs and removes a potential barrier to your getting the job. To make your résumé fit on one page, you can omit this category. However, include REFERENCES if you're having trouble filling the page.

Ethics and Legal Dealing with No-Comment Reference Policies*

The task for candidates looking for strong references became more difficult in the late 1980s and 1990s when companies began adopting no-comment reference policies in response to lawsuits by (a) employees who felt references caused them not to get jobs and (b) employers claiming references were responsible for their hiring candidates who acted criminally or caused the legal liability.

No-comment policies mean that references limit comment to confirming candidates' titles and dates of employment. Or all inquiries are referred to HR. The policies can be as disastrous for employers as for employees.

To protect yourself,

- Ask about company policy
- If policy permits, ask a colleague or supervisor if he/she is willing to use home contact information for reference purposes
- Inform potential employers of policy so that they are better prepared to get and interpret any comment

*Based on "How to determine a company's reference policy," retrieved April 22, 2008, http://www.ehow.com/how_2065260_determine-companys-reference-policy.html; Robert S. Adler, "Encouraging employers to abandon their 'no comment' policies regarding job references: A reform proposal," *Washington and Lee Law Review* (1996), retrieved April 22, 2008; Ralph L. Quinones & Arthur Gross Schaefer, "The legal, ethical, and managerial implications of the neutral employment reference policy," *Employee Responsibilities and Rights Journal*, 10.2 (1997), 173–189.

If you do not want your current employer to know you are job hunting, omit the category in the résumé and say in the letter, "If I become a finalist for the job, I will supply the names of current references."

While some argue that you should never say "References available on request" since no job applicant will refuse to supply references, others argue that it is appropriate. It can allow you time to select and contact the right reference for a specific job and prepare them well in advance with updated materials should they be contacted after the interview.

When you list references (typically on a separate page) provide at least three, including at least one professor and at least one employer or adviser—someone who can comment on your work habits and leadership skills. Don't use relatives or roommates, even if you've worked for them. If you're changing jobs, include your current superior. See Figure 13.6. See also "Choosing Your References" below and ▸▸"Letters of Recommendation" later in this chapter.

Always ask the person's permission to list him or her as a reference (see "Dealing with No-Comment Reference Policies" above). In the case of a professor or instructor, be aware of how your classroom or other conduct may have endeared you to him or her—or not![27] Don't ask, "May I list you as a reference?" Instead, say, "Can you speak positively about my work?" Jog the person's memory by taking along or e-mailing copies of work you did for him or her and a copy of your current résumé. Keep your list of references up to date. If it's been a year or more since you asked someone, ask again—and tell the person about your recent achievements. Make it easy for your references to write the best possible letters by listing your relevant skills and qualifications. Together with your résumé, the references can help secure that interview or appointment.

How an Average Student Created an Excellent Résumé

Allyson was convinced that she had nothing to put on her résumé. In a conference, her professor asked Allyson to describe exactly what she'd done. Allyson's "baby-sitting" was actually house management and child care. But a summer job at Harvard had consisted of changing beds and cleaning rooms for conference guests.

Her five summers of work at a law firm sounded more promising. She went to the library, formulated medical and legal questions, and searched for answers. The information she found helped the firm win a $7-million out-of-court

On the Job Choosing Your References

Because your references can help make or break a deal, choose with care:

- People who can represent your work or academic experience (employers interested in both)
- People who can vouch for your character
- People who have known you for at least 1–2 years
- Former teachers, professors, supervisors, employers, high school counsellors, colleagues, coaches, volunteer administrators
- References who can credibly comment on skills relevant to the targeted position
- Those who have agreed to write a positive reference and have detailed knowledge of your skills
- Those who are not constrained by company "no-comment" reference policies designed to protect against legal liability
- Those with outstanding communication skills!

settlement. But Allyson was in advertising and wanted to go into copywriting, not market research. The experience was certainly worth putting on her résumé, but the kind of thinking she'd done as a law clerk wasn't the kind of thinking she needed to demonstrate to an ad agency.

Some of the items under ACHIEVEMENTS were interesting. The Locker Room was a restaurant in town where Allyson had had dinner. Its menu said the restaurant "had a long history." In fact, the restaurant was new; it was the *building* that was old. Allyson approached the owner, told him several of the things that were wrong with the menu, and offered to rewrite it. The owner told her he'd pay her for doing that and also invited her to submit ideas for ads.

The professor was impressed. The whole anecdote might work in a job application letter, while the résumé could highlight the fact that Allyson had written menu and advertising copy for a real business (not just a class). "What you need," the instructor said, "is a skills résumé" (Figure 13.7).

ONLINE RÉSUMÉS

Most large companies request e-mail or online résumés or scan résumés into an electronic job-applicant tracking system.[28] Prepare a scannable version of your résumé for any company that asks for it.

Figure 13.7 A Skills Résumé for a Graduate Entering the Job Market

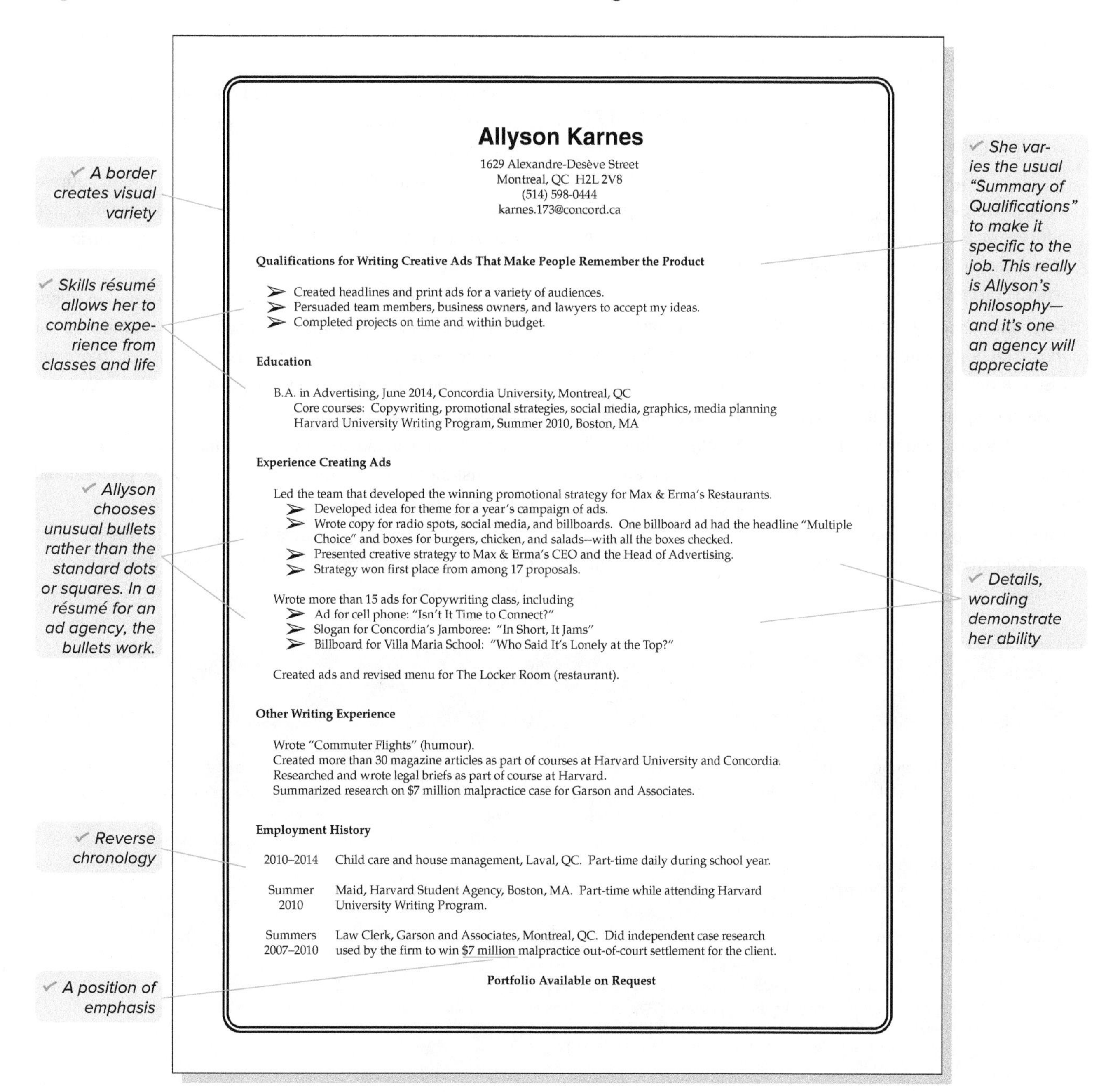

Allyson Karnes

1629 Alexandre-Desève Street
Montreal, QC H2L 2V8
(514) 598-0444
karnes.173@concord.ca

Qualifications for Writing Creative Ads That Make People Remember the Product

- Created headlines and print ads for a variety of audiences.
- Persuaded team members, business owners, and lawyers to accept my ideas.
- Completed projects on time and within budget.

Education

B.A. in Advertising, June 2014, Concordia University, Montreal, QC
Core courses: Copywriting, promotional strategies, social media, graphics, media planning
Harvard University Writing Program, Summer 2010, Boston, MA

Experience Creating Ads

Led the team that developed the winning promotional strategy for Max & Erma's Restaurants.
- Developed idea for theme for a year's campaign of ads.
- Wrote copy for radio spots, social media, and billboards. One billboard ad had the headline "Multiple Choice" and boxes for burgers, chicken, and salads--with all the boxes checked.
- Presented creative strategy to Max & Erma's CEO and the Head of Advertising.
- Strategy won first place from among 17 proposals.

Wrote more than 15 ads for Copywriting class, including
- Ad for cell phone: "Isn't It Time to Connect?"
- Slogan for Concordia's Jamboree: "In Short, It Jams"
- Billboard for Villa Maria School: "Who Said It's Lonely at the Top?"

Created ads and revised menu for The Locker Room (restaurant).

Other Writing Experience

Wrote "Commuter Flights" (humour).
Created more than 30 magazine articles as part of courses at Harvard University and Concordia.
Researched and wrote legal briefs as part of course at Harvard.
Summarized research on $7 million malpractice case for Garson and Associates.

Employment History

2010–2014 Child care and house management, Laval, QC. Part-time daily during school year.

Summer 2010 Maid, Harvard Student Agency, Boston, MA. Part-time while attending Harvard University Writing Program.

Summers 2007–2010 Law Clerk, Garson and Associates, Montreal, QC. Did independent case research used by the firm to win $7 million malpractice out-of-court settlement for the client.

Portfolio Available on Request

Using your social media skills to advantage is increasingly relevant to the job search, including résumé writing. Faced with floods of information, recruiters and applicants are turning not only to LinkedIn but also to Twitter or six-second Vine videos. From the perspective of Vala Afshar, then chief marketing officer of networking company Enterasys, "The Web is your CV and social networks are your references." For making your mark, Kathryn Minshew, founder of the TheMuse.com, recommends the tweet as "the new elevator pitch."[29]

Here are some basic guidelines of e-mail job-hunting etiquette:

- Don't use your current employer's e-mail system for your job search. You'll leave potential employers with the impression that you spend company time on writing résumés and other non-work-related activities.
- Set up a free, Internet-based e-mail account using services such as Hotmail or Yahoo! to manage correspondence related to your job hunt.
- Avoid using silly or cryptic e-mail addresses. Instead of bubbles@hotmail.com, opt for something more business-like: yourname@hotmail.com.
- Understand that e-mail isn't confidential. Don't put an address or phone number on your e-résumé. Instead write "Confidential Résumé" and list a personal e-mail address where you can be reached.
- Send individual, targeted messages rather than mass mailings. You don't want a coveted employer to see that you're also sending your résumé to 20 other companies.
- Write a simple subject line that makes a good first impression: Résumé—Kate Sanchez. A good subject line will improve the chances that your résumé is actually read.
- Prepare a résumé that looks good on a computer screen. Computer systems vary widely and have differently installed fonts, printer drivers, and word processing software.
- Use a plain-text résumé. Save your fully formatted résumé in your word processing program as "text" or "rich-text format" (rtf)—a document type that's compatible with all systems. It's important to heed the specific directions of employers that you are e-mailing. Also mention the types of files in a brief cover letter in your message. (See ⏩ Figure 13.13 later in this chapter.)

With the popularity of the Web, you may want to post your résumé online. If you don't know hypertext markup language (HTML), the behind-the-scenes programming that displays Web pages in your browser, you can save your résumé as HTML in Word or WordPerfect. However, be aware that the HTML editors in word-processing programs create messy codes that computer programmers deplore. If you're claiming the ability to code Web pages as one of your skills and abilities, use real HTML.

- Include an e-mail link at the top of the résumé under your name.
- Omit your street addresses and phone numbers. Employers who find your résumé on the Web will have the technology to e-mail you.
- Consider having links under your name and e-mail address to the various parts of your résumé. Use phrases that give the viewer some idea of what you offer: e.g., *Marketing Experience.*
- Link to other pages that provide more information about you (profiles on LinkedIn, Facebook, and/or Twitter, a list of courses, a document you've written), but not to organizations (your university, an employer) that shift emphasis away from your credentials.
- Be professional. Link to other pages you've created (a blog, for instance) only if they convey the same professional image as your résumé.
- Put your strongest qualification immediately after your name and e-mail address. If the first screen doesn't interest readers, they won't scroll through the rest of the résumé.

Ethics and Legal Managing Online Reputations*

According to a December 2010 survey of business executives, 80% are turning to social networking sites to attract workers and to conduct background checks. The City of Calgary, for example, has posted Dilbert-style videos on YouTube.

Attending to a professional online presence is all the more important. Take care of your personal brand.

Employment lawyer Charles Caulkins warns corporate clients that using video and photo materials may open them to accusations of discrimination based on appearance.

Job candidates may also find their trust in job sites violated. Thieves and scam artists mine and misuse personal data, sending phishing e-mails that endanger privacy.

In 2007 Monster.com revealed that hackers had compromised 1.3 million records.

*Based on Joe Light, "Recruiters rewriting the online playbook," *Report on Business*, January 21, 2011, B14; Bridget Carey, "A professional presence online: Reputation management has become important for job seekers," *National Post*, March 19, 2008, WK5; Ross Kerber, "Online job hunters grapple with misuse of personal data," *Saint John Telegraph Journal*, November 17, 2007, E1.

- Specify the job you want. Recruiters respond negatively to scrolling through an entire résumé only to find that the candidate is in another field.[30]
- Specify city and province for educational institutions and employers.
- Use lists, indentations, and white space to create visual variety.
- Most commercial and many university sites offer lists of applicants, with a short phrase after each name. Craft this phrase to convince the recruiter to click on your résumé.
- Proofread the résumé carefully.

Be prepared during the job interview to create HTML or Java text or provide writing samples. Fifty percent of candidates with electronic portfolios as evidence of their skills received job offers; 35% were offered better jobs than expected.[31]

Scannable Résumés

Increasingly, large companies scan paper résumés to search them by keyword to match job descriptions. See Figure 13.8. To increase the chances that the résumé is scanned correctly,

- Use a standard typeface: Helvetica, Futura, Optima, Times Roman, New Century Schoolbook, Courier, Univers, or Bookman.[32]
- Use 12- or 14-point type.
- Use a ragged right margin rather than full justification. Scanners can't always handle the extra spaces between words and letters that full justification creates.
- Don't italicize or underline words—even titles of books or newspapers that grammatically require such treatment.
- Check text to make sure letters are not touching; use Times New Roman or Helvetica to avoid the problem.
- Don't use lines, boxes, script, leader dots, or borders.
- Don't use two-column formats.
- Put each phone number on a separate line.
- Use plenty of white space.
- Don't fold or staple the pages.
- Don't write anything by hand on your résumé.
- Send a laser copy or a high-quality photocopy. Stray marks defeat scanners.

To increase the number of matches, or hits,

- Prepare a traditional chronological résumé. Don't be "creative." It doesn't matter where information is; the system can find it anywhere.
- Use a *Keywords* summary under your name, address, and phone number. In it, put not only degrees, job field or title, and accomplishments but also personality traits and attitude: *dependability, skill in time management, leadership, sense of responsibility.*[33]
- Use industry buzzwords and jargon, even if you're redundant. For example, "Web page design and HTML coding" will "match" either "Web" or "HTML" as a keyword.
- Use specific, concrete nouns. Some systems don't handle verbs well, and tracking systems "key in" primarily on nouns.
- Use common headings such as *Summary of Qualifications, Strengths, Certifications,* and so forth as well as *Education, Experience,* and so on.
- Mention specific software programs (e.g., *Dreamweaver*) you've used.
- Be specific and quantifiable. "Managed $2-million building materials account" will generate more hits than "manager" or "managerial experience."

Technology Tips Unfiltered Résumés*

Companies are losing billions of dollars a year to the time wasted on spam, so they have installed filters to block spam. Unfortunately, some messages being blocked are legitimate messages containing résumés.

To lessen the chance of a résumé being blocked by a spam filter:

- Try not to use words that filters are likely to block, including cash, expand, free, mortgage, singles, and trial. Avoid exclamation points, too.
- Put the résumé in the body of the message instead of attaching it (unless the company requests an attachment).
- Avoid using coloured backgrounds.
- Send your résumé to one recipient per message. Avoid services that will "blast" your résumé to thousands of companies.
- Use a specific subject line ("Adept project manager with CRM experience").
- Test your message and résumé by sending it to yourself, perhaps at a different address where you set filtering at various levels. Make sure it gets through your own filters before you send it to a company.

Also, just as companies may filter out your résumé, your own e-mail service may filter out important messages from recruiters. Read addresses and subject lines carefully before deleting anything in your spam folder.

*Based on Michael Trust, "How to stop your résumé from becoming spam," retrieved June 14, 2011, from http://www.careerealism.com/stop-resume-spam/; Kris Maher, "Stringent spam filters mistakenly block e-mailed résumés," *The Wall Street Journal*, April 13, 2004, downloaded at http://online.wsj.com; and Sharon Gaudin, "False positives: Spam's casualty of war costing billions," *Earthweb*, August 7, 2003, downloaded at http://itmanagement.earthweb.com.

Figure 13.8 A Scannable Résumé

Use 12- or 14-point type in a standard typeface. Here, Times Roman is used.

Don't use columns. Scanners can't handle them.

In keywords, use labels and terms that employers might use in a job listing

Give as much information as you like. The computer doesn't care how long the document is.

Jerry A. Jackson

Keywords: family financial management; investment sales; computer modelling; competitive; self-starter; hard worker; responsible; collegiate athletics; sales experience; willing to travel

Campus Address
1636 Highland Street
Guelph, ON N1G 1W2
(519) 555-5718
E-mail address: Jackson.2495@guelphu.ca
Created a Web page on saving for life goals, such as a home, children's education, and retirement: http://www.guelphu.ca/students/Jackson.2495/home.htm

Permanent Address
45 East Main Street
Moncton, NB E1C 1E6
(506) 555-7793

Summary of Qualifications
High energy. Played sports during four years of university. Started two businesses.
Sales experience. Sold both clothing and investments successfully.
Presentation skills. In individual and group presentations, spoke to groups ranging from 2 to 75 people. Gave informative, persuasive, and inspirational talks.
Knowledgeable about stocks and bonds, especially energy and telecommunication companies.
Computer experience. Microsoft Word, Excel, SPSS, PowerPoint, and Dreamweaver. Experience creating Web pages.

Education
B.Comm. in Financial Management, June 2014, University of Guelph—Guelph, ON
"B" Grade Point Average
Comprehensive courses related to major provide not only the basics of family financial management but also skills in communication, writing, speaking, small groups, and computer modelling
Accounting I and II
Business and Professional Writing
Business Information Systems
Business Law
Computer Programming
Investment Finance
Economics I and II
Personal Financial Planning
Portfolio Management

(continued)

× Weak: Microsoft Front Page

✓ Better: Used Microsoft Front Page to design an interactive Web page for a national fashion retailer, with links to information about style trends, current store promotions, employment opportunities, and an online video fashion show.

- Put everything in the résumé rather than "saving" some material for the cover letter. While some applicant-tracking systems can search for keywords in cover letters and other application materials, most extract information only from the résumé.

Experts differ on whether candidates should phone to follow up. Taunee Besson advises phoning the administrator or verifier of the tracking system just once to be sure that your résumé arrived.[34]

LO4

HOW JOB LETTERS DIFFER FROM RÉSUMÉS

The job application letter (ideally one page) accompanies your résumé. Although the two documents overlap slightly, they differ in several ways:

- A résumé is adapted to a position; the letter is adapted to the needs of a particular organization.

Figure 13.8 A Scannable Résumé *(concluded)*

Omit bold and italics. Some scanners can handle bullets, but they aren't needed in a scannable résumé.

Sports Experience
Intramural Hockey Team (Division Champions, Winter 2013)
Men's Division I Lacrosse (Provincial Champions, 2012)

Work Experience
Financial Sales Representative, Primerica Company, Guelph, ON, February 2012–present.
Work with clients to plan investment strategies.
Research and recommend specific investments, including stocks, bonds, mutual funds, and annuities.

Entrepreneur, Moncton, NB and Guelph, ON, September 2010–January 2012.
Created a saleable product, secured financial backing, found a manufacturer, supervised production, and sold product—12 dozen T-shirts at a $5.25 profit each—to help pay for university expenses.

Landscape Maintenance Supervisor, Moncton, NB, Summers 2005–2010.
Formed a company to cut lawns, put up fences, fertilize, garden, and paint houses.
Hired, fired, trained, motivated, and paid employees to complete jobs.

Collector and Repair Worker, ACN Inc., Moncton, NB, Summers 2005–2008.
Collected and counted up to $10,000 a day.
Worked with technicians troubleshooting and repairing electronic and coin mechanisms of video and pinball games, cigarette machines, and jukeboxes.

Don't right justify margins. Doing so creates extra spaces, which confuse scanners.

- The résumé summarizes all your qualifications. The letter shows how your qualifications can help the organization meet its needs, how you differ from other applicants, and how much you know about the organization.
- The résumé uses short, parallel phrases (« Chapter 3) and sentence fragments. The letter uses complete sentences in well-written paragraphs to weave "a narrative; it tells a story."[35]

Writing a letter is good preparation for a job interview, since the letter is your first step in showing a specific company what you can do for it. You-attitude (« Chapter 2) is key. Focus not on your interests but on the recruiter's interests. Paragraphs beginning with pronouns such as "I" and "my" send a strong signal about whose interests dominate! And remember the advice of Todd Defren, CEO of Shift Communications, "Grammatical errors are perfectly acceptable—so long as you don't mind if we immediately *trash your letter.*"[36]

LO5

ORGANIZING JOB APPLICATION LETTERS

In your letter, focus on

- Major requirements of the job for which you're applying
- Qualifications that separate you from other applicants
- Points that show your knowledge of the organization
- Qualities that every employer is likely to value: the ability to write and speak effectively, to solve problems, to get along with people

Two different hiring situations call for two different kinds of application letters. Write a **solicited letter** (Figure 13.9) when you know that the company is hiring: you've seen an ad, you've been advised to apply by a professor or friend, you've read in a trade publication that the company is expanding. This situation is similar to a persuasive direct request (« Chapter 9): you can indicate immediately that you are applying for the position. See Figure 13.10.

Figure 13.9 How to Organize a Solicited Job Application Letter

1. State that you're applying for the job (phrase the job title as your source phrased it). Tell where you learned about the job (ad, referral, etc.). Include any reference number mentioned in the ad. Briefly show that you have the major qualifications required by the ad: a degree, professional certification, job experience, etc. Summarize your other qualifications briefly in the same order in which you plan to discuss them in the letter.
2. Develop your major qualifications in detail. Be specific about what you've done; relate your achievements to the work you'd be doing in this new job. This is not the place for modesty!
3. Develop your other qualifications, even if the ad doesn't ask for them. (If the ad asks for a lot of qualifications, pick the most important three or four.) Show what separates you from the other applicants who will also answer the ad. Demonstrate your knowledge of the organization.
4. Ask for an interview; tell when you'll be available to be interviewed and to begin work. End on a positive, forward-looking note.

Figure 13.10 A Solicited Letter from a Graduating Senior

1072 Adams Street, Apt. 23
London, ON N4A 5B3

April 17, 2015

Mr. Robert H. Catanga, Senior Accountant
IBM Corporation
1717 Central
New York, NY 10021

Dear Mr. Catanga:

Well prepared with diverse academic and professional experience, technical and interpersonal skills. I am applying for the Accounting position announced on IBM's Web site (jof17747). After receiving an Honours Business Administration degree from Richard Ivey School of Business this May, I plan to take the CA exam next December.

Courses in the accountancy curriculum at Ivey have given me not only the necessary theoretical background but also extensive practical experience in General Ledgers, Accounts Payable, and Travel Expenses. I have worked many cases and problems using computer data, including preparing simulated accounting records for hypothetical firms.

These true-to-life cases gave me the opportunity to interpret all sorts of data in order to prepare accurate financial statements. For instance, I've learned the best measures for fixed assets and property controls, how to figure inter/intra-company and travel expenses, and the best methods of matching revenues with expenditures. These I could then analyze and compare to past statements to identify trends and recommend ways that costs could be reduced so that the business could be run even more efficiently.

Courses in management communication have taught me how to provide reports, financial statements, and visuals to show how accounting information is related to management needs. I can use Excel and create computer graphics to provide the reliable accounting data that IBM needs to continue growing each year. Visit my Web page (www.ivey/business/students/mckenna/report.htm) to see my report on choosing the best method to accelerate depreciation.

Three years' experience with Imperial Insurance has also given me the opportunity to take leadership and show responsibility. Although I was hired as a part-time assistant, my supervisor frequently asked for my recommendations of ways to get work done more efficiently. In fact, I developed a procedure for making out arbitration reports that saved so much time that I was asked to teach it to the other employees in my department.

The enclosed résumé summarizes my qualifications. I can come to New York for an interview now that examinations are over. I can begin work in September and look forward to discussing with you ways in which I can help IBM continue its tradition of excellence.

Sincerely,

Tracey McKenna

Tracey McKenna

Encl.: Résumé

✓ Tracey has had only course work and one part-time job. But by being specific about what she's done in class and on the job, she creates a positive impression.

✓ In ¶ 1, show you have the qualifications the ad lists.

✓ These terms come from the job listing

✓ The ad asked for experience with spreadsheets and computer graphics

✓ Referring to her Web page suggests her technological savvy

✓ Phrase from the CEO's letter in the annual report, which Tracey read on the Web

✓ One way to refer to résumé

✓ You don't have to note the enclosure, but doing so is a nice touch if you have room at the bottom of the page

✓ Block format is good for letters of application

✓ Tell where you learned about the job. If the job has a number, provide it

✓ Many courses provide practice with simulated cases—you may be able to use Tracey's strategy, too

✓ Relates what she has done to what she could do for the company

✓ She gets a lot of mileage out of her part-time job by being specific

✓ Nice allusion to inclusion of IBM in *In Search of Excellence*

Sometimes, however, the advertised positions may not be what you want, or you may want to work for an organization that has not announced openings in your area. Then you write a **prospecting letter** to tap in to the hidden job market. (The metaphor is drawn from prospecting for gold.) The prospecting letter is like a problem-solving persuasive message (◂◂ Chapter 9). See Figure 13.11.

In both solicited and prospecting letters you should

- Address the letter to a specific person.
- Indicate the specific position for which you're applying.
- Be specific about your qualifications.
- Show what separates you from other applicants.
- Show a knowledge of the company and the position.
- Use the language of the ad, organization, and industry.
- Refer to your résumé (which you would enclose with the letter).
- Ask for an interview.

First Paragraphs of Solicited Letters

Note how the following paragraph picks up several of the characteristics of the ad:

Figure 13.11 How to Organize a Prospecting Letter

1. Catch the reader's interest.
2. Create a bridge between the attention-getter and your qualifications. Focus on what you know and can do. Since the employer is not planning to hire, he or she won't be impressed with the fact that you're graduating. Summarize your qualifications briefly in the same order in which you plan to discuss them in the letter. This summary serves as an organizing device for your letter.
3. Develop your strong points in detail. Be specific. Relate what you've done in the past to what you could do for this company. Show that you know something about the company. Identify the specific niche you want to fill.
4. Ask for an interview and tell when you'll be available for interviews. (Don't tell when you can begin work.) End on a positive, forward-looking note.

Ad: Architectural Technology Trainer at Mohawk College of Applied Arts and Technology. Candidate must possess a Bachelor's degree in Engineering or Architecture. Will be responsible for providing in-house leadership/training to professionals. . . . Candidate should have at least six months' experience. Prior teaching experience not required.
Letter: Scheduled to receive a Bachelor of Engineering degree from Carleton University in December, I am applying for your position in Architectural Technology. In addition to two years' experience teaching word processing and computer accounting courses to adults, I have developed leadership skills in the volunteer guide program at the National Gallery of Canada.

Your **summary sentence** or **paragraph** covers everything you will talk about and serves as an organizing device for your letter.

With a good background in standard accounting principles and procedures, I also have a working knowledge of some of the special accounting practices of the oil industry. This working knowledge is based on practical experience in the oil fields: I've pumped, tailed rods, and worked as a roustabout.

Let me put my creative eye, artistic ability, and experience to work for McLean Design.

Good word choices can help set your letter apart from the scores or even hundreds of letters the company is likely to get in response to an ad. The following first paragraph of a letter in response to an ad by Imperial Insurance Company shows a knowledge of the firm's advertising slogan and sets itself apart from the dozens of letters that start with "I would like to apply for. . . ."

The Imperial Insurance Company is famous for its "Good Hands Policy." I would like to lend a helping hand to many Canadians as a financial analyst for Imperial, as advertised in *The Globe and Mail.* I have an Honours Business Administration degree from the Ivey School, University of Western Ontario, and I have worked with figures, computers, and people.

Note that the last sentence forecasts the organization of the letter, preparing for paragraphs about the student's academic background and (in this order) experience with "figures, computers, and people."

First Paragraphs of Prospecting Letters

In a prospecting letter, asking for a job in the first paragraph is dangerous: unless the company plans to hire but has not yet announced openings, the reader is likely to throw the letter away. Instead, catch the reader's interest. Then in the second paragraph you can shift the focus to your skills and experience, showing how they can be useful to the employer.

See the first two paragraphs of a letter applying to be a computer programmer for an insurance company:

Computers alone aren't the answer to demands for higher productivity in the competitive insurance business. Merging a poorly written letter with a database of customers just sends out bad letters more quickly. But you know how hard it is to find people who can both program computers and write well.

My education and training have given me this useful combination. I'd like to put my associate's degree in computer technology and my business experience writing to customers to work in FarmCredit's service approach to insurance.

Showing What Separates You from Other Applicants

Your knowledge of the company can separate you from other applicants (Figure 13.12). You can also use coursework, an understanding of the field, and experience in jobs and extracurricular events. Be specific but concise. Usually three to five sentences will enable you to give enough specific supporting details.

This student uses both coursework and summer jobs to set herself apart from other applicants:

My university courses have taught me the essential accounting skills required to contribute to the growth of Monsanto. Since you recently adopted new accounting methods for fluctuations in foreign currencies, you will

Figure 13.12 A Prospecting Letter from a Career Changer

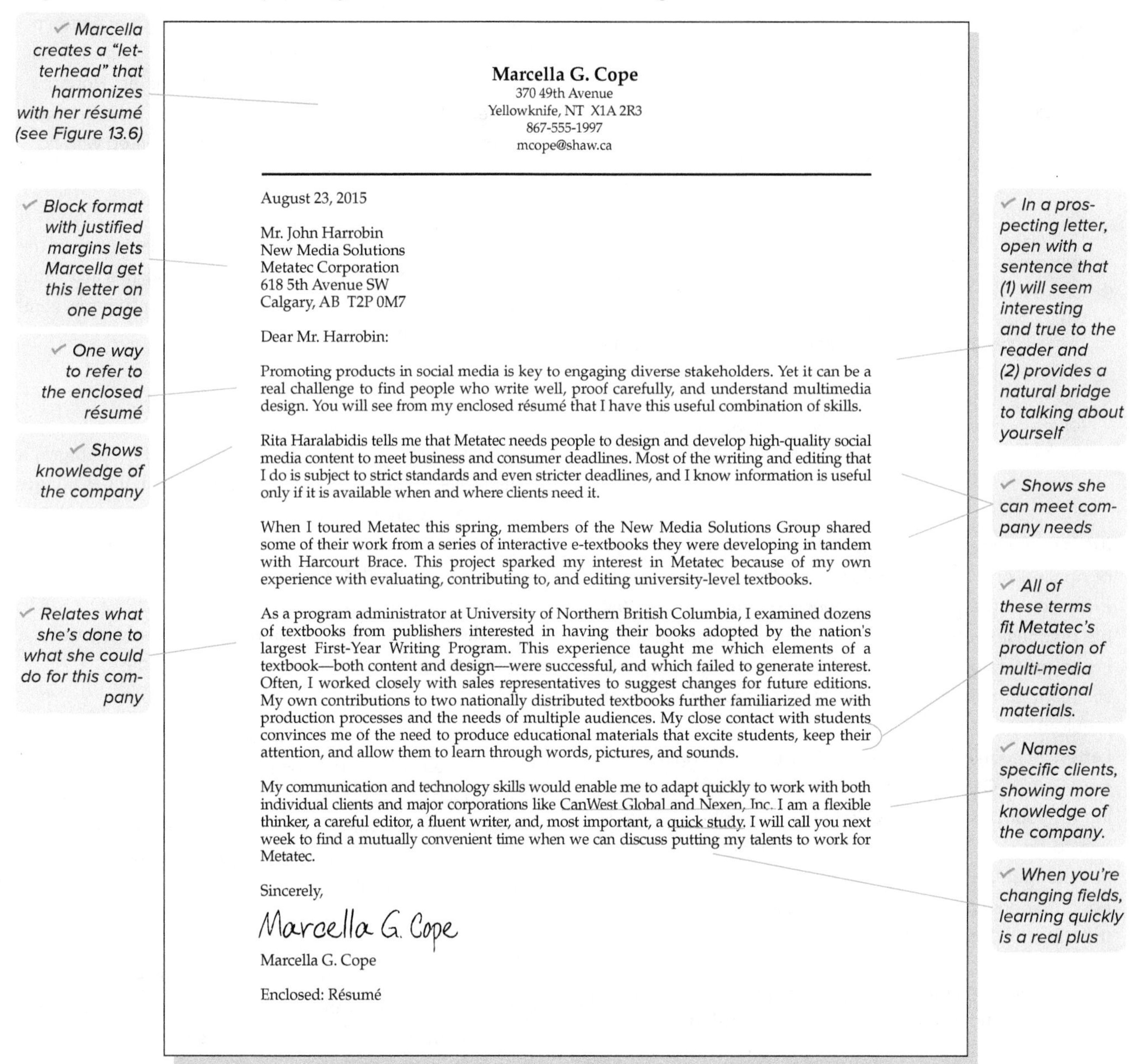
Marcella G. Cope
370 49th Avenue
Yellowknife, NT X1A 2R3
867-555-1997
mcope@shaw.ca

August 23, 2015

Mr. John Harrobin
New Media Solutions
Metatec Corporation
618 5th Avenue SW
Calgary, AB T2P 0M7

Dear Mr. Harrobin:

Promoting products in social media is key to engaging diverse stakeholders. Yet it can be a real challenge to find people who write well, proof carefully, and understand multimedia design. You will see from my enclosed résumé that I have this useful combination of skills.

Rita Haralabidis tells me that Metatec needs people to design and develop high-quality social media content to meet business and consumer deadlines. Most of the writing and editing that I do is subject to strict standards and even stricter deadlines, and I know information is useful only if it is available when and where clients need it.

When I toured Metatec this spring, members of the New Media Solutions Group shared some of their work from a series of interactive e-textbooks they were developing in tandem with Harcourt Brace. This project sparked my interest in Metatec because of my own experience with evaluating, contributing to, and editing university-level textbooks.

As a program administrator at University of Northern British Columbia, I examined dozens of textbooks from publishers interested in having their books adopted by the nation's largest First-Year Writing Program. This experience taught me which elements of a textbook—both content and design—were successful, and which failed to generate interest. Often, I worked closely with sales representatives to suggest changes for future editions. My own contributions to two nationally distributed textbooks further familiarized me with production processes and the needs of multiple audiences. My close contact with students convinces me of the need to produce educational materials that excite students, keep their attention, and allow them to learn through words, pictures, and sounds.

My communication and technology skills would enable me to adapt quickly to work with both individual clients and major corporations like CanWest Global and Nexen, Inc. I am a flexible thinker, a careful editor, a fluent writer, and, most important, a quick study. I will call you next week to find a mutually convenient time when we can discuss putting my talents to work for Metatec.

Sincerely,

Marcella G. Cope

Marcella G. Cope

Enclosed: Résumé

need people knowledgeable in foreign currency translation to convert currency exchange rates. In two courses in international accounting, I compiled simulated accounting statements of hypothetical multinational firms in countries experiencing different rates of currency devaluation. Through these classes, I acquired the skills needed to work with the daily fluctuations of exchange rates and at the same time formulate an accurate and favourable representation of Monsanto.

A company as diverse as Monsanto requires extensive record keeping as well as numerous internal and external communications. Both my summer jobs and my coursework prepare me to do this. As Office Manager for Shaw Cable, I was in charge of most of the bookkeeping, report, and letter writing for the company. I kept accurate records for each workday, and I often entered over 100 transactions in a single day. In business and technical writing I learned how to write persuasive letters and memos and how to present extensive data in reports in a simplified style that is clear and easy to understand.

In your résumé, you may list activities, offices, and courses. In your letter, give more detail about what you did and show how that experience will help you contribute to the employer's organization more quickly.

When you discuss your strengths, don't exaggerate. No employer will believe that a new graduate has a "comprehensive" knowledge of a field. Indeed, most employers believe that six months to a year of on-the-job training is necessary before most new hires are really earning their pay. Specifics about what you've done will make your claims about what you can do more believable and ground them in reality.

The Last Paragraph

In the last paragraph, indicate when you'd be available for an interview. If you're free anytime, you can say so. But it's likely that you have responsibilities in class and work. If you'd have to go out of town, there may be only certain days of the week or certain weeks that you could leave town for several days. Use a sentence that fits your situation.

> I could come to London for an interview any Wednesday or Friday.
>
> I'll be attending the Administrative Science Association's November meeting and will be available for interviews there.

Should you wait for the employer to call you, or should you call the employer to request an interview? In a solicited letter, it's safe to wait to be contacted: you know the employer wants to hire someone, and if your letter and résumé show that you're one of the top applicants, you'll get an interview. In a prospecting letter, call the employer. Because the employer is not planning to hire, you'll get a higher percentage of interviews if you're aggressive.

End the letter on a positive note that suggests you look forward to the interview and that you see yourself as a person who has something to contribute, not as someone who just needs a job.

> I look forward to discussing with you ways in which I could contribute to Big Rock's continued growth.

You may be required to submit your job application letter via e-mail; Figure 13.13 provides an example.

INTERVIEWING IN THE 21ST CENTURY

Job interviews are scary, even when you've prepared thoroughly. But when you are prepared, you can harness the adrenaline to work for you, so that you put your best foot forward and get the job you want. Knowing what recruiters may or may not ask is part of that preparation.[37]

Interviews are changing as interviewers respond to interviewees who are prepared to answer the standard questions. Today, many employers have these expectations of interviewees:

- **Be more assertive.** One employer says he deliberately tells the company receptionist to brush off callers who ask about advertised openings. He interviews only those who keep calling and offer the receptionist reasons they should be interviewed.
- **Follow instructions to the letter.** The owner of a delivery company tells candidates to phone at a precise hour. Failing to do so means that the person couldn't be trusted to deliver packages on time.[38]

On the Job Productive and Engaged*

Mandatory retirement age is in the news. The Ontario government abolished the 65 age limit effective December 12, 2006, making the announcement at Home Depot, a store known for its policy of hiring staff over 50. Representing over 20% of staff, these older employees have proven a source of solid know-how for customers.

On January 1, 2008, British Columbia joined Saskatchewan and Newfoundland and Labrador adding to the long list of jurisdictions that have scrapped mandatory retirement. Nova Scotia completed the list in July 2009.

Research suggests that businesses and organizations get "the most productive and engaged employees" staying on the job. The percentage of those over 65 in the workforce has risen from 6% in the late 1990s to 12% in 2012, and companies are offering flexible arrangements to retain them. Even those over 80 are finding work a "much-needed, and energizing, social outlet."

Still, despite the trend, the average age of retirement fell to 62.3 in 2003 from 65 in the late 1970s. After Quebec abolished mandatory retirement, early retirements actually rose in number, over-65s dropping from 8.3% of the workforce to 5.7%.

A 2011 Royal Bank of Canada survey found that 40% of retired Canadians had to leave the work force before they had planned to do so. Daniel Rubin of Rubin, Thomlinson LLP Toronto, warns that there may be no "smoking gun where they'll say, 'You're old and we don't want to retain you any more'—it's more subtle than that."

Amendments to the Canadian Human Rights Act and the Canadian Labour Code on December 16, 2012, ended mandatory retirement for federally regulated employers except where inconsistent with occupational requirements.

*Based on Employment and Social Development Canada, "Work—Employment rate," retrieved June 21, 2014, from http://www4.hrsdc.gc.ca/.3ndic.1t.4r@-eng.jsp?iid=13; Government of Canada, "Eliminating the mandatory retirement age," retrieved June 21, 2014, from http://actionplan.gc.ca/en/initiative/eliminating-mandatory-retirement-age; Jennifer Myers, "When the exit door awaits," *The Globe and Mail,* May 13, 2011, B20; Rob Ferguson, "Mandatory retirement on its way out," *The Toronto Star,* June 7, 2005, retrieved July 1, 2005, from http://www.thestar.com; Wallace Immen, "Post-65 workers 'productive and engaged,'" *The Globe and Mail,* March 18, 2005, C1; Randy Chapnik Myers, "Past 80 and still going strong," *The Globe and Mail,* April 9, 2008, C1–2; "Retiring mandatory retirement," CBC News, retrieved April 22, 2008, http://www.cbc.ca/news/background/retirement/mandatory_retirement.html.

Figure 13.13 An E-Mail Application Letter

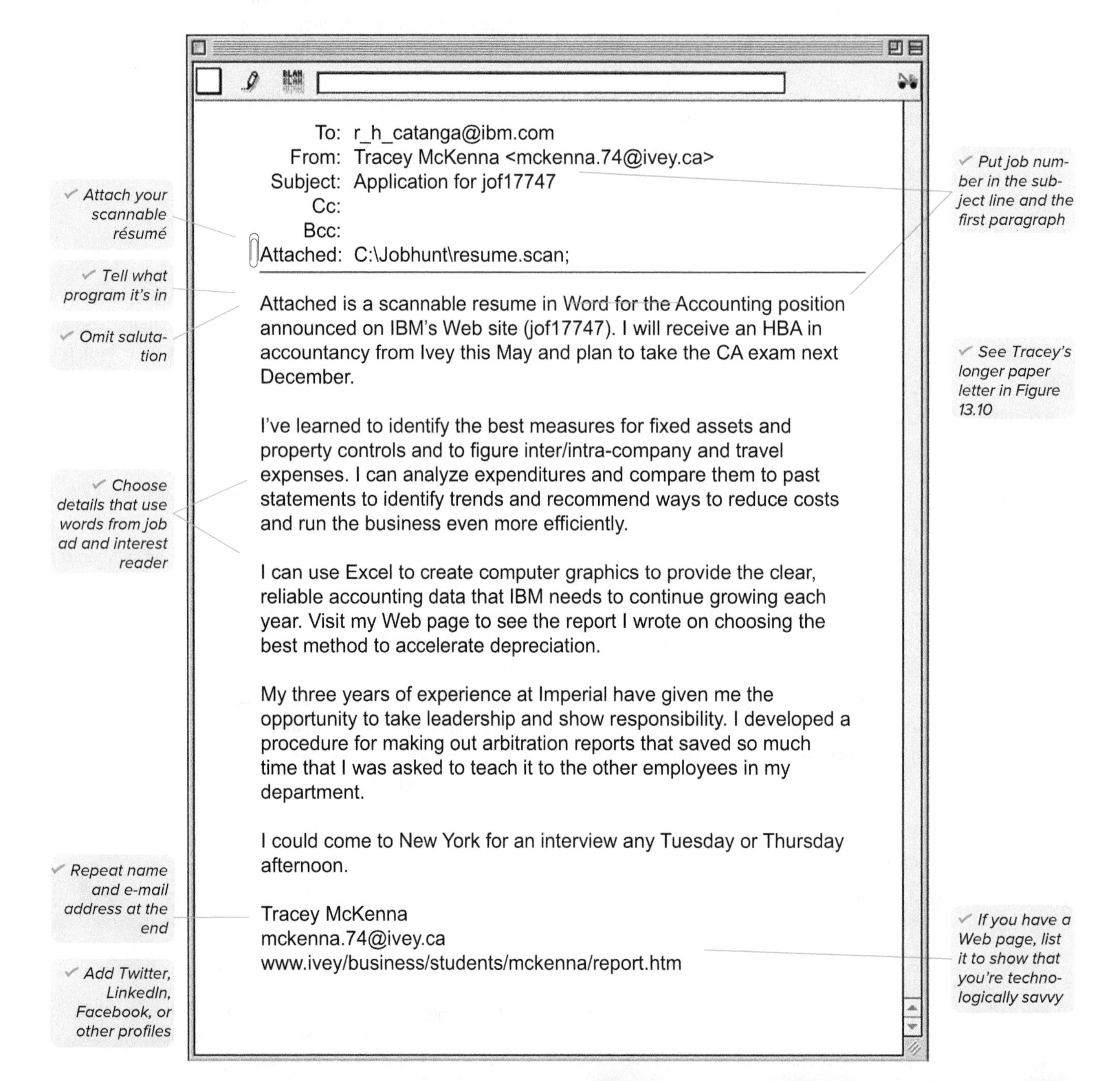

To: r_h_catanga@ibm.com
From: Tracey McKenna <mckenna.74@ivey.ca>
Subject: Application for jof17747
Cc:
Bcc:
Attached: C:\Jobhunt\resume.scan;

Attached is a scannable resume in Word for the Accounting position announced on IBM's Web site (jof17747). I will receive an HBA in accountancy from Ivey this May and plan to take the CA exam next December.

I've learned to identify the best measures for fixed assets and property controls and to figure inter/intra-company and travel expenses. I can analyze expenditures and compare them to past statements to identify trends and recommend ways to reduce costs and run the business even more efficiently.

I can use Excel to create computer graphics to provide the clear, reliable accounting data that IBM needs to continue growing each year. Visit my Web page to see the report I wrote on choosing the best method to accelerate depreciation.

My three years of experience at Imperial have given me the opportunity to take leadership and show responsibility. I developed a procedure for making out arbitration reports that saved so much time that I was asked to teach it to the other employees in my department.

I could come to New York for an interview any Tuesday or Thursday afternoon.

Tracey McKenna
mckenna.74@ivey.ca
www.ivey/business/students/mckenna/report.htm

- **Participate in many interviews.** Candidates for jobs with Electronic Arts, a maker of computer games, first answer questions online. Then they have up to five phone interviews—some asking candidates to solve problems or program functions. Candidates who get that far undergo "the gauntlet": three days of onsite interviewing.[39]
- **Be approved by the team you'll be joining.** In companies with self-managed work teams, the team has a say in who is hired.
- **Have one or more interviews by phone, computer, or video.** Investing in more interviews to get the best candidate, more than half of employers in a 2011 survey said they are using phone interviews more and 41% use panel interviews.[40] Since 2005 the proportion of initial interviews

Video interviewing is an art that takes careful preparation and practice.

Technology Tips What's in Your E-Portfolio?*

Putting together your e-portfolio—a purposeful collection of electronic evidence of your abilities and achievements in text, image, multimedia—is a useful source of learning as well as a valuable job search tool even if the corporate world hasn't kept pace with university and college interest in and programs for e-portfolios. Contents can include reports and presentations, learning blogs, wikis, tweets, Web sites, video, feedback from peers and instructors, certificates, images, and résumés and cover letters that can be readily searched and navigated.

While some students have uncovered new opportunities and career goals, others have confirmed their aptitudes and professional direction. For researchers and employers, e-portfolios are proving "richer media than regular resumes—think outline versus visually rich, interactive website."

Managers report getting "a better feel for who the person is" with their specific evidence of skills.

In one case, 2,000 tweets in a candidate's Twitter account got him the job. It proved to be a powerful portfolio that beat out "the pile of résumés by giving [him] a presence and a personal brand."

Stefan Strohmeier recognizes e-portfolios' value in uncovering competencies and "relevant personality traits," although he argues that customizing for specific organizations as well as interpreting information remains onerous and "authentication measures" are needed to address fakes and "ghost-writing."

*Based on Melissa Korn, "E-portfolios fail to find audience," *Report on Business*, February 12, 2014, B19; Charlotte Brammer, "Electronic portfolios: For assessment and job search," Proceedings of the 2007 Association for Business Communication Annual Convention, retrieved June 15, 2011, from http://businesscommunication.org/wp-content/uploads/2011/04/01ABC07.pdf; Stefan Strohmeier, "Electronic portfolios in recruiting? A conceptual analysis of usage," *Journal of Electronic Commerce Research*, 11.4 (2010), 268–280; Wallace Immen, "Tweet your way to a job," *The Globe and Mail*, May 19, 2011, B16–18.

conducted by video has increased from 10% to 30%.[41] Emilie Cushman of Toronto's Kira Talent claims increases as high as 60 percent.[42] One client is Queen's University in Kingston, ON, that turned to video interviews to reduce misleading applications and help navigate 1,300 to 1,400 applications for 70 seats in its MBA program.[43] Video interviews focus more than 50% of attention on appearance and presentation, 40% on voice tone and inflection, and 10% on what you actually say. They also magnify inadvertent or nervous gestures.[44]

- **Take one or more tests,** including drug tests, psychological tests, aptitude tests, computer simulations, and essay exams where you're asked to explain what you'd do in a specific situation. McMaster University in Hamilton has developed an online test to identify medical students "with the character to match their cognitive powers." The test focuses on "good decision-making, ethics, communication skills and cultural sensitivity." This two-hour test (relying on video scenarios giving students five minutes for three questions) complements the Multiple Mini Interviews begun in 2004 that challenge students with "live scenarios" at as many as 12 interview stations.[45]
- **Provide—at the interview or right after it—a sample of the work you're applying to do.** You may be asked to write a memo or a proposal, calculate a budget on a spreadsheet, or make a presentation (see "What's in Your E-Portfolio?"). Your class experience and projects will serve you well.

All the phoning required in 21st-century interviews places a special emphasis on phone skills. If you get voice mail, leave a concise message—complete with your name and phone number. Even if you've called 10 times, keep your voice pleasant.

LO6

DEVELOPING AN INTERVIEW STRATEGY

Develop an overall strategy based on your answers to these three questions:

1. **What about yourself do you want the interviewer to know?** Pick two to five points that represent your strengths for that particular job. For each strength, think of a specific action or accomplishment to support it. For example, be ready to show how you helped an organization save money or serve customers better.

   At the interview, listen to every question to see if you could make one of your key points as part of your answer. If the questions don't allow you to make your points, bring them up at the end of the interview.
2. **What disadvantages or weaknesses do you need to minimize?** Expect that you may be asked to explain weaknesses or apparent weaknesses in your record: lack of experience, so-so grades, and gaps in your record.
3. **What do you need to know about the job and the organization to decide whether or not you want to accept this job if it is offered to you?** Plan *in advance* the criteria on which you will base your decision (you can always change the criteria).

TAKING CARE OF THE DETAILS

Wearing inappropriate clothing or being late can cost you a job. Put enough time into planning details so that you can move on to substantive planning.

If you're interviewing for a management or office job, wear a business suit. What kind of suit? If you've got good taste and a good eye for colour, follow your instincts. If not, learn from people inside the organization. Check out the Web site, annual report, Facebook, or other sources that signal how people dress and behave.

Take care of all the details. Check your heels to make sure they aren't run down; make sure your shoes are shined. Have your hair cut or styled conservatively. Jewellery and makeup should be understated. Personal hygiene must be impeccable. Avoid cologne and perfumed aftershave lotions. Be aware that many people respond negatively to smoking. Cover any body art and take out any nose or lip rings.[46]

Bring extra copies of your résumé. If your campus placement office has already given the interviewer a data sheet, present the résumé at the beginning of the interview: "I thought you might like a little more information about me."

Bring something to write on and something to write with. It's OK to bring in a small notepad with the questions you want to ask on it.

Bring copies of your work or a portfolio: an engineering design, a copy of a memo you wrote on a job or in a business writing class, an article you wrote for the campus paper. You don't need to present these unless the interview calls for them, but they can be very effective (see ◀◀ "What's in Your E-Portfolio?").

Bring the names, addresses, and phone numbers of references if you didn't put them on your résumé. Bring complete details about your work history and education, including dates and street addresses, in case you're asked to fill out an application form.

If you can afford it, buy a briefcase to carry these items. At this point in your life, an inexpensive vinyl briefcase is acceptable.

Rehearse everything you can: Put on the clothes you'll wear and practise entering a room, shaking hands, sitting down, and answering questions. Ask a friend to interview you. Saying answers out loud is surprisingly harder than saying them in your head.

DURING THE INTERVIEW

Be yourself. There's no point in assuming a radically different persona. If you do, you run the risk of getting into a job that you'll hate. Furthermore, you have to be a pretty good actor to come across convincingly if you try to be someone other than yourself. Yet keep in mind that all of us have several selves. Be your best self at the interview.

Interviews can make you feel vulnerable and defensive; to counter this, review your accomplishments—the things that make you especially proud. You'll make a better impression if you have a firm sense of your own self-worth.

Every interviewer repeats the advice that your mother probably gave you: sit up straight, don't mumble, look at people when you talk. Interviews are not the place for profanities, especially for women who face "greater career risks," even if there are those who argue that swearing can be galvanizing in team settings or more acceptable in cultural settings such as Britain.[47]

Office visits that involve meals and semi-social occasions call for sensible choices. When you order, choose something that's easy and not messy to eat. Watch your table manners. At dinner or an evening party, decline alcohol if you don't drink. If you do drink, accept just one drink—you're still being evaluated, and you can't afford to have your guard down. Be aware that some people respond negatively to applicants who drink hard liquor.

In the *opening* (two to five minutes), good interviewers will try to set you at ease. Some interviewers will open with easy questions about your major or interests. Others open by telling you about the job or the company. If this happens, listen so you can answer questions later to show that you can do the job or contribute to the company.

The *body* of the interview (10 to 25 minutes) is an all-too-brief time for you to highlight your qualifications and find out what you need to know to decide if you want to accept a follow-up interview or office trip. Expect questions that give you an opportunity to showcase your strong points and questions that probe any weaknesses evident from your résumé. ("You were neither in school nor working last fall. What were you doing?") Normally the interviewer will also try to sell you on the company and give you an opportunity to raise questions.

In the *close* of the interview (two to five minutes), the interviewer will usually tell you what happens next: "We'll be bringing our top candidates to the office in February. You should hear from us in three weeks." One interviewer reports that he gives applicants his card and tells them to call him. "It's a test to see if they are committed, how long it takes for them to call, and whether they even call at all."[48]

Close with an assertive statement. Depending on the circumstances, you could say: "I've certainly enjoyed learning more about General Electric." "I hope I get a chance to visit your Mississauga office. I'd really like to see the new computer system you talked about." Or "This job seems to be a good match between what you're looking for and what I'd like to do."

ANSWERING TRADITIONAL INTERVIEW QUESTIONS

First interviews seek to screen out less qualified candidates rather than to find someone to hire. Negative information will hurt you less if it comes out in the middle of the interview and is preceded and followed by positive information. If you blow a question near the end of the interview, don't leave until you've said something positive—perhaps restating one of the points you want the interviewer to know about you.

As Figure 13.14 shows, successful applicants use different communication behaviours than do unsuccessful applicants

Figure 13.14 The Communication Behaviours of Successful Interviewees

BEHAVIOUR	UNSUCCESSFUL INTERVIEWEES	SUCCESSFUL INTERVIEWEES
Statements about the position	Had only vague ideas of what they wanted to do; changed "ideal job" up to six times during the interview.	Specific and consistent about the position they wanted; were able to tell why they wanted the position.
Use of company name	Rarely used the company name.	Referred to the company by name four times as often as unsuccessful interviewees.
Knowledge about company and position	Made it clear that they were using the interview to learn about the company and what it offered.	Made it clear that they had researched the company; referred to specific brochures, journals, or people who had given them information.
Level of interest, enthusiasm	Responded neutrally to interviewer's statements: "OK," "I see." Indicated reservations about company or location.	Expressed approval of information provided by the interviewer non-verbally and verbally; "That's great!" Explicitly indicated desire to work for this particular company.
Non-verbal behaviour	Made little eye contact; smiled infrequently.	Made eye contact often; smiled.
Picking up on interviewer's cues	Gave vague or negative answers even when a positive answer was clearly desired ("How are your math skills?").	Answered positively and confidently—and backed up the claim with a specific example of "problem solving" or "toughness."
Response to topic shift by interviewer	Resisted topic shift.	Accepted topic shift.
Use of industry terms and technical jargon	Used almost no technical jargon.	Used technical jargon: "point of purchase display," "NCR charge," "two-column approach," "direct mail."
Use of specifics in answers	Gave short answers—10 words or less, sometimes only one word; did not elaborate. Gave general responses: "fairly well."	Supported claims with specific personal experiences, comparisons, statistics, statements of teachers and employers.
Questions asked by interviewee	Asked a small number of general questions.	Asked specific questions based on knowledge of the industry and the company. Personalized questions: "What would my duties be?"
Control of time and topics	Interviewee talked 37% of the time, initiated subjects 56% of the comments.	Interviewee talked 55% of the total interview time, initiated 36% of the time.

Source: Based on research reported by Lois J. Einhorn, "An Inner View of the Job Interview: An Investigation of Successful Communicative Behaviors," *Communication Education* 30 (July 1981), 217–228; and Robert W. Elder and Michael M. Harris, eds., *The Employment Interview Handbook* (Thousand Oaks, CA: Sage, 1999), 300, 303, 327–328.

who are overly vague. Successful applicants are more likely to use the company name during the interview, support their claims with specific details, and ask specific questions about the company and the industry. In addition to practising the content of questions, try to incorporate these tactics.

The following questions frequently come up at interviews. Do some unpressured thinking before the interview so that you'll be able to come up with answers that are responsive, honest, and paint a good picture of you. Choose answers that fit your qualifications and your interview strategy.

1. **Tell me about yourself.** Don't launch into an autobiography. Instead, state the things about yourself that you want the interviewer to know. Give specifics to prove each of your strengths.
2. **What makes you think you're qualified to work for this company? Or, I'm interviewing 120 people for two jobs. Why should I hire you?** This question may feel like an attack. Use it as an opportunity to state your strong points: your qualifications for the job, the things that separate you from other applicants.
3. **What two or three accomplishments have given you the greatest satisfaction?** Pick accomplishments that you're proud of, that create the image you want to project, and that enable you to share something you want the interviewer to know about you. Focus on the problem-solving and thinking skills that made the achievement possible.
4. **Why do you want to work for us? What is your ideal job?** Even if you're interviewing just for practice, make

sure you have a good answer—preferably two or three reasons why you'd like to work for that company.

If you're interested in this company, do some research so that what you ask for is in the general ballpark of the kind of work the company offers.

5. **What college or university subjects did you like best and least? Why?** This question may be an icebreaker; it may be designed to discover the kind of applicant they're looking for. If your favourite class was something outside your major, prepare an answer that shows that you have qualities that can help you in the job you're applying for: "My favourite class was a seminar on the Canadian novel. We got a chance to think on our own, rather than just regurgitate facts; we made presentations to the class every week. I found I really like sharing my ideas with other people and presenting reasons for my conclusions about something."
6. **Why are your grades so low?** If your grades aren't great, be ready with a non-defensive explanation. If possible, show that the cause of low grades now has been solved or isn't relevant to the job you're applying for: "My father almost died last year, and my schoolwork really suffered." "When I started, I didn't have any firm goals. Since I discovered the field that was right for me, my grades have all been B's or better."
7. **What have you read recently? What movies have you seen recently?** These questions may be icebreakers; they may be designed to probe your intellectual depth. The term you're interviewing, read at least one book or magazine (regularly) and see at least one movie that you could discuss at an interview.
8. **Show me some samples of your writing.** Employers no longer take mastery of basic English for granted, even if the applicant has a degree from a prestigious university.

   The year you're interviewing, go through your old papers or reports and select the best, rekeying or reformatting them if necessary, so that you'll have samples ready if you're asked for them.
9. **Where do you see yourself in five years?** Employers ask this question to find out if you are a self-starter or if you passively respond to what happens. You may want to have several scenarios for five years from now to use in different kinds of interviews. Or you may want to say, "Well, my goals may change as opportunities arise. But right now, I want to. . . ."
10. **What are your interests outside work? What campus or community activities have you been involved in?** While it's desirable to be well rounded, naming ten interests is a mistake: the interviewer may wonder when you'll have time to work.

    If you mention your fiancé, spouse, or children in response to this question ("Well, my fiancé and I like to go sailing"), it is perfectly legal for the interviewer to ask follow-up questions ("What would you do if your spouse got a job offer in another town?"), even though the same question would be illegal if the interviewer brought up the subject first.
11. **What have you done to learn about this company?** An employer may ask this to see what you already know about the company (if you've read the recruiting literature, the interviewer doesn't need to repeat it). This question may also be used to see how active a role you're taking in the job search process and how interested you are in this job.
12. **What adjectives would you use to describe yourself?** Use only positive ones. Be ready to illustrate each with a specific example of something you've done.
13. **What is your greatest strength?** Employers ask this question to give you a chance to sell yourself and to learn something about your values. Pick a strength related to work, school, or activities: "I'm good at working with people." "I'm good at solving problems." "I learn quickly." "When I say I'll do something, I do it." Be ready to illustrate each with a specific example of something you've done.
14. **What is your greatest weakness?** Use a work-related negative, even if something in your personal life really is your greatest weakness. Interviewers won't let you get away with a "weakness" like being a workaholic or just not having any experience yet. Instead, use one of the following strategies:

    a. Discuss a weakness that is not related to the job you're being considered for and will not be needed even when you're promoted. (Even if you won't work with people or give speeches in your first job, you'll need those skills later in your career, so don't use them for this question.) End your answer with a positive that is related to the job:

    [For a creative job in advertising:] I don't like accounting. I know it's important, but I don't like it. I even hire someone to do my taxes. I'm much more interested in being creative and working with people, which is why I find this position interesting.

    b. Discuss a weakness that you are working to improve:

    In the past, I wasn't a good writer. But last term I took a course in business writing that taught me how to organize my ideas and how to revise. I may never win a Pulitzer Prize, but now I'm a lot more confident that I can write effective reports and proposals.

15. **Why are you looking for another job?** Stress what you're looking for in a new job, not why you want to get away from your old one.

If you were fired, say so. There are three acceptable ways to explain why you were fired:

a. It wasn't a good match. Add what you now know you need in a job, and ask what the employer can offer in this area.

b. You and your supervisor had a personality conflict. Make sure you show that this was an isolated incident, and that you normally get along well with people.

c. You made mistakes, but you've learned from them and are now ready to work well. Be ready to offer a specific anecdote proving that you have indeed changed.

16. **What questions do you have?** This question gives you a chance to cover things the interviewer hasn't brought up; it also gives the interviewer a sense of your priorities and values. Don't focus on salary or fringe benefits. Better questions are

    - What would I be doing on a day-to-day basis?
    - What kind of training program do you have? If, as I'm rotating among departments, I find that I prefer one area, can I specialize in it when the training program is over?
    - How do you evaluate employees? How often do you review them? Where would you expect a new trainee (banker, staff accountant) to be three years from now?
    - How are interest rates (a new product from competitors, imports, demographic trends, government regulations, etc.) affecting your company?
    - How would you describe the company's culture?
    - This sounds like a great job. What are the drawbacks?

You won't be able to anticipate every question you may get. (One interviewer asked students, "What vegetable would you like to be?" Another asked, "If you were a cookie, what kind of cookie would you be?"[49]) Check with other people who have interviewed recently to find out what questions are being asked in your field.

LO7

BEHAVIOURAL, SITUATIONAL, AND STRESS INTERVIEWS

Many companies, dissatisfied with hires based on responses to traditional questions, are now using behavioural or situational interviews. **Behavioural interviews** ask the applicant to describe actual behaviours, rather than plans or general principles. Thus, instead of asking "How would you motivate people?" the interviewer might ask, "Tell me what happened the last time you wanted to get other people to do something." Follow-up questions might include, "What exactly did you do to handle the situation? How did you feel about the results? How did the other people feel? How did your superior feel about the results?"

In your answer, describe the situation, tell what you did, and what happened. Think about the implications of what you did and be ready to talk about whether you'd do the same thing next time or if the situation were slightly different. For example, if you did the extra work yourself when a team member didn't do his or her share, does that fact suggest that you prefer to work alone? If the organization you're interviewing with values teams, you may want to go on to show why doing the extra work was appropriate in that situation but that you can respond differently in other situations.

Situational interviews put you in a situation that allows the interviewer to see whether you have the qualities the company is seeking.

Amy's Ice Cream stores sell entertainment. To find creative, zany employees, Amy Miller gives applicants a white paper bag and a week to do something with it. People who produce something unusual are hired.

Situational interviews may also be conducted using traditional questions but evaluating behaviours other than the answers. Greyhound hired applicants for its customer-assistance centre who made eye contact with the interviewer and smiled at least five times during a 15-minute interview.[50]

A **stress interview** deliberately puts the applicant under stress. If the stress is physical (for example, you're given a chair where the light is in your eyes), be assertive: move to another chair or tell the interviewer that the behaviour bothers you.

Usually the stress is psychological. A group of interviewers fire rapid questions. A single interviewer probes every weak spot in your record and asks questions that elicit negatives. If you get questions that put you on the defensive, *rephrase* them in less inflammatory terms, if necessary, and then *treat them as requests for information.*

Q: Why did you major in physical education? That sounds like a pretty Mickey Mouse major.

A: You're asking whether I have the academic preparation for this job. I started out in physical education because I've always loved sports. I learned that I couldn't graduate in four years if I officially switched my major to business administration because the requirements were different in the two programs. But I do have 21 hours in business administration and 9 hours in accounting. And my sports experience gives me practical training in teamwork, motivating people, and management.

Respond assertively. The candidates who survive are those who stand up for themselves and who explain why indeed they are worth hiring.

AFTER THE INTERVIEW

What you do after the interview can determine whether you get the job. One woman wanted to switch from banking, where she was working in corporate relations, to advertising. The ad agency interviewer expressed doubts about her qualifications. Immediately after leaving the agency, she tracked down a particular book the interviewer had mentioned he was looking for but had been unable to find. She presented it to him—and was hired.[51]

After a first interview, make follow-up phone calls to reinforce positives from the first interview, to overcome any negatives, and to get information you can use to persuade the interviewer to hire you.

A letter after an onsite visit (Figure 13.15) is essential to thank your hosts for their hospitality as well as to send in receipts for your expenses (where such requests are invited). The letter should

- Remind the interviewer of what he or she liked in you.
- Counter any negative impressions that may have come up at the interview.
- Use the jargon of the company and refer to specific things you learned during your interview or saw during your visit.
- Be enthusiastic.
- Refer to the next move, whether you'll wait to hear from the employer or whether you want to call to learn about the status of your application.

Be sure the letter is well written and error free. Whereas some argue that the personal touch of a hand-written card can help seal the deal, others argue for an e-mail showing "someone who was fast and responsive."[52] When 90% of senior executives confirm "thoughtful follow-up" letters influence their hiring decisions, be sure to invest time and care to leave the best impression.[53]

LO8

PERFORMANCE APPRAISALS

At regular intervals, supervisors evaluate, or appraise, the performance of their subordinates. In most organizations, employees have access to their files; sometimes they must sign the appraisal to show that they've read it. Sometimes employees are invited to write an evaluation of their own performance. The superior normally meets with the subordinate to discuss the appraisal.

Some organizations use 360-degree appraisals; that is, appraisals that have multiple sources surrounding the employee (superiors, subordinates, peers, the employee, and even external stakeholders such as clients and suppliers). Often used for training and development purposes, some argue that they complement rather than replace traditional appraisals.

Appraisals both protect the organization and motivate the employee. These two purposes may conflict. Most of us will see a candid appraisal as negative; we need praise and reassurance to believe that we're valued and can do better. But the praise that motivates someone to improve can come back to haunt the company if the person does not eventually do acceptable work. An organization is in trouble if it tries to fire someone whose evaluations never mention mistakes.

Avoid labels (*wrong, bad*) and inferences (see ◀◀ Chapter 1). Instead, cite specific observations that describe behaviour.

✗ Inference:	Sam is an alcoholic.
✗ Vague observation:	Sam calls in sick a lot. Subordinates complain about his behaviour.
✓ Specific observation:	Sam called in sick a total of 12 days in the last two months. After a business lunch with a customer last week, Sam was walking unsteadily. Two of his subordinates have said that they would prefer not to make sales trips with him because they find his behaviour embarrassing.

Figure 13.15 Follow-up Letter after an Office Visit

405 West College, Apt. 201
Antigonish, NS B2G 1L3

April 2, 2015

Mr. Robert Land, Account Manager
Sive Associates
378 Norman Boulevard
Montreal, QC H3B 4A3

Dear Mr. Land:

After visiting Sive Associates last week, I'm even more sure that writing direct mail is the career for me.

I've always been able to brainstorm ideas, but sometimes, when I had to focus on one idea for a class project, I wasn't sure which idea was best. It was fascinating to see how you make direct mail scientific as well as creative by testing each new creative package against the control. I can understand how pleased Linda Hayes was when she learned that her new package for *Canadian Art* beat the control.

Seeing Kelly, Luke, and Gene collaborating on the Sesame Street package gave me some sense of the tight deadlines you're under. As you know, I've learned to meet deadlines, not only for my class assignments, but also in working on the *Antigonish Review*. The award I won for my feature on the provincial election suggests that my quality holds up even when the deadline is tight!

Thank you for your hospitality while I was in Montreal. You and your wife made my stay very pleasant. I especially appreciate the time the two of you took to help me find information about apartments that are accessible to wheelchairs. Montreal seems like a very livable city.

My expenses totalled $474. Enclosed are receipts for my plane fare from Halifax to Montreal ($367), the taxi to the airport in Montreal ($50), and the bus from Antigonish to Halifax ($57).

I'm excited about a career in direct mail and about the possibility of joining Sive Associates. I look forward to hearing from you soon!

Sincerely,

Gina Focasio

Gina Focasio
(902) 555-2948

Encl.: Receipts for Expenses

Refers to the things she saw and learned during the interview

Reminds interviewer of her strong points

Inserts request for reimbursement before final paragraph to de-emphasize it: ends with focus on the job.

Be positive, not pushy. She doesn't assume she has the job.

Sam might be having a reaction to a physician-prescribed drug; he might have a mental illness. A supervisor who jumps to conclusions creates ill will, closes the door to solving the problem, and may provide grounds for legal action against the organization.

Be specific in an appraisal.

✗ Too vague:	Sue does not manage her time as well as she could.
✓ Specific:	Sue's first three weekly sales reports have been three, two, and four days late, respectively; the last weekly sales report for the month is not yet in.

Without specifics, Sue won't know that her boss objects to late reports. She may think that she is being criticized for spending too much time on sales calls or for not working 80 hours a week. Without specifics, she might change the wrong things in a futile effort to please her boss.

Figure 13.16 shows a performance appraisal for a member of a collaborative business communication group who is doing good work.

Letters of Recommendation

In an effort to protect themselves against lawsuits, some companies state only how long they employed someone and the position that person held. Such bare-bones letters have themselves been the target of lawsuits when employers did not reveal relevant negatives (see ◀◀ "Dealing with No-Comment Reference Policies" earlier in this chapter). Whatever the legal

Figure 13.16 A Performance Appraisal

To: Barbara Buchanan

From: Brittany Papper BAP

Date: February 13, 2015

Subject: Your Performance Thus Far in Our Collaborative Group

You have been a big asset to our group. Overall, our business communication group has been one of the best groups I have ever worked with, and I think that only minor improvements are needed to make our group even better.

What You're Doing Well

You demonstrated flexibility and compatibility at our last meeting before we turned in our proposal on February 12 by offering to key the proposal since I had to study for an exam in one of my other classes. I really appreciated this because I really did not have the time to do it. I will definitely remember this if you are ever too busy with your other classes and cannot key the final report.

Another positive critical incident occurred February 5. We had discussed researching the topic of sexual discrimination in hiring and promotion at MacLennan Insurance. As we read more about what we had to do, we became uneasy about reporting the information from our source who works at MacLennan. I called you later that evening to talk about changing our topic to a less personal one. You were very understanding and said that you agreed that the original topic was a touchy one. You offered suggestions for other topics and had a positive attitude about the adjustment. Your suggestions ended my worries and made me realize that you are a positive and supportive person.

Your ideas are a strength that you definitely contribute to our group. You're good at brainstorming ideas, yet you're willing to go with whatever the group decides. That's a nice combination of creativity and flexibility.

Areas for Improvement

Two minor improvements could make you an even better member.

The first improvement is to be more punctual to meetings. On February 5 and February 8 you were about 10 minutes late. This makes the meetings last longer. Your ideas are valuable to the group, and the sooner you arrive the sooner we can share in your suggestions.

The second suggestion is one we all need to work on. We need to keep our meetings positive and productive. I think that our negative attitudes were worst at our first group meeting February 5. We spent about half an hour complaining about all the work we had to do and about our busy schedules in other classes. In the future if this happens, maybe you could offer some positive things about the assignment to get the group motivated again.

Overall Compatibility

I feel that this group has gotten along very well together. You have been very flexible in finding times to meet and have always been willing to do your share of the work. I have never had this kind of luck with a group in the past and you have been a welcome breath of fresh air. I don't hate doing group projects any more!

✓ Subject line indicates that memo is a performance appraisal

✓ Overall evaluation

✓ These headings would need to be changed in a negative performance appraisal

✓ Specific observations provide dates, details of performance

✓ Other strengths

✓ Specific recommendations for improvement

✓ Specific behaviour to be changed

✓ Positive, forward-looking ending

climate, there may be times when you want to recommend someone for an award or for a job.

Letters of recommendation must be specific. General positives that are not backed up with specific examples and evidence are seen as weak recommendations. Letters of recommendation that focus on minor points also suggest that the person is weak.

Either in the first or the last paragraph, summarize your overall evaluation of the person. Early in the letter, perhaps in the first paragraph, show how well and how long you've known the person. In the middle of the letter, offer specific details about the person's performance. At the end of the letter, indicate whether you would be willing to rehire the person and repeat your overall evaluation.

SUMMARY OF KEY POINTS

- The job search process has three parts—know yourself, know job trends, and know the job search process—that involve repeated efforts at self-evaluation, targeting careers, researching, networking, calling, answering ads, and writing letters and résumés to secure an interview.
- A résumé must fill at least one page. Use two pages if you have extensive activities and experience.
- A *chronological résumé* summarizes what you did in a timeline (starting with the most recent events, and going backward in reverse chronology). It emphasizes degrees, job titles, and dates. It is useful when your education and experience prepare you for the position, you have impressive job titles, offices, or honours, and you have shown good progress.
- A *skills or functional résumé* emphasizes the skills you've developed and used, rather than the job in which or the date when you used them. Your accomplishments make up for the relative lack of experience.
- A version of the skills résumé, a *targeted résumé* highlights abilities and achievements that relate to a specific job target. It signals that you have taken care to adjust your strategy for a particular job.
- A résumé typically contains this information: *Name and Contact Information, Career Objective, Summary of Qualifications, *Education, Honours, *Experience, Activities, References (those marked with an asterisk are essential).
- A résumé adapted to a position summarizes all your qualifications; the letter adapted to the needs of a particular organization shows how your qualifications meet the organization's needs. The résumé uses short, parallel phrases; the letter uses complete sentences in well-written paragraphs.
- When organizing a job application letter, include the following.
  - Address the letter to a specific person.
  - Indicate the specific position for which you're applying.
  - Be specific about your qualifications.
  - Show what separates you from other applicants.
  - Show a knowledge of the company and the position.
  - Use the language of the ad, organization, and industry.
  - Refer to your résumé (which you would enclose with the letter).
  - Ask for an interview.
- Develop an overall interview strategy based on your answers to these three questions:
  1. What two to five facts about yourself do you want the interviewer to know?
  2. What disadvantages or weaknesses do you need to overcome or minimize?
  3. What do you need to know about the job and the organization to decide whether or not you want to accept this job if it is offered to you?
- *Behavioural interviews* ask the applicant to describe actual behaviours, rather than plans or general principles. *Situational interviews* put you in a situation that allows the interviewer to see whether you have the qualities the company is seeking.
- In a *stress interview*, the interviewer deliberately creates physical or psychological stress. Change the conditions that create physical stress. Meet psychological stress by rephrasing questions in less inflammatory terms and treating them as requests for information.
- Performance appraisals should cite specific observations, not inferences, and contain specific suggestions for improvement.

EXERCISES AND PROBLEMS

GETTING STARTED

13.1 ANALYZING YOUR ACCOMPLISHMENTS

List the 10 accomplishments that give you the most personal satisfaction. These could be things that other people wouldn't notice. They can be things you've done recently or things you did years ago.

Answer the following question for each accomplishment:

1. What skills or knowledge did you use?
2. What personal traits did you exhibit?
3. What about this accomplishment makes it personally satisfying to you?

As Your Professor Directs,

a. Share your answers with a small group of other students.

b. Summarize your answers in a blog or an e-mail to your professor.

c. Present your answers orally to the class.

13.2 DEVELOPING ACTION STATEMENTS

Use 10 of the verbs from Figure 13.5 to write action statements describing what you've done in paid or volunteer work, in classes, in extracurricular activities, or in community service. As your professor directs, peer grade answers.

13.3 CHANGING VERBS TO NOUNS

Revise the action statements you created for Problem 13.2, changing the verbs to nouns so that you could use the same information in a scannable résumé. As your professor directs, peer grade answers.

RÉSUMÉ ASSIGNMENTS

13.4 WRITING A RÉSUMÉ

Write the kind of résumé (chronological, skills, functional, targeted, or a new creation) that best represents your qualifications. Write a paper version that you could submit to an employer or hand to an interviewer for an interview.

As Your Professor Directs,

a. Write a résumé for the field in which you hope to find a job.

b. Write two different resumes for two different job paths that you are interested in pursuing.

c. Adapt your résumé to a specific company you hope to work for.

d. Create an online or scannable version of your résumé.

LETTER ASSIGNMENTS

13.5 WRITING A SOLICITED LETTER

Write a letter of application in response to an announced opening for a full-time job (not an internship) that a new graduate could hold.

Turn in a copy of the listing. If you use option (a), (b), or (d) below, your listing will be a copy. If you choose option (c), you will write the listing and can design your ideal job.

a. Respond to an ad in a newspaper, in a professional journal, in the placement office, or on the Web. Use an ad that specifies the company, not a blind ad. Be sure that you are fully qualified for the job.

b. Take a job description and assume that it represents a current opening. Use a directory to get the name of the person to whom the letter should be addressed.

c. If you have already worked somewhere, you may assume that your employer is asking you to apply for full-time work after graduation. Be sure to write a fully persuasive letter.

d. Respond to one of the listings below. Use a directory to get the name and address of the person to whom you should write.

1. Enterprise Rent-A-Car has an immediate opening for an entry-level staff accountant. Responsibilities will include but are not limited to A/P, A/R, Bank Recs, and journal entries. To qualify you must possess a four-year accounting degree, strong written and oral skills, and a strong desire to succeed.
2. KPMG seeks international human resources trainees to interact with corporate human resources, expatriates, payroll, relocation, and accounting functions. Bachelor's degree in an international field a plus. Personal expatriate experience preferred but not required. Must have computer skills. Please refer to job number MMGE-3W7LAY in your correspondence.
3. Bose Corporation seeks public relations/communications administrative associate (Job Code 117BD). Write, edit, and produce the in-house newsletter using desktop publishing software. Represent the company to external contacts (including the press). Provide administrative support to the manager of PR by scheduling meetings, preparing presentations, tabulating and analyzing surveys, and processing financial requests. Excellent organizational, interpersonal, and communication skills (both written and oral) required. Must be proficient in MS Office and Filemaker Pro.
4. A local non-profit organization seeks a Coordinator of Volunteer Services. Responsibilities for this full-time position include coordinating volunteers' schedules, recruiting and training new volunteers, and evaluating existing programs. Excellent listening and communication skills required.

13.6 ANALYZING FIRST PARAGRAPHS OF PROSPECTING LETTERS

All of the following are first paragraphs in prospecting letters written by new graduates. Evaluate the paragraphs on these criteria:

- Is the paragraph likely to interest the reader and motivate him or her to read the rest of the letter?
- Does the paragraph have some content that the student can use to create a transition to talking about his or her qualifications?
- Does the paragraph avoid asking for a job?

1. For the past two and one-half years I have been studying turf management. On August 1, I will graduate from _____ University with a BA in Ornamental Horticulture. The type of job I will seek will deal with golf course maintenance as an assistant superintendent.
2. Ann Gibbs suggested that I contact you.
3. Whether to plate a two-inch eyebolt with cadmium for a tough, brilliant shine or with zinc for a rust-resistant, less expensive finish is a tough question. But similar questions must be answered daily by your salespeople. With my experience in the electroplating industry, I can contribute greatly to your constant need of getting customers.
4. What a set of tractors! The new 9430 and 9630 diesels are just what is needed by today's farmer with his ever-increasing acreage. John Deere has truly done it again.
5. Prudential Insurance Company did much to help my academic career as the sponsor of my National Merit Scholarship. Now I think I can give something back to Prudential. I'd like to put my education, including a B.Comm. degree in finance from _____ University, to work in your investment department.

6. Since the beginning of Delta Electric Construction Co. in 1993, the size and profits have grown steadily. My father, being a shareholder and vice-president, often discusses company dealings with me. Although the company has prospered, I understand there have been a few problems of mismanagement. I feel with my present and future qualifications, I could help ease these problems.

COMMUNICATING AT WORK

13.7 WRITING A PERFORMANCE APPRAISAL FOR A MEMBER OF A COLLABORATIVE GROUP

During your collaborative writing group meetings, keep a log of events. Record specific observations of both effective and ineffective things that group members do. Then evaluate the performance of the other members of your group. (If there are two or more other people, write a separate appraisal for each of them.)

In your first paragraph, summarize your evaluation. Then in the body of your memo, give the specific details that led to your evaluation by answering the following questions:

- What specifically did the person do in terms of the task? Brainstorm ideas? Analyze the information? Draft the text? Suggest revisions in parts drafted by others? Format the document or create visuals? Revise? Edit? Proofread? (In most cases, several people will have done each of these activities together. Don't overstate what any one person did.) What was the quality of the person's work?
- What did the person contribute to the group process? Did he or she help schedule the work? Raise or resolve conflicts? Make other group members feel valued and included? Promote group cohesion? What roles did the person play in the group?

Support your generalizations with specific observations. The more observations you have and the more detailed they are, the better your appraisal will be.

As Your Professor Directs,

a. Write a mid-term performance appraisal for one or more group members. In each appraisal, identify positive contributions and the two or three things the person could improve during the second half of the term.

b. Write a performance appraisal for one or more group members at the end of term. Identify and justify the grade you think each person should receive for the portion of the grade based on group process.

c. Give a copy of your appraisal to the person about whom it is written.

13.8 ASKING A PROFESSOR FOR A LETTER OF RECOMMENDATION

You're ready for the job market and you need letters of recommendation.

As Your Professor Directs,

a. Assume that you've orally asked a professor for a recommendation, and he or she has agreed to write one. "Why don't you write up something to remind me of what you've done in the class? Tell me what else you've done, too. And tell me what they're looking for. Be sure to tell me when the letter needs to be in and whom it goes to."

b. Assume that you've been unable to talk with the professor whose recommendation you want. When you call, no one answers the phone; you stopped by once and no one was in. Write asking for a letter of recommendation.

c. Assume that the professor is no longer on campus. Write him or her a letter asking for a recommendation.

Hints:

- Be detailed about the points you'd like the professor to mention.
- How well will this professor remember you? How much detail about your performance in his or her class do you need to provide?

- Specify the name and address of the person to whom the letter should be written; specify when the letter is due. If there's an intermediate due date (for example, if you must sign the outside of the envelope to submit the recommendation to law school), say so.

13.9 GATHERING INFORMATION ABOUT AN INDUSTRY

Use six recent issues of a trade journal to report on three to five trends, developments, or issues that are important in an industry.

As Your Professor Directs,

a. Share your findings with a small group of other students.

b. Summarize your findings in a memo to your professor.

c. Present your findings to the class.

d. Join with a small group of other students to write a report summarizing the results of this research.

13.10 GATHERING INFORMATION ABOUT A SPECIFIC ORGANIZATION

Gather information about a specific organization, using several of the following methods:

- Check the organization's Web site and social media.
- Read the company's annual report.
- Pick up relevant information at the Chamber of Commerce.
- Read articles in trade publications and *The Globe and Mail* or *National Post* that mention the organization.
- Get the names and addresses of its officers from a directory or the Web.
- Read recruiting literature provided by the company.

As Your Professor Directs,

a. Share your findings with a small group of other students.

b. Summarize your findings in a memo to your professor.

c. Present your findings orally to the class.

d. Write a paragraph for a job letter using (directly or indirectly) the information you found.

13.11 PREPARING AN INTERVIEW STRATEGY

Based on your analysis in Problem 13.10, prepare an interview strategy.

1. List two to five things about yourself that you want the interviewer to know before you leave the interview.
2. Identify any weaknesses or apparent weaknesses in your record and plan ways to explain them or minimize them.
3. List the points you need to learn about an employer to decide whether to accept an office visit or plant trip.

As Your Professor Directs,

a. Share your strategy with a small group of other students.

b. Describe your strategy in a memo to your professor.

c. Present your strategy orally to the class.

13.12 PREPARING ANSWERS TO QUESTIONS YOU MAY BE ASKED

Prepare answers to 10 of the interview questions listed in this chapter and to any other questions that you know are likely to be asked of job hunters in your field or on your campus.

As Your Professor Directs,

a. Write down the answers to your questions and turn them in.

b. Conduct mini-interviews in a small group of students. In the group, let student A be the interviewer and ask five questions from the list. Student B will play the job candidate and answer the questions, using real information about student B's field and qualifications. Student C will evaluate the content of the answer. Student D will observe the nonverbal behaviour of the interviewer (A); student E will observe the nonverbal behaviour of the interviewee (B).

   After the mini-interview, let students C, D, and E share their observations and recommend ways that B could be even more effective. Then switch roles. Let another student be the interviewer and ask five questions of another interviewee, while new observers note content and nonverbal behaviour. Continue the process until everyone in the group has had a chance to be "interviewed."

c. Assume that you are an independent behavioural psychologist hired to conduct screening interviews and interview yourself (silently, if you like). Then write a report to the organization considering the applicant, identifying each strength, weakness, and other characteristics. Support each claim with one or more behavioural examples. Write about yourself in the third person.

(Option c based on a problem written by William J. Allen, University of La Verne and University of Phoenix.)

Appendix A WRITING CORRECTLY

Learning Outcomes

LO1 Define and explain the logic of grammar

LO2 Discuss how to identify and correct common punctuation errors

LO3 Explain the uses of punctuation within sentences

LO4 List uses of special punctuation marks

LO5 Distinguish words that are often confused

LO6 Describe the proofreading process

LO1

USING GRAMMAR

Good writers invest in editing and proofreading after the revision process, knowing that correctness is a vital source of their credibility (◂◂ Chapter 3). With the possible exception of spelling, grammar (or the rules of combination of a language) is the aspect of writing that writers seem to find most troublesome. Faulty grammar is often what executives are objecting to when they complain that university graduates or MBAs "can't write." They often assume that the writers do not know or understand what is conventionally agreed to be good or bad writing.

If you like to think that only executives of a certain age care about the rules of grammar, you'd be wrong. For 43% of 1,700 online daters surveyed, bad grammar was "a 'major' turn-off." More positively, 35% found good grammar to be "sexy."[1] Professional writers also feel the sting of alert readers' criticisms. *The Globe and Mail* public editor Sylvia Stead lists readers' grammar "pet peeves" as verb tense, incorrect pronouns, redundancies ("past history" or "factual reality"), abbreviations, and dangling participles.[2]

If spontaneity and sincerity are at a premium in a social media environment, a conversational style is no "license for sloppiness." According to Rueben Bronee, executive director of British Columbia's Public Service Initiative, "Clarity and simplicity are just as important to our writing today as they were 50 years ago."[3] Achieving both simplicity and spontaneity takes planning and preparation (◂◂ Chapter 1).

Although grammar-checkers can help, we've seen in ◂◂ Chapter 3 that they do not catch all errors. They may also be overly prescriptive, focused more on the technical than the social aspects of writing. Hence it is worth investing in mastering grammar and mechanics so that you can draft, revise, edit, and proofread independently.

Although concern with correctness too early in the writing process can lead to writer's block, grammatical correctness is an important way that writers signal the logic of their documents. Grammar establishes the logical connections between parts of a sentence, showing, for example, cause and effect: *This happens because. . . .* Attending to grammar as well as logical and rhetorical considerations is necessary to get your message across, to control how people access and respond to your writing, and to enhance persuasive power.

Most writers make a small number of grammatical errors repeatedly. Their readers may well find these errors distracting and even irritating. Keep a record of errors that your professors, employers, or peers identify as barriers to communication. Check out advice in this appendix for help in creating the professional image you want to convey in everything you write.

Sentence Types

Sentences are composed of the basic building blocks of subjects (nouns or the who/what is acting) and verbs (the acting or doing). Good, readable writing mixes sentence types and lengths. **Simple sentences** have one **main** or **independent clause:**

We will open a new store this month.

A main clause is a complete sentence with subject and verb. A **subordinate** or **dependent clause**—When the store opens—contains a subject and verb but is not a complete statement and cannot stand by itself.

Compound sentences have two main clauses joined with *and, but, or,* or another conjunction (a joining word that indicates relations between words, phrases, or clauses). Compound sentences work best when the ideas in the two clauses are closely related.

We have hired staff, and they will complete their training next week.

We wanted to have a local radio station broadcast from the store during its grand opening, but the DJs were already booked.

Complex sentences have one main and one **subordinate** or **dependent clause;** they are good for showing logical relationships.

When the store opens, we will have balloons and specials in every department.

Because we already have a strong customer base in the northwest, we expect the new store to be just as successful as the store in the Granville Mall.

Compound-complex sentences have two or more independent clauses and at least one dependent clause.

Because we already had a strong customer base in the northwest, we expected the new store to be successful, but it never had the drawing power of the store in the Granville Mall.

Agreement

Subjects and verbs *agree* when they are both singular or both plural.

✕ Incorrect: The accountants who conducted the audit was recommended highly.

✓ Correct: The accountants who conducted the audit were recommended highly.

Subject–verb agreement errors often occur when other words come between the subject and the verb. Edit your draft by finding the subject and the verb of each sentence.

Canadian usage treats company names and the words *company, board,* and *government* as singular nouns—unless the company or board is not acting as a unit.

✓ Correct (Canadian): Uniglobe Carefree Travel Group trains its agents well.

✓ Correct: The board are arguing about the strategic direction.

If following the rule feels awkward, reword to avoid the problem.

✓ Correct: The board members are arguing about the strategic direction.

Use a plural verb when two or more singular subjects are joined by *and.*

✓ Correct: Larry McGreevy and I are planning to visit the client.

Use a singular verb when two or more singular subjects are joined by *or, nor,* or *but.*

✓ Correct: Either the shipping clerk or the superintendent has to sign the order.

In either–or/neither–nor cases, use a plural verb if the subject closest to the verb is plural.

✓ Correct: Neither the professor nor her students were impressed by the behaviour.

Use a singular verb when a singular subject is followed by a phrase beginning with *as well as, together with, in addition to, along with.* These phrases do not change a singular subject to plural.

✓ Correct: The supervisor, together with her assistants, attends to customer needs.

When the sentence begins with *Here* or *There,* make the verb agree with the subject that follows the verb.

✓ Correct: Here is the booklet you requested.

✓ Correct: There are the blueprints I wanted.

Errors in **noun–pronoun agreement** occur if a pronoun is of a different number or person than the word it refers to.

× Incorrect: All drivers of leased automobiles are billed $100 if damages to his automobile are caused by a collision.

✓ Correct: All drivers of leased automobiles are billed $100 if damages to their automobiles are caused by collisions.

× Incorrect: A manager has only yourself to blame if things go wrong.

✓ Correct: As a manager, you have only yourself to blame if things go wrong.

The following words require a singular pronoun:

a person	each	neither
anybody	either	nobody
anyone	everybody	none
anything	everyone	someone

✓ Correct: Everyone should bring his or her copy of the manual to the next session on changes in the law.

If *his* or *her* feels awkward, use words (*people,* for instance) that take plural pronouns.

Each pronoun must refer to a specific word. If a pronoun does not refer to a specific term, add a word to correct the error.

× Incorrect: We will open three stores in the suburbs. This will bring us closer to our customers.

✓ Correct: We will open three new stores in the suburbs. This strategy will bring us closer to our customers.

Make sure *this* and *it* refer to a specific noun in the previous sentence. If either refers to an idea, add a noun ("this strategy") to make the sentence grammatically correct.

Use *who* and *whom* to refer to people and *which* to refer to objects. *That* can refer to anything: people, animals, organizations, and objects.

✓ Correct: The new Executive Director, who moved here from Burnaby, is already making friends.

✓ Correct: The information that she wants will be available tomorrow.

✓ Correct: This confirms the price that I quoted you this morning.

Dangling and Misplaced Modifiers

A **modifier** is a word or phrase that gives more information about the subject, verb, or object in a clause. A **dangling modifier** is not clearly related to the word it limits or modifies. Reword the modifier so that it is grammatically correct and logically modifies the subject.

× Incorrect: Confirming our conversation, the truck will leave Monday. [The speaker is doing the confirming. But the speaker isn't in the sentence.]

× Incorrect: At the age of eight, I began teaching my children about Canadian business. [This sentence says that the author was eight when he or she had children who could understand business.]

× Incorrect: Being a first-year manager, it's difficult to bring much to the discussion. [It is not a first-year manager.]

Correct a dangling modifier in one of these ways:

- Recast the modifier as a subordinate clause.

  ✓ Correct: As I told you, the truck will leave Monday.

  ✓ Correct: When they were eight, I began teaching my children about Canadian business.

  ✓ Correct: Because I am a first-year manager, it's difficult to bring much to the discussion.

- Revise the main clause so its subject or object can be modified by the now-dangling phrase.

  ✓ Correct: Confirming our conversation, I have scheduled the truck to leave Monday.

  ✓ Correct: At the age of eight, my children began learning about Canadian business.

  ✓ Correct: Being a first-year manager, I find it difficult to bring much to the discussion.

Whenever you use a verb or adjective that ends in *-ing,* ensure it modifies the grammatical subject of your sentence. If it doesn't, reword the sentence.

A **misplaced modifier** appears to modify an element of the sentence other than the writer intended.

× Incorrect: Customers who complain often alert us to changes we need to make. [Does the sentence mean that customers must complain frequently to teach us something? Or is the meaning that frequently we learn from complaints?]

Correct a misplaced modifier by moving it closer to the word it modifies or by adding punctuation to clarify your meaning. If a modifier modifies the whole sentence, use it as an introductory phrase or clause; follow it with a comma.

✓ Correct: Often, customers who complain alert us to changes we need to make.

Parallel Structure

Items in a series or list (whether the list is horizontal or vertical) must have the same grammatical (or **parallel**) structure (see also ◂◂ Chapter 3). If possible, put lists vertically to make them easier to see. If the list items are complete sentences, begin with a capital letter and end with a period. Note that the list in parallel structure must fit grammatically into the umbrella sentence that introduces the list.

× Not Parallel:

In the second month of your internship, you will do the following:

1. Learn how to resolve customers' complaints.
2. Supervision of desk staff.
3. Interns will help plan store displays.

✓ Parallel:

In the second month of your internship, you will do the following:

1. Learn how to resolve customers' complaints.
2. Supervise desk staff.
3. Plan store displays.

✓ Also parallel:

Duties in the second month of your internship include resolving customers' complaints, supervising desk staff, and planning store displays.

× Not parallel:

To improve project management processes, the business needs:

- adequate financing and project plans
- clear dispute resolution processes
- to improve frequency of progress reports

✓ Parallel:

To improve project management processes, the business needs:

- adequate financing and project plans
- clear dispute resolution processes
- regular progress reports

Parallel structure helps you make your writing tighter, smoother, and more forceful.

× Not parallel:

Providing visual aids will shorten the report, relieve the monotony, aid in highlighting statistical relationships, and the report will be made more readable.

✓ Parallel:

Visual aids will shorten the report, relieve the monotony, highlight statistical relationships, and improve readability.

LO2

UNDERSTANDING PUNCTUATION

Punctuation marks are road signs to help readers predict what comes next. (See Figure A.1.)

When you move from the subject to the verb, no comma is needed. When you end an introductory phrase or clause, the comma tells readers the introduction is over and you're turning to the main clause. When words interrupt the main clause, like this, commas tell the reader when to turn off the main clause for a short side route and when to return.

Some people have been told to put commas where they'd take breaths. That's bad advice. How often you'd take a breath depends on how big your lung capacity is, how fast and how loud you're speaking, and the emphasis you want. Commas aren't breaths. Instead, like other punctuation, they're road signs.

Figure A.1 What Punctuation Tells the Reader

MARK	TELLS THE READER
Period	We're stopping.
Semicolon	What comes next is closely related to what I just said.
Colon	What comes next is an example, formal statement, or list.
Dash	What comes next is a dramatic example of or a shift from what I just said.
Comma	What comes next is a slight turn, but we're going in the same basic direction.

International Punctuation Matters

The success of Lynne Truss's 2004 book *Eats, Shoots & Leaves: The Zero Tolerance Approach to Punctuation* has shown a healthy appetite worldwide for the story of punctuation. Winner of the Book of the Year in Britain, Truss's book takes a humorous approach to the history of punctuation and the rules governing the use of apostrophes, commas, dashes, hyphens, colons, and semicolons. It has sold more than 3 million copies.

We have seen that a sentence contains at least one main clause or complete statement. A subordinate or dependent clause contains both a subject and verb but cannot stand by itself. A phrase is a group of words that does not contain both a subject and a verb.

Main clauses

Your order will arrive Thursday.

He dreaded talking to his supplier.

I plan to enroll for summer school classes.

Subordinate clauses

if you place your order by Monday

because he was afraid the product would be out of stock

when I graduate next spring

Phrases

With our current schedule

As a result

After talking to my adviser

A clause with one of the following words will be subordinate: after, although, though, because, since, before, until, if, when, whenever, while, as.

Using the correct punctuation will enable you to avoid these major sentence errors: comma splices, run-on sentences, fused sentences, and sentence fragments.

Comma Splices

A **comma splice** or **comma fault** occurs when two main clauses are joined only by a comma (instead of by a comma and a coordinating conjunction).

× Incorrect: The contest will start in June, the date has not been set.

Correct a comma splice in one of the following ways:

- If the ideas are closely related, use a **semicolon** rather than a comma. If they aren't closely related, start a new sentence.

  ✓ Correct: The contest will start in June; the exact date has not been set.

- Add a coordinating conjunction.

  ✓ Correct: The contest will start in June, but the exact date has not been set.

- Subordinate one of the clauses.

  ✓ Correct: Although the contest will start in June, the exact date has not been set.

Remember that you cannot use a comma before the following conjunctive adverbs or transitional expression: however, therefore, nevertheless, moreover. Instead, either use a semicolon to separate the clauses or start a new sentence.

× Incorrect: Computerized grammar checkers do not catch every error, however, they may be useful as a first check before an editor reads the material.

✓ Correct: Computerized grammar checkers do not catch every error. However, they may be useful as a first check before an editor reads the material.

Run-on Sentences

A **run-on sentence** strings together several main clauses using *and, but, or, so,* and *for.* Run-on sentences and comma splices are "mirror faults." A comma splice uses only the comma and omits the coordinating conjunction, while a run-on sentence uses only the conjunction and omits the comma. Correct a short run-on sentence by adding a comma. Separate a long run-on sentence into two or more sentences. Consider subordinating one or more of the clauses.

× Incorrect: We will end up with a much smaller markup but they use a lot of this material so the volume would be high so try to sell them on fast delivery and tell them our quality is very high.

✓ Correct: Although we will end up with a much smaller markup, volume would be high since they use a lot of this material. Try to sell them on fast delivery and high quality.

Fused Sentences

A **fused sentence** results when two sentences or more are fused, or joined with neither punctuation nor conjunctions. To fix the error, add the punctuation, add a conjunction, or subordinate one of the clauses.

× Incorrect: The advantages of intranets are clear the challenge is persuading employees to share information.

✓ Correct: The advantages of intranets are clear; the challenge is persuading employees to share information.

✓ Also correct: Although the advantages of intranets are clear, the challenge is persuading employees to share information.

Sentence Fragments

In a **sentence fragment,** a group of words that is not a complete sentence is punctuated as if it were a complete sentence.

× Incorrect: Observing these people, I have learned two things about the program. The time it takes. The rewards it brings.

To fix a sentence fragment, either add whatever parts of the sentence are missing or incorporate the fragment into the sentence before it or after it.

✓ Correct: Observing these people, I have learned that the program is time consuming but rewarding.

LO3

PUNCTUATION WITHIN SENTENCES

Good writing means knowing how to use the following punctuation marks: apostrophes, colons, commas, dashes, parentheses, periods, and semicolons.

Apostrophes

Whereas some people cannot distinguish an *its* from an *it's*, others confuse plurals and possessives. Use an apostrophe in a contraction to indicate that a letter or number has been omitted.

We're trying to renegotiate the contract.

The '90s were years of restructuring for our company.

It's hard to imagine that you once feared presenting.

To indicate possession, add an **apostrophe** and an *s* to singular nouns and plurals that do not end in *s*.

The corporation's head office is in Hamilton, Ontario.

This year's sales will be higher than last year's.

The children's needs will be met by the new design features.

They agreed to meet in the woman's office on Fridays.

James's presentation proved a success with the interview committee.

When adding an apostrophe and *s* sounds awkward—in the case of Classical and biblical names, for instance—it is acceptable to use only an apostrophe for the possessive form.

Many of Aristophanes' plays are as political as they are satirical.

Jesus' teachings continue to motivate many.

With many nouns, the placement of the apostrophe indicates whether the noun is singular or plural. Plural nouns that end in an *s* take only an apostrophe to form the possessive.

The program should increase the participant's knowledge. [Only one participant]

The program should increase the participants' knowledge. [More than one participant]

The companies' employees worked well together on the joint venture. [More than one company]

Where possession is joint, use the possessive form for the last name only. Where possession is separate or individual, use the possessive form for each.

Have you visited Leroy and Diana's new condominium?

John's and Rachell's expectations of the workshop were different.

Note that possessive pronouns (*his, hers, its, ours, theirs*) do not take apostrophes. An exception is *one's*.

His promotion was announced today.

The book is hers.

The dog ate from its new bowl.

One's greatest asset is the willingness to work hard.

Colons

A colon announces to the reader what it introduces or illustrates. Use a colon to introduce a formal quotation or statement.

The board defined the meaning of the co-operative to the people: The co-operative is a place where community members can express their identities, their aspirations, and their self-determination. Since the founding meeting, they have talked about caring and sharing, about acting for the collective, and about doing things for themselves.

Use a colon to introduce appositives (nouns or noun phrases to qualify or explain nouns or pronouns).

The survey found that only 67% had a formal crisis communication plan even after the devastating storm that hit New Orleans: Hurricane Katrina.

Use a colon to separate a main clause and introduce a list that explains the last element in the clause. The items in the list are specific examples of the word that appears immediately before the colon.

Please order the following supplies:

printer cartridges
company letterhead
company envelopes

When the list is presented vertically, some authorities suggest capitalizing the first letter of each item in the list. When the list is run in with the sentence, don't capitalize the first letter after the colon.

Please order the following supplies: printer cartridges, company letterhead, and company envelopes.

Do not use a colon when the list is grammatically part of the main clause.

× Incorrect: The rooms will have coordinated decors in natural colours such as: eggplant, moss, and mushroom.

✓ Correct: The rooms will have coordinated decors in natural colours such as eggplant, moss, and mushroom.

✓ Also correct: The rooms will have coordinated decors in a variety of natural colours: eggplant, moss, and mushroom.

If the list is presented vertically, some authorities suggest introducing the list with a colon even though the words preceding the colon are not a complete sentence.

Use a colon to join two independent clauses when the second clause explains or restates the first clause.

Selling is simple: give people the service they need, and they'll come back with more orders.

In formal business writing and in works cited use a colon in these situations

Dear Dr. Thomas:

The meeting starts at 9:00 a.m.

The ratio is 2:1

CEO Speak: The Language of Corporate Leadership

Toronto: McGraw-Hill Ryerson

BusinessWeek 5 June 2015: 114–28. Print; *International Journal of Business Communication* 51(2014): 109–117. Print (MLA style)

Commas

The comma introduces, inserts, coordinates, and links. Use commas to separate the main clause from an introductory clause or phrase, the reader's name, or words that interrupt the main clause. Note that commas both precede and follow the interrupting information.

When she was ready to run, her companion had lost interest.

By providing visuals, you can shorten the report, relieve monotony, and enhance readability.

R. J. Garcia, the new sales manager, comes to us from the Hamilton office.

The financial officer, for example, could not be reached for comment.

A **non-essential clause** gives extra information that is not needed to identify the noun it modifies. Because non-essential clauses give extra information, they need extra commas.

Sue Decker, who wants to advance in the organization, has signed up for the company training program in sales techniques.

The essays, which are reasonable, will be submitted on time. [The essays will be submitted on time.]

Do not use commas to set off information that restricts the meaning of a noun or pronoun. **Essential clauses** give essential, not extra, information.

The essays that are reasonable will be submitted on time. [Only those essays considered reasonable will be submitted on time.]

Anyone who wants to advance in the organization should take advantage of on-the-job training.

Do not use commas to separate the subject from the verb, even if you would take a breath after a long subject.

× Incorrect: Laws require that anyone collecting $5,000 or more on behalf of another person, apply to schools and private individuals as well to charitable groups and professional fundraisers.

✓ Correct: Laws require that anyone collecting $5,000 or more on behalf of another person apply to schools and private individuals as well to charitable groups and professional fundraisers.

Use a comma before the coordinating conjunction (*and, but, for, nor, or, so, yet*) in a compound sentence.

This policy eliminates all sick-leave credit of the employee at the time of retirement, and payment will be made only once to any individual.

Do not use commas to join independent clauses without a conjunction. Doing so produces comma splices.

Use commas to separate items in a series. Using a comma (Oxford or serial) before the final *and* clarifies which items are part of the series. See the On the Job box "For or Against the Oxford Comma?"

On the Job For or Against the Oxford Comma?*

What is the Oxford comma? Is it necessary or not? Does it reduce ambiguity, or add to it? Why do people care so much? Warren Clements is right to suggest we "underestimate the Oxford comma at [our] peril." In a 2011 *Globe and Mail* poll, 65% used the Oxford comma, while 24% did not. Only 11% "didn't care."

The Oxford or serial comma inserted before the final "and" in a list of more than two items has both a Facebook page and a TED-Ed video!

In addition to the Oxford University Press, where its use originated, the Oxford comma is the rule for the Chicago Manual of Style, Modern Language Association of America, American Psychological Association, American Medical Association, as well as grammar guides such as Strunk and White and Fowler. The Associated Press and *The Globe and Mail* do not follow the rule.

*Based on Warren Clements, "Separatives, connectives(,) and the Oxford comma," *The Globe and Mail*, July 9, 2011, R6; Warren Clements, "Underestimate the Oxford comma at your peril," *The Globe and Mail*, July 16, 2011, R4; Kristin Piombino, "Infographic: The Oxford comma debate," posted February 19, 2013, retrieved June 24, 2014, from http://www.ragan.com/Main/Articles/46247.aspx; TED-Ed, "The Oxford comma debate," retrieved June 24, 2014, from http://ed.ted.com/lessons/grammar-s-great-divide-the-oxford-comma-ted-ed; The Oxford Comma Facebook page, retrieved June 24, 2014, from https://www.facebook.com/pages/The-Oxford-Comma/48254769340.

Ethics and Legal Costly Commas*

Commas can make a big difference in intended meanings, Rogers Communications Inc. has found. One comma in a 14-page contract has proven costly in Rogers's dispute with Aliant Inc. over Aliant's attempt to cancel the contract and increase rates for the use of Aliant utility poles in Atlantic Canada.

Page 7 of the contract states that the agreement "shall continue in force for a period of five (5) years from the date it is made, and thereafter for successive five (5) year terms, unless and until terminated by one year prior notice in writing by either party."

Rogers thought the contract secured the company for five years and for further five-year terms—unless a one-year notice is given. Regulators at the Canadian Radio-television Telecommunications Commission (CRTC), however, determined in 2006 that "the rules of punctuation" make clear that the second comma "allows for the termination of the [contract] at any time, without cause, upon one year's written notice."

Keen to avoid what has become known as the million-dollar comma error, Rogers appealed—only to win the battle and lose the war. The CRTC in August 2007 agreed that the French version of the agreement (which had received regulatory approval) was clear that the contract could not be terminated within the five-year term. But the CRTC concluded that it had no authority to intervene on the question of power poles. Hence the CRTC neither gave Rogers the relief sought nor upheld its ruling that Aliant be responsible for the increased fees for one year. A costly lesson for Rogers!

*Based on Grant Robertson, "Comma quirk irks Rogers," *The Globe and Mail,* August 6, 2006; Ian Austen, "The comma that costs 1 million dollars (Canadian)," *The New York Times,* October 24, 2006; Goodmans Update, "The comma case redux," retrieved February 14, 2008, from http://goodmans.ca/docs%5CLitigationCommaRedux.pdfr.

I received the property, offices, and houses. [Means all property as well as offices and houses.]

I received the property, offices and houses. [Means the property is limited to the offices and houses.]

The company pays the full cost of hospitalization insurance for eligible employees, spouses, and unmarried dependent children under age 23.

Dashes

Use dashes—keyed with two hyphens or inserted from a word-processer's symbols—to emphasize an insertion or a break in thought.

All the indicators—from the promising sustainability figures to the improved vulnerability performance—were welcomed by the auditor.

The Toronto Maple Leafs—including goal-scorers Phil Kessel, James van Riemsdyk, and Nazem Kadri—enjoyed the goaltending heroics of James Reimer in the win over the Montreal Canadiens.

Ryertex comes in 30 grades—each with a special use.

They planned carefully, hired more staff, worked long hours—and still missed their deadline.

The dash can be effective so long as it is not overused. Too many dashes make for choppy writing.

Parentheses

Use **parentheses** to set off words, phrases, or sentences used to explain or comment on the main idea.

For the thinnest Ryertex (.038 cm) only a single layer of the base material may be used, while the thickest (25.4 cm) may contain over 600 greatly compressed layers of fabric or paper. By varying the fabric used (cotton, glass, or nylon) or the type of paper, and by changing the kind of resin (phenolic, melamine, silicone, or epoxy), we can produce 30 different grades.

Any additional punctuation goes outside the second parenthesis when the punctuation applies to the whole sentence. Punctuation goes inside when it applies only to the words in the parentheses.

Moore's law has had a dramatic effect on computer graphics (Figure 4.5).

Please check the invoice to see if credit should be issued. (A copy of the invoice is attached.)

Periods

Use a period at the end of a sentence. Leave one space before the next sentence (see the Technology Tips feature "Much Ado about Spacing?"). Use periods in abbreviations where conventionally required.

Mr. Ms. Mrs. Dr. Rev. e.g. (for example) i.e. (that is) etc. (and so forth)

The periods are typically omitted in degree designations.

BComm MBA PhD

Semicolons

Using a semicolon suggests that two ideas are very closely connected. Using a period and a new sentence is also correct but implies nothing about how closely related the two sentences are. In this case, a semicolon could be replaced by a period and a capital letter. It has a sentence on both sides.

Use semicolons to join two independent clauses when they are closely related.

The accounting team had finished presenting; the marketing team had not yet begun.

Use semicolons before conjunctive adverbs (consequently, hence, however, indeed, meanwhile, moreover) and transitional expressions (after all, as a result, for example, in addition, in other words) in compound sentences.

The department must reduce spending; for example, it could reduce subsidies.

Technology Tips Much Ado about Spacing?*

Columnist Russell Smith comments that Canadians make for a "nation of language obsessives." What got people excited and filling his e-mail box? How many spaces to put after a period! Responses to his January 21, 2011, column numbered more than for any column he had written in the past five years and showed just how "emotionally people feel about change."

Most of his respondents still used two spaces because that is what they had learned and they "could not unlearn the habit now," although typographers and proofreaders argued strongly for the one period.

The issue came to the forefront with an article on the writing of Julian Assange of WikiLeaks by Farhad Manjoo of Slate.com, who complained that two spaces were "ugly" and plain "wrong." He was mystified that Assange could cling to such an "obsolete tradition" linked to the early history of type when typographic convention (as well as MLA and Chicago) specify one space.

*Based on Russell Smith, "To double space or not? That is the question," *The Globe and Mail*, January 21, 2011, retrieved from http://m.theglobeandmail.com/news/arts/russell-smith/to-double-space-or-not-that-is-the-question/article1876000/?service=mob; Russell Smith, "A nation of language obsessives has roared," *The Globe and Mail*, January 27, 2011, R1; Farhad Manjoo, "Space invaders: Why you should never, ever use two spaces after a period," *Slate*, January 13, 2011, retrieved from http://www.slate.com/id/2281146/; Eileen Burmeister, "The rule stands: One space after a period. Period," posted January 29, 2013, retrieved June 24, 2014, from http://www.ragan.com/Main/Articles/46131.aspx.

> We'll do our best to fill your order promptly; however, we cannot guarantee a delivery date.

Use semicolons to separate items in a series when the items themselves contain commas.

> The final choices for the new plant are Toronto, Ontario; Halifax, Nova Scotia; Calgary, Alberta; and Burnaby, British Columbia.

LO4

SPECIAL PUNCTUATION MARKS

Quotation marks, square brackets, and ellipses are used when you quote material.

Quotation Marks

Use quotation marks around direct quotations and around the names of brochures or pamphlets (italics in MLA style), story and song titles, and articles in periodicals.

> According to Marshall McLuhan, "We shape our tools and afterwards our tools shape us."
>
> The brochure "How to Cope with Chemotherapy" was as useful to the family as to the patient.
>
> Enclosed are 30 copies of our pamphlet "Saving Energy."
>
> Leslie Feist's "1234" became enormously popular after being featured in an iPod commercial.
>
> "What is it about people in uniforms" is Wallace Immen's *Globe and Mail* article about levels of trust enjoyed by professionals in Canada.

Use quotation marks around words you think misleading.

> The students complained about the "anti-business" approach of the ethics professor.

Square Brackets

Use square brackets to insert additions or changes in quoted material.

> "Some people say they are more proud, more impressed, have a greater sense of the courageousness of [Canadian Forces] members, and less a sense of dilapidated machinery," according to a November 2007 Decima study.

Ellipses

Ellipses are spaced dots. Key three spaced periods for an ellipsis to indicate missing words within a quotation (a period and the three ellipses at the end of a sentence). You do not need ellipses to mark missing elements before and after the quoted excerpt. The use of ellipses helps shorten the quoted material to focus only on important elements.

> In *CA Magazine*, Jeremy Miller suggests that the most cost-effective compensation for company employees is "psychic income. It is the satisfaction employees get from the work they do, the customers they help, the recognition they get and the people they work with. . . . Companies that offer their employees psychic income are better equipped to improve performance than those that do not."[4]

In advertising and direct mail, use ellipses to imply the pace of spoken comments.

> If you've ever wanted to live on a tropical island . . . cruise to the Bahamas . . . or live in a castle in Spain . . .
>
> . . . you can make your dreams come true with Exotic Vacations.

LO5

WORDS THAT ARE OFTEN CONFUSED

Writers (and readers) often have difficulties with words that look (homonyms) or sound (homophones) alike but have very different meanings. When you are editing, take care to check that you haven't confused the following:

accept (receive) and *except* (exclude)

adept (skilled) and *adopt* (take as one's own)

advice (noun: counsel) and *advise* (verb: to give counsel or advice) *affect* (verb: to influence) and *effect* (verb: to produce; noun: result)

a lot (many) and *allot* (divide or give to)

already (adverb: by now) and *all ready* (phrase: completely prepared)

altogether (adverb: completely) and *all together* (phrase: in a group)

amount (for things that cannot be counted numerically: amount of interest) and *number* (for things that can be counted: number of questions)

baited (harass, annoy, entice) and *bated* (from *abated* meaning restrained or held)

between (used with two) and *among* (used with more than two)

cite (quote), *site* (location), and *sight* (seeing)

compose (make up) and *comprise* (consist of)

cutback (noun: decrease) and *cut back* (verb: prune or reduce)

discreet (tactful) and *discrete* (distinct)

fewer (for objects that can be counted numerically: fewer people) and *less* (for objects counted in other ways: less unemployment)

flair (noun: style) and *flare* (verb: to blaze; noun: flame)

forward (ahead) and *foreword* (introductory remarks at beginning of a book or report)

good (adjective: beneficial) and *well* (adverb: in an acceptable manner)

hanged (people and animals) and *hung* (pictures, doors, juries)

hanger (noun: item for hanging clothes) and *hangar* (noun: building for aircraft)

imply (suggest) and *infer* (deduce)

lie (recline, tell falsehood) and *lay* (put object on something)

loose (not tight) and *lose* (to have something disappear, forfeit)

maybe (adverb: perhaps) and *may be* (verb phrase: could be)

mute (silent) and *moot* (debatable)

outset (start) and *onset* (beginning of unpleasant situation or operation; attack)

peaked (reached highest point or value) and *piqued* (aroused)

personal (adjective: individual) and *personnel* (noun: staff, employees)

precede (verb: to go before), *proceed* (verb: to continue), and *proceeds* (noun: money from transaction)

principal (adjective: main; noun: person in charge and money lent at interest) and *principle* (rule, code of conduct)

stationary (not moving) and *stationery* (paper)

then (at that time) and *than* (introducing second element in a comparison)

LO6

PROOFREADING SYMBOLS

The final stage of the writing process involves careful proofreading that aims to catch what the spell-checker and grammar-checkers cannot (see ◀◀ Chapter 3 for proofreading tips). This is your final opportunity to catch those embarrassing—PMS (premenstrual syndrome) for PSM (process safety management program), add for ad, anal for Alan, pubic for public—and potentially costly errors (see the Ethics and Legal boxes in this appendix).[5]

Use the conventional proofreading symbols in Figure A.2 to make corrections when you are working on a hard copy.

Figure A.2 Proofreading Symbols

- delete
- insert a letter
- start a new paragraph here
- stet (leave as it was before the marked change)
- spell out
- transpose (reverse)
- lower case (don't capitalize)
- capitalize
- set in italic type
- move to left
- move to right
- centre
- move up
- move down
- leave a space
- close up
- align vertically
- insert comma
- insert apostrophe
- insert quotation marks
- insert period
- insert semicolon
- insert colon
- insert hyphen

Ethics and Legal Costly Typos*

A recipe calling for "salt and freshly ground black people" proved costly for an Australian publisher. Penguin Group Australia had to destroy 7,000 copies of the *Pasta Bible* and pay $18,500 for a reprint when the error was uncovered.

Head of Publishing Robert Sessions defended proofreaders for missing "a misprint that he suggested came from a spell-check program," explaining the error was "quite forgivable" in a book in which almost every recipe included black pepper.

The official Web site included a sincere apology for the error and "for any offence this error may have caused readers."

*Based on Richard Lea, "Penguin cookbook calls for 'freshly ground black people,'" *The Guardian,* April 19, 2010, retrieved from http://www.guardian.co.uk/books/2010/apr/19/penguin-cook-book; "Cook-book misprint costs Australian publishers dear," retrieved May 20, 2011, from http://news.bbc.co.uk/2/hi/8627335.stm; "The typo that pulped 7,000 books," April 18, 2010, retrieved April 21, 2010, from http://www.theglobeandmail.com/books/the-typo-that-pulped-7000-books/artcile1538567/.

SUMMARY OF KEY POINTS

- *Grammar* (or the rules of combination of a language) is the aspect of writing that writers seem to find most troublesome. Grammatical correctness is an important way that writers signal the logic of their documents. Grammar establishes the relationship between words and the logical connections between parts of a sentence. Attending to grammar as well as logical and rhetorical considerations is necessary to get your message across, to control how people access and respond to your writing, and to enhance persuasive power.
- *Punctuation marks* are road signs to help readers predict what comes next: whether we're stopping (*period*), moving to something closely related (*semicolon*), introducing an example (*colon*), shifting from what has been said (*dash*), or making a slight turn while proceeding in the same basic direction (*comma*).
- *Comma splices* are caused by splicing or joining two main clauses with a comma. Correct by substituting a semicolon (if ideas are closely related) or a period for the comma; inserting a coordinating conjunction (and, but, or, nor, for, so, yet); or subordinating one of the clauses.
- *Run-on sentences* string together several main clauses using conjunctions but without commas. Correct a short run-on by inserting a comma. Separate a long one into two or more sentences.
- A *fused sentence* results when two sentences or more are fused, or joined with neither punctuation nor conjunctions. To fix the error, add the punctuation, add a conjunction, or subordinate one of the clauses.
- A *sentence fragment* punctuates a group of words that is not a complete sentence as if it were a complete sentence. To correct, either add whatever parts of the sentence are missing or incorporate the fragment into the sentence before it or after it.
- Good writing means knowing how to use the following punctuation marks: apostrophes, colons, commas, dashes, parentheses, periods, and semicolons.
- *Apostrophes* signal possessives and contractions. A *colon* tells the reader what it is introducing or illustrating. A *comma* introduces, inserts, coordinates, and links. *Dashes* emphasize an insertion or a break in thought. *Parentheses* set off words, phrases, or sentences used to explain or comment on the main idea. *Periods* mark the end of a sentence and appear in some abbreviations. *Semicolons* join two main clauses that are closely related, precede conjunctive adverbs in compound sentences, and separate items in a series when the items themselves contain commas.
- Quotation marks, square brackets, and ellipses are used when you quote material.
- Writers (and readers) often have difficulties with words that look or sound alike but have very different meanings. When you are editing, take care to check for commonly confused words.
- *Proofreading* is your final opportunity to catch those embarrassing and potentially costly errors. Use the conventional proofreading symbols to make corrections when you are working on a hard copy.

EXERCISES AND PROBLEMS

A.1 CHECKING PUNCTUATION AND GRAMMAR

Identify and correct the errors in the following passages.

a. Company's are finding it to their advantage to cultivate their suppliers. Partnerships between a company and it's suppliers can yield hefty payoffs for both company and supplier. One example is Bailey Controls, an Ontario headquartered company. Bailey make control systems for big factories. They treat suppliers almost like departments of their own company. When a Bailey employee scans a bins bar code the supplier is instantly alerted to send more parts.

b. Entrepreneur Trip Hawkins appears in Japanese ads for the video game system his company designed. "It plugs into the future! he says in one ad, in a cameo spliced into shots of U.S kids playing the games. Hawkins is one of several US celebrieties and business people whom plug products on Japanese TV. Jodie Foster, harrison ford, and Charlie Sheen adverstises canned coffee beer and cigarettes respectively.

A.2 PROVIDING PUNCTUATION

Provide the necessary punctuation in the following sentences. Note that not every box requires punctuation.

1. The system ☐ s ☐ user ☐ friendly design ☐ provides screen displays of work codes ☐ rates ☐ and client information.
2. Many other factors also shape the organization ☐ s ☐ image ☐ advertising ☐ brochures ☐ proposals ☐ stationery ☐ calling cards ☐ etc.
3. Charlotte Ford ☐ author of ☐ Charlotte Ford ☐ s ☐ Book of Modern Manners ☐ says ☐ Try to mention specifics of the conversation to fix the interview permanently in the interviewer ☐ s ☐ mind and be sure to mail the letter the same day ☐ before the hiring decision is made ☐
4. What are your room rates and charges for food service ☐
5. We will need accommodations for 150 people ☐ five meeting rooms ☐ one large room and four small ones ☐ coffee served during morning and afternoon breaks ☐ and lunches and dinners.
6. The current student page of Georgian College ☐ s Web site has a link to Turnitin ☐ an on ☐ line plagiarism prevention tool ☐ to help students improve their research and writing skills.
7. Most computer packages will calculate three different sets of percentages ☐ row percentages ☐ column percentages ☐ and table percentages ☐
8. In today ☐ s ☐ economy ☐ it ☐ s almost impossible for a firm to extend credit beyond it ☐ s regular terms.
9. The Department of Transportation does not have statutory authority to grant easements ☐ however ☐ we do have authority to lease unused areas of highway right ☐ of ☐ way.
10. The program has two goals ☐ to identify employees with promise ☐ and to see that they get the training they need to advance.

A.3 CREATING AGREEMENT

Revise the following sentences to correct errors in noun–pronoun and subject–verb agreement.

1. If there's any tickets left, they'll be $17 at the door.
2. A team of people from marketing, finance, and production are preparing the proposal.
3. Image type and resolution varies among clip art packages.
4. Your health and the health of your family is very important to us.
5. If a group member doesn't complete their assigned work, it slows the whole project down.
6. Baker & Baker was offended by the ad agency's sloppy proposal, and they withdrew their account from the firm.
7. The first step toward getting out of debt is not to add any more to it. This means cutting up your old credit card.

8. Contests are fun for employees and creates sales incentives.
9. The higher the position a person has, the more professional their image should be.
10. A new employee should try to read verbal and nonverbal signals to see which aspects of your job are most important.

A.4 IMPROVING MODIFIERS

Revise the following sentences to correct dangling and misplaced modifiers.

1. Originally a group of four, one member dropped out after the first meeting due to a death in the family.
2. Examining the data, it is apparent that most of our sales are to people on the northwest side of the city.
3. As a busy professional, we know that you will want to take advantage of this special offer.
4. Often documents end up in files that aren't especially good.
5. By making an early reservation, it will give us more time to coordinate our trucks to better serve you.

A.5 CREATING PARALLEL STRUCTURE

Revise the following sentences to create parallel structure.

1. To narrow a Web search,
   - Put quotation marks around a phrase when you want an exact term.
   - Many search engines have wild cards (usually an asterisk) to find plurals and other forms of a word.
   - Reading the instructions on the search engine itself can teach you advanced search techniques.
2. Men drink more alcoholic beverages than women.
3. Each issue of *Hospice Care* has articles from four different perspectives: legislative, health care, hospice administrators, and inspirational authors.
4. The university is one of the largest employers in the community, brings in substantial business, and the cultural impact is also big.
5. These three tools can help competitive people be better negotiators:
   1. Think win–win
   2. It's important to ask enough questions to find out the other person's priorities, rather than jumping on the first advantage you find.
   3. Protect the other person's self-esteem.

These three questions can help co-operative people be better negotiators:

1. Can you develop a specific alternative to use if negotiation fails?
2. Don't focus on the bottom line. Spend time thinking about what you want and why you need it.
3. Saying "You'll have to do better than that because . . ." can help you resist the temptation to say "yes" too quickly.

A.6 IMPROVING PARALLEL STRUCTURE

Revise each of the following sentences to create parallelism.

1. The orientation session will cover the following information:
   - Company culture will be discussed.
   - How to use the equipment.
   - You will get an overview of key customers' needs.
2. Five criteria for a good Web page are content that serves the various audiences, attention to details, and originality. It is also important to have effective organization and navigation devices. Finally, provide attention to details such as revision date and the Webmaster's address.

3. When you leave a voice mail message,
   - Summarize your main point in a sentence or two.
   - The name and phone number should be given slowly and distinctly.
   - The speaker should give enough information so that the recipient can act on the message.
   - Tell when you'll be available to receive the recipient's return call.

A.7 CORRECTING SENTENCE ERRORS

Revise the following sentences to correct comma splices, run-on sentences, fused sentences, and sentence fragments.

1. Members of the group are all experienced presenters, most have had little or no experience using PowerPoint.
2. Proofread the letter carefully and check for proper business format because errors undercut your ability to sell yourself so take advantage of your opportunity to make a good first impression.
3. Some documents need just one pass others need multiple revisions.
4. Videoconferencing can be frustrating. Simply because little time is available for casual conversation.
5. Entrepreneurs face two main obstacles. Limited cash. Lack of business experience.
6. The margin on pet supplies is very thin and the company can't make money selling just dog food and the real profit is in extras like neon-coloured leashes, so you put the dog food in the back so people have to walk by everything else to get to it.
7. The company's profits jumped 15%. Although its revenues fell 3%.
8. The new budget will hurt small businesses it imposes extra fees it raises the interest rates small businesses must pay.
9. Our phones are constantly being used. Not just for business calls but also for personal calls.
10. Businesses are trying to cut travel costs, executives are taking fewer trips and flying out of alternate airports to save money.

A.8 USING PLURALS AND POSSESSIVES

Choose the right word for each sentence.

1. Many Canadian (companies, company's) are competing effectively in the global market.
2. We can move your (families, family's) furniture safely and efficiently.
3. The (managers, manager's) ability to listen is just as important as his or her technical knowledge.
4. A (memos, memo's) style can build goodwill.
5. (Social workers, Social worker's) should tell clients about services available in the community.
6. The (companies, company's) benefits plan should be checked periodically to make sure it continues to serve the needs of employees.
7. Information about the new community makes the (families, family's) move easier.
8. The (managers, manager's) all have open-door policies.
9. (Memos, Memo's) are sent to other workers in the same organization.
10. Burnout affects a (social workers, social worker's) productivity as well as his or her morale.

A.9 EDITING FOR GRAMMAR AND USAGE

Revise the following sentences to eliminate errors in grammar and usage.

1. The number of students surveyed that worked more than 20 hours a week was 60%.
2. Not everyone is promoted after six months some people might remain in the training program a year before being moved to a permanent assignment.

3. The present solutions that has been suggested are not adequate.
4. At times while typing and editing, the text on your screen may not look correct.
5. All employees are asked to cut back on energy waste by the manager.
6. The benefits of an online catalogue are
   a. We will be able to keep records up-to-date;
   b. Broad access to the catalogue system from any networked terminal on campus;
   c. The consolidation of the main catalogue and the catalogues in the departmental and branch libraries;
   d. Cost savings.
7. You can take advantage of several banking services. Such as automatic withdrawal of a house or car payment and direct deposit of your paycheque.
8. As a first-year, business administration was intriguing to me.
9. Thank you for the help you gave Joanne Jackson and myself.
10. I know from my business experience that good communication among people and departments are essential in running a successful corporation.

A.10 CHOOSING THE RIGHT WORD

Choose the right word for each sentence.

1. The audit revealed a small (amount, number) of errors.
2. Diet beverages have (fewer, less) calories than regular drinks.
3. In her speech, she (implied, inferred) that the vote would be close.
4. We need to redesign the stand so that the catalogue is eye level instead of (laying, lying) on the desk.
5. (Their, There, They're) is some evidence that (their, there, they're) thinking of changing (their, there, they're) policy.
6. The settlement isn't yet in writing; if one side wanted to back out of the (oral, verbal) agreement, it could.
7. In (affect, effect), we're creating a new department.
8. The firm will be hiring new (personal, personnel) in three departments this year.
9. Several customers have asked that we carry more campus merchandise, (i.e., e.g.,) pillows and mugs with the university seal.
10. We have investigated all of the possible solutions (accept, except) adding a turning lane.

GLOSSARY

A

acknowledgment responses Nods, smiles, frowns, and words that let a speaker know someone is listening.

active listening Feeding back the literal meaning or the emotional content or both so that the speaker knows that the listener has heard and understood.

AIDA plan A four-part indirect persuasive pattern involving gaining **A**ttention, creating **I**nterest, building **D**esire, and motivating **A**ction. It is also referred to as the **AIRA** plan when the emphasis is on reducing **R**esistance before motivating action.

alliteration A sound pattern occurring when several words begin with the same sound.

apostrophe Punctuation mark indicating (1) omission of letters or numbers in contractions or (2) possession.

argument The reasons or logic offered to persuade the audience.

B

background (or history of the problem) Section of a report that explains factors leading to the problem addressed in the report. It is a useful record for later readers who may not have ready access to the situation that gave rise to the report.

bar chart A visual consisting of parallel bars or rectangles that represent specific sets of data.

behavioural interviews Job interviews that ask candidates to describe actual behaviours they have used in the past in specific situations.

bias-free language Language that does not discriminate against people on the basis of sex, physical condition, race, age, or any other category.

blind copies Copies sent to other recipients that are not listed on the original letter or memo.

blindering Limiting options unnecessarily when more than two possible positions exist (after the blinders horses wear).

block format In letters, a format in which inside address, date, and signature block are lined up at the left margin. In résumés, a format in which dates are listed in one column and job titles and descriptions in another. This format emphasizes work history.

blogs Short for Web log; a Web page with links as well as comment and content typically presented in reverse chronological order and updated regularly by an individual. Blogs often invite others to comment on entries but they are not editable by others. They can be personal (like journal or diary entries), corporate, or political.

blueprints Overviews or forecasts that tell the reader what will be discussed in a section or an entire report.

body The body of a report is the main part (after the front matter and before the conclusions and recommendations) that introduces the report, gives background or history, presents and interprets data, analyzes causes, and assesses solutions. Some organizations count the executive summary as part of the body, while others count as the body only the section after the introduction and background.

buffer A neutral or positive statement designed to allow the writer to bury, or buffer, the negative message.

build goodwill To create a good image of yourself and of your organization—the kind of image that makes people want to do business with you.

bullets Large round dots or squares that set off items in a list. When you are giving examples, but the number is not exact and the order does not matter, use bullets to set off items.

business plans Documents written to gain capital for new business venture.

businessese A kind of jargon including unnecessary words. Some words were common 200–300 years ago but are no longer part of spoken English. Some have never been used outside business writing. All of these terms should be omitted.

bypassing Miscommunication that occurs when two people use the same symbol to mean different things.

C

central selling point A super reader benefit, big enough to motivate readers by itself, but also serving as an umbrella to cover other benefits and to unify the message.

channel overload The inability of a channel to carry all the messages that are being sent.

channels The physical means by which a message is sent. Written channels include memos, letters, and billboards. Oral channels include phone calls, speeches, and face-to-face conversations.

chartjunk Decoration that is irrelevant to a visual and that may be misleading.

chronological résumé A résumé that lists what you did in a timeline, starting with the most recent events and going backward in reverse chronology.

citation Attributing a quotation, summary, or idea to a source in the body of the report.

claims The parts of an argument that the speaker or writer wants the audience to agree with.

clip art Predrawn images that you can import into your newsletter, sign, or graph.

closed body positions Include keeping the arms and legs crossed and close to the body; suggest physical and psychological discomfort, defending oneself, and shutting the other person out. Also called a defensive body position.

cloud computing Network-based applications, platforms, and infrastructure offering on-demand services, including running applications, sharing information, storing data, on the Internet (dubbed "the cloud" for this purpose).

cold list A list used in marketing of people with no prior connection to your group.

collection letters Ask customers to pay for goods and services received.

colon A punctuation mark used primarily to introduce the words that follow it: a list, a formal quotation, or formal statement, for example.

comma A punctuation mark that introduces, coordinates, links, or inserts words, phrases, or clauses in a sentence.

comma splice or comma fault Using a comma to join two independent clauses. To correct, use a semicolon, subordinate one of the clauses, or use a period and start a new sentence.

communication theory A theory explaining what happens when we communicate and where miscommunication can occur.

community of practice A group of people who work together, share a sense of purpose, engage in learning together, produce meaning, develop identities, and add value to an organization. People may belong to more than one community of practice within an organization.

complex sentences Sentences with one main clause and one subordinate clause.

complimentary closes Words after the body of the letter and before the signature. *Sincerely* and *Cordially* are the most commonly used complimentary closes in business letters.

compound sentences Sentences with two main clauses joined by a conjunction.

compound-complex sentences Have two or more independent clauses and at least one dependent clause.

conclusions Section of a report that restates the main points.

confirmation bias The process whereby people who have formed stereotypes perceive examples that reinforce or confirm their biases, while overlooking examples that would disprove their biases.

connotations The emotional colourings or associations that accompany a word.

conversational style Patterns such as speed and volume of speaking, pauses between speakers, whether questions are direct or indirect. When different speakers assign different meanings to a specific pattern, miscommunication results.

coordination The third stage in the life of a task group, when the group finds, organizes, and interprets information, and examines alternatives and assumptions. This is the longest of the four stages.

counterclaim In logic, a statement whose truth would negate the truth of the main claim.

credibility The audience's response to the source of the message as a believable one.

crop To trim a photograph to fit a specific space. Photographs are also cropped to delete visual information that is unnecessary or unwanted.

cultural competence See *intercultural competence.*

culture The unconscious patterns of behaviour and beliefs that are common to a people, nation, or organization.

cycle Sending a document from writer to superior to writer to yet another superior for several rounds of revisions before the document is approved.

D

dangling modifier A phrase that modifies a word that is not actually in a sentence. To correct a dangling modifier, recast the modifier as a subordinate clause or revise the sentence so its subject or object can be modified by the now-dangling phrase.

data Facts or figures from which conclusions can be drawn.

decoding Extracting meaning from symbols.

defensive body positions See *closed body positions.*

demographic characteristics Measurable features of an audience that can be counted objectively: age, sex, race, education level, income, etc.

denotation A word's literal or "dictionary" meaning. Most common words in English have more than one denotation. Context usually makes it clear which of several meanings is appropriate.

dependent clause See *subordinate clause.*

descriptive executive summaries Lists of the topics an article or report covers that tell how thoroughly each topic is treated but do not summarize what is said about each topic.

deviation bar charts Bar charts that identify positive and negative values, or winners and losers.

dingbats Small symbols such as arrows, pointing fingers, and so forth that are part of a typeface.

direct mail A form of direct marketing that asks for an order, inquiry, or contribution directly from the reader.

direct request pattern A pattern of organization that makes the request directly in the first and last paragraphs.

directed subject line A subject line that makes clear the writer's stance on the issue.

discourse community A group of people who share assumptions about what channels, formats, and styles to use for communication, what topics to discuss and how to discuss them, and what constitutes evidence.

documentation Providing full bibliographic information so that interested readers can go to the original source of material used in the report.

dot chart A chart that shows correlations or other large data sets. Dot charts have labelled horizontal and vertical axes.

dot planning A way for large groups to set priorities; involves assigning coloured dots to ideas.

E

early letter A collection letter that is gentle. Assumes that the reader intends to pay but has forgotten or has met with temporary reverses.

editing Checking the draft to see that it satisfies the requirements of good English and the principles of business writing. Unlike revision, which can produce major changes in meaning, editing focuses on the surface of writing.

emotional appeal Making the audience want to do what the writer or speaker asks.

empathy The ability to put oneself in someone else's shoes, to feel with that person.

enclosures Documents that accompany a letter.

encoding Putting ideas into symbols.

enunciate To voice all the sounds of each word while speaking.

essential clauses Clauses not set off by commas that give necessary information that restricts or limits the nouns they modify.

ethnocentrism The tendency to assess other cultures by criteria specific to one's own culture and to believe other cultures are inferior.

evaluating Measuring the draft against your goals and the requirements of the situation and audience. Anything produced during each stage of the writing process can be evaluated, not just the final draft.

evidence Facts or data the audience already accepts.

executive summary A summary of a report, specifying the recommendations and the reasons for them.

external audiences Audiences who are not part of the writer's organization.

external documents Documents that go to people outside the organization.

extranets Web pages for customers and suppliers.

extrinsic motivators Benefits that are "added on"; they are not a necessary part of the product or action.

eye contact Looking another person directly in the eye.

F

Facebook A social networking site that has been connecting people since 2004, Facebook reached 1.3 billion active users in 2014. The platform allows for personal profiles, information exchange, group formation, and increasing business uses.

fact sheets Present data about businesses, organizations, industries, events, and issues in brief, clear, relevant, and usable ways. Used to provide a summary introduction to an organization (as well as its services and products), break down information into manageable parts, and answer questions people may have.

feasibility report A report that evaluates two or more possible alternatives and recommends one of them. Doing nothing is always one alternative.

feedback The receiver's response to a message.

figures Any visuals that are not tables.

fixed typeface A typeface in which each letter has the same width on the page. Sometimes called typewriter typeface.

Flickr A photo and video hosting Web site where online communities can share their images. Organized by tags identifying topics and places, for instance, it is a useful image research tool for bloggers and other social media users.

fonts Unified styles of type; come in several sizes and usually several styles.

form letter A prewritten, fill-in-the-blank letter designed to fit standard situations.

formal meetings Meetings run under strict rules, like the rules of parliamentary procedure summarized in Robert's Rules of Order.

formalization The fourth and last stage in the life of a task group, when the group makes and formalizes its decision.

formation The second stage in the life of a task group, when members choose a leader and define the problem they must solve.

frozen evaluation An assessment that does not take into account the possibility of change.

full justification Margins that end evenly on the right side of the page.

functional (topic) headings See *headings.*

functional résumé Stresses individual areas of competence and accomplishment, while subordinating work and educational experience.

fused sentence The result when two or more sentences are joined with neither punctuation nor conjunctions.

G

gatekeeper The audience with the power to decide whether your message is sent on to other audiences. Some gatekeepers are also initial audiences.

gathering Physically getting the background data you need. It can include informal and formal research or simply getting the letter to which you're responding.

generic headings See *headings.*

getting feedback Asking someone else to evaluate your work. Feedback is useful at every stage of the writing process, not just during composition of the final draft.

glossary A list of terms used in a report with their definitions.

good appeal An appeal in direct marketing that offers believable descriptions of benefits, links the benefits of the product or service to a need or desire that motivates the reader, makes the reader want to read the letter, and motivates the reader to act.

good mailing list A mailing list used in direct marketing that has accurate addresses and is a good match to the product.

good product A product that appeals to a specific segment of people, is not readily available in stores, is mailable, and provides an adequate profit margin.

good service or cause A service or cause that fills an identifiable need.

goodwill The value of a business beyond its tangible assets, including its reputation and patronage. Also, a favourable condition and overall atmosphere of trust that can be fostered between parties conducting business.

goodwill endings Focus on the business relationship you share with your reader.

goodwill presentations Presentations that entertain and validate the audience.

grapevine An organization's informal informational network that carries gossip and rumours as well as accurate information.

grid system A means of designing layout by imposing columns on a page and lining up graphic elements within the columns.

grouped bar chart A bar chart that allows the viewer to compare several aspects of each item or several items over time.

groupthink The tendency for groups to put such a high premium on agreement that they directly or indirectly punish dissent.

guide headings The elements at the top of a memo or e-mail that introduce who the memo is from, to whom it is addressed, date, and subject. The order may be altered according to the preference of business, organization, or individual. Some organizations have special letterhead for memos; some use the memo templates in word-processing programs.

guided discussions Presentations in which the speaker presents the questions or issues that both speaker and audience have agreed on in advance. Instead of functioning as an expert with all the answers, the speaker serves as a facilitator to help the audience tap its own knowledge.

H

headings Words or short phrases that group points and divide a letter, memo, or report into sections. Topic, generic, or functional headings describe topics or functions (background, budget, recommendations); informative or talking heads add information and interest.

hearing Perceiving sounds. (Not the same thing as listening.)

hidden job market Jobs that are never advertised but that may be available or may be created for the right candidate.

hidden negatives Words that are not negative in themselves, but become negative in context.

histograms Bar charts using pictures, asterisks, or points to represent a unit of the data.

history of the problem See *background.*

I

impersonal expressions Sentences that attribute actions to inanimate objects, designed to avoid placing blame on a reader.

independent clause See *main clause.*

indirect approach A pattern of organization that gives the reasons first to prepare the reader for and to explain negative messages. It is appropriate for bad news, unreceptive audiences, ideas requiring persuasion, and sensitive matter communicated to superiors.

inference A statement that has not yet been verified but whose truth or falsity could be established, either now or in the future.

infinitive The form of the verb that is preceded by *to.*

infographic A graphic visual representation of complex data to make patterns and connections clear and accessible in media, educational, and other contexts.

inform To explain something or tell the audience something.

informal meetings Loosely run meetings in which votes are not taken on every point.

information (closure) report Summarizes completed work or research that does not typically result in actions or recommendations.

information interview An interview in which you talk to someone who works in the area you hope to enter to find out what the day-to-day work involves and how you can best prepare to enter that field.

information overload A condition in which a human receiver cannot process all the messages he or she receives.

informational messages In a group, messages focusing on the problem, data, and possible solutions.

informative executive summaries Present the logical skeleton of the article: the thesis or recommendation and its proof. Used to give the most useful information in the shortest space.

informative message Message to which the reader's basic reaction will be neutral.

informative presentations Used to inform or teach the audience.

inside address The reader's name and address; put below the date and above the salutation in most letter formats.

initial audience The audience that assigns the message and routes it to other audiences.

Instagram An online photo and video sharing and social networking service. Acquired by Facebook in 2012, it boasted 150 million monthly active users by December 2013.

interactive presentation A conversation in which the seller uses questions to determine the buyer's needs, probe objections, and gain provisional and then final commitment to the purchase.

intercultural competence The ability to communicate sensitively with people from other cultures and countries, based on an understanding of cultural differences.

internal audiences Audiences in the writer's organization.

internal documentation Providing information about a source in parentheses in the text rather than in endnotes or footnotes.

internal report Reports written by employees for use only in their organization.

interpersonal communication Communication between people.

interpersonal messages In a group, messages promoting friendliness, co-operation, and group loyalty.

interpret To determine the significance or importance of a message.

interview a structured conversation with someone able to give you useful information

intranets Web pages that are just for employees.

intrapreneurs Innovators who work within organizations.

intrinsic motivators Benefits that come automatically from using a product or doing something.

introduction The part of a report that states the purpose and scope of the report. The introduction may also include limitations, assumptions, methods, criteria, and definitions.

J

jargon Exists as two types: (1) the specialized terminology of a technical field, and (2) businessese, outdated words that do not have technical meanings and are not used in other forms of English.

Johnson box In the 1940s, in an effort to add impact to his sales letters, direct mail copywriter Frank H. Johnson developed the Johnson box. Placed before the salutation, the Johnson rectangular box highlights the offer without readers having to read masses of copy first.

judgment See *opinion.*

justification reports Justify the need for a purchase, an investment, a new personnel line, or a change in procedure.

K

key word outline Highlights key words in an outline, clarifying main ideas in ways useful for short presentations or online or other concise communications.

Koofers A student information-sharing service that covers class selection, professor rating, and exam and study material sharing.

L

late letters Collection letters that threaten legal action if the bill is not paid.

letters Short documents using block letter format that go to readers outside an organization.

letterhead Stationery with the organization's name, logo, address, and telephone number printed on the page.

limit In logic, a modification of an argument in response to a counterclaim.

limitations Problems or factors that limit the validity of the recommendations of a report.

line graph A visual consisting of lines that show trends or allow the viewer to interpolate values between the observed values.

LinkedIn A social networking tool increasingly used in business for professional networking and posting jobs. In 2014, it claimed 300 million professional users and promised "inside connections."

listening Decoding and interpreting sounds correctly.

M

main clause A group of words that can stand by itself as a complete sentence. Also called an *independent clause.*

memos Documents using memo format sent to readers in an organization.

middle letters Collection letters that are more assertive than an early letter. May offer to negotiate a schedule for repayment if the reader is not able to pay the whole bill immediately, remind the reader of the importance of good credit, educate the reader about credit, or explain why the creditor must have prompt payment.

minutes Record of a meeting, listing the items discussed, the results of votes, and the individuals responsible for carrying out follow-up steps.

mirror question In a research interview, a question that paraphrases the content of the last answer.

misplaced modifier A word or phrase that appears to modify another element of the sentence than the writer intended.

mixed executive summary A hybrid executive summary: part summary, part description.

mixed punctuation Using a colon after the salutation and a comma after the complimentary close in a letter.

modifier A word or phrase giving more information about another word in a sentence.

monochronic cultures Cultures in which people do only one important activity at a time.

monologue presentation A presentation in which the speaker speaks without interruption. The presentation is planned and is delivered without deviation.

Myers-Briggs Type Indicator A scale that categorizes people on four dimensions: introvert-extravert; sensing-intuitive; thinking-feeling; and perceiving-judging.

N

negative message A message in which basic information conveyed is negative; the reader is expected to be disappointed or angry.

news release Also called a media or press release, a news release is sent to the media to announce, for example, a press conference or product recall; a promotion, partnership, or product name change; a major sponsorship or philanthropic event; or a new business, product, or service. The release must have news value and answer journalists' questions (who, what, when, why, and how) with carefully chosen headline, brief quotations to humanize the story, content organized from the most to least important, and contact information.

noise Any physical or psychological interference in a message.

non-ageist Refers to words, images, or behaviours that do not discriminate against people on the basis of age.

non-essential clause A clause that gives additional information that does not identify or restrict the meaning of the noun it modifies.

non-racist Refers to words, images, or behaviours that do not discriminate against people on the basis of race.

non-sexist language Language that treats both sexes neutrally, that does not make assumptions about the proper gender for a job, and that does not imply that one sex is superior or takes precedence over the other.

nonverbal communication Communication that does not use words.

noun–pronoun agreement Having a pronoun be the same number (singular or plural) and the same person (first, second, or third) as the noun it refers to.

O

observation In semantics, a statement that you yourself have verified.

omnibus motion A motion that allows a group to vote on several related items in a single vote. Saves time in formal meetings with long agendas.

open body positions Include keeping the arms and legs uncrossed and away from the body. Suggests physical and psychological comfort and openness.

open punctuation Using no punctuation after the salutation and the complimentary close.

open-source Open-source software makes available for public use its source code on the assumption that transparency and access will enable collaboration, peer review, and a better and cheaper product. The Open Source Initiative (OSI) is a non-profit corporation that advocates for the open source advantage.

opinion A statement that can never be verified, since it includes terms that cannot be measured objectively. Also called a *judgment.*

organizational culture The values, attitudes, and philosophies shared by people in an organization that shape its messages and its reward structure.

orientation The first stage in the life of a task group, when members meet and begin to define their task.

outsourcing Going outside the company for products and services that once were made by the company's employees.

P

paired bar charts Bar charts that show the correlation between two items.

parallel structure Putting words or ideas that share the same role in the sentence's logic in the same grammatical form.

paraphrase To repeat in your own words the verbal content of what the previous speaker said.

parentheses Brackets that set off words, phrases, or sentences used to explain or comment on the main idea. Also used to insert sources in in-text citations.

passive verb A verb that describes action done to the grammatical subject of the sentence.

people-first language Language that focuses on the person, not the condition.

perception The ability to see, hear, taste, smell, and touch.

persona The "author" or character who allegedly writes a letter; the voice that a writer assumes in creating a document.

personal space The distance someone wants between him- or herself and other people in ordinary, non-intimate interchanges.

persuade To motivate and convince the audience to act.

persuasive presentation A presentation that motivates the audience to act or to believe.

pictograms Bar charts that use images to create the bars.

pie chart A circular chart whose sections represent percentages of a given quantity.

Pinterest A site that hosts photo and video sharing among online communities.

pitch Measures whether a voice uses sounds that are low or high.

plagiarism (from Latin *plagiarius:* kidnapper) The unacknowledged use of another's ideas and/or expression. To plagiarize is to pass off as your own something borrowed from someone else.

planning All the thinking done about a subject and the means of achieving your purposes. Planning takes place not only when devising strategies for the document as a whole, but also when generating "mini-plans" that govern sentences or paragraphs.

podcasts Digital media files broadcast over the Internet and played on computers or mobile media players. People can subscribe to and download podcasts available on Web sites.

polarization In logic, trying to force the reader into a position by arguing that there are only two possible positions, one of which is clearly unacceptable.

polite listening Listening that is mechanical and inattentive to the message because it is focused on the listener's own thoughts, speech, or response.

polychronic cultures Cultures in which people do several things at once.

positive or good-news message Message to which the reader's reaction will be positive.

primary audience The audience who will make a decision or act on the basis of a message.

primary research Gathering new information.

pro-and-con pattern A pattern of organization for reports that presents all the arguments for an alternative and then all the arguments against it.

probe A question that follows up an original question to get at specific aspects of a topic.

problem-solving pattern A pattern of organization that describes a problem that affects the reader before offering a solution to the problem.

procedural messages Messages focusing on a group's methods: how it makes decisions, who does what, when assignments are due.

proofreading Checking the final copy to see that it's free from typographical errors.

proportional typeface A typeface in which some letters are wider than other letters (for example, *w* is wider than *i*).

proposals Documents that suggest a method for finding information or solving a problem; help an organization decide whether to change, how to change, or how to implement a change that is agreed on.

prospecting letter A job application letter written to companies that have not announced openings but where you'd like to work.

psychographic characteristics Human characteristics that are qualitative rather than quantitative: values, beliefs, goals, and lifestyles.

psychological description Description of a product or service in terms of reader benefits.

psychological reactance Phenomenon occurring when a reader reacts to a negative message by asserting freedom in some other arena.

Q

questionnaire List of questions for people to answer in a survey.

R

ragged right margins Margins that do not end evenly on the right side of the page.

reader benefits Benefits or advantages that the reader gets by using the writer's services, buying the writer's products, following the writer's policies, or adopting the writer's ideas. Reader benefits can exist for policies and ideas as well as for goods and services.

rebuttal In logic, the refutation of a counterclaim.

recommendations Section of a report that specifies items for action.

reference line A subject line that refers the reader to another document (usually a numbered one, such as an invoice).

referral interview Interviews scheduled to learn about current job opportunities in a field and to get referrals to other people who may have the power to create a job. Useful for tapping into unadvertised jobs and the hidden job market.

release date Date a report will be made available to the public.

request To ask the audience to take an easy or routine action.

requests for proposals (RFPs) Announcements issued by a government agency or company inviting the submission of proposals.

résumé A persuasive summary of one's qualifications for employment.

response rate The percentage of people who respond to a survey.

reverse chronology Starting with the most recent job or degree and going backward. Pattern of organization used for chronological résumés.

revising Making changes in the draft: adding, deleting, substituting, or rearranging. Revision can be changes in single words, but more often it means major additions, deletions, or substitutions, as the writer measures the draft against purpose and audience and reshapes the document to make it more effective.

rhyme Repetition of the final vowel sounds, and if the words end with consonants, the final consonant sounds.

rhythm Repetition of a pattern of accented and unaccented syllables.

rule of three The rule explaining that when a series of three items are logically parallel, the last will receive the most emphasis.

run-on sentence A sentence containing several main clauses strung together with *and, but, or, so,* or *for.*

S

salutation The greeting in a letter: "Dear Ms. Smith."

sans serif Literally, without serifs. Typeface whose letters lack bases or little extensions. Helvetica and Geneva are examples of sans serif typefaces.

Scheedule A calendar app or calendar "reinvented for students" that permits users to add classes to schedules, track interesting events, and see what friends are doing.

secondary audience The audience affected by the decision or action. These people may be asked by the primary audience to comment on a message or to implement ideas after they've been approved.

secondary research Retrieving information that someone else gathered.

segmented, subdivided, or stacked bars Bars in a bar chart that sum components of an item.

semantics or general semantics The study of the ways behaviour is influenced by the words and other symbols used to communicate.

sentence fragment A group of words that are not a complete sentence but that are punctuated as if they were a complete sentence.

sentence outline An outline using complete sentences that lists the sentences proving the thesis and the points proving each of those sentences. A sentence outline is the basis for an executive summary.

serif The little extensions from the main strokes on the r and g and other letters. Times Roman and Courier are examples of serif typefaces.

semicolon A punctuation mark used to join closely related independent clauses not joined by a coordinating conjunction; before conjunctive adverbs (*consequently, however, indeed*); before transitional expressions (*in addition, as a result*) in compound sentences; and between items in a series when the items contain commas.

signpost An explicit statement of the place that a speaker or writer has reached: "Now we come to the third point."

simple sentences Sentences with one main clause.

situational interviews Job interviews in which candidates are asked to describe what they would do in specific hypothetical situations.

skills résumé A résumé organized around the skills you've used, rather than the date or the job in which you used them.

Skype A software application that can be used on your computer, television, mobile, or phone; since 2003 Skype has been allowing people to work and play together, to hold virtual meetings or keep in touch with family and friends.

social accounting A means by which businesses and organizations can monitor, evaluate, and account for economic, social, and environmental effects of business practices. Also known as social auditing, CSR reporting, sustainability reporting.

social intranets Using social media tools and Web 2.0 technologies, support broad knowledge sharing and collaboration across distance and organizational silos.

social media Electronic tools or platforms (including Facebook and Twitter) supporting social interaction in online conversations and communities, allowing consumers and businesses to communicate and interact quickly and regularly.

solicited letter A job letter written when you know that the company is hiring.

standard agenda A seven-step process for solving problems.

stereotyping Distorting unfair generalizations and labels to make people conform to unfair mental images.

storyboard A visual representation of the structure of a document, with a rectangle representing each page or unit. An alternative to outlining as a method of organizing material.

strategy A plan for reaching your specific goals with a specific audience.

stress Emphasis given to one or more words in a sentence.

stress interview A job interview that deliberately puts the applicant under stress, physical or psychological. Here it's important to change the conditions that create physical stress and to meet psychological stress by rephrasing questions in less inflammatory terms and treating them as requests for information.

structured interview Type of interview where the interviewer uses a detailed list of questions.

subject line The title of the document, used to file and retrieve the document. A subject line tells readers why they need to read the document and provides a framework in which to set what you're about to say.

subordinate clause A group of words containing a subject and a verb but that cannot stand by itself as a complete sentence. Also called a *dependent clause.*

summary sentence or paragraph A sentence or paragraph listing in order the topics that following sentences or paragraphs will discuss.

survey A research method for questioning a large group of people.

T

tables Numbers or words arrayed in rows and columns.

talking or informative heads See *headings.*

target audience The audience one tries to reach with a mailing: people who are likely to be interested in buying the product, using the service, or contributing to the cause.

targeted résumé Highlights abilities and achievements that relate to specific job targets.

thank-you note A note thanking someone for helping you.

tone The implied attitude of the author toward the reader and the subject.

tone of voice The rising or falling inflection that indicates whether a group of words is a question or a statement, whether the speaker is uncertain or confident, whether a statement is sincere or sarcastic.

topic or functional heads See *headings.*

topic sentence A sentence that introduces or summarizes the main idea in a paragraph. A topic sentence may be either stated or implied, and it may come anywhere in the paragraph.

transitions Words, phrases, or sentences that show the connections between ideas.

transmission Sending a message.

truncated code Symbols such as asterisks that turn up other forms of a keyword in a computer search.

truncated graphs Graphs with part of the scale missing.

Twitter A social networking and microblogging service operated by Twitter Inc. allowing users to share messages or tweets limited to 140 characters.

U

umbrella paragraph Lists in order and foreshadows the points that will be made in a report.

unity Using only one idea or topic in a paragraph or other piece of writing.

unstructured interview Type of interview where the interviewer has three or four main questions and other questions build on what the interviewee says.

V

verbal communication Communication that uses words; may be either oral or written.

vested interest The emotional stake readers have in something if they benefit from keeping things just as they are.

vicarious participation An emotional strategy in fundraising letters based on the idea that by donating money, readers participate vicariously in work they are not able to do personally.

Vine Since January 2013, this mobile app has enabled users to create and share short videos (maximum 6 seconds) to tell stories and create communities. Likes, comments, and revines are measures of impacts.

VoIP (Voice over Internet Protocol) A protocol designed to transmit voice via the Internet or other data network. VoIP is used by wireless, long-distance, and cable providers. VoIP capacity allows users to call and receive calls from land lines and cell phones from their computers.

volume The loudness or softness of a voice or other sound.

W

watchdog audience An audience that has political, social, or economic power and that may base future actions on its evaluation of a message.

webinar A presentation, workshop, or seminar delivered over the Web. It typically includes audience interaction supported by telephone or VoIP technology.

white space The empty space on the page. White space emphasizes material that it separates from the rest of the text.

wikis A powerful social networking software tool valuable for community building and for collaborative learning, brainstorming, and writing. A wiki is a Web site where users without special software or sophisticated knowledge of information technology can post and edit text, video, and sound.

WikiRoster A crowd-sourced service for students to communicate and connect, to see students enrolled in classes and synchronize schedules, and to discuss and share resources.

wild card Symbols such as asterisks that turn up other forms of a keyword in a computer search. See also *truncated code.*

wordiness Taking more words than necessary to express an idea.

writing The act of putting words on paper or on a screen, or of dictating words to a machine or a secretary.

Y

you-attitude A style of writing that looks at things from the reader's point of view, emphasizes what the reader wants to know, respects the reader's intelligence, and protects the reader's ego. Using *you* probably increases you-attitude in positive situations. In negative situations or conflict, avoid *you* since that word will attack the reader.

YouTube A video-sharing Web site created in 2005 on which viewers can share and view user-produced videos.

NOTES

Chapter 1

1. Natasha Artemeva, "Toward a Unified Social Theory of Genre Learning," *Journal of Business and Technical Communication*, 22.2 (2008): 160–85.
2. Charles Rubin, "You Are What You Write," Guerrilla Marketing International. http://www.gmarketing.com/articles/read/103/You_Are_What_You_Write.html, retrieved October 22, 2008.
3. Gillian Shaw, "'Soft Skills' Can Pack a Punch," *The StarPhoenix*, December 31, 2004, F16. Postmedia News, a division of Postmedia Network Inc.
4. Robyn D. Clarke, "A New Labor Day," *Black Enterprise*, February 2001, 98.
5. Anne Fisher, "The High Cost of Living and Not Writing Well," *Fortune*, December 7, 1998, 244.
6. Michael Bloom, Marjorie Burrows, Brenda Lafleur, Robert Squires, *The Economic Benefits of Improving Literacy Skills in the Workplace* (Ottawa: Conference Board of Canada, September 2007).
7. Elaine Viets, "Voice Mail Converts Boss into a Secretary," *The Columbus Dispatch*, August 10, 1995, 3E; Rochelle Sharpe, "Work Week," *The Wall Street Journal*, September 26, 1995, A1.
8. *The Chartered Professional Accountant Competency Map*. Retrieved February 6, 2014, from http://unification.cpacanada.ca/wp-content/uploads/2012/10/CompetencyMap.pdf.
9. Terrence Belford, "Engineers Need 'Soft' Skills," *The Globe and Mail*, January 13, 2003, B10.
10. Dean Beeby, "Tangle of Rules and Procedures Strangles Federal Government Tweets," *The Globe and Mail*, February 3, 2014, A2.
11. "New Survey Shows Canadian Productivity Drain," CCN Matthews, retrieved February 6, 2014, from http://www.marketwired.com/press-release/new-survey-shows-canadian-productivity-drain-589690.htm.
12. Jennifer Myers, "Literacy Gets a New Job Emphasis," *The Globe and Mail*, March 6, 2010, B15.
13. Bloom, et al., *The Economic Benefits of Improving Literacy Skills*.
14. Elizabeth Allen, "Excellence in Public Relations & Communication Management," IABC/Dayton Awards Banquet. Dayton, OH, July 12, 1990.
15. "Canadian Relay Swimmers Fall Short," CBC Olympics, retrieved August 13, 2008, from http://www.cbc.ca/olympics/swimming/story/2008/08/12/olympics-swimming-men-day-five.html.
16. Henry Mintzberg, *The Nature of Managerial Work* (New York: Harper & Row, 1973), 32, 65.
17. Jeff Buckstein, "Hurt It through the Grapevine," *The Globe and Mail*, May 25, 2007, C1. See also Joe Labianca, "It's Not 'Unprofessional' to Gossip at Work," *Harvard Business Review* 88.9 (2010): 28–29; Travis J. Grosser, Virginie Lopez-Kidwell, Giuseppe (Joe) Labianca, "Hearing It through the Grapevine: Positive and Negative Workplace Gossip," *Organizational Dynamics* 41 (2012): 52–61.
18. John Kotter, *The General Managers* (1982), summarized in Alan Deutschman, "The CEO's Secret of Managing Time," *Fortune*, June 1, 1992, 140.
19. Melissa Dark, "The Gleam of Gold," *Communication World*, January–February 2011, 5.
20. Rahim Mosahab, Osman Mahamad, and T. Ramayah, "Service Quality, Satisfaction and Loyalty: A Test of Mediation," *International Business Research* 3.4 (2010): 72–80; Toddi Gutner and Mike Adams, *A Leadership Prescription for the Future of Quality: A Report from the Conference Board Quality Council*, accessed February 6, 2014, http://www.nist.gov/baldrige/about/upload/Leadership_Prescription_The_Conference_Board.pdf.
21. James R. Rosenfield, "Tackling the Tough Topics," *Direct Marketing*, June 2001, 4.
22. Nicholas G. Carr, "The Economics of Customer Satisfaction," *Harvard Business Review*, March–April 1999, 17–18.
23. Jörgen Sandberg, "Understanding Competence at Work," *Harvard Business Review*, March 2001, 24–28.
24. Andy Holloway, "Top CEO: WestJet's Clive Beddoe," *Canadian Business* 77.9, April 26–May 9, 2004, 43; "WestJet's Ongoing Commitment to Caring for the Community," *Up! Magazine*, January 2011, 14; Brent Jang, "WestJet Charts a Bold New Path, Ever Mindful of Its No-Frills Past," *Report on Business Weekend*, March 27, 2010, B4.
25. Adapted from RBC, Women Entrepreneurs, accessed February 8, 2014, http://www.rbcroyalbank.com/sme/women/statistics.html; Roma Luciw, "Stay-at-Home Moms Stay the Business Course," *The Globe and Mail*, March 3, 2007, B10. On the Mompreneur Networking Group Inc. and *The Mompreneur Magazine*, see www.themompreneur.com.
26. CYBF, About Us, http://www.cybf.ca/about/; CYBF, *Empowering Canada's Young Entrepreneurs:* 2012–13 Annual Review, accessed February 4, 2014, from http://www.cybf.ca/wp-content/uploads/2013/09/CYBF_AR_2012-13_EN.pdf.
27. Canadian Council for Aboriginal Business (in partnership with Environics), *Promise and Prosperity: The Aboriginal Business Survey*, accessed February 8, 2014, https://www.ccab.com/uploads/File/Promise-and-Prosperity-The-Aboriginal-Business-Survey.pdf; Small Business Accelerator, Demographic Information on Aboriginal Entrepreneurs and Businesses, accessed February 8, 2014, http://www.sba-bc.ca/community/blog/demographic-information-aboriginal-entrepreneurs-and-businesses; Canadian Council for Aboriginal Business, "The State of Aboriginal Entrepreneurs," retrieved February 5, 2011, from http://www.ccab.com/uploads/File/One%20Pagers/A-Snapshot-of-Aboriginal-Entrepreneurs.pdf; Business Development Bank of Canada (BDC), "Aboriginal Entrepreneur," retrieved April 1, 2008, from http://www.bdc.ca/en/i_am/aboriginal_entrepreneur/default.htm; Isobel M. Findlay and Wanda Wuttunee, "Aboriginal Women's Community Economic Development," *IRPP Choices* 13.4 (August 2007).
28. Adapted from Canadian Centre for Social Entrepreneurship, http://www.bus.ualberta.ca/ccse; Sherrill Johnson, "Literature Review on Social Entrepreneurship," http://www.bus.ualberta.ca/ccse/Publications/Publications/Lit.ReviewSENovember2000.rtf, accessed October 22, 2008.
29. Sara Kehaulani Goo, "Building a 'Googley' Workforce: Corporate Culture Breeds Innovation," *Washington Post*, October 21, 2006, D01; Wallace Immen, "Diversity on Teams Powers Innovation, Creativity, Poll Finds," *The Globe and Mail*, September 28, 2007, C01; Kira Vermond, "Going Green Can Attract and Keep Employees," *Report on Business Weekend*, January 19, 2008, B16.
30. Statistics Canada, Outsourcing and Innovation, accessed February 8, 2014, http://www41.statcan.gc.ca/2008/0193/ceb0193_001-eng.htm; Canada, Innovation in Canada: Outsourcing, accessed March 22, 2008, http://innovation.gc.ca/gol/innovation/site.nsf/en/in03589.html.
31. Adapted from BC Biomedical Laboratories, BC Biomedical News, accessed February 6, 2014, http://www.bcbio.com/news; Jim Sutherland, "Unbeatable: Even After Cuts in Funding, BC Biomedical Is Our No. 1 Employer for the Third Year in a Row. Here's How They Do It." *Report on Business*, January 2005, 46–47.
32. Toronto Board of Trade, *Lifting All Boats: Promoting Social Cohesion and Economic Inclusion in the Toronto Region* (Toronto: Board of Trade, 2010).

33. Pete Engardio, "Smart Globalization," *BusinessWeek,* August 27, 2001, 132–136; Michael Arndt and Pete Engardio, "Diebold," *BusinessWeek,* August 27, 2001, 138.

34. Joel Kranc, "Chris Hadfield's Call for Collaboration," *Report on Business,* January 29, 2014, B16; CBC News, "Astronaut Chris Hadfield Guarded $5 Polymer Note before Space Debut," January 13, 2014, accessed February 8, 2014, http://www.cbc.ca/news/politics/astronaut-chris-hadfield-guarded-5-polymer-note-before-space-debut-1.2491549; CBC News, "Chris Hadfield, Retired Canadian Astronaut, Lands CBC Gig," January 17, 2014, accessed February 8, 2014, http://www.cbc.ca/news/technology/chris-hadfield-retired-canadian-astronaut-lands-cbc-gig-1.2500829; CTV News, "Chris Hadfield to Play with WSO This Fall," February 4, 2014, accessed February 8, 2014, http://windsor.ctvnews.ca/chris-hadfield-to-play-with-wso-this-fall-1.1670339.

35. Adapted from Amanah, About Us, accessed February 9, 2014, http://www.amanah.com/about-us/; Shannon Boklaschuk, "Internet Help for Arabian Firms," *StarPhoenix,* December 31, 2003, posted Canadian Youth Business Foundation Web site, http://www.cybf.ca/cl_saskatoon2.html, retrieved September 8, 2005.

36. "On Trial," *BusinessWeek,* January 12, 2004, downloaded from Infotrac at http://www.businessweek.com/magazine; and Nanette Byrnes, "Reform: Who's Making the Grade," *BusinessWeek,* September 22, 2003, http://www.businessweek.com/magazine/content/03_38/b3850070_mz056.htm, retrieved October 22, 2008.

37. 2013 Edelman Trust Barometer, accessed February 8, 2014, http://www.edelman.com/insights/intellectual-property/trust-2013/.

38. Matthew McClearn, "Did Anybody Even Read This?" *Canadian Business,* May 24–June 6, 2004, 14; Clarke, "A New Labor Day," 96; Tony Schwartz, "While the Balance of Power Has Already Begun to Shift, Most Male CEOs Still Don't Get It," *Fast Company,* December 1999, 366; and Pamela Kruger, "Jobs for Life," *Fast Company,* May, 2000, 236–252.

39. Adapted from McClearn, "Did Anybody Even Read This?"; Steve Maich, "Selling Ethics at Nortel: The Company's Paeans to Integrity Drip with Irony to Shareholders," *Maclean's,* January 24, 2005, 32.

40. Adapted from Jane Gadd, "Is Ethics the New Bottom Line?" *The Globe and Mail,* March 8, 2005, E6.

41. "Time Escapes: Workaholics and Time Perception," *Canadian Social Trends,* Vol. 83, May 2007 (Statistics Canada 11-008-XWE).

42. Linda Duxbury and Christopher Higgins, "Revisiting Work–Life Issues in Canada: The 2012 National Study on Balancing Work and Caregiving in Canada," accessed February 8, 2014, http://newsroom.carleton.ca/wp-content/files/2012-National-Work-Long-Summary.pdf.

43. Sue Shellenbarger, "Work–Life Balance? It's Working," *The Globe and Mail,* October 19, 2007, C3; Virginia Galt, "A Sea Change Is about to Hit the Workplace: Are You Ready?" *Report on Business,* January 6, 2007, B9; Kira Vermond, "Punching In on the Variable Clock," *Report on Business,* March 22, 2008, B14.

44. Clarke, "A New Labor Day," 96; Tony Schwartz, "While the Balance of Power Has Already Begun to Shift, Most Male CEOs Still Don't Get It," *Fast Company,* December 1999, 366; and Pamela Kruger, "Jobs for Life," *Fast Company,* May 2000, 236–252.

45. Virginia Galt, "Workaholics Have to Learn to Just Say No," *The Globe and Mail,* October 13, 2007, B18.

46. J. McFarland, "Start Spreading the (Good) News, Conference Board Tells Business," *The Globe and Mail,* May 27, 2004, http://www.theglobeandmail.com/servlet/ArticleNews/TPPrint/LAC/, retrieved May 29, 2004.

47. A. Arnot, "The Triple Bottom Line," *CGA Magazine,* January/February 2004, http://www.cga-canada.org/en-ca/AboutCGA-Canada/CGAMagazine/2004/Jan-Feb/Pages/ca_2004_01-02_ft3.aspx, retrieved October 24, 2008.

48. D. J. Manning, "Benefits of Environmental Stewardship," *Review of Business,* 25.2 (2004), 9.

49. Arnot, "The Triple Bottom Line."

50. P. Raynard, "Coming Together: A Review of Contemporary Approaches to Social Accounting, Auditing, and Reporting in Non-Profit Organisations," *Journal of Business Ethics,* 17.13 (1998), 1471–1479.

51. G. Monbiot, cited in R. Frost, "Corporate Social Responsibility and Globalization: A Reassessment, 2004," *CW Online,* International Association of Business Communicators, http://www.iabc.com/cw/private/cwb/2004/0204/reassessment.htm, retrieved July 16, 2004.

52. James Cowan, "The Companies We Trust," *Canadian Business,* May 10, 2010, 28–29.

53. Turnbull and Stamnes presentations to Canadian Co-operative Association Congress, 2003.

54. Janet McFarland and Elizabeth Church, "Crisis Management Moving Up on the Boardroom Agenda," *The Globe and Mail,* October 15, 2004, B1–B5.

55. Gillian Shaw, "F-Bombs or Friendly Words? Are Social Media Making Us Rude?" *The Vancouver Sun,* October 21, 2013, accessed February 6, 2014, http://blogs.vancouversun.com/2013/10/21/f-bombs-or-friendly-words-is-social-media-making-us-rude/; Leah Eichler, "Sorry to Be Rude, But My Phone Needs Me," *Report on Business Weekend,* October 5, 2013, B16; Ann-Frances Cameron and Jane Webster, "Multicommunicating: Juggling Multiple Conversations in the Workplace," *Information Systems Research* 24.2 (2013): 352–371.

56. Canada Helps.org. What We Do. Accessed February 8, 2014, https://www.canadahelps.org/Info/Default.aspx?sid=3&cid=16&aid=&pls=ss.

57. Brian Caulfield, "Talk Is Cheap. And Good for Sales, Too," *Business 2.0,* April 2001, 114; Elizabeth Allen, "Excellence in Public Relations & Communication Management," IABC/Dayton Awards Banquet, Dayton, OH, July 12, 1990.

58. Ryan Williams, "Social Media Tools Are Making Their Way into Corporate Intranets—And Redefining Internal Communication Research in the Process," *Communication World,* January–February 2011, 28–30.

59. Jennifer Reingold and Marcia Stepanek, "The Boom," *BusinessWeek,* February 14, 2000, 116.

60. Virginia Galt, "'Drive-by Interruptions' Taking a Toll on Production," *The Globe and Mail,* April 21, 2007; Roberto Rocha, "Information Overload Hurts Productivity," *The StarPhoenix,* August 29, 2009, F14; Nicholas Carr, "Is Google Making Us Stupid?" *The Atlantic Monthly,* July/August 2008; Peter Nicholson, "Information-rich and Attention-poor," *The Globe and Mail,* September 12, 2009, A15.

61. Josh Fischman, "Students Stop Surfing After Being Shown In-Class Laptop Use Lowers Test Scores," *The Chronicle of Higher Education,* March 16, 2009, retrieved from http://chronicle.com/blogs/wiredcampus/students-stop-surfing-after-being-shown-how-in-class-laptop-use-lowers-test-scores/4576; Carrie B. Fried, "In-Class Laptop Use and Its Effects on Student Learning," *Computers & Education,* 50.3 (2008), retrieved June 26, 2011, from http://portal.acm.org/citation.cfm?id=1342673.

62. Jonathan Pollinger, "Making Your Intranet Social," *CW Bulletin,* December 2010, retrieved January 24, 2011, from http://www.iabc.com/cwb/archive/2010/1210/Pollinger.htm; Stephen Schillerwein, "Social Intranets: The Magic Is in the Culture, Not the Tools," *CW Bulletin,* December 2010, retrieved January 24, 2011, from http://www.iabc.com/cwb/archive/2010/1210/Schillerwein.htm; Gail E. Johnson, "Face-to-Face Communication: There's an App for That," *CW Bulletin,* December 2010, retrieved January 24, 2011, from http://www.iabc.com/cwb/archive/2010/1210/Johnson.htm; *Edelman Trust Barometer 2009,* retrieved January 25, 2011, from http://www.edelman.com/trust/2009/.

63. G. Sciadis, "Our Lives in Digital Times," Connectedness Series, Statistics Canada, November 2006 (Catalogue no. 56F0004MIE, no. 14); John Izzo, "In Your Face—Far More Effective," *The Globe and Mail* August 15, 2008, C1.

Chapter 2

1. Audiences 1, 3, and 4 are based on J. C. Mathes and Dwight Stevenson, *Designing Technical Reports: Writing for Audiences in Organizations,* 2nd ed. (New York: Macmillan, 1991), 40. The fifth audience is suggested by Vincent J. Brown, "Facing Multiple Audiences in Engineering and R&D Writing: The Social Context of a Technical Report," *Journal of Technical Writing and Communication,* 24, no. 1 (1994): 67–75.

2. Isabel Briggs Myers, *Introduction to Type* (Palo Alto, CA: Consulting Psychologists Press, 1980). The material in this section follows Myers's paper.

3. Marty Parker, "Cultural Fit More Important Than Skills When Hiring," *Financial Post,* July 8, 2010, C6; Jean Hitchcock and Johnny Hagerman, "Does the Devil Wear Prada or Flip-Flops?" *Marketing Health Services,* 32. No. 2 (2010): 32.

4. Vancity homepage, accessed February 12, 2014, https://www.vancity.com/.

5. Calvin Leung, "Culture Club: Building Up Employee Values Lifts Corporate Morale and Results," *Canadian Business,* October 9–22, 2006, 115–20.

6. Renée Huang, "In a Digital World, Face Time Reaps Big Rewards," *Report on Business,* December 8, 2010, B9.
7. Keith Naughton, "How Ford's F-150 Lapped the Competition," *BusinessWeek,* July 29, 1996, 74–76; Bob McHugh, "Scions of the Times for Gen Y-ers: Toyota Promises a Different Buying Experience for a New Group of Consumers," *The Province* [Vancouver, BC], September 22, 2010, retrieved February 9, 2011, from http://search.proquest.com/docview/754979233/12D768AA7C466CA5A05/10?accountid=14739.
8. Calvin Leung, "On Target: Businesses Are Discovering the Value of Marketing to Older Consumers," *Canadian Business,* August 18, 2008, 45–46; Gabrielle Sándor, "Attitude (Not Age) Defines the Mature Market," *American Demographics,* January 1994, 18–21.
9. Susan Krashinsky, "Cogeco's TV Test: Same Show, Different Ad," *Report on Business,* December 7, 2010, B9.
10. SRIC-BI, "Representative VALS Projects," SRIC-BI Web site, www.sric-bi.com, retrieved June 2, 2004.
11. Kate Wilkinson, "Tim Hortons Ranks among 100 Most-Loved Companies in the World," *Canadian Business,* October 21, 2013, retrieved February 14, 2014, http://www.canadianbusiness.com/companies-and-industries/tim-hortons-well-loved-companies/; Andy Holloway, Zena Olijnyk, Thomas Watson, "The Countdown Continues," *Canadian Business,* 88–89, cited in Kitty O. Locker, Stephen Kyo Kaczmarek, and Kathryn Braun, *Business Communication: Building Critical Skills* (Toronto: McGraw-Hill Ryerson, 2005), 35; James Cowan, "The Companies We Trust," *Canadian Business,* May 10, 2010, 28–29.
12. Denise Deveau, "Social Networking Enhances Job," Saskatoon *StarPhoenix,* September 19, 2009, F14.
13. Marina Strauss, "Tweet to Lululemon: Smaller Sizes Please," *The Globe and Mail,* June 10, 2010, B1–2.
14. Marina Strauss, "Does This Blouse Make Sears Look Plugged-in?" *Report on Business,* April 22, 2011, B4.
15. Russell Working, "Perrier's First YouTube Campaign Creates Sensation," posted June 24, 2011, retrieved from http://www.ragan.com/Main/Articles/43170.aspx.
16. Virginia Galt, "Method Not As Important As the Message," *The Globe and Mail,* February 28, 2011, B15.
17. Robin Stephenson, "10 Ways Nonprofits Should Use Twitter," posted April 27, 2011, retrieved from http://www.ragan.com/Main/Articles/42891.aspx.
18. Mark Schaefer, "15 Best Nonprofit Blogs in The World," posted on May 17, 2011, retrieved from http://www.ragan.com/Main/Articles/42978.aspx.
19. Linda Driskill, "Negotiating Differences among Readers and Writers" (Paper presented at the Conference on College Composition and Communication, San Diego, CA, March 31–April 3, 1993).
20. Tripp Frohlichstein, "United Airlines Flubs Response to Computer Outage," posted June 20, 2011, retrieved June 27, 2011, from http://www.ragan.com/Main/Articles/43161.aspx.
21. John F. Helliwell and Haifang Huang, "How's the Job? Well-Being and Social Capital in the Workplace," *Industrial & Labor Relations Review,* 63, no. 2 (2010): 205–27.
22. Cf. Tove Helland Hammer and H. Peter Dachler, "A Test of Some Assumptions Underlying the Path-Goal Model of Supervision: Some Suggested Conceptual Modifications," *Organizational Behavior and Human Performance,* 14 (1975): 73.
23. Edward E. Lawler, III, *Motivation in Work Organizations* (Monterey, CA: Brooks/Cole, 1973), 59. Lawler also notes a third obstacle: people may settle for performance and rewards that are just OK. Offering reader benefits, however, does nothing to affect this obstacle.
24. Charles Montgomery, "And the Pursuit of Happiness," *Report on Business,* October 2007, 24–26.
25. Kevin Leo, "Effective Copy and Graphics," DADM/DMEF Direct Marketing Institute for Professors, Northbrook, IL, May 31–June 3, 1983.
26. Rachel Spilka, "Orality and Literacy in the Workplace: Process- and Text-Based Strategies for Multiple Audience Adaptation," *Journal of Business and Technical Communication,* 4, no. 1 (January 1990): 44–67.
27. Spencer E. Ante, Amir Efrati, and Anupreeta Das, "Red-Hot Twitter Valued at $10-billion," *Report on Business,* February 10, 2011, B9.
28. Sue Shellenbarger, "Companies Are Finding It Really Pays to Be Nice to Employees," *The Wall Street Journal,* July 22, 1998, B1.
29. Jim Collins, "Level 5 Leadership: The Triumph of Humility and Fierce Resolve," *Harvard Business Review,* January 2001, 66–76; Alan M. Webber, "Danger: Toxic Company," *Fast Company,* November 1998, 152–159.
30. Charles Burck, "Learning from a Master," *Fortune,* December 27, 1993, 144; Kathy Casto, "Assumptions about Audience in Negative Messages," Association for Business Communication Midwest Conference, Kansas City, MO, April 30–May 2, 1987; and John P. Wanous and A. Colella, "Future Directions in Organizational Entry Research," *Research in Personnel/Human Resource Management,* ed. Kenneth Rowland and G. Ferris (Greenwich, CT: JAI Press, 1990).
31. Annette N. Shelby and N. Lamar Reinsch, Jr., "Positive Emphasis and You-Attitude: An Empirical Study," *Journal of Business Communication,* 32, no. 4 (October 1995): 303–327.
32. Margaret Baker Graham and Carol David, "Power and Politeness: Administrative Writing in an 'Organized Anarchy,'" *Journal of Business and Technical Communication,* 10, no. 1 (January 1996): 5–27.
33. John Hagge and Charles Kostelnick, "Linguistic Politeness in Professional Prose: A Discourse Analysis of Auditors' Suggestion Letters, with Implications for Business Communication Pedagogy," *Written Communication,* 6, no. 3 (July 1989): 312–339.
34. Métis National Council, "Who Are the Métis?" http://www.metisnation.ca/who/definition.html, retrieved April 2, 2008.
35. For a fuller account, see Margery Fee and Janice McAlpine, *Oxford Guide to Canadian English Usage* (Don Mills, ON: Oxford University Press, 1997).
36. Brad Edmondson, "What Do You Call a Dark-Skinned Person?" *American Demographics,* October 1993, 9.
37. Statistics Canada, "Growth in Disability Rates from 2001 to 2006," retrieved February 14, 2011, from http://www.statcan.gc.ca/pub/89-628-x/2007002/4125018-eng.htm; Isobel M. Findlay, Julia Bidonde, Maria Basualdo, and Alyssa McMurtry, *South Bay Park Rangers Employment Project for Persons Living with a Disability* (Saskatoon: Centre for the Study of Co-operatives and Community-University Institute for Social Research, 2009); Michael J. Prince, "Canadian Disability Policy: Still a Hit-or-Miss Affair," *Canadian Journal of Sociology,* 29.1 (2004), http://muse.jhu.edu/demo/Canadian_journal_of_sociology/vo29/29.1prince.pdf, retrieved March 10, 2005.
38. Marilyn A. Dyrud, "An Exploration of Gender Bias in Computer Clip Art," *Business Communication Quarterly,* 60, no. 4 (December 1997): 30–51.

Chapter 3

1. See especially Linda Flower and John R. Hayes, "The Cognition of Discovery: Defining a Rhetorical Problem," *College Composition and Communication,* 31 (February 1980): 21–32; Rose, *Writer's Block;* and the essays in two collections: Charles R. Cooper and Lee Odell, *Research on Composing: Points of Departure* (Urbana, IL: National Council of Teachers of English, 1978), and Mike Rose, ed., *When a Writer Can't Write: Studies in Writer's Block and Other Composing-Process Problems* (New York: Guilford Press, 1985).
2. Rebecca E. Burnett, "Content and Commas: How Attitudes Shape a Communication-Across-the-Curriculum Program," Association for Business Communication Convention, Orlando, FL, November 1–4, 1995.
3. W. Ross Winterowd and John Nixon, *The Contemporary Writer: A Practical Rhetoric,* 3rd ed. (San Diego: Harcourt Brace Jovanovich, 1989), 37.
4. Mike Rose, *Writer's Block: The Cognitive Dimension,* published for Conference on College Composition and Communication (Carbondale, IL: Southern Illinois University Press, 1984), 36.
5. Anne Mangen and Jean-Luc Velay, "Digitizing Literacy: Reflections on the Haptics of Writing," *Advances in Haptics,* ed. Mehrdad Hosseini Zadeh (InTech, 2010), 385–401; Nicholas Carr, "Is Google Making Us Stupid?" *The Atlantic Monthly,* July/August 2008; Peter Nicholson, "Information-rich and Attention-poor," *The Globe and Mail,* September 12, 2009, A15; Jakob Nielsen, "Be Succinct! (Writing for the Web)," *Alertbox,* March 15, 1997, retrieved March 3, 2011, http://www.useit.com/alertbox/9703b.html.
6. Yoram Eshet-Alkalai and Nitza Geri, "Does the Medium Affect the Message? The Effect of Congruent Versus Incongruent Display on Critical Reading," *Human Systems Management,* 29, no. 4 (2010): 243–251.
7. Peter Elbow, *Writing with Power: Techniques for Mastering the Writing Process* (New York: Oxford University Press, 1981), 15–20.

8. See Gabriela Lusser Rico, *Writing the Natural Way* (Los Angeles: J. P. Tarcher, 1983), 10.
9. Rachel Spilka, "Orality and Literacy in the Workplace: Process- and Text-Based Strategies for Multiple Audience Adaptation," *Journal of Business and Technical Communication*, 4, no. 1 (January 1990): 44–67.
10. Jakob Nielsen, "How Users Read on the Web," *Alertbox*, October 1, 1997, retrieved March 3, 2011, from http://www.useit.com/alertbox/9710a.html.
11. Fred Reynolds, "What Adult Work-World Writers Have Taught Me about Adult Work-World Writing," *Professional Writing in Context: Lessons from Teaching and Consulting in Worlds of Work* (Hillsdale, NJ: Lawrence Erlbaum Associates, 1995), 18–21.
12. Raymond W. Beswick, "Communicating in the Automated Office," American Business Communication Association International Convention, New Orleans, LA, October 20, 1982.
13. Robert L. Brown, Jr., and Carl G. Herndl, "An Ethnographic Study of Corporate Writing: Job Status as Reflected in Written Text," *Functional Approaches to Writing: A Research Perspective*, ed. Barbara Couture (Norwood, NJ: Ablex, 1986), 16–19, 22–23.
14. Linda Flower, *Problem-Solving Strategies for Writing*, 3rd ed. (New York: Harcourt Brace Jovanovich, 1989), 38.
15. James Suchan and Robert Colucci, "An Analysis of Communication Efficiency between High-Impact and Bureaucratic Written Communication," *Management Communication Quarterly*, 2, no. 4 (May 1989): 464–473.
16. Hilvard G. Rogers and F. William Brown, "The Impact of Writing Style on Compliance with Instructions," *Journal of Technical Writing and Communication*, 23, no. 1 (1993): 53–71.
17. Thomas N. Huckin, "A Cognitive Approach to Readability," *New Essays in Technical and Scientific Communication: Research, Theory, Practice*, ed. Paul V. Anderson, R. John Brockmann, and Carolyn R. Miller (Farmingdale, NY: Baywood, 1983), 93–98.
18. Harris B. Savin and Ellen Perchonock, "Grammatical Structure and the Immediate Recall of English Sentences," *Journal of Verbal Learning and Verbal Behavior*, 4 (1965): 348–353; and Pamela Layton and Adrian J. Simpson, "Deep Structure in Sentence Comprehension," *Journal of Verbal Learning and Verbal Behavior*, 14 (1975): 658–664.
19. E. B. Coleman, "The Comprehensibility of Several Grammatical Transformations," *Journal of Applied Psychology*, 48, no. 3 (1964): 186–190; Keith Rayner, "Visual Attention in Reading: Eye Movements Reflect Cognitive Processes," *Memory and Cognition*, 5 (1977): 443–448; and Lloyd Bostian and Ann C. Thering, "Scientists: Can They Read What They Write?" *Journal of Technical Writing and Communication*, 17 (1987): 417–427.
20. Arn Tibbetts, "Ten Rules for Writing Readably," *Journal of Business Communication*, 18, no. 4 (Fall 1981): 55–59.
21. Myer Siemiatycki, Tim Rees, Roxana Ng, and Khan Rahi, "Integrating Community Diversity in Toronto: On Whose Terms?" CERIS Working Paper no. 14, 2001, at http://ceris.metropolis.net/Virtual%20Library/community/siemiatycki2.html, retrieved March 8, 2005; *The New Canada*, special issue of *Canadian Geographic*, January–February 2001.
22. George Bush, Washington, DC, November 27, 2002, cited in *Slate's The Complete Bushisms*, http://www/slate.com, retrieved October 22, 2008.
23. Sign in front of a Kentucky Fried Chicken franchise in Bloomington, IN, July 13, 1984.
24. Philip B. Crosby, *Quality Is Free: The Art of Making Quality Certain* (New York: New American Library, 1979), 79–84.
25. Jaguar ad, *The Wall Street Journal*, September 29, 2000, A20.
26. Erika L. Kirby and Lynn M. Harter, "Speaking the Language of the Bottom Line: The Metaphor of 'Managing Diversity,'" *Journal of Business Communication*, 40.1 (2003), 28–49.
27. Richard C. Anderson, "Concretization and Sentence Learning," *Journal of Educational Psychology*, 66, no. 2 (1974): 179–183.
28. Nicole Henderson, "Web Writing Untangled: 5 Tips to Get Noticed—and Read—Online," *CW Bulletin*, retrieved June 27, 2011, from http://www.iabc.com/cwb/archive/2010/0910/Henderson.htm.
29. Barb Sawyers, "6 Tips to Turn Your Web Writing into a Conversation," *CW Bulletin*, retrieved June 27, 2011, from http://www.iabc.com/cwb/archive/2010/0910/Sawyers.htm.
30. Guidelines based on Change Sciences Group, "Writing for the Web: Best Practices," Change Sciences Research Brief (Irvington, NY: Change Sciences Group, 2003), downloaded at http://www.changesciences.com; Jakob Nielsen, "Writing Style for Print vs. Web," *Alertbox*, June 9, 2008, retrieved March 5, 2011, from http://www.useit.com/alertbox/print-vs-online-content.html; Jakob Nielsen, P.J. Schemenaur, and Jonathan Fox, "Writing for the Web," retrieved April 11, 2008, http//www.sun.com/980713/webwriting/.
31. Janice C. Redish and Jack Selzer, "The Place of Readability Formulas in Technical Communication," *Technical Communication*, 32, no. 4 (1985): 46–52.
32. Susan D. Kleimann, "The Complexity of Workplace Review," *Technical Communication*, 38, no. 4 (1991): 520–526.
33. This three-step process is modelled on the one suggested by Barbara L. Shwom and Penny L. Hirsch, "Managing the Drafting Process: Creating a New Model for the Workplace," *Bulletin of the Association for Business Communication*, 57, no. 2 (June 1994): 1–10.
34. Eileen Chadnick, "Step Out of a Judging Mindset to Give the Most Effective Feedback," *The Globe and Mail*, February 2, 2011, B18.
35. Mangen and Velay, "Digitizing Literacy: Reflections on the Haptics of Writing."
36. James Suchan and Ronald Dulek, "A Reassessment of Clarity in Written Managerial Communications," *Management Communication Quarterly*, 4, no. 1 (August 1990): 93–97.

Chapter 4

1. Jocelyn Canfield, "Why Design Matters," *Communication World Bulletin 5.11*, November 2007; Linda Reynolds, "The Legibility of Printed Scientific and Technical Information," *Information Design*, ed. Ronald Easterby and Harm Zwaga (New York: John Wiley & Sons, 1984), 187–208.
2. Charles Kostelnick and Michael Hassett, *Shaping Information: The Rhetoric of Visual Conventions* (Carbondale, IL: Southern Illinois University Press, 2003).
3. "ISL Develops Custom 'Fund-Racer' Application," retrieved March 15, 2014, from www.isl.ca/en/home/about/news/isl-helps-raise-funds-for-mental-health-foundation.aspx.
4. See Roger Boisjoly, Online Ethics Center at the National Academy of Engineering, at www.onlineethics.org/cms/7123.aspx.
5. David Akin, "Canada Must Act Fast to Replace Ageing Isotope Reactor: Panel, *National Post*, July 28, 2008, http://www.nationalpost.com/news/story.html?id=686004, retrieved July 29, 2008; David Ljunggren, "Report Rips AECL over Chalk River Fiasco," *National Post*, July 28, 2008, http://www.nationalpost.com/news/story.html?id=685943, retrieved July 29, 2008.
6. George A. Miller, "The Magical Number Seven, Plus or Minus Two: Some Limits on Our Capacity for Processing Information," *Psychological Review*, 63, no. 2 (March 1956): 81–97.
7. Once we know how to read English, the brain first looks to see whether an array of letters follows the rules of spelling. If it does, the brain then treats the array as a word (even if it isn't one, such as *tweal*). The shape is processed in individual letters only when the shape is not enough to suggest meaning. Jerry E. Bishop, "Word Processing: Research on Stroke Victims Yields Clues to the Brain's Capacity to Create Language," *The Wall Street Journal*, October 12, 1993, A6.
8. David Matis, "The Graphic Design of Text," *Intercom*, February 1996, 23.
9. Robert Everett-Green, "Helvetica: Lean, Clean, Ubiquitous," *The Globe and Mail*, March 1, 2014, A13.
10. See the *First Drafts of History* video at http://www.theglobeandmail.com/news/news-video/video-first-drafts-of-history-the-globe-and-mail-celebrates-170-years/article17311609/. See too "A Reader's Guide to the New *Globe and Mail*," retrieved March 7, 2011, from http://www.newsdesigner.com/blog/images/april07/tguide.pdf; "New-look Globe Wins Top Redesign Award," *The Globe and Mail*, February 23, 2011, A3.
11. Russell N. Baird, Arthur T. Turnbull, and Duncan McDonald, *The Graphics of Communication: Typography, Layout, Design, Production*, 5th ed. (New York: Holt, Rinehart & Winston, 1987), 37.
12. Philip M. Rubens, "A Reader's View of Text and Graphics: Implications for Transactional Text," *Journal of Technical Writing and Communication*, 16, nos. 1–2 (1986): 78.
13. M. E. Wrolstad, "Adult Preferences in Typography: Exploring the Function of Design," *Journalism Quarterly*, 37 (Winter 1960): 211–223; summarized in Rolf F. Rehe, "Typography: How to Make It Most Legible," Design Research International, Carmel, IN, 57.
14. Elizabeth Keyes, "Typography, Color, and Information Structure," *Technical Communication*, 40, no. 4 (November 1993):

652; and Joseph Koncelik, "Design, Aging, Ethics, and the Law" (Paper presented in Columbus, OH, May 6, 1993).

15. *Make Poverty History* homepage, http://www.makepovertyhistory.org, retrieved October 24, 2008; "Make Poverty History: First Nations Plan for Creating Opportunity," http://www.afn.ca/article.asp?id=2903, retrieved April 20, 2008. See too the Facebook page at http://www.facebook.com/topic.php?uid=2209726698&topic=1564.
16. Brian O'Mara-Croft, "Every Picture Tells a Story," *Communication World*, September–October 2008, 22–25.
17. The Building Alberta Plan 2014. Budget Address 2014 delivered by Honourable Doug Horner, President of Treasury Board and Minister of Finance, March 6, 2014, retrieved from http://finance.alberta.ca/publications/budget/budget2014/speech.pdf.
18. Gene Zelazny, *Say It with Charts: The Executive's Guide to Successful Presentations*, 4th ed. (New York: McGraw-Hill, 2001), 52.
19. Stephen H. Wildstrom, "A Picture Is Worth 1,000 Charts," *BusinessWeek*, January 20, 2003, downloaded from http://www.businessweek.com on November 29, 2005; "Market Map 1000," SmartMoney.com, downloaded on March 8, 2011.
20. W. S. Cleveland and R. McGill, "Graphical Perception: Theory, Experiments, and Application to the Development of Graphic Methods," *Journal of the American Statistical Association*, 79, nos. 3 & 7 (1984): 531–553; cited in Jeffry K. Cochran, Sheri A. Albrecht, and Yvonne A. Greene, "Guidelines for Evaluating Graphical Designs: A Framework Based on Human Perception Skills," *Technical Communication*, 36, no. 1 (February 1989): 27.
21. Peter Robinson, "More Than Meets the Eye," *Archivaria*, 1, no. 2 (1976): 33–43; Suzanne Salvo, "True Lies—Manipulating Images: Is It Ethical?" *Communication World*, September–October 2008, 26–30; Michael Posner, "Photo Fakery," *The Globe and Mail*, May 7, 2011, A10–11.
22. T.L.G. Thorell and W. J. Smith, *Using Computer Color Effectively: An Illustrated Reference* (Englewood Cliffs, NJ: Prentice Hall, 1990), 13.
23. Edward R. Tufte, *The Visual Display of Quantitative Information* (Cheshire, CT: Graphics Press, 1983), 113.
24. Salvo, "True Lies—Manipulating Images: Is It Ethical?" 30.
25. Thophilus Addo, "The Effects of Dimensionality in Computer Graphics," *Journal of Business Communication*, 31, no. 4 (October 1994): 253–265.
26. "Design Guidelines for Homepage Usability," retrieved March 9, 2011, from http://www.useit.com/homepageusability/guidelines.html.
27. "Sociable Design—Introduction," retrieved March 9, 2011, from http://jnd.org/dn.mss/sociable_design_-_introduction.html.
28. ISL, "Web Design and Development," retrieved March 10, 2011, from http://www.isl.ca/en/home/services/webdesigndevelopment/default.aspx.
29. Angelo Fernando, "Prep Your Story for the 'Timeless Web,'" *Communication World*, May–June 2010, 10–11.
30. Marilyn A. Dyrud, "An Exploration of Gender Bias in Computer Clip Art," *Business Communication Quarterly*, 60, no. 4 (December 1997): 30–51.
31. Suzanne Salvo, "Visually Speaking: The Human Element," *Communication World Bulletin* 3.10, October 2005.
32. Jakob Nielsen, "Why You Only Need to Test with 5 Users," *Jakob Neilsen's Alertbox*, March 19, 2000, www.useit.com/alertbox/20000319.html, retrieved October 24, 2008.
33. ISL Web Marketing and Development. Retrieved September 19, 2011, from http://www.isl.ca/en/home/ourwork/maritime-innsresorts.aspx.

Chapter 5

1. Terry Eagleton, *The Idea of Culture* (Oxford: Blackwell, 2000); Raymond Williams, *Keywords: A Vocabulary of Culture and Society* (London: Fontana, 1976).
2. Brenda Arbeláez, statement to Kitty Locker, December 12, 1996. See also Aleksandra Vuckovic, "Intercultural Communication: A Foundation of Communicative Action," *Multicultural Education & Technology Journal*, 2, no. 1 (2008): 47–59; Daphne A. Jameson, "Reconceptualising Cultural Identity and Its Role in Intercultural Business Communication," *Journal of Business Communication*, 44, no. 3 (2007): 199–235.
3. Citizenship and Immigration Canada, "Facts and Figures 2012—Immigration Overview: Permanent and Temporary Residents," retrieved March 25, 2014, from http://www.cic.gc.ca/english/resources/statistics/facts2012/permanent/10.asp; Murray Whyte, "Forgotten in Media's Culture Gap," *Toronto Star*, June 24, 2006, http://friendscb.org/News/Friends_News/archives/articles06240604.asp, retrieved October 24, 2008.
4. Statistics Canada, "Study: Projections of the Diversity of the Canadian Population," *The Daily*, March 9, 2010, retrieved March 11, 2011, from http://www.statcan.gc.ca/daily-quotidien/100309/dq100309a-eng.htm; Myer Siemiatycki, Tim Rees, Roxana Ng, and Khan Rahi, "Integrating Community Diversity in Toronto: On Whose Terms?" CERIS Working Paper no. 14, 2001, retrieved March 8, 2005, from http://ceris.metropolis.net/Virtual%20Library/community/siemiatycki.html; *The New Canada*, special issue of *Canadian Geographic*, January–February 2001; Jill Mahoney, "Visible Majority by 2017," *The Globe and Mail*, March 23, 2005, A1; Jill Mahoney and Caroline Alphonso, "How the Lines Between Races Are Blurring," *The Globe and Mail*, March 24, 2005, A3.
5. Karl Moore, "Multicultural Canada Breeds Managers with Global Outlook," *The Globe and Mail*, August 21, 2002, B9.
6. Douglas Coupland, *Generation X: Tales for An Accelerated Culture* (New York: St. Martin's Press, 1991); "Generation X," *Wikipedia: The Free Encyclopedia*, http://www.wikipedia.org/wiki/Generation_X, retrieved October 24, 2008; Barbara Moses, "Coddled, Confident and Cocky: The Challenge of Managing Gen Y," *The Globe and Mail*, March 11, 2005, C1–2.
7. Isobel M. Findlay and Jantina Kowbel, "Engaging an Age-Diverse Workplace: Revisiting a Business Opportunity and Challenge," *Journal of Business & Financial Affairs*, 2, no. 2 (2013): 1–3
8. Wallace Immen, "Generation Y in It for the Long Haul," *Globe Careers*, September 22, 2010, B20; RSM Richter, "Don't Believe the Workplace Stereotypes," retrieved March 16, 2011, from http://www.rsmrichter.com/pressrelease.aspx?ID=163.
9. Becky Johns, "Stop Griping about Millennials, and Start Teaching Us," posted February 4, 2011, retrieved February 7, 2011, from http://www.ragan.com/Main/Articles/42679.aspx.
10. Michael McCullough, "Too Afraid to Fly? Why 40% of Canadian Firms Do No Business Abroad," *Canadian Business*, July 19, 2010, 44–45.
11. Richard Blackwell, "Canadian Builds Global Ad Empire," *Report on Business*, March 14, 2005, B1; McCall MacBain Foundation homepage, retrieved March 25, 2014, from http://www.mccallmacbain.org/.
12. Zena Olijnyk, et al., "Canada's Global Leaders: 40 Canadians Who've Become International Business Power Players," *Canadian Business*, March 28–April 10, 2005, 37–64.
13. Dean Elmuti, Benjamin Tück, and Frederike Kemper, "Analyzing Cross-Cultural Adaptability among Business Students: An Empirical Investigation," *International Journal of Management*, 25, no. 3 (2008): 551–568; Max Williams, "Canadian CEOs Ignorant of International Business?" October 5, 2010, retrieved March 16, 2011, from http://www.businessreviewcanada.ca/sectors/tsq-canada/canadian-ceos-ignorant-international-business.
14. Andrea Mandel-Campbell, "Wake-Up Call: Why Canadian Companies Must Develop Global Strategies," *Canadian Business*, October 8, 2007, 58–62; Graham Silnicki, "China Has Been Rocked by Scandals Involving Everything from Tainted Drugs to Poison Dog Food: Now Canadians Are Helping the Largest Exporter in the World to Get Back on Track," *Canadian Business*, April 14, 2008, 50–55.
15. United Nations Educational, Scientific and Cultural Organization (UNESCO), Universal Declaration on Cultural Diversity, retrieved March 26, 2014, from http://www.ohchr.org/EN/ProfessionalInterest/Pages/CulturalDiversity.aspx.
16. Richard Davis, "The Trouble with Typecasting on the Job," *The Globe and Mail*, July 23, 2004, C1–2; Rosemary Barnes, "Encouraging Diversity Key to Success," *The Globe and Mail*, September 11, 2004, B13; Virginia Galt, "Visible Minorities Build a Diverse Work Force," *The Globe and Mail*, September 18, 2004, B9.
17. Doug Sanders, "Lazy and Untrustworthy? It Depends on the Economy," *The Globe and Mail*, October 6, 2007, F3.
18. Foreign Affairs, Trade and Development Canada, "Canada's State of Trade: Trade and Investment Update 2012," retrieved March 27, 2014, from http://www.international.gc.ca/economist-economiste/performance/state-point/state_2012_point/2012_5.aspx?lang=eng.
19. Laura Macdonald, "The North American Relationship Is Stale," *Ottawa Citizen*, February 19, 2014, retrieved from http://www.ottawacitizen.com/business/North+-American+relationship+stale/9521728/story.html; Neil Reynolds, "Canada's Disrespect

for Mexico Is a Bad Bet on the Future," *Report on Business,* March 9, 2011, B2.

20. Kevin Carmichael and Tavia Grant, "Missed Opportunities: Latin America Is Booming, But Canadian Businesses Are Barely in the Game," *Report on Business,* March 26, 2011, B1–4.
21. Ha-Joon Chang, *Bad Samaritans: The Myth of Free Trade and the Secret History of Capitalism.* London and New York: Bloomsbury Press, 2007, p. 176.
22. Harvey J. Krahn and Graham S. Lowe, *Work, Industry, and Canadian Society* (Toronto: Nelson, 2002), 411–14.
23. Brian Milner, "As China Booms, Japan Stalls," *Report on Business,* February 15, 2011, B3.
24. John Doyle, "What We Learn from Watching Japan-Watchers," *The Globe and Mail,* March 16, 2011, R3.
25. Geneviève Hilton, "Becoming Culturally Fluent," *Communication World,* Nov.–Dec. 2007, 34–36
26. Cathryn Atkinson, "A World of Good for Your Résumé," *The Globe and Mail,* March 16, 2011, E5.
27. See, for instance, Conference Board of Canada, *Saskatchewan in the Spotlight: Acquisition of Potash Corporation of Saskatchewan Inc.—Risks and Opportunities,* retrieved March 17, 2011, from http://us-cdn.creamermedia.co.za/assets/articles/attachments/29986_potash_study_-_final_report.pdf; CBC News, "Potash Corp Sale Could Cost Sask. Billions," retrieved March 16, 2011, from http://www.cbc.ca/news/canada/saskatchewan/story/2010/10/04/sk-bhp-potashcorp-1010.html; Terence Corcoran, "Let BHP Buy Potash Corp," *Financial Post,* September 14, 2010, retrieved March 17, 2011, from http://opinion.financialpost.com/2010/09/14/terence-corcoran-let-bhp-buy-potash-corp/; Jeremy Torobin and Andy Hoffman, "Potash Bid a Test of Takeover Rules," and Gordon Pitts and Brenda Bouw, "BHP's Prairie Appeal: Mine Global, But Act Local," *Report on Business,* August 18, 2010, B1–B4.
28. Clare Woodcraft, "Letter from the Middle East," *Communication World,* Nov.–Dec. 2006, 27–29.
29. Emile Hokayem, "Enough!" *The Globe and Mail,* February 29, 2011, F1–7.
30. John Allemang, "The Exponential Power of the Public Square," *The Globe and Mail,* February 26, 2011, A8–9.
31. Evgeny Morozov, "So, You Think the Internet Will Set You Free? Think Again," *The Globe and Mail,* February 29, 2011, F7; Jerrold J. Merchant, "Korean Interpersonal Patterns: Implications for Korean/American Intercultural Communication," *Communication,* 9 (October 1980): 65.
32. Sheema Khan, "A Revolution Leaves Women Behind," *The Globe and Mail,* April 7, 2011, A17.
33. Hokayem, "Enough," F6; Naomi Wolf, "The Middle East's Feminist Revolution," *The Globe and Mail,* March 2, 2011, A13.
34. Wolf, "The Middle East's Feminist Revolution," A13.
35. "Female Entrepreneurs in Middle East and North Africa Defy Expectations," http://www.worldbank.org/WBSITE/EXTERNAL/NEWS/0,,contentMDK:21589991~pagePK:64257043~piPK:437376~theSitePK:4607,00.html, retrieved April 15, 2008.
36. Edward T. Hall, *The Hidden Dimension* (Garden City, NY: Doubleday, 1966).
37. Daphne A. Jameson, "Reconceptualizing Cultural Identity and Its Role in Intercultural Business Communication," *Journal of Business Communication,* 44 (2007): 199–235. For a critique of G. Hofstede's concept of culture as similarly overly focused on national aggregates of characteristics and hence "intellectually numbing" in its "effect on the treatment of culture and international marketing," see Nigel Holden, "Why Marketers Need a New Concept of Culture for the Global Knowledge Economy," *International Marketing Review,* 21, no. 6 (2004): 563–572.
38. Tara Perkins, "How to Succeed in China Today," *The Globe and Mail,* October 13, 201, E8. See too "Chinese Business Culture," retrieved March 17, 2011, from http://chinese-school.netfirms.com/guanxi.html; Cultural China, "History and Literature: Humanistic Spirit," retrieved March 17, 2011, from http://history.cultural-china.com/en/43History984.html.
39. Carolynne Wheeler, "China's Food Inflation Leaving a Bad Taste," *Report on Business,* February 16, 2011, B12; Mark McKinnon, "China's Drought Situation 'Grim,'" *The Globe and Mail,* February 17, 2011, B15; Mark MacKinnon, "The Cultural Revolution," *The Globe and Mail,* July 31, 2010, F4; Mark MacKinnon, "The Year of the Angry Rabbit," *The Globe and Mail,* February 2011, F6–7; Jason Kirby, "China's Coming Collapse," *Canadian Business,* March 14, 2011, 26–35; Eric Reguly, "China's Troubled Shift to a Green Economy," *The Globe and Mail,* October 26, 2013, B4.
40. Claudia Hammond, *Time Warped: Unlocking the Mysteries of Time Perception.* Toronto: Anansi International, 2012.
41. Edward Twitchell Hall, *Hidden Differences: Doing Business with the Japanese* (Garden City, NY: Anchor-Doubleday, 1987), 25.
42. Lawrence B. Nadler, Marjorie Keeshan Nadler, and Benjamin J. Broome, "Culture and the Management of Conflict Situations," in *Communication, Culture, and Organizational Processes,* ed. William B. Gudykunst, Lea P. Stewart, and Stella Ting-Toomey (Beverly Hills, CA: Sage, 1985), 103.
43. Lauren McKeon, "Tied to Home," *Canadian Business,* April 14, 2008, 33–34.
44. Anne Fisher, "Ask Annie: Overseas, U.S. Businesswomen May Have the Edge," *Fortune,* September 28, 1998, 304.
45. Royal Commission on Aboriginal Peoples, *Looking Forward, Looking Back.* Volume 1. (Ottawa: Minister of Supply and Services Canada, 1996), 615–623.
46. James (Sakej) Youngblood Henderson, Marjorie L. Benson, and Isobel M. Findlay, *Aboriginal Tenure in the Constitution of Canada* (Scarborough: Carswell, 2000), 257–279.
47. Mi'kmaq Spirit, "Talking Circles," retrieved March 18, 2011, from http://www.muiniskw.org/pgCulture2c.htm.
48. Public Health Agency of Canada, "Getting Information to Aboriginal Seniors," retrieved March 18, 2011, from http://www.phac-aspc.gc.ca/seniors-aines/publications/public/various-varies/communicating_aboriginal/reaching05-eng.php#how.
49. David Matsumoto, *The New Japan: Debunking Seven Cultural Stereotypes* (Yarmouth, ME: Intercultural Press, 2002), 28–29, 40–41, 144–45.
50. Laray M. Barna, "Stumbling Blocks in Intercultural Communication," in *Intercultural Communication,* ed. Larry A. Samovar and Richard E. Porter (Belmont, CA: Wadsworth, 1985), 331.
51. Scott Maniquet, "Montreal Demonstrators Throw Shoes to Protest George W. Bush Speech," *National Post Posted,* October 22, 2009, retrieved March 17, 2011, from http://network.nationalpost.com/np/blogs/posted/archive/2009/10/22/montreal-demonstrators-throw-shoes-to-protest-george-w-bush-speech.aspx.
52. Kitty O. Locker, Stephen Kyo Kaczmarek, and Kathryn Braun, *Business Communication: Building Critical Skills,* 2nd Canadian Ed. (Toronto: McGraw-Hill Ryerson, 2005), 56.
53. Canadian Criminal Justice Association, "Aboriginal People and the Justice System," retrieved March 18, 2011, from http://www.ccja-acjp.ca/en/abori4.html.
54. Michael Argyle, *Bodily Communication* (New York: International University Press, 1975), 89.
55. Jerrold J. Merchant, "Korean Interpersonal Patterns: Implications for Korean/American Intercultural Communication," *Communication,* 9 (October 1980): 65.
56. Ray L. Birdwhistell, *Kinesics and Context: Essays on Body Motion Communication* (Philadelphia: University of Philadelphia Press, 1970), 30–31.
57. Glenna Dod and Gergana Kuneva, "Yes or No: Communication Barriers between Bulgaria and the United States," ABC Canadian, Eastern US, Southeastern US Joint Regional Conference, Nashville, TN, March 30–April 1, 2000.
58. Roger E. Axtell, *Gestures: The Do's and Taboos of Body Language around the World* (New York: Wiley, 1998); Paul Ekman, Wallace V. Friesen, and John Bear, "The International Language of Gestures," *Psychology Today,* 18, no. 5 (May 1984): 64.
59. Baxter, 1970, reported in Marianne LaFrance, "Gender Gestures: Sex, Sex-Role, and Nonverbal Communication," in *Gender and Nonverbal Behavior,* ed. Clara Mayo and Nancy M. Henley (New York: Springer-Verlag, 1981), 130.
60. Nine-Curt, "Hispanic-Anglo Conflicts," 238.
61. Brenda Major, "Gender Patterns in Touching Behavior," in *Gender and Nonverbal Behavior,* ed. Clara Mayo and Nancy M. Henley (New York: Springer-Verlag, 1981), 26, 28.
62. Mike McKeever to Kitty Locker, June 25, 2001.
63. Natalie Porter and Florence Gies, "Women and Nonverbal Leadership Cues: When Seeing Is Not Believing," in *Gender and Nonverbal Behavior,* ed. Clara Mayo and Nancy M. Henley (New York: Springer-Verlag, 1981), 48–49.
64. Argyle, *Bodily Communication,* 92.

65. Mariko Sanchanta, "Japanese Workers Sweat Over Summer Dress Code," *The Globe and Mail,* June 27, 2011, B8.

66. Carl Quintanilla, "Work Week," *The Wall Street Journal,* August 13, 1996, A1; Mary Ritchie Key, *Paralanguage and Kinesics* (Metuchen, NJ: Scarecrow, 1975), 23; Fred Hitzhusen, conversation with Kitty Locker, January 31, 1988; and William Horton, "The Almost Universal Language: Graphics for International Documents," *Technical Communication,* 40, no. 4 (1993): 687.

67. L. G. Thorell and W. J. Smith, *Using Computer Color Effectively: An Illustrated Reference* (Englewood Cliffs, NJ: Prentice Hall, 1990), 12–13; William Horton, "The Almost Universal Language: Graphics for International Documents," *Technical Communication,* 40, no. 4 (1993): 687; and Thyra Rauch, "IBM Visual Interface Design," *The STC Usability PIC Newsletter,* January 1996, 3.

68. David Stipp, "Mirror, Mirror on the Wall, Who's the Fairest of Them All?" *Fortune,* September 9, 1996, 87.

69. Deborah Tannen, *That's Not What I Meant!* (New York: William Morrow, 1986).

70. Daniel N. Maltz and Ruth A. Borker, "A Cultural Approach to Male–Female Miscommunication," in *Language and Social Identity,* ed. John J. Gumperz (Cambridge: Cambridge University Press, 1982), 202.

71. Rosenzweig & Co., 3rd annual *Report on Women at the Top Levels of Corporate Canada* (January 2008); Stefanie Kranjec, "Fewer Women in Top Corner Offices in Canada," Reuters, http://www.reuters.com/article/lifestyleMolt/idUSN1554583020080115, retrieved April 12, 2008; Canadian Labour Congress, *Women in the Workforce: Still a Long Way from Equality* (March 2008), http://canadianlabour.ca/updir/womensequalityreportEn.pdf, retrieved April 14, 2008; Barbara Moses, "Still Wanted: Female-Friendly Workplaces," *Globe Careers,* January 14, 2005, C1–2.

72. Sheryl Sandberg, *Lean In: Women, Work, and the Will to Lead* (New York: Alfred A. Knopf, 2013). See Kate Carraway, "Don't Hate Sheryl Sandberg. Join Her," *The Globe and Mail,* March 15, 2013, retrieved from http://www.theglobeandmail.com/arts/books-and-media/book-reviews/dont-hate-sheryl-sandberg-join-her/article9818240/; Vanessa Garcia, "Why I Won't Lean In," *Huffington Post,* July 19, 2013, retrieved from http://www.huffingtonpost.com/vanessa-garcia/why-i-wont-lean-in_b_3586527.html.

73. Janet McFarland, "Canada's Firms Outpace Peers for Women Directors," *The Globe and Mail,* February 5, 2014, B1, B8.

74. Leah Eichler, "Face It, the 'Beauty Premium' Exists at Work," *Report on Business Weekend,* January 11, 2014, B15; Naomi Wolf, "In the Business Media, a CEO Remains a Lady First," *The Globe and Mail,* January 4, 2014, F2.

75. Barbara Annis, "We Need Gender Intelligence, Not Myths, in the Workplace," *The Globe and Mail,* October 13, 2010, A21.

76. Muriel Saville-Troike, "An Integrated Theory of Communication," in *Perspectives on Silence,* ed. Deborah Tannen and Muriel Saville-Troike (Norwood, NJ: Ablex, 1985), 10–11.

77. A. Jann Davis, *Listening and Responding* (St. Louis: Mosby, 1984), 43.

78. Alan M. Perlman, "World English: Communicating with International Audiences," *Communication World Bulletin,* January 2005.

79. Marilyn A. Dyrud, "An Exploration of Gender Bias in Computer Clip Art," *Business Communication Quarterly,* 60.4 (December 1997), 30–51.

80. Kitty O. Locker, Stephen Kyo Kaczmarek, and Kathryn Braun, *Business Communication: Building Critical Skills,* 2nd Canadian Ed. (Toronto: McGraw-Hill Ryerson, 2005), 67; Lisa Tyler, "Communicating about People with Disabilities: Does the Language We Use Make a Difference?" *Bulletin of the Association for Business Communications,* 53.3 (September 1990), 65.

Chapter 6

1. Dana Mattiolo, "Web Meeting This Week? Think Before You Scratch," *Report on Business Weekend,* June 14, 2008, B18.

2. *Managing Across Distance in Today's Economic Climate: The Value of Face-to-Face Communication.* A Report by Harvard Business Review Analytic Services, retrieved March 20, 2011, from http://www.imex-frankfurt.com/documents/harvard-business-review_Oct09.pdf.

3. Zosia Bielski, "How Online Social Schedulers are Reinventing the Classroom," *The Globe and Mail,* August 30, 2013, L2.

4. Richard Hammond, "Party Lines, Wikis, and Project Management," *Online,* September–October 2007, 30–33, www.onlinemag.net, retrieved August 15, 2008.

5. Nicole Martin, "Keep Your Eyes on the Enterprise: Emails, Wikis, Blogs, and Corporate Risk," *EContent,* July–August 2007, 54–59.

6. Martin, 54.

7. Natasha Nicholson, "Communicating with a Remote Workforce," *CW Bulletin,* May 2010, retrieved June 28, 2011, from http://www.iabc.com/cwb/archive/2010/0510/#feature1; Alison Davis, "Using Social Media to Keep Remote Workers Connected," *CW Bulletin,* May 2010, retrieved June 28, 2011, from http://www.iabc.com/cwb/archive/2010/0510/Davis.htm.

8. Tom Harris, "Listen Carefully," *Nation's Business,* June 1989, 78; L. K. Steil, L. I. Barker, and K. W. Watson, *Effective Listening: Key to Your Success* (Reading, MA: Addison-Wesley, 1983); and J. A. Harris, "Hear What's Really Being Said," *Management-Auckland,* August 1998, 18, qtd. in Mary Ellen Guffey, Kathleen Rhodes, and Patricia Rogin, *Business Communication: Process and Product,* 4th Canadian Ed. (Toronto: Thomson Nelson, 2005), 72.

9. "Listening Factoids," International Listening Association, retrieved September 25, 2005, from http://www.listen.org/Templates/factoids.htm.

10. For a full account of the accident, see Andrew D. Wolvin and Caroline Gwynn Coakely, *Listening,* 3rd ed. (Dubuque, IA: William C. Brown, 1988), 10–11.

11. Thomas Gordon with Judith Gordon Sands, *P.E.T. in Action* (New York: Wyden, 1976), 83.

12. "Listen Up and Sell," *Selling Power,* July/August 1999, 34.

13. Thomas J. Knutson, "Communication in Small Decision-Making Groups: In Search of Excellence," *Journal for Specialists in Group Work,* 10, no. 1 (March 1985): 28–37. The next four paragraphs summarize Knutson's analysis.

14. Khalid Al-Rawi, "Cohesiveness within Teamwork: The Relationship to Performance Effectiveness-Case Study," *Education, Business and Society: Contemporary Middle Eastern Issues,* 1 No.2 (2008): 92–106.

15. Lenard C. Huff, Joanne Cooper, and Wayne Jones, "The Development and Consequences of Trust in Student Project Groups," *Journal of Marketing Education,* 24, no. 1 (April 2002): 24–34.

16. Huff et al., "The Development and Consequences of Trust," 24.

17. Ed Catmull, "How Pixar Fosters Collective Creativity," *Harvard Business Review,* September 2008, 64–72. In his *Creativity Inc.: Overcoming the Unseen Forces that Stand in the Way of True Inspiration* (New York: Random House, 2014), Catmull (writing with Amy Wallace) addresses the challenges of becoming part of Disney and the conservativism that comes with success.

18. For a fuller listing of roles in groups, see David W. Johnson and Frank P. Johnson, *Joining Together: Group Theory and Group Skills,* 6th ed. (Englewood Cliffs, NJ: Prentice Hall, 1997), 20–21.

19. Beatrice Schultz, "Argumentativeness: Its Effect in Group Decision-Making and Its Role in Leadership Perception," *Communication Quarterly,* 30, no. 4 (Fall 1982): 374–375; Dennis S. Gouran and B. Aubrey Fisher, "The Functions of Human Communication in the Formation, Maintenance, and Performance of Small Groups," in *Handbook of Rhetorical and Communication Theory,* ed. Carroll C. Arnold and John Waite Bowers (Boston: Allyn and Bacon, 1984), 640; Curt Bechler and Scott D. Johnson, "Leadership and Listening: A Study of Member Perceptions," *Small Group Research,* 26, no. 1 (February 1995): 77–85; and Scott D. Johnson and Curt Bechler, "Examining the Relationship between Listening Effectiveness and Leadership Emergence: Perceptions, Behaviors, and Recall," *Small Group Research,* 29, no. 3 (August 1998): 452–471.

20. H. Lloyd Goodall, Jr., *Small Group Communications in Organizations,* 2nd ed. (Dubuque, IA: William C. Brown, 1990), 39–40.

21. Dotmocracy. Retrieved May 8, 2014, from http://www.audiencedialogue.net/dotmocracy.html.

22. Greg Miller, "Social Savvy Boosts the Collective Intelligence of Groups," *Science,* 330 (October 1, 2010), 22; Ingrid Peritz and Adrian Morrow, "For Collective Smarts, Include Women," *The Globe and Mail,* October 1, 2010, A4.

23. See, for example, the issue on Age of Change, *Communication World,* March–April 2008; Poppy Lauretta McLeod, Sharon Alisa Lobel, Taylor H. Cox, Jr., "Ethnic Diversity and Creativity in Small Groups," *Small Group Research,* 27, no. 2 (May 1996): 248–264; and Leisa D. Sargent and Christina Sue-Chan, "Does Diversity Affect Efficacy? The Intervening Role of Cohesion and Task Interdependence," *Small Group Research,* 32 (2001): 426–450.

24. Canadian Bureau for International Education, *A World of Learning: Canada's Performance and Potential in International Education,* 2013. Retrieved May 8, 2014, from https://mp.cbie.ca/mpower/event/loadevent.action?e=47#home; James Bradshaw, "Canada Aggressively Courts Foreign Students. How to Help Them Fit In," *The Globe and Mail,* August 28, 2013, A6–7.
25. Huff et al., "The Development and Consequences of Trust," 27–31.
26. Nance L. Harper and Lawrence R. Askling, "Group Communication and Quality of Task Solution in a Media Production Organization," *Communication Monographs,* 47, no. 2 (June 1980): 77–100.
27. Rebecca E. Burnett, "Conflict in Collaborative Decision-Making," in *Professional Communication: The Social Perspective,* ed. Nancy Roundy Blyler and Charlotte Thralls (Newbury Park, CA: Sage, 1993), 144–162.
28. Kimberly A. Freeman, "Attitudes Toward Work in Project Groups as Predictors of Academic Performance," *Small Group Research,* 27, no. 2 (May 1996): 265–282.
29. David S. Jalajas and Robert I. Sutton, "Feuds in Student Groups: Coping with Whiners, Martyrs, Saboteurs, Bullies, and Deadbeats," *Mastering Management Education: Innovations in Teaching Effectiveness,* ed. Charles M. Vance (Newbury Park, CA: Sage, 1993), 217–227.
30. Alan Sharland, "How to Adopt a No-Blame Approach to Workplace Conflict," *CW Bulletin,* August 2009, retrieved July 1, 2011, from http://iabc.com/cwb/archive/2009/0809/sharland.htm.
31. Nancy Schullery and Beth Hoger, "Business Advocacy for Students in Small Groups," Association for Business Communication Annual Convention, San Antonio, TX, November 9–11, 1998.
32. "Survey Finds Workers Average Only Three Productive Days per Week," March 15, 2005, retrieved September 25, 2005, from http://www.microsoft.com/presspass/press/2005/mar05/03-15ThreeProductiveDaysPR.mspx.
33. Frank Buchar, "Stifle Yawns: Wake Up Your Meetings," *Globe Careers,* June 4, 2004, C1.
34. Cleveland D. Bonner, "How Cloud Computing Is Fueling Innovation," *Forbes,* retrieved May 10, 2014, from http://www.forbes.com/sites/ibm/2014/05/09/how-cloud-computing-is-fueling-innovation/.
35. Jonathan Stoller, "How to Make a Cross-Functional Team Work," *The Globe and Mail,* April 17, 2014, B10.
36. Lisa Ede and Andrea Lunsford, *Singular Texts/Plural Authors: Perspectives on Collaborative Writing* (Carbondale, IL: Southern Illinois Press, 1990), 60.
37. Paul Benjamin Lowry, Aaron Curtis, and Michelle Rene Lowry, "Building a Taxonomy and Nomenclature of Collaborative Writing to Improve Interdisciplinary Research and Practice," *Journal of Business Communication,* 41.1 (January 2004), 66–99, http://job.sagepub.com/cgi/reprint/41/1/66, retrieved October 24, 2008.
38. Rebecca Burnett, "Characterizing Conflict in Collaborative Relationships: The Nature of Decision-Making during Coauthoring." PhD dissertation, Carnegie-Mellon University, Pittsburgh, PA, 1991.
39. Kitty O. Locker, "What Makes a Collaborative Writing Team Successful? A Case Study of Lawyers and Social Service Workers in a State Agency," in *New Visions in Collaborative Writing,* ed. Janis Forman (Portsmouth, NJ: Boynton, 1991), 37–52.
40. Ede and Lunsford, *Singular Texts/Plural Authors,* 66.
41. Jo Mackiewicz and Kathryn Riley, "The Technical Editor as Diplomat: Linguistic Strategies for Balancing Clarity and Politeness," *Technical Communication,* 50.1 (February 2003), 83–94, downloaded from http://www.ingentaconnect.com, November 29, 2005.
42. Meg Morgan, Nancy Allen, Teresa Moore, Dianne Atkinson, and Craig Snow, "Collaborative Writing in the Classroom," *The Bulletin of the Association for Business Communication,* 50, no. 3 (September 1987): 22.

Chapter 7

1. Shannon Proudfoot, "One-Third of Canadians Admit Sending Dicey E-Mails," *Montreal Gazette,* June 25, 2008, http://www.canada.com/montrealgazette/news/story.html?id=65db0c5d-67b2-4f60-919f-7dc35918fc01, retrieved August 20, 2008; Christopher B. Sullivan, "Preferences for Electronic Mail in Organizational Communication Tasks," *The Journal of Business Communications,* 32, no.1 (January 1995): 46–64.
2. Erin Anderssen. "Crushed," *The Globe and Mail,* March 29, 2014, F1, F6–7; Erin Anderssen, "Inbox of Burden," *The Globe and Mail,* March 31, 2014, L1–L4.
3. Jason Markusoff, "Nenshi on Redford, Council, $52 Million and Where Taxes Are Going": Year-End Interview, Part 1, *Calgary Herald,* December 16, 2013, retrieved from http://blogs.calgaryherald.com/2013/12/16/nenshi-on-redford-council-52-million-and-where-taxes-are-going-year-end-interview-part-1/.
4. Rick Spence, "Putting Emotion into Your Emails Can Spell Success," *National Post,* August 31, 2010, B2.
5. Lisa Stephens, "Generation Text Sends Wrong Message," *Report on Business,* November 26, 2010, B16.
6. For more detailed advice, see the *Postal Guide* on the Canada Post Web site at https://www.canadapost.ca.
7. Anna Pitts, "The 4 Most Essential Components of an Email," Ragan.com, February 8, 2013; retrieved May 18, 2014, from http://www.ragan.com/Main/Articles/46190.aspx.
8. Erich Schwartzel, "Your E-mail Signoff Says a Lot about You," *The Globe and Mail,* February 2011, B20.
9. In a study of 483 subject lines written by managers and MBA students, Priscilla S. Rogers found that the average subject line was 5 words; only 10% of the subject lines used 10 or more words ("A Taxonomy for Memorandum Subject Lines," *Journal of Business and Technical Communication,* 4, no. 2 [September 1990]: 28–29).
10. A 2004 study of 650 e-mail marketers found that lines under 50 text characters had open rates 12.5% higher than those over 50 text characters. *Daily News* for Monday, October 4, 2004, http://www.internetretailer.com/dailyNews.asp?id=13051, retrieved May 5, 2005. A 2009 study of more than a billion e-mails confirmed that short subject lines "outperform" longer ones, although "content and brand messaging" can be equally important. Misty Harris, "E-mail Subject Line Size Significant, Study Finds," Saskatoon *StarPhoenix,* February 7, 2009, F18.
11. Matt Wilson, "Report: Email Drives More Sales than Social Media," Ragan.com, posted August 21, 2012, retrieved May 18, 2014, from http://www.ragan.com/Main/Articles/45397.aspx?format=2. See also Shelly Kramer, "Report: Consumers Prefer to Reach Brands via Email," Ragan.com, February 6, 2013, retrieved May 18, 2014, from http://www.ragan.com/Main/Articles/46175.aspx.
12. Harris, "E-Mail Subject Line."
13. Shel Holtz, "Next-Generation Press Releases," *CW Bulletin,* September 2009, retrieved April 2, 2011, from http://www.iabc.com/cwb/archive/2009/0909/Holtz.htm.
14. Deborah Tannen, *That's Not What I Meant: How Conversational Style Makes or Breaks Your Relationships with Others* (New York: Morrow, 1986), 108.
15. Richard C. Whitely, *The Customer-Driven Company* (Reading, MA: Addison-Wesley, 1991), 39–40.
16. Ruth King, "Five Things You Should Never Say to Customers," *Journal of Light Construction,* October 2003, downloaded from http://www.jlconline.com.
17. An earlier version of this problem, the sample solutions, and the discussion appeared in Francis W. Weeks and Kitty O. Locker, *Business Writing Cases and Problems* (Champaign, IL: Stipes, 1980), 40–44.

Chapter 8

1. Brent Jang, "Jetsgo Ditches in Red Ink," *The Globe and Mail,* March 12, 2005, A1–A6; Brent Jang, "Jetsgo Sent Jets to Quebec for Safe Haven from Creditors," *Report on Business,* March 15, 2005, B1–B8; Brent Jang, "Leblanc on Sorrow, Remorse and His Little 'White Lie,'" *Report on Business,* March 18, 2005, B1–B2; Keith MacArthur, "An Airline Addict Hits His Fourth Wall," *Report on Business,* March 12, 2005, B4; Richard Bloom and Colin Freeze, "Workers Find That Jobs Have Flown," *Report on Business,* March 12, 2005, B5.
2. Shawn McCarthy, "Shuttered Meat Plant to Reopen after Standoff with Food Inspectors," *The Globe and Mail,* October 14, 2012, retrieved from www.theglobeandmail.com/news/national/shuttered-meat-plant-to-reopen-after-standoff-with-food-inspectors/article4611938/.
3. Bill Curry, "XL Foods Recall Was Product of Preventable Errors, Review Finds," *The Globe and Mail,* June 5, 2013, retrieved from globeandmail.com/news/politics/xl-foods-recall-was-product-of-preventable-errors-review-finds/article12363508/.
4. Bryan Weismiller, "Danielle Smith Takes Heat for 'Retweet" on Feeding Tainted Beef to Homeless," *Calgary Herald,* October 22, 2012, retrieved from calgaryherald.

com/health/Danielle+Smith+takes+heat+retweet+feeding+tainted+beef+homeless/7422418/story.html.

5. Gary Mason, "What the Mounties' Saviour Must Do to Regain Canada's Trust," *The Globe and Mail,* February 10, 2011, A15.
6. Joann S. Lublin, "More Companies Cut Little Perks," *The Wall Street Journal,* January 4, 2001, B4.
7. Kitty O. Locker, "Factors in Reader Responses to Negative Letters: Experimental Evidence for Changing What We Teach," *Journal of Business and Technical Communication,* 13, no. 1 (January 1999): 21.
8. Jacquie McNish, "Compromise, or 'the Canadian Way,' in Governance," *Report on Business,* March 25, 2005, B4.
9. Locker, "Factors in Reader Responses," 25–26.
10. Sharon S. Brehm and Jack W. Brehm, *Psychological Reactance: A Theory of Freedom and Control* (New York: Academic Press, 1981), 3.
11. "Tim Hortons Pulls Ad That Offended Family of Murder Victim," *Report on Business,* September 17, 2005, B7.
12. Jan Wong, "Fifteen Minutes of Shame," *The Globe and Mail,* May 7, 2005, F1–8; Jacquie McNish, "E-Mails Penetrate Closed Doors," *The Globe and Mail,* January 26, 2004, B1–4; Erin Pooley, "Not for Your Eyes Only," *Canadian Business,* January 31–February 13, 2005, 36.
13. David Parkinson, "A Train Wreck? Greenspan Says He Didn't See It Coming," *The Globe and Mail,* November 8, 2008, B2.
14. Rob Carrick, "A Simple Sorry Would Have Been Nice," *The Globe and Mail,* February 5, 2009, retrieved April 16, 2011, from http://www.theglobeandmail.com/globe-investor/investment-ideas/article10989.ece.
15. Carrick, "A Simple Sorry."
16. Archana Verma, "Navigating the Financial Crisis," *Communication World,* January–February 2009, 4–7.
17. Verma, "Navigating the Financial Crisis," 5–6.
18. Paul Sanchez, "Assessing the Impact," *Communication World,* March–April 2009, 4–6.
19. Deborah Tannen, *Talking from 9 to 5: Women and Men in the Workplace: Language, Sex, and Power* (New York: Avon, 1994), 43–52.
20. Will and Ian Ferguson, *How to Be a Canadian* (Douglas & McIntyre, 2001).
21. Leslie N. Vreeland, "SEC 'Cop' Has Eye on Mutual Funds," *Columbus Dispatch,* July 21, 1987, 3F.
22. Frederick M. Jablin and Kathleen Krone, "Characteristics of Rejection Letters and Their Effects on Job Applicants," *Written Communication,* 1, no. 4 (October 1984): 387–406; and Carlos Tejada, "Work Week," *The Wall Street Journal,* October 23, 2001, A1.
23. Elizabeth A. McCord, "The Business Writer, the Law, and Routine Business Communication: A Legal and Rhetorical Analysis," *Journal of Business and Technical Communication,* 5, no. 2 (1991): 183.
24. Catherine Schryer, "Walking a Fine Line: Writing Negative Letters in an Insurance Company," *Journal of Business and Technical Communication* 14 (October 2000): 445–497.
25. Gabriella Stern, "Companies Discover That Some Firings Backfire into Costly Defamation Suits," *The Wall Street Journal,* May 5, 1993, B1.

Chapter 9

1. Alan Farnham, "You're So Vain," *Fortune,* September 9, 1996, 78–80.
2. Helen Leggatt, "Sweet Smell of Success for Old Spice Video Campaign," *Biz Report: Social Marketing,* retrieved April 21, 2011, from http://www.bizreport.com/2010/07/sweet-smell-of-success-for-old-spice-social-campaign.html; Simon Houpt, "The Man Your Man Could Smell Like," *The Globe and Mail,* December 13, 2010, B4–5.
3. Susan Krashinsky, "A Sunday Shift: The Rise of Real-Time Ads," *The Globe and Mail,* January 31, 2014, B5.
4. James Cowan, "Viral Ads That Smell as Good as This Guy," *Canadian Business,* May 10, 2010, 85.
5. Jay A. Conger, "The Necessary Art of Persuasion," *Harvard Business Review,* May–June 1998, 88.
6. Adapted from Andy Holloway, "Massaging the Message: A New Breed of Marketer Turns Conventional Brand Wisdom Upside Down," *Canadian Business,* March 15–28, 2004, 65–66.
7. Keith McArthur, "Teens, Moms Targeted in Oven-Ready Pizza War," *The Globe and Mail,* February 21, 2005, B4.
8. Paul M. Connell, Merrie Brucks, and Jesper H. Nielsen. "How Childhood Advertising Exposure Can Create Biased Product Evaluations That Persist into Adulthood," *Journal of Consumer Research,* June 2014.
9. Susan Krashinsky, "A New Generation of Moms Meets An old Favourite," *Report on Business,* April 18, 2014, B7.
10. Newfoundland and Labrador Tourism homepage, retrieved June 1, 2014, from http://www.newfoundlandlabrador.com/.
11. James Suchan and Ron Dulek, "Toward a Better Understanding of Reader Analysis," *Journal of Business Communication,* 25, no. 2 (Spring 1988): 40.
12. Frances Harrington, "Formulaic Patterns versus Pressures of Circumstances: A Rhetoric of Business Situations," Conference on College Composition and Communication, New Orleans, LA, March 17–19, 1986.
13. Thomas H. Davenport and John C. Beck, "Getting the Attention You Need," *Harvard Business Review,* September–October 2000, 124.
14. Priscilla S. Rogers, "A Taxonomy for the Composition of Memorandum Subject Lines: Facilitating Writer Choice in Managerial Contexts," *Journal of Business and Technical Communication,* 4, no. 2 (September 1990): 21–43.
15. Nicole Stewart, *Missing in Action: Absenteeism Trends in Canadian Organizations.* Ottawa: Conference Board of Canada, September 2013, retrieved from http://www.conferenceboard.ca/e-library/abstract.aspx?did=5780; Linda Nguyen, "Canadian Economy Loses $16.1B Annually Due to Absenteeism: Conference Board," *The Star.com,* retrieved May 31, 2014, from http://www.thestar.com/business/economy/2013/09/23/absenteeism_cost_canada_lost_166_billion_study.html.
16. Brian Morton, "Workplace Fitness Cited for Bottom-Line Benefits," *Vancouver Sun,* reprinted in Saskatoon *StarPhoenix,* July 30, 2005, F11.
17. Yuri Kageyama, "A Day at Japan's New Mall: Buy Clothes, a Few CDs . . . Maybe a New Lexus," *The Globe and Mail,* March 26, 2008, B11.
18. John Lorinc, "The Medicare Myth That Refuses to Die," *The Globe and Mail,* August 9, 2008, F3.
19. Daniel J. O'Keefe, *Persuasion* (Newbury Park, CA: Sage, 1990), 168; Joanne Martin and Melanie E. Powers, "Truth or Corporate Propaganda," *Organizational Symbolism,* ed. Louis R. Pondy, Thomas C. Dandridge, Gareth Morgan, and Peter J. Frost (Greenwich, CT: JAI Press, 1983), 97–107; and Dean C. Kazoleas, "A Comparison of the Persuasive Effectiveness of Qualitative versus Quantitative Evidence: A Test of Explanatory Hypotheses," *Communication Quarterly,* 41, no. 1 (Winter 1993): 40–50.
20. "Phoning Slow Payers Pays Off," *Inc.,* July 1996, 95.
21. Adapted from "2004 Facts about Newspapers," Newspaper Association of America, http://www.naa.org/info/facts04/canada-allmedia.html, retrieved May 6, 2005; Barrie McKenna, "Snail Mail Corp. Tries to Break Out of Its Shell, *The Globe and Mail,* January 21, 2011, B1–6.
22. "Dead Letter Office," *Canadian Business,* October 2013, 44–46; Barrie McKenna, "Canada Post's Losses Mount," *Report on Business,* May 6, 2014, B3.
23. Bill Bradley, Paul Jansen, and Les Silverman, "The Non-profit Sector's $100 Billion Opportunity," *Harvard Business Review,* May 2003, 94–103.
24. Sandra Yin, "Mail Openers," *American Demographics,* October 2001, 20–21.
25. John D. Beard, David L. Williams, and J. Patrick Kelly, "The Long versus the Short Letter: A Large Sample Study of a Direct-Mail Campaign," *Journal of Direct Marketing,* 4, no. 12 (Winter 1990): 13–20.
26. Ray Jutkins, "All about Post and Post Post Scripts—A Key Element in Direct Mail," *Direct Marketing,* January 1997, 44.
27. Eileen Daspin, "How to Give More," *The Wall Street Journal,* October 2, 1998, W1, W4.
28. Beth Negus Viveiros, "No Laughing Matter: Use of Humour in Direct Mail Marketing," *Direct,* January 2003, downloaded from LookSmart's FindArticles, www.findarticles.com.
29. Maxwell Sackheim, *My First Sixty-Five Years in Advertising* (Blue Ridge Summit, PA: Tab Books, 1975), 97–100.

Chapter 10

1. For a useful taxonomy of proposals, see Richard C. Freed and David D. Roberts, "The Nature, Classification, and Generic Structure of Proposals," *Journal of Technical Writing and Communication,* 19, no. 4 (1989): 317–351
2. Nicholas Carr, "Is Google Making Us Stupid?" *The Atlantic Monthly,* July/August 2008, retrieved April 28, 2011, from http://www.theatlantic.com/magazine/

archive/2008/07/is-google-making-us-stupid/6868/.

3. Jeff Beer, "In Search of Growth," *Canadian Business*, February 28, 2011, 14–16; Amir Efrati, "Violators Feel Sting of Google's Admonition," *The Globe and Mail*, March 3, 2011, B11; Jason Madger, "Google's Risky Business," *Montreal Gazette*, February 19, 2011.
4. Susan Krashinsky, "Publishers Go 'Native' with Advertising," *The Globe and Mail*, October 4, 2013, B4.
5. Amy Mitchell, "State of the News Media 2014," Pew Research Journalism Project, retrieved June 3, 2014, from http://www.journalism.org/2014/03/26/state-of-the-news-media-2014-overview/.
6. Marian Burright, "Database Reviews and Reports: Google Scholar—Science and Technology," retrieved May 1, 2011, from http://www.library.ucsb.edu/istl/06-winter/databases2.html; Trent University Library, "Google and other Internet Search Engines," retrieved May 1, 2011, from http://www.trentu.ca/admin/library/help/google.html.
7. Peter Nicholson, "Information-rich and Attention-poor," *The Globe and Mail*, September 12, A15.
8. Palmer Morrel-Samuels, "Getting the Truth into Workplace Surveys," *Harvard Business Review*, February 2002, 111–118.
9. Morrel-Samuels, "Getting the Truth," 111–118.
10. David B. Wolfe, "Targeting the Mature Mind," *American Demographics*, March 1994, 34.
11. Janice M. Lauer and J. William Asher, *Composition Research: Empirical Designs* (New York: Oxford University Press, 1986), 66.
12. Irving Crespi, quoted in W. Joseph Campbell, "Phone Surveys Becoming Unreliable, Pollsters Say," *Columbus Dispatch*, February 21, 1988, 8F.
13. Palmer Morrel-Samuels, "Web Surveys' Hidden Hazards," *Harvard Business Review*, July 2003, 16–17; Jakob Nielsen, "Keep Online Surveys Short," *Alertbox*, http://www.useit.com, February 2, 2004.
14. Joshua Macht, "The New Market Research," *Inc.*, July 1998, 90–92.
15. Gerry Khermouch, "Consumers in the Mist," *BusinessWeek*, January 26, 2001, 92–94.
16. Michael Schrage, "Take the Lazy Way Out? That's Far Too Much Work," *Fortune*, February 5, 2001, 212.
17. Jakob Nielsen, "Risks of Quantitative Studies," *Alertbox*, March 1, 2004, retrieved October 24, 2008. From http://www.useit.com/alertbox/20040301.html.
18. "The Incredible Shrinking Failure Rate," *Inc.*, October 1993, 58.
19. Bill Curry and Tavia Grant, "How Kijiji's Job Listings Drove Ottawa's Skills-Shortage Claims," *The Globe and Mail*, March 26, 2014, A1, A4; Daniel Tencer, "Feds Ditch Kijiji Data, and Look What Happens to Job Vacancies," Huffington Post Canada, May 5, 2014, retrieved from http://www.huffingtonpost.ca/2014/05/05/feds-ditch-kijiji-data-job-vacancies_n_5268037.html.
20. Bill Curry, "Auditor-General Seeks More Detailed Job Data," *The Globe and Mail*, May 7, 2014, A10.
21. Bill Curry, "Budget Cuts Blamed for Statscan Data Gaps," *The Globe and Mail*, May 10, 2014, A6.
22. "Whirlpool: How to Listen to Consumers," *Fortune*, January 11, 1993, 77.
23. Peter Lynch with John Rothchild, *One Up on Wall Street: How to Use What You Already Know to Make Money in the Market* (New York: Fireside-Simon & Schuster, 2000), 189.
24. Patricia Sullivan, "Reporting Negative Research Results," and Kitty O. Locker to Pat Sullivan, June 8, 1990.
25. George A. Miller, "The Magical Number Seven, Plus or Minus Two: Some Limits on Our Capacity for Processing Information," *Psychological Review*, 63, no. 2 (March 1956): 81–97.
26. Karen Birchard, "Canada's Simon Fraser Suspends 44 Students in Plagiarism Scandal," *The Chronicle of Higher Education*, October 2002, retrieved September 25, 2005, from http://chronicle.com/daily/2002/10/2002102404n.htm; Holly Moore, "Cheating Students Punished by the 1000s, But Many More Go Undetected," CBC News, February 25, 2014, retrieved from http://www.cbc.ca/news/canada/manitoba/cheating-students-punished-by-the-1000s-but-many-more-go-undetected-1.2549621.
27. Nicole Wahl, "Online Database Pinpoints Plagiarism," *News @ University of Toronto*, retrieved September 25, 2005, from http://www.newsandevents.utoronto.ca/bin3/0211 21a.asp.
28. Stuart H. Loory and Petya Stoeva, "Journalism's Chronic Crisis: Corruption of Its Honesty," *Global Journalist Magazine*, 2004 Fourth Quarter, retrieved September 25, 2005, from http://www.globaljournalist.org/magazine/2004-4/chronic-crisis.html.
29. Kristin Rushowy, "Globe Disciplines Margaret Wente Over Plagiarism Accusations," *The Star.com*, September 24, 2012, retrieved from http://www.thestar.com/news/gta/2012/09/24/globe_disciplines_margaret_wente_over_plagiarism_accusations.html.
30. Margaret Wente, "A Columnist Defends Herself," *The Globe and Mail*, September 25, 2012, A13.
31. Margaret Wente, "The Consultant vs. the Professor," *The Globe and Mail*, October 1, 2012, A17.
32. Wahl, 1; Zoe Cormier, "Stolen Words: The Internet Has Made Plagiarizing Easier Than Ever. But Detection Methods Have Gone High-Tech Too," *U of T Magazine*, Winter 2009, retrieved June 6, 2014, from http://www.magazine.utoronto.ca/winter-2009/u-of-t-plagiarism-academic-dishonesty-zoe-cormier/; LaPointe quoted in Loory and Stoeva, 4.
33. Trip Gabriel, "Plagiarism Lines Blur for Students in Digital Age," *New York Times*, August 1, 2010, retrieved August 8, 2010, from http://www.nytimes.com/2010/08/02/education/02cheat.html.
34. Canadian Heritage, "Fair Dealing in Canada," retrieved May 1, 2011, from http://www.canadianheritage.gc.ca/pc-ch/org/sectr/ac-ca/pda-cpb/publctn/cch-2007/102-eng.cfm. Most Canadian universities have published guidelines on the effect of 2012 Supreme Court of Canada rulings expanding fair dealing provisions.
35. Creative Commons, About, retrieved June 6, 2014, from creativecommons.org/about; on the Canadian affiliate of Creative Commons, see Canada—Creative Commons at http://creativecommons.org/tag/ca.

Chapter 11

1. Christine Peterson Barabas, *Technical Writing in a Corporate Culture: A Study of the Nature of Information* (Norwood, NJ: Ablex Publishing, 1990), 327.

Chapter 12

1. Steffan Postaer, "The Rules of Presenting," *Adweek*, February 24, 2003.
2. Dan Gilmore, "Putting on a Powerful Presentation," *Hemispheres*, March 1996, 31–32.
3. Florence L. Wolff, Nadine C. Marsnik, William S. Tracey, and Ralph G. Nicholas, *Perceptive Listening* (Englewood Cliffs, NJ: Prentice Hall, 1983), 154.
4. Linda Driskill, "How the Language of Presentations Can Encourage or Discourage Audience Participation," paper presented at the Conference on College Composition and Communication, Cincinnati, OH, March 18–21, 1992.
5. Anne Fisher, "Willy Loman Couldn't Cut It," *Fortune*, November 11, 1996, 210.
6. Doug Mollenhauer, "A Convenient Lesson for Presenters," *The Globe and Mail*, February 23, 2007, C1–2.
7. "D. Simon Jackson, The Spirit Bear Coalition," retrieved May 19, 2011, from http://www.spiritbearyouth.org/?page_id=78.
8. Jim Gray, "Jokes Often No Laughing Matter," *The Globe and Mail*, August 28, 2009, B15.
9. Robert S. Mills, conversation with Kitty Locker, March 10, 1988.
10. Roy Alexander, *Power Speech: Why It's Vital to You* (New York: AMACOM, 1986), 156.
11. Phil Theibert, "Speechwriters of the World, Get Lost!" *The Wall Street Journal*, August 2, 1993, A10.
12. "A Study of the Effects of the Use of Overhead Transparencies on Business Meetings," Wharton Applied Research Center, reported in Martha Jewett and Rita Margolies, eds., *How to Run Better Business Meetings: A Reference Guide for Managers* (New York: McGraw-Hill, 1987), 109–110; and Tad Simmons, "Multimedia or Bust," Presentations, February 2000, 44, 48–50.
13. University of Minnesota/3M Study, reported in Martha Jewett and Rita Margolies, eds., *How to Run Better Business Meetings: A Reference Guide for Managers* (New York: McGraw-Hill, 1987), 115.
14. Jim Gray, "The 18-Minute Presentation," *The Globe and Mail*, March 12, 2011, B19.
15. Peter Norvig, "The Gettysburg PowerPoint Presentation," retrieved June 20, 2014, from http://norvig.com/Gettysburg/. You can also watch Peter Norvig talk about his PowerPoint on YouTube at http://www.youtube.com/watch?v=d34cl5JiwD8.
16. Andrew Wahl, "PowerPoint of No Return," *Canadian Business*, November 23, 2003, 131; Virginia Galt, "Glazed Eyes a Major Peril of Using PowerPoint," *The Globe and Mail Report on Business*, June 4, 2005, B10;

Ian Parker, "Absolute PowerPoint," *The New Yorker,* May 28, 2001, 76.

17. Jim Gray, "The Perils of PowerPoint Slides," *The Globe and Mail,* September 6, 2002, http://www.hrpa.ca/HRPA/HRResourceCentre/KnowledgeCentre/newscluster3/The+Perils+of+PowerPoint+Slides.htm, retrieved October 24, 2008.
18. Edward Tufte, "PowerPoint Is Evil," *Wired News,* 11.9, September 2003, http://www.cis.rit.edu/research/DQE_materials/Wired-Article.pdf, retrieved October 24, 2008.
19. See, for example, Chris Clark, "Comparison Chart—PowerPoint and Prezi," posted March 22, 2011, retrieved from http://ltlatnd.wordpress.com/2011/03/22/comparison-chart-powerpoint-and-prezi/; Diane Hamilton, "What Is Prezi? How Does It Compare to PowerPoint?" posted November 5, 2010, retrieved from http://drdianehamilton.wordpress.com/2010/11/05/what-is-prezi-how-does-it-compare-to-powerpoint/; Maddie Grant, "Prezi Just Got Even Cooler," posted September 16, 2010, retrieved from http://www.socialfish.org/2010/09/prezi-just-got-even-cooler.html.
20. Stephen E. Lucas, *The Art of Public Speaking,* 2nd ed. (New York: Random House, 1986), 248.
21. Edward J. Hegarty, *Humor and Eloquence in Public Speaking* (West Nyack, NY: Parker, 1976), 204.
22. Kami Griffiths and Chris Peters, "10 Steps for Planning a Successful Webinar," posted January 27, 2009, retrieved May 19, 2011, from http://www.techsoup.org/learningcenter/training/page11252.cfm.
23. Dana Lacey, "Collaboration Tools Replace Business Travel: Anyone Can Dial In from Any Location," *National Post,* June 14, 2010, F5. On the costs of different Web conferencing platforms, see Sandy Klowak, "A Cubicle as Big as the World," *Winnipeg Free Press,* June 17, 2010, B8.
24. Griffiths and Peters, "10 Steps."
25. Renée Huang, "Face Time Reaps Big Rewards," *The Globe and Mail,* December 8, 2010.
26. David Benady, "Look Who's Talking," *Marketing Week,* August 12, 2004, http://findarticles.com/p/articles/mi_go1550/is_/ai_n6330921?tag=artBody;col1, retrieved October 24, 2008.
27. The comparison is taken from Jim Martin, "National Debt: Pennies to Heaven," *The Wall Street Journal,* February 22, 1988, 18.
28. Some studies have shown that previews and reviews increase comprehension; other studies have found no effect. For a summary of the research, see Kenneth D. Frandsen and Donald R. Clement, "The Functions of Human Communication in Informing: Communicating and Processing Information," *Handbook of Rhetorical and Communication Theory,* ed. Carroll C. Arnold and John Waite Bowers (Boston: Allyn and Bacon, 1984), 340–41.
29. Toastmasters International, "Fear Factor," retrieved June 20, 2014, from http://www.toastmasters.org/MainMenuCategories/FreeResources/NeedHelpGivingaSpeech/FearFactor.aspx.
30. Toastmasters International, "What You Should Have Said," retrieved June 20, 2014, from http://www.toastmasters.org/MainMenuCategories/FreeResources/NeedHelpGivingaSpeech/FearFactor/WhatYouShouldHaveSaid.aspx.
31. Jim Gray, "Public Speaking—Hint: It's Not about You," *The Globe and Mail,* June 11, 2003, retrieved December 7, 2007, from http://www.mediastrategy.ca.
32. S. A. Beebe, "Eye Contact: A Nonverbal Determinant of Speaker Credibility," *Speech Teacher,* 23 (1974): 21–25; cited in Marjorie Fink Vargas, *Louder Than Words* (Ames: Iowa State University Press, 1986), 61–62.
33. J. Wills, "An Empirical Study of the Behavioral Characteristics of Sincere and Insincere Speakers," Ph.D. diss., University of Southern California, 1961; cited in Vargas, *Louder Than Words,* 62.
34. James Gray, "In a World of Words, the Eyes Have It," *The Globe and Mail,* December 5, 2003, http://www.hrpa.ca/HRPA/HRResourceCentre/KnowledgeCentre/newscluster3/In+a+World+of+Words+The+Eyes+Have+It.htm, retrieved October 24, 2008.
35. "Presentation Lessons from *The King's Speech,*" posted February 28, 2011, retrieved May 19, 2011, from http://www.m62.net/presentation-skills/presentation-tips/presentation-lessons-from-the-kings-speech/.
36. Susan Young, "5 Royal Communication Lessons from *The King's Speech,*" posted February 4, 2011, retrieved from http://www.ragan.com/Main/Articles/42677.aspx.
37. George W. Fluharty and Harold R. Ross, *Public Speaking* (New York: Barnes & Noble, 1981), 162–163.
38. Ralph Proodian, "Mind the Tip of Your Tongue," *The Wall Street Journal,* May 4, 1992, A20.
39. Lucas, *The Art of Public Speaking,* 243.
40. Ralph Proodian, "Raspy Throat? Read This, Mr. President," *The Wall Street Journal,* January 25, 1993, A14.
41. Michael Waldholz, "Lab Notes," *The Wall Street Journal,* March 19, 1991, B1.
42. Jim Gray, "Orator Obama: Lessons for Leaders," *The Globe and Mail,* August 29, 2008, B13.
43. Jim Gray, "The Magic of Movement," *The Globe and Mail,* September 5, 2003, retrieved October 24, 2008 from http://www.hrpa.ca/HRPA/HRResourceCentre/KnowledgeCentre/newscluster3/The+Magic+of+Movement.htm.
44. Speaking-Tips.com, "Hand Gestures," December 2003, http://www.speaking-tips.com/Articles/Hand-Gestures.aspx, retrieved October 24, 2008.
45. James Gray, "How to Handle the Audience Bully," *The Globe and Mail,* January 16, 2004, C1.

Chapter 13

1. Smooch Repovich Reynolds, "Career Branding: The Misunderstood Professional Asset," *CW Bulletin,* November 2010, retrieved from http://www.iabc.com/cwb/archive/2010/1110/Reynolds.htm.
2. Jacqueline Nelson, "Millennials Value Workplace Culture: Study," *Report on Business,* May 7, 2014, B18. See also Leah Eichler, "For Younger Workers Perks Trump Pay," *Report on Business Weekend,* September 14, 2013, B17; Aaron Hurst, "Six Ways to Help Millennials Find Purpose," *Report on Business,* June 6, 2014, B12; Deborah Aarts, "Give Staff Freedom without Creating Chaos," *Canadian Business,* April 2014, 16.
3. Carl Quintanilla, "Coming Back," *The Wall Street Journal,* February 22, 1996, R10.
4. LeAne Rutherford, "Five Fatal Résumé Mistakes," *Business Week's Guide to Careers,* 4, no. 3 (Spring/Summer 1986): 60–62.
5. Phil Elder, "The Trade Secrets of Employment Interviews," Association for Business Communication Midwest Convention, Kansas City, MO, May 2, 1987.
6. Although some internships are well paid means for business to access talent, some are a modern version of "slave labour" that should be banned. See, for example, James Cowan, "Time to Ban Unpaid Internships," *Canadian Business,* April 2014, 38.
7. Denise Deveau, "A Matter of Degrees," *Financial Post,* September 2, 2009, D3.
8. Lane Wallace, "Multicultural Critical Theory. At B-School?" *New York Times,* January 9, 2010, retrieved from http://www.nytimes.com/2010/01/10/business/10mba.html?emc=eta1. See also Erin Millar, "The Rise of the Generalists," *Canadian University Report 2014.*
9. Lee Rainie and Barry Wellman, *Networked: The New Social Operating System* (Cambridge, MA: MIT, 2012).
10. Joe Light, "In Hunt for Talent, Companies Polish Their 'Employer Brand,'" *Report on Business Weekend,* May 21, 2011, B18.
11. Brian Fugere, "Movies with a Message," *Communication World,* January–February 2009, 40–41.
12. Jennifer Lewington, "What Companies Look for in New Hires," *The Globe and Mail,* March 13, 2014, E10.
13. Omar El Akkad, "Please Tell Canadians to Send Their CVs In," *Report on Business,* February 16, 2011, B7; Omar El Akkad, "Google's Big Bright Bet on Canada," *Report on Business,* May 19, 2011, B3.
14. Joe Light, "Recruiters Rewriting the Online Playbook," *Report on Business,* January 21, 2011, B14.
15. Leah Eichler, "Want the Job? You Need to Play the Hiring Game," *Report on Business Weekend,* December 7, 2013, B16.
16. Dakshana Bascaramurty, "Wanted: Summer Job, for Me," *The Globe and Mail,* June 14, 2011, L1–2.
17. Pierre Mornell, *Games Companies Play: The Job Hunter's Guide to Playing Smart & Winning Big in the High-Stakes Hiring Game* (Berkeley, CA: Ten Speed Press, 2000), 25.
18. Dennis Nishi, "Scoring Unlisted Jobs," *The Wall Street Journal,* December 10, 2010, retrieved from http://online.wsj.com/article/SB10001424052748704368004576028183800807692.html.
19. Virginia Galt, "The New 'Stealth' Recruiting Tool: Online Social Sites," *The Globe and Mail,* November 23, 2007, C1; Wallace Immen, "Why the Race for a Job Just Got Slower," *Report on Business,* May 6, 2011, B18.
20. Kristin Piombino, "Social Media Costs Candidates Their Jobs, Report Says," posted July 10, 2013, retrieved from http://www.ragan.com/Main/Articles/46973.aspx.

21. Jennifer Valentino-Devries, "How Facebook Can Lead to Bias in Hiring," *Report on Business,* December 11, 2013, B18.
22. Elizabeth Blackburn-Brockman and Kelly Belanger, "One Page or Two? A National Study of CPA Recruiters' Preferences for Résumé Length," *The Journal of Business Communication,* 38 (2001): 29–45.
23. Davida H. Charney, Jack Rayman, and Linda Ferreira-Buckley, "How Writing Quality Influences Readers' Judgments of Résumés in Business and Engineering," *Journal of Business and Technical Communication,* 6, no. 1 (January 1992): 38–74.
24. See, for example, resources on workplace issues and labour law at Employment and Social Development Canada at http://www.esdc.gc.ca/eng/home.shtml. Or check out the Canadian Human Rights Commission's Guide to Screening and Selection in Employment at http://www.esdc.gc.ca/eng/home.shtml.
25. Jenny Lee, "Freshen Up That Online Résumé with Original Keywords," *Vancouver Sun,* January 3, 2011, retrieved from http://www.twitlinker.com/blog/2011/01/freshen-up-that-online-resume-with-original-keywords-2.html.
26. Vincent S. Di Salvo and Janet K. Larsen, "A Contingency Approach to Communication Skill Importance: The Impact of Occupation, Direction, and Position," *The Journal of Business Communication,* 24, no. 3 (Summer 1987): 13.
27. Lorra Brown, "10 Ways to Annoy a College Professor (and Lose a Reference)," posted February 26, 2013, retrieved from http://www.ragan.com/Main/Articles/46278.aspx.
28. Kitty O. Locker, Gianna M. Marsella, Alisha C. Rohde, and Paula C. Weston, "Electronic Résumés: Lessons from Fortune 500, Inc. 500, and Big Six CPA Firms," Association for Business Communication Annual Convention, Chicago, IL, November 6–9, 1996.
29. Rachel Emma Silverman and Lauren Weber, "The New Résumé: It's 140 Characters," WSJ.com, April 9, 2013, retrieved June 19, 2014, from http://online.wsj.com/article/SB10001424127887323820304578412741852687994.html.
30. Locker, Marsella, and Rohde, "Electronic Résumés."
31. Charlotte Brammer, "Electronic Portfolios: For Assessment and Job Search," Proceedings of the 2007 Association for Business Communication Annual Convention, retrieved June 14, 2011, from http://businesscommunication.org/wp-content/uploads/2011/04/01ABC07.pdf.
32. Beverly H. Nelson, William P. Gallé, and Donna W. Luse, "Electronic Job Search and Placement," Association for Business Communication Convention, Orlando, FL, November 1–4, 1995.
33. Resumix, "Preparing the Scannable Resume," retrieved June 14, 2011, from http://www.1stresumes.com/articles/resumix-scannable-resume.htm.
34. Taunee Besson, *The Wall Street Journal National Employment Business Weekly: Résumés,* 3rd ed. (New York: John Wiley and Sons, 1999), 263.
35. Michael Sebastian, "5 Memorable Cover Letters That Went Viral," posted March 8, 2013, retrieved from http://www.ragan.com/Main/Articles/463445.aspx.
36. Todd Defren, "Open Letter to Millennials—PR Industry Edition," posted April 18, 2013, retrieved June 20, 2014, from http://www.ragan.com/Main/Articles/46559.aspx.
37. Review Canadian Human Rights Commission's Guide to Screening and Selection in Employment at http://www.esdc.gc.ca/eng/home.shtml.
38. Thomas Petzinger, Jr., "Lewis Roland's Knack for Finding Truckers Keeps Firm Rolling," *The Wall Street Journal,* December 1, 1995, B1.
39. Bill Breen and Anna Muoio, "PeoplePalooza," *Fast Company,* November 2000, 88.
40. Wallace Immen, "Why the Race for a Job Just Got Slower."
41. Wallace Immen, "Lights, Camera. . .Can I Have a Job?" *The Globe and Mail,* March 2, 2007, C1.
42. Ivor Tossell, "Hire Education," *Report on Business,* November 2013, 20–22.
43. Paul Attfield, "Applicants Get Ready for Their Close-Ups," *Report on Business Education,* March 13, 2014, E2.
44. Immen, "Lights, Camera."
45. James Bradshaw, "Brains Alone Won't Get You into Med School," *The Globe and Mail,* December 13, 2010, A11.
46. Defren, "Open Letter to Millennials."
47. Joann S. Lublin, "Running Afoul of Workplace Language Rules," *Report on Business,* June 1, 2012, B14.
48. Rachel Emma Silverman, "Why Are You So Dressed Up? Do You Have a Job Interview?" *The Wall Street Journal,* April 17, 2001, B1.
49. The Catalyst Staff, *Marketing Yourself* (New York: G. P. Putnam's Sons, 1980), 179.
50. Christopher Conte, "Labor Letter," *The Wall Street Journal,* October 19, 1993, A1.
51. *Marketing Yourself,* 101.
52. L. M. Sixel, "Before Social Media, There Were Social Niceties," *Report on Business,* April 20, 2011, B18.
53. Joann Lublin, "Thoughtful Thank-Yous Carry Clout," *The Globe and Mail,* February 22, 2008, C2.

Appendix A

1. Michael Sebastian, "43 Percent of Singles Say Bad Grammar Is a Turnoff," posted February 7, 2013, retrieved June 20, 2014, from http://www.ragan.com/Main/Articles/46183.aspx.
2. Sylvia Stead, "Fluent in the Language of Errors," *The Globe and Mail,* January 25, 2014, F8.
3. Matt Wilson, "Are Internal Commas on a Slippery Slope of Informality?" posted July 11, 2011, retrieved June 24, 2014, from http://www.ragan.com/Main/Articles/43259.aspx?format=2.
4. "Beyond Cold Cash," *CA Magazine,* May 2006, http://www.camagazine.com/3/0/6/6/7/index1.shtml, retrieved May 21, 2007.
5. Lindsay Miller, "My Raganites Share Typo Horror Stories," posted April 11, 2011, retrieved from http://www.ragan.com/Main/Articles/41902.aspx.

PHOTO CREDITS

Chapter 1

Page 1: Blend Images/Ariel Skelley/ Getty Images; page 2: © Bayne Stanley; page 13: © DAN RIEDLHUBER/Reuters/Corbis; page 14: Blend Images/Inti St Clair/Getty Images; page 15 (top): Cornell University Photography; page 15 (bottom): © Sean Kilpatrick/The Canadian Press; page 19: Hiroko Masuike/The New York Times/Redux Pictures.

Chapter 2

Page 25: Shock/Dreamstime.com/ GetStock.com; page 26: Reprinted with permission of Regina Leader Post; page 28: Courtesy of Safe Harbour Respect for All; page 29: Sophie Harrington, Enactus Canada; page 31 (top): © Richard Lam/The Canadian Press; page 31 (bottom): Courtesy of Faye, Scott, and Sydney Whyte; page 41: Kitty O. Locker, by permission of Joseph-Beth Booksellers; page 47: AP Images/Rob Carr.

Chapter 3

Page 52: © Chris Ryan/age fotostock; page 53: Darren Jacknisky, Bluefish Studios/Uzma Rayani, Sameer Bhojani and Saira Bhojani; page 60: Courtesy of PotashCorp; page 69: Bear Dancer Studios/Mark Dierker.

Chapter 4

Page 78: © Digital Vision/Punchstock; page 79: ISL Web Marketing & Development/Jive Photographic; page 80: Jen Polegatto, Web Designer, ISL Digital Marketing.

Chapter 5

Page 102: Image Source/Getty Images; page 103: Photograph by Mathieson & Hewitt Photography; page 105: © Michael Hillman; page 106 (top): Getty Images/Comstock Images; page 106 (bottom): Steve Russell/ GetStock.com; page 109: Helene Rogers/GetStock.com; page 110: photo by Maria Chu; page 111: http://www.naaf.ca/image-galleries (photo 7 of 24 from 2008); page 117: http://www.populationmedia.org/where/jamaica/.

Chapter 6

Page 124: Comstock Images/Getty Images; page 125: Couvrette/Ottawa; page 129: JJM Stock Photography/ Travel/GetStock.com; page 130: Courtesy of Mosaic.net International, Inc.; page 131: Monkeybusinessimages/Dreamstime.com.

Chapter 7

Page 144: ©Jose Luis Pelaez Inc/ Blend Images LLC; page 145: Courtesy of Mayor Naheed Nenshi; page 147: laif/Redux/Christoph Goedan.

Chapter 8

Page 171: ©James Hardy/Photo Alto; page 172: © Fred Lum/The Globe and Mail/The Canadian Press; page 174: Courtesy of Danielle Smith; page 181: Courtesy of CBC Halifax; page 182 (top): Courtesy of Novartis Consumer Health Canada, Inc.; page 182 (bottom): Richard Lautens/ GetStock.com; page 184: Courtesy of Pacific Cycle.

Chapter 9

Page 194: © Colin Anderson/Blend Images LLC; page 195: Courtesy of Clarence Louie and Donald Triggs; page 197: Courtesy of Mondelēz Canada; page 198: © Chris Young/ The Canadian Press; page 214 (top): Courtesy of Volunteer Richmond Information Services; page 214 (bottom): Chris Howes/Wild Places Photography/Alamy.

Chapter 10

Page 224: Alistair Berg/Getty Images; page 225: ©Geoff Robins/ The Canadian Press; page 227: © Karen Moskowitz; page 229: Reprinted by permission of Ashley Hutcheson; page 235: Rim Light/ PhotoLink/PhotoDisc, Volume 21 Retail, Shopping and Small Business; page 240: Curtis Lantinga, Photographer.

Chapter 11

Page 250: Duane Osborn/Somos Images/Corbis; page 251: Courtesy of Vancity.

Chapter 12

Page 287: © Digital Vision/Punchstock; page 288: © Adrian Wyld/The Canadian Press; page 289: Ron Verzuh, Canadian Union of Public Employees (CUPE); page 291: Courtesy of Simon Jackson; page 293: © Junebug Clark/ Photo Researchers; page 295: © Fred Chartrand/The Canadian Press; page 301: Hong Kong Economic and Trade Office in Toronto.

Chapter 13

Page 307: Jose Luis Pelaez, Inc./ Getty Images; page 308: Laura Arsie Photography; page 315: © Mark Lennihan/AP/The Canadian Press; page 332: ©Andersen Ross/Blend Images LLC; page 337: Amy's Ice Creams.

Appendix A

Page AP-1: Yuri_arcurs/Dreamstime.com/GetStock.com.

ORGANIZATION INDEX

A

B

C

D

E

F

G

V

W

X

Y

SUBJECT INDEX

D

E

F

Q

R

S

Y

Z